Globalization of Japanese Real Estate Appraisal

英語で読む証券化対象不動産の鑑定評価の実務
Practical Guidance on Investment (Securitized) Real Estate Appraisal

編著　(社)日本不動産鑑定協会
　　　証券化鑑定評価委員会
　　　証券化グローバル化対応委員会
JAPANESE ASSOCIATION OF REAL ESTATE APPRAISAL

グローバル化への対応が求められている
不動産証券化関係業務従事者のバイブル！

住宅新報社

Globalization of Japanese Real Estate Appraisal

英語で読む
証券化対象
不動産の
鑑定評価の
実務

Practical
Guidance
on Investment
(Securitized)
Real Estate
Appraisal

編　著　(社)日本不動産鑑定協会
　　　　証券化鑑定評価委員会
　　　　証券化グローバル化対応委員会
JAPANESE ASSOCIATION OF REAL ESTATE APPRAISAL

住宅新報社

Remarks upon the publication of "Practical Guidance on Investment (Securitized) Real Estate Appraisal"

It is a great pleasure for me to announce that "Practical Guidance on Investment (Securitized) Real Estate Appraisal" has now been published.

Real estate securitization in Japan has a history only just over 10 years, but as a result of the efforts of all the parties involved, a great deal has been achieved during this period. Securitization refers to the structure by which the real estate market is connected to the financial and capital markets. Sound development of securitization market has played a vital role in diversifying the investment opportunities for both individual and institutional investors. The smooth injection of funds into the real estate business enhances the value of real estate, which is necessary to support the development of Japan's economy and to invigorate economic activities. The real estate appraisal system in Japan plays an important part in the development of the real estate securitization business, which is important for the national economy, and we have been making every effort not just to maintain but to enhance the reliability of the real estate market through the use of appropriate appraisal practices.

The growth of the real estate securitization business was hit by the global financial crisis, but it has been showing signs of recovery from the second half of last year. As the real estate investment market becomes increasingly globalised, it has become necessary to attract investment from overseas as well as from the domestic market in order to ensure the strength of the Japanese economy. In fact, it is now more necessary than ever for all the people involved with overseas investors to understand our real estate investment market and to have the confidence to invest.

Until now there was no document in English explaining the overall investment real estate appraisal system, and therefore the Japanese Association of Real Estate Appraisal has decided to publish this book to support overseas investors to better understand the Japanese real estate investment market and gain confidence in investing in the market.

We are more than happy for this book to be used not only by overseas investors but also by all those involved in the real estate securitization business, and to contribute to the further development of the investment real estate market.

Finally, I would like to express my warmest thanks and appreciation to all of those who have been involved in the compilation of this book.

Tomikichi Kanbe
Chairman
Japanese Association of Real Estate Appraisal
June 2011

『英語で読む証券化対象不動産の鑑定評価の実務』刊行にあたって

　このたび、『英語で読む証券化対象不動産の鑑定評価の実務』を発刊するはこびとなりました。
　わが国における不動産証券化の取組みは10有余年の短い歴史を重ねたに過ぎませんが、関係者の大変な努力によって短期間に大きな実績を上げてまいりました。不動産と金融・資本市場を結びつける仕組みが不動産の証券化ですが、この分野の健全な発展は個人投資家はもとより機関投資家にとっても投資機会の多様化に欠くべからざるものです。不動産に資金をスムースに循環させることにより不動産の価値向上を実現することが、国民経済の発展とわが国の経済活動の活性化に必要です。このように国民経済にとって重要な役割を果たしている不動産証券化事業の堅実な発展のために、わが国に定着した不動産鑑定評価制度がその一翼を担っており、これまで適切な鑑定評価の実践をとおして不動産投資市場の信頼性の維持向上に努めてまいりました。
　不動産証券化事業は、世界的な金融不安の影響によりその成長の歩みが緩みましたが、昨年後半より回復の途につきつつあります。不動産投資市場のグローバル化が加速、進展するなかでわが国の確固たる地位を築くためには、国内はもとより広く海外からの投資を呼込むことが必要です。そのためには、海外投資家等の関係者にわが国の不動産投資市場を理解してもらい、投資への信頼を持ってもらうことがなによりも必要となります。
　これまで、投資用不動産鑑定評価の全体を把握できる英語の著作がありませんでしたが、日本不動産鑑定協会では、日本の不動産投資市場に対する海外投資家の理解を促進し、信頼をいただくために本書を著すこととといたしました。
　本書が海外投資家はもとより、不動産証券化の関係者各位の皆さんに活用され、不動産投資市場の一層の発展に資することができれば幸いです。

　末筆ながら、本書の編集にあたり多くの方々のご協力を賜りましたことを、心から御礼申し上げます。

2011年6月
社団法人日本不動産鑑定協会
会長　神　戸　冨　吉

Foreword

The Japanese real estate market is becoming increasingly globalised in two important aspects. .
First, the amount of investment towards Japanese real estate from overseas is increasing. Recently, there has been strong activity by overseas investors, notably from Asian countries. Looking back at land prices during the mini bubble period and subsequent collapse at the time of Lehman Shock in 2008, the only areas considered to have been seriously affected were the areas where REITs and other real estate funds had been investing. A high proportion of such investments in real estate funds are from overseas and therefore it may be said that Japanese land prices are partly affected by the movements of overseas investors. Under such environment, Japanese real estate appraisers who have issued appraisal reports for overseas investors have found it difficult to explain some of the concepts of value unique to Japan, such as "market value based on special considerations" .

In addition, there has been pressure on the Japanese real estate market to become more globalised with respect to the accounting system. Following the introduction of Note on fair value of investment and rental property from March 2010, the accounting system in Japan is moving towards the International Financial Reporting Standard (IFRS), with the possible compulsory adoption of the IFRS in 2012. As a result of this internationalization of accounting standards, it is necessary for Japanese real estate appraisal standards to be brought into line with international standards. Under such environment, the Japanese government has introduced Valuation Guidelines in January 2011, which are to be applied as the new real estate valuation guidelines along with Real Estate Appraisal Standards. Yet there remains an area for discussion in which Real Estate Appraisal Standards is still incompatible with the International Valuation Standards (IVS) which is the basis for real estate valuations in most overseas countries, and therefore the Japanese Association of Real Estate Appraisal (hereafter referred to as the "JAREA") is undertaking a comparative investigation on behalf of the Japanese government.

The other globalization trend is for Japanese to invest in overseas real estate. This trend has temporarily ceased during the recent financial crisis. However, in the longer term, it is clear that such movement as J-REITs interest toward investing in overseas real estate will continue to grow. Looking at REIT worldwide, there are hardly any countries other than Japan where portfolios tend to be limited to domestic real estates. The "Guidelines for Appraising Overseas Investment Real Estate" was implemented in January 2008 to be the standard for Japanese appraisers for the valuation of overseas real estates. In May 2008, the Tokyo Stock Exchange eased the regulation of J-REITs' investment of overseas real estate.

まえがき

　日本の不動産マーケットは、二つの意味でグローバル化が着実に進行してきています。その一つの動きは、海外から日本に対する不動産投資が増えていることです。最近では日本の投資用不動産ファンドに対する投資家として海外投資家の存在感が増し、特にアジアからの投資家も増加してきています。2008年のリーマンショック前後のミニバブルとその崩壊のときの地価の動きを見てみますと、このとき大きな影響を受けたのは、J-REIT等不動産ファンドが物件を購入していた地域であったと言えます。その不動産ファンドへの投資家の大きな割合を海外からの投資家が占めていますので、今や日本の地価の一部を海外投資家が動かしていると言っても過言ではありません。こういう動きの中で、海外からの投資家に対して鑑定評価書を発行した日本の不動産鑑定士は、日本独自の価格概念である「特定価格」などを説明するときに大変苦労してきました。

　また、日本の不動産は、会計制度の面からもグローバル化を迫られています。日本の会計制度は国際財務報告基準（IFRS）に近づいてきており、2010年3月期からは賃貸等不動産の時価開示がはじまり、2012年には、IFRSを強制適用（アドプション）するかどうか決まる予定です。会計基準の国際化とともに、それに適合するように日本の不動産を対象とした評価基準も変えていく必要があるので、既に国もこれに対応して、2010年1月に不動産鑑定評価基準と並び新しい不動産評価基準である価格等調査ガイドラインを施行しました。なお、海外のほとんどの国の不動産の評価基準が準拠している国際評価基準（IVS）と日本の鑑定評価基準の整合性が課題になっており、㈳日本不動産鑑定協会（以下「鑑定協会」）では、国からの委託業務で、その比較研究を行っています。

　もう一方のグローバル化の動きは、日本の投資家が海外不動産に投資する動きです。リーマンショックでこの動きが一時止まってしまいましたが、特にJ-REITが海外不動産を組み入れるという動きは、中長期的な目で見れば必ず進展すると考えられます。世界各国のREITを見てもポートフォリオを自国の不動産だけにとどめているものは日本以外にほとんどありません。日本の不動産鑑定士が海外不動産を評価する際の基準として「海外投資不動産鑑定評価ガイドライン」が2008年1月に定められ、同年5月東京証券取引所等の有価証券上場規程により禁止されていたJ-REITによる海外不動産の組み入れが可能になりました。

There was a Japanese real estate globalization boom around 1990, during the bubble era, but this was predominately a move from Japan to other countries, in which Japanese investors bought overseas real estate. On the other hand, Japanese real estate was not attractive to attract investment from overseas. At that time, Japanese investors bought overseas real estate only through the distorted vision of the economic bubble, whereas the current globalization trend has led by real estate securitization through J-REIT since around 2000, and is a two way process both into and out of Japan, built on the reliability of the Japanese real estate investment market. It is, therefore considered to be an enduring trend and not a short term move.

In the JAREA, in addition to the International Committee (chair Keiko Maekawa), such working groups as Globalization of Securitization Sub-committee (chair Shinji Muraki) working under the Securitization Appraisal Committee (chair Takaji Kumakura) and the Real Estate Appraisal Business Future Vision Research Group II (chair Katsue Okuda) have been working to correspond to the globalization of Japanese real estate. This book incorporates "Guidelines Regarding Appraisal of Securitized Properties" translated by the Globalization of Securitization Sub-committee of the Appraisal Association, and a translation of the "Valuation Guidelines" from the Ministry of Land, Infrastructure, Transport and Tourism(hereafter referred to as the "MLIT") as well as translations of the "Real Estate Appraisal Standards" and the "Public Notice of Land Prices Act".

In the real estate business, words and expressions in common use can take special meanings as a result of legal systems and customs relating to real estate systems, and therefore translating into another language have not been easy. To translate a word in one language into another language requires a thorough understanding of background such as legal systems of both countries. Some individual translators think it better to translated directly and literally while adding notes, while others translate freely using their own words and expressions with keeping the concepts close to the original. Although it is not necessary to standardize translated terminology perfectly for readers, standardization of translated terminology helps their better understating. In this book, consistent English terminology has been used to the extent possible in translating each individual Japanese words, while the chart in the appendix endeavors to explain the main differences between the terminologies.

This book has been compiled mainly to cater to the needs of overseas investors considering investment in Japanese real estate in mind but, in addition, it is expected to be equally useful not only to Japanese appraisers but also to those involved in the real estate securitization business in Japan, including real estate funds, as a comprehensive reference source to help them explain the real estate appraisal system to overseas investors to further their understanding of real estate valuation in Japan. We will be delighted if this book

日本の不動産のグローバル化の波は、90年バブル前後にもありましたが、そのときは日本の投資家が海外で不動産を購入する内から外の動きが主であり、日本の不動産は投資対象として海外投資家にとって魅力あるものではありませんでした。当時はまさにバブル状態の中での日本の投資家による海外不動産投資でしたが、最近のグローバル化の波は、2000年前後に始まった不動産証券化を通じてJ-REITが創設され、国内の不動産投資市場が整備されたうえでの、外から内、内から外と両方向へ向けてのグローバル化であるため、一時的ではない本物の動きであると思われます。

　鑑定協会では、国際委員会（委員長前川桂子）のほか、証券化鑑定評価委員会（委員長熊倉隆治）の証券化グローバル化対応専門委員会（委員長村木信爾）、不動産鑑定業将来ビジョン研究会Ⅱ（委員長奥田かつ枝）等により日本の不動産のグローバル化に対処してきました。本書は、鑑定協会の証券化グローバル化対応専門委員会にて、新たに翻訳しました「証券化対象不動産に関する実務指針」や、国土交通省の「価格等調査ガイドライン」の翻訳のほか、「不動産鑑定評価基準」「地価公示法」の翻訳も取り入れています。

　一般に不動産ビジネスにおいてよく使われている単語には法制度や不動産に関する慣習がベースになり特別な意味が込められているので、別の言語で翻訳することは簡単な作業ではありません。双方の国の法制度等を十分に理解したうえで、対象の言葉と自国の言葉を置き換えることが必要です。翻訳者によっては、文字通り表面的に訳し、別途説明をつける方がよいと考えるでしょうし、逆に、できるだけ意訳して、原語に近い意味で、自国語で表現する翻訳者もいます。訳語を完全に統一する必要はないと思いますが、統一できるものは統一した方が読み手にとって利便性が高まります。本書の中では、できるだけ同じ言葉に対する訳語を統一するよう努めましたが、必ずしも同じではなく、主な相違点を別添の表でまとめています。

　本書は、主に海外から日本の不動産投資を検討している投資家を意識して編集されたものですが、日本の不動産鑑定士のみならず、不動産ファンド等、国内の日本の不動産証券化関係のビジネスにかかわる人にとっても、不動産評価に関して整理して理解が深まり、また海外投資家に日本の不動産鑑定評価について説明する際に、ワンストップで参照できる座右の書となりうるものだと思います。本書が、海外投資家の日本の不動産についての理解を進め、かつグローバル化に対応できる不動産鑑定士の人材育成においても役にたつ

serves to help overseas investors better understand the Japanese real estate system, while at the same time contributing to the personal development of Japanese real estate appraisers in this time of globalization.

Finally, I would again like to extend my grateful thanks to the MLIT, the Japan Real Estate Institute, Ogata Appraisal Corporation, and the members of the Globalization of Securitization Sub-committee and International Committee in JAREA: (Takaji Kumakura, Shinji Muraki, Kazuya Wakimoto, Takeshi Ichikawa, Shigeko Mizutani, Masaharu Fuse, Tomoo Takeuchi, Kiyoshi Sasagawa, Kaori Arai, Katsue Okuda), as well as the secretariat of the JAREA (Seiichi Washizu, Kanako Ito).

On behalf of the compiler, Shinji Muraki, Chair of the Globalization of Securitization Sub-Committee, Japanese Association of real Estate Appraisal.

ことができれば幸いです。

　最後に、本書刊行に快く全面的にご協力いただきました、国土交通省、一般財団法人日本不動産研究所、㈱緒方不動産鑑定事務所、および㈳日本不動産鑑定協会の証券化グローバル化対応専門委員会、国際委員会で本書の内容の執筆、翻訳、編集等に携わっていただきました委員（鑑定協会：熊倉隆治、村木信爾、脇本和也、市川丈、水谷賀子、布施正浩、武内朋生、笹川清、新井香里、奥田かつ枝）、日本不動産鑑定協会事務局の方々（鷲巣誠一、伊藤愛奈子）（順不同）に改めて御礼申しあげます。

（編著者を代表して㈳日本不動産鑑定協会　証券化グローバル化対応専門委員会委員長
　村木信爾　記）

Table of Contents

Remarks upon the publication of "Practical Guidance on Investment (Securitized) Real Estate Appraisal"

Foreword

I. **Overview of Real Estate Appraisals in Japan** *1*

II. **Specific Standards Chapter 3 of Real Estate Appraisal Standards** *39*

III. **Basic Policy on Revaluation of Securitized Real Estate** *63*

IV. **Guidelines Regarding Appraisal of Securitized Properties** *71*

V. **Reference Materials** *203*

   1. Act on Real Estate Appraisal *205*

   2. Land Price Publication Act *227*

   3. Real Estate Appraisal Standards and Guidance Notes on the Real Estate Appraisal Standards *247*

   4. General Guideline for Real Estate Appraisers on Determination of Purpose and Scope of Valuation and Contents of Report *357*

   5. Guidance Notes on the General Guideline for Real Estate Appraisers on Determination of Purpose and Scope of Valuation and Contents of Report *387*

   6. Guidelines for Appraisal of Overseas Investment Real Estate *411*

   7. Guidelines Regarding Valuation Practice for Appraisal Firms *439*

   8. Japanese-English Glossary *479*

   9. Related taxation issues etc *485*

総　目　次

『英語で読む証券化対象不動産の鑑定評価の実務』刊行にあたって

まえがき

Ⅰ．日本の不動産鑑定評価制度の概要 …………1
Ⅱ．不動産鑑定評価基準（各論第3章） …………39
Ⅲ．証券化対象不動産の継続評価の実施に関する基本的考え方 ………63
Ⅳ．証券化対象不動産の鑑定評価に関する実務指針 …………71
Ⅴ．参考資料 …………203

1．不動産の鑑定評価に関する法律　*205*
2．地価公示法　*227*
3．不動産鑑定評価基準及び不動産鑑定評価基準運用上の留意事項　*247*
4．不動産鑑定士が不動産に関する価格等調査を行う場合の業務の目的と範囲等の確定及び成果報告書の記載事項に関するガイドライン　*357*
5．不動産鑑定士が不動産に関する価格等調査を行う場合の業務の目的と範囲等の確定及び成果報告書の記載事項に関するガイドライン運用上の留意事項　*387*
6．海外投資不動産鑑定評価ガイドライン　*411*
7．不動産鑑定業者の業務実施態勢に関する業務指針　*439*
8．日英用語対照表　*479*
9．関連税制等　*485*

Contents of this book, and references:

I. Overview of Real Estate Appraisals in Japan (extracts from JAREA documents and MLIT website)

II. Specific Standards Chapter 3 of Real Estate Appraisal Standards (translated by Japan Real Estate Institute, published previously)

III. Basic Policy on Revaluation of Securitized Real Estate (translated by MLIT)

IV. Guidelines Regarding Appraisal of Securitized Properties (translated by the Globalization of Securitization Sub-committee of JAREA)

V. Reference Materials

  1. Act on Real Estate Appraisal (as II)

  2. Land Price Publication Act (translated by Ogata Appraisal Corporation)

  3. Real Estate Appraisal Standards and Guidance Notes on the Real Estate Appraisal Standards (From "Internationalization of Real Estate Appraisal" published by Jutaku Shimposha translated by the Japan Real Estate Institute and JAREA : Note 1)

  4. General Guideline for Real Estate Appraisers on Determination of Purpose and Scope of Valuation and Contents of Report (translated by MLIT)

  5. Guidance Notes on the General Guideline for Real Estate Appraisers on Determination of Purpose and Scope of Valuation and Contents of Report (translated by MLIT)

  6. Guidelines for Appraisal of Overseas Investment Real Estate (translated by MLIT)

  7. Guidelines Regarding Valuation Practice for Appraisal Firms (translated by the Globalization of Securitization Sub-committee of the Appraisal Association)

  8. Japanese - English Glossary

  9. Related taxation issues etc (translated by MLIT, from MLIT website)

Note 1: Except the parts of the revision of Real Estate Appraisal Standards implemented in January 1.2010, and the revision of Guidance Note on Real Estate Appraisal Standards implemented in April 1.2010. These revisions are translated by JAREA.

Note 2: Copyright and other translation rights in each case owned by the organizations in parenthesis.

【本書の構成及び出典】

Ⅰ．日本の不動産鑑定評価制度の概要
（㈳日本不動産鑑定協会執筆及び国土交通省ホームページ等より引用）

Ⅱ．不動産鑑定評価基準（各論第三章）
（一般財団法人日本不動産研究所訳：『不動産鑑定評価の国際化』（㈱住宅新報社刊）より引用）

Ⅲ．証券化対象不動産の継続評価の実務に関する基本的考え方（国土交通省訳）

Ⅳ．証券化対象不動産の鑑定評価に関する実務指針（㈳日本不動産鑑定協会・証券化グローバル化対応専門委員会訳）

Ⅴ．参考資料
1．不動産の鑑定評価に関する法律（一般財団法人日本不動産研究所訳：上記Ⅱと同じ）
2．地価公示法（㈱緒方不動産鑑定事務所訳）
3．不動産鑑定評価基準及び不動産鑑定評価基準運用上の留意事項（一般財団法人日本不動産研究所及び㈳日本不動産鑑定協会訳：注1）
4．不動産鑑定士が不動産に関する価格等調査を行う場合の業務の目的と範囲等の確定及び成果報告書の記載事項に関するガイドライン（国土交通省訳）
5．不動産鑑定士が不動産に関する価格等調査を行う場合の業務の目的と範囲等の確定及び成果報告書の記載事項に関するガイドライン運用上の留意事項（国土交通省訳）
6．海外投資不動産鑑定評価ガイドライン（国土交通省訳）
7．不動産鑑定業者の業務実施態勢に関する業務指針（㈳日本不動産鑑定協会・証券化グローバル化対応専門委員会訳）
8．日英用語対照表（同上）
9．関連税制等（国土交通省訳、国土交通省ホームページ等）

(注1) 平成22年1月1日施行の不動産鑑定評価基準の改定部分及び平成22年4月1日施行の不動産鑑定評価基準運用上の留意事項の改定部分を除く。これらの改定部分については、㈳日本不動産鑑定協会訳。

(注2) 上記カッコ内の団体が英語翻訳文の著作権を有する。

I

Overview of Real Estate Appraisals in Japan

日本の不動産鑑定評価制度の概要

System of Real Estate Appraisal in Japan

		Private/General (1)	Securitized Real Estate (2)
	Characteristics	← Private	
	Background of Client		Investors of Real Estate
	Client	Individuals, Private corporation, etc.	J-REIT・privately placed real estate investment funds・financial institution
			Real Estate
	Types of Appraisal	General purpose Consulting for investment Simple price estimation etc.	Securitized Real Estate Revaluation of Securitized Real Estate
(a) Applicable Laws	Act on Real Estate Appraisal		
	Other Laws		Act on Securitization of Assets Act on Investment Trust and Investment Corporations
(b) Valuation Standards (MLIT)	Real Estatate Appraisal Standards etc.		S.Chapter 3 / S.Chapter 3
	(Reseach without expressing value)		
	Valuation Guidelines, etc.		
			Basic Policy on Revaluation of Securitized Properties
			Guidelines for Appraising Overseas Investment Real Estate
(c) Guidelines (JAREA)	Guideline, Guidance Notes, etc. (JAREA)	Appraisals of Collateral Real Estate etc.	Guidelines Regarding Appraisal of Securitized Properties
			Valuation of Securitization Properties Administrative Instructions for Appraisal Firms
			Guidelines Regarding Valuation

Finantial Statements (3)	Public (4)			
				Public →
Investors in General	General Public			
Private corporation (Financial Statements)	National Government, Local Government, etc.			

Appraisal

					Public notice of land prices	Land price survey	Public Auction
Financial Statements	Contribution in kind	Buy & Sale	Compensation for Loss	Fixed Assets Tax Inheritance Tax			
	Companies Act		Compulsory Purchase of Land Act	Law concerning tax	Public Notice of Land Prices Act	National Land Use Planning Act	Civil Execution Act
					Guidance Notes		

Basic Policy on Valuation for Financial Statements

Operating Guidance Regarding Valuation for Financial Statements

Practice for Appraisal Firms

日本における不動産評価の体系

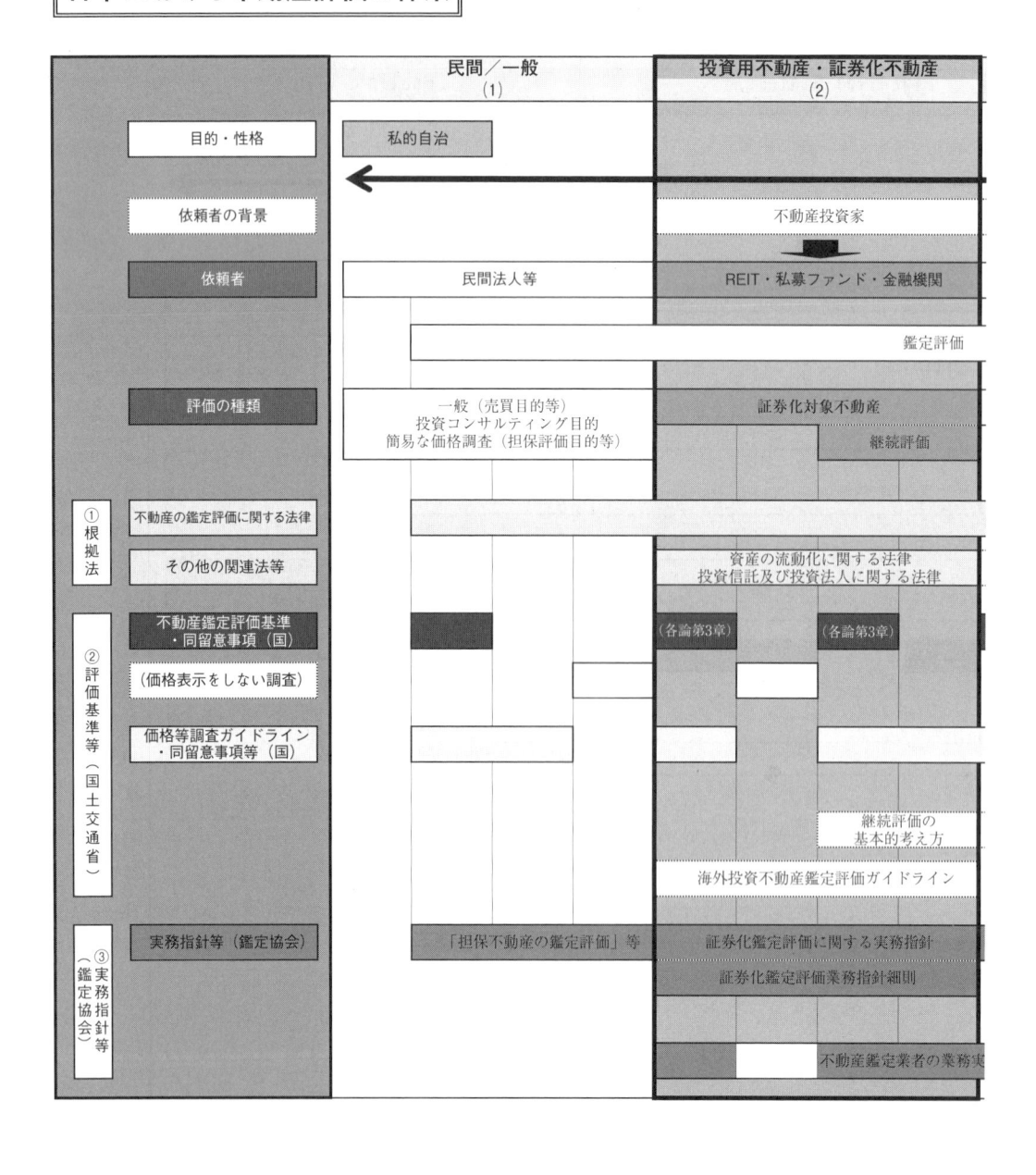

		民間／一般 (1)	投資用不動産・証券化不動産 (2)
	目的・性格	私的自治 ←	
	依頼者の背景		不動産投資家
	依頼者	民間法人等	REIT・私募ファンド・金融機関
			鑑定評価
	評価の種類	一般（売買目的等） 投資コンサルティング目的 簡易な価格調査（担保評価目的等）	証券化対象不動産 継続評価
①根拠法	不動産の鑑定評価に関する法律		
	その他の関連法等		資産の流動化に関する法律 投資信託及び投資法人に関する法律
②評価基準等（国土交通省）	不動産鑑定評価基準・同留意事項（国）		（各論第3章）　（各論第3章）
	（価格表示をしない調査）		
	価格等調査ガイドライン・同留意事項等（国）		
			継続評価の基本的考え方
			海外投資不動産鑑定評価ガイドライン
③実務指針等（鑑定協会）	実務指針等（鑑定協会）	「担保不動産の鑑定評価」等	証券化鑑定評価に関する実務指針 証券化鑑定評価業務指針細則
			不動産鑑定業者の業務実

財務諸表のための価格調査 (3)	公　共 (4)					
				公共性		
	一般投資家	一般国民				
	民間法人（財務諸表目的）	国・地方自治体等				
等業務				地価公示	地価調査	競売
財表価格調査	現物出資不動産	売買目的等	損失補償	固定資産税 相続税路線価		
	会社法	土地収用法	税　法	地価公示法	国土利用計画法	民事執行法
				地価公示業務実施の手引		
財表価格調査の基本的考え方						
財表価格調査に関する実務指針						
実施態勢に関する業務指針						

1. Real Estate Appraisals in Japan - Outline

Before describing valuation of securitized real estate, we provide herewith overview of the real estate appraisals in Japan by classifying different types of appraisals based on its purpose and potential clients.

We have also refered to applicable laws and guidelines for each type of appraisal classified.

Within this chapter, for details of each classification, please see section 2 of this chapter (Major Laws and Guidelines on Securitized Real Estate Appraisal).

(1) Valuation for non-public (general) purpose

(Potential client: individuals, general corporations, financial institutions, etc)

① Purpose and Type of Valuation

Purpose of valuation requests includes references for 1) acquisition/sales of real estate by individuals or general corporations, 2) corporate split/M&A by general corporations or 3) mortgage lending purpose for financial institutions.

② Applicable Laws

If the request is within the scope of real estate appraisal, it is undertaken in accordance with the Act on Real Estate Appraisal. Under this law, the appraisal of real estate is stipulated in Article 3 Clause 1, and adjacent/peripheral services in Article 3 Clause 2.

③ Appraisal Standards and Guidelines (by MLIT)

Following standards and guidelines are established by MLIT.

1) Real Estate Appraisal Standards

Real Estate Appraisal Standards (including Guidance Notes on Real Estate Appraisal Standards) are the operating standards which real estate appraisers follow and abide by when conducting real state appraisals in Japan.

2) Valuation Guidelines

When real estate appraisers conduct valuation not fully compliant with the Real Estate Appraisal Standards, he/she must follow "General Guidline for Real Estate Appraisers on Determination of Purpose and Scope of Valuation and Contents of Report" (hereafter referred to as "Valuation Guidelines" and including Guidance Notes on Valuation Guidelines).

④ Guidelines and Guidance Notes (by the JAREA)

The JAREA publishes operating guidances, guidance notes and research reports in relation to appraisals under activities of each committee within the JAREA. For example, there is a research report of "Appraisals of Collateral Real Estate" in relation to valuation of mortgages.

1. 日本における不動産評価の体系

　証券化対象不動産の鑑定評価について詳細を述べる前に、以下、日本における不動産に関する鑑定評価について、依頼目的、依頼者の観点で分類し、分類されたそれぞれの種類の評価に応じて適用される根拠法やガイドライン等に言及する。
　詳細は、本章２．「証券化対象不動産の鑑定評価に関する主な法律・鑑定評価基準等」参照。

(1) 一般的評価（公共目的以外）

（依頼者：個人・一般民間法人・金融機関等）

① 評価目的、評価の種類
　評価依頼目的は、１）個人や一般法人の不動産の取得、売却参考、２）会社分割、M&Aの際の参考、３）金融機関の担保目的等がある。

② 根拠法
　不動産鑑定評価に該当する場合、「不動産鑑定評価に関する法律（以下「不動産鑑定法」という）」が適用される。同法においては、第３条第１項に規定する不動産の鑑定評価と、同条第２項にいわゆる隣接・周辺業務が規定されている。

③ 鑑定評価基準、ガイドライン等（国土交通省）
　国土交通省によって作られた以下の基準、ガイドラインがある。
　１）不動産鑑定評価基準
　　不動産鑑定評価基準（留意事項を含む）は、日本において不動産鑑定士が鑑定評価を行う際に順守しなければならないものである。

　２）価格等調査ガイドライン
　　「不動産鑑定士が不動産に関する価格等調査を行う場合の業務の目的と範囲等の確定及び成果報告書の記載事項に関するガイドライン」（以下（留意事項を含み「価格等調査ガイドライン」という））は、不動産鑑定士が不動産鑑定基準に完全には準拠しない評価を行うときに従うべきルールである。

④ 実務指針、留意事項等（㈳日本不動産鑑定協会）
　㈳日本不動産鑑定協会においては、各委員会活動において鑑定評価上の実務指針、留意事項、研究成果物等を発表している。一般の評価では、例えば担保評価に関する研究成果物として「担保不動産の鑑定評価」等がある。

(2) *Valuation of Securitized Real Estate*

(Potential clients: J-REIT, privately placed real estate investment funds, financial institutions)

① Purpose and Type of Valuation

This valuation is applicable when subject for valuation is regarded as "Securitized Real Estate" as specified in Specific Standards Chapter 3 of the Real Estate Appraisal Standards.
Parties for the securitization scheme are the potential clients for this type of valuation.
In the case of listed REITs, a summary of the appraisal report is included in its financial report.

② Applicable Laws

In addition to Act on Real Estate Appraisal, Act on Securitization of Assets and Act on Investment Trust and Investment Corporation also apply.

③ Appraisal Standards and Guidelines (by MLIT)

a. Specific Standards Chapter 3 of Real Estate Appraisal Standards

Specific Standards Chapter 3 of the Real Estate Standards is applied. The Real Estate Appraisal Standards has been revised and reissued in 2007 adding new chapter, Specific Standards Chapter 3. Specifics Standards Chapter 3 incorporates such articles as 1) the subject for securitized real estate, 2) proactive use of engineering report, and 3) clarification of process for applying discounted cash flow analysis and standardizing income and expense items.

b. Valuation Guidelines

The Valuation Guidelines may also be applicable to valuation for securitized real estate.
If the valuation is revaluation of securitized real estate, the "Basic Policy on Revaluation of Securitized Properties" which stipulates such matters as valuation procedures for conducting revaluation, applies.

c. Guidelines for Appraisal of Overseas Investment Real Estate

The standard method of appraising overseas investment real estate by Japanese real estate appraisers is given in the "Guidelines for Appraisal of Overseas Investment Real Estate"

④ Guidelines and Guidance Notes (by the JAREA)

a. Guidelines Regarding Appraisal of Securitised Properties

The Guidelines is set forth by the JAREA as a basic guidelines which the real estate appraisers should follow when conduciting appraisals for securitized real estates, with taking into account of the Real Estate Appraisal Standards (including Guidance Notes)

b. Guidelines Regarding Valuation Practice for Appraisal firms

The Guidelines is published by the JAREA as a basic guidelines for real estate appraisal firms in conducting its business and to check the appropriateness of its operational practices.

(2) 証券化対象不動産向け評価

（依頼者：J-REIT、私募不動産投資ファンド、金融機関）

① 評価目的、評価の種類

　この評価は、評価対象が不動産鑑定評価基準各論第三章に規定されている「証券化対象不動産」に該当するときに行われる。証券化スキームの関係者はこのタイプの評価の依頼者となりうる。

　なお、上場リートの場合は、有価証券報告書等において不動産鑑定評価書の概要が毎期公表されている。

② 根拠法

　不動産鑑定法に加え、資産の流動化に関する法律と投資信託及び投資法人に関する法律が適用される。

③ 鑑定評価基準、ガイドライン等（国土交通省）

a. 不動産鑑定評価基準（各論第3章）

　不動産鑑定評価基準においては、平成19年に改正新設された各論第3章がこれに該当し、1）証券化対象不動産の範囲、2）エンジニアリング・レポートの活用、3）DCF法の適用過程の明確化・収益費用項目の統一などが盛り込まれている。

b. 価格等調査ガイドライン等

　証券化対象不動産の評価においても価格等調査ガイドラインが適用される。また、証券化対象不動産の再評価の際に、継続的な価格調査を行う場合における一定のルールとして、調査手順などを定めた「証券化対象不動産の継続評価の実施に関する基本的考え方」が適用される。

c. 海外投資不動産鑑定評価ガイドライン

　「海外投資不動産鑑定評価ガイドライン」は、日本の不動産鑑定士が、海外における投資用不動産についての鑑定評価行う際に適用される標準的手法について示すものである。

④ 実務指針、留意事項等（㈳日本不動産鑑定協会）

a. 証券化対象不動産の鑑定評価に関する実務指針

　不動産鑑定士が証券化対象不動産の鑑定評価を行う際には、不動産鑑定評価基準及び同基準運用上の留意事項を踏まえ、原則として準拠すべき指針として、鑑定協会が定めたものである。

b. 証券化鑑定評価に関する業務指針

　不動産鑑定業者が、鑑定業等実務を行うにあたり指針とすべきものとして、かつ当該実務の適正さを確認するための指針として鑑定協会が公表するものである。鑑定業等実務を行う際には、原則として準拠するものである。

(3) Valuation of Real Estate for Financial Statements

(Potential clients: general corporations)
① **Purpose and Type of Valuation**
　Valuation for impairment of fixed assets, measurement of inventories, and note on fair value of investment and rental property as a result of the convergence to IFRS (International Financial Reporting Standards),and business combinations and related matters, contribution in kind related to Companies Act, come into this category.
② **Applicable Laws**
　Companies Act
③ **Appraisal Standards and Guidelines (by MLIT)**
　Real Estate Appraisal Standards, Valuation Guidelines, Basic Policy on Valuation for Financial Statements are to be applied.
④ **Guidelines and Guidance Notes (by the JAREA)**
　The JAREA has established and published guidance named "Operating Guidance Regarding Valuation for Financial Statements.* The purpose of the guidance is Impaired fixed assets accounting, Inventory assets accounting Note on fair value of investment and rental property and valuation for business combination

(4) Valuation for Public Purposes

(Clients: national government, local government, etc)
　These valuations are undertaken by the national and local government for public purposes including Public Notice of Land Prices, Land Price Surveys, inheritance and fixed asset tax assessment, compensation of loss from public works, auctions, etc.

① **Public Notice of Land Prices (Publication of Land Price)**
　Land prices in the public notice are the normal price of standard land as of January 1 every year, publicly announced by the Land Appraisal Committee in March, under the Public Notice of Land Prices Act (the Land Price Publication Act)(Law No. 49, 1969). The purpose of the public notice (Land Price Publication) is to provide a guideline for general transaction prices of lands, to help in evaluating acquisition prices of public use lands, and to serve as a standard for land appraisal by real estate appraisers and others, thus contributing to determination of appropriate land prices.
　In addition to these functions, Land prices in the public notice are utilized as a guideline for appraisal of inheritance tax and fixed assets tax, for the purpose of balancing and adjusting the evaluated values of public lands. At the same time, those prices are also used for real estate for sale in corporate accounting. In this way, the importance of the Public Notice of Land Prices has been increasing.
　To determine the price in the public notice, the Land Appraisal Committee requires appraisals from two or more real estate appraisers, reviews the results, adjusts them if

---

* "Current Price Valuation for Corporate Accounting" by Japanese Association of Real Estate Appraisal, pub Jutaku Shinposha, June 30, 2010

(3) 財務諸表作成目的の評価

(依頼者：一般民間法人)

① 評価目的、評価の種類

　固定資産の減損会計、棚卸資産の時価会計、国際財務報告基準のコンバージェンスの影響を受けて、2010年3月決算から始まった賃貸等不動産の期末時価の注記のための評価や、会社法上の現物出資に伴う評価、企業結合の際の評価もこの範疇に入る。

② 根拠法
・会社法

③ 鑑定評価基準、ガイドライン等（国土交通省）

　不動産鑑定評価基準、価格等調査ガイドライン、財表価格の評価の基本的考え方、が適用される。

④ 実務指針、留意事項等（(社)日本不動産鑑定協会）

　固定資産の減損、棚卸資産の評価、賃貸等不動産の時価等の注記、企業結合等に関する価格調査について、「財務諸表のための価格調査に関する実務指針」として、鑑定協会が定め、公表したものである。*

(4) 公的評価

(依頼者：国、地方自治体等)

　地価公示、地価調査、相続税、固定資産税などの徴税、公共事業に基づく損失補償、競売等、国、地方公共団体が行う評価で、公共目的のものである。

① 地価公示

　地価公示は、地価公示法（昭和44年法律第49号）にもとづいて、土地鑑定委員会が、毎年1月1日時点における標準地の正常な価格を3月に公示するものであり、一般の土地の取引価格に対して指標を与え、公共用地の取得価格の算定に資するとともに、不動産鑑定士等が土地についての鑑定評価を行う場合の規準等となることにより、適正な地価の形成に寄与することを目的としている。

　また、公示価格は、これらの役割に加え、公的土地評価の均衡化・適正化の観点から、相続税評価や固定資産税評価の目安として活用されているとともに、企業会計の販売用不動産の時価評価の基準としても活用されるなど、地価公示制度の重要性が高まっている。

　公示価格の判定は、地価公示法第2条に基づいて、土地鑑定委員会が、2人以上の不動産鑑定士の鑑定評価を求め、その結果を審査し、必要な調整を行って、当該標準地の1平方メートル当たりの正常な価格を判定している。根拠法は地価公示法である。

---

* (社)日本不動産鑑定協会編著『企業会計のための時価評価』(株)住宅新報社刊、平成22年6月30日）

necessary, and ascertains normal prices per square meter of the land in question, under Article 2 of Public Notice of Land Prices Act.

Applicable law is Public Notice of Land Prices Act

(note) Land Price Publication Act in V-2 is the same as Public Notice of Land Prices

② **Land Price Surveys**

Land Price Survey refers to the determination of standard land prices as of July 1 every year by all prefectural governors according to the Order for Enforcement of the National Land Use Planning Act Clause 9. It serves as the standard for price assessment relating to land transaction restrictions and for setting the price of land purchased by local governments, with the aim of facilitating land price determination.

Applicable law is National Land Use Planning Act

③ **Valuation for inheritance tax (inheritance tax street-based value)**

The purpose of the Valuation is for inheritance tax and gift tax, requested by Director of National Tax Bureau, National Tax Agency. Price reference date is January 1 each year (published July 1).

The price standard is about 80% of Land Prices in Public Notice. Applicable law is Inheritance Tax Act.

Valuation standards used are Basic Circular of Fixed Property Valuation Standards.

④ **Valuation for fixed assets tax (Fixed assets tax street-based value)**

The purpose of the Valuation is for determining fixed assets tax, requested by Ministy of Internal Affairs and Communications or municipal mayors. Price reference date is January 1 (surveyed at 3 year intervals)

The price standard is about 70% of Land Prices in Public Notice. Applicable law is Local Tax Act. Valuation standards used are Fixed Assets Valuation Standards.

⑤ **Valuation for loss compensation purposes**

The purpose of the Valuation is to calculate compensation for losses associated with the compulsory purchase of land for public purposes, requested by national government and local governments. The applicable law is The Compulsory Purchase of Land Act.

Valuation standards is 'Compensation Standard for Losses associated with the Compulsory Purchase of Land for Public Purposes'

⑥ **Valuation for auction**

The purpose of the valuation is for setting the standard price for sale at auction, requested by District courts. A real estate auction refers to a situation when a creditor files suit to recover a debt in accordance with the Civil Execution Act and the court initiates the procedures to sell the real estate. This generally includes both compulsory auctions and secured real estate auctions. Applicable law is Civil Execution Act. Official valuation standards is not available.

(5) *Other*

In addition to the above valuations for a public purpose, the government issues land price information in the form of the "Real Estate Transaction Price Information (Gener-

② 地価調査

　地価調査とは、国土利用計画法施行令第9条にもとづき、都道府県知事が毎年7月1日における標準価格を判定するものである。土地取引規制に際しての価格審査や地方公共団体等による買収価格の算定の規準となることにより、適正な地価の形成を図ることを目的としている。根拠法は国土利用計画法である。

③ 相続税評価（相続税路線価）

　相続税及び贈与税課税のための評価である。実施機関は、国税庁・国税局長であり、価格時点は毎年1月1日時点（7月頃発表）である。評価額の水準は、公示価格の8割程度とされている。根拠法は相続税法であり、評価基準は「財産評価基本通達」である。

④ 固定資産税評価（固定資産税路線価）

　固定資産税課税のための評価であり、実施機関は総務省・市町村長である。価格時点は1月1日時点である（3年に1度評価替）。評価額の水準は公示価格の7割程度とされている。根拠法は地方税法であり、評価基準は「固定資産評価基準」である。

⑤ 損失補償目的の評価

　公共用地の取得に伴う損失補償の際に必要となる不動産評価であり、実施機関は国、地方公共団体等である。根拠法は土地収用法であり、評価基準は「公共用地の取得に伴う損失補償基準」である。

⑥ 競売のための評価

　競売制度における「売却基準価額」算定のための不動産評価で、実施機関は各地方裁判所である。不動産競売とは、民事執行法に基づき、債権回収のために、債権者が裁判所に対して申立てを行うと、その不動産を裁判所が売却する手続である。強制競売と担保不動産競売を併せて一般にこのように呼ぶ。根拠法は、民事執行法である。公式的な評価基準はない。

(5) その他

　以上の公的評価のほかに国は、以下の「不動産取引価格情報（土地総合情報システム）」や「主要都市の高度利用地地価動向報告〜地価LOOKレポート」により、地価の情報を開示している。

al Land Information System)" and the "Major Cities Intensively Developed Land Price Movement Information – Land Price LOOK Report".

① Real Estate Transaction Price Information (General Land Information System)

Since April 2006, information on actual real estate transaction prices is collected through a questionnaire from those who conduct actual real estate transactions and published quarterly to enhance the reliability and transparency of the real estate market and to facilitate smooth and efficient real estate transactions. All localities subject to the public notification of land prices etc (almost all of Japan) are covered in this survey and the reported information includes location (municipality and sub-division), date of transaction, transaction price (to 2 significant figures), land area, plot shape, building use, construction type, floor area, year completed, road frontage, nearest railway station, town planning zone, percentage of plot built on, total floor area as a percentage of plot area, other.

② Major Cities Intensively Developed Land Price Movement Information – Land Price LOOK Report

The Major Cities Intensively Developed Land Price Movement Information (Land Price LOOK Report) clarifies land price movements for land in major cities that tend to show price movements in advance of other areas, such as intensively used land, by determining land price movements on a quarterly basis. The report covers the three major metropolitan areas, Greater Tokyo, urban Kansai and Greater Nagoya, within which 150 locations in the central metropolitan areas (including designated major cities) where intensively developed land used for high rise apartments, shops, offices etc is concentrated and which tends to show price trends in advance of other areas. The survey collects information on prices of the specific locations and real estate market trends from relevant sources in each district including real estate related businesses and financial institutions.

① 不動産取引価格情報（土地総合情報システム）
　不動産市場の信頼性・透明性を高め、不動産取引の円滑化、活性化を図るため、平成18年4月より、不動産取引当事者へのアンケート調査に基づく不動産の実際の取引価格に関する情報を四半期毎に提供している。対象地域は全国の地価公示対象区域等（ほぼ全国）で、提供内容は所在地（※町・大字レベル）、取引時期、取引価格（※有効数字2桁）、土地の面積・形状、建物の用途・構造、床面積、建築年、前面道路、最寄駅、都市計画、建ぺい率、容積率　等である。

② 主要都市の高度利用地地価動向報告～地価 LOOK レポート
　主要都市の高度利用地地価動向報告（地価 LOOK レポート）とは、主要都市の地価動向を先行的に表しやすい高度利用地などの地区について、四半期毎に地価動向を把握することにより先行的な地価動向を明らかにするもの。調査対象は、三大都市圏（東京圏、近畿圏、中部圏）、地方中心都市（政令指定市等）等における、地価動向を先行的に表しやすい高層住宅等や店舗、事務所等が高度に集積している高度利用地等の150地点の土地で、調査内容は、対象地点の地価、不動産関連業者、金融機関等の地元不動産関係者からの不動産市場の動向に関する情報である。

2. Major Laws and Guidelines on Securitised Real Estate Appraisal

(1) Applicable Laws

① Act on Real Estate Appraisal

(Law No 152, July 16, 1963, latest version law No 10, March 31, 2006)

Japanese real estate appraisers are licensed on a national basis to conduct real estate appraisals, and the law specifies that people other than licensed real estate appraisers are not allowed to conduct real estate appraisals. A summary of the Act on Real Estate Appraisal and the Japanese real estate appraisal business is as follows.

(note) Real Estate Appraisal Act in V-1 is the same as Act on Real Estate Appraisal

a. Real Estate Appraiser

There is a license system for real estate appraisers to license them to conduct real estate appraisals, and those who pass the national examination for real estate appraiser and complete their training are qualified as Japanese real estate appraisers registered in the MLIT register of appraisers.

Licensed real estate appraisers in their capacity as licensed real estate appraisers investigate and analyze the various factors which affect the objective value of real estate and alternatively they can provide commercial consultancy with regard to real estate transactions and investment in so far as their business activities in this area are not constrained by other laws.

Real estate appraisers are required to conduct business as specified in clause 3 (hereafter referred to as "appraisal etc business") conscientiously and in good faith and should not bring the profession of real estate appraiser into disrepute.

MLIT or the Governor of a Prefecture may admonish a registered real estate appraiser who violates these sanctions and order the cessation of business or suspend their registration for a defined period.

b. Real Estate Appraisal Business

A real estate appraisal business is a business entity which conducts real estate appraisals as required by clients in return for remuneration, which may be conducted by the business owner or by employees of the business. Businesses with offices in more than one prefecture which are registered in the register of real estate appraisal companies at the MLIT, while others which are registered in the register in the prefecture, are allowed to conduct this business. Registration as a real estate appraisal business is valid for 5 years.

Duties for a real estate appraisal business are as follows:

a. Assignment of Real Estate Appraisers

A real estate business shall employ one or more real estate appraisers exclusively in each office (law clause 35).

b. Reporting

A real estate appraisal business shall submit a report of its business performance to the MLIT or to the appropriate prefectural governor before January 31 each year.

2. 証券化対象不動産の鑑定評価に関する主な法律・鑑定評価基準等

(1) 根拠法

① 「不動産の鑑定評価に関する法律」（不動産鑑定法）
（昭和38年7月16日法律第152号、最終改正：平成18年3月31日法律第10号）

日本の不動産鑑定士は不動産を評価する国家資格である。そして、不動産鑑定士以外の人は法律上評価を行うことができない。この理由で、法律上の不動産鑑定士と日本の不動産鑑定士等に関する概要は以下の通り定義される。

a. 不動産鑑定士

不動産鑑定評価を行う者の資格として、不動産鑑定士の資格制度があり、不動産鑑定士試験に合格した者が、実務修習を終了し、国土交通省に備える不動産鑑定士名簿への登録を受けると不動産鑑定士となる。

不動産鑑定士は、不動産鑑定業者の下において不動産鑑定業務を行うとともに、不動産鑑定士の名称を用いて、不動産の客観的価値に作用する諸要因に関して調査若しくは分析を行い、又は不動産の利用、取引若しくは投資に関する相談に応じることを業とすることができる。ただし、他の法律においてその業務を行うことが制限されている事項については、この限りでない。

不動産鑑定士は、良心に従い、誠実に第三条に規定する業務を行うとともに、不動産鑑定士の信用を傷つけるような行為をしてはならない。

国土交通大臣は、不当な鑑定評価等を行った不動産鑑定士に対して、期間を定めて業務の禁止又は登録の消除をすることができる。

b. 不動産鑑定業者

不動産鑑定業とは、自ら行うと他人を使用して行うとを問わず、他人の求めに応じて報酬を得て、不動産の鑑定評価を業として行うことをいい、2以上の都道府県に事務所を設ける者は国土交通省に、その他の者は都道府県に、それぞれ備える不動産鑑定業登録簿に登録されて、不動産鑑定業を営むことができる。不動産鑑定業者の登録の有効期間は5年である。

不動産鑑定業者の義務として以下のものがある。

a. 不動産鑑定士の設置等
　不動産鑑定業者は、その事務所ごとに専任の不動産鑑定士を1人以上置かなければならない（不動産鑑定法35条）

b. 書類の提出義務
　毎年1月31日までに過去1年間における事業実績の概要を記載した書面と、毎年1月1日における事務所ごとの不動産鑑定士の氏名を記載した書面を国土交通大臣又は都道府県知事に提

The report includes the outlines of its business performance for the previous calendar year and a report detailing the name(s) of all real estate appraisers employed at each office as of January 1 each year (law clause 28, ministerial ordinance clause 36).

c. Prohibition on Real Estate Appraisals by Non- Real Estate Appraisers.

People who are not appraisers are not allowed to conduct appraisals. (law clause 36).

d. Confidentiality

Real estate appraisers and real estate appraisal companies are prohibited from disclosing confidential information obtained in the course of business without good reason, this prohibition continuing to apply after the real estate appraisal business is closed or the appraiser ceases to conduct business.

e. Appraisal Report

The appraisal report is a document describing the result of an appraisal of real estate with the purpose of explaining the appraiser's assessment and opinion based on their professional expertise and experience and the extent of their responsibility, and must have the official seal of the appraiser involved on it.

Sanctions: The MLIT may prohibit from conducting business or cancel the registration of an appraiser who has conducted an appraisal illegally, etc, for a defined period.

② **Act on Securitization of Assets**

This law establishes a system for the securitization of assets using a special purpose company or a special purpose trust and ensures that the securitization using this system is conducted appropriately while facilitating investment by general investors by protecting the purchasers of the various securities issued as part of an asset securitization. It thus aims to support the sound development of the national economy.

③ **Act on Investment Trust and Investment Corporation**

This law protects people who are not themselves direct investors but invest in securities issued by investment trusts or investment corporations who invest their investors' money, and establishes a system to distribute the resulting return to each investor while ensuring the investment fund operates under the system in an appropriate manner. At the same time it facilitates investment in securities by individual investors, aiming to support the sound development of the national economy.

It is stipulated in the Act on Securitization of Assets and the Act on Investment Trust and Investment Corporation that where the particular asset to be acquired is real estate, the price survey should be based on an appraisal conducted by a real estate appraiser. The JAREA has produced the "Operating Guidance for Valuation of Specified Assets Conducted by Real Estate Appraisers under Act on Securitization of Assets"

④ **Public Notice of Land Prices Act (Land Price Publication Act in V-2)**

This law contributes to the determination of appropriate land prices by providing reference prices for the buying and selling of land through the publication of standard prices for typical plots of land in and around major cities and assists in the calculation of appropriate compensation for land to be acquired and developed in the public interest.

出しなければならない（不動産鑑定法28条、省令36条）。

c. 不動産鑑定士でないもの等による鑑定評価の禁止
　不動産鑑定士でない者は、不動産鑑定業者の業務に関し、不動産の鑑定評価を行ってはならない（不動産鑑定法36条）。
d. 秘密を守る義務
　不動産鑑定士及び不動産鑑定業者は、正当な理由がなく、業務に関して知り得た秘密を他に漏らしてはならず、不動産鑑定士でなくなった後及び不動産鑑定業を廃止した後においても同様である。

e. 鑑定評価書
　鑑定評価書は、不動産の鑑定評価の成果を記載した文書であり、不動産鑑定士が自己の専門的学識と経験に基づいた判断と意見を表明し、その責任を明らかにすることを目的とするものであり、関与した不動産鑑定士が署名押印しなければならない。
　国土交通大臣又は都道府県知事は、登録を受けた不動産業者が処分に違反した場合等に、戒告を与え、期間を定めて業務の停止または登録の消除をすることができる。

② 資産の流動化に関する法律
　この法律は、特定目的会社又は特定目的信託を用いて資産の流動化を行う制度を確立し、これらを用いた資産の流動化が適正に行われることを確保するとともに、資産の流動化の一環として発行される各種の証券の購入者等の保護を図ることにより、一般投資家による投資を容易にし、もって国民経済の健全な発展に資することを目的としている。

③ 投資信託及び投資法人に関する法律
　この法律は、投資信託又は投資法人を用いて投資者以外の者が投資者の資金を主として有価証券等に対する投資として集合して運用し、その成果を投資者に分配する制度を確立し、これらを用いた資金の運用が適正に行われることを確保するとともに、この制度に基づいて発行される各種の証券の購入者等の保護を図ることにより、投資者による有価証券等に対する投資を容易にし、もって国民経済の健全な発展に資することを目的としている。
　上記 b.「資産の流動化に関する法律」及び c.「投資信託及び投資法人に関する法律」）においては、特定資産が不動産であるときは、当該資産の取得等の際に、不動産鑑定士による鑑定評価を踏まえて価格等の調査を行わなければならないことが規定されている。
　鑑定協会では、資産流動化法における特定資産の価格等の調査を不動産鑑定士が行う場合の実務上の手続きや留意点等について『「資産の流動化に関する法律（資産流動化法）」における不動産鑑定士が行う特定資産の価格等の調査に関する実務指針』を取りまとめている。

④ 地価公示法
　都市及びその周辺の地域等において、標準地を選定し、その正常な価格を公示することにより、一般の土地の取引価格に対して指標を与え、及び公共の利益となる事業の用に供する土地に対する適正な補償金の額の算定等に資し、もって適正な地価の形成に寄与することを目的とする。

(2) Real Estate Appraisal Standards, Guidelines(MLIT)

① Real Estate Appraisal Standards

The real estate appraisal standards which is the unified standard and shall be the basis for sanctions against an appraiser, was established in 1964 when Act on Real Estate appraisal was established. It has been revised several times since then.

Specific Chapter 3 regarding Securitized Real Estate was added to the Standards in 2007, with the main resulting changes being as follows.

(1) Securitized Real Estate was defined as,
  (a) the real estate, in the transactions conducted by J-REIT,
  (b) the real estate in the transactions related to Real Estate Specified Joint Enterprise
  (c) the rights considered to be securities (such as trust beneficiary rights etc) according to the Financial Instruments and Exchange Act.

(2) In the appraisal of securitized real estate, the client is generally required to submit an Engineering Report and the real estate appraiser in person will assess its content and employ it in the production of his appraisal.

(3) Because real estate appraisers and real estate business are required higher lebel of accountability, in estimating the value indicated by income approach of securitized real estate, the discounted cash flow method (DCF method) shall be used and the report shall include not only the explanation of terminal capitalization rate, discount rate, estimation of revenue and expenses in each items of a cash flow sheet, but also the process and reasoning that the value have been obtained in terms of the DCF method.

In addition, the items of revenue and expenses in a cash flow sheet of DCF method were standardized and defind in detail in Specific Chapter 3.

② Guidance Notes on the Real Estate Appraisal Standards

The Guidance Notes refers to the real estate appraisal standards and covers the most important points in the Standards.

③ Valuation Guidelines

When a real estate appraiser makes an appraisal of real estate, it is in principle to be based on the Real Estate Appraisal Standards., but is recognized that as a result of the diversity of client needs, the needs for the survey which is not based on the Real Estate Appraisal Standards is increasing. This may result in some problems that a simple request for a low cost and quick result does not correspond to the client's needs or the various uses, and that the simple price survey is used in ways not recognized by the real estate appraiser or real estate appraisal business.

The MLIT has compiled "Valuation Guidelines" as a guideline to facilitate valuations being conducted appropriately by real estate appraisers, which came into force on January 1 2010.

The Valuation Guidelines covers the procedure to be followed by the real estate appraiser when conducting a valuation, whether the procedure is of the realestate appraisal stipulated in Act on Real Estate Appraisal clause 3, article 1 or that is of the ad-

(2) 鑑定評価基準、ガイドライン等（国土交通省）

① 不動産鑑定評価基準

　不動産鑑定評価基準は、不動産鑑定評価の拠り所となる統一的基準であるとともに、不動産鑑定法による処分の判断根拠となるもので、不動産鑑定法の発足とともに昭和39年に制定され、数度の改正を経て現在に至っている。

　平成19年のいわゆる証券化対象不動産対象の各論第3章を追加した改正での主なポイントは、以下の通りである。

(1) 証券化対象不動産の範囲として、(a) Ｊリートが行う不動産取引、(b) 不動産特定共同事業に係る不動産取引、(c) 金融商品取引法の規定により有価証券とみなされる権利（信託受益権など）と定義されたこと

(2) 証券化対象不動産の鑑定評価に当たっては、原則として依頼者にERの提出を求め、不動産鑑定士が主体的にその内容を分析・判断した上で、鑑定評価に活用することが義務づけられたこと

(3) 不動産鑑定士により一層の説明義務が課せられるようになったため、証券化対象不動産の収益価格算定に当たっては、DCF法の適用が義務づけられ、また、最終還元利回り・割引率・収益費用予測等の説明に加え、これらを採用して収益価格を求める過程及びその理由の記載も義務づけられた。このほか、DCF法の費用収益項目の統一と項目の定義の明確化がなされた。

② 不動産鑑定評価基準運用上の留意事項

　不動産鑑定評価基準運用上の留意事項は、不動産鑑定評価基準の運用にあたり、特に留意すべき事項について定めたものである。

③ 価格等調査ガイドライン

　不動産鑑定士が不動産の鑑定評価を行う場合、原則として不動産鑑定評価基準に則るが、依頼者ニーズの多様化により、不動産鑑定評価基準によらない価格等調査のニーズの増大が想定される。これに対し、低コスト・短期間で結果を得たいがために、依頼目的や結果の利用範囲等に見合わない簡便なものが依頼されたり、簡便な価格等の調査が不動産鑑定士・不動産鑑定業者が認識していた範囲を超えて利用され、トラブルが発生する可能性がある。

　国土交通省では、不動産鑑定士が行う価格等調査全般について、その適正な実施を図るためのルールである「価格等調査ガイドライン」を策定し、平成22年1月1日から施行されている。

　価格等調査ガイドラインは、不動産の鑑定評価に関する法律第3条第1項に規定する不動産の鑑定評価であるか、同条第2項に規定するいわゆる隣接・周辺業務であるかを問わず、価格等調査を行う場合に、不動産鑑定士が従うべき業務の方法等を示すものであり、不動産鑑定評価基準に則った鑑定評価を行う場合は、不動産鑑定評価基準のほか、価格等調査ガイドラインに従うものである。また、他の不動産鑑定業者が依頼者から受注した価格等調査業務の全部又は一部について価格等調査を当該他の不動産鑑定業者から再受注する場合の当該再受注する価格等調査については、価格等

jacent/peripheral service stipulated in article 2 of the same clause. When an appraisal based on the real estate appraisal standards is conducted, the Valuation Guidelines are followed as well as the real estate appraisal standards.

Also, when a real estate appraisal business receives an order for a valuation from a client all or part of which is to be subcontracted to another real estate appraisal business, the Valuation Guidelines may not apply to the subcontracted valuation. However, the procedures detailed under the Valuation Guidelines are to be adopted as far as possible. Also Public Notice of Land Prices, Land Price Surveys, valuation for inheritance tax, valuations for fixed asset tax, etc requested by national or local governments shall be based on their respective acts and not on the Valuation Guidelines since the requirements are stipulated in the respective acts.

Two Basic Policies concepts mensioned (below ④ & ⑤) for the porpose of implementing Valuations for use for financial statements and revaluation of securitized real estate were issued by MLIT with which real estate appraisers are considered to comply at present in relation to the Valuation Guidelines.

④ Basic Policy on Valuation for Financial Statements

This Policy apply to the valuation that an appraiser conducts for the preparation of finanancial statements in accordance with Valuation Guidelines, regarding 1)Impairment of fixed assets, 2) Measurement of inventories, 3)Note on fair value of investment and rental property, 4)Business combinations and related matters, etc. For the valuation within the scope of the policy, either "Fundamental Value Estimation" or "Deemed Value Estimation" is carried out for each purpose above.

Fundamental Value Estimation means a method of estimation of value for real estate that is a reasonably estimated based on the method specified in the "Real Estate Appraisal Standards" or a similar method. A similar method refers to the use of international valuation standards for example. When updating a valuation, if an appraisal approach that is recognized to be relatively convincing or in the indices that are considered to appropriately reflect the market value since the last appraisal compliant with the Real Estate Appraisal Standards or any other Fundamental Value Estimation, it is acceptable to estimate the Market value by making appropriate adjustments accordingly, depending on the type of the subject property.

Deemed Value Estimation means a method of estimation of value for real estate (other than when carring out a Fundamental Value Estimation), required under the Accounting Standards etc., which is the value applied the appraisal method selectively or the value based on some valuation, an assessed value reflecting market value appropriately, value by Public Notice of Land Prices, Land Price Surveys, valuation for inheritance tax(inheritance tax street-based value), valuation for fixed assets tax(fixed assets tax street-based value)

This method of estimation can be used, to judge whether the total value of the investment and rental properties in a certain company is important for it or not, and be used for the real estate of less importance among all the investment and rental properties in the company, which are to be disclosed.

調査ガイドラインは適用しない。ただし、必要に応じ、価格等調査ガイドラインに準じた措置を取るよう努めるものとする。また、国又は地方公共団体が依頼する地価公示、都道府県地価調査、路線価、固定資産税評価等、別に法令等に定めるものは、当該法令等に従うものとし、価格等調査ガイドラインは適用しない。

また、財務諸表のための価格調査の実施と証券化対象不動産の継続評価の実施に関する２つの目的別基本的考え方が国土交通省から発表された（以下④⑤参照）。これは不動産鑑定士が価格等調査ガイドラインについて、現時点において遵守することが望ましいと考えられる事項である。

④ 財務諸表のための価格調査の実施に関する基本的考え方

この「基本的考え方」は、不動産鑑定士が価格等調査ガイドライン等に従って価格調査を行う場合に、１）固定資産の減損、２）棚卸資産の評価、３）賃貸等不動産の時価等の注記、４）企業結合等、に関する基準、指針等（以下「企業会計基準等」という。）に関して財務諸表の作成に利用される目的で適用される。

この「基本的考え方」が適用される評価においては、「原則的時価算定」と「みなし時価算定」という評価方法が、上記それぞれの目的で適用される。

原則的時価算定とは、賃貸等不動産に関する合理的に算定された価格は、「不動産鑑定評価基準」による方法又は類似の方法に基づいて算定するもので、類似の方法とは、国際評価基準等を採用する場合などである。また、時点修正において、直近の原則的な時価算定を行ったときから一定の評価額や適正に市場価格を反映していると考えられる指標に重要な変動が生じていない場合には、当該評価額、指標（収益還元法の適用等）を用いて調整した金額をもって当期末における原則的時価算定における時価とみなすことができる。

みなし時価算定とは、企業会計基準等において求めることとされている不動産の価格を求めるため、鑑定評価手法を選択的に適用し、又は一定の評価額や適切に市場価格を反映していると考えられる査定価格等の評価額、公示価格、都道府県基準地価格、路線価による相続税評価額、固定資産税評価額など指標等に基づき、企業会計基準等において求めることとされている不動産の価格調査（原則的時価算定に該当するものを除く。）をいう。賃貸等不動産の総額の重要性が乏しいか否かを判断する場合や、開示対象となる賃貸等不動産のうち重要性が乏しいものについて適用可能である。

⑤ Basic Policy on Revaluation of Securitized Real Estate

This stipulates the general rule for valuation procedures etc when conducting a revaluation of securitized real estate for which a previous valuation has been completed based on the real estate appraisal standards etc. It applies to surveys undertaken for the purpose of continuously identifying the period end price etc of real estate for the valuation of securitized real estate and for the formation of financial statements.

⑥ Guidelines for Appraisal of Overseas Investment Real Estate

As globalization progresses in the real estate market, inward investment in real estate from overseas and investment in overseas real estate by Japanese companies and investors are increasing, REIT markets are opening in country after country, and international competition in the real estate market is increasingly severe. Also, Japanese real estate business are directing their attention to investment in overseas real estate with a view to diversifying the risk associated with concentrating their real estate investment in the domestic market, and therefore in 2008 the Tokyo Stock Exchange removed from the securities listing regulations the prohibition on overseas real estate being incorporated into J-REIT real estate investments.

The Guidelines for Appraisal of Overseas Investment Real Estate, in view of the progressive globalization of the real estate market, inward investment in real estate from overseas and increasing investment in overseas real estate by Japanese companies and investors, explain how to collaborate and cooperate with overseas real estate appraisers from the point of view of investor protection and how to improve the reliability of appraisals of investments in overseas real estate.

(V-6. refer to Overseas Real Estate Appraisal Guidelines)

(3) Guidelines and Guidance Notes (by the JAREA)

The JAREA has published the points to be complied with when conducting valuation.

① Guidelines Regarding Appraisal of Securitized Properties

This is published by the JAREA as guidelines regarding appraisal of securitized properties for real estate appraisers and also to confirm the appropriateness of appraisals. Actual appraisal activities should in principle adhere to the guidelines, with the reason given for any deviation from the guidelines or adherence to alternative methods.

The guidelines are to serve as a reference document for a wide range of purposes including for those in the securities business making use of an appraisal (as guidance to confirm its suitability).

As the guidelines describes the principle important points to follow when appraising real estate for securitization, it should be noted that it does not cover all aspects of the business , and for matters which are not covered in this guidelines, the Real Estate Appraisal Standards(including Guidance Notes) and some established business practices are to be followed.

The "Operating Guidance in Relation to Appraisal of Securitized Real Estate" issued in March 2007 serves as operating guideline in relation to Specified Chapter 3 of Real Estate Appraisal Standards revised in April 2007 and the Guidance Notes on the Real

⑤ 証券化対象不動産の継続評価の実施に関する基本的考え方

過去に不動産鑑定評価基準等に則った鑑定評価が行われた証券化対象不動産について、継続的な価格調査を行う場合における一定のルールとして、調査手順などを定めたものである。証券化対象不動産の評価や財務諸表作成のための評価において、不動産の期末時価等を継続的に把握することを目的とする調査に適用される。

⑥ 海外投資不動産鑑定評価ガイドライン

不動産市場のグローバル化が進む中、海外からの国内不動産への投資や国内企業や投資家による海外不動産への投資も活発化するとともに、各国でリート市場の開設が相次ぎ、不動産分野における国際間競争が厳しくなってきている。国内の不動産事業者も、不動産投資の国内集中に伴うリスクを分散させる観点から、海外不動産への投資に目を向けたため、有価証券上場規程によりJリートの運用対象資産に海外不動産を組み入れることを禁止していた東京証券取引所はこれを2008年に解禁した。

海外投資不動産鑑定評価ガイドラインは、このような不動産市場のグローバル化が進行する中、海外からの国内不動産への投資や国内企業・投資家による海外不動産への投資が活発化に伴い、海外不動産への投資を行う場合において、投資家保護及び鑑定評価の信頼性の向上の観点から適正な鑑定評価が行われるよう、海外現地の不動産鑑定人との連携・共同作業のあり方、鑑定評価の手法等を示すものである。
（Ⅴ－6．海外投資不動産鑑定評価ガイドライン参照）

(3) 実務指針、留意事項等（㈳日本不動産鑑定協会）

鑑定協会では、価格等調査にあたって遵守すべき事項について、次のとおり公表を行っている。

① 証券化対象不動産の鑑定評価に関する実務指針

不動産鑑定士が、鑑定評価等実務を行うにあたり指針とすべきものとして、かつ当該実務の適正さを確認するための指針として㈳日本不動産鑑定協会が公表するものである。鑑定評価等実務を行う際には、原則として準拠するものとし、準拠できない場合又は他の方法に拠る場合には、その根拠を明示しなければならない。

本実務指針は、さらに、鑑定評価を活用する証券化市場関係者をはじめとする広範な関係者の参考資料（その適正さを確認するための指針等）としての位置づけも有する。

なお、本実務指針は、証券化対象不動産の鑑定評価を行うに当たって特に留意すべき事項について記載したものであるため、すべての実務に対応しているものではないことに留意するとともに、本実務指針に記載していない事項については、不動産鑑定評価基準及び不動産鑑定評価基準運用上の留意事項並びに従来からの実務慣行に従うこととなる。

平成19年3月に策定した「証券化対象不動産の価格に関する鑑定評価の実務指針」は、平成19年4月に改正された不動産鑑定評価基準各論第3章及びこれに係る不動産鑑定評価基準運用上の留意事項の実務的な解説の性格を有し、その内容は『新・要説　不動産鑑定評価基準』（日本不動産鑑定協会編、住宅新報社刊、平成19年11月）の不動産鑑定評価基準各論第3章に包含された。

また、不動産鑑定協会の内部規定である「証券化対象不動産の価格に関する鑑定評価手法適用上

Estate Appraisal Standards and its contents have been incorporated into Specified Chapter 3 given in "New Edition Guideline – Real Estate Appraisal Standards" by JAREA, pub Jutaku Shinposha, November, 2007.

Furthermore, the Association's bye-law "Guidance Notes in the Application of Appraisal Procedures Regarding the Price of Securitized Real Estate" (March 2007) has been found to be being used as a reference document not only by real estate appraisers and appraisal businesses but also by those involved in the securitization market. Therefore, it has been integrated and rearranged based on current best practice and a review of appraisal procedures and reissued as Guidelines Regarding Appraisal of Securitized Properties in June 2009. This has now been revised several times based upon Valuation Guidelines issued in August 2009, and "Basic Policy on Revaluation of Securitized Real Estate" etc.

② **Business Guidance**

The Japanese Association of Real Estate Appraisal has issued "Business Guidance for Implementation by Real Estate Appraisal Businesses" and its Guidance Notes, for the conduct of business and to confirm the appropriateness of appraisals. These should be followed in principle when conducting valuation. In particular, they cover how to handle inappropriate clients's requests, requests for materials and the order of engineering reports to clients when starting valuations, as well as details of the real estate appraisers to be involved, the valuation system for multiple subject sites, and the treatment of the draft of appraisal reports etc. They also cover standards of quality control and information control.

の留意事項」（平成19年3月）が、不動産鑑定士又は不動産鑑定業者のみならず、証券化市場関係者の参考資料として事実上活用されてきたとの指摘も見られた。このため、これらを統合し、昨今の運用状況及び検討結果も踏まえて鑑定評価の手順に沿って再整理した「証券化対象不動産の鑑定評価に関する実務指針」を平成21年6月に策定した。平成21年8月策定された「価格等調査ガイドライン」、「証券化対象不動産の継続評価の実施に関する基本的考え方」、「継続評価の基本的考え方」等も踏まえて、以後数度改訂されている。

② 業務指針

不動産鑑定業者が、鑑定業等実務を行うにあたり指針とすべきものとして、かつ当該実務の適正さを確認するための指針として、「不動産鑑定業者の業務実施態勢に関する業務指針」および「証券化対象不動産の鑑定評価業務を実施する場合における不動産鑑定業者の業務実施態勢に関する業務指針細則」を公表している。鑑定業等実務を行う際には、原則として準拠するものとする。その内容は、価格等調査業務の受託に関しては、不適切な依頼要請への対応、受託時における資料提供の協力の要請、エンジニアリング・レポートの依頼内容を記載した書面の提出の要請が定められ、価格等調査業務の実施に関しては、関与不動産鑑定士、複数不動産の評価体制、鑑定評価書のドラフト等について定められている。その他、品質管理や情報管理について定められている。

3. Implementation of Real Estate Appraisal System

The relationships between real estate appraisers, real estate businesses, who both actually conduct appraisals, and the Appraisal Association, the MLIT or individual prefectures, who supervise the appraisal system, and outline descriptions of real estate appraisers, real estate businesses and the appraisal association are as follows.

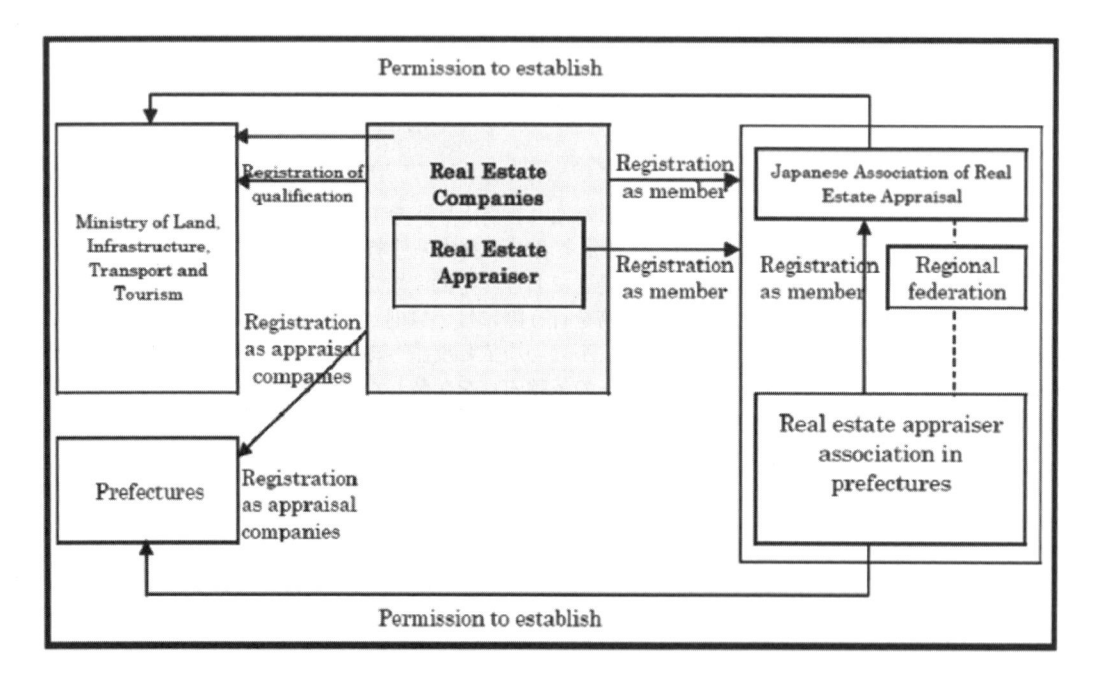

```
                        Permission to establish
   ┌─────────────────────────────────────────────────────────────┐
   │                    Registration of    ┌──────────────┐   Registration   ┌──────────────────────┐
   │   Ministry of Land,  qualification    │ Real Estate  │   as member      │ Japanese Association │
   │   Infrastructure,   ◄─────────────    │  Companies   │ ────────────►    │ of Real Estate       │
   │   Transport and                       ├──────────────┤                  │ Appraisal            │
   │   Tourism                             │ Real Estate  │   Registration   ├────────────┬─────────┤
   │                     Registration      │  Appraiser   │   as member      │Registration│ Regional│
   │                     as appraisal      └──────────────┘ ────────────►    │as member   │federation│
   │                     companies                                           └────────────┴─────────┘
   │   ┌──────────────┐  Registration                                        ┌──────────────────────┐
   │   │  Prefectures │  as appraisal                                        │ Real estate appraiser│
   │   │              │  companies                                           │ association in       │
   │   └──────────────┘                                                      │ prefectures          │
   │                                                                         └──────────────────────┘
                        Permission to establish
```

(1) Real Estate Appraisers and Real Estate Businesses

The number of Real Estate Appraisal Businesses which conducted real estate appraisals during 2010 are shown in the table below. In a few cases a business has offices in two or more prefectures employing several appraisers, but in most cases appraisers are self-employed individuals conducting appraisals within one prefecture.

3．不動産鑑定評価を実施する体制

　不動産鑑定評価を実施する不動産鑑定士・不動産鑑定業者、鑑定協会並びにこれらを指導・監督する国土交通省又は都道府県の関係と、不動産鑑定士・不動産鑑定業者、鑑定協会の概要は次の通りである。

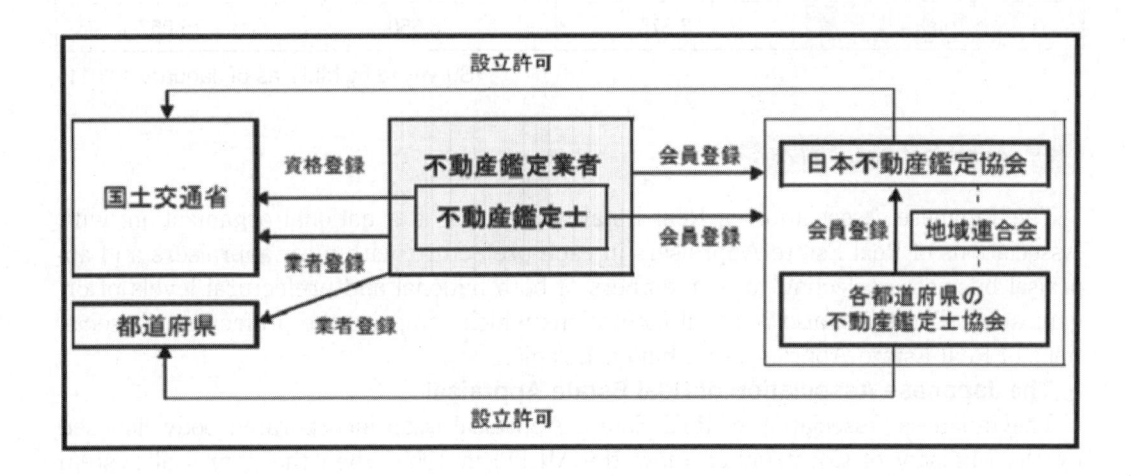

```
                          設立許可
     ┌─────────────────────────────────────────┐
     │                                         ▼
┌─────────┐  資格登録  ┌─────────────┐  会員登録  ┌─────────────┐
│         │ ◄────────  │ 不動産鑑定業者 │ ────────► │ 日本不動産   │
│ 国土交通省│           ├─────────────┤           │ 鑑定協会     │
│         │ ◄────────  │ 不動産鑑定士  │ ────────► ├──────┬──────┤
└─────────┘  業者登録  └─────────────┘  会員登録  │会員登録│地域連合会│
                                                  └──┬───┴──────┘
┌─────────┐  業者登録                                │
│ 都道府県 │ ◄──────────────────                    ▼
│         │                                   ┌─────────────┐
└─────────┘                                   │ 各都道府県の │
     ▲                                        │不動産鑑定士協会│
     │          設立許可                        └─────────────┘
     └─────────────────────────────────────────┘
```

(1) 不動産鑑定士・不動産鑑定業者

　平成22年1月1日から同年12月31日までに、鑑定評価業務を行った不動産鑑定業者数等は次頁表の通りであり、2以上の都道府県に事務所を置いて複数の不動産鑑定士が従事する鑑定業者は僅かで、1つの都道府県内において不動産鑑定士自らが不動産鑑定業者となっている個人業者がほとんどである。

Classification	Number of appraisal business	Number of appraisal office	The number of practicing appraiser
Registration at minister	81 (2.4%)	242 (6.8%)	1,025 (20.3%)
Registration at governor	3,294 (97.6%)	3,308 (93.2%)	4,032 (79.7%)
Total	3,375	3,550	5,057

(Surveyed by MLIT as of January 1,2011)

(2) *Appraisal Associations*

The Japanese Association of Real Estate Appraisal is a national organization, with Associations of Real Estate Appraisers in each prefecture, with most appraisers and appraisal businesses electing to be members of both national and prefectural levels of organization. There are also regional federations which comprise the prefectural Associations of Real Estate Appraisers within each region.

① **The Japanese Association of Real Estate Appraisal**

The Japanese Association of Real Estate Appraisal is an incorporated body licensed by the Ministry of Construction (now the MLIT) in 1965 when the appraisal system was established, with 5,843members as at the end of February 2011.

Its main functions includes drawing up appraisal operating guidance, conducting research into appraisal theory and land price surveys, in accordance with the real estate appraisal standards etc. In addition it is defined in Act on Real Estate Appraisal as the sole training institute.

② **Associations of Real Estate Appraisers**

Associations of Real Estate Appraisers have been established in all prefectures, in most cases as incorporated bodies licensed by each prefecture. Their functions are almost the same as the Japanese Association of real Estate Appraisers.

業者区分	業者数	事務所数	従事する不動産鑑定士数
大臣登録	81 (2.4%)	242 (6.8%)	1,025 (20.3%)
知事登録	3,294 (97.6%)	3,308 (93.2%)	4,032 (79.7%)
合　計	3,375	3,550	5,057

(平成23年1月1日現在　国土交通省調べ)

(2) 鑑定協会

　鑑定協会には、全国組織である日本不動産鑑定協会と都道府県毎の組織である不動産鑑定士協会があり、不動産鑑定士及び不動産鑑定業者のほとんどが両協会の会員（強制加入ではない）となっている。また、不動産鑑定士協会の地域団体である地域連合会がある。

① 日本不動産鑑定協会

　鑑定協会は、鑑定評価制度発足とともに、昭和40年に建設省（現：国土交通省）の許可を受けて設立された社団法人であり、平成23年2月末現在の総会員数は5,843人である。
主な事業として、不動産鑑定評価基準等に基づく実務指針等の策定・鑑定評価理論の研究・地価の調査等を行っているほか、不動産鑑定法に定める唯一の実務修習機関となっている。

② 不動産鑑定士協会

　不動産鑑定士協会は、全ての都道府県に設立されており、そのほとんどは各都道府県の許可を受けて設立された社団法人となっている。事業内容は、鑑定協会とほぼ同様となっている。

4. Real Estate Securitization and Real Estate Appraisal

The real estate market for investment has developed greatly in Japan over a decade as a result of the expansion of real estate securitization including J-REIT, private funds, etc. Real estate appraisal is widely used in connection with the securitization of real estate and the two are closely related.

The relationship between real estate securitization and real estate appraisal is broadly as follows.

(1) Summary of Real Estate Securitization

Real estate securitization in Japan is classified broadly as follows:
- (i) "J-REIT" as specified in the "Act on Investment Trust and Investment Corporation".
- (ii) "Special purpose companies" called "TMK : Tokutei Mokuteki Kaisha"as specified in the "Act on Securitization of Assets ".
- (iii) Businesses where a securitization scheme is defined in law, for example "Real Estate Special Joint Ventures" as specified in the "Real Estate Specified Joint Enterprise Act ".
- (iv) Businesses where a securitization scheme is not defined in law such as Limited Liability Companies called "TK(Tokumei Kumiai)-GK(Goudou Kaisha)" under the "Companies Act" and "Silent Partnerships" under the "Commercial Law" which combine as "silent partnership limited liability companies".

For reference, the basic J-REIT system is as follows. An investment corporation, in which investors have invested, entrusts its funds to an asset management company to manage their investment in real estate. There are currently 35 such corporations listed on the Tokyo Stock Exchange.

4．不動産証券化と不動産鑑定評価

　日本の不動産投資市場は、ここ数年、J-REIT やプライベートファンド等不動産証券化の拡大により飛躍的に発展してきた。また、不動産証券化に際しては不動産鑑定評価を活用する場合が多く、両者は密接な関係を有している。
　日本における不動産証券化の概要と不動産鑑定評価との関係は次の通りである。

(1) 不動産証券化の概要

日本における不動産証券化は、主に、
- (ⅰ)「投資信託及び投資法人に関する法律」に基づく「J-REIT」
- (ⅱ)「資産の流動化に関する法律」に基づく「特定目的会社（TMK：Tokutei Mokuteki Kaisya）」
- (ⅲ)「不動産特定共同事業法」に基づく「不動産特定共同事業」のように法律で証券化スキームが規定されているものと
- (ⅳ)「会社法」の合同会社と「商法」の匿名組合出資を組み合わせた「TK（Tokumei Kumiai）-GK（Goudou Kaisya）」と呼ばれるスキーム等のように法律で証券化スキームが規定されていないものがある。

　参考までに、「J-REIT」の基本的な仕組みは以下の通りであり、投資家がビークルである投資法人に出資した金銭を、投資法人から委託を受けた資産運用会社が、主として不動産に対する投資として運用する仕組みとなっている。現在35法人が東京証券取引所等に上場している。

＜Organizational Structure of J-REIT＞

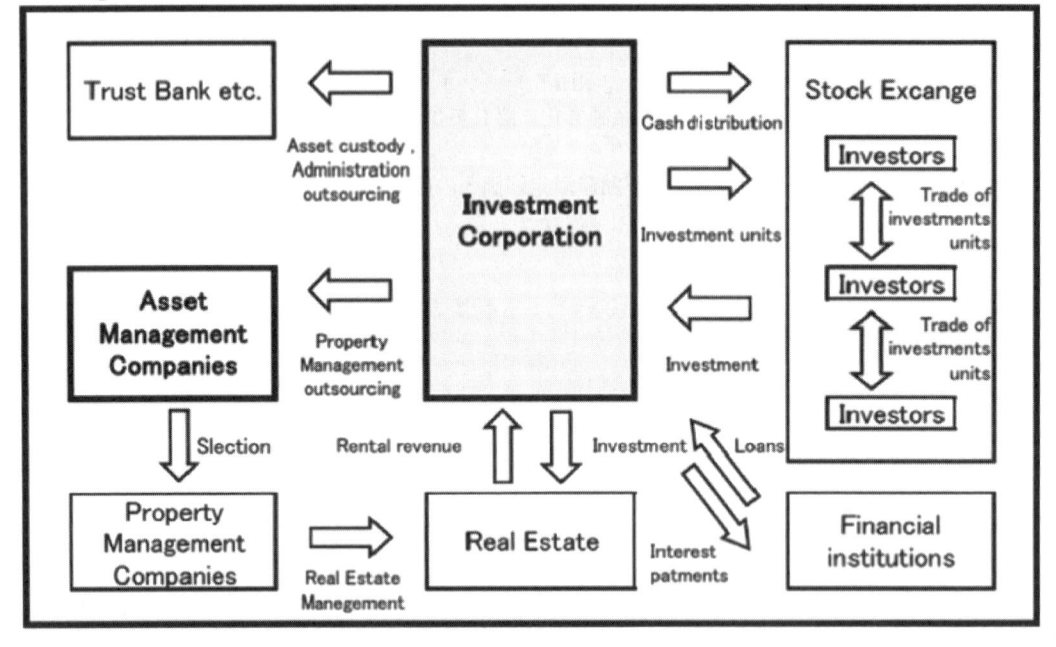

```
Trust Bank etc.  ←  Asset custody,        Investment    ⇒ Cash distribution   Stock Excange
                    Administration        Corporation                          Investors ⇅ Trade of investments units
                    outsourcing                         ⇒ Investment units     Investors ⇅ Trade of investments units
Asset
Management       ←  Property                            ←  Investment          Investors
Companies           Management
                    outsourcing
    ↓Slection       Rental revenue   ↑↓ Investment   Loans
Property                                                        Financial
Management       ⇒  Real Estate      Real Estate    Interest    institutions
Companies           Manegement                      patments
```

(2) Relationship between Securitization of Real Estate and Real Estate Appraisal

Among those involved in the securitization of real estate, the main organizations to request appraisals of real estate are asset management companies, with most real estate appraisals being required for the following purposes.

① **Appraisals required by law**

Among the schemes above, according to (i) the "Act on Investment Trust and Investment Corporation" and (ii) the "Act on Securitization of Assets", a real estate appraisal is required for J-REIT etc under these acts for assets that are real estate.

② **Appraisals not required by law, but commercially required**

In cases other than (1) above, appraisal is not required by law. However, in cases of securitization, real estate appraisal is frequently required. In addition the asset management company is required to register as a financial transaction company in accordance with the "Financial Instruments and Exchange Act" as amended in 2007. In addition, it is inspected by monitoring organizations such as the Securities and Exchange Surveillance Commission of the Financial Services Agency and real estate appraisals are an important feature of these inspections and supervision. Real estate appraisal is thus frequently required for management purposes.

<J-REITの基本的な仕組み>

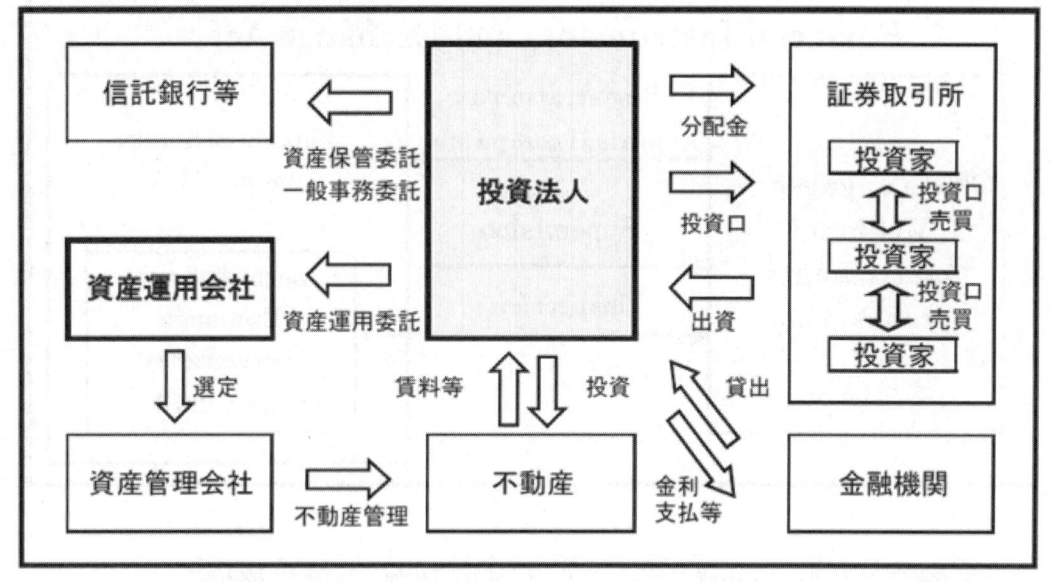

(2) 不動産証券化と不動産鑑定評価の関係

　不動産証券化関係者のうち、主として不動産鑑定評価を依頼するのは資産運用会社であるが、不動産証券化に当たっては、次の通り不動産鑑定評価が必要となることが多い。

① 法律によって必要な鑑定評価
　前記のスキームのうち、(i)「投資信託及び投資法人に関する法律」と(ii)「資産の流動化に関する法律」においては、これらの規制下にある J-REIT 等の運用資産が不動産である場合には不動産鑑定評価が義務付けされている。

② 法律には義務はないが運用上必要な鑑定評価
　一方、(1)以外については、法律による義務はないが、不動産証券化の商慣行上、不動産鑑定評価を活用する場合が多い。また、平成19年に改正された「金融商品取引法」により、資産運用会社は同法による金融商品取引業者としての登録が義務づけられ、金融庁に置かれた証券取引等監視委員会の検査対象になるなど、不動産鑑定評価が、監督や検査においても重要視されている。これらのことから、不動産鑑定評価が、運用上必要となる場合が多くなっている。

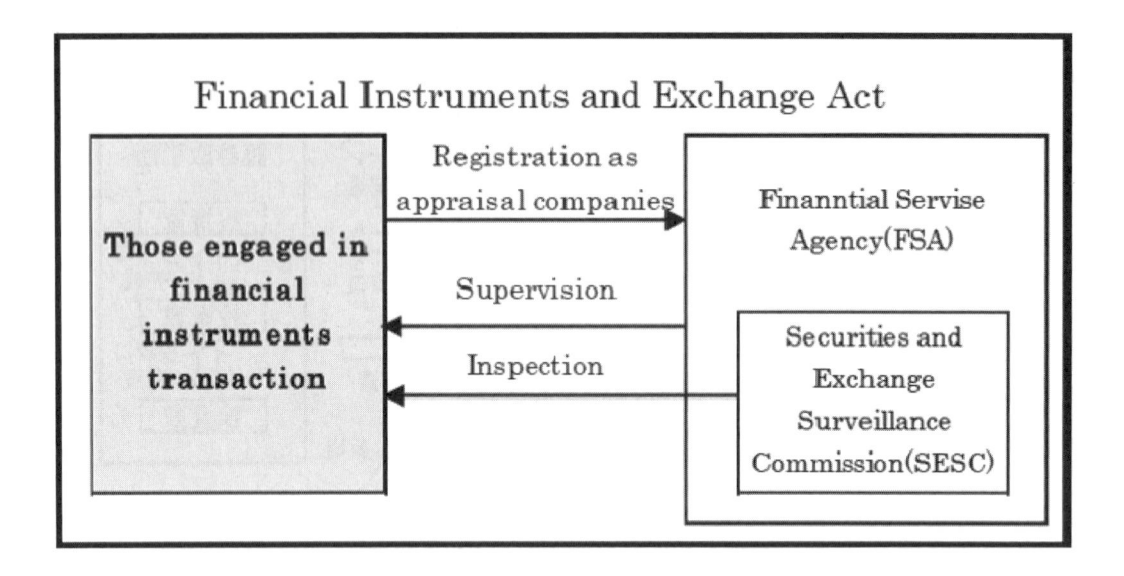

Financial Instruments and Exchange Act

```
Those engaged in           Registration as
financial          ──appraisal companies──▶   Finanntial Servise
instruments                                    Agency(FSA)
transaction        ◀────Supervision─────
                                               Securities and
                   ◀────Inspection──────       Exchange
                                               Surveillance
                                               Commission(SESC)
```

(3) Government Monitoring of Appraisal of Real Estate for Securitization

The MLIT monitors the appraisal process for the purposes of ensuring compliance with regulations and improving the market reliability of appraisals.

(4) On-site inspection of Real Estate Appraisal Businesses by Government

The MLIT has been conducting on-site inspections of real estate appraisal businesses since 2008. In 2010 the Ministry issued the "Policy for Conducting On-site Inspections of Businesses Appraising Real Estate, 2010", based on the "Outline for Inspecting the Business Operation of Real Estate Appraisal Businesses" for inspecting real estate appraisal businesses involved with conducting appraisals of securitized real estate.

(5) Sanctions to be Applied in the Event of Unlawful Appraisals or Other Violations

The sanctions in the laws relating to real estate appraisal for unlawful appraisal and violations are the basis for applying disciplinary sanctions to real estate appraisers and supervisory sanctions to real estate appraisal businesses.

```
┌─────────────────────────────────────────────────┐
│              金融商品取引法                      │
│  ┌─────────┐     業者登録      ┌──────────┐   │
│  │金融商品取│ ───────────────▶ │  金融庁  │   │
│  │引業者   │     指導・監督    │          │   │
│  │         │ ◀───────────────  ├──────────┤   │
│  │         │       検査        │証券取引等│   │
│  │         │ ◀───────────────  │監視委員会│   │
│  └─────────┘                   └──────────┘   │
└─────────────────────────────────────────────────┘
```

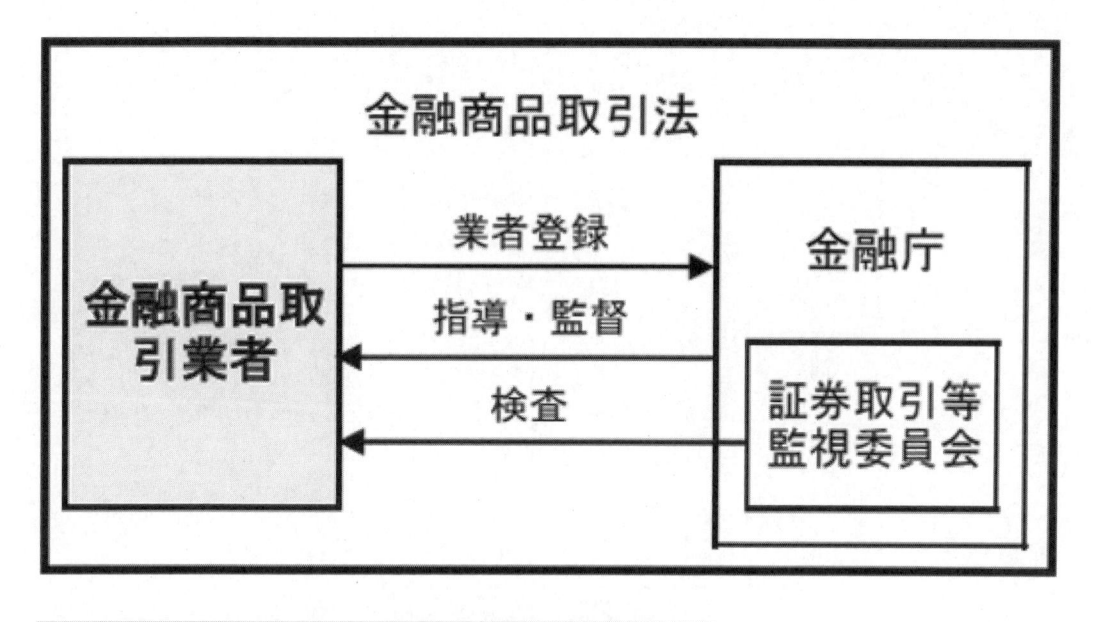

(3) 国による証券化対象不動産の鑑定評価モニタリング

　国土交通省では、その規定の運用状況を把握し、市場における鑑定評価の信頼性を向上させることを目的に、鑑定評価モニタリングを実施している。

(4) 国による不動産鑑定業者への立入検査

　国土交通省では、平成20年度より不動産鑑定業者への立入検査を実施している。平成22年度は、「不動産鑑定業者の業務等の検査実施要綱」に基づき「平成22年度における不動産鑑定業者に対する立入検査の実施方針」を定め、証券化対象不動産の鑑定評価を行った不動産鑑定業者を対象に検査を実施することとしている。

(5) 不当な鑑定評価等及び違反行為に係る処分基準

　不当な鑑定評価等及び違反行為に係る処分基準は、不動産の鑑定評価に関する法律に基づき、不動産鑑定士に対する懲戒処分又は不動産鑑定業者に対する監督処分を行う際の基準となるものである。

II

Specific Standards Chapter 3 of Real Estate Appraisal Standards

不動産鑑定評価基準（各論第 3 章）

This chapter Ⅱ is part of the chapter Ⅴ-3, "Real Estate Appraisal Standards". It is established in a separated chapter in order to set the Appraisal of the Securitized Real Estate in particular.

このⅡは、本書Ⅴ-3の不動産鑑定評価基準の一部である。証券化対象不動産の鑑定評価について特別に定める目的で設けられているため、本書ではⅡとして別立てにしたものである。

CHAPTER 3. APPRAISAL OF REAL ESTATE VALUE SUBJECT TO SECURITIZATION

Section 1. Basic Approach to Securitization-Properties

I Definition of Securitization-Properties

In this chapter, the term "securitization-properties" refers to properties (including those held under trust beneficiary rights), which are subject to or likely to become subject to a real estate transaction of any of the following types.

(1) Assets undergoing liquidation as specified in the *Asset Liquidation Law (Shisan Ryudoka Ho)*; real estate transactions involving investment trusts as specified in the *Investment Trust and Investment Corporation Law (Toshin Ho or Kaisei SPC Ho)* ; or real estate transactions undertaken by investment corporations as defined in that law.

(2) Real estate transactions related to contracts involving real estate syndication as defined in the Real Estate Syndication Act (Fudosan Kyodo Jigyo Ho).

(3) Real estate transactions generating income or profit, and undertaken for the main purpose of fulfilling obligations on securities as specified in the *Financial Instruments Trading Law (Kinsho Ho)*, Article 2, Paragraph 1, No. 5, No. 9 (which deals only with stock corporations established for the sole purpose of real estate trading, including limited companies (yugen kaisha), which survive as stock corporations under Article 2, Paragraph 1 of the *Law Concerning the Coordination, Etc. of Relevant Laws Relating to the Enforcement of the Corporation Act)*, No. 14, or No. 16, or property rights considered to be securities under Paragraph 2, No. 1, 3, or 5 of that article.

The appraisal of securitization properties must be conducted as is prescribed in this chapter. A statement to this effect must be included in the appraisal report.

Even when appraising properties other than securitization properties, it is important that the appraiser endeavor to conduct the appraisal as is prescribed in this chapter for appraisals of a large-scale rental property held for investment purposes, and whenever it is considered necessary to protect the investor, purchaser, or other interested party.

II Responsibility of LREAs

(1) LREAs must always conduct appraisals in a manner giving full consideration to the proper procedures for the appraisal of securitization properties, while recognizing that they (LREAs) exert a significant influence on the decision making, not only of the persons requesting the appraisal of securitization properties (hereinafter referred to as "clients") but also of a wide range of investors and others, and also keeping in mind that they (LREAs) bear the important responsibility of upholding the public reputation of the real estate appraisal profession.

(2) When appraising a property for securitization purposes, the LREA should seek to facilitate the securitization, etc., of the property by providing the client with explanations of the data, procedures, and other matters related to the appraisal, thereby enhancing the client's understanding, and obtaining his cooperation. The LREA must also take care as to the way information is presented in the appraisal report in order

第3章　証券化対象不動産の価格に関する鑑定評価

第1節　証券化対象不動産の鑑定評価の基本的姿勢
Ⅰ　証券化対象不動産の範囲
　この章において「証券化対象不動産」とは、次のいずれかに該当する不動産取引の目的である不動産又は不動産取引の目的となる見込みのある不動産（信託受益権に係るものを含む。）をいう。
(1) 資産の流動化に関する法律に規定する資産の流動化並びに投資信託及び投資法人に関する法律に規定する投資信託に係る不動産取引並びに同法に規定する投資法人が行う不動産取引
(2) 不動産特定共同事業法に規定する不動産特定共同事業契約に係る不動産取引
(3) 金融商品取引法第2条第1項第5号、第9号（専ら不動産取引を行うことを目的として設置された株式会社（会社法の施行に伴う関係法律の整備等に関する法律第2条第1項の規定により株式会社として存続する有限会社を含む。）に係るものに限る。）、第14号及び第16号に規定する有価証券並びに同条第2項第1号、第3号及び第5号の規定により有価証券とみなされる権利の債務の履行等を主たる目的として収益又は利益を生ずる不動産取引

　証券化対象不動産の鑑定評価は、この章の定めるところに従って行わなければならない。この場合において、鑑定評価報告書にその旨を記載しなければならない。
　証券化対象不動産以外の不動産の鑑定評価を行う場合にあっても、投資用の賃貸大型不動産の鑑定評価を行う場合その他の投資家及び購入者等の保護の観点から必要と認められる場合には、この章の定めに準じて、鑑定評価を行うよう努めなければならない。

Ⅱ　不動産鑑定士の責務
(1) 不動産鑑定士は、証券化対象不動産の鑑定評価の依頼者（以下単に「依頼者」という。）のみならず広範な投資家等に重大な影響を及ぼすことを考慮するとともに、不動産鑑定評価制度に対する社会的信頼性の確保等について重要な責任を有していることを認識し、証券化対象不動産の鑑定評価の手順について常に最大限の配慮を行いつつ、鑑定評価を行わなければならない。
(2) 不動産鑑定士は、証券化対象不動産の鑑定評価を行う場合にあっては、証券化対象不動産の証券化等が円滑に行なわれるよう配慮しつつ、鑑定評価に係る資料及び手順等を依頼者に説明し、理解を深め、かつ、協力を得るものとする。また、証券化対象不動産の鑑定評価書については、依頼者及び証券化対象不動産に係る利害関係者その他の者がその内容を容易に把握・比較することができるようにするため、鑑定評価報告書の記載方法等を工夫し、及び鑑定評価に活用した資料等を明示することができるようにするなど説明責任が十分に果たされるものとしなければならない。

to make the content of the appraisal report on the securitization property easier for the client, persons holding interests in the securitization property, and others to understand and use in comparisons with reports on other properties. The LREA must be fully accountable, ensuring that the data and other informational materials used in the appraisal are available for disclosure.

(3) Whenever several LREAs are working jointly on the appraisal of a securitization-property, the roles of each LREA must be clearly defined, and all of the LREAs must work as a team to complete the appraisal assignment, sharing information on the overall appraisal and maintaining close and thorough collaboration.

Section 2. Drafting a Work Plan for the Appraisal

I   Verifying the data needed to develop the work plan

When drafting a work plan for the appraisal, the LREA should verify with the client in advance matters related to the appraisal of a securitization property, in order to develop an appropriate and reasonable work plan that allows competent and reliable implementation of the appraisal. The verified information should be reflected in the work plan for the appraisal, and the plan should be changed whenever any change occurs in the information specified. Matters that should be verified include:

(1) Purpose of the request for the appraisal and background as to why the request was made.

(2) Classification of the subject property transaction under (1), (2), or (3) of Section 1, I above.

(3) Main subjects covered in the engineering report (an investigative report on the condition of the securitization property, conducted by a person having specialized knowledge of buildings, mechanical and electrical [M&E] systems, environmental matters, etc.; the same applies in Section 3 below), data needed to apply DCF analysis, and other relevant documents; and the time when these documents will be available.

(4) Whether there are explanatory comments from the preparer of the engineering report.

(5) Scope of the field surveys, including visual inspection of the interior of the subject property.

(6) Other matters needed to develop the work plan for the appraisal.

II   Records of verified information

After verifying the matters listed in (1) through (6) of Section 2, I (1) above, records must be prepared for each of these items, and these records must be attached to the appraisal report as appendices. Included among these records are:

(1) Date verified

(2) Name of the LREA who verified the information

(3) Name and occupation of the person who provided the verification

(4) Content of the information confirmed, and whether it has been reflected in the work plan for the appraisal

(5) Details of any changes in the appraisal procedures or changes in the content of the

(3) 証券化対象不動産の鑑定評価を複数の不動産鑑定士が共同して行う場合にあっては、それぞれの不動産鑑定士の役割を明確にした上で、常に鑑定評価業務全体の情報を共有するなど密接かつ十分な連携の下、すべての不動産鑑定士が一体となって鑑定評価の業務を遂行しなければならない。

第2節　処理計画の策定
I　処理計画の策定に当たっての確認事項
処理計画の策定に当たっては、あらかじめ、依頼者に対し、証券化対象不動産の鑑定評価に関する次の事項を確認し、鑑定評価の作業の円滑かつ確実な実施を行うことができるよう適切かつ合理的な処理計画を策定するものとする。この場合において、確認された事項については、処理計画に反映するとともに、当該事項に変更があった場合にあっては、処理計画を変更するものとする。
(1) 鑑定評価の依頼目的及び依頼が必要となった背景
(2) 対象不動産が第1節Ⅰ(1)、(2)又は(3)のいずれに係るものであるかの別
(3) エンジニアリング・レポート（建築物、設備等及び環境に関する専門的知識を有する者が行った証券化対象不動産の状況に関する調査報告書をいう。以下同じ。）、ＤＣＦ法等を適用するために必要となる資料その他の資料の主な項目及びその入手時期
(3) エンジニアリング・レポートを作成した者からの説明の有無
(5) 対象不動産の内覧の実施を含めた実地調査の範囲
(6) その他処理計画の策定のために必要な事項

Ⅱ　確認事項の記録
第2節Ⅰ(1)から(6)までの事項の確認を行った場合には、それぞれ次の事項に関する記録を作成し、及び鑑定評価報告書の附属資料として添付しなければならない。
(1) 確認を行った年月日
(2) 確認を行った不動産鑑定士の氏名
(3) 確認の相手方の氏名及び職業
(4) 確認の内容及び当該内容の処理計画への反映状況
(5) 確認の内容の変更により鑑定評価の作業、内容等の変更をする場合にあっては、その内容

report, etc., which were made as a result of changes in the verified information

III Purpose of the request for the appraisal, and the relationship between the client and the parties involved in the securitization of the property

In many cases, a wide variety of parties are involved and hold complex interests in a securitization-property. The appraisal report must state the purpose of the request for the appraisal of the securitization property, the background as to why the request was made, and the following items concerning the interests of the client with regard to the securitization property.

(1) Whether the client holds interests in the securitization of the property (parties such as an originator, arranger, asset manager, lender, equity investor, special purpose company [SPC], corporate investor, or funding agency [referred to below as parties involved in the securitization"] should be identified).

(2) Whether the client has capital ties or business connections to any of the parties involved in the securitization; and if so, the details of those relationships.

(3) The details of any other special interests between the client and any of the parties involved in the securitization.

Section 3. Investigating Property-Specific Value Influences acting on the Securitization-Property

I Investigation of property-specific value influences acting on the subject property

In the investigation of property-specific value influences acting on a securitization property, there must be a reliable and detailed confirmation of information about the physical and legal characteristics of the securitization property. The field survey for the requested appraisal of the securitization property, including the visual inspection of the interior of the subject property, must be conducted in the presence of the client (or persons designated by the client); and the data needed for the appraisal, including the identification of associated rights and interests, restrictions under public statute, the presence of toxic substances such as asbestos, determination of earthquake resistance, and the history of remodeling, expansion, etc., must be verified by means such as interviews with the manager, etc., of the subject property.

II Property inspection

The LREA must include the following matters relating to the field survey in the appraisal report.

(1) Date of the field survey.

(2) Name of the LREA who performed the field survey.

(3) Names and occupations of witnesses to the survey and managers of the subject property.

(4) Scope of the field survey (including whether or not the interior was visually inspected) and matters verified in the field survey.

(5) If it was not possible to perform any part of the field survey, the reasons must be stated.

Ⅲ　鑑定評価の依頼目的及び依頼者の証券化関係者との関係
　　証券化対象不動産については、関係者が多岐にわたり利害関係が複雑であることも多く、証券化対象不動産の鑑定評価の依頼目的及び依頼が必要となった背景等並びに依頼者と証券化対象不動産との利害関係に関する次の事項を鑑定評価報告書に記載しなければならない。
(1)　依頼者が証券化対象不動産の証券化に係る利害関係者（オリジネーター、アレンジャー、アセットマネジャー、レンダー、エクイティ投資家又は特別目的会社・投資法人・ファンド等をいい、以下「証券化関係者」という。）のいずれであるかの別
(2)　依頼者と証券化関係者との資本関係又は取引関係の有無及びこれらの関係を有する場合にあっては、その内容
(3)　その他依頼者と証券化関係者との特別な利害関係を有する場合にあっては、その内容

第3節　証券化対象不動産の個別的要因の調査等

Ⅰ　対象不動産の個別的要因の調査等
　　証券化対象不動産の個別的要因の調査等に当たっては、証券化対象不動産の物的・法的確認を確実かつ詳細に行うため、依頼された証券化対象不動産の鑑定評価のための実地調査について、依頼者（依頼者が指定した者を含む。）の立会いの下、対象不動産の内覧の実施を含めた実地調査を行うとともに、対象不動産の管理者からの聴聞等により権利関係、公法上の規制、アスベスト等の有害物質、耐震性及び増改築等の履歴等に関し鑑定評価に必要な事項を確認しなければならない。

Ⅱ　実地調査
　　不動産鑑定士は、実地調査に関し、次の事項を鑑定評価報告書に記載しなければならない。
(1)　実地調査を行った年月日
(2)　実地調査を行った不動産鑑定士の氏名
(3)　立会人及び対象不動産の管理者の氏名及び職業
(4)　実地調査を行った範囲（内覧の有無を含む。）及び実地調査により確認した内容
(5)　実地調査の一部を実施することができなかった場合にあっては、その理由

III Handling of the engineering report, and the property investigation by the LREA

(1) In the appraisal of a securitization property, the LREA must ask the client to submit the engineering report required for the appraisal, and after analyzing and evaluating its content, the LREA must incorporate its conclusions in the appraisal. However, if no engineering report is submitted, or if its content is considered to be inadequate for use in the appraisal, the LREA must then take action such as conducting an independent investigation to substitute for the engineering report and thereby fulfill the requirements of the assignment; and the appraisal report must describe the results of that investigation as well as the reasons why it is considered to be appropriate.

(2) For example, the engineering report could be lacking or inadequate for use in reappraising a securitization property, which has previously been appraised, or the securitization property may be an empty lot (or one on which the buildings are to be demolished).

(3) The appraisal report must include a statement of what decision was made as to whether or not to use the content of the engineering report in the appraisal, along with the reasons for that decision. For all the items listed in the following table, the information specified must be included in the appraisal report. Appendix 1 provides a sample format for an appraisal report. The same applies in the case of the second statement at III (1) above (beginning with " however").

Item	Content
Basic information about the engineering report	· Name, etc., of the preparer of the engineering report · Date of the investigation undertaken for the engineering report, and date when the engineering report was prepared
How the engineering report was obtained, and how it was handled in the appraisal	· Party providing the engineering report (name, occupation, etc.) · Date obtained · Whether explanatory comments were obtained from the preparer of the engineering report · How the engineering report was handled in the appraisal
Method of investigation of property-specific influences , which is required for the appraisal	Statement as to whether the engineering report was used for the investigation of property-specific influences, or whether the LREA investigated these influences himself (the investigation may have also been done by another expert, at the request of the LREA): Property-specific influences to be investigated include: · Regulations and restrictions under public and private statutes (including the state of compliance with the law) · Renovation plan · Replacement cost · Building environment with regard to toxic substances, including asbestos · Soil pollution

Ⅲ　エンジニアリング・レポートの取扱いと不動産鑑定士が行う調査
(1)　証券化対象不動産の鑑定評価に当たっては、不動産鑑定士は、依頼者に対し当該鑑定評価に際し必要なエンジニアリング・レポートの提出を求め、その内容を分析・判断した上で、鑑定評価に活用しなければならない。ただし、エンジニアリング・レポートの提出がない場合又はその記載された内容が鑑定評価に活用する資料として不十分であると認められる場合には、エンジニアリング・レポートに代わるものとして不動産鑑定士が調査を行うなど鑑定評価を適切に行うため対応するものとし、対応した内容及びそれが適切であると判断した理由について、鑑定評価報告書に記載しなければならない。
(2)　エンジニアリング・レポートの提出がない場合又はその記載されている内容が不十分である場合として想定される場合を例示すれば、既に鑑定評価が行われたことがある証券化対象不動産の再評価をする場合、証券化対象不動産が更地である場合（建物を取り壊す予定である場合を含む。）等がある。
(3)　エンジニアリング・レポートの内容を鑑定評価に活用するか否かの検討に当たっては、その判断及び根拠について、鑑定評価報告書に記載しなければならない。この場合においては、少なくとも次の表の項目ごとに、それぞれ同表に掲げる内容を鑑定評価報告書に記載しなければならない。この場合における鑑定評価報告書の様式の例は、別表１のとおりとする。なお、(1)ただし書きの場合においても、同様とする。

項　　目	内　　容
エンジニアリング・レポートの基本的属性	・エンジニアリング・レポートの作成者の名称等 ・エンジニアリング・レポートの調査が行われた日及び作成された日
エンジニアリング・レポートの入手経緯、対応方針等	・入手先（氏名及び職業等） ・入手した日 ・エンジニアリング・レポートの作成者からの説明の有無等 ・入手したエンジニアリング・レポートについて鑑定評価を行う上での対応方針等
鑑定評価に必要となる専門性の高い個別的要因に関する調査	次に掲げる専門性の高い個別的要因に関する調査について、エンジニアリング・レポートを活用するか又は不動産鑑定士の調査を実施（不動産鑑定士が他の専門家へ調査を依頼する場合を含む。）するかの別 ・公法上及び私法上の規制、制約等（法令遵守状況調査を含む。） ・修繕計画 ・再調達価格 ・有害な物質（アスベスト等）に係る建物環境 ・土壌汚染 ・地震リスク ・耐震性 ・地下埋設物

	・Earthquake risk ・Earthquake resistance ・Buried structures or objects
LREA's conclusions about the method of investigation of property-specific influences, which is required for the appraisal	Decisions on whether to use the content of the engineering report or an investigation by the LREA of property-specific influences, along with the reasons for that decision, etc.

(4) Because the engineering report may need to be revised or supplemented owing to changes in the market environment for real estate securitization, the LREA must maintain close contact with the preparer of the engineering report, and must also endeavor to improve his own knowledge and understanding of engineering reports.

Section 4. Application of DCF method

When appraising the value of a securitization property by the income approach, DCF method must be applied. In addition, it is also appropriate to apply direct capitalization method for verification.

Ⅰ Clarifying the procedure for applying DCF method

(1) The appraisal report must include statements regarding the suitability of the data used to determine the property's value by the income approach. Along with the reasons for the conclusion, these statements must indicate the following:

① Whether the data that was obtained from the client for the subject property, such as the income and expense amounts, has been used without modification.

② Whether the data that was obtained from the client for the subject property, such as the income and expense amounts, has been adjusted or modified.

③ Whether the LREA himself has obtained data for the subject property, such as the income and expense amounts.

(2) When DCF method is used to determine the value by the income approach, in addition to explaining the selection of the terminal capitalization rate, discount rate, forecasts of future income and expenses, and other individual items that have been assessed, the appraisal report must lay out the procedure by which that data was used to determine the value by the income approach and the reasons for using that procedure, clearly indicating such factors as the possibility of change in the economic situation, the specific comparables which were examined, and the logical consistency. When several LREAs work jointly to appraise a group of securitization properties, they must endeavor to ensure logical consistency among all of the subject properties with regard to the selection of terminal capitalization rates, discount rates, forecasts of future income and expenses, and other data used in applying DCF method.

鑑定評価に必要となる専門性の高い個別的要因に関する調査についての不動産鑑定士の判断	専門性の高い個別的要因に関する調査に関する対応について、エンジニアリング・レポートの記載内容を活用した場合、不動産鑑定士の調査で対応した場合等の内容、根拠等

(4) エンジニアリング・レポートについては、不動産証券化市場の環境の変化に対応してその内容の改善・充実が図られていくことにかんがみ、エンジニアリング・レポートを作成する者との密接な連携を図りつつ、常に自らのエンジニアリング・レポートに関する知識・理解を深めるための研鑽に努めなければならない。

第4節　DCF法の適用等

証券化対象不動産の鑑定評価における収益価格を求めるに当たっては、DCF法を適用しなければならない。この場合において、併せて直接還元法を適用することにより検証を行うことが適切である。

I　DCF法の適用過程等の明確化

(1) DCF法の適用に当たっては、DCF法による収益価格を求める際に活用する資料を次に定める区分に応じて、その妥当性や判断の根拠等を鑑定評価報告書に記載しなければならない。
　① 依頼者から入手した対象不動産に係る収益又は費用の額その他の資料をそのまま活用する場合
　② 依頼者から入手した対象不動産に係る収益又は費用の額その他の資料に修正等を加える場合
　③ 自らが入手した対象不動産に係る収益又は費用の額その他の資料を活用する場合

(2) DCF法による収益価格を求める場合に当たっては、最終還元利回り、割引率、収益及び費用の将来予測等査定した個々の項目等に関する説明に加え、それらを採用して収益価格を求める過程及びその理由について、経済事情の変動の可能性、具体的に検証した事例及び論理的な整合性等を明確にしつつ、鑑定評価報告書に記載しなければならない。また、複数の不動産鑑定士が共同して複数の証券化対象不動産の鑑定評価を行う場合にあっては、DCF法の適用において活用する最終還元利回り、割引率、収益及び費用の将来予測等について対象不動産相互間の論理的な整合性を図らなければならない。

(3) 鑑定評価報告書には、DCF法で査定した収益価格（直接還元法による検証を含む。）と原価法及び取引事例比較法等で求めた試算価格との関連について明確にしつつ、鑑定評価額を決定した理由について記載しなければならない。

(4) DCF法の適用については、今後、さらなる精緻化に向けて自己研鑽に努めることにより、説明責任の向上を図る必要がある。

(3) The appraisal report must contain a clear statement of the relationship between the value indicated by the income approach, using DCF method (including verification by direct capitalization), and the indicated value using the cost approach, and sales comparison approach; and the appraisal report must also state the reasons for concluding the final opinion of value.

(4) The LREA must strive for greater accountability, endeavoring to improve his own knowledge and understanding in order to achieve further proficiency in the application of DCF method.

II Uniformity in income and expense items in DCF method

(1) When using DCF method to determine the value by the income approach, the income and expense amounts for the securitization property (hereinafter referred to as "income and expense items") must be entered in the appraisal report for each of several continuous time periods, classified according to the items shown in the following table. Each of the income and expense items should be accompanied by a breakdown of how the figures were calculated. When entering this data in the appraisal report, each item in the "Item" column of the following table should be defined as specified in the table.

	Item	Definition
Effective gross income	Potential gross income	When all or a portion of the subject property is rented or operated by a contractor, the recurring income (assuming full occupancy).
	Income from common area charges	Income collected under contracts with tenants for that portion of the recurring expenses in the maintenance, management, and operation of the subject property (including expenses for electricity, water, gas, regional heating and air conditioning, etc.), which apply to the common areas.
	Utility fee income	Income collected under contracts with tenants for that portion of the recurring expenses for electricity, water, gas, regional heating and air conditioning, etc., in the operation of the subject property, which apply to leased areas (assuming full occupancy).
	Parking fee income	Income from leasing the subject property's parking spaces to tenants, or from renting parking spaces by the hour.
	Other income	Other income from facility installation fees for signs, antennas, vending machines, etc., and income from lump-sum payments, which are not refundable, such as key money and renewal fees.
	Vacancy allowance	Decrease in each income item, based on predicted vacancies, periods it will take to replace tenants, etc.
	Collection losses allowance	Decrease in each income item, based on predicted debt collection losses.
Operating expenses	Maintenance and management expenses	Recurring expenses for the maintenance and management of the subject property, including building and mechanical and electrical (M&E) system management, security, and cleaning.
	Utility expenses	Expenses for electricity, water, gas, regional heating and air conditioning, etc., incurred in the operation of the subject property.
	Repair expenses	That portion of the expenditures for building and M&E system repair, renovation, etc., of the subject property, which is a recurring expense

Ⅱ　DCF法の収益費用項目の統一等

(1)　DCF法の適用により収益価格を求めるに当たっては、証券化対象不動産に係る収益又は費用の額につき、連続する複数の期間ごとに、次の表の項目（以下「収益費用項目」という。）に区分して鑑定評価報告書に記載しなければならない（収益費用項目ごとに、記載した数値の積算内訳等を付記するものとする）。この場合において、同表の項目の欄に掲げる項目の定義は、それぞれ同表の定義の欄に掲げる定義のとおりとする。

	項　目	定　義
運営収益	貸室賃料収入	対象不動産の全部又は貸室部分について賃貸又は運営委託をすることにより経常的に得られる収入（満室想定）
	共益費収入	対象不動産の維持管理・運営において経常的に要する費用（電気・水道・ガス・地域冷暖房熱源等に要する費用を含む）のうち、共用部分に係るものとして賃借人との契約により徴収する収入（満室想定）
	水道光熱費収入	対象不動産の運営において電気・水道・ガス・地域冷暖房熱源等に要する費用のうち、貸室部分に係るものとして賃借人との契約により徴収する収入（満室想定）
	駐車場収入	対象不動産に附属する駐車場をテナント等に賃貸することによって得られる収入及び駐車場を時間貸しすることによって得られる収入
	その他収入	その他看板、アンテナ、自動販売機等の施設設置料、礼金・更新料等の返還を要しない一時金等の収入
	空室等損失	各収入について空室や入替期間等の発生予測に基づく減少分
	貸倒れ損失	各収入について貸倒れの発生予測に基づく減少分
運営費用	維持管理費	建物・設備管理、保安警備、清掃等対象不動産の維持・管理のために経常的に要する費用
	水道光熱費	対象不動産の運営において電気・水道・ガス・地域冷暖房熱源等に要する費用
	修繕費	対象不動産に係る建物、設備等の修理、改良等のために支出した金額のうち当該建物、設備等の通常の維持管理のため、又は一部がき損した建物、設備等につきその原状を回復するために経常的に要する費用
	プロパティマネジメントフィー	対象不動産の管理業務に係る経費
	テナント募集費用等	新規テナントの募集に際して行われる仲介業務や広告宣伝等に要する費用及びテナントの賃貸借契約の更新や再契約業務に要する費用等

		for ordinary building and M&E system maintenance and management, etc., or is expended to restore damaged building and M&E system portions to their original condition.
	Property management fees	Expenses for management services in the subject property.
	Tenant recruitment expenses, etc.	Expenses for rental agency services, advertising, etc., to recruit new tenants; and expenses for lease renewal or repeat leasing contracts with existing tenants.
	Real estate taxes	Property taxes (on land, buildings, and depreciable assets) and city planning taxes (on land and buildings).
	Casualty insurance premiums	Premiums for fire insurance on the subject property and accessory equipment; liability insurance for losses by third parties, etc., due to subject property defects or management failures, etc.
	Other expenses	Other expenses for ground rent, road occupancy and utilization, etc.
Net Operating Income		Operating income minus operating expenses.
Operating profit on lump-sum payments		Operating profit on security deposits and other lump-sum payments, which are f refundable deposits.
Capital expenditures		That portion of expenditures for building and M&E system repair, renovation, etc., which is recognized as increasing the value of the building, M&E system, etc., or strengthening its durability.
Net Cash Flow(Adjusted NOI)		Net operating income, plus operating profit on lump-sum payments, minus capital expenditures.

(2) When using DCF analysis to determine the value by the income approach, the LREA must identify and explain the income and expense items and their definitions to the client before obtaining the requisite data, and must check that each income and expense item corresponds to its specified definition.

(3) Appendix 2 is a sample format for an appraisal report when DCF analysis is applied. This format may be revised as is necessary to conform to the specific appraisal situation, based on factors such as the purpose and the category of the securitization property.

	公租公課	固定資産税（土地・建物・償却資産）、都市計画税（土地・建物）
	損害保険料	対象不動産及び附属設備に係る火災保険、対象不動産の欠陥や管理上の事故による第三者等の損害を担保する賠償責任保険等の料金
	その他費用	その他支払地代、道路占用使用料等の費用
運営純収益		運営収益から運営費用を控除して得た額
一時金の運用益		預り金的性格を有する保証金等の運用益
資本的支出		対象不動産に係る建物、設備等の修理、改良等のために支出した金額のうち当該建物、設備等の価値を高め、又はその耐久性を増すこととなると認められる部分に対応する支出
純収益		運営純収益に一時金の運用益を加算し資本的支出を控除した額

(2) ＤＣＦ法の適用により収益価格を求めるに当たっては、収益費用項目及びその定義について依頼者に提示・説明した上で必要な資料を入手するとともに、収益費用項目ごとに定められた定義に該当していることを確認しなければならない。

(3) ＤＣＦ法を適用する際の鑑定評価報告書の様式の例は、別表２のとおりとする。証券化対象不動産の用途、類型等に応じて、実務面での適合を工夫する場合は、同表２に必要な修正を加えるものとする。

Appendix 1

LREA		Affiliation	

Basic information about the engineering report and its acquisition

Basic information about the engineering report and its acquisition		Preparer	Client
	A		
	B		
	C		
	D		

How the submitted engineering report was handled in the appraisal; whether an additional investigation by the LREA was needed; results of the investigation by LREA, etc.	

Results of the investigation and preparer comments (Enter A, B, C, or D in the "Preparer" column)	Explanatory comments from the preparer	Item	Was the engineering report used, or did LREA conduct an investigation?
1. Building condition survey		Location overview	
		Building overview	
		M&E system overview	
		Structural overview	
		Regulations and restrictions under public and private statutes (state of compliance with the law)	
		Renovation/renewal history and plans	
		Emergency repair/renewal expenses	
		Short-term repair/renewal expenses	
		Long-term repair/renewal expenses	
		Replacement cost	
2. Building environment survey		Asbestos (Phase 1)	
		PCBs	
		Other	
3. Soil pollution risk assessment		Soil survey (Phase 1)	
4. Earthquake risk assessment		Simple analysis	
		Detailed analysis	

Buried structures or objects			
Building environment survey		Asbestos (Phase 2)	
Soil pollution risk assessment		Soil survey (Phase 2)	
		Environmental assessment, etc.	
Earthquake resistance survey		Earthquake resistance determination by architects, etc.	

Note: "Phase 1" indicates investigating the possible presence of toxic substances or pollutants by performing field surveys, collecting and analyzing data, and conducting interviews; "Phase 2" indicates confirming the presence or absence of toxic substances or pollutants by taking samples and conducting chemical analyses. "Simple analysis" indicates analysis by means of statistical methods, while "detailed analysis" indicates the use of analytical techniques.

Date of form completion		Name of property		Location of property	

Date investigated	Date prepared	Obtained from	Date obtained

Items used in appraisal, and reasons for doing so

別表1

	不動産鑑定士		所属	

エンジニアリング・レポートの基本的属性・入手経緯

		作成者	委託者
エンジニアリング・レポートの基本的属性・入手経緯	A		
	B		
	C		
	D		

提出されたエンジニアリング・レポートについて、鑑定評価を行う上での対応方針、不動産鑑定士の調査の必要性・内容等	

調査内容及び作成者 (※作成者欄には上記A、B、C又はDを記載)	作成者からの説明	項目	エンジニアリング・レポートの活用又は不動産鑑定士の調査の別
1 建物状況調査		立地概要調査	
		建物概要調査	
		設備概要調査	
		構造概要調査	
		公法上及び私法上の規制、制約等(法令遵守状況調査を含む。)	
		更新・改修履歴とその計画の調査	
		緊急修繕更新費	
		短期修繕更新費	
		長期修繕更新費	
		再調達価格	
2 建物環境調査		アスベスト(フェーズⅠ)	
		PCB	
		その他の項目	
3 土壌汚染リスク評価		土壌調査(フェーズⅠ)	
4 地震リスク評価		簡易分析	
		詳細分析	

地下埋設物			
建物環境調査		アスベスト(フェーズⅡ)	
土壌汚染リスク評価		土壌調査(フェーズⅡ)	
		環境アセスメント等	
耐震性調査		建築士等による耐震診断	

(注)「フェーズⅠ」とは現地調査・資料収集分析・ヒアリングによる有害又は汚染物質の可能性の調査、「フェーズⅡ」とは試料採取と化学的分析による有害又は汚染物質の有無の確認を行う調査。「簡易分析」とは統計的な手法による分析、「詳細分析」とは解析的な手法による分析。

記入日		物件名称		物件所在地	

調査年月日	作成年月日	入手先	入手年月日

鑑定評価において活用した事項とその根拠

Appendix 2

Identification of the subject property

Land	Location and block number	Land category	Lot area			
Building	Location	House number	Structure	Purpose	Floor area	Date co

			1	2	·	·	·	·	·	·	·
(a)	Effective gross income	Potential gross income									
(b)		Income from common area charges									
(c)		Rental income, including income from common area charges [(a)+(b)]									
(d)		Utility fee income									
(e)		Parking fee income									
(f)		Other income									
①		(c) + (d) + (e) + (f)									
		Vacancy allowance for (c) and (d)									
		Vacancy allowance for (e) and (f)									
(g)		Total vacancy allowance									
(h)		Collection losses allowance									
②	Effective gross income [①−(g)−(h)]										
(i)	Operating expenses	Maintenance and management expenses									
(j)		Utility expenses									
(k)		Repair expenses									
(l)		Property management fees									
(m)		Tenant recruitment expenses, etc.									
(n)		Real estate taxes — Land									
		Real estate taxes — Buildings									
		Real estate taxes — Depreciable assets									
(o)		Casualty insurance premiums									
(p)		Other expenses									
③		Operating expenses [(i)+(j)+(k)+(l)+(m)+(n)+(o)+(p)]									
④	Net operating income [②−③]										
(q)		Operating profit on lump-sum payments									
(r)		Capital expenditures									
⑤	Net cash flow [④+(q)−(r)]										
		(Reference)									
		Operating efficiency ratio (OER)									
		Balance of lump-sum payments (refundable deposits)									
		Compound present value rate									
(s)		Present value									
(t)		Total for (s) column									

Value indicated by the income approach ((t)+(x)) *	

(u)	Sale value ⑤ for n+1 years / z
(v)	Sale expenses
(w)	Reversionary value (u)-(v)
(x)	Current reversionary value
(y)	Discount rate
(z)	Terminal capitalization rate

n	Year after expiration of the preservation period (n+1)	Grounds for assessment			Additional comments
		Assessment method			
		If data obtained from the client or other informational materials were used, were any modifications made, or did the LREA use data which he had obtained himself? State the grounds for those decisions.	Anticipated changes		

	Reasons for conclusion	Additional comments
%		
%		

別表2

対象不動産の表示

土地	所在及び地番		地目		地目			
建物	所在		家屋番号		構造	用途	床面積	新築

				1	2	・	・	・	・	・	・
①	運営収益	(a)	貸室賃料収入								
		(b)	共益費収入								
		(c)	（共益費込み貸室賃料収入）[(a)+(b)]								
		(d)	水道光熱費収入								
		(e)	駐車場収入								
		(f)	その他収入（　　　）								
			(c)+(d)+(e)+(f)								
			(c)(d)空室等損失								
			(e)(f)空室等損失								
		(g)	空室等損失合計								
		(h)	貸倒損失								
②	運営収益　[①−(g)−(h)]										
③	運営費用	(i)	維持管理費								
		(j)	水道光熱費								
		(k)	修繕費								
		(l)	プロパティマネジメントフィー								
		(m)	テナント募集費用等								
		(n)	公租公課　土地								
			建物								
			償却資産								
		(o)	損害保険料								
		(p)	その他費用								
			運営費用 [(i)+(j)+(k)+(l)+(m)+(n)+(o)+(p)]								
④	運営純収益　[②−③]										
		(q)	一時金の運用益								
		(r)	資本的支出								
⑤	純収益　[④+(q)−(r)]										
	（参考）										
	OEM（運用費用／運営収益）										
	預り一時金（敷金・保証金等）残高										
	複利現価率										
(S)	現在価値										
(t)	(S)欄合計										

収益価格((t)+(x))　※

(u)	売却価額（(n+1)年度の⑤÷(z)）
(v)	売却費用
(w)	復帰価格〈(u)−(v)〉
(x)	復帰価格現在価値
(y)	割引率
(z)	最終還元利回り

	年月日				

	保有期間満了時点翌年 (n+1)	査定根拠			
n		査定方法		変動予測	補足
		依頼者から入手した資料又はその他の史料を採用する場合、修正を加える場合、自らが入手した資料を採用する場合の別及びその根拠			

	査定根拠	補足
%		
%		

III

**Basic Policy on Revaluation
of Securitized Real Estate**

December 24, 2009
Ministry of Land, Infrastructure, Transport and Tourism

証券化対象不動産の継続評価の実施に関する基本的考え方

平成21年12月24日　国土交通省

I. Purpose

This Policy provides the basic rule of revaluation of securitized real estate that a real estate appraiser periodically performs in order to obtain the value to be indicated in an asset operation report for each business period and to recognize the value for financial purposes, such as making financial statements according to Article 129, paragraph 2 of the Act on Investment Trust and Investment Corporations (Act No. 198 of 1951), based on the General Guideline for Real Estate Appraisers on Determination of Purpose and Scope of Valuation and Contents of Report (hereinafter referred to as the "Guideline").

II. Scope of Application

This Policy shall apply to revaluation of securitized real estate, excluding the one that falls under I-4-(i) or (iii)[1] of the Guideline.

III. Valuation Method

Valuation to which this Policy applies shall be carried out in accordance with (1) through (4) below as well as the Real Estate Appraisal Standards (hereinafter referred to as the "Standards").[2,3]

(1) Interior inspection

If a real estate appraiser has performed in the past a field survey (including an interior inspection[4]) of the subject property, and no significant changes have been found[5] in property-specific value influences, he/she may omit an interior inspection from among the items set

---

[1] (i) Cases where the value conclusion is only for internal use by the client.

(iii) Cases where all of the recipients of disclosure/submission have agreed that the value conclusion is not to be published.

[2] The value estimated by applying this Policy is considered to be the property value required under the Accounting Standards, which are prescribed in II of the Basic Policy on Valuation for Financial Statements.

[3] In this case, it is necessary to confirm the method of asset valuation indicated in the investment corporation constitution prescribed in Article 66 of the Act on Investment Trust and Investment Corporations.

[4] If a number of real estate appraisers are involved in the valuation of certain property, not all of them need to have performed a field survey. It would be sufficient that any one of them has performed a field survey in the past.

[5] The determination on the presence or absence of significant changes shall be made after clarifying the following matters by a field survey, confirmation with the client, and analysis of data:

i) The presence or absence of merger or split of parcels, land development work with changes in land characteristics, and renovation or repair of buildings (excluding minor ones).

ii) Material changes in regulations or limitations under public or private law (including legal compliance conditions), repair plans, replacement cost, hazardous substances such as asbestos with regard to the building environment, soil contamination, earthquake risk, seismic adequacy, and underground installations.

iii) The presence or absence of movements of primary tenants occupying the majority of the rentable space and amendment to the land lease agreement (except minor ones such as revision of small amount in rent).

Ⅰ．目的
　この基本的考え方は、「不動産鑑定士が不動産に関する価格調査を行う場合の業務の目的と範囲等の確定及び成果報告書の記載事項に関するガイドライン」（以下「価格等調査ガイドライン」という。）に従って、同一の証券化対象不動産（不動産鑑定評価基準各論第3章に定める証券化対象不動産をいう。以下同じ。）を対象に不動産鑑定士が継続調査（投資信託及び投資法人に関する法律（昭和26年法律第198号）第129条第2項に基づき、各営業期間に係る資産運用報告書に記載する当期末現在における不動産の価格を求めることを目的とする調査その他財務諸表の作成や企業会計上の要請、財務状況の把握等を目的に継続的に不動産の価格を把握することを目的とする調査をいう。以下同じ。）として行う価格調査（不動産の鑑定評価に関する法律（昭和38年法律第152号）第3条第1項の業務として行う不動産の価格を文書又は電磁的記録に表示する調査をいう。以下同じ。）の基本的考え方を示すものである。

Ⅱ．適用範囲
　この基本的考え方は、継続調査として行う証券化対象不動産を対象とした価格調査（価格等調査ガイドラインⅠ.4.①又は③[1]に該当するものを除く。）に適用する。

Ⅲ．価格調査の実施の指針
　この基本的考え方が適用される価格調査については、以下の(1)から(4)までに規定するところによるほか、不動産鑑定評価基準に則って行うものとする。[2,3]

　(1) 内覧の実施
　　　価格調査の対象とする不動産について、内覧の実施を含めた実地調査を過去に自ら行った[4]ことがあり、かつ、当該不動産の個別的要因（不動産鑑定評価基準各論第3章第3節Ⅲの表に

---

[1] ①調査価格等が依頼者の内部における使用にとどまる場合、③調査価格等が公表されない場合ですべての開示・提出先の承諾が得られた場合

[2] この基本的考え方の適用によって算出された価格は、企業会計基準等（「財務諸表のための価格調査の実施に関する基本的考え方」Ⅱ.に規定する企業会計基準等をいう。）において求めることとされている不動産の価格に該当するものと考えられる。

[3] この場合において、投資信託及び投資法人に関する法律第66条に規定する規約（投資法人規約）に記載された資産評価の方法を確認すべきことに留意する必要がある。

[4] 複数の不動産鑑定士がある不動産の価格調査に関与する場合においては、当該複数の不動産鑑定士全員が実地調査を過去に自ら行っている必要はなく、当該複数の不動産鑑定士のうちのいずれかが当該不動産の実地調査を過去に自ら行ったことがあれば足りる。

[5] 個別的要因についての重要な変化の有無に関する判断は、例えば以下に掲げる事項を実地調査、依頼者への確認、要因資料の分析等により明らかにした上で行う。
　①敷地の併合や分割（軽微なものを除く。）、区画形質の変更を伴う造成工事（軽微なものを除く。）、建物に係る増改築や大規模修繕工事（軽微なものを除く。）等の実施の有無、②公法上若しくは私法上の規制・制約等（法令遵守状況を含む。）、修繕計画、再調達価格、建物環境に係るアスベスト等の有害物質、土壌汚染、地震リスク、耐震性、地下埋設物等に係る重要な変化、③賃貸可能面積の過半を占める等の主たる借主の異動、借地契約内容の変更（少額の地代の改定など軽微なものを除く。）等の有無

forth in Chapter 3, Section 3 (Investigating Property-Specific Value Influences Acting on the Securitized Property) of the Specific Principles of the Standards.

(2) Methods to be applied

If no significant changes have been found[6] in property-specific value influences or in general and area-specific value influences such as land value indices (e.g., official land prices, sales prices, rents, and yields) in light of the use and location of the subject property since the last appraisal compliant with the Standards (limited to the Standards after the enforcement of Chapter 3 of the Specific Principles[7]; the same shall apply hereinafter) , at least the income capitalization approach shall be adopted from among the valuation methods (meaning the appraisal approaches set forth in Chapter 7 of the General Principles of the Standards; the same shall apply hereinafter) . The capitalization approach shall be applied in accordance with Chapter 7, Section 1, IV (Income Capitalization Approach) of the General Principles and Chapter 3, Section 4 (Application of DCF Method) of the Specific Principles of the Standards. However, if the subject property is a vacant lot (including the case where buildings are scheduled to be demolished) or a non-rental property, whose capitalized value is not necessarily viewed as a key factor, at least those approaches that were recognized to be relatively convincing in adjusting the estimated value in the last appraisal compliant with the Standards shall be adopted, and the said approaches shall be applied in accordance with Chapter 7, Section 1 (Appraisal Approaches for Determining Value) of the General Principles and Chapter 1 (Appraisal of Value) of the Specific Principles of the Standards.

(3) Valuation on the assumption that construction of the property with any uncompleted buildings would have been completed

In the case of valuation on the assumption that construction of the property with any uncompleted buildings would have been completed, the subject of valuation shall be appropriately determined according to the progress of the completed part of the buildings and the assumptions added. The Valuation shall comply with the Standards except for the parts of Chapter 5, Section 1 (Identification of the Subject Property) and Chapter 8, Section 4 (Identification of the Subject Property) of the General Principles of the Standards, which provide for the confirmation of the physical characteristics and the legal estate in the subject proper-

---

[6] It includes the case where, after the announcement of addition of Chapter III to the Specific Principles of the Standards (published by the vice-minister of the Ministry of Land, Infrastructure, Transport and Tourism on April 2, 2007), the valuation has been carried out under the said chapter prior to its enforcement.

[7] The determination on the presence or absence of significant changes shall be made after clarifying the following matters by a field survey, confirmation with the client, and analysis of data:

Property-specific value influences: Matters set forth in footnote 5.

General and area-specific value influences:

i) Amendment to tax, law, and regulations concerning real estate (excluding minor ones).

ii) Changes in the scope of the market area, the standard use in the neighborhood and the market characteristics concerning the subject property.

iii) Fluctuations in the suitability of the subject property in terms of economic factors.

掲げる専門性の高い個別的要因を含む。）に重要な変化がないと認められる場合[5]においては、不動産鑑定評価基準各論第3章第3節（証券化対象不動産の個別的要因の調査等）のうち、内覧の実施については省略することができる。

(2) 適用する手法

不動産鑑定評価基準（不動産鑑定評価基準各論第3章施行後のものに限る[6]。以下同じ。）に則った鑑定評価が行われた時点と比較して、当該不動産の個別的要因並びに当該不動産の用途や所在地に鑑みて公示価格その他地価に関する指標や取引価格、賃料、利回り等の一般的要因及び地域要因に重要な変化がないと認められる場合[7]においては、鑑定評価手法（不動産鑑定評価基準総論第7章の鑑定評価の方式をいう。以下同じ。）のうち、少なくとも収益還元法は適用するものとし、同手法の適用に当たっては、不動産鑑定評価基準総論第7章第1節Ⅳ（収益還元法）及び不動産鑑定評価基準各論第3章第4節（ＤＣＦ法の適用等）に則るものとする。ただし、対象不動産が更地である場合（建物を取り壊す予定である場合を含む。）や、賃貸用不動産以外の不動産であって必ずしも収益価格が重視されないものである場合には、直近に行われた不動産鑑定評価基準に則った鑑定評価における試算価格の調整において相対的に説得力が高いと認められた鑑定評価手法は少なくとも適用するものとし、当該鑑定評価手法の適用に当たっては、不動産鑑定評価基準総論第7章第1節（価格を求める鑑定評価の手法）及び不動産鑑定評価基準各論第1章（価格に関する鑑定評価）に則るものとする。

(3) 未竣工建物を含む不動産の竣工を前提として行う価格調査

未竣工建物を含む不動産について建物の竣工を前提として行う価格調査を行う場合においては、建物の既施工部分の進捗状況及び付加された想定上の条件に応じて価格調査の対象となる部分を適切に確定するものとする。また、不動産鑑定評価基準第5章第1節（対象不動産の確定）及び第8章第4節（対象不動産の確認）のうち、当該未竣工建物に係る物的確認及び権利の態様の確認以外の部分について、不動産鑑定評価基準に則るものとする。

---

[6] 不動産鑑定評価基準各論第3章追加（平成19年4月2日国土交通事務次官通知）後、同章の施行までに同章を適用した鑑定評価が行われた場合を含む。

[7] 個別的要因並びに一般的要因及び地域要因についての重要な変化の有無に関する判断は、例えば以下に掲げる事項を実地調査、依頼者への確認、要因資料の分析等により明らかにした上で行う。

個別的要因：脚注5に掲げる事項。

一般的要因及び地域要因：不動産に関連する税制又は法令等の改正（いずれも軽微なものを除く。）、同一需給圏の範囲若しくは近隣地域の標準的使用又は対象不動産に係る市場の特性に係る変化、対象不動産の経済的要因からの適応状態に係る変動等

ty.

(4) Matters to be stated in the report
   (i) In the case of valuation with different procedures from the Standards, such as omitting an interior inspection based on (1) above and omitting part of the appraisal methods based on (2) above, the matters in III-1) and 2) of the Guideline shall be stated.
   (ii) If it is considered that there have been no significant changes listed in (1) and (2) above, the reason of the consideration shall be stated in the report.
   (iii) In the case of eliminating any part of the valuation methods that were adopted in the last appraisal compliant with the Standards based on (2) above, the adopted method shall be clearly stated, instead of the value type specified in Chapter 5, Section 3 of the General Principles of the Standards, with regard to the matters in II-4-(4) and III-4-(4)[8] of the Guideline.

---

[8] Valuation method or the type of value.

(4) 成果報告書の記載事項等
　① (1)に基づく内覧の省略、(2)に基づく一部の鑑定評価手法の省略その他不動産鑑定評価基準に定める手順と異なる手順で価格調査を行った場合には、価格等調査ガイドラインⅢ．1)及び2)の記載を行うものとする。
　② (1)及び(2)に掲げる重要な変化がないと認められると判断した場合には、その根拠を成果報告書に記載しなければならない。
　③ (2)に基づき直近に行われた不動産鑑定評価基準に則った鑑定評価において適用された鑑定評価手法の一部を適用しない場合には、価格等調査ガイドラインⅡ．4．(4)の明記及びⅢ．4．(4)[8]の記載については、不動産鑑定評価基準総論第5章第3節に定める価格の種類ではなく、適用した鑑定評価手法を明記又は記載するものとする。

8　価格等を求める方法又は価格等の種類

IV

Guidelines Regarding Appraisal of Securitized Properties

証券化対象不動産の鑑定評価に関する実務指針

Table of Contents

December 2009
Japanese Association of Real Estate Appraisal
Committee on Appraisal of Securitized Properties

Purpose ·· 78
Background ·· 78
Ⅰ. **Scope of Application** ·· 82
  1. **Significance of Appraisal of Securitized Properties** ······················· 82
    1) **Key Features of Securitized Properties** ·· 82
    2) **Purposes of Appraisal of Real Estate Securitization** ···················· 84
  2. **Scope of Appraisal for Securitized Properties** ································· 84
  3. **When application of Specific Standards Chapter 3 is not required though the subject can be categorized as a "securitized property"** ·· 86
Ⅱ. **Ethic** ·· 90
  1. **Basic Attitude** ·· 90
  2. **Accountability** ·· 90
Ⅲ. **Confirmation Required at the Time of Valuation Request** ················· 92
  1. **Purposes of Valuation and Scope of Work** ······································ 92
    1) **Client and Parties for Submission of Final Appraisal Report** ······· 92
    2) **Purpose of Valuation, Parties for Disclosure of Appraisal Value, and Publication Appraisal value** ··· 96
    3) **Special Interests** ·· 96
    4) **Basic Elements of Valuation** ··· 96
    5) **Appraisal Process** ·· 106
    6) **Possibility of the Difference in the Result with Values Estimated based on the Appraisal Standards (only if not based on the Appraisal Standards)** ·· 108
  2. **Items to be Confirmed with Client for Valuation Schedule** ··········· 108
    1) **Major Contents of Engineering Report and Date the Engineering Report is Obtained** ··· 108
    2) **Required Information for Application of DCF Method and Date it is Obtained** ·· 110
    3) **Explanation from those who Prepared Engineering Report** ······· 110
Ⅳ. **Investigation of the Subject Property** ·· 112

目　次

平成21年12月
社団法人日本不動産鑑定協会
証券化鑑定評価委員会

目　的	79
策定の背景	79
Ⅰ　適用範囲	83
1　証券化対象不動産の鑑定評価の意義	83
(1)　不動産証券化の対象となる不動産の特性	83
(2)　不動産証券化における鑑定評価の目的	85
2　対象とする鑑定評価の範囲	85
3　形式的に「証券化対象不動産」に該当しても基準各論第3章等を適用しないことができる場合	87
Ⅱ　倫理	91
1　基本姿勢	91
2　説明責任	91
Ⅲ　受付時確認事項	93
1　業務の目的と範囲等の確定	93
(1)　依頼者及び成果報告書の提出先	93
(2)　依頼目的、鑑定評価額が開示される範囲又は公表の有無等	97
(3)　利害関係等	97
(4)　鑑定評価の基本的事項	97
(5)　鑑定評価の手順	107
(6)　不動産鑑定評価基準に則った鑑定評価と結果が異なる可能性がある旨（不動産鑑定評価基準に則らない場合に限る）	109
2　処理計画策定のための依頼者との確認事項	109
(1)　エンジニアリング・レポート等の主な項目及び入手時期	109
(2)　DCF法等を適用するために必要となる資料等の主な項目及び入手時期	111
(3)　エンジニアリング・レポートを作成した者（以下「ER作成者」という。）等からの説明の有無	111
Ⅳ　対象不動産の調査	113

1. Market Research	112
2. Site Inspection	112
3. Gathering Information	114
1) Information to be gathered	114
2) Engineering Report	114
4. Unclear Value Influences	118

Ⅴ. **Analysis of Value Influences** 120
  1. General Value Influences 120
  2. Specific Value Influences 120
    1) Land 120
    2) Buildings 126
    3) Building and its site 134

Ⅵ. **Application of Appraisal Approaches** 138
  1. Valuation Policy 138
  2. Income Capitalization Approach 140
    1) Income and Expense Items 140
    2) DCF Method 140
    3) DCF Method (development of a leasehold property) 160
    4) Direct Capitalization Method 164
    5) Conclusion of Value Indicated by Income Capitalization Approach 166
    6) Trade Related Property 168
  3. Reconciliation of Indicated Value 168

Ⅶ. **Appraisal Report** 172
  1. Basic Items 172
    1) Identification of Subject Property 172
    2) Special Interests 172
    3) Management Method based on Asset Securitization Plan 174
  2. Information and Issues to be Confirmed 174
    1) Site Inspection 174
    2) Engineering Report 176
  3. Analysis of Value Influences 182
    1) General Value Influences 182
    2) Area-Specific Value Influences 182
    3) Property-Specific Value Influences 182
    4) Unknown Issues 186
  4. Application of Valuation Method 186
  5. Reconciliation of Indicated Values 186
  6. Appraisal Value 188

	1　市場調査	113
	2　実地調査	113
	3　資料収集	115
	(1)　収集すべき資料	115
	(2)　エンジニアリング・レポート	115
	4　不明事項	119
Ⅴ	価格形成要因の分析	121
	1　一般的要因分析等	121
	2　個別的要因分析	121
	(1)　土地	121
	(2)　建物	127
	(3)　建物及びその敷地	135
Ⅵ	鑑定評価手法の適用	139
	1　評価方針	139
	2　収益還元法	141
	(1)　収益費用項目	141
	(2)　DCF法	141
	(3)　DCF法（開発賃貸型）	161
	(4)　直接還元法	165
	(5)　収益価格の決定	167
	(6)　事業経営の影響の大きい用途の不動産の場合	169
	3　試算価格の調整	169
Ⅶ	鑑定評価報告書	173
	1　基本的事項	173
	(1)　対象不動産の確定	173
	(2)　利害関係	173
	(3)　資産流動化計画等による運用方法	175
	2　資料及び確認事項	175
	(1)　実地調査	175
	(2)　エンジニアリング・レポート	177
	3　価格形成要因の分析	183
	(1)　一般的要因	183
	(2)　地域要因	183
	(3)　個別的要因	183
	(4)　不明事項	187
	4　鑑定評価手法の適用	187
	5　試算価格の調整	187
	6　鑑定評価額	188

  1) **If value is increased due to merger with adjacent property** ············188
  2) **If market value based on special considerations and market value are concluded to be equal** ············188
  3) **If value of land and building are to be separately shown** ············188
 7. **Appendix** ············188
 8. **Draft Report** ············190
Ⅷ. **Periodic Valuation** ············194
 1. **General Considerations in Periodic Valuation** ············194
 2. **Considerations in Periodic Valuation for an Appraisal not Compliant with the Appraisal Standards** ············196
  1) **Internal Inspection** ············196
  2) **Approaches to be Applied** ············196
  3) **Contents of the Final Report** ············196
 3. **Valuation not compliant with the Appraisal Standards other than Periodic Valuation** ············198
  1) **Properties including uncompleted buildings assuming completion** ············198
  2) **When not compliant with the Appraisal Standards for a valid reason** ············198

(1)　隣接不動産の併合等により増分価値が生じる場合 …………………………189
　　(2)　特定価格と正常価格が一致すると判断される場合 …………………………189
　　(3)　土地建物の内訳価格を記載する場合 ……………………………………………189
　7　付属資料 ……………………………………………………………………………189
　8　ドラフト ……………………………………………………………………………191

Ⅷ　継続評価等 ……………………………………………………………………………195
　1　継続評価における一般的留意事項 ………………………………………………195
　2　価格調査として継続評価を行う場合における留意事項 ………………………197
　　(1)　内覧の実施 ………………………………………………………………………197
　　(2)　適用する手法 ……………………………………………………………………197
　　(3)　成果報告書の記載事項 …………………………………………………………197
　3　継続評価以外の価格調査 …………………………………………………………199
　　(1)　未竣工建物を含む不動産の竣工を前提とする場合 …………………………199
　　(2)　やむを得ず不動産鑑定評価基準に則ることができない場合 ………………199

Purpose

The Guidelines Regarding Appraisal of Securitized Properties (hereinafter the "Guidelines") are publicized by the Japanese Association of Real Estate Appraisal (hereinafter the "Association") for licensed real estate appraisers and real estate appraisal firms to comply with when conducting appraisal work for securitized properties based on the Real Estate Appraisal Standards and Guidance Notes on the Real Estate Appraisal Standards[1]. The Guidelines also serve as a reference (to verify the validity of value) for the wide range of parties who use the appraisal value, such as those concerned with the securitization market.

The Guidelines explain issues to which appraisers should pay particular attention when conducting appraisal work for securitized properties. As such, it should be noted that the Guidelines do not explain all processes. For issues not specified in the Guidelines, appraisers should comply with the Appraisal Standards and Guidance Notes on the Real Estate Appraisal Standards, as well as common appraisal practices.

Valuation not complying with these Guidelines should not immediately be deemed as unsuitable, but it should at least be able to rationally be explained for its reasons.

Background

"Valuation Guidelines Regarding Value of Securitized Properties" determined in March 2007 (and partially revised in June 2007), had a characteristic as a practical guide for actual practices of Specific Standards Chapter 3 of the Appraisal Standards and relevant Guidance Notes on the Real Estate Appraisal Standards (hereinafter "Specific Standards Chapter 3 and relevant Notes"). The contents of these valuation guidelines were included in Specific Standards Chapter 3 section of the "New Instruction: Real Estate Appraisal Standards" (edited by the research committee of the Japanese Association of Real Estate Appraisal; published by Jutaku-Shimpo-Sha, Inc., November 2007).

It was also pointed out that the Association's internal rules, "Guidance Notes on the Application of Valuation the Approaches regarding Value of Securitized Properties" (March 2007) have been used as a reference not only by licensed real estate appraisers and real estate appraisal firms, but also by participants in the securitization market.

Therefore, we consolidated and organized such documents in accordance with the appraisal process based on recent practices and considerations, and determined the "Guidelines Regarding Appraisal of Securitized Properties" (hereinafter the "Current Guidelines") in June 2009.

While the Association was working to determine such guidelines, the Ministry of Land, Infrastructure, Transport and Tourism published the Real Estate Appraisal Committee Report, "Improving Valuation to Meet Changes in Society," prepared by the National Land Development Council, and asked licensed real estate appraisers and real estate appraisal firms to improve the quality and trust of valuation in order to maintain stable growth of the

---

[1] Released by the administrative vice minister of the Ministry of Land, Infrastructure, Transport and Tourism on April 2, 2007

目　的

　証券化対象不動産の鑑定評価に関する実務指針（以下「本実務指針」という。）は、不動産鑑定士及び不動産鑑定業者が証券化対象不動産の価格に関する鑑定評価の実務を行うに当たり、不動産鑑定評価基準及び不動産鑑定評価基準運用上の留意事項[※1]を踏まえ、原則として準拠すべき指針として、社団法人日本不動産鑑定協会（以下「当協会」という。）が公表するものである。さらに、鑑定評価を活用する証券化市場関係者をはじめとする広範な関係者の参考資料（その適正さを確認するための指針等）としての位置づけも有することとなるものである。

　なお、本実務指針は、証券化対象不動産の鑑定評価を行うに当たって特に留意すべき事項について記載したものであるため、すべての実務に対応しているものではないことに留意するとともに、本実務指針に記載していない事項については、不動産鑑定評価基準及び不動産鑑定評価基準運用上の留意事項並びに従来からの実務慣行に従うこととなる。

　また、本実務指針に準拠していないことをもって直ちに不適切であることを意味するものではないが、少なくともその理由について合理的に説明できる必要がある。

策定の背景

　平成19年3月に策定した「証券化対象不動産の価格に関する鑑定評価の実務指針」（平成19年6月一部改正）は、平成19年4月に改正された不動産鑑定評価基準各論第3章及びこれに係る不動産鑑定評価基準運用上の留意事項（以下「基準各論第3章等」という。）の実務的な解説の性格を有し、その内容は「新・要説　不動産鑑定評価基準」（㈳日本不動産鑑定協会調査研究委員会編　住宅新報社　平成19年11月）の不動産鑑定評価基準各論第3章に包含された。

　また、当協会の内部規定である「証券化対象不動産の価格に関する鑑定評価手法適用上の留意事項」（平成19年3月）が、不動産鑑定士又は不動産鑑定業者のみならず、証券化市場関係者の参考資料として事実上活用されてきたとの指摘も見られた。

　このため、これらを統合し、昨今の運用状況及び検討結果も踏まえて鑑定評価の手順に沿って再整理した「証券化対象不動産の鑑定評価に関する実務指針」（以下「現実務指針」という。）を平成21年6月に策定した。

　当協会がかかる指針の策定に向けた検討を進める一方、国土交通省では平成21年3月に国土審議会土地政策部会分科会不動産鑑定評価部会報告書「社会の変化に対応したよりよい鑑定評価に向けて」を公表し、今後の不動産投資市場の安定的な成長のために、鑑定評価の質の向上、信頼性の向上を図るよう不動産鑑定士及び不動産鑑定業者に求めた。この報告書を受けて、同省は平成21年8月「不動産鑑定士が不動産に関する価格等調査を行う場合の業務の目的と範囲等の確定及び成果報告書の記載事項に関するガイドライン」（以下「価格等調査ガイドライン」という。）を、同年12月には「証券化対象不動産の継続評価の実施に関する基本的考え方」（以下「継続評価の基本的考え方」という。）を策定したところである。

　本実務指針は、このような状況にかんがみ、現実務指針の内容に加え、価格等調査ガイドライン及び継続評価の基本的考え方からの要請も取り入れ、再度改定することとなったものである。

　なお、本実務指針と不動産鑑定評価基準、ガイドライン、実務指針、業務指針等の位置づけを整

1　平成19年4月2日国土交通省事務次官通知

real estate investment market. In response to this report, the ministry determined the "General Guidelines for Real Estate Appraisers on Determination of Purpose and Scope of Valuation and Contents of Report " (hereinafter the "Valuation Guidelines") in August 2009, and "Basic Policy on Periodic Valuation of Securitized Properties" (hereinafter the "Basic Policy of Periodic Valuation") in December 2009.

Given such circumstances, the Guidelines are determined by revising the Current Guidelines and add the requirements specified in the Valuation Guidelines and Basic Policy of Periodic Valuation.

The chart below summarizes the position of the Guidelines, Real Estate Appraisal Standards, Valuation Guidelines, and other relevant guidelines.

Chart: Position of Appraisal Standards, Valuation Guidelines, and the Guidelines

Ministry of Land, Infrastructure, Transport and Tourism | Japanese Association of Real Estate Appraisal

Real Estate Appraisal Committee Report - "Improving Valuation to Meet Changes in Society," prepared by the National Land Development Council

Valuation Guidelines
(including Considerations for Operations of the Guidelines)

Appraisal complies with the Appraisal Standards

Appraisal does not comply with the Appraisal Standards
(In some cases a valuation may be regarded as an appraisal under relevant laws)

Estimating Value is the Ultimate Objective

a. Cannot comply with the Appraisal Standards
   a) Forced by circumstances
   b) Given the condition that it cannot comply

b. Does not comply, although it could
   a) Estimate value for revaluation purpose of the same securitized property by the same appraiser
   -Omission of internal inspection
   -Application only of DCF method of income capitalization approach

Specific Standards Chapter 3, etc.
(In the case of appraisal for securitized properties)

Estimating Value is not the Ultimate Objective

a. Consulting use and utilization of real estate
b. Due diligence for collateral properties
c. Opinion on time adjustment, etc.

Mainly Concerned with Appraisers

1. Guidelines for role of appraisers and business alliance of appraisal firms
   (Section in relation to role of appraisers)
2. Guidelines in relation to management of Opinion of Value Guidelines
   (Example of written format)
   -Example of report

Mainly Concerned with Appraisal Firms

1. Guidelines regarding business operation of appraisal firms
2. Guidelines regarding role of appraisers and business alliance of appraisal firms
   (Section in relation to business alliance with appraisal firms)
3. Guidelines regarding Preparing Engagement agreements for valuation assignments
4. Guidelines regarding management of Valuation Guidelines
   (Example)
   - Confirmation to Determine Purposes and Scope of Work

1. Guidelines regarding Appraisal of Securitized Properties ("Guidelines")
2. Guidelines regarding business operation of appraisal firms
   (Operational guidelines bylaw regarding business operation of appraisal firms when conducting appraisal of securitized properties)

"Basic Policy on Periodic Valuation of Securitized Properties"

理すると、下表のようになる。

(表) 不動産鑑定評価基準、価格調査等ガイドライン、本実務指針等の位置づけ

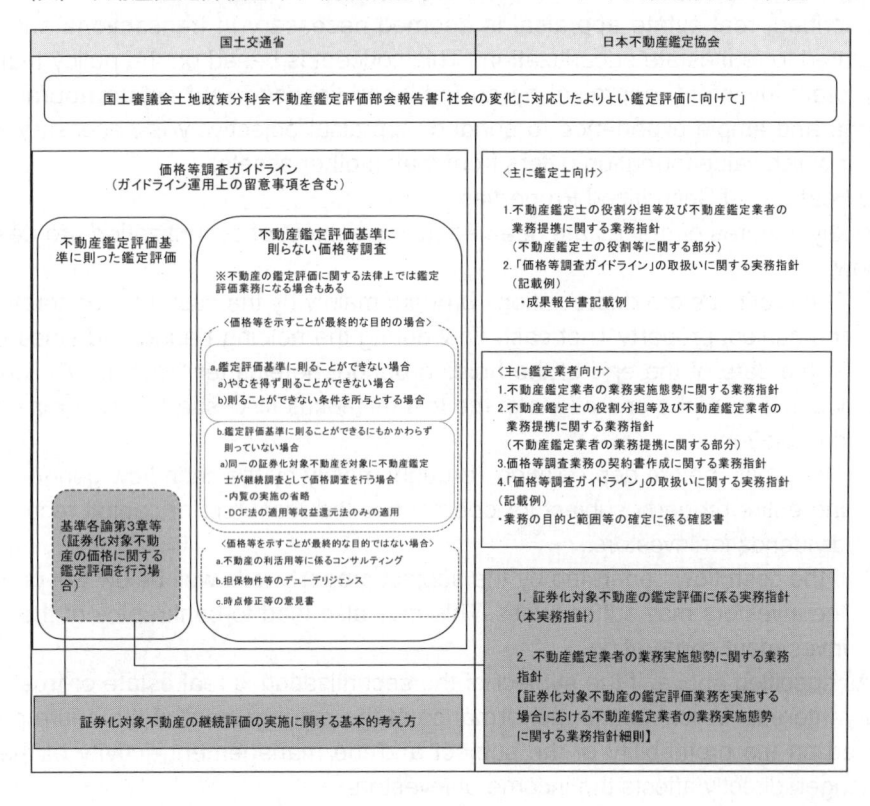

国土交通省	日本不動産鑑定協会
国土審議会土地政策分科会不動産鑑定評価部会報告書「社会の変化に対応したよりよい鑑定評価に向けて」	
価格等調査ガイドライン（ガイドライン運用上の留意事項を含む） **不動産鑑定評価基準に則った鑑定評価** 基準各論第3章等（証券化対象不動産の価格に関する鑑定評価を行う場合） **不動産鑑定評価基準に則らない価格等調査** ※不動産の鑑定評価に関する法律上では鑑定評価業務になる場合もある 〈価格等を示すことが最終的な目的の場合〉 a.鑑定評価基準に則ることができない場合 　a)やむを得ず則ることができない場合 　b)則ることができない条件を所与とする場合 b.鑑定評価基準に則ることができるにもかかわらず則っていない場合 ・同一の証券化対象不動産を対象に不動産鑑定士が継続評価として価格調査を行う場合 ・内覧の実施の省略 ・DCF法の適用等収益還元法のみの適用 〈価格等を示すことが最終的な目的ではない場合〉 a.不動産の利活用等に係るコンサルティング b.担保物件等のデューデリジェンス c.時点修正等の意見書	〈主に鑑定士向け〉 1.不動産鑑定士の役割分担等及び不動産鑑定業者の業務提携に関する業務指針（不動産鑑定士の役割等に関する部分） 2.「価格等調査ガイドライン」の取扱いに関する実務指針 （記載例） ・成果報告書記載例 〈主に鑑定業者向け〉 1.不動産鑑定業者の業務実施態勢に関する業務指針 2.不動産鑑定士の役割分担等及び不動産鑑定業者の業務提携に関する業務指針（不動産鑑定業者の業務提携に関する部分） 3.価格等調査業務の契約書作成に関する業務指針 4.「価格等調査ガイドライン」の取扱いに関する実務指針 （記載例） ・業務の目的と範囲等の確定に係る確認書 1.証券化対象不動産の鑑定評価に係る実務指針（本実務指針） 2.不動産鑑定業者の業務実施態勢に関する業務指針 【証券化対象不動産の鑑定評価業務を実施する場合における不動産鑑定業者の業務実施態勢に関する業務指針細則】
証券化対象不動産の継続評価の実施に関する基本的考え方	

I. Scope of Application

1. Significance of Appraisal of Securitized Properties

In the securitization schemes of J-REIT and private funds, the major securitization schemes in Japan, the entity that provides funds by equity or debt financing and that which manages the funds are separated. Real estate appraisal objectively estimates the value of investment property or value changes during the holding period and provides convincing information to the investors in order for them to determine validity of the investment decisions made by asset managers or to determine potential conflicts of interest between concerned parties. By doing so, real estate appraisal takes on a significant role in ensuring the trust of the entire real estate securitization market.

As described, real estate appraisal is deemed necessary in transactions and procedures related to real estate securitization[2]. This concept is based on the policy that, in order to protect investors, appraisal by an unbiased licensed real estate appraiser with knowledge and ample experience to conduct appraisal objectively is necessary for real estate, for which value formation differs from that of other assets.

1) Key Features of Securitized Properties

   The key features of real estate deemed as the subject of securitization are described below:

   (a) The profit (before depreciation) brought mainly by the cash flow generated from the subject property (net cash flow during the holding period and sales income at the date of the end of the holding period; hereinafter "cash flow") forms the foundation of the operations of the tokutei mokuteki kaisha (TMK) or investment corporation.

   (b) The profit (before depreciation) brought mainly by the cash flow generated from the entire property subject for operation is the resource for capital recovery and dividends for investors.

   (c) If the cash flow generated by the subject property falls well below the projection, the investors may suffer a loss. This may also lead to bankruptcy of the TMK or investment corporation.

   As specified above, if the subject of the securitization is real estate or trust beneficiary interests in real estate, performance of the management of the entire property, based on the profitability of the subject and the management activity of the asset manager, directly affects the income of investors.

   Accordingly, profitability of securitized properties (including trust assets) basically

---

[2] In Specific Standards Chapter 3 and relevant Notes, in order to protect investors, "real estate securitization" includes a wide range of cases not only regarding when an owner removes cash-generating property from the balance sheet and issues liquid investment products but also includes investments to SPC etc. and sales of small-lot real estate ownership. Accordingly, "real estate securitization" herein does not require off-balance accounting; that is, the scheme under the Act Concerning Designated Real Estate Joint Enterprises in which the real estate is included in the balance sheet is also the subject of Specific Standards Chapter 3 and relevant Notes.

I　適用範囲

1　証券化対象不動産の鑑定評価の意義

　わが国における証券化の主要なスキームであるJ-REITやプライベートファンドなどの証券化スキームでは、出資や融資等の形態で資金を提供する主体とその資金を運用する主体が分離されている。不動産鑑定評価は、投資対象である不動産等の資産の取引価格あるいは運用期間中の当該資産の価値の増減について客観的に評価し、資金運用者による投資意思決定の妥当性や利害関係者間等の取引における利益相反の有無等を判定する有力な材料を資金提供者等に提供することにより、不動産証券化市場全体の信頼性を確保する上で極めて重要な役割を担っている。
　このように不動産証券化に関連する取引や手続き[2]において不動産鑑定評価が必要とされる理由は、価格形成が一般の財と相違する不動産について、投資家保護等の観点から客観的な評価を行い得る専門的知識と豊富な経験を有する中立的な不動産鑑定士による鑑定評価が必要であるとの考え方に基づいている。

(1)　不動産証券化の対象となる不動産の特性

　不動産証券化の対象となる不動産は、以下のような特性を有するものと考えられる。
　ア　対象不動産の生み出すキャッシュフロー（投資期間中の純収益（期間収益）と転売時点の売却に伴う収益をいい、以下「キャッシュフロー」という。）を主要な源泉とする利益（償却前）が、特定目的会社や投資法人等の運営の基盤となる。
　イ　運用対象となる不動産全体の生み出すキャッシュフローを主要な源泉とする利益（償却前）が、投資家にとっての元本回収及び配当の原資となる。
　ウ　対象不動産の生み出すキャッシュフローが予測を大きく下回る場合、投資家が損失を蒙り、さらには特定目的会社や投資法人等の破綻に繋がるような事態も生じ得る。
　このように、証券化の対象資産が不動産又は不動産を信託財産とする信託受益権である場合は、運用対象となる対象不動産の収益力と資産の運用者による不動産全体の運用の巧拙が投資家の収益に直結することとなる。
　このため、証券化の対象となる不動産（信託財産である場合を含む。）は、一般にその収益力が価格形成面で極めて重要な役割を果たすものである。

---

[2] 基準各論第3章等においては、投資家保護等の観点から、「不動産証券化」について、不動産の所有者がキャッシュフローを生み出す不動産をバランスシートから切り離し、流動性の高い投資商品を発行する場合だけでなく、不動産を取得しようとする者がSPC等に出資等を行ったり、不動産の所有権を小口化して販売したりするケース等も含めたものとして広く捉えている。したがって、会計上のオフバランスを要件とはせず、例えば、オンバランスで処理される不動産特定共同事業法のスキームも対象とされている。

assumes a significant role in value formation of such property.
2) Purposes of Appraisal of Real Estate Securitization

Appraisal of property in securitization is positioned as an important indicator in terms of investor protection and examples herein:

(a) The appraisal value estimated based on the potential cash flow generated from the subject property and the materials and analyses used in the appraisal can be an important indicator for investors when making investment decisions.

(b) The appraisal value is used as an indicator for the asset manager and contributors to the investment when they make investment decisions.

(c) In transaction between parties for conflict of interests, the appraisal value is used as a reference to verify fairness of the sales price of the property.

(d) In order to determine the net present value of the securities, especially those unlisted on the stock market, the appraisal value of the property is used as a reference.

(e) When rating agencies allocate ratings for investment corporation bonds or specified bonds in relation to debt finance, the items included in the appraisal report are used as an important reference.

(f) For listed securities, the Financial Instruments and Exchange Act requires inclusion of the appraisal value in the security registration statement. For private securities, the appraisal value is used as a reference in determining the underwriting amount.

(g) If information related to the appraisal value of the subject property in each year-end result during the holding period is to be disclosed, the appraisal report is used.

2. Scope of Appraisal for Securitized Properties

The securitized properties, as specified in Specific Standards Chapter 3 and relevant Notes, refers to properties that are the subject of a real estate transaction (not only limited to sales/purchase but also fund-raising including equity, debt, bond purchase, etc.), properties that are the subject for potential real estate transaction, properties held by special-purpose company[3] or investment corporation (hereinafter "SPC, etc.") as a result of real estate transaction (including those related to trust beneficiary interest), that falls into

---

[3] Special-purpose company (SPC) refers to a TMK as specified in Article 2-3 of the Asset Securitization Law of Japan and entity operating a business equivalent to a TMK, in which a change of business type is limited.

[4] Article 2-1-5: corporate bond; Article 2-1-9: stocks or stock warrants; Article 2-1-14: beneficiary securities of trust beneficiary as specified in the Trust Act; Article 2-1-16: mortgage securities as specified in the Mortgage Certificate Act (no. 15, 1931)

[5] Article 2-2-1: beneficiary interest in trust asset; Article 2-2-3: rights of members of general partnership or limited partnership companies or rights of employees of limited liability companies; Article 2-2-5: interests based on association contract as specified in Article 667-1 of the Civil Code or based on an anonymous association contract as specified in Article 535 of the Commercial Code, where the investor can earn dividends generated from the subject business ("equity in group investment scheme")

(2) 不動産証券化における鑑定評価の目的

不動産証券化における対象不動産の鑑定評価は、投資家保護の観点を含め、次の諸点で重要な位置付けを持つ。

ア 対象不動産からどの程度のキャッシュフローが期待できるかという観点から求められる鑑定評価額、その判断資料、判断過程等は投資家の投資判断の重要な指標となる。

イ 鑑定評価額は、運用者や投資対象不動産の拠出者の意思決定に当たっての重要な指標として活用される。

ウ 利益相反取引において、適正な取引価格であることの参考資料として不動産の鑑定評価が利用される。

エ 発行証券の基準価格の算定に当たり、特に上場されていないものについて、対象となる不動産の鑑定評価額が参考とされる。

オ 発行される投資法人債や特定社債等のデットファイナンスについて格付機関による格付けがなされる場合に、鑑定評価書の記載事項が重要な参考資料とされる。

カ 鑑定評価額は、上場される証券については金融商品取引法上の有価証券届出書の記載事項とされている。また、私募のときは引受価格の決定における参考資料とされる。

キ 運用期間中の各決算期に対象不動産の鑑定評価額に関する情報開示を行う場合に、鑑定評価書が利用される。

2 対象とする鑑定評価の範囲

基準各論第3章等に規定する「証券化対象不動産」とは、次のいずれかに該当する不動産取引(売買だけでなく、出資や貸付、債券等の購入等の資金調達にかかわる行為も含む。)の目的である不動産、不動産取引の目的となる見込みのある不動産又は不動産取引の結果、特別目的会社[3]や投資法人等(以下「SPC等」という。)が保有することになった不動産(信託受益権に係るものを含む。)をいう。

不動産取引の目的となる見込みのある不動産とは、以下のアからエに掲げる取引を行うことが予定されている、又は当該取引を行うことが意図されている場合における当該取引の目的となっている不動産を指す。現に証券化されている不動産だけでなく、依頼者へ確認できる範囲で、これから証券化される不動産をも適用対象とする趣旨である。

従前に鑑定評価が行われたものを再評価する場合を含め、これらの不動産取引を規定する法律に基づく情報開示を目的とする場合など、過去に証券化されたSPC等が保有する不動産に係る鑑定評価も対象となる。なお、証券化対象不動産に係る賃料を求める鑑定評価は対象としない。

ア 資産の流動化に関する法律(平成10年法律第105号。以下「資産流動化法」という。第2条第2項に規定する資産流動化に係る不動産取引

---

[3] 特別目的会社とは、資産流動化法第2条第3項に規定する特定目的会社及び事業の内容の変更が制限されているこれと同様の事業を営む事業体をいう。

either of the following:

Properties for potential real estate transaction are those for which the following (a) through (d) is scheduled or intended. This means that not only properties already under a securitization scheme but also those that will be securitized are also included.

Appraisal of securitized properties includes those securitized in the past and owned by an SPC, etc. such as revaluation of previously valued property and valuation required for disclosure of information based on relevant laws for real estate transactions. Appraisal that estimates rent of securitized properties is, however, not included.

(a) Real estate transaction related to asset securitization as specified in Article 2-2 of the Asset Securitization Law of Japan (no. 105; 1998)

(b) Real estate transaction related to a trust investment as specified in Article 2-3 of the Investment Trust and Investment Corporation Law and real estate transaction conducted by an investment corporation as specified in Article 2-12 of the same law

(c) Real estate transaction related to joint enterprise agreements as specified in Article 2-3 of the Act Concerning Designated Real Estate Joint Enterprises (no. 198; 1994)

(d) Income- or profit-generating transaction of real estate primarily for the purpose of repayment of securities[4] as specified in Articles 2-1-5, 2-1-9*, 2-1-14, and 2-1-16, and securities equivalents[5] as stipulated in Articles 2-2-1, 2-2-3, and 2-2-55 of the Financial Instruments and Exchange Act (*This case only includes those associated with corporations whose business is real estate transactions. "Corporation" here includes a yugen kaisha currently operating as a kabushiki kaisha as stipulated in Article 2-1 of the Act on Arrangement of Relevant Acts Incidental to Enforcement of the Companies Act.)

3. **When application of Specific Standards Chapter 3 is not required though the subject can be categorized as a "securitized property"**

Even if the subject can be formally categorized as a securitized property as specified in Specific Standards Chapter 3 and relevant Notes, if appraisal without application of Specific Standards Chapter 3 does not damage the profit of third parties, including investors, with reference to the purpose of valuation (such as when the appraisal does not require greater explanation and accuracy than those prepared based on other chapters), the application of Specifics Chapter 3 is not required. Examples of such cases are specified herein. However, even in such cases, if the subject is a large-scale lease property, appraisers should try to apply Specific Standards Chapter 3 to the greatest extent possible by obtaining an engineering report and applying the DCF method, etc.

(a) Real estate transaction as specified in Article 3-1-I (3) (abovementioned 2.(d)) but it is obvious that a securitization scheme is not used[6] in the transaction

---

[6] Such as where the future cash flow (including the income from sale of the property) generated from the property (including derivative assets) is not the only source of income in the fundraising, and also, no SPC, etc. (including scheduled and expected) aiming at holding the subject property to raise funds exists.

イ　投資信託及び投資法人に関する法律（昭和26年法律第198号。以下「投信法」という。）第2条第3項に規定する投資信託に係る不動産取引及び同条第12項に規定する投資法人が行う不動産取引

ウ　不動産特定共同事業法（平成6年法律第77号）第2条第3項に規定する不動産特定共同事業契約に係る不動産取引

エ　金融商品取引法第2条第1項第5号、第9号〔専ら不動産取引を行うことを目的として設置された株式会社（会社法の施行に伴う関係法律の整備等に関する法律第2条第1項の規定により株式会社として存続する有限会社を含む。）に係るものに限る。〕、第14号及び第16号に規定する有価証券[※4]並びに同条第2項第1号、第3号及び第5号の規定により有価証券とみなされる権利[※5]の債務の履行等を主たる目的として収益又は利益を生ずる不動産取引

3　形式的に「証券化対象不動産」に該当しても基準各論第3章等を適用しないことができる場合

　基準各論第3章等に規定する「証券化対象不動産」に形式的に該当する場合においても、その依頼目的等から当該鑑定評価の説明力、精度を基準各論第3章等以外の規定に準拠した鑑定評価以上に向上させることを必要としないなど、必ずしも基準各論第3章等を適用しなくても投資家をはじめとする第三者の利益を害するとは認められないと判断される場合には、基準各論第3章等を適用しないことができる。このような場合を例示すれば、次のとおりである。ただし、このような場合においても対象不動産が賃貸大型不動産の場合においては、エンジニアリング・レポートの取得やDCF法の適用等、可能な限り基準各論第3章等を準用するよう努めなければならない。

ア　不動産鑑定評価基準各論第3章第1節Ⅰ(3)（前記2エ）のうち、証券化の仕組みを用いていないこと[※6]が明確な不動産取引の場合。

4　第5号：社債券。第9号：株券又は新株予約証券。第14号：信託法に規定する受益証券発行信託の受益証券。第16号：抵当証券法（昭和6年法律第15号）に規定する抵当証券

5　第1号：信託の受益権。第3号：合名会社若しくは合資会社の社員権又は合同会社の社員権。第5号：民法第667条第1項に規定する組合契約や商法第535条に規定する匿名組合契約等に基づく権利等のうち、出資者が出資対象事業から生ずる配当等を受けることができる権利（いわゆる集団投資スキーム持分）。

(b) If the appraisal of a property for which the buyer is not yet determined is requested by the owner who is not planning for securitization, and later the property is purchased by concerned parties for a securitization scheme

(c) If the appraisal is related to derivatives, such as securitization of loans (e.g., housing loans) backed by non-investment properties[7]

(d) If the purpose of the valuation is to secure collateral or debt collection, and it is obvious that the appraisal report will only be used internally by the client, and the client determines that the appraisal is to estimate the value of the subject property as collateral and does not require a appraisal report based on Specific Standards Chapter 3 and relevant Notes[8]

(e) If the purpose of the request is for acquisition of property owned by a SPC, etc, and it is obvious that the securitization scheme will not be used after the acquisition[9]

If Specific Standards Chapter 3 and relevant Notes is not applied, the appraiser should inform the client that the appraisal report cannot be used for transactions related to securitization, and acquire the client's consent. The appraiser should also specify in the appraisal report that "this report cannot be used for transactions related to securitization."

---

[7] Since the source of repayment of the loan is not the income generated from the subject property, general valuation of collateral property is considered sufficient.

[8] Such as cases where the client is the security interest holder. (Securitization of such debt is excluded.)

[9] If the valuation is requested when the client is considering purchasing the subject, sufficient information for application of Specific Standards Chapter 3 and relevant Notes may not be available. In such cases, if it is obvious that the securitization scheme will not be used, it is also deemed acceptable not to apply Specific Standards Chapter 3 and relevant Notes for investor protection.

イ 証券化目的のない売主からの買主未定の売却目的の鑑定評価依頼において、後日、証券化関係者が購入することとなった場合。
ウ 住宅ローン等の収益目的でない不動産を担保不動産とするローン債権の証券化等派生商品に係る鑑定評価の場合[7]。
エ 依頼目的が担保徴求や債権回収等の場合において、鑑定評価書が依頼者の内部でのみ利用されることが明確で、依頼者が、対象不動産について基準各論第3章等適用の鑑定評価書については必要とせずに担保価値の把握等を行うものと判断している場合[8]。
オ 依頼目的がSPC等の保有する不動産の購入である場合において、購入後証券化の仕組みを用いないことが明確である場合[9]。

なお、基準各論第3章等を適用しない場合には、依頼者に当該鑑定評価書は証券化関連の取引には利用できない旨の了解を得るとともに、鑑定評価書に「不動産証券化の取引等に関して当該鑑定評価書を用いることができない」旨を記載する必要がある。

---

[6] 不動産（派生資産を含む）の将来のキャッシュフロー（売却収入を含む）のみを裏付けとした資金調達を行わないこと、かつ、そのための当該不動産の保有を目的とするSPC等が存しないこと（予定又は見込みを含む。）。

[7] ローン債権の返済原資が対象不動産の収益でないため、通常の担保目的の鑑定評価として行えば足りると考えられる。

[8] 依頼者が担保権者の場合（ただし、当該債権を対象とする証券化商品の場合は除く。）。

[9] 購入の検討段階の評価依頼においては、基準各論第3章等を適用するための必要十分な資料が必ずしも全て入手できない場合があるが、証券化の仕組みを用いないことが明確な場合であれば、投資家保護の観点からも基準各論第3章等を適用しなくても問題ないと考えられる。

II. Ethic

1. Basic Attitude

It must be recognized that if inappropriateness of an appraisal of securitized property results in damaging the sound management of an investment corporation and the like, significant damage may be caused to a wide range of investors. As such, full consideration must be given throughout each process of the appraisal of a securitized property, such as gathering data, confirming the subject property, analyzing value influences (influences on the value of real estate), and applying appraisal approaches. Along with that, the appraisal value (market value or market value based on special considerations [*tokutei kakaku*]), in which the subject property's profitability is properly reflected, must be obtained based on a detailed investigation.

In the appraisal of a securitized property, the subject property is individually valued. The appraisal does not go as far as estimating the value of the property on the premise of managing it as a whole with another property, or commenting on the actual transaction prices of the securitized products

2. Accountability

An appraisal report on securitized property is used as a reference by multiple parties with interest regarding investment in or financing for the subject property. Therefore, the appraiser or appraisal firm must be careful that the investigations or verification provided in the appraisal are comprehensible for these and other parties, in addition to the client. Also, for investment decisions, the appraisal report must provide specific verification of the figures presented in the investigations or appraisal to enable investors to make comparisons with other securitized properties appraisal reports. The appraiser must also be careful in the way information is presented in the report and the report must fulfill its accountability; such as by specifying the information used in the appraisal.

Though the appraiser, in principle, uses investigative data provided by other experts, including engineering reports, the appraiser's decision on utilization of such data must be explained.

Additionally, when a single client requests appraisal of multiple properties at one time, further accountability is required for uniformity and consistency among the requested reports regarding identification of the subject property's value influences (difference in value influences, yields, etc.), and application of appraisal approaches.

Ⅱ　倫理

1　基本姿勢

　証券化対象不動産の鑑定評価が適正を欠いた結果、投資法人等の運営の健全性を害した場合には、これにより不特定多数の投資家に多大の損害を与えるおそれがあることに留意し、証券化対象不動産の鑑定評価に当たっては、資料の収集、対象不動産の確認、価格形成要因の分析、鑑定評価手法の適用等、鑑定評価の手順の各段階において常に最大限の配慮を行い、詳細な調査に基づいて対象不動産の収益力を的確に反映した適正な市場価値又は投資採算価値を表わす鑑定評価額（正常価格又は特定価格）を求める必要がある。

　なお、証券化対象不動産の鑑定評価は、あくまでも対象不動産単独の評価を行うものであり、他の不動産と一体として運用した場合の価格や、証券市場においてその価格が形成される証券価格の評価にまで立ち入るものではない。

2　説明責任

　証券化対象不動産に係る鑑定評価書は、証券化対象不動産への投資、融資に係る多くの利害関係者の参考資料として用いられるので、不動産鑑定士及び不動産鑑定業者は、依頼者のみならず証券化対象不動産に係る利害関係者その他の者が鑑定評価の調査内容や判断根拠を把握することができるようにする必要がある。さらに、投資判断のため、他の証券化対象不動産の鑑定評価書との比較を行えるように、調査内容や鑑定評価で用いた数値等の判断根拠をより具体的に明示するとともに、鑑定評価報告書の記載方法等を工夫し、鑑定評価に採用した資料等を明示するなど説明責任が十分に果たされるものとする必要がある。

　また、基本的にはエンジニアリング・レポート等他の専門家による調査結果を活用することになるが、当該調査結果の活用の有無について判断した結果について、説明を行う必要がある。

　さらに、同一の依頼者から同時に複数物件の鑑定評価を依頼された場合には、各対象不動産の価格形成要因に対する判断（増減価要因の格差や利回り等）や評価手法の適用方法等について、複数の鑑定評価報告書相互間の統一性や整合性の確保を行うことなどの一層の説明責任が求められる。

III. Confirmation Required at the Time of Valuation Request

The influence of appraisal associated with securitized properties is extensive. Therefore, the appraiser in charge of confirming the valuation request must pay attention to the client and the subject property regarding the below issues before accepting the request.

- The appraiser should explain that detailed investigation, data gathering, and confirmation of the subject property are required for conducting appraisal for securitized properties, as well as the importance of information and procedure for the appraisal. Such is necessary to improve the understanding of the client and gains its cooperation.
- The appraiser should try to obtain appropriate information from the client by confirming with the client if the data is the most recent and whether it is adequate and genuine. If the client provisionally provides a draft report or past data, the appraiser should confirm the date of submission of the final report or the latest data.
- During the appraisal process, person not in charge of the appraisal of the subject property may in some cases receive the valuation request, hold discussions with the client, and/or draft a schedule for appraisal of multiple properties. However, even in such a case, it is the role of the appraiser to confirm the request and valuation details with the client, request information from the client, and draft an appropriate schedule for appraisal.

1. Purposes of Valuation and Scope of Work

In accordance with the valuation guidelines designated by the Ministry of Land, Infrastructure, Transport, and Tourism, the appraisal firm is obligated to issue a document called the "Confirmation to Determine Purposes and Scope of Work" (hereinafter the "Confirmation Letter"), which clearly specifies the purposes of valuation and scope of work to the client before concluding the valuation contract. This Confirmation Letter should be finalized by confirming with the client via the request screening conducted by the appraiser in charge of confirming the valuation request.

The purposes of valuation and scope of work may not necessarily be determined in complete detail by the date of contract conclusion. These often have to be changed in accordance with the result of the site inspection, etc. In such cases, the appraiser in charge of confirming the valuation request must confirm the revised Confirmation Letter. The appraiser in charge of confirming the valuation request is involved in the appraisal process by determining the basic elements and process, and therefore, this appraiser should sign and seal in the final appraisal report.

To determine the purposes of valuation and scope of work, the appraiser in charge of confirming the valuation request should check the following:

1) **Client and Parties for Submission of Final Appraisal Report**
    - Client

        To the extent possible using information provided by the client, it is required to check the role of the client in the securitization scheme (namely, how the client is in-

Ⅲ 受付時確認事項

　証券化対象不動産に係る不動産の鑑定評価はその影響が広範に及ぶため、確定担当不動産鑑定士は、依頼者及び対象不動産について、以下の事項を踏まえて鑑定評価依頼の受付を行う必要がある。
　ア　不動産鑑定士は、依頼者に対し証券化対象不動産の鑑定評価を行うためには、より詳細な調査、資料収集、対象不動産の確認作業が必要となること、及び鑑定評価に係る資料、手順等の重要性を説明して、依頼者の理解を深め、かつ協力を得る必要がある。
　イ　不動産鑑定士は、依頼者から入手する資料について、それが最新のデータであるのか、不備はないのか、真正なものであるかなどについて、依頼者に確認し適切な資料の入手に努めなければならない。依頼者から暫定的にドラフトや過去のデータの提示を受けた場合には、最終版や最新のデータの提示時期を確認する必要がある。
　ウ　鑑定評価作業において、鑑定評価の受付や依頼者との協議及び複数不動産の鑑定評価の処理計画の策定は、対象不動産の鑑定評価を担当する不動産鑑定士以外の者が行う場合もあるが、依頼者への依頼内容及び評価内容の確認、資料の要請並びに適切な処理計画の策定は不動産鑑定士の役割である。

1　業務の目的と範囲等の確定

　国土交通省が定めた価格等調査ガイドラインにより、不動産鑑定業者は、契約の締結までに業務の目的と範囲等を明記した文書等である「業務の目的と範囲等の確定に係る確認書」(以下「確認書」という。)を依頼者に交付することが義務づけられたが、この確認書は、確定担当不動産鑑定士が受付行為を通じて依頼者に確認の上で確定するものである。
　業務の目的と範囲等については、契約の締結までに必ずしも全ての内容を確定できるとは限らず、実地調査等を踏まえ変更になることが多く、この場合、変更後の確認書の確定も、確定担当不動産鑑定士が行うものである。確定担当不動産鑑定士は、鑑定評価の基本的事項及び手順を決定することで鑑定評価業務に関与することになるため、成果報告書である鑑定評価書への署名押印が必要となる。
　確定担当不動産鑑定士が業務の目的と範囲等の確定にあたり、確認すべき事項は以下のとおりである。

(1)　依頼者及び成果報告書の提出先
　　1）依頼者
　　　依頼者から確認できる範囲で、鑑定評価の依頼者の証券化関係者の中での位置付け、すなわち依頼者が証券化対象不動産証券化手続きにどのように係わっているのかについて、依頼者と

volved in the securitization procedures) by confirming whether the client has any capital or business ties or other special interests with parties involved in the securitization. If these exist, their details need to be identified[10].

The above mentioned identification is assumed that it is not asking for the details of the interests. For example, the appraiser should basically need to identify the securitization scheme diagram to understand the subject property's structure of securitization, and use the diagram to understand the names of concerned parties or person in the securitization (including those expected to be involved) who are directly related to the client in the transaction of the subject property.

The concerned parties in the securitization, as in Specific Standards Chapter 3 and relevant Notes, including the SPC, etc. are: originator who uses the securitization to remove the properties owned by the SPC from the balance sheet[11]; arranger who arranges the securitization scheme and negotiates with relevant parties for fund-raising for the originator[12]; asset manager entrusted by investors to manage the assets; lender who provides financing to the SPC[13]; equity investor who invests in the SPC[14]; bond-holder who sells/purchases or holds bonds issued by the SPC; trustee such as a trust and banking company entrusted with management and disposal of real estate; and the fund specified in Article 1-8 of Cabinet Office Regulations regarding disclosure of information of specified securities (no. 22; 1993; Ministry of Finance)[15].

- Parties for Submission of Appraisal Report

    The final version of an appraisal report of a securitized property may be submitted not only to the client but also to third parties via the client. Financial institutions (lender, etc.) and investors are examples of parties for submission.

    Confirmation of the parties for submission and how the parties should be written as addressees on the appraisal report should be made in accordance with the purpose of the valuation. Details of these parties, such as their individual exact names, may not necessarily be required. In some cases, information that is useful in understanding how the report will be used, such as the reason for submission or attributes of the parties, may be sufficient[16].

---

[10] According to the Valuation Guidelines, the "client" includes not only the named client but also the asset manager who is the actual client in the valuation of securitized properties.

[11] The originator is the original owner of the securitized property.

[12] The arranger assumes an important role: considers the overall structure of the securitization and constructs the basic scheme to carry it out by negotiating with parties concerned, including the originator, investor, and lender.

[13] A lender herein refers to an investing financial institution that mainly provides non-recourse loans

[14] Equity refers to capital that is calculated by deducting the debt from the total assets. Stock issued by companies, securities equivalent to this (investment securities issued by an investment corporation, or specified shares and preferred shares issued by TMK), and investment in anonymous associations or voluntary partnerships fall into this category. Equity investors refer to those who invest in such securities.

[15] A fund herein refers to a fund managed by the issuer of the investment trust securities for the holders of such securities. The fund invests mainly in securities, real estate, and other specified assets (those specified in Article 2-1 of the Investment Trust and Investment Corporation Law).

他の証券化関係者との資本関係や取引関係、その他特別の利害関係及びこれらの関係がある場合にはその内容を確認する必要がある[10]。

この確認は、詳細な利害関係の確認まで求めているものではないと考えられるので、例えば、対象不動産がどのような証券化スキームにより証券化の対象となっているのかについて、当該証券化スキームを理解しうる図表等により確認し、その中での当該不動産取引等において依頼者と直接関与する証券化関係者の名称や氏名（予定されている者を含む。）を確認する。

なお、基準各論第3章等にいう証券化関係者とは、SPC等のほか、SPC等が保有する不動産のオフバランスを目的として証券化の仕組みを利用する者であるオリジネーター[11]、オリジネーター等のために証券化の仕組みづくりや資金調達等のための関係者間の調整等を実施するアレンジャー[12]、投資家からの委託を受けて資産運用を行うアセットマネジャー、SPC等に対して融資を行うレンダー[13]、SPC等に出資を行うエクイティ投資家[14]、SPC等の社債を売買又は保有する社債権者、不動産に係る管理処分信託を受託する信託銀行等の信託受託者、特定有価証券の内容等の開示に関する内閣府令（平成5年大蔵省令第22号）第1条第8号に掲げるファンド[15]等を含む。

2）鑑定評価書の提出先

証券化対象不動産に係る成果報告書である鑑定評価書は、依頼者だけではなく、依頼者を通じて第三者に提出される場合があり、この場合における提出先としては、金融機関（レンダー等）や投資家などが考えられる。

提出先の確定及び明記は、依頼目的等に応じ、必ずしも個別具体的な提出先の名称等は必要ではなく、提出の目的や提出先の属性等利用目的の把握に資するものでも足りる[16]。

---

10 価格等調査ガイドラインによれば、依頼者とは、依頼名義人のほか、証券化対象不動産の鑑定評価の場合の実質的な依頼者となるアセットマネジャー等を含む。
11 証券化する不動産の原所有者
12 不動産証券化のためのストラクチャー全体を検討し、証券化を実現させるための基本的な枠組みをオリジネーター、投資家、レンダー等の関係者と協議しながら構築していく重要な役割を担う。
13 投資家のうち、主にノンリコース・ローンを実行する金融機関のことをいう。
14 エクイティとは、総資産から負債（デット）を差し引いた資本のことを指し、会社の発行する株式やそれに準ずる証券（投資法人が発行する投資証券や特定目的会社が発行する特定出資・優先出資証券等）、あるいは匿名組合・任意組合への出資等がこれに該当し、エクイティ投資家はこれら証券投資・出資を行う投資家である。
15 ファンドとは、投資信託証券の発行者が当該投資信託証券の所有者のために主として有価証券、不動産その他の特定資産（投信法第2条第1項に規定する特定資産をいう。）に対する投資として運用する財産をいう。
16 成果報告書の記載についても、提出の目的や提出先の属性等利用目的の把握に資するもので足りる。

2) **Purpose of Valuation, Parties for Disclosure of Appraisal Value, and Publication Appraisal value**
   - Purposes of Valuation
      The purposes of the valuation must include not only vague descriptions such as "for estimation of asset value" or "for reference for sales," but also confirm with the client and include the background of why the client requires the valuation, securitization scheme (including planned securitization), details of transaction (acquisition, sales, mortgage, disclosure of prices, etc.), role of the client, and potential conflict of interest in concerned parties. Details of the above, whether Specific Standards Chapter 3 and relevant Notes is applied (and also which of the categories specified in Article 3-1-1 of the chapter this valuation falls into), and its reasons should all be detailed in the appraisal report.
   - Parties for Disclosure of Appraisal Value and Publication
      Since the appraisal of securitized properties is based on the Appraisal Standards, it is not required to be identified or specified in the appraisal report of the parties for disclosure of the appraisal value or of publication.
      Auditing firms, certified public accountants, lawyers, financial institutions (lenders), and investors are some examples of parties for disclosure other than the client in the appraisal of securitized properties. Public documents such as the asset management report are example of publication of appraisal value.

3) **Special Interests**
   - Interests of appraisers or the appraisal firm regarding the subject property
   - Ties between the client and appraiser or appraisal firm
   - Ties between the parties for disclosure/submission and appraiser or appraisal firm
   - Ties between the client and concerned parties in securitization
      · Roles of the client in securitization of the subject property, such as whether the client is the originator, arranger, asset manager, lender, equity investor, TMK, investment firm, or fund
      · Whether there are capital or business ties or other special interests between the client and concerned parties in the securitization; and if so, give the details

4) **Basic Elements of Valuation**
   - Subject Property
      Determine the land and/or building(s), and ownership and other rights to be valued.
      Whether a property is investment-grade or not is determined based on the asset management policy, and so is the selection of investment-grade property. Therefore the appraiser does not directly determine whether the subject property is investment-grade or not. However, upon receiving a valuation request for securitized properties, the appraiser should pay attention to the investment-grade decision of the asset manager and referring to the purpose and background of the request, should take

---

[16] Also in the final valuation report, giving information that is useful in understanding how the report is sufficient, such as the reason for submission or attributes of the parties.

(2) 依頼目的、鑑定評価額が開示される範囲又は公表の有無等

1) 依頼目的
　　鑑定評価の依頼目的については、「資産評価」や「売買の参考」といった抽象的な内容だけではなく、依頼者に対して依頼が必要となった背景、証券化スキーム（予定を含む。）、取引等の内容（取得、売却、担保提供、価格開示等）、依頼者の立場、利害関係等について確認する必要がある。なお、当該各確認の内容、基準各論第3章等の適用の有無（不動産鑑定評価基準各論第3章第1節Ⅰのどの項目に該当するか。）とその理由について鑑定評価報告書に記載しなければならない。

2) 鑑定評価額が開示される範囲又は公表の有無等
　　証券化対象不動産の鑑定評価は、不動産鑑定評価基準に則った鑑定評価であるため、鑑定評価額が開示される範囲又は公表の有無等の確定及び明記は必ずしも求められていない。
　　なお、証券化対象不動産の鑑定評価における依頼者以外の開示先としては、監査法人又は公認会計士、弁護士、金融機関（レンダー等）、投資家などが考えられ、また鑑定評価額等の公表方法としては、資産運用報告等各種開示資料への掲載が考えられる。

(3) 利害関係等
　1) 不動産鑑定士又は不動産鑑定業者の対象不動産に関する利害関係等
　2) 依頼者と不動産鑑定士又は不動産鑑定業者との間の関係
　3) 開示・提出先と不動産鑑定士又は不動産鑑定業者との間の関係
　4) 依頼者の証券化関係者との関係
　　ア　依頼者が証券化対象不動産の証券化に係る利害関係者（オリジネーター、アレンジャー、アセットマネジャー、レンダー、エクイティ投資家又は特定目的会社・投資法人・ファンド等をいい、以下「証券化関係者」という。）のいずれかであるかの別
　　イ　依頼者と証券化関係者との資本関係、取引関係その他特別な利害関係の有無及びこれらの関係を有する場合にあっては、その内容

(4) 鑑定評価の基本的事項
　1) 対象不動産
　　鑑定評価の対象となる土地又は建物等、所有権及び所有権以外の権利を確定する。
　　証券化対象不動産は、運用方針に照らして個々の不動産の投資適格性が判断され、選択されるので、不動産鑑定士は対象不動産の投資適格性を直接的に判断する立場にはない。しかしながら、不動産鑑定士が証券化対象不動産の鑑定評価の依頼を受け付けるに当たっては、投資適格性に関する運用者の判断等も踏まえ、鑑定評価の依頼目的及び依頼が必要になった背景に照らして、適切であるかについて十分に留意する。

note whether the valuation request is appropriate or not.
- Premises of Subject Identification

   Investor protection is important in appraisal of securitized properties. Therefore it is not permitted to simply add limiting conditions, but the valuation should, in principle, be based on "as is" in status[17], which means it is based on the current physical conditions and usufructuary right, and generally not including security rights that do not affect the value of the property.

   If the building is under construction, the subject to be valued should only be the land, unless the building is near completion and deemed an appropriate subject for valuation[18].

- Date of Value

   The site inspection of the securitized properties should be conducted on a day as close to the date of value as possible since the valuation is based on "as is" in status.

   The date of value should be set, considering the condition changes of the subject property, within the days available for the appraiser to analyze and judge the value influences confirmed at the site inspection. A date of value in the future (i.e., a prospective value opinion) should be within approximately seven days of the date of completion of the appraisal process, if in the case that providing a prospective value opinion is inevitable.

- Basis of Value
  - Securitization Scheme under the Asset Securitization Law of Japan or Investment Trust and Investment Corporation Law

     If the securitization scheme is based on the Asset Securitization Law of Japan or Investment Trust and Investment Corporation Law (hereinafter the "designated scheme") and falls into one of the categories detailed in (a) through (e), the subject property is deemed to be the objective for investment carried out through the SPC. Therefore, because the SPC operates leasing or development for some period of time, cash flow may be limited or the value for typical investors may differ from the market value that may include value of owner-occupancy which may be estimated from the point of view other than of profitability. As such, in order to protect investors, the appraiser should estimate the value that shows investment profitability based on the value indicated by the income capitalization approach that appropriately reflects the profitability of the subject property assuming such limita-

---

[17] In the valuation of property where the influence of the operation is large, such as a hotel, commercial facility, hospital, or logistics facility (trade related property), it is difficult to value without assumption of specific business operation. Accordingly, essentially, such property is valued based on the current operator, employees, competitiveness, and other conditions. It is also important to state clearly which asset belongs to the owner, tenant, or hotel management operator (in the case of a hotel building). In order to do so, it is recommended that the appraiser not only interviews the property owner and manager, but asks the client to provide the asset ledger and confirm what was found during the interview.

[18] Such as cases when the building is near completion and ready to obtain a certificate of inspection, as well as when it is possible to identify and confirm the items regarding the subject property as specified in Article 5-1 of the General Topics of the Appraisal Standards. (In principle, this is when the certificate of inspection is issued or tentative use is permitted.)

2）対象確定条件

　証券化対象不動産の鑑定評価に当たっては、投資家保護の観点が重要であるため、安易に評価条件を付することは許されず、原則として現状を所与として鑑定評価を行う必要がある[17]。現状を所与とするとは、物理的な現状及び現状の用益権の存在を所与とすることをいうものであり、一般的に不動産の価値自体に対する影響はない担保権の存在等を含めるものではない。

　なお、建物が建築中の土地の場合は、建築中の建物が鑑定評価の対象として認められる程度に完成している場合[18]を除き、鑑定評価の対象となるのは、土地部分のみである。

3）価格時点

　証券化対象不動産の鑑定評価における実地調査を行った日（実地調査日）は、現状を所与とした評価の観点から、可能な限り価格時点に近い日に設定するものとする。

　また、価格時点は、対象不動産の変動状況を考慮し、実地調査により確認した価格形成要因の分析や判定が可能な範囲で設定するものとし、やむを得ず鑑定評価を行った日を基準として将来時点とする場合にはおおむね7日以内とする。

4）価格の種類

　ア　資産流動化法又は投信法に基づくスキーム

　　資産流動化法又は投信法に基づくスキーム（以下「法定スキーム」という。）において以下の㈦から㈺の場面で鑑定評価を行う場合は、対象不動産がSPC等を通じた投資の目的とされるという性格から、SPC等により一定期間の賃貸等の運用や開発が行われることにより、キャッシュフローが制約を受けたり、投資採算価値が自己利用等による収益性以外の価値判断を含む市場価値とかい離したりすることがあるため、投資家保護のために、それらの制約等を前提に対象不動産の収益力を適切に反映する収益価格に基づいた投資採算価値を表す価格を求める必要がある。

　　これらの場合には、法令等により不動産鑑定士による鑑定評価に基づく開示資料の作成が求められ、かつ、資産流動化計画等により投資家に開示される対象不動産の運用方法等のSPC等による運用、開発等を所与とする必要があることから、必ずしも最有効使用を前提とするものではないため特定価格として求める必要がある。特定価格を求める場合には、資産流動化法又は投信法による運用方法[19]を前提とすることについて鑑定評価報告書に記載するものとする。

---

[17] ホテル、商業施設、病院、物流施設など、事業経営の影響が大きい用途の不動産においては、事業の特性により、特定の事業者を前提としないで、評価を行うことは困難であるため、原則運営者、人員構成、施設競争力などの現状を所与として評価を行う。また、オーナー、賃借人、ホテルマネジメント会社（ホテルの場合）等の資産区分を明確に行い、物件の特定を行う必要がある。その際、所有者や施設管理者へのヒアリングのみならず、依頼者へ資産台帳を徴求して確認するのが望ましい。

[18] 工事完了検査済証の取得が可能な状態で、建物が不動産鑑定評価基準総論第5章第1節鑑定評価の基本的事項における対象不動産の確定、確認が可能な程度に完成している場合（原則として検査証の交付または仮使用の承認を受けている場合）。

[19] 投資法人等の資産の一部としてということではなく、あくまでも対象不動産単独としての運用方法を前提とする。

tions.

In such cases, it is required by law to prepare documents for disclosure based on the valuation conducted by the appraiser, and required that the management and development of the subject property be based on those disclosed by the SPC to investors via the asset securitization plan. Therefore, the value is not necessarily estimated assuming the highest and best use. Accordingly, the basis of value to be estimated is market value based on special considerations. In order to conduct this estimate, the valuation is based on the management policy[19] specified under the Asset Securitization Law of Japan or Investment Trust and Investment Corporation Law, and this should be shown in the appraisal report.

(a) Valuation related to the acquisition of specified assets in securitization under the Asset Securitization Law of Japan (Article 40-1-8, 122-1-18, and 226-1-2 of the Asset Securitization Law of Japan and Article 107-4 of the ordinance for enforcement)

(b) Upon public offering of securities under the Asset Securitization Law of Japan, if the value of the subject property is to be listed in the security registration statement as managed assets or as part of specified trust assets (5-2 and 5-4 of the attached format of the Cabinet Office Regulations regarding disclosure of information of specified securities)

(c) Upon acquisition of real estate by the asset manager of an investment trust or investment company as specified assets, if the valuation is conducted based on the appraisal work conducted by an appraiser (Article 11-2, 54, 201-2 of the Investment Trust and Investment Corporation Law)

(d) Upon public offering of securities, if the value of investment property is to be listed in the security registration statement as an investment result (4 and 4-3 of attached format of the Cabinet Office Regulations regarding disclosure of information of specified securities)

(e) If the value of the real estate is to be listed in the asset management report prepared by the asset manager as disclosure of year-end fair value of specified assets during the holding period (Article 14-1, 54, and 129-2 of the Investment Trust and Investment Corporation Law; Article 58-1-8 and 73-1-7 of Ordinance regarding Calculation of Investment Company)

If the case that the assemblage or component market value is the basis of value to be estimated, such as if the valuation is related to a purchase of interest in land to merge the leasehold interest and ownership interest in land, or if it is related to a purchase of adjacent property to merge with the subject property, the basis of value should be market value based on special considerations. The limiting conditions regarding this should be detailed in the appraisal report.

However, in the case of a sale of securitized properties, the potential sales value should be estimated based on an ordinary market where the mentioned investment

---

[19] The valuation should be based on the management policy of a single subject property, not as a part of the assets held by the investment corporation.

(ア) 資産流動化法に基づく証券化における、特定資産の取得に関する価格調査等（資産流動化法第40条第1項第8号、第122条第1項第18号、第226条第1項第2号、規則第107条第4号）
(イ) 資産流動化法に基づく証券化における証券の公募が行われる際に、有価証券届出書に管理資産又は特定信託財産を構成する資産内容として、当該不動産の価格を記載する場合（特定有価証券の内容等の開示に関する内閣府令別紙様式第五号の二、第五号の四）
(ウ) 運用者が、投資信託又は投資法人について、特定資産として不動産の取得をした際に、不動産鑑定士による鑑定評価を踏まえた価格調査を行う場合（投信法第11条第2項、第54条、第201第2項）
(エ) 証券についての公募が行われるとき、有価証券届出書に、投資状況等として投資不動産の価格を記載する場合（特定有価証券の内容等の開示に関する内閣府令別紙様式第四号、第四号の三）
(オ) 運用期間中の各決算期に特定資産の適正な価格に関する情報開示として、運用者が作成する資産運用報告書に不動産の評価額が記載される場合（投信法第14条第1項、第54条、投資信託財産の計算に関する規則第58条第1項第8号、投信法第129条第2項、投資法人の計算に関する規則第73条第1項第7号）

なお、借地権と底地の併合を目的とする売買に関連する場合や隣接不動産の併合を目的とする売買に関連する場合など、限定価格の要件に該当する場合であっても求める価格の種類は特定価格とすることとし、当該要件に即した内容は鑑定評価報告書で説明するものとする。

ただし、証券化対象不動産を譲渡する場合は、前記の運用等の制約のない一般的な不動産市場での売却可能価格を判断するためのものであるので正常価格を求めるものとし、また、前記(ア)から(オ)であってもバルク処分型の仕組みで対象不動産が賃貸用不動産以外であって一定期間の保有を前提としていない場合など、投資家に開示される対象不動産の運用方法等がない場合には、投資対象としての運用等を行うものではなく、特定価格の要件を満たさないことから正常価格を求めるものとする。これらの場合に限定価格の要件に該当する場合には限定価格を求めるものとする。

予定される運用方法が最有効使用と一致し、投資採算を重視して価格形成される市場に属する不動産は、多くはDCF法による収益価格を標準として正常価格を求めることとなる[20]ので、投資採算価値を表す価格（特定価格）と正常価格とで、結果として求められた価格に相違がないことが多いが、このような場合も、結果として価格が一致するということであり、あくまで鑑定評価で求める価格は特定価格となる（この場合でも正常価格は付記する。）。

---

20 特定価格の試算価格の調整については後記Ⅷ3 参照。

restrictions do not exist and, accordingly, the basis of value should be market value. Also, even if the valuation falls into one of the categories detailed in (a) through (e), if there is no management policy of the subject property to be disclosed to investors, such as bulk sales of non-lease property not expected to be held, the valuation does not satisfy the conditions of market value based on special considerations since it is not managed as a subject for investment; therefore the basis of value should be market value. If it falls into conditions of assemblage value, the basis of value should be assemblage or component market value.

If the property's management policy matches the highest and best use and its value is generated placing emphasis on investment profitability, the basis of value to be estimated is market value in most cases and is estimated based on the value indicated by the DCF method of the income capitalization approach[20]. Accordingly, market value based on special considerations that shows the investment profitability often results in the same figure as market value. Please note however that even if the outcomes are the same, the basis of value which should be estimated should be market value based on special considerations. (In such cases, market value should also be shown in the report.)

· Scheme other than the Designated Scheme

If a scheme other than the designated scheme (hereinafter a "non-designated scheme") is used in the securitization, due to the reasons specified below, it is deemed as valuation in which the "purposes of valuation are derived from public demand specified in laws"[21]. Accordingly, the basis of value should be the same as the designated scheme[22], meaning if it is for the acquisition of a property by a SPC or disclosure of the current value during the holding period, market value based on special considerations is the basis of value to be estimated. If market value based on special considerations is estimated, it is based on assumptions that the property is managed by a SPC, and this should be detailed in the appraisal report.

(a) The private fund market including non-designated schemes satisfies the valuation objectives derived from public demand specified in laws to protect investors, similar to that of the designated scheme.

(b) The non-designated scheme is also offering investment opportunities to investors based on the asset management plan, and there are only few differences between the designated and non-designated schemes since change of an asset securitization plan is currently flexible.

(c) Other than the real estate in relation to Asset Securitization Law of Japan or

---

[20] See VIII.3 for reconciliation of the indicated market values based on special considerations.

[21] Though the non-designated scheme has been regarded as not satisfying the requirements of market value based on special considerations ("purposes of such valuation are derived from public demand specified in laws") as specified in Article 5-3-I-3 of the General Topics of the Appraisal Standards, we changed this statement. Note however that even before our change, some appraisal firms had regarded the non-designated scheme as satisfying the requirements of market value based on special considerations.

[22] Except for cases of collateral securities where general valuation of collateral (market value) is sufficient

イ　法定スキーム以外のスキーム

法定スキーム以外のスキーム（以下「法定外スキーム」という。）を用いた場合においても、以下の理由により「法令等による社会的要請を背景とする評価目的」がある場合と判断される[21]ので、求める価格は、SPC等が対象不動産を取得する場合や保有時の時価開示の場合には特定価格を求めるなど、法定スキームを用いた場合と同様とする[22]。特定価格を求める場合、SPC等による運用等を前提とすることについて鑑定評価報告書に記載するものとする。

(ア) 法定外スキームを含むプライベートファンド市場は、法定スキームと同様の投資家保護という法令等による社会的要請を背景とする評価目的を満たすと認められること。

(イ) 一定の運用計画等を前提に投資家を募る仕組みであることには変わりがなく、また、昨今では、資産流動化計画の変更も容易に行われるなど、法定スキームと法定外スキームにおける制度上の差異が少なくなってきていること。

(ウ) 不動産鑑定評価基準各論第3章において、資産流動化法及び投信法のほか、金融商品取引法に規定する有価証券等や不動産特定共同事業法に規定する不動産特定共同事業契約等に係る不動産が、証券化対象不動産として規定されたこと。

(エ) 結果として、正常価格を付記することとなるため、特に正常価格と異なる場合には、運用計画の制約等による価格の違いを明確に投資家に説明できることとなること。

---

[21] これまで法定外スキームを用いた証券化に係る鑑定評価については、不動産鑑定評価基準総論第5章第3節Ⅰ3「特定価格」の要件である「法令等による社会的要請を背景とする評価目的」を満たさないものとして扱ってきたが、その扱いを変更する。なお、一部の鑑定業者においては、法定外スキームを用いた証券化に係る鑑定評価においても特定価格の要件を満たすものとして取り扱ってきた。

[22] 抵当証券等、正常価格として通常の担保目的の鑑定評価として行えば足りる場合を除く

Investment Trust and Investment Corporation Law, real estate related to securities under the Financial Instruments and Exchange Law or related to joint enterprise agreements under the Act Concerning Designated Real Estate Joint Enterprises are newly designated as securitized properties in Specific Standards Chapter 3

(d) Ultimately, the market value must also be shown in the appraisal report, and if it significantly differs from the market value based on special considerations, the differences in value caused by limitations of the management plan can then be clearly explained to the investor.

· Other

In the case of estimating market value based on special considerations, if the asset securitization plan or trust asset securitization plan is determined, conditions which are deemed legal and feasible should be taken into account as valuation condition as it is,. If there are illegal or impractical conditions or the asset securitization plan or trust asset securitization plan has not yet been determined, valuation condition should be set and applied assuming a management policy that is deemed appropriate for investment of the subject property. In such a case, this should be detailed in the appraisal report.

● Assumptions

In the appraisal of securitized properties, area-specific or property-specific assumptions that do not conform to the current conditions should basically not be made. If some unclear value influences exist after investigation by professionals due to data limitation or inadequacy, assumption that such issues have been solved or excluded from the value influences must not be made. Accordingly, including the case when existence of such issues is unclear, the appraiser should make a reasonable estimation of the value influences based on the obtained data within the range of the appraiser's ability[23].

However, assumptions are acceptable if as described herein:

(a) For the case that the subject building has just been completed and tenants have yet to occupy it, but the planned lease agreement or documents equivalent to this have been concluded, , the valuation based on the assumption that it will be leased as specified in the planned lease agreements, confirming that the planned lease conditions are feasible.

(b) For the case that the subject property consists of multiple condominium units in a building and its site, the valuation based on transaction of the property as a whole.

(c) For the case that soil contamination or sprayed asbestos measurement is in progress and near completion, and that the measurement works are at a stage enough to identify and confirm the completed status of the property, the valuation based on the completion of such measurement works.

---

[23] Resulting from the investigation by the appraiser, if that issue is deemed to not be a substantial value influence, it is acceptable to exclude it from the value influences in the valuation.

ウ　その他

　　特定価格を求める場合において、資産流動化計画又は資産信託流動化計画等については、それらが策定されている場合はその内容を検討し、それが合法的で実現性が認められると判断される事項については、当該事項を考慮した条件を所与とし、そうでない事項及び資産流動化計画又は資産信託流動化計画等が策定されていない場合は、対象不動産に応じて投資対象として適切と判断できる運用方法を鑑定評価の条件を設定し適用する。この場合は鑑定評価報告書にその旨を記載する。

5）想定上の条件等

　証券化対象不動産の鑑定評価においては、原則として地域要因や個別的要因について現況と異なる想定上の条件等を付加してはならない。特に、専門家の調査を行っても資料収集の限界や資料の不備等により対象不動産の価格形成要因について不明事項が存する場合には、当該事項について問題が解消したもの、又は当該事項を考慮外とする条件を付加して鑑定評価を行うことはできない。したがって、当該事項の存否の端緒が確認できない場合を含め、調査し得た範囲から不動産鑑定士の調査分析能力の範囲内で価格形成要因について合理的な推定を行って鑑定評価を行う必要がある[23]。

　ただし、想定上の条件等を付すことができる場合を例示すれば、以下のとおりである。

ア　竣工直後でテナントが未入居の場合等に、予定賃貸借契約若しくはこれに準ずる書面がある場合に、当該賃貸借条件の実現性があるものと判断のうえ、当該賃貸借条件どおり賃貸されるものとして鑑定評価を行う場合

イ　一棟の建物に属する複数の区分所有建物及びその敷地について、一括売買を前提として一体として鑑定評価を行う場合

ウ　土壌汚染や吹付アスベスト等の対策工事が実施中である場合で、工事完了後の不動産として対象不動産の確定、確認が可能な程度に工事が完了している場合に、当該対策工事が完了したものとして鑑定評価を行う場合

---

[23] 調査の結果、当該事項が価格形成に大きな影響を与えないと判断されるときには、当該事項を価格形成要因から除外して鑑定評価を行うことができる。

- Differences with Valuation based on the Appraisal Standards, and their Validity

    The appraisal of securitized properties is based on the Appraisal Standards, and therefore it is not applicable for this section.

5) **Appraisal Process**
    - Appraisal Schedule

        If valuation at one time of multiple properties is requested within a certain period, the proposal for appraisal schedule should be made in accordance with the attributes and volume of process of each property, and adjustment should be made so that the valuation can be accurately conducted.

    - Site Inspection

        Determine whether the site inspection will be conducted, and if it will be conducted, determine how it will be carried out including whether it will be accompanied by a guide (including the guide or building manager's position), and whether internal inspection will be conducted.

        In addition, in site inspection for appraisal of securitized properties, building completion drawings is required in order to verify the building's internal design; as such, internal inspection is necessary. However, there may be cases that internal inspection is not possible due to occupancy conditions. Therefore, it is important to confirm in advance the area available for internal inspection. In such cases, the appraiser should determine how to estimate the area that could not be inspected and the required documents necessary for such estimate. The area that was inspected should be clearly described in the appraisal report[24]. The appraiser should confirm with the client whether there are any improvements implemented by tenants and whether it is in compliance, and how these can be confirmed.

    - Gathering and Organizing Data

        In the appraisal of securitized properties, the list of required documents for application of Specific Standards Chapter 3 and relevant Notes need to be provided in advance to the client. The appraisal must not be conducted appraisals simply using the documents provided by the client. Here are some examples of required documents. Not all these documents are available in some cases. Also note that if other documents are required for the valuation, the appraiser should ask the client to provide them.

        (a) Documents related to the securitization scheme of the subject property (diagram that illustrates names of concerned parties in the securitization, explanatory documents, permission letter, notification documents, etc.)

        (b) Documents that show the management policy of the subject property disclosed to the investors of the securitization plan

        (c) Location map or guide map of the subject property

        (d) Certificate of all items of registry, copy of registry, copy of cadastral map, building floor plan

        (e) List of tenants and rent (rent roll)

---

[24] If internal inspection is not available and sufficient information for estimation for the valuation cannot be obtained, the valuation request should be declined.

6）不動産鑑定評価基準に則った鑑定評価との主な相違点及びその妥当性

　証券化対象不動産の鑑定評価は、不動産鑑定評価基準に則った鑑定評価であるため、本項目に該当しない。

(5) 鑑定評価の手順

1）処理計画の策定

　一定の期間に大量の不動産の鑑定評価が同時に依頼される場合においても、対象不動産ごとに作業の性質、量に応じた処理計画の立案を行い、鑑定評価を的確に実施できるようスケジュールを調整する必要がある。

2）実地調査の有無及びその方法

　対象不動産の実地調査の有無及び実地調査を行う場合の立ち会いの有無、内覧の有無（立会人又は管理者の属性を含む。）等対象不動産の実地調査の方法を確定する。

　なお、証券化対象不動産の鑑定評価における実地調査は、建物竣工図等を用いて建物内部と照合を行う必要があることから、建物の内覧を行うことが必須である。ただし、建物の入居者等、占有状況等によっては建物内部への立入調査ができない場合があるので、対象不動産の内覧が可能なその範囲を予め依頼者に確認を行う。この場合、内覧が出来ない部分の推定方法及び推定に必要な資料等の検討を行うとともに、鑑定評価報告書で内覧した範囲を明確にする必要がある[24]。さらに、テナントが行った工事部分の有無及びその違法性の確認方法についても依頼者に確認する必要がある。

3）資料の収集及び整理の方法

　証券化対象不動産の鑑定評価においては、あらかじめ必要資料リストを提供して、基準各論第3章等を適用するために必要となる資料を依頼者に求めなければならず、安易に提供された資料のみを用いて鑑定評価を行ってはならない。主な必要資料を例示すれば以下のとおりであるが、必ずしもすべての資料が整っているとは限らず、また、この他にも必要と思われる資料がある場合には案件に即して適切に徴求する必要があることに留意する。

　ア　対象不動産に係る証券化のスキーム関連資料（証券化関係者名等を含む当該証券化スキームを説明した図表及び説明資料、許認可、届出資料等）
　イ　資産流動化計画等の投資家に開示される対象不動産の運用方法がわかる資料
　ウ　対象不動産の位置図、案内図
　エ　全部事項証明書又は登記簿謄本、公図写し、建物図面
　オ　テナント及び賃料等の一覧（レントロール）
　カ　賃貸借契約書（各区画、駐車場、看板等）
　キ　建物竣工図（建築概要、設備概要、内外部仕上表、配置図、平面図、立面図）
　ク　建築確認通知書写、検査済証写
　ケ　固定資産税・都市計画税の証明書等
　コ　保険料に関する資料

---

[24] 内覧が行えず、鑑定評価を行うに十分な確認を行うために推定するに足る資料が得られないときは、鑑定評価を謝絶する。

(f) Lease agreements (exclusive areas, parking, signage)
(g) Building completion drawings (outline of the building and equipment, list of materials used for the internal and external parts of the building, layout map, floor plan, elevation plan)
(h) Copy of building confirmation certificate, building examination certificate
(i) Certificate of fixed asset tax and city planning tax
(j) Documents related to insurance premiums
(k) Engineering report
(l) Agreements related to management
(m) Documents related to utility income and expenses
(n) Ground lease agreements
(o) Letters of agreement, code of management (in the case of jointly owned building or condominiums)
(p) Documents related to boundary confirmation
(q) Security registration statement and annual security report (if the client is a listed investment company)

Required documents may not necessarily be available at the time of valuation request. They should be obtained appropriately in accordance with the procedures of the appraisal work. If necessary, the appraiser should personally order the required documents.

- Application of Appraisal Approaches

  Determine the approaches (cost approach, sales comparison approach, income capitalization approach) to be applied. Also, if any other approaches are to be applied, determine which of such approach to be applied.

- Differences with Valuation based on the Appraisal Standards, and their Validity

  The appraisal of securitized properties is based on the Appraisal Standards, and therefore it is not applicable for this section.

6) **Possibility of the Difference in the Result with Values Estimated based on the Appraisal Standards (only if not based on the Appraisal Standards)**

The appraisal of securitized properties is based on the Appraisal Standards, and therefore it is not applicable for this section.

2. Items to be Confirmed with Client for Valuation Schedule

In order to determine an appropriate valuation schedule, the appraiser should confirm with the client beforehand the contents of documents, date they were obtained, and coverage of site inspection and its date, as described in (1) through (3).

These documents may not necessarily be available at the time of valuation request. They should be obtained appropriately in accordance with the procedures of the valuation work.

1) **Major Contents of Engineering Report and Date the Engineering Report is Obtained**

The engineering report refers to the report related to the conditions of a securitized properties (property-specific value influences that require professional analysis, such as underground objects and seismic issues) investigated by building and structure pro-

サ　エンジニアリング・レポート
　　　シ　管理に関する契約書等
　　　ス　水道光熱費関係の収支に関する資料
　　　セ　借地契約書等
　　　ソ　協定書、管理規約等（共同ビル、区分所有建物の場合）
　　　タ　境界確定に関する資料
　　　チ　有価証券届出書及び有価証券報告書（依頼者が上場投資法人の場合）
　　　　なお、必要資料は、必ずしも受付時に全て整っているものではないため、業務の進捗状況に応じて、適切に入手するものとする。また、必要に応じて不動産鑑定士自らが発注して取得する。

　4）適用する鑑定評価手法
　　　原価法、取引事例比較法、収益還元法の各手法の適用の有無及び他の手法を適用する場合の当該手法を確定する。

　5）不動産鑑定評価基準に則った鑑定評価との主な相違点及びその妥当性
　　　証券化対象不動産の鑑定評価は、不動産鑑定評価基準に則った鑑定評価であるため、本項目に該当しない。

(6) **不動産鑑定評価基準に則った鑑定評価と結果が異なる可能性がある旨（不動産鑑定評価基準に則らない場合に限る）**
　　証券化対象不動産の鑑定評価は、不動産鑑定評価基準に則った鑑定評価であるため、本項目には該当しない。

2　処理計画策定のための依頼者との確認事項

　不動産鑑定士は、適切な処理計画の策定のため次の(1)から(3)の事項について、これらの資料の内容や入手時期及び実地調査等の範囲や日時等について、あらかじめ依頼者に確認する必要がある。
　なお、これらの事項は、受付時にすべて確認できるものでもないことから、業務の進捗状況に応じて、適切に対応するものとする。

(1)　エンジニアリング・レポート等の主な項目及び入手時期

　　エンジニアリング・レポートとは、証券化対象不動産の鑑定評価に当たって対象不動産の個別的要因等の確認等に必要となる、建築物・設備等及び環境に関する専門的知識を有する者が行った証券化対象不動産の状況（地下埋設物、耐震性等に関する内容を含む専門性の高い個別的要因）に関する調査報告書をいい、具体的には不動産鑑定評価基準各論第3章別表1[※25]に例示された

fessionals. This report is required for the confirmation of property-specific value influences of the subject in appraisal of securitized properties. More specifically, the report includes items listed in Appendix 1 of Specific Standards Chapter 3[25]. However, in some cases, items not listed in Appendix 1 may be required and those items should be included in the engineering report.

In order to clarify property-specific value influences of a subject in appraisal of securitized properties, the appraiser should ask the client for documents such as professionally prepared engineering reports[26]. If the appraiser examines the content and coverage of the engineering report held by the client or scheduled to be conducted and finds them insufficient for valuation, the appraiser should inquire with the client about additional investigation. The engineering report must be obtained before conducting appraisal, with sufficient time secured for understanding of the contents. If the subject property is a special-purpose facility such as a large-scale shopping center, hotel, or assisted-living residence for seniors, the appraiser should confirm with the client whether the client has a market report prepared by other professionals, and if client has the report, ask the client to provide the report[27].

2) **Required Information for Application of DCF Method and Date it is Obtained**

It is required to confirm in advance with the client the coverage and expected date the information to be provided. Information to be provided by the client include rent roll, lease agreements, data of actual operating expenses, management agreement, building completion drawings necessary for confirmation of the subject property and application of appraisal approaches such as cost approach, construction agreement, surveyed land map, and confirmation of boundary[28].

3) **Explanation from those who Prepared Engineering Report**

The appraiser should confirm with the client in advance the way to ask for explanation from professionals who prepared the engineering report[29], as there may be cases that there are differences with the contents of engineering report with that of confirmed at site inspection, or unclear descriptions be found in the report, The same applies for analyses, such as market reports, prepared by other professionals.

---

[25] Appendix 1 of Specific Standards Chapter 3 is a list of contents of the engineering report, the appraiser's own study, and items in the engineering report used in the valuation and the rationale, described by the appraiser at his/her own responsibility.

[26] Upon accepting a valuation request associated with securitized properties, the appraisal firm should ask the client to submit the contents of the engineering report now under preparation or the request of a scheduled engineering report that lists the report's content.

[27] Even for a special-purpose facility, it is likely to be valued as a lease property. In order to determine the affordable rent level, market analysis of the industry is required.

[28] If unified documents (templates) are used for the lease agreements, etc., confirmation of all written lease agreements may not be necessary. In such a case, the client should make this clear, and then the appraiser should check some of the agreements, and find whether there is any separate special contract.

[29] If subcontract of part of the engineering report (soil contamination, etc.) has been requested, the parties receiving and accepting the request should also be included as preparers of the report.

ものが含まれる。ただし、鑑定評価に当たっては不動産鑑定評価基準各論第3章別表1に例示されたもの以外にも更なる専門家の調査が必要な場合があり、これらもすべてエンジニアリング・レポートに含むものとする。

　証券化対象不動産の鑑定評価として求められる対象不動産の個別的要因を明確にするために、エンジニアリング・レポート等の専門家による確認資料を依頼者に要求する必要がある[26]。この際、すでに依頼者が保有又は実施を依頼しているエンジニアリング・レポートの内容・範囲を確認し、鑑定評価を行うのに不足すると判断される場合には、追加調査の可否を確認する。エンジニアリング・レポートは、鑑定評価を行う日以前で、その内容を把握するのに必要な期間を確保できる時期に入手しなければならない。また、対象不動産が大規模ショッピングセンター、ホテル、老人ホーム等の特殊な用途の場合には、他の専門家が行ったマーケットレポート等の市場分析資料の有無を確認し、当該資料が有る場合には提供を求める必要がある[27]。

(2) DCF法等を適用するために必要となる資料等の主な項目及び入手時期

　収益費用項目の査定に必要な賃貸借契約状況の一覧表、賃貸借契約書等、運営費用の実績表、管理等に関する契約書等及び対象不動産の確認や原価法等の適用に必要な建物竣工図面、請負契約書、土地測量図面、境界確認書類等について、依頼者より提示される資料等の範囲及び入手時期を事前に確認する必要がある[28]。

(3) エンジニアリング・レポートを作成した者（以下「ER作成者」という。）等からの説明の有無

　後日、対象不動産の確認を行った結果、エンジニアリング・レポートの内容と相違がある場合や不明瞭な記載がある場合などに備えて、必要に応じてER作成者[29]からの説明を聞く方法について事前に確認しておくことが必要である。また、マーケットレポート等他の専門家が行った市場分析資料についても同様である。

---

[25] 不動産鑑定評価基準各論第3章別表1 とは、依頼者から提示されたエンジニアリング・レポートの内容、不動産鑑定士の調査内容及び鑑定評価において活用した事項とその根拠を不動産鑑定士の責任において記載した一覧表である。

[26] 証券化対象不動産に係る鑑定評価の受託に際し、不動産鑑定業者は、鑑定評価の依頼者から別途実施中若しくは実施予定のエンジニアリング・レポートの作成業務内容について記載したエンジニアリング・レポート依頼内容報告書の提出を求める必要がある。

[27] 特殊な用途の場合も賃貸型として鑑定評価を行うことが多いと思われるが、この場合においても賃料負担力の判断をするために当該事業の市場分析が必要となる。

[28] 賃貸借契約書等が統一された契約書フォーム（雛形）を用いて作成されている場合は、依頼者よりその旨の表明を受けて代表例の確認と個別の契約における特約等の有無の確認を十分に行うことにより、賃貸借契約書等のすべてを確認することが必ずしも必要でない場合もある。

[29] エンジニアリング・レポートの一部（土壌汚染等）の調査が再委託された場合には、その受託者もER作成者に含まれる。

IV. Investigation of the Subject Property

In appraisal of securitized properties, a wider and deeper investigation of the subject property, regarding, for instance, physical, legal, economic, and environmental aspects, must be conducted and this needs to be reflected properly in the appraisal.

Especially for real estate with uses largely influenced by the business operation, such as hotels, large-scale commercial facilities, and hospitals (trade related property), gathering and analyzing information on such operations is needed in order to verify the capability of the occupancy cost, even if it is a leasing property. Also, verification of the relevant rights or on-site physical identification must be conducted discreetly since business types vary, and renovation or expansion is commonplace.

1. Market Research

In appraisal of securitized properties, the appraiser should pay attention to influences that largely affect the behavior of market participants, especially regarding the matters shown below. The present and future influence of the following on the market participants' action must be analyzed and include the relation to the financial market along with sufficient market research utilizing a range of market research reports.

1) General real estate investment and securitized real estate market conditions: investment real estate trends, entering into/withdrawing from the market by funds, investors' expected yield, financing environment
2) Market participants: whether the typical market participants concerned in the subject property are well-financed funds, small- to medium-scale real estate companies, or individuals
3) Primary market area: properties for potential buyers of the subject property to compare with in terms of area, use, scale, etc.

2. Site Inspection

Not only when the subject property is to be securitized, but also if it has already been under securitization scheme, a site inspection including an internal inspection needs be conducted in the presence of the client or building manager designated by the client, to identify any considerable value influences. However, when the subject property is a vacant lot or a leased fee interest in land for which a sole inspection by an appraiser can be sufficiently conducted such attendance for the inspection is not necessarily required. In a site inspection particular attention must be paid to the following:

1) For appraisal of a building under construction on the condition that the appraisal report will be issued with appraisal value concluded after completion of the building, another site inspection is needed after the building completion.
2) When part of the subject property cannot be inspected because the space is being leased, is in business operation, etc., but the specifications or maintenance status can likely be assumed from other similar available spaces or exclusive areas, the inspection may be omitted by performing the following: an internal inspection of other

Ⅳ　対象不動産の調査

　証券化対象不動産の鑑定評価では、対象不動産に関して物理的側面、法律的側面、経済的側面、環境的側面等について、一般の鑑定評価以上に広範かつ詳細な調査を行って、その結果を不動産の鑑定評価に適切に反映させる必要がある。

　特に、ホテル、大規模商業施設、病院等の事業経営の影響が大きな用途の不動産の場合には、賃貸の形態をとる場合であっても、賃料負担力の検証等のため当該事業についての資料収集及び分析を行う必要がある。また、事業形態が多種にわたることや、改装、増築等がなされている場合も多いため、権利関係の確認や現地の物的確認は慎重に行う必要がある。

1　市場調査

　証券化対象不動産の鑑定評価においては、不動産投資市場における市場参加者の行動に大きな影響を及ぼす要因に着目すべきであり、特に以下の点等について金融市場等との関連を含め、各種の市場調査レポート等も活用して十分な市場調査を行った上で、それらが不動産投資市場の市場参加者の行動にどのような影響を及ぼしているか、また、今後及ぼすであろうかについて分析する必要がある。

　　ア　一般的な不動産投資、不動産証券化市場における市況感：投資用不動産の需給動向、ファンド等の参入・退出状況、投資家の要求する利回り、資金調達環境等
　　イ　市場参加者：対象不動産に係る典型的な市場参加者は、資金力のあるファンド等か、中小規模の不動産会社や個人かなど
　　ウ　同一需給圏：対象不動産の想定される主要な需要者が比較検討する不動産は、どのような地域、用途、規模の不動産かなど

2　実地調査

　対象不動産が新規に証券化される場合だけでなく、既に証券化されている場合であっても、依頼者や依頼者の指示を受けた対象不動産の管理者等の立会いのもと、建物の内覧も含めた実地調査を行い、価格形成要因に大きな影響を与える要因について実地に確認する必要がある。ただし、対象不動産が更地や底地であって立ち会いなしでの不動産鑑定士の単独調査によっても十分な調査を行うことが可能な場合には必ずしも立会いを要しない。

　実地調査において留意すべき主な点を例示すれば、以下のとおりである。

　　ア　建築中の建物について完成後に鑑定評価額の決定を行って鑑定評価書を発行することを条件に鑑定評価を行う場合には、完成後に改めて実地調査を行う必要がある。
　　イ　対象不動産の一部が、賃貸中、営業中等で内覧が行えない場合で、仕様、管理状況等が内覧できる他の区画とほぼ同一あるいは他の専用部分等から推測可能と判断できる場合には、当該部分を推定できる他の建物内の代表的な部分（自用又は空室区画等）の内覧、竣工図面、賃貸借契約書等による確認、管理者や賃借人等からのヒアリング等により推定することにより当該区画の実地調査を省略することができる。

typical areas (owner-occupied or vacant spaces, etc.) of the building from which the uninspected space can be assumed; verifying the completion drawings and lease contracts; and interviewing the building manager or tenants.

3) At a site inspection, the following should be checked and taken into consideration by interviewing the building manager of the subject property: building users and use status; discrepancies in leased area between the lease contracts and actual leased area; boundary indicators and encroachment; repair history of the building; expansion/renovation/alteration; building compliance; soil contamination; asbestos use in the building; storage of PCB.

4) When there is a building scheduled for demolition, the site inspection should be conducted to estimate the demolition cost and maintenance cost necessary until demolition, and inspection should be made on such factors as use of asbestos and storage of PCB.

3. Gathering Information
1) Information to be gathered

Any ambiguous[30] content in the information provided by the client must be clarified with the client. Also, if client-provided information is still in draft form, the final version of the document must be provided by the date of completion of the appraisal process, with sufficient time kept to review it. If there are differences between the draft and final versions, the content of the final version must be reflected in the appraisal. This will not, however, apply to documents such as expected lease agreements or property management agreements, where it is apparent that the final version of the agreement is only applicable after the date of completion of the appraisal process.

Information to be received as a final version can be in PDF format.

2) Engineering Report

Engineering report is obtained by the client for the purpose of investment decisions and is not originally prepared for appraisal. Consequently, even those in accordance with[31] BELCA guidelines[32] may not be sufficient[33] for usage in the appraisal. Though preparation of engineering report should be in accordance with BELCA guidelines, it does not have compelling force over the preparer of the report.

Therefore, in the appraisal of securitized properties, the appraiser must explain to the client about the required content of the engineering report[34] for the appraisal so that the report optimally fulfills its purpose. The appraiser needs to understand the contents of the report in order to recognize specific value influences and take responsibility for his/her analysis and judgment before utilizing it. The appraiser also needs to verify the engineering report by interviewing other professionals when necessary. If there is any risk of a non-investment grade regarding building compliance or seismic adequacy, the possibility of correction must be checked and, if it exists, the expected cost or payer must be confirmed by the client and reflected in the appraisal.

---

[30] Specific terms and conditions, discrepancies in the average price or ratio between the subject and comparables, and inconsistency between the provided data and subject property's status or other data

ウ　実地調査の際には、対象不動産の管理者等へのヒアリング等を行うなどして、対象不動産の使用者及び使用状況、賃貸借契約書の対象範囲と実際の賃貸部分の相違の有無、敷地境界標と越境の有無、建物の修繕履歴・増改築・用途変更等の有無、建物の違法性、土壌汚染、建物のアスベスト使用、PCB保管の有無等に留意する。

エ　取り壊し予定の建物が存する場合には、取壊費用及び取り壊しまでの管理費用の査定が可能な範囲（アスベスト使用の有無やPCB保管の有無等）で建物についての実地調査を行うことが必要である。

3　資料収集

(1)　収集すべき資料

依頼者より受け取った資料の内容について不明な点がある場合[30]は、依頼者に確認する必要がある。また、依頼者から受領した資料がドラフトの場合は、原則として鑑定評価を行った日以前で、その内容を把握するのに必要な期間を確保できる時期に最終版を取得し、ドラフトとの相違を確認して、相違がある場合には、その内容に応じた鑑定評価を行う必要がある。ただし、あらたな賃貸借契約やPM契約等が予定されている場合であって、これらの契約の締結が鑑定評価を行った日以降であることが明らかな場合にはこの限りでない。

なお、最終版として受領する資料はPDFファイルであっても差し支えない。

(2)　エンジニアリング・レポート

エンジニアリング・レポートは、依頼者が投資判断等の目的で取得するものであり、そもそも鑑定評価のために作成されたものではないため、BELCAのガイドライン[31]に準拠[32]したエンジニアリング・レポートであっても、鑑定評価に活用する内容として不十分な場合もある[33]。

---

[30] 特異な契約条件、類似不動産の標準的な金額や比率との乖離、対象不動産の状況や他の資料との不整合等

[31] 「不動産投資・取引におけるエンジニアリング・レポート作成に係るガイドライン（2007年版）」（社団法人建築・設備維持保全推進協会、社団法人日本ビルヂング協会）

[32] BELCAのガイドラインに準拠したエンジニアリング・レポートとは、ⅰ建物状況調査、ⅱ建物環境調査（フェーズⅠ）、ⅲ土壌汚染リスク評価（フェーズⅠ）、ⅳ地震リスク評価を指す。フェーズⅠとは、いわゆるサンプリング調査（フェーズⅡ）に進む前の段階の、現地目視調査・依頼者からの資料や公表資料の収集分析・関係者や現地管理人からのヒアリングによる調査を指す。

[33] 例えば、土壌汚染リスク評価報告書（フェーズⅠ）で「土壌汚染の可能性があるため、詳細調査を推奨する」とされているのに、フェーズⅡの詳細調査が未実施な場合。また、建物環境調査リスク評価報告書（フェーズⅠ）で「吹き付けアスベスト使用の可能性があるため、詳細調査を推奨する」とされているのに、フェーズⅡの詳細調査が未実施な場合。このような場合は、依頼者に追加調査を要請する必要がある。また、耐震性調査や地下埋設物の調査は、BELCAのガイドラインに準拠したエンジニアリング・レポートではないが、これらの調査を行っている場合には、原則として依頼者から提示を受けるべきである。

However, even if no engineering report is submitted or the report's effective date is old and the contents are inadequate for use in the appraisal, the securitized properties can be valued as per the appraiser's judgment; provided that reasonable assumptions regarding value influences can be made within the appraiser's analytical ability. Typical cases are as follows:

(a) The subject property is a building scheduled for demolition and its site (However, engineering reports on soil contamination risk assessment and asbestos in the building scheduled for demolition are needed in order to estimate the demolition cost)

(b) For periodic valuation, if no significant changes in value influences regarding the building, such as expansion, renovation, major repair work, major amendments in the relevant regulations, etc. have occurred and the previously provided data including the engineering report can be used[35]

(c) Detached houses or units of apartment buildings where multiple value influences can be obtained by the appraiser's investigation

So-called bulk transactions[36] or transactions of value-enhanced properties[37] are different in character from usual securitized properties transactions. As such, if no engineering report is submitted by the client, a careful risk analysis is needed in the course of value influence analysis. In such a case, the details of such analysis must be included in the appraisal report.

Any unclear or vague content in the engineering report needs clarification by the preparer of the engineering report via the client.

---

[31] "Guidelines for Engineering Report" (2010 edition) (Building and Equipment Long-life Cycle Association, Japan Building Owners and Managers Association)

[32] Engineering reports compliant with BELCA guidelines refer to:

i. Building condition survey; ii. Building environment survey (phase I) ; iii. Soil contamination risk assessment (phase I) ; iv. Earthquake risk assessment

Phase I indicates preliminary investigations toward sampling analysis (phase II), including: external onsite inspection, gathering and analyzing provided and published information, and interviewing concerned parties and the building manager.

[33] For instance, when a detailed phase II investigation is not conducted despite the soil contamination risk assessment report (phase I) recommending that further investigation is necessary due to the possibility of soil contamination or the building environmental survey recommending further investigation due to the possibility of sprayed asbestos. In such cases, the client is required to conduct extra investigation. Also, though seismic adequacy and underground object surveys are not regarded as engineering reports compliant with BELCA guidelines, when those surveys are conducted, the reports should in principle be provided by the client.

[34] The engineering report's scope of work and coverage regarding the subject property to be surveyed must be sufficient for the valuation.

[35] Even if no major changes are found in specific value influences on the building, it is desirable to request that the client reacquire an engineering report, in the case that approximately three to five years have passed since the issuance of the engineering report...

エンジニアリング・レポートの作成に際しては、BELCA が発行するガイドラインに準拠すべきとされるものの、ER 作成者に対して強制力のあるものではない。

したがって、証券化対象不動産の鑑定評価に当たっては、不動産鑑定士は、依頼者に対し、鑑定評価に必要なエンジニアリング・レポートの内容[※34]を説明し、できる限り内容の充足したエンジニアリング・レポートを入手する必要があり、個別的要因の把握に必要な範囲で、エンジニアリング・レポートの内容を十分理解し、主体的に自らの責任を持ってこれを分析及び判断した上で、活用しなければならない。さらに、必要に応じて他の専門家による意見を聴取してエンジニアリング・レポートの検証を行うよう努める必要がある。その際に、建物の違法性や耐震性等に関し投資適格性を欠く可能性がある場合には、是正の見込みの有無を確認し、是正する場合の見込み費用や費用負担先について、依頼者に確認するなどして鑑定評価に反映する必要がある。

なお、依頼者よりエンジニアリング・レポートの提出がない場合やエンジニアリング・レポートの調査時点が古い場合など、その記載内容が鑑定評価を行う上で不十分な場合であっても、不動産鑑定士の判断により、自己の調査分析能力の範囲内で価格形成要因に係る合理的な推定を行うことができる場合には、証券化対象不動産の鑑定評価を行うことができる。その主な場合を例示すれば、以下のとおりである。

　ア　対象不動産が取り壊し予定の建物及びその敷地である場合（ただし、土壌汚染リスク評価や取り壊し費用算定のための取り壊し予定建物のアスベストについてのエンジニアリング・レポートは必要である。）

　イ　継続評価の場合で、増改築工事又は大規模修繕の実施、関連法令等の大規模な変更等建物に関する価格形成要因の大きな変更がない場合など、以前に提示を受けたエンジニアリング・レポート等の資料が活用できる場合[※35]

　ウ　戸建住宅や 1 戸の居住用マンション等で不動産鑑定士による調査によって多くの価格形成要因の把握が可能な場合

いわゆるバルク取引[※36]や、バリューアップ型不動産取引[※37]は、通常の証券化不動産取引と性格を異にするため、依頼者よりエンジニアリング・レポートの提出がない場合には、価格形成要因の分析においてリスク分析を十分に行わなければならない。このような場合には、その分析内容を鑑定評価報告書に記載しなければならない。

エンジニアリング・レポートの内容について、不明な点や不明瞭な記載がある場合は、依頼者を通じて ER 作成者に確認する必要がある。

---

[34] エンジニアリング・レポートの業務範囲、調査対象不動産の範囲が鑑定評価を行うにあたって充分な内容である必要がある。

[35] 建物に係る個別的要因に大きな変更がない場合でも、エンジニアリング・レポートの作成後おおむね 3 年から 5 年経過しているときには、エンジニアリング・レポートの再取得を依頼者に要請することが望ましい。

[36] ここで想定するバルク取引とは、投資家が、不動産の個別的要因の詳細を確認せず、個別的要因が不明なこと自体をリスクと見込んで、複数の不動産を一度に購入する取引をいう。

[37] ここで想定するバリューアップ型不動産取引とは、投資家が、違法性等に瑕疵がある可能性がある不動産を購入し、購入後、瑕疵を治癒して売却し、売却益を得る取引をいう。バリューアップ取引の中には、バルク取引と同様、投資家が、不動産の個別的要因の詳細を確認せず、個別的要因が不明なこと自体をリスクと見込んで、購入する場合もある。

4. Unclear Value Influences

Unclear value influences that are judged to significantly affect the value of the property must be explained to the client and measures to clarify them need to be confirmed by the client. If it is judged that reasonable assumptions cannot be made due to factors such as a lack of required information for value influence analysis, the appraisal should be refused.

---

[36] The assumed bulk transactions here are multiple properties purchased at one time by investors without identifying the property's specific value influences, assuming the uncertainty as a risk.

[37] The assumed value-enhanced real estate transactions here are those investors' purchasing real estate that involves potential defects in compliance, etc. to gain sales profit by selling the real estate after correcting the defect. In some cases of value-enhanced transactions, investors purchase real estate without identifying the property's specific value influences assuming the uncertainty as a risk, as in bulk transactions.

4　不明事項

　価格形成に大きな影響があると判断される価格形成要因について、不明事項が存在する場合は、依頼者にその不明事項について説明し、当該不明事項を明らかにするための方策等について確認する必要がある。当該不明事項について、価格形成要因の分析に必要な資料が整わないなど合理的な推定ができないと判断された場合には、鑑定評価を謝絶すべきである。

V. Analysis of Value Influences

1. General Value Influences

The market for securitized properties is considered to be more vulnerable to financial market volatility, such as interest-rate changes, than the conventional real estate market. Consequently, it is necessary to fully analyze the present and potential influence of such market factors over the behaviors of market participants of the real estate investment market[38].

In order to value trade related property (hotels, commercial facilities, hospitals, or logistics facilities), the following are taken into account: business profitability, competitive facilities, alternative tenants, building versatility, ratio of building frame and facilities. Other specific issues are to be considered for valuation: for hotels; occupancy rates, room charges, brand value of the management company; for commercial facilities; possibility of reconstruction (existing non-conforming building issues due to revision of relevant regulations); for logistics facilities; influence of Ports and Harbors Act and other regulations on logistics companies' operations, particularity of the facilities.

2. Specific Value Influences

In the appraisal of securitized properties, it is important to verify specific value influences via a site inspection or engineering report, etc.

1) **Land**
   (a) Soil Contamination
   - Investigations

     When soil contamination is found with the subject property, the soil, in principle, needs to be removed or purified, and those countermeasures often require substantial cost, which largely affects the value of the property. Therefore, in appraisal, it is essential to determine the influence of soil contamination on the value.

     In the appraisal of securitized properties, one of the engineering reports defined by BELCA, "Soil Contamination Risk Assessment Report (Phase I)" is generally provided by the client. The appraiser will judge if the contents of the assessment report match the engineering report, and utilize it after close examination.

     In the appraisal of securitized properties, conclusions about soil contamination as a value influence are required and a Phase II investigation (soil/groundwater environmental survey including a sampling survey) needs to be conducted unless there is judged to be little need to consider soil contamination as a value influence based on a Phase I investigation (study of data) by an expert, and the appraiser's own study. Also, depending on the results of a Phase II investigation, Phase III (planning/implementation of countermeasure) may be required with a survey and

---

[38] The yield gap, the difference between the yield on investment properties and 10-year government bonds, for instance, is an important index for real estate investors. Analyzing the level, trends, and factors of yield gap is considered to be an essential analysis of general value influences.

V 価格形成要因の分析

1 一般的要因分析等

証券化対象不動産の属する市場は、従来の不動産に比べ金利等の金融市場の変動の影響をより大きく受けるものと考えられる[38]ので、それらが不動産投資市場の市場参加者の行動にどのような影響を及ぼしているか、又は今後及ぼすであろうかについて十分に分析する必要がある。

なお、ホテル、商業施設、病院、物流施設等の事業経営の影響が大きい用途の不動産においては、事業としての収益性、競合施設の状況、代替テナントの可能性、建物の汎用性、建物の躯体・設備の割合のほか、ホテル評価においては稼働状況、宿泊料金、マネジメント会社のブランド等、商業施設評価においては再建築の可能性（関連法令の改正の影響による既存不適格建物の問題）、物流施設評価においては適用される港湾法その他の法令が物流業者の事業展開に及ぼす影響、設備の特殊性等に留意する。

2 個別的要因分析

証券化対象不動産の鑑定評価においては、実地調査、エンジニアリング・レポート等を活用し、個別的要因の確認を行うことが重要である。

(1) 土地

1) 土壌汚染

① 調査

対象不動産に土壌汚染が認められる場合には、原則として、土壌の搬出（除去）、浄化等の措置を行う必要があり、その措置工事には多額の費用を要する場合が多く、対象不動産の価格に大きな影響を与えることが一般的である。したがって、鑑定評価に当たっては、土壌汚染の価格への影響を判断する必要がある。

証券化対象不動産の鑑定評価では、通常、BELCAの定義するエンジニアリング・レポートの一つである「土壌汚染リスク評価報告書（フェーズⅠ）」を、依頼者から提供されることが一般的であるため、エンジニアリング・レポートの内容がその内容に合致しているか否かを自ら判断し、十分吟味のうえ、活用する。

証券化対象不動産の鑑定評価においては、土壌汚染の価格に与える影響についての結論を求められるため、原則として価格形成要因から除外することは許されず、専門家によるフェーズⅠ調査（資料等調査）及び不動産鑑定士の独自調査の結果を踏まえ、土壌汚染が存する端緒がないなど、土壌汚染の価格形成への影響が大きくないと判断できる場合以外は、フェーズⅡ調査（サンプリング調査を伴う土壌・地下水環境調査）を実施することが必要となる。また、フェーズⅡの結果によっては、フェーズⅢ（対策工事の設計と実施）までの調査及び措置工事が必要な場合があり、対策措置を完了した状態での鑑定評価が求められることもあ

---

[38] 例えば、投資用不動産の利回りと10年国債利回り等の開差であるイールドギャップは、不動産投資を行う投資家の重要な判断指標となっており、イールドギャップの大きさや動向、及びその原因の分析は、一般的要因の分析として重要なものといえる。

measures and appraisal with all the countermeasures completed.
- Application to the Appraisal
  - For the case that there is judged to be little influence on the value little based on the appraiser's own study

    If there is judged to be little influence on the value based on a Phase I level investigation and the appraiser's own study, soil contamination can be excluded from value influences. In this case, the appraisal will be the same as the case in which absence of contamination is confirmed. Even so, it is necessary to specify in the appraisal report that the influence on the value is little based on the engineering report and appraiser's own study.
  - For the case that soil contamination is found present

    If presence of soil contamination is verified based on a Phase II or higher level of investigation by a professional institution and its estimate for the cost of countermeasures is available, it is possible to provide appraisal with the removal cost taken into consideration. It should be further noted that the appraiser may have to consider the stigma of soil contamination affecting the value of the subject property.
  - For the case that soil contamination is found absent

    If the results of a Phase II level investigation meet all environmental standards, the appraisal is regarding as verifying the absence of soil contamination. In this case, the above result will be stated in the appraisal report and soil contamination will be excluded from value influences for conducting appraisal.

(b) Buried Archaeological Artifacts
- Surveys

    If the subject property is in an area recognized as containing buried archaeological artifacts as per the Cultural Properties Protection Law, a notification is required for land excavation, civil engineering work, etc. Also, if conducting excavation decided on by a board of education in response to the notification, the cost is generally borne by the landowner. If any important remains are discovered in the course of a survey, a further survey for the purpose of protecting the remains will be required.

    The cost of excavation surveys or cessation and prohibition of civil engineering work, design changes, and restrictions on land use (referring not only to costs but also including restrictions on use and loss of time), are post-investment, unexpected costs for investors. Therefore, in appraisal of securitized properties, the subject property's inclusion in an area recognized as containing buried archaeological artifacts must be surveyed.

    The appraiser must investigate the following: whether the subject property is in an area recognized by the relevant board of education as containing buried archaeological artifacts; whether a survey is requested on a best-effort basis; whether an excavation survey has already been instructed; study of the availability of past excavation surveys and measures taken, and if there is an ongoing excavation, the cessation/prohibition period of civil engineering must be checked.

る。
② 鑑定評価への反映
（ⅰ）独自調査により価格に対する影響が大きくないと判断できる場合
　エンジニアリング・レポートのフェーズⅠレベルの調査と不動産鑑定士による独自調査の結果を受けて、価格に対する影響が大きくないと判断できる場合には、土壌汚染を価格形成要因から除外できる。この場合には、土壌汚染がないことが判明している場合の鑑定評価と同様の評価をすることになるが、その場合であっても、エンジニアリング・レポート及び独自調査の内容を受けて価格に対する影響が大きくない旨の鑑定評価報告書への記載が必要である。
（ⅱ）土壌汚染があることが判明している場合
　土壌汚染の存在が専門調査機関によるフェーズⅡレベル以上の調査に基づいて判明しており、専門調査機関による対策費用の見積書がある場合には、除去費用を考量した鑑定評価が可能となる。なお、心理的嫌悪感等による価格形成への影響を考慮しなければならない場合があることに留意する。
（ⅲ）土壌汚染がないことが判明している場合
　フェーズⅡレベルの調査の結果、環境基準をすべて満たしていた場合は、鑑定評価においては、土壌汚染がないことが判明している場合に該当する。このような場合には、当該調査結果の概要を鑑定評価報告書へ記載し、土壌汚染を価格形成要因から除外して鑑定評価を実施することになる。

2）埋蔵文化財
① 調査
　対象不動産が文化財保護法に定める「周知の埋蔵文化財包蔵地」に該当する場合には、土木工事等で土地を掘削する場合には届出が必要であり、また、届出に基づき教育委員会等が発掘調査を実施する場合には、発掘調査に要する費用は通常土地所有者の負担となる。発掘調査の結果、重要な遺跡の出土に至れば、さらに遺跡保護のための調査が必要となる。
　発掘調査に要する費用や土木工事の停止・禁止、設計変更や土地利用上の制限（以下、これら費用のみならず利用制約や時間ロスを含めて「発掘調査に係わる費用」という。）は、投資家にとって、投資後の予期せぬ支出に該当する。したがって、証券化対象不動産の鑑定評価に当たっては、周知の埋蔵文化財包蔵地に該当するかどうか調査を行う必要がある。
　不動産鑑定士は、所轄の教育委員会等で対象不動産が「周知の埋蔵文化財包蔵地」に該当するかどうか、努力義務としての調査要請があり得るか、既に発掘調査等の指示が出ているかどうか、過去に発掘調査が実施された場合はその履歴や措置状況、遺跡の調査中であれば土木工事の停止・禁止期間等について調査する必要がある。

- Application to the Appraisal

    Even if the subject property is included in an area recognized as containing buried archaeological artifacts, if no land excavation is expected, there is no risk of costs incurred for test drilling or an excavation survey. Consequently, if the specific value influence of being in an area containing buried archaeological artifacts (including when the adjacent land is such an area; the same will apply hereinafter) is judged to have no significant effect on the value of the subject property—such as when no construction or expansion plan for the building is reasonably assumed, including when the building has a long remaining useful life and no reconstruction is planned—the appraisal can be conducted without consideration of its value influence. For securitization development property, when the subject property is included in an area containing recognized as containing buried cultural archeological artifacts, appraisal can be conducted as long as the period and costs for test drilling and an excavation survey can reasonably be estimated.

(c) Underground Objects
- Surveys

    When underground objects exist beneath the subject property, including foundation piles of former buildings, basements, underground tanks, bomb shelters, waste substances, or human remains, measures such as removal or backfill of the underground objects are required, which will lead to design changes or restrictions on land use that become unexpected costs for investors (referring not only to costs but also including restrictions on use and loss of time). Therefore, in the appraisal of securitized properties, it is necessary to conduct a survey to check for the presence of underground objects. If an underground object containing hazardous substances is discovered, it needs to be handled as a soil contamination issue.

    A full-scale survey often goes beyond the appraiser's abilities since it requires use of radar, and ultimately needs a drilling survey. However, the appraiser must to the extent possible survey for the possibility of underground objects by: studying past land uses based on old maps; obtaining a summary of the property explaining material facts; interviewing the client, etc.

- Application to the Appraisal

    Even when the presence of an underground object is likely, if no land excavation is expected, the risk of underground objects generally will not become evident. Consequently, if it is judged to have no significant effect on the value of the subject property—such as when no construction or expansion plan for the building is reasonably assumed, including when the building has a long remaining useful life and no reconstruction is planned—the appraisal can be conducted without consideration of its value influence.

    If the presence of underground objects is discovered in securitization of a development property, the cost regarding the objects will be estimated, and if the amount is large enough to affect the value of the property, an appropriate deduction is needed. In order to appropriately estimate such cost, a survey and estimate by another expert is generally necessary.

② 鑑定評価への反映

「周知の埋蔵文化財包蔵地」であっても、土地を掘削する予定がなければ、試掘調査及び発掘調査に係わる費用が生じる危険性はない。したがって、建物の残存耐用年数が長く建替えの予定がない場合を含め、建物の新設、増築等の予定がないと合理的に判断できる場合など、埋蔵文化財包蔵地等（隣接地等が埋蔵文化財包蔵地である場合を含む。以下同じ。）という個別的要因が、価格形成に大きな影響を与えることがないと判断できれば価格形成要因から除外して鑑定評価を行うことができる。一方、開発型証券化等の場合で対象不動産が周知の埋蔵文化財包蔵地等に該当する場合には、試掘調査及び発掘調査に係る期間、費用等が合理的に見積もることができる場合には鑑定評価を行うことができる。

3）地下埋設物
① 調査

対象不動産の地下に、従前建物の基礎杭、地下室等の地下施設、地下タンク、防空壕、廃棄物、人骨等の地下埋設物がある場合、当該埋設物の除去や埋め戻し等の措置が必要になり、設計変更や土地利用上の制限を受けたりするなど、投資家にとって、予期せぬ支出となる場合がある（以下、これら地下埋設物の措置に係わる費用のみならず利用制約や時間ロスを含めて「地下埋設物に係る措置費用」という。）。したがって、証券化対象不動産の鑑定評価に当たっては、地下埋設物が存在するかどうかについての調査を行う必要がある。なお、地下埋設物に有害物質を含む場合には、土壌汚染の問題として取り扱う必要がある。

地下埋設物の有無を本格的に調査するには、レーダーでの探索や、最終的には掘削による調査が必要なため、不動産鑑定士の調査能力を超えていることが多いが、不動産鑑定士は、古地図で従前の使用方法を調査するほか、売買時の重要事項説明書の記載概要の入手や依頼者へのヒアリングにより、地下埋設物存在の可能性をできる限り調査する必要がある。

② 鑑定評価への反映

地下埋設物の存在が予想される場合でも、土地を掘削する予定がなければ、通常、地下埋設物のリスクが顕在化することはない。したがって、建物の残存耐用年数が長く建替えの予定がない場合を含め、建物の新設、増築等の予定がないと合理的に判断できる場合など、価格形成に大きな影響を与えることがないと判断できれば価格形成要因から除外して鑑定評価を行うことができる。

開発型証券化で地下埋設物の存在が確認された場合には、地下埋設物に係る措置費用について査定し、その金額が価格に影響を与える程度に大きい場合には、これを適切に減価することが必要となる。なお、地下埋設物に係る措置費用を適切に査定するには、一般的には他の専門家による調査及び見積りが必要となる。

2) **Buildings**
   (a) Compliance
   ● Surveys

   Non-compliant buildings are not only unethical but may also incur unexpected costs or decreased income during operation. For instance, illegal buildings as per the Building Standards Act may be instructed to take measures subject to Article 9, paragraph 1 of the act: "Measures needed to correct violations regarding removal, relocation, renovation, expansion, repair, remodeling, use prohibition, use restriction, and other violations of the above stipulations and conditions." Also, lack of compliance even to expected efforts stipulated in ordinances or guidelines may incur a risk of reputation damage.

   Consequently, it is necessary to verify that the subject property conforms to public regulations.

   The compliance status survey is an essential element of the "Building Condition Survey Report," one of the engineering reports defined by BELCA. As such, the appraiser must verify the contents of the provided engineering report and utilize it. If questions or discrepancies with the appraiser's survey are found in the course of referring to the engineering report, the appraiser must confirm the contents with the engineering report's preparer via the client and an additional survey may be asked accordingly. When restrictions under private law regarding the subject property are difficult to judge, it may be necessary to seek the opinion of a professional such as a lawyer to determine them or judge the specific influences.

   ● Application to the Appraisal

   If any compliance issues exist or emergency repair is needed, an appraisal will be conducted when the problems are confirmed to be corrected (or at least the realization including the intent to correct the problems is confirmed).

   In appraisal of a building with a compliance issue or an item for emergency repair left uncorrected, the appraiser must estimate the cost regarding those corrections (not only construction cost but also the cost of the tenant's vacation for the construction period and income decrease must be included). If the amount is large enough to affect the property's value an appropriate deduction of value equivalent to such cost is needed. Since such costs for correction are generally difficult to estimate by appraisers only, the appraiser, in principle, needs to request the client to receive a professional estimate of the cost, such as from preparer of engineering report. Even if some correction is expected, if the cost is small for the appraisal value and judged to have no significant effect on the value of the subject property, the appraisal can be conducted without consideration of its value influence.

   In contrast, when the building is scheduled for demolition, compliance or emergency repair items normally do not need to be surveyed. However, in the event of demolition and redevelopment after more than one year of building operation, compliance of the current pre-demolition building needs to be surveyed, in principle.

   (b) Analysis of Seismic Adequacy and Earthquake Risk

(2) 建物
 1) 遵法性
  ① 調査
　　遵法性に欠ける建物は、社会倫理に反するだけでなく、事業運営上、思わぬ支出や収入の減少を生じさせる場合がある。例えば、建築基準法に違反する建物は、同法第9条第1項により、「除却、移転、改築、増築、修繕、模様替え、使用禁止、使用制限その他これらの規定又は条件に対する違反を是正するために必要な措置」を講じられる可能性がある。また、条例、要綱等に記載された努力規定であっても、規定を遵守していないことによる風評リスク等が生じる場合もある。
　　したがって、対象不動産の建物が公法上の規制に合致したものであるかどうかを確認する必要がある。
　　法令遵守状況調査については、BELCAの定義するエンジニアリング・レポートの1つである「建物状況調査報告書」の必須項目となっているため、依頼者から提供されたエンジニアリング・レポートの内容を自ら判断し、活用する。なお、エンジニアリング・レポートを参照する過程で、疑問が生じたり、不動産鑑定士の調査結果と異なっている場合には、依頼者を通じてER作成者に内容を確認し、必要に応じ追加調査を要請する必要がある。また、対象不動産に係る私法上の制約等について、判断が容易でない場合には、弁護士等の他の専門家の意見を求めて、確認や個別的要因の判断を行う必要が生じる場合もある。

  ② 鑑定評価への反映
　　遵法性に問題がある又は緊急修繕の必要がある場合には、原則としてその問題が是正されるのを確認（少なくとも是正を行う意思を含む実現性を確認）した上で鑑定評価を行うものとする。
　　遵法性に問題がある又は緊急修繕事項の是正の必要があるが未だ是正されていない建物について鑑定評価を行う場合には、当該是正に要する費用（単に工事費だけでなく、工事期間中のテナント退去に要する費用や収入の減少等も含む。）を査定し、その金額が価格に影響を与える程度に大きいと判断される場合には、是正に要する費用相当分を減価する必要がある。是正に要する費用の見積りは、一般的には不動産鑑定士単独では困難であることが多いため、原則として、ER作成者等他の専門家による見積りを依頼者に要請する。なお、是正される見込みのある場合でも、是正に要する費用が鑑定評価額に比して小さく、対象不動産の価格形成に大きな影響を与えないと判断できる場合には、価格形成要因から除外して鑑定評価を行うこともできる。
　　一方、建物の取壊しを予定している場合には、通常、遵法性や緊急修繕事項を調査する必要はないが、建物を1年以上運用してから取り壊して開発する場合などは、原則どおり、取壊し前の建物の遵法性を調査する必要がある。

 2) 耐震性及び地震リスクに関する分析

- Surveys

In order to determine investment grade, for properties that have a high probability of significant damage in the event of an earthquake, earthquake insurance and retrofitting are needed to be considered. Since these issues may largely affect the property's value, both seismic adequacy and earthquake risk must be surveyed in the appraisal of securitized properties.

・Seismic Adequacy

Engineering reports defined by BELCA include a structural overview in the building condition survey but not a seismic adequacy survey. As such, judging from the completion date the appraiser must determine whether the building was constructed based on the former seismic standards. If the result shows the building was constructed based on the former standards,[39] the appraiser will provide surveys focusing on interviews with the client to figure out whether the building underwent a seismic assessment subject to the Act on Promotion of Seismic Retrofitting of Buildings, and if it did, the report of the assessment results will be utilized as an engineering report on the seismic assessment.

This assessment is, especially from a life protection standpoint, a building survey/assessment based on the regulations that promote seismic retrofitting of buildings designed subject to the former seismic standards (Act on Promotion of Seismic Retrofitting of Buildings[40]).This is not included in the engineering reports defined by BELCA and its implementation is only encouraged[41] under the above act.

・Earthquake Risk

Earthquake risk is used as an index for economic options based on the cost-effectiveness of the measures regarding assets with clear economic value. Since it indicates earthquake damage with a monetary value, it features estimation of the scale of the damage or vulnerability of the building from an economic stand point.

Analysis is necessary for the results of earthquake risk assessment such as PML[42] to determine the need for earthquake insurance and seismic reinforcement work for the building. Since earthquake risk assessment is included in the engineering reports defined by BELCA, the appraiser must verify and utilize the contents of the engineering report provided by the client that was prepared by

---

[39] The seismic standards effective before the order for revision of the Building Standards Act as of June 1, 1981, are referred to as the old seismic standards. The judgment if the construction confirmation was applied for before or after the revision is normally made based on the completion date. However, determination of the time of construction confirmation is not always easy and some buildings that applied for the confirmation before the revision were designed in accordance with the revised act in advance. Therefore, it must be noted that for buildings constructed around the year of the revision, the confirmation cannot be merely based on the completion date.

[40] The official name is the Act on Promotion of Seismic Retrofitting of Buildings (Law number: Act No. 123 of 1995)

[41] Under the Act on Promotion of Seismic Retrofitting of Buildings, Article 6, seismic assessment is required on a best-effort basis for the specified buildings constructed in accordance with the old seismic standards.

① 調査
　　地震が起こる確率が高く、地震が起きた際の損害額が甚大となる可能性が高い不動産は、投資適格性を判断するに当たり、地震保険の付保、耐震補強工事の実施等の検討が必要となる。これらは不動産の価格に対して大きな影響を与える可能性があるため、証券化対象不動産の鑑定評価に当たっては、耐震性や地震リスクの調査を行う必要がある。

（i）耐震性
　　BELCA の定義するエンジニアリング・レポートには関連項目として建物状況調査に構造概要調査があるが耐震性の調査は含まれないため、まず建物の竣工年から、旧耐震基準[39]に基づく建物かどうかを判定することが必要である。その結果、旧耐震基準に基づく建物であった場合は、さらに耐震改修促進法に準拠した耐震診断が実施されているかどうかを依頼者へのヒアリングを中心に調査し、実施している場合には、依頼者の協力の下、耐震診断結果の報告書を耐震性調査におけるエンジニアリング・レポートとして活用する。
　　耐震診断は、特に人命確保の観点から、旧耐震基準にて設計された建築物の耐震改修を促進するための法制度（いわゆる耐震改修促進法[40]）に基づく建物の調査・診断である。これは、BELCA の定義するエンジニアリング・レポートの範囲外であり、耐震改修促進法においてその実施が努力義務[41]とされているものである。

（ii）地震リスク
　　「地震リスク」とは、経済的価値が明確な資産に対し、対策の費用対効果に基づいた経済選択の指標として用いられる。地震被害に伴う損失を貨幣価額で表記することから、被害の大きさや建物の脆弱性を、経済的尺度で把握できるという特徴がある。
　　PML 値[42]等地震リスク分析結果が地震保険付保及び耐震補強工事の必要性からみてどの程度であるかを分析する。地震リスク分析は、BELCA の定義するエンジニアリング・レポートに含まれるため、依頼者から提供された地震リスクの専門家の作成したエンジニアリング・レポートを自ら判断し、活用する。

---

[39] 昭和56 年 6 月 1 日建築基準法施行令改正以前の耐震性基準を、旧耐震基準と称する。竣工年月から建築確認申請が改正後のものであるかどうかを推測して判断を行うことが多いが、建築確認時期の推定は必ずしも容易ではなく、また、改正年前に確認申請された建物でも、先取りして新耐震基準に準拠して設計されたものもあるため、改正年前後の竣工の建物については、竣工年月のみでの確認は行えないことに留意が必要である。
[40] 正式名称は「建築物の耐震改修の促進に関する法律」（平成 7 年法律第123号）
[41] 耐震改修促進法第 6 条において、旧耐震基準の特定建築物について耐震判断の実施が努力義務となっている。
[42] 証券化不動産においては、50年間で超過確率10％（再現期間475年相当）の損失率の PML 値を算定することが慣例的な評価基準となっている。なお、PML 値とは、対象不動産の地震による経済的損失を予測する地震リスク分析の確率値である。

an expert on earthquake risk.
- Application to the Appraisal
  - Seismic Adequacy

    If the subject property was built based on the former seismic standards and its seismic assessment in accordance with the Act on Promotion of Seismic Retrofitting of Buildings resulted in lack of seismic adequacy requiring reinforcement, the effect of the relevant cost on the value of the property must be taken into account[43].

    Additionally, if as a result of the assessment in accordance with the Act on Promotion of Seismic Retrofitting of Buildings, a building turns out to be significantly lacking seismic adequacy but no retrofitting is expected, appraisal with application of Specific Standards Chapter 3 and relevant Notes cannot be provided since investors generally judge such a property as a non-investment grade.

  - Earthquake Risk

    When the PML of a property exceeds a certain level[44], earthquake insurance is often provided, in which case the insurance cost must be estimated and the effect on the value of the property must be taken into account.

    Additionally, if seismic reinforcement is judged as needed, the effect of the relevant cost on the subject property must be taken into account.

(c) Asbestos
- Surveys

  If the use of airborne asbestos is confirmed in the subject property, countermeasures such as removal or containment must be taken. These countermeasures often require significant cost that considerably affects the value of the property, so the presence of asbestos must be surveyed during appraisal.

  Asbestos used in forming materials poses no risk of dispersal unless it is significantly deteriorated or damaged. It therefore is not considered to directly pose health hazards other than in the event of building demolition.

  Asbestos is an essential topic of the "Building Environment Risk Assessment Survey Report (Phase I)," one of the engineering reports defined by BELCA. Therefore the appraiser must evaluate the contents of the provided engineering report and utilize them. If questions or discrepancies concerning the appraiser's survey are found in the course of referring to the engineering report, the appraiser must confirm the contents with the report's preparer via the client, and an additional survey may be asked accordingly.

---

[42] Estimating a 10% probability of being exceeded in a 50-year time span (return period of 475 years) is a common measure for securitized properties.

PML refers to probable maximum loss; the subject property's anticipated value of the monetary loss during a seismic event indicated as a percentage.

[43] If no seismic assessment has been conducted, the valuation is assumed to be a case with an unknown matter.

[44] In valuation practice, the standard level is usually around 15%-20%.

② 鑑定評価への反映
（ⅰ）耐震性
　　対象不動産が旧耐震基準に基づく建物で、耐震改修促進法に準拠した耐震診断が実施されており、当該耐震診断結果によって、耐震性に問題があって耐震補強工事が必要な場合には、耐震補強工事に要する費用等が価格に与える影響を考慮する必要がある[※43]。
　　なお、耐震改修促進法に準拠した耐震診断の結果、耐震性に著しく問題があることが判明したが、耐震補強工事の実施の予定がない建物は、取り壊しを前提とする以外は、通常、投資家から投資適格性に欠けると判断されるため、基準各論第3章等適用の鑑定評価の対象とすることはできない。

（ⅱ）地震リスク
　　一定水準[※44]のPML値を超過すると、地震保険が付保されるケースが多いため、このような場合には、地震保険の費用を査定し、当該保険費用が価格に影響を与える程度を考慮する。
　　なお、耐震補強工事が必要と判断される場合には、耐震補強工事に要する費用等が価格に与える影響を考慮する必要がある。

3）アスベスト
① 調査
　　対象不動産に飛散性のアスベスト含有吹付け材の使用が認められる場合には、除去、封じ込め等の措置を行う必要があり、その措置工事には多額の費用を要する場合が多く、対象不動産の価格に大きな影響を与えることが一般的である。したがって、鑑定評価に当たっては、アスベストの有無について調査する必要がある。
　　なお、成形材に使用されているアスベストは、劣化、損傷等が著しい場合を除き、飛散のおそれはないため、建物取り壊しの場合以外は、健康被害には直結しないと考えられている。
　　アスベストについては、BELCAの定義するエンジニアリング・レポートの1つである「建物環境リスク評価報告書（フェーズⅠ）」の必須項目である。アスベストについての調査に当たっては、依頼者から提供されたエンジニアリング・レポートを自ら判断し、活用する。なお、エンジニアリング・レポートを参照する過程で、疑問が生じたり、不動産鑑定士の調査結果と異なっている場合には、依頼者を通じてER作成者に内容を確認し、必要に応じて追加調査を要請する必要がある。
　　不動産鑑定士が行う調査を例示すれば、以下のとおりである。
　ア　建物の構造及び用途、防火地域か否か等
　イ　施工時期（築年、吹き付け等を行った改修時期等）
　ウ　エンジニアリング・レポートの調査において、現地調査（目視）を行ったのか、サンプリング調査まで行ったのか
　エ　設計図書等による内装、外装等の使用材料の確認

---

43 耐震診断が行われていない場合には、不明事項が存する場合として対応する。
44 実務上、おおむね15〜20％程度が目安とされることが多い。

Examples of surveys conducted by appraisers are as follows:
- Building structure and use, whether the area is a fire protection district
- Year constructed (completion date, renovation date when the spraying took place)
- Whether the engineering report surveys include only a site inspection (external inspection) or also a sampling inspection
- Verification of the interior/exterior materials used based on the design drawings and specifications
- Interviewing with concerned parties
- Public investigation regarding asbestos based on the relevant regulations

- Application to the Appraisal

The BELCA guidelines state: "The problem is not the use itself of sprayed materials. Assessment will be made by judging whether appropriate countermeasures are taken in the case asbestos dispersal is feared." Consequently, when the engineering report only describes as far as the "sprayed materials may contain asbestos" and not referring to the possibility of dispersal, it must be determined via the client. Also, in the appraisal of securitized properties, if there is possible presence of asbestos, separate analysis of sampling materials is often conducted regardless of the risk of dispersal. As such, whether there is a separate analysis or not should also be checked.

If the result of analysis state the "use of sprayed asbestos was confirmed" countermeasures such as removal or containment are generally required. However, if there is judged to only be a small effect on the property value, such as when possibility of asbestos dispersal is extremely low and the condition is stable based on the engineering report, the above countermeasures are not necessarily conducted. In the appraisal, the following should be considered: cost for countermeasures, tenants' vacation cost for the countermeasure construction period, decrease in occupancy rate, cost for restoration work of the refractory coating after the countermeasures, difficulty in lease-up (hereinafter "cost for countermeasures"). When the effect of the cost for countermeasures on the value of the subject property is considerable, the property must be valued with an appropriate deduction for the amount equivalent to the above cost. Since such a countermeasure cost is generally difficult to estimate only by appraisers, the appraiser, in principle, needs to request the client to have estimation conducted by other experts.

As such, if sprayed asbestos is present, the appraisal will take place after the completion, in principle, of its removal or containment. If the completion of such countermeasures is after the date of appraisal, however, appraisal can be conducted under the assumption that countermeasures have been taken for sprayed asbestos, provided that their feasibility is confirmed.

(d) PCB
- Surveys

Transfer or succession of PCB waste is prohibited by law. Therefore, in securitization, the former owner of the building generally removes the waste from the site or properly disposes of it before transfer of the property. Also, if any PCB-contain-

オ　関係者へのヒアリング
　　カ　法令等に基づく石綿に係る公的調査の有無及び内容

② 鑑定評価への反映
　BELCAのガイドラインの考え方では、「アスベスト吹付け材が使用されているから問題があるのではなく、あくまで飛散のおそれのある場合についてのみ然るべき対応がなされているかを判断して評価する。」ということであるため、「吹付け材にアスベストの含有の可能性がある」という記載にとどまり、飛散のおそれに関する評価がなされていない場合には、依頼者を通じてその点についての確認をする必要がある。また、証券化対象不動産の鑑定評価においては、アスベスト含有の可能性があるものに関しては、飛散のおそれの有無にかかわらず、別途、試料採取し分析調査がなされる場合も少なくないため、その点に関する確認も必要である。
　分析調査の結果、「吹付けアスベスト使用が確認された」と記載されていた場合には、原則として、除去、封じ込め等の措置工事が必要となる。ただし、吹付けアスベストであっても、エンジニアリング・レポートの記載内容等により、飛散のおそれが極めて少なく安定した状態で健康被害のおそれがない場合など、価格に対する影響が大きくないと判断できる場合は、この限りではない。
　鑑定評価においては、措置工事に要する費用、措置工事中のテナント退去に要する費用、稼働率の低下、措置工事終了後の耐火被覆の復旧工事費用、テナント募集の困難等（以下「措置費用等」と称する。）を考慮し、措置費用等が対象不動産の価格に影響を与える程度が大きい場合には、措置費用等相当額を適切に減価して評価する必要がある。措置費用等の見積りは、一般的には不動産鑑定士単独では困難であることが多いため、原則として、他の専門家による見積りを依頼者に要請する。
　したがって、吹付けアスベストが存する場合には、除去、封じ込め等の工事完了後に鑑定評価することが原則である。ただし、除去、封じ込め等の工事完了日が鑑定評価を行った日以降となる場合には、当該工事が行われることの確実性が確認できる場合には、吹付けアスベストについては措置済みという条件を付して鑑定評価することができる。

4）PCB
① 調査
　PCB廃棄物は法律により、譲渡又は譲受けが禁止されている。そのため、証券化においては建物の前所有者が、譲渡前にPCB廃棄物を敷地外に適正に移動又は廃棄する場合がほとんどである。また、使用中のPCBが含有されている電気工作物がある場合は、法律にし

ing electric facilities are in use, a notification must be submitted to the relevant Bureau of Economy in accordance with the law and a daily inspection to prevent oil leakage, etc. is necessary.

PCB is an essential topic of the "Building Environment Risk Assessment Survey Report (Phase I)," one of the engineering reports defined by BELCA. Therefore in the inspection for facilities containing PCB, the appraiser must conduct a site inspection, interview the building manager, and evaluate the contents of the provided engineering report and utilize them. If questions or discrepancies concerning the appraiser's survey are found in the course of referring to the engineering report, the appraiser must confirm the contents with the report's preparer via the client, and the appraiser should ask the client for additional survey if necessary.

- Application to the Appraisal

    Since transfer or succession of PCB waste is prohibited by law, such waste is normally removed at the time of transfer of the property. Even if there is PCB present at the time of internal inspection, appraisal can be conducted under the assumption that the PCB has been removed, provided the feasibility of the removal is confirmed with the client. PCB waste must be disposed of by a licensed operator, or other such party by July 15, 2016, in accordance with the Law Concerning Special Measures against PCB Waste (entered into force in 2001). Standard rates exist for the disposal.

    If PCB is not removed at the time of transfer of the property and is left within the property remaining as the transferor's possession, the cost for securing the space for PCB waste or for the relevant countermeasures must be reflected in the appraisal value.

    If, however, the cost is small for the appraisal value and is considered to have little effect on the value of the subject property, the appraisal can be conducted without consideration of its value influence.

3) **Building and its site**
   (a) Terms and Conditions
   - Investigations

        Regarding the terms and conditions of the lease and cash flow statement, the appraiser must be provided with information for verification, including: income-related contracts such as the lease contract, rent roll, and management cost-related contract, agreements among rights holders, memorandums, and management by-laws. The relevant rights should also be verified with a copy of the register.

        Special attention must be paid to studying the following: lease terms and conditions (restrictions on use, presence of a fixed-term lease, solidity of the lease terms and conditions, conditions for breaking the lease, etc.), the lessee's attributes and credibility, and the operation and services of the management company, since the study is the foundation of the application of the DCF method and may be related to the building's compliance.

        For instance, the difference among weekly rental apartments, monthly rental apartments, offices for SOHO, and ordinary apartments is not based on the structure of the building but on the management, including the lease terms and condi-

たがい所轄の経済産業局に届出し、漏油等の不具合が生じないように日常点検を実施する必要がある。

PCBについては、BELCAの定義するエンジニアリング・レポートの1つである「建物環境リスク評価報告書（フェーズⅠ）」の必須項目であるので、PCB使用機器の有無の調査においては、実地調査及び依頼者や建物管理者へのヒアリングに加え、エンジニアリング・レポートを自ら判断し、活用する。なお、エンジニアリング・レポートを参照する過程で、疑問が生じたり、不動産鑑定士の調査結果と異なっていたりする場合には、依頼者を通じてER作成者に内容を確認し、必要に応じて追加調査を要請する必要がある。

② 鑑定評価への反映

PCB廃棄物は、法律により譲渡又は譲受が禁止されているため、譲渡時には撤去されるのが通常である。内覧時に存在していても、撤去されることの確実性が確認できる場合は、依頼者に確認のうえ、撤去されたものとして鑑定評価を行うことができる。なお、PCB廃棄物は平成13年に施行されたPCB特別措置法により、平成28年7月15日までに、許可を受けた業者に委託するなどして、処分しなければならないこととされている。また、処理料金については基準価格が決められている。

譲渡時に撤去されず、譲渡人の所有でありながら、対象不動産内に残置される場合は、PCB廃棄物置場の確保等に起因する収益費用や措置に伴う収益費用等を評価額に反映させる必要がある。

ただし、当該収益費用等が鑑定評価額と比較して小さく、対象不動産の価格形成に大きな影響を与えないと判断できる場合には、価格形成要因から除外して鑑定評価を行うことができる。

(3) 建物及びその敷地

1）契約関係

① 調査

賃貸借契約内容及び収支状況については、依頼者から賃貸借契約書や賃貸借契約一覧表（レントロール）等の収益に関する契約、管理契約等の費用に関する契約、権利者間の協定書、覚書、管理規約等の提示を受け確認する。なお、権利関係は登記事項証明書等でも確認する。

賃貸借契約の内容（用途制限、定期借家契約であるかどうか、賃貸条件の確実性、中途退去時の条件等）、借主の属性や信用力、管理委託先や管理サービスの内容等の調査は、DCF法適用の基礎であり、建物の遵法性にも関連する場合もあるため、特に留意する。

例えば、ウィークリーマンション、マンスリーマンション、SOHO向けオフィスと通常のマンションの違いは、建物の構造ではなく、賃貸借契約等の運営方法による違いに起因するものであるが、これによって建築基準法その他の関連規定や行政における取り扱いが異なることがある[45]。したがって、内覧時には対象建物の運営状況に留意し、賃貸借契約内容等を確認する必要がある。また、レントロールを確認し、稼動状況や総賃貸可能床面積に占

---

[45] ウィークリーマンションは通常、住宅ではなくホテルと見做されるため、条例等による住宅附置義務や住宅附置による容積割り増しの要件を充足しない一方、旅館業法の適用を受ける。

tions. This means they may each be treated differently under the Building Standards Act and other relevant regulations or by the political administration[45]. Consequently, the appraiser must pay attention to the management status of the subject property at the time of internal inspection, and check the lease terms and conditions. Also, the occupancy status or the leased area ratio of key tenants for the net rentable area should carefully be checked with the rent roll.

Some lease contracts may include a free rent period, but this can often not be confirmed by only checking the rent roll and it needs to be confirmed by the client. Such confirmation must be made through written communication for the record, such as documents and email. The record of date of confirmation, name of the contact person, etc. must be stored.

- Application to the Appraisal

    Relevant rights regarding the subject property and specific value influences based on the terms and conditions must be properly reflected in the appraisal, especially upon application of the DCF method.

(b) Major Repair Plans

- Investigations

    In the survey and projection for repair work plans, the appraiser determines the estimation referring to information provided by the client, such as data on the repair history and engineering report.

    Repair plans are an essential topic of the "Building Condition Survey Report," one of the engineering reports defined by BELCA. Therefore the appraiser must verify the contents of the provided engineering report carefully and utilize them. If questions or discrepancies concerning the appraiser's survey are found in the course of referring to the engineering report, the appraiser must confirm the contents with the report's preparer via the client, and the appraiser should ask the client for additional survey if necessary.

- Application to the Appraisal

    Based on the appropriate repair plan, ordinary repair expenses and those included in the CAPEX (major repair expenses) must be estimated separately, which becomes the foundation when applying the DCF or direct capitalization method.

    In order to maintain a building, major repairs are generally essential every 10-15 years. Even if a major repair is not included in the holding period via the DCF method, it is necessary to reflect the expenses for after the holding period in the revisionary value. The reflection can be made as follows: include the annualized average amount in the annual expenses for the following year of the holding period when estimating the revisionary value; consider the expense in the terminal cap rate.

---

[45] Weekly rental apartments are generally deemed as hotels, not residences. Therefore, obligation to provide certain dwelling units in a building by ordinance or extra FAR for the provided dwelling units is not applied to such apartments, but they are subject to the Inns and Hotels Act.

める主たる借主の賃貸面積の割合にも留意する。
　一部の賃貸借契約にフリーレントが付されている場合もあるが、一般にフリーレントについては賃貸借契約書のみの確認では把握できないことが多いため、その存否について依頼者への確認が必要である。確認については文書、電子メール等記録に残る媒体で行い、当該確認の日時、確認相手等についての記録を残しておくことが必要である。

② 鑑定評価への反映
　鑑定評価に当たっては、対象不動産に係わる権利関係や契約関係に基づく個別的要因が評価額に適切に反映されるよう、特にDCF法の適用の際には留意する。

2) 大規模修繕計画
① 調査
　修繕計画の調査と想定に当たっては、エンジニアリング・レポートをはじめ、修繕履歴等の依頼者の提示資料等を参考に、不動産鑑定士が自ら判断する。
　すなわち、修繕計画は、BELCAの定義するエンジニアリング・レポートの1つである「建物状況調査報告書」の必須項目であるため、依頼者から提供されたエンジニアリング・レポートの内容を十分吟味のうえ、活用する。なお、エンジニアリング・レポートを参照する過程で、疑問が生じたり、不動産鑑定士の調査結果と異なっている場合には、依頼者を通じてER作成者に内容を確認し、必要に応じ追加調査を要請する必要がある。

② 鑑定評価への反映
　適切な修繕計画に基づき、日常的な費用に相当する修繕費と資本的支出に相当する修繕費（大規模修繕費）を区別して査定し、DCF法、直接還元法等鑑定評価手法適用の基礎とする。
　一般的に、建物の維持、保全等のためには10～15年に一度の大規模修繕が不可欠であるが、DCF法の分析期間中に大規模修繕が見込まれない場合であっても、復帰価格には、分析期間以降の大規模修繕費を反映させることが必要になる。
　この反映方法としては、復帰価格算定に当たっての費用に分析期間翌年の年間ベースに平準化した費用を計上する方法、最終還元利回りに織り込む方法等がある。

VI. Application of Appraisal Approaches

1. Valuation Policy

In order to estimate the market value, appraisal approaches that are appropriate for the type of subject property are applied based on the Appraisal Standards. For properties that are within a market where a majority of potential buyers are interested for investment purposes under securitization scheme, the DCF method should be applied in accordance with Specific Standards Chapter 3 and relevant Notes, and the value must be estimated with attention paid to the guidelines stated in 2 and beyond.[46] If the subject property is vacant land assumed for development (securitization of development property), the DCF method (development of a leasehold property) is applied instead of the ordinary DCF method[47].

In order to estimate market value based on special considerations (which shows the investment profitability), the required management plan, such as the asset securitization plan or the investment policy stated in the security registration statement, should be reflected as given conditions, and the investment profitability should be estimated based on these plans. Accordingly, the appraisal value needs to be determined based on the value indicated by the DCF method[48,49]. If market value based on special considerations and market values are considered equal, the application approaches that estimate the value of one or the other can be omitted.

In any case, however, for property or securitization scheme which do not place importance on the value indicated by the income capitalization approach, for instance the property is a detached house that is not a leasehold property and it is obvious that the property is acquired for resale, or it is vacant land and will certainly be developed as a condominium and to be sold, the appraisal value should be determined in accordance with the type of property and securitization scheme, based on the value indicated by the appropriate appraisal approaches, and the result verified with values indicated by other

---

[46] In the valuation of securitized properties, generally the final appraisal value is determined based on the value indicated by the DCF method of the income capitalization approach, and the result is verified with the value indicated by the direct capitalization method. However, the degree of verification with other indicated values may differ depending on the method preferred in the market to which the subject property belongs and accuracy of information used in the individual appraisal process.

[47] In the direct capitalization method, the land residual method that is used in the normal valuation of vacant land is applied.

[48] See 2. 3) for the valuation of development of a leasehold property.

[49] If the management plan of the subject property conforms to the subject's highest and best use and also if the value of the property is formed based on the subject's investment profitability in the market to which the subject property belongs, the estimated market value is in many cases equal to the market value based on special considerations. However, in some cases, the management plan's assumptions and future projections used in the estimation of the market value based on special considerations may differ from assumptions used in the estimation of market value. Therefore, the market value based on special considerations should not merely be estimated by estimating the market value first and then verifying the investment profitability.

Ⅵ 鑑定評価手法の適用

1 評価方針

　正常価格を求める場合には、不動産鑑定評価基準に基づき対象不動産の種類に応じた適切な手法を適用することとなるが、特に証券化等による投資目的の需要者が中心となる市場に属する不動産については、基準各論第3章等にしたがい、DCF法を適用した上で、2以下の点に留意して評価を行う必要がある[46]。なお、開発を前提に更地等を対象不動産とする開発型証券化の場合には、通常のDCF法に代わりDCF法（開発賃貸型）を適用する[47]。

　特定価格（投資採算価値を表す価格）を求める場合には、その要件である資産流動化計画、有価証券届出書の投資方針等の運用計画等を所与のものとし、当該運用計画等に基づく投資採算価格を求める必要があることから、DCF法を適用して求められたDCF法による収益価格を標準として[48]鑑定評価を行う必要がある[49]。なお、特定価格と正常価格が一致すると判断される場合には、一方の価格を求める手法適用を省略することもできる。

　ただし、いずれの場合でも、対象不動産が賃貸用不動産以外の戸建て住宅等で当該不動産の転売を目的とすることが明らかな場合や、分譲マンションとして開発し販売することが明らかな更地の場合など、必ずしも収益価格が重視されないような不動産及び証券化の仕組みである場合には、対象不動産の種類及び証券化の仕組みに応じて、適切な鑑定評価手法を適用して求められた試算価格を標準とし、それ以外の鑑定評価手法によって求められた試算価格による検証を行って鑑定評価額を決定する必要がある。

　また、複数の不動産鑑定士が共同して複数の証券化対象不動産の鑑定評価を行う場合にあっては、DCF法等の適用において採用する利回り、割引率、収益及び費用の将来予測等や取引事例比較法等における補修正率等について対象不動産相互間の論理的な整合性を図るなど、説明責任の向上を図らなければならない。

---

[46] 証券化対象不動産の鑑定評価においては、多くの場合は、DCF法による収益価格を中心に、直接還元法による収益価格等による検証を行って鑑定評価額を決定することとなると考えられるが、対象不動産の属する市場において重視される手法や、個々の鑑定評価作業における資料の精度等により、直接還元法による収益価格をはじめ他の試算価格との調整度合いは異なる。

[47] 直接還元法としては、通常の更地評価の際に用いる直接還元法による土地残余法を適用する。

[48] 開発型の場合には、後記2(3)参照。

[49] 運用計画が対象不動産の最有効使用と一致し、対象不動産の属する市場が投資採算価値を標準として価格が形成されている場合には、結果として特定価格と正常価格は一致することが多い。ただし、評価の前提となる運用計画や将来予測等は正常価格を求める場合と異なる場合もあるので、特定価格は、単に正常価格を求めてその投資採算性をチェックして求めるものではない。

approaches.

Also, when two or more appraisers jointly conduct valuation of multiple securitized properties, accountability must be improved by ensuring logical consistency between each subject property of the adopted cap rate, discount rate, and estimation of future cash flows in the DCF method and adjustments of comparables in the sales comparison method.

2. **Income Capitalization Approach**

1) **Income and Expense Items**

If the DCF method is applied for a leasehold property, the income and expense items should, in principle, be in accordance with those same items and their definitions stipulated in Specific Standards Chapter 3 and relevant Notes. The definitions of each item are detailed in the Appendix "Income and Expense Items (Comparison with Expenses in Accounting)" which is prepared referring to the classification in "Real Estate Management: Journal and Accounting Entries and Explanation," prepared by the Japan Building Owners and Managers Association and the Tokyo Building Owners and Managers Association as a reference and reflecting the Appraisal Standards and actual conditions of the appraisal.

In order to ensure consistency and comparability between each method, the same income and expense items must also be used in the direct capitalization method. If the data obtained is not based on the definitions of standard income and expense items, this should be clearly described in the report.

In the estimation of the net operating income, interest on deposit and CAPEX such as costs for large-scale maintenance, not recognized as operating cash flow in accounting, should not be included. In the estimation of value indicated by the income capitalization approach, however, the net cash flow (NCF) that includes the interest on deposit and CAPEX such as costs for large-scale maintenance should be used.

In the DCF method (including the DCF method for development of a leasehold property), sales of the subject property are assumed after the holding period in some cases but not in others. In either case, for the appraisal of securitized properties, the reversionary value should be estimated by deducting the sales cost from the potential sales price.

2) **DCF Method**

● Operating Income

The operating income is estimated by estimating the potential income of the subject property assuming full occupancy, and deducting vacancy loss and collection loss from the estimated potential income.

The common area maintenance ("CAM") charges are often deemed as including rent equivalents. It is also often difficult to differentiate between the charges for the lease area and common area. Accordingly, in current market practices it is becoming more common to include CAM charges in rental income for analysis, and the expenses that match with the received charges are included in the expenses in the cash flow. Based on this, the "CAM income" was added to the income items.

2 収益還元法
(1) 収益費用項目

賃貸用不動産についてDCF法を適用する場合の収益費用項目については、原則として基準各論第3章等に記載されている項目、定義等にしたがう必要がある。各項目の定義は、社団法人日本ビルヂング協会連合会、社団法人東京ビルヂング協会連合会編「不動産経営管理業務　出納・会計項目一覧及び解説」中分類等を参考に、不動産鑑定評価基準や鑑定評価実務の実態を踏まえ、『別表「収益費用項目表（会計上の費用との対比表）」』のとおりとする。

また、手法間の整合性や比較可能性確保のため、直接還元法についても同様の収益費用項目とする。この場合に、標準項目以外の定義で収集されたデータが入手された場合には、標準項目と違う定義を用いていることを必ず明記する必要がある。

運営純収益の算定に当たっては、会計上営業損益に含まれない一時金の運用益等、大規模修繕費等の資本的支出を含まないものとする。ただし、収益価格の査定においては、一時金の運用益等、大規模修繕費等の資本的支出を考慮した純収益を用いる必要がある。

なお、DCF法（開発賃貸型を含む）の適用方法として、保有期間後の売却を想定する場合と売却を想定しない場合とがあるが、証券化対象不動産の鑑定評価においては、復帰価格は、売却予測価格から売却費用を控除して求めるものとする。

(2) DCF法
① 運営収益

対象不動産が満室の場合に得られる収入を査定し、これから空室等損失、貸倒れ損失を差し引き、運営収益を求める。

共益費には実質的に賃料に相当する部分が含まれると判断されることが多いこと、費用の計上に当たり賃貸部分と共用部分で区別することが困難な場合が多いことなどから、昨今の市場慣行として、収益を共益費を含めた賃料収入により分析し、費用においても見合いの費用を計上することが多くなっていることを踏まえ、「共益費収入」という項目を設けている。

空室等損失、貸倒れ損失は、各収益項目の稼動率の状況がそれぞれ適切に反映されるように設定する。

共益費収入と維持管理費及び水道光熱費収入（附加使用料）と水道光熱費（費用）について

The occupancy rate conditions of each income item should be appropriately reflected in the vacancy loss and collection loss.

Regarding the CAM income and utility income received (additional charges) and maintenance cost and utility expenses paid (expenses), basically, if the subject property is an office building both the income received and expenses paid for the entire building, including those for the exclusive area, are included in the cash flow. If the subject property is a residential building, basically, both the income received and expenses paid for the common area are included in the cash flow. Note that the expense ratio differs depending on the method used. Therefore when comparing the expense ratio, attention must be paid to what the income and expenses cover.

· Rental Income

The rental income determines the gross rent and per-sqm or per-*tsubo* rent of each rentable area based on lease agreements, rent roll, and management reports.

The Year 1 rental income is estimated based on the assumption that the rent for the currently leased area will be the same as the current rent and that the owner-occupied or vacant area will be newly leased up. If a rent revision for the currently leased area, however, is obvious, as stated in the contract or because a cancellation notice is submitted, the rent should be estimated in the same manner as that of the owner-occupied or vacant spaces. As for the Year 2 and after, rental income is estimated taking into account of lease term of each tenant, change in rental level for new leases and renewal conditions of ongoing rents.

In determining the rentable area of the subject property, it must be verified with the completion drawings at site inspection or must be confirmed with the property manager about whether the rentable area includes such area as the common area (rest rooms, etc.). It is also required to confirm the rentable area if the areas specified in the rent roll and lease agreements are different or the completion drawings list the size of the exclusive areas.

In order to estimate the Year 1 rental income, attention should be paid to the following:

(a) To examine the current rent level, determine the new rent for the owner-occupied or vacant spaces, and project the rent for future periods, lease comparables of nearby properties similar to the subject are analyzed, and the new-lease rent level for the subject property by each use is determined accordingly. In such cases the analysis is generally based on the rent including the CAM charge.

(b) If the subject property is for a business use, such as a large-scale commercial facility, hotel, or assisted living residence for seniors, and if it is deemed necessary to examine the current rent level based on the financial performance of business operated in the subject property, the affordable rent level should be estimated by first analyzing the business operation.

は、対象不動産がオフィスの場合は、原則として、専用部分を含むビル全体の収益費用を両建てする方法を標準とする。一方、対象不動産が住宅の場合は、共用部分に係る収益費用を両建てする方法を原則とする。なお、選択した手法によって、経費率が変わるために、経費率の比較を行う場合には、計上している収益費用の対象範囲を確認することが必要であることに留意する。

i 貸室賃料収入

貸室賃料収入は、賃貸借契約、レントロール、管理運営報告書等に基づき各貸室について総額及び単価（円／㎡、円／坪）について確認する。

初年度の貸室賃料収入は、現に賃貸されている部分については価格時点における実際支払賃料とし、自用又は空室部分については新規に賃貸借することを想定して査定する。ただし、現に賃貸されている部分について約定又は解約予告等により、新規賃料への変更が明確である場合には自用又は空室部分と同様に査定する。翌期以降については、テナント毎の契約期間等を考慮し、新規賃料水準の変動状況及び継続賃料の改定状況を総合的に勘案して査定する。

なお、対象不動産の賃貸範囲については、現地調査において竣工図面との照合や管理者へのヒアリングにより共用部分（トイレ等）を含むものであるかどうかなどの確認を行う必要がある。また、レントロールの面積と賃貸契約書の面積が異なる場合や竣工図等において専用面積の記載がある場合等においては、賃貸面積の確認を行う必要がある。

初年度の貸室賃料収入の査定に当たって留意する点を例示すれば、以下のとおりである。

ア　現行の賃料水準の把握、自用又は空室部分における新規賃料の把握及び翌期以降の将来予測のために、まず、周辺類似不動産の賃貸事例を分析し、対象不動産の用途別の新規賃料水準を把握する。この場合、共益費込みの賃料水準で分析するのが一般的である。

イ　対象不動産が、大規模商業施設、ホテル、老人ホーム等の事業用不動産の場合で、現行の賃料水準を、当該不動産における事業収支を前提に把握する必要が認められる場合には、当該事業分析を行って負担可能賃料水準を分析のうえ行う。

ウ　賃貸借契約がマスターリースの場合、当該マスターリース賃料を用いることとなるが、転借人の支払賃料水準についても分析する。

エ　対象不動産が、店舗等の場合で賃料に歩合制を加味している場合には、歩合部分について、過去の実績や同業種の営業状況等を分析して査定する。

オ　開発型証券化において、竣工後建物の貸室賃料収入を査定する場合には、予定賃貸借契約等において賃料が定まっている場合には、原則として当該賃料とし、定まっていない場合には、竣工時点において新規に賃貸借することを想定して査定する。

(c) If it is a master-lease agreement, the rental income is estimated based on the master-lease rent. The sublease rent level should, however, also be analyzed.

(d) If the subject property is a retail store and its rent is based on sales, the rental income should be estimated by analyzing historical data and sales of similar business operations.

(e) To estimate the rental income of the building after its completion in the appraisal of securitized properties assumed for development, if the rent is listed in the planned lease agreement, etc, this rent should basically be used. If the rent is not yet determined, the rent should be estimated assuming it will be leased upon completion of the building.

· CAM Income

CAM income refers to the "income collected under agreements with the lessee for the ordinary expenses required for maintenance and management of the subject property (including utility and regional heating and cooling expenses), which apply to the common area." CAM income estimates gross and per-sqm or per-*tsubo* CAM income of each rentable area based on lease agreements, rent roll, and management reports.

CAM income is estimated in the same manner as rental income. If rental income and CAM income are not differentiated between and the gross amount (rental income including CAM) is stated in the agreement, the CAM income is estimated as included in the rental income.

In order to project future changes, revision of CAM income should, in principle, not be assumed when commodity prices are stable. If CAM income is stated as the gross amount (rental income including CAM) the projection should be made with a conservative view compared to the revision of the rent only. However, if there is rationale for revision in CAM charges, such as a plan for facility renovation, this should be reflected in the estimation.

· Utility Reimbursement

Utility reimbursement refers to the "income collected under agreements with the lessee for the expenses for electricity, water, gas, regional heating and cooling, etc., in the management of the subject property, which apply to the rentable area." The projection should be based on the historical data, but if the vacancy rate assumption differs from that, the cash flow may result in differences. Accordingly, the utility reimbursement must be projected in accordance with the vacancy rate assumption.

As in the estimation of the maintenance cost and utility expenses, whether the utility reimbursement applies to the rentable area and common area or only to the common area, must be checked, and care must be taken to not include income that should be included in the CAM income.

If the regional heating and cooling system is installed, the cost for this could be high and the amount collected from the lessee differs depending on the management policy. Accordingly, confirmation must be made on whether such a sys-

ⅱ　共益費収入

　共益費収入は、「対象不動産の維持管理・運営において経常的に要する費用（電気、水道、ガス、地域冷暖房熱源等に要する費用を含む）のうち、共用部分に係るものとして賃借人との契約により徴収する収入」を指し、賃貸借契約、レントロール、管理運営報告書等に基づき各貸室について総額及び単価（円／㎡、円／坪）について確認する。

　共益費収入の査定方法は、貸室賃貸収入と同様である。なお、貸室賃料収入と共益費収入が区別されておらず、共益費込み貸室賃料収入として総額が約定されている場合には、共益費込み貸室賃料収入として査定する。

　将来予測に当たっては、共益費収入部分については、原則として物価安定期においては改定を見込むべきではない。また、総額として把握されている場合には、貸室賃料のみの更改に比較し保守的な観点から予測を行う。ただし、施設更新に伴う改定等の合理的な予定がある場合には、これらを反映して査定する。

ⅲ　水道光熱費収入

　水道光熱費収入は、「対象不動産の運営において電気、水道、ガス、地域冷暖房熱源等に要する費用のうち、貸室部分に係るものとして賃借人との契約により徴収する収入」を指し、その予測は原則として過年度収支等を参考に行うが、想定する空室率が異なる場合には、過年度の収支と必ずしも一致しないため、想定した空室率に即した収入予測を行わなければならない。

　また、水道光熱費収入については、維持管理費や水道光熱費と同じく、当該収入の対象範囲が貸室部分に係るものと共用部分に係るものであるのか、後者のみであるのか等を確認し、共益費収入として計上すべきものとのダブりがないように注意することが必要である。

　地域冷暖房を採用している場合は、高額でありかつ、対象不動産の運営方針の違いにより請求金額に差異があるために、依頼者に採用の有無、運営方針等についての確認が必要である。

tem is installed and, if so, its management policy must also be confirmed.
- Parking Income

    Parking income estimates the gross parking income and per car rate of each parking space based on the lease agreements, rent roll, and management reports.

    For monthly and hourly parking spaces the market parking rate must be determined for each. Monthly parking income is estimated based on the historical data, but whether the future condition will be the same as the historical data must be analyzed by taking market trends into account and appropriately estimating the income.
- Other Income

    If it is collected monthly under agreements, other income is estimated in the same manner as the rental income in accordance with the income items. If income of an irregular deposit (key money, etc.) is expected, other income is estimated in accordance with the actual timing of the potential deposit or by calculating the annual average amount based on the average tenant turnover period. For other cases the historical data should be used as a reference.

    Other major income includes the following:
    (a) Antennas
    (b) Advertising facilities, such as signage
    (c) Vending machines
    (d) Non-refundable deposit that could be deemed as prepayment, such as key money (pay attention to its attributes) and cancellation penalty; these should be included in the income for the year they are received

    Other income should be estimated based on the historical data, with attention paid to whether it will be transferred to the new owner. It is necessary to confirm with the client on details of the other income in the historical data when estimating other income.

    In order to estimate the income generating from antennas, advertising facilities such as signage, and vending machines, a full check must be made with the client about the continuity of agreements on which the income is based and their relevant compliance issues, and the assets must be confirmed at the site inspection.

    Key money (including amortization of deposit) is estimated as interest on deposit and income from amortization of the deposit. In Specific Standards Chapter 3 and relevant Notes, however, it has been changed to be included in other income and separated from refundable deposits, such as the security deposit. Generally, key money received by the previous owner will not be transferred to the new owner upon sale of the property. Accordingly, as long as the lease agreement continues, key money is not included in the cash flow.
- Vacancy Loss

ⅳ　駐車場使用料収入

　　駐車場収入は賃貸借契約、レントロール、管理運営報告書等に基づき各駐車部分について総額及び単価（円／台）について確認する。

　　月極と時間貸しがある場合には各々の使用料の市場水準を把握することが必要となる。時間貸し駐車場収入については過年度の実績が参考となるが、過年度実績における賃貸状況が将来と同じ状態になるかどうかについては市場動向を踏まえ、的確に見積ることが必要である。

ⅴ　その他収入

　　その他収入は、収入項目にしたがって、月極で約定されている場合には、賃貸料収入と同様に査定する。また、権利金の一時金収入等のように不定期に収入が見込まれるものについては、実際に収入が見込まれる期に応じて査定するか又はテナントの平均回転期間を考慮した年平均額として査定する。また、それ以外の場合には過年度実績等を参考に査定する。

　その他収入の主なものを例示すれば、以下のとおりである。
　ア　アンテナ収入
　イ　看板等の広告施設収入
　ウ　自動販売機設置料収入
　エ　礼金、権利金（その性格に留意する。）等の前払い的性格を有する一時金や解約違約金等の一時金収入（これらは収受年度の収益として計上する。）

　　その他収入については、新所有者における承継の可否等に留意のうえ、過年度実績を参考に見積もることとし、見積もりに際しては過年度実績がどのような状況のもとで積み上げられたかを確認する必要がある。

　　アンテナ収入や看板等の広告施設収入、自動販売機設置料収入については、それらの収入の前提となる契約関係の継続性やそれらの設置に係る違法性等について十分依頼者に確認するとともに、現地調査において対象資産の確認を行うことが必要である。

　　従来、一時金の運用益及び償却益等として査定してきた権利金（保証金の償却部分を含む）等については、基準各論第3章等では、その他収入の一つとして、保証金等の預かり金的性格の一時金とは異なる取り扱いに変更されている。なお、前所有者が授受した権利金等は、一般的に売買の際には新所有者に引き継がれないので、当該賃貸借契約が継続している間は計上しないこととなる。

ⅵ　空室等損失

Year 1 vacancy loss is estimated taking into account the current vacancy rate and expected lease-up of vacant spaces in Year 1. Vacancy loss for Year 2 and beyond is estimated taking into account the ordinary occupancy of nearby comparable properties and vacancy assuming tenant turnover. The vacancy loss of parking and other income may not necessarily change in accordance with the occupancy of the rentable area, and as such, it should be estimated separately.

In a case of a lease to a single tenant or of a master lease, the vacancy loss should be estimated as the annual average amount assuming tenant turnover caused by lease expiration or cancellation, or if the vacancy loss is not estimated the vacancy risk should be reflected in the yield such as discount rate.

· Collection Loss

Collection loss is projected based on the actual past default of the current lessee and its related credit.

It is recognized as a deduction from the income. This cost occurs when unpaid rent could not later be collected and it therefore is difficult to accurately reflect this loss in expense items such as property management fees estimated based on the operating income.

Collection loss typically occurs when the lessee goes bankrupt and cancellation of the lease is not allowed during judicial proceedings, and after approximately three months the security deposit can no longer cover the restoration cost and unpaid rent. Therefore collection loss can be projected by estimating the possibility of such a case. In the actual valuation, collection loss is not recognized in many cases because it is considered to be covered by the security deposit. It should be determined, however, considering the lessee's credit, supply-demand of the area, and amount of security deposit.

● Operating Expenses

Operating expenses estimate the maintenance cost, utility expenses, minor repair cost, property management fees, leasing cost, property tax, insurance premiums, and other expenses based on the occupancy assumptions. In the case of a lease to a single tenant or of a master lease, not all expense items are necessarily borne by the owner. Accordingly, reference to the lease agreements and appropriate estimation of the expenses borne by the owner are required.

· Maintenance Cost

Maintenance cost refers to the cleaning (exterior wall and common area), facility (maintenance of elevators, cold-hot water machine, air conditioner filter, and firefighting equipment), sanitary, and security costs. These are estimated based on the occupancy assumption derived from the historical data, and comprehensively considering the management plan and typical cost level of comparable properties. It is also important to examine the provided data for any outliers by gathering a considerable volume of comparables and analyzing the per-tsubo or per-sqm cost (net rentable area or gross building area) of each cost mentioned herein in accordance with the subject property's scale and age. The maintenance cost must be determined at an appropriate level that can provide sufficient

初年度の空室等損失は、現行空室率を参考に、初年度において見込まれる入居可能性を考慮して査定する。翌期以降は、周辺類似不動産における平均的な稼働状況を参考にテナントの入替えに伴う空室を勘案して査定する。なお、駐車場収入やその他収入においては、必ずしも貸室の稼働状況と連動しないために、各収入に応じた空室等損失を査定する。
　　また、一棟貸しやマスターリースの場合は、契約期間満了や途中解約等による入替えを考慮した年平均額として査定するか、空室等損失として査定しない場合には割引率等において空室リスクとして考慮する。

　vii　貸倒れ損失
　　貸倒れ損失は、現行賃借人の過去の貸倒れ実績及び賃借人の信用力に基づき予測する。
　　収益に連動する控除項目として扱うが、当該費用は後日未収金が回収できないことによって発生するものであるために、収益に連動するプロパティマネジメントフィー等には正確な反映は困難となる。
　　貸倒れ損失は、賃借人が倒産し、裁判の手続きに入り、契約解除できなくなり、3ヶ月ほどの後、原状回復費用と、未払い賃料を敷金、保証金等でまかなえなくなった事例において発生するのが典型的であり、このような事例の発生確率を考慮することにより査定することもできる。実務上、保証金等により担保されているとして計上しない場合も多いが、賃借人の信用、地域の需給動向、保証金の多寡等を考慮して判断する必要がある。

② 運営費用
　　運営費用は、想定した稼働状況に基づく、維持管理費、水道光熱費、修繕費、プロパティマネジメントフィー、テナント募集費用等、公租公課、損害保険料、その他費用を査定する。なお、一棟貸しやマスターリース等の場合には、すべての項目が必ずしも所有者負担ではないため、賃貸借契約書等により所有者が負担すべき費用を適切に査定する必要がある。

　i　維持管理費
　　維持管理費は、清掃費（外壁及び共用部分清掃業務等）、設備費（EV保守点検、冷温水発生装置点検、空調機フィルター交換、消防設備点検等）、環境衛生費、警備費等であり、過去の実績等を参考に想定した稼働状況に基づき、今後の管理運営計画、類似不動産の費用水準等を総合的に勘案して査定する。また、多数の事例を収集し、対象不動産の規模、経年に応じ、できるだけ前記維持管理費の内訳別に面積単価（賃貸面積又は延面積）によって分析し、依頼者から受領したデータを検証し、異常値がないか確認することが必要であり、想定する運営収益が得られるような維持管理を行える適正な水準で設定する必要がある。

maintenance to generate the assumed operating income.
- Utility Expenses

    Utility expenses estimate the utility cost required for the entire building based on the occupancy assumptions derived from the historical data. Note that they can be divided into two: the cost for the common area in which the influence of occupancy is limited and the cost for the exclusive area in which the influence of occupancy is substantial. The utility expenses are recognized as expenses that match the received utility reimbursement in some cases, and as expenses for the common area that are covered by the received CAM charge in other cases. (Generally speaking, there is no item as utility expenses for residential properties. Utility expenses for the common area are covered by the CAM income and those for the exclusive area are borne by each lessee.)
- Minor Repair Cost

    Minor repair cost is estimated taking into account the historical data, management plan, and typical cost level of comparable properties.

    Costs recognized as expenses in the profit and loss statement fall under this item. Minor repair cost is sometimes required for restoration of a residential leasehold property when the lessee vacates. Such costs must be estimated by referring to the historical data.

    In the estimation process, the minor repair cost and the large-scale maintenance cost (CAPEX) may be recognized as a combined amount and the cost level is estimated as a percentage of the reproduction cost of the building. Even in such case, it is important to appropriately separate the minor repair cost and CAPEX amount.
- Property Management Fees (PM Fees)

    PM fees are estimated assuming a fee level based on the current property management agreements, taking into account the continuity of the property management company and typical cost level of comparable properties. In a broad sense the property management (PM) includes the building management (BM: PM in a narrow sense), construction management (CM: determination and implementation of medium- and long-term repair and maintenance plan), and leasing management (LM: finding tenants, concluding agreements, management). Accordingly, the fees can be categorized as BM, CM, and LM. PM fees refer to the cost for the management to arrange on-site requirements; the on-site cost is not included. (Note that in J-REIT, PM is often used in a narrow sense (BM). Irrespective of its name, its purpose and contents must be revealed and its amount must be determined accordingly.)

    PM in a broad sense may cover BM, CM, and LM (fees are high in such cases). For the valuation it is important to find out what the PM fees cover.
- Leasing Cost

    Leasing cost refers to the "expenses needed for brokerage and advertising in a new leasing, and those required for renewal and re-contracting of lease agreements with tenants." It is estimated based on the timing of expected new leasing

ⅱ 水道光熱費
　　水道光熱費は、過年度実績等を参考に想定した稼働状況に基づき、建物一棟全体に要する水道光熱費を査定する。水道光熱費は、稼働状況にあまり影響を受けない共用部分に係るものと稼働状況に大きく影響を受ける専用部分に係るものとに分かれることに留意する。水道光熱費には、水道光熱費収入に対応する費用として計上するものと共用部分に係る水道光熱費で共益費の一部によってまかなわれるものとがある（住宅の場合は一般に水道光熱費という項目がなく、共益費収入で共用部分の水道光熱費はまかなわれ、専用部分の費用は個別に支払われる。）。

ⅲ 修繕費
　　修繕費は、過去の実績を参考に、今後の管理運営計画、類似不動産の費用水準等の観点から検討し、予測を行う。
　　損益計算上、修繕費として費用処理されるものが対象となる。居住用賃貸不動産の場合には、賃借人退去時に原状回復等のための修繕費用が必要となることがあるために、これらの支出について過去の実績を参考に見積もることが必要である。
　　この際、大規模修繕費（資本的支出）と合算で、建物の再調達原価に対して何％程度の工事費であるかどうか等の支出水準を把握する場合もあるが、その場合にあっても、修繕費と大規模修繕費（資本的支出）とに適切に区分する必要がある。

ⅳ プロパティマネジメントフィー（PMフィー）
　　プロパティマネジメントフィーは、現行の管理運営委託契約書等に基づくフィー水準を前提に、PM会社の継続性の観点や類似不動産の費用水準等の観点から検討し、予測を行う。広義のプロパティマネジメント（PM）はBM（ビルメンテナンス：狭義のPM）、CM（コンストラクションマネジメント、中長期的な改修及び修繕計画の策定及び実施）、LM（リーシングマネジメント及びテナントの誘致、契約、管理等）の管理統括業務で、PMフィーは、BMフィー、CMフィー、LMフィーに分類できる。現場の費用は別で、現場を手配する統括業務である（ただし、J－REITではPMが狭義（BM）で使われる場合が多い。呼び方に係わらず業務の内容について確認し金額を把握することが必要である。）。
　　PM（広義）は、BM、CM、LM実務と兼ねている場合がある（この場合のフィーは高額になる。）。鑑定評価に当たっては、PMフィーの対象となる業務を確認する必要がある。

ⅴ テナント募集費用等
　　テナント募集費用等とは、「新規テナントの募集に際して行われる仲介業務や広告宣伝等に要する費用及びテナントの賃貸借契約の更新や再契約業務に要する費用等」を指し、実際に新規テナントの募集が見込まれる期に応じて査定するか、又はテナントの平均回転期間を

or on the annual average based on the average tenant turnover.

This cost may, however, not be necessary in a market that favors owners. Accordingly, the leasing cost borne by the owner should be estimated taking into account the lease market trend. Also note that the additional PM fees may be required for rent revision during the lease term.

· Tax

The tax estimates the tax imposed on the subject property and borne by the owner, such as fixed asset tax.

Fixed Asset Tax and City Planning Tax

The actual amount, in principle, is included in the Year 1 cash flow. If the actual amount is unknown it is estimated based on the actual taxation conditions. For Year 2 and beyond, the tax should be appropriately estimated within the foreseeable range, paying attention to changes in assessed value. The foreseeable special exemptions of the tax base must also be reflected. In addition, the building tax, in principle, does not increase and the same amount may be used in the cash flow; or it can be estimated applying an officially used formula such as reduction rate adjustment for age deterioration.

Tax on Depreciable Assets

For the Year 1 cash flow, the tax associated with the subject property is estimated based on depreciable asset declaration. For the Year 2 cash flow and beyond, the tax is estimated taking into account conditions of replacements in previous years.

· Insurance Premiums

Though insurance premiums differ depending on the amount of indemnity and whether it contains a special contract that covers the total reproduction cost, they are estimated based on the actual amount and referring to the standard coverage and premiums.

Also note that owners state different coverage levels for earthquake insurance in their investment policy or in the management standards, and earthquake risk insurance is not necessarily common. Accordingly, earthquake insurance premiums are for the most part not included in the expenses. If the subject property's probability of maximum loss (PML) exceeds the standard level, however, and it is highly likely that the earthquake risk is covered by insurance premiums, this cost must be included in the expenses or the cost equivalent must be reflected in the yields such as discount rate. It is also important to view the management plan of the subject property because it might be appropriate to assume above-standard PML to be remedied by seismic retrofitting.

· Other Expenses

The other expenses include the following:

Ground Lease Fee Ground Rent

考慮した年平均額として査定する。
　　ただし、賃貸人に有利な市場環境等の場合には必ずしも発生しないこともあるため、賃貸市場の動向を鑑み、賃貸人負担分を査定する。なお、PMフィーとして契約期間中の賃料改定等に関する費用が発生する場合があることに留意する。

vi　公租公課
　　固定資産税等、対象不動産を課税対象とし、所有者負担となる公租公課について査定する。

（ⅰ）固定資産税、都市計画税
　　　初年度は、原則として実額を計上し、実額が不明な場合には、課税実態を考慮して査定する。翌期以降は、評価替え年度を踏まえて、予測できる範囲で適切に査定する。また、課税標準の特例等各種軽減措置については、予測可能な範囲で適切に反映する必要がある。なお、建物については、基本的に上昇することはないため同額とするか、若しくは「経年減点補正率」等、公的機関で使われている計算式を用いて予測することができる。

（ⅱ）償却資産に対する固定資産税
　　　初年度は、償却資産申告書等によって対象不動産に属する部分を査定する。翌期以降は、過年度における更新状況等を勘案して査定する。

vii　損害保険料
　　損害保険料は、価額協定特約の有無、免責額等により異なるが、標準的な付保額、保険料等を参考として、実額に基づいて査定する。
　　また、地震保険は、投資方針や運用基準において、所有者ごとに付保基準は異なり、必ずしも地震保険を付保することが一般化していないため、原則として費用には含めないこととする。ただし、一定水準のPML値を超える場合で、地震保険の付保の可能性が高い場合には、当該保険料を費用に計上するか、又は当該費用相当額を割引率等で考慮する必要がある。なお、耐震改修によって措置することを想定することが妥当な場合もあるため、対象不動産の運営計画を確認することも必要である。

viii　その他費用
　　その他費用の主なものを例示すれば、以下のとおりである。

（ⅰ）支払地代

Use the actual rent paid for ground lease after examining the ground lease agreement. For Year 2 cash flow and beyond, the fee is estimated taking into account the possibility of fee revision.

Road Occupancy Charges

Road occupancy charges refer to charges required for signage boards, and other such items that protrude from the building above the road. In order to estimate the occupancy charges of public assets such as roads and rivers, use the actual occupancy charges after examining the occupancy agreement. For Year 2 cash flow and beyond, the charges are estimated taking into account the possibility of charge revision.

Management Association Fee

The management association fee is paid by each condo-owner and collected by the management association to cover the maintenance of the entire condominium building and the utility expenses for the common area. If this fee is included within other expenses, it should be paid special attention not to doubly count this fee in the abovementioned items such as building maintenance fees and utility expenses (for the common area). Also note that the fee and renovation reserve should be confirmed with the management association. If coverage of the CAM charges and the management association fee are unclear, this should also be confirmed.

Renovation Reserve

Renovation reserve is paid by each condo-owner and collected by the management association to cover the minor repair cost and CAPEX of the entire condominium building (mainly the common area). It is, in principle, estimated based on the historical data and engineering report. If the accumulated renovation reserve level is low, however, and additional collection is estimated separately for special renovation in the future, this amount should be included in the minor repair expenses and CAPEX.

· Expenses not Included in the Operating Expenses

Trust Fee and Asset Management Fee

The trust fee for the real estate securitization, management cost of the SPC, etc., and asset management fee are not specific costs associated with the property, and accordingly are not included in the operating expenses. If these expenses are in actuality deemed to be part of the maintenance cost, minor repair cost, or property management fee, they must be included in the operating expenses and it is important to determine them irrespective of their name.

Acquisition Expenses

Expenses required for acquisition of the subject property, such as brokerage fee and acquisition tax, are not included in the operating expenses for consisten-

　　　　支払地代は、借地契約の内容を確認のうえ実額を計上する。翌期以降は賃料改定の可能性等を勘案して査定する。

(ⅱ) 道路等占用使用料
　　　　道路等占有使用料は、建物から道路の上空にせり出して設置される看板等の道路占用使用料のことである。道路や河川等公共物の占用使用料は、契約内容を確認のうえ実額を計上する。翌期以降は占用使用料改定の可能性等を勘案して査定する。

(ⅲ) 管理組合費
　　　　管理組合費とは、区分所有建物において一棟全体の建物保守管理費、共用部分の水道光熱費等に充当するために各区分所有者より管理組合が徴収するものである。これを計上する場合には、通常前記建物保守管理費と電気料と水道料（共用部分）が計上されないことに留意するとともに、修繕積立金とともに管理組合等で確認する必要がある。なお、共益費と管理組合費の範囲が不明確な場合はこれを確認する必要がある。

(ⅳ) 修繕積立金
　　　　修繕積立金とは、区分所有建物において一棟全体（主に共用部分）の修繕費や資本的支出に該当するために各区分所有者より管理組合が徴収するものである。原則として、過年度実績やエンジニアリング・レポート等を参考に査定する。ただし、修繕積立金累計額等の水準が低い場合などで、将来における特別修繕のための追加的徴収に相当する部分を別途査定した場合には、当該部分を修繕費と資本的支出に計上する。

ⅸ　運営費用として見込まない費用
（ⅰ）信託報酬、アセットマネジメントフィー
　　　　不動産証券化に伴う信託報酬やSPC等の管理費用、アセットマネジメントフィーは、いずれも不動産に関する固有のコストではないため、運営費用として計上しない。なお、これらの費用のうち、実質的に対象不動産の維持管理費、修繕費、プロパティマネジメントフィー等と判断される場合には、当該費用については運営費用に含む必要があるので、名目にとらわれずに判断する必要がある。

（ⅱ）不動産の取得に係る費用
　　　　対象不動産の取得に係る仲介手数料や不動産取得税等は、他の鑑定評価手法との整合性の観点から、運営費用として計上しない。

cy with other appraisal approaches.

Business Tax
Business tax is usually borne by the business owner (lessee). Therefore it is, in principle, not included in the operating expenses.

Consumption Tax
Consumption tax (including local consumption tax, same applies hereinafter) is, in principle, not included in inflows or outflows.

- Net Operating Income

Net operating income is estimated by deducting operating expenses from operating income.

- Interest on Refundable Deposit, etc.

The refundable deposit influences the actual rent amount. Therefore, regardless of the conditions for earning interest, it is, in principle, estimated as the interest equivalent amount for the year-end balance. If the subject property is a building on leasehold land and deposit is paid to the owner of the leased land, the unearned interest caused by this opportunity loss is estimated.

The interest rate used in the estimation of interest equivalent earned or lost on deposit is estimated comprehensively considering the operational and fund-raising aspects because the interest rate contains both of these.

In the DCF method, the refundable deposit is, in principle, not included in the year it is actually received. The interest equivalent earned on deposit is instead included. This concept on interest rate and its rationale should be included in the appraisal report.

The interest rate during the holding period of the DCF method is estimated based on the interest rate level as of the date of value and taking into account the restrictions on management of the deposit specified in the lease agreement. The interest rate for the direct capitalization method or for the estimation of the reversionary value in the DCF method assuming stabilized cash flow is estimated based on the super-long term stabilized interest rate level and taking into account the restrictions on management of the deposit specified in the lease agreements.

- Capital Expenditure (CAPEX)

CAPEX refers to the "amount spent on repair and renovation of the building and facilities, which are recognized as increasing the value or strengthening the durability of the subject property[50]." CAPEX is estimated taking into account the historical repair and renovation records and the long-term repair and maintenance cost in the engineering report, in accordance with the timing of the expenditures or as an annual average amount considering the holding period.

---

[50] According to the BELCA guidelines, repair and maintenance is "replacement of deteriorated construction materials and equipment with new ones. Generally speaking, improvement of the facility is not the objective. Deteriorated materials and equipment are replaced by equivalent items.

(iii) 事業所税

　　事業所税は通常、事業主（賃借人）が負担するものなので、原則として費用として計上しない。

(iv) 消費税

　　消費税等（地方消費税を含む。以下同じ。）は、原則として収益及び費用いずれにおいても計上しない。

③ 運営純収益

　運営収益から運営費用を控除して、運営純収益を査定する。

④ 一時金（預かり金）の運用益等

　預かり金的性格を有する一時金は、実際支払賃料の額に影響を与えることから、実際の運用実態にかかわらず、原則として、毎期の残高に対する運用益相当額として査定する。また、借地権付建物の場合で、底地所有者に同様の一時金を預託している場合には、運用益獲得機会の喪失相当額として査定する。

　運用益相当額又は運用益獲得機会の喪失相当額の査定における運用利回りは、資金の運用的側面と調達的側面双方を有するため、これらを総合的に勘案して査定する。

　DCF法等における一時金（預かり金）は、実際の授受の期に計上する方法ではなく、運用益等相当額を計上する方法によることを原則とし、運用利回りの考え方及び査定根拠を鑑定評価報告書に記載する。

　DCF法の保有期間中における運用利回りは、当該時点における運用利回り水準を基本に、また、直接還元法及びDCF法の復帰価格査定において収益費用の標準化を前提とする場合は超長期における標準的な運用利回り水準を基本に、賃貸借契約等による預かり金の運用制約の程度を勘案して査定する。

⑤ 資本的支出

　資本的支出とは、「対象不動産に係る建物、設備等の修理、改良等のために支出した金額のうち当該建物、設備等の価値を高め、又はその耐久性を増すこととなると認められる部分に対応する支出」を指し[50]、過去の修繕履歴やエンジニアリング・レポート記載の長期修繕更新費等を参考に、支出が見込まれる期に応じて査定するか又は保有期間を考慮した年平均額として査定する。

---

50 なお、BELCAのガイドラインによれば、更新とは「劣化した建築材料や設備機器等を新しいものに取り替えること。一般的には機能の向上は目的とはせず、従来使用されていきた素材・機器と同等の仕様とする。」とされている。

- Net Cash Flow (NCF)

  NCF is estimated by adding or deducting the interest on deposit and deducting the CAPEX from the net operating income.

- Reversionary Value at End of Holding Period

  Reversionary value is based on the assumption that the subject property will be sold at the end of the holding period. It is estimated by deducting the sales cost from the potential sales price.

  · Holding Period

  The holding period should be determined for the subject property in accordance with the generally acceptable holding period in real estate investment. Note that if the subject property is a building on fixed-term leasehold land, the holding period is subject to the restriction of the remaining term of the ground lease agreement.

  It is considered unnecessary to use the same holding period. Note that regardless of the holding period, the estimated value results are the same as long as the discount rate and terminal capitalization rate are appropriate.

  The holding period must be within the period in which highly accurate projection of the NCF changes is possible.

  · Potential Sales Price

  The potential sales price is estimated by capitalizing the NCF of the year after the holding period at the terminal capitalization rate. Consistency must be ensured with this NCF and the single-period NCF used in the direct capitalization method.

  · Sales Cost

  Sales cost, in principle, includes the brokerage fee equivalent. If the subject property is a building on leasehold land and it is deemed common to pay/collect a transfer acceptance fee, this should be included in the sales cost. However, if the contract states that this fee is not paid, it should not be included.

  · Reversionary Value

  Reversionary value is estimated by deducting the sales cost from the potential sales price.

- Projection

  Cash flow projection involves uncertainty and the results often vary depending on decision made by licensed real estate appraisers. In the appraisal of securitized properties the appraiser must understand and analyze how a rational market participant estimates future cash flow and makes decisions assuming that the value of the subject property is estimated based on the investment profitability derived from the expected potential cash flow.

  It is important to effectively use the data available as of the timing of the projection and to project objectively and rationally. To ensure that the decision related to the projection matches the activity of typical market participants based on rational decisions, continual attention needs to be paid to trends of market participants in valuing the subject property.

⑥　純収益

　　運営純収益に、一時金の運用益等を加算又は控除し、資本的支出を控除して、純収益を査定する。

⑦　保有期間末の復帰価格

　　復帰価格は、保有期間末において対象不動産の売却を想定し、予測される売却価格から売却費用を控除して査定する。

　　ⅰ　保有期間

　　　　保有期間は、不動産投資において一般的と認められる保有期間を対象不動産に即して設定する。ただし、定期借地権付建物の場合の保有期間は、借地契約の残存期間の制約を受けることに留意する。

　　　　保有期間を一定期間で統一する必要はないものと思われるが、保有期間が異なる場合であっても、採用する割引率や最終還元利回りが適切である限り、求められる価格は変わらないものであることに留意する。

　　　　保有期間は、純収益の変動について、相対的に精度の高い予測ができる期間内であることが必要である。

　　ⅱ　売却価格

　　　　売却価格は、保有期間翌年において予測される純収益を最終還元利回りで還元して査定する。この場合の純収益は、直接還元法において採用した一期間の純収益の考え方との整合性をはかる必要がある。

　　ⅲ　売却費用

　　　　売却費用は、原則として仲介手数料等相当額を見込むものと査定する。なお、借地権付建物の場合で、譲渡承諾料等が慣行的に授受されると判断される場合には、当該譲渡承諾料等も含むものとする。ただし、譲渡承諾料等について、契約により支払わない旨の約定がある場合を除く。

　　ⅳ　復帰価格

　　　　売却価格から売却費用を控除して、復帰価格を査定する。

⑧　予測

　　収益費用の予測には不確実性が伴うために、予測主体によって判断が大きく分かれることも少なくない。証券化対象不動産の鑑定評価においては、当該不動産の価格が、将来において獲得することができるであろう収益を見通した上での収益性及び投資採算性を基準として形成されることを前提に、合理的に行動する典型的な市場参加者が収益費用の将来動向をどのように予測して行動するかの把握及び分析に努めなければならない。

　　また、予測時点において入手可能な情報を有効に活用し、客観性と合理性を有する予測を行うことが重要であり、予測に関する判断が、典型的な市場参加者が合理的な判断のもとで行うであろうところと整合するように、市場参加者の動向を常に注視しながら鑑定評価を行う必要がある。

　　収益費用の将来予測に当たっては、市場分析で詳細に分析した対象不動産と同用途の不動産に係る市場における需給状況や賃料の推移等の把握を起点とし、一般的要因の分析で把握及び

The market supply-demand conditions and rent changes of comparables in which their use is the same as the subject are analyzed in the market analysis section and this should be the base for the projection of future cash flow. Cash flow should be estimated carefully taking into account current and forecasted macroeconomic conditions such as economic climate, prices, and interest rates discussed in the analysis of general value influences and supply- and demand-side value influences that affect real estate supply-demand conditions in the same primary market area.

- Yields
  - Discount Rate

    Discount rate is the expected rate of return to discount each year's NCF to the date of value. It is estimated based on the return of financial assets deemed to be the standard rate of return for investment or the return of real estate deemed as the reference rate of return for real estate investment, and comprehensively considering the rate of return adjusted with property-specific influences (uncertainty of NCF), the rate of return of comparable properties within the same primary market area, and investor survey results. If several subject properties are to be valued at once, the discount rate should be estimated by recognizing the differences caused by area- or property-specific influences, taking into account the risk of changes in future cash flow based on these differences, and paying attention to consistency.

    It is required to describe in the appraisal report how the interest rate trend, market analysis results, and uncertainty of future cash flow of the subject property are reflected during the estimation of the discount rate, using the data used as a rationale if possible.

  - Terminal Capitalization Rate

    The terminal capitalization rate (capitalization rate used for estimation of potential sales price) is estimated based on the capitalization rate at the date of value and reflecting premiums caused by future uncertainty and changes in asset value that is not reflected in the NCF to be capitalized.

    Generally speaking, the terminal capitalization rate is likely to be higher than the capitalization rate at the date of value due to the risk assumptions specified below:

    Risk of decline in property value caused by aging
    Risk associated with estimating NCF after the holding period
    Risk associated with sales, etc.

3) **DCF Method (development of a leasehold property)**

The DCF method (development of a leasehold property) is a appraisal approach applied for vacant land (in some cases including buildings assuming demolition) in the securitization of development property; a DCF method containing components of the development method. More specifically, this method estimates the value of vacant land considering the investment profitability, based on assumption of a building to be

検討した景気、物価、金利等のマクロ経済の現状と見通し及び同一需給圏における不動産の需給状況に影響を及ぼす需要面及び供給面の要因を踏まえた上で、慎重な姿勢で行うべきである。

⑨　各種利回り
　ⅰ　割引率
　　割引率は、各期の純収益と復帰価格を価格時点に割引くための期待収益率であり、投資の標準とされている金融資産の利回りや不動産投資利回りの目安となっている不動産の利回りに、対象不動産の個別性（純収益の不確実性）を加味して求めた利回り、同一需給圏内の類似不動産の取引事例の利回り、投資家へのアンケート結果等を総合的に勘案して査定する。複数の対象不動産を一時に鑑定評価する場合には、個別の不動産の地域要因や個別的要因の格差を把握し、それらの格差に基づく将来収益の変動リスクについて検討し、整合性に留意して割引率を査定することが必要である。
　　割引率の査定については、金利動向、市場分析結果、対象不動産の純収益の不確実性等をどのように反映させたかについて、判断根拠とした資料とともに、できるだけ明確に鑑定評価報告書に記載する必要がある。

　ⅱ　最終還元利回り
　　最終還元利回り（売却予測価格を求めるための還元利回り）は、価格時点の還元利回りに、将来の不確実性及び還元対象となる純収益に反映されない資産価格の変動にともなうプレミアムを、加減して査定する。
　　なお、最終還元利回りは、一般的には、以下のリスクが想定されるため還元利回りより大きくなる場合が多いと考えられている。
　　　ア　期間の経過による不動産の価値下落のリスク
　　　イ　保有期間後の純収益の見積もりリスク
　　　ウ　売却等に係るリスク

(3)　DCF法（開発賃貸型）
　DCF法（開発賃貸型）は、開発型証券化において、更地（取り壊し前提の建物等を含む場合もある。）に適用する手法であり、開発法的要素を加味したDCF法といえる。具体的には、更地に建物を建築し、テナントへ賃貸のうえ、主として賃貸不動産としてSPC等に売却することを前提に、投資家の投資採算性を考慮した更地価格を求める手法である。
　投資家の投資採算性を考慮するために、価格時点から建築期間中及び竣工後建物のキャッシュ

constructed on the vacant land, leased to tenants, and then sold to the SPC or other entity as a leasehold property.

In order to reflect investment profitability, the value of the subject vacant land as of the date of value is estimated by projecting cash flow from the date of value to the construction and completion of the building, and discounting to the present value.

The DCF method (development of a leasehold property) is based on sale of a property immediately after completion in some cases or based on sale after a certain period after completion. In either case, logically, the estimated value should not result in difference. Accordingly, the timing of the sales should be assumed in accordance with the management plan of the SPC or the highest and best use of the subject property.

If the subject property is to be sold immediately after completion, the potential sales price (gross sales price) is estimated by applying DCF method as a tenant-occupied building and its site, and verifying the result with the direct capitalization method.

- Yields

  The yields applied are defined as follows:
  - Return on investment capital: This rate is used to discount the cash flow generated from the date of value to completion of the building to the present value.
  - Discount rate: This rate is used to discount the cash flow generated from the land and building after completion of the building to the present value or value at the time of sales.
  - Terminal capitalization rate: In order to estimate the sales price (gross sales price) by the DCF method, the reversionary value is estimated first. This rate is used for the reversionary value estimation in the DCF method.
  - Capitalization rate: In order to estimate the sales price (gross sales price) by the direct capitalization method, this rate is used.

- Determining the Time Horizon
  - Development Period

    The period between the date of value and completion of the building should be determined by taking an in-depth look at the subject property's development plan. The issues confirmed with the client should be detailed on the appraisal report and carefully examined for validity.

  - Holding Period

    The period between the date of value through to the completion of the building and sale of the land and building is determined in accordance with the timing of the sale. If the land and building are sold after a certain period after completion of the building and leased to tenants, the period toward completion is called the development period and the period after and that toward sale is called the holding period. If the land and building are sold immediately after completion of the building, the development period and holding period are the same.

- Expenses
  - Land acquisition expenses

フローを予測し、それらの現在価値により価格時点における対象不動産（更地）の価格を求めるものである。

DCF法（開発賃貸型）は、竣工後直ちに転売を見込む場合と竣工後一定期間保有し転売する場合が想定されるが、いずれの場合であっても求める価格は、理論的に異なるところではない。したがって、SPC等における運用計画又は最有効使用の判断に則して想定する必要がある。

竣工後直ちに転売を見込む場合に、売却価格（販売総額）の査定に当たっては、貸家及びその敷地としてのDCF法を適用し、直接還元法を併用して検証を行うものとする。

① 採用する利回り
　採用する利回りについては、以下により区別を行う。
　ア　投下資本収益率：価格時点から建物竣工までのキャッシュフローを現在価値に割り引くために用いる利回り
　イ　割引率：竣工時点以降に土地及び建物から得られるキャッシュフローを現在価値又は売却時の価値に割り引くために用いる利回り
　ウ　最終還元利回り：売却価格（販売総額）をDCF法によって求める際に当該DCF法における復帰価格を求める場合に用いられる利回り
　エ　還元利回り：売却価格（販売総額）を求めるために、直接還元法を適用する際に用いる利回り

② 期間の設定
　ⅰ　開発期間
　　価格時点から建物竣工までの期間は、個別不動産の開発計画について詳細に検討した上で判断を行う。依頼者等に確認した内容については鑑定評価報告書に記載するとともに、その妥当性を慎重に吟味する。
　ⅱ　保有期間
　　価格時点から建物竣工後土地建物の売却を行うまでの期間については、建物竣工、テナント賃貸、一時保有等の期間を得た後で売却する場合は、建物竣工までが開発期間、売却期間までが保有期間となる。建物の竣工後ただちに土地及び建物を売却する場合は、開発期間と保有期間は一致する。

③ 費用
　ⅰ　土地取得費用

The land acquisition expenses (brokerage fees, acquisition tax, registration and license tax, etc.) are not included in the cash flow.
- Expenses incurred during the development period
    (a) Construction cost (building, facilities attached to the building, structures, design and supervision, etc.)
    (b) Selling and general and administrative expenses
    (c) Property tax on land
    (d) Other expenses
    If an investigation cost for soil contamination measures or buried archeological artifacts is required it should be estimated appropriately in accordance with the value influences of the subject property.
    In real estate securitization, fees are sometimes paid under the name of the project management to the asset manager (normally the developer) who promotes the development project. This is recognized in the return on investment capital as a so-called profit of the developer; therefore it is not included in the expenses to be deducted.
- Building acquisition expenses
    The building acquisition expenses (acquisition tax, registration and license tax, attorney fee, stamp tax, etc.) are included in the cash flow.
- Sales cost
    The sales cost (brokerage fees, transfer acceptance fees, transfer registration fees) is included in the cash flow.

● Other Notes

The DCF method (development of a leasehold property) includes a series of assumptions. Accordingly, the figures applied for appraisal process require rationale. The return on investment capital, development period, rent assumptions, capitalization rate upon completion, and discount rate for the holding period should also be determined as a whole and not separately.

4) **Direct Capitalization Method**

If the DCF method (including DCF method for development of a leasehold property) is applied, the direct capitalization, in principle, should also be applied. However, if the land residual technique is applied for the securitization of development property, it is acceptable not to apply the direct capitalization method as long as there are justifiable exceptions, such as difficulty in determining cash flow in detail and reflecting the influence of the timing of payments because the subject is a large-scale development for which expansion takes a long time.

● Net Cash Flow (NCF)

The NCF of a single period used in the direct capitalization method may in some cases be the subject property's Year 1 NCF to ensure consistency with the NCF used in the DCF method; in other cases it is the NCF deemed as the standard level for the subject property to ensure consistency with the discount rate and terminal capitalization rate used in the DCF method. In either case, the NCF should, in principle, be estimated by reflecting the future change in NCF on the capitalization rate

　　　　　　土地取得費用（仲介手数料、不動産取得税、登録免許税等）は、含めない。

　　　ii　開発期間中の費用
　　　　ア　建築費（建物、建物付属設備、構築物、設計監理費等）
　　　　イ　販売費及び一般管理費
　　　　ウ　土地の公租公課
　　　　エ　その他費用
　　　　　土壌汚染対策費用や埋蔵文化財の調査費用が発生する場合など対象不動産の価格形成要因に即して適切に見込むことが必要である。
　　　　　なお、不動産証券化においてプロジェクトマネジメントと称して、一定のフィーが開発事業を推進するアセットマネジャー（通常ディベロッパーであることが多いと考えられる。）に支払われることがあるが、これらは、いわゆるディベロッパーの利潤として投下資本収益率等で考慮されるため、控除する費用項目には計上しない。

　　　iii　建物取得に係る費用
　　　　不動産取得税、登録免許税、司法書士報酬、印紙税等を考慮する。

　　　iv　売却費用
　　　　仲介手数料、借地権の譲渡承諾料、名義書換料等を考慮する。

　④　その他適用上の留意事項
　　DCF法（開発賃貸型）は想定事項を多く含む手法である。このため、採用する数値については、判断根拠が必要であり、また、投下資本収益率、開発期間、想定賃料、竣工時の還元利回りや保有期間の割引率等について、それぞれを単独で設定するものではなく、一体として考える必要がある。

(4) 直接還元法

　DCF法（開発賃貸型を含む）を適用する場合には、原則として直接還元法を併用する必要がある。ただし、開発型証券化における土地残余法については、開発規模が大きく開発期間が長期にわたり、キャッシュフローの詳細な検討とそれらの支出時期が価格に及ぼす影響を反映することが困難な場合など、適用しないことに合理的な理由がある場合には適用しないことができる。

　①　純収益
　　直接還元法における一期間の純収益は、DCF法における純収益との整合性を図る観点からDCF法の初年度純収益を用いる場合と、DCF法における割引率や最終還元利回りとの整合性を図る観点から対象不動産において標準的と思われる純収益を用いる場合のいずれかの方法により査定する。いずれの場合においても、原則として将来における純収益の変動を還元利回りに織り込み、価格時点における純収益として査定する必要がある。
　　なお、価格時点における純収益が、一時的な要因で市場標準と乖離している場合には、価格

and be estimated as NCF at the date of value.

If the NCF at the date of value is temporarily apart from the market level, it is acceptable to revise the NCF to the standard level of the subject property. In such case, estimated value applying the actual NCF as of the date of value or applying the standardized level of NCF will logically results in the same; it should be adjusted by the capitalization rate.

- Capitalization Rate

In order to estimate the capitalization rate for the direct capitalization method with comparable data, the comparable securitized properties and the yield levels by area and uses indicated by the interview with investors must be taken into account. In the estimation of the capitalization rate the appraiser should describe the comparables and survey results used during the estimation in the appraisal report as much as possible.

If the capitalization rate is estimated based on the return of financial assets deemed as the standard rate of return for investment or the return of real estate deemed as the reference rate of return for real estate investment, and reflecting the differences of uncertainty of the NCF (risk premiums) caused by location, property rights, conditions of building, and status of lessee, note that these factors all have affects over the others; therefore the risk premiums can be too large if all the risk premiums are simply added up. Therefore the estimated capitalization rate must be verified by gathering enough comparable data of properties similar to the subject and comparing the capitalization rate for the comparables and the estimated capitalization rate.

Also note that if a different method is used in the estimation of the capitalization rate, a different method is accordingly used in the estimation of the NCF.

5) **Conclusion of Value Indicated by Income Capitalization Approach**

The value indicated by the DCF method (including DCF method for development of a leasehold property) that uses the NCF adjusted with the detailed future changes and the discount rate based on the projected future NCF changes and changes in risk premiums should, in principle, be the base value when concluding income value of a securitized property.

The direct capitalization method, however, is a simple method in estimating income value that uses the capitalization rate estimated with the market rate of return, reflecting actual conditions of the market. The value indicated by the direct capitalization method is no less accurate than the DCF method (including DCF method for development of a leasehold property) in such case as that NCF is not projected to change significantly. Accordingly, it should be noted that not all cases should the base value be that of a value indicated by the DCF method (including DCF method for development of a leasehold property).

If the value indicated by the two methods results in significant difference, there may be an error in one of the appraisal processes and this should be comprehensively reviewed.

時点における純収益を対象不動産の標準的なものに修正する方法もある。この際、価格時点における純収益をそのまま用いる場合であっても標準化を行う場合であっても求める価格は理論的には同じであり、適用する還元利回りにおいて調整することが必要となることに留意する。

② 還元利回り

　直接還元法で用いる還元利回りを、取引事例等から求めるためには、証券化対象不動産等の取引事例、投資家へのヒアリング等による地域別、用途別の利回り水準の把握が必要となっている。不動産鑑定士は、できるだけこれらの事例やアンケート結果を鑑定評価報告書に明示して、還元利回りの査定を行う必要がある。

　対象不動産に適用する還元利回りを、標準的な金融資産の利回り又は不動産投資の標準とされる不動産の利回りに、立地条件、権利関係、建物の状況、賃借人の状況等に係る純収益の不確実性の格差（リスクプレミアム）を加減して求める場合は、これらの要因は、互いに影響しあっているために、単純にそれぞれのリスクプレミアムを足し上げていくと過大になることがあるため、できる限り対象不動産と類似の不動産の取引事例を多数収集し、その還元利回りとの比較を行うことによって、求められた還元利回りを検証する必要がある。

　なお、純収益の査定方法によって、還元利回りの査定方法も異なることに留意する。

(5) 収益価格の決定

　証券化対象不動産の収益価格の決定に当たっては、純収益の詳細な変動予測を反映し、対象不動産に係る将来の純収益変動予測と当該予測の変動リスクに基づく割引率を適用して求めるDCF法（開発賃貸型を含む）による収益価格を、原則として標準とする。

　ただし、直接還元法は、還元利回りを市場利回り等から査定して収益価格を求めるというわかりやすい手法であり、市場の実態を反映した価格といえ、純収益が大きく変動しないと予測されるような場合には求められた価格の精度もDCF法（開発賃貸型を含む）と比べ劣らないので、必ずしもすべての場合にDCF法（開発賃貸型を含む）による収益価格を標準とすべきとしているものではないことに留意する。

　なお、二つの手法により求めた価格に大きな開差がある場合は、いずれかの手法の適用過程に誤りがある場合が想定されるため、再吟味を十分に行うことが必要である。

6) **Trade Related Property**

In the case of a property in which the value is largely influenced by the business operations, such as a hotel or commercial facility (trade related property), the business form in many cases are based on lease agreements concluded between the lessor (owner) and lessee, and the income value can be estimated if the rent and appropriate capitalization rate are determined. However, risks such as default due to tenant bankruptcy, rent reduction, finding new tenants after the end of the lease term, and credit of the tenant, must be reflected in the capitalization rate and estimation of future cash flow. Accordingly, the financial results of a business that is operated by the tenants should be analyzed to verify the risk as a real estate and operational cash flow.

- Verification

    In the estimation of each income and expense item, the appropriate stabilized rent and cost level in the medium- and long-term should be verified by to the extent possible taking the standpoints of affordable rent for the tenants and data on comparables via the method described below.
    (a) Verification using the ratio of rent to gross sales or operating income
    (b) Consistency of each income and expense item in the actual historical cash flow of the subject property (for at least three years) and the cash flow plan
    (c) Verification of each income and expense item using nationwide, regional, or local statistics such as average data
    (d) Comparison of each income and expense item of the subject property and that of competitors, if available
    (e) Estimation of projection of future supply-demand in the market, by utilizing data of population changes, trend in company locations, new business entrants, and macro economical data

- Business-Specific Income and Expense Items

    Attention must be paid to the type of rent (fixed rent, turnover rent), type of tenant (single, multiple), sales promotion cost, type of lease, hotel or commercial facility-specific property management coverage and its fees, and how to reflect specific income and expense items unique to such businesses.

    Note that the expense rate results in differences depending on the type of lease, such as for a shell lease, and the capitalization rate and discount rate are affected by the credit of the tenants and business operators, and also take into account how the fixed-term land lease and fixed-term building lease agreements are treated.

3. **Reconciliation of Indicated Value**

In estimating market value based on special considerations, the final appraisal value should, in principle, be determined based on the income value by adopting the value indicated by DCF method as the base value and examine the result with that of the direct capitalization method, and reconciled with values indicated by the sales comparison approach and cost approach.

For securitization of development property, the final appraisal value should be deter-

(6) 事業経営の影響の大きい用途の不動産の場合

　ホテル、商業施設等事業経営の影響が大きい用途の不動産の場合においても、事業形態は、賃貸人（オーナー）と賃借人間における賃貸借方式を採用する場合が大半であり、賃料と適切な還元利回りが決まれば収益価格は算出できるが、賃借人の倒産等によるデフォルトリスク、賃料値下げリスク、賃貸借契約期間終了後の新賃借人を見つけるリスク、クレジットリスク等を還元利回りや今後のキャッシュフローのシナリオに織り込む必要があるため、原則として、当該事業そのものの事業収支を検討することにより不動産としてのリスクや事業収支を検証する必要がある。

① 検証の観点および方法

　収益、費用各項目の査定においてテナントの賃料負担力の観点、事例の比較等の観点より、可能な限り以下のような方法で、中長期的かつ安定的な賃料、経費水準の妥当性を検証する。
ア　総売上や営業利益に対する賃料の比率からの検証
イ　対象不動産の過年度（少なくとも過去３年程度）の収益費用各項目の実績値及び計画値との整合
ウ　地域あるいは地方、全国ベースの平均値等の統計を利用して収益・費用の各項目を検証
エ　競合不動産のデータが手に入る場合は、その収益・費用の各項目の数値を比較
オ　対象エリアの人口動態、企業立地動向及び新規参入者の動向やマクロ経済データを利用して、各マーケットの需給に関する将来を予測して査定。

② 事業に特有な収益費用項目等の扱い

　固定賃料、歩合賃料等の賃料徴収の形態、シングルテナント、マルチテナント等のテナントのタイプ、販売促進費の扱い、リースの方式、ホテルや商業施設等特有のＰＭ業務及びＰＭフィー等、これらの事業に特有な収益費用項目の扱いに留意する。
　また、スケルトン貸しかどうかなど賃貸借形式によって経費率が異なること、テナント、事業者の信用力等によって還元利回りや割引率が影響されること、また、定期借地契約や定期借家契約の取り扱いにも留意する。

3　試算価格の調整

　特定価格（投資採算価値を表す価格）を求める場合には、原則として、DCF法により求めた価格を標準とし、直接還元法により検証を行って求めた収益価格に基づき、比準価格及び積算価格による検証を行って鑑定評価額を決定する。
　開発型証券化の場合には、DCF法（開発賃貸型）を標準とし、直接還元法（土地残余法）による検証を行って求めた収益価格に基づき、比準価格（可能な場合は積算価格も）による検証を行って鑑定評価額を決定する。また、開発後賃貸等を行わず一括売却する前提の場合には、開発法によ

mined based on the income value by adopting the value indicated by DCF method for development of a leasehold property as the base value and examine the result with that of the direct capitalization method [land residual technique]) and verified with the value indicated by the sales comparison approach (and cost approach, if possible). If it is based on sale of the land and building after development and not assuming leasing before sale, the final appraisal value should be determined based on the value indicated by development method as the base value and examine the result with that of the direct capitalization method [land residual technique]) and verified with the value indicated by the sales comparison approach (and cost approach, if possible).

In the appraisal of securitized properties, the values indicated by the income capitalization approach and cost approach sometimes result in large differences. In such cases, the cause for the large difference should be clarified through market analysis from the standpoints described below. In the review of indicated values, attention should be paid to the consistency in value influences by examining such points as to whether the profitability is appropriately reflected in the value of land and building indicated by the cost approach.

- Whether real estate is often sold and purchased for investment purposes and such transactions is considered to be the typical case when estimating the market value of real estate in the area
- Whether the attributes and funding ability of typical buyers are different in the transaction of building and its site and vacant land alone
- Whether the vacant land is generally purchased for development purposes aiming at investment in the land and building after development

る価格を標準とし、直接還元法（土地残余法）により検証を行って求めた価格に基づき、比準価格（可能な場合は積算価格も）による検証を行って鑑定評価額を決定する。

　証券化対象不動産の鑑定評価においては、収益価格と積算価格等の間に大きな乖離が生じる場合があるが、このような場合には市場分析における次のような視点を通じ乖離の原因究明を行う必要がある。また、各試算価格の再吟味に当たっては、原価法適用における土地価格や建物価格が収益性を適切に反映したものとなっているかなど、価格形成要因の反映の整合性に留意する。

　　ア　投資目的での不動産取引が珍しくなく、そのような取引を基準として地域における不動産価格の水準感が形成されているか。
　　イ　複合不動産と更地の取引では典型的な買い手の属性や資金力等が異なるか。
　　ウ　開発後の土地建物に対する投資を視野に入れた開発目的の更地の取引が一般的に行われているか。

VII. Appraisal Report

The contents of an appraisal report are the full results of the valuation delivered by the appraisal firm to the client. An appraisal report of securitized properties is influential not only to the client but also to third parties, including general investors. Moreover, it is a foundation for the development of a fair real estate investment market. Because of these factors, it should be prepared with particular care, leaving no room for misunderstanding. Specifically, the appraiser should be able to adequately explain the rationale of the determination of the final appraisal value to the client and third parties.

Also note that since the valuation of securitized properties is conducted in accordance with the Appraisal Standards, the appraisal report should contain items specified in Article 38 of the Rules of Practice of Real Estate Appraisal Act (based on Article 39-1 of the Act), Article 9 of the General Topics and Specific Standards Chapter 3 of Appraisal Standards.

1. Basic Items

1) Identification of Subject Property

If the subject property consists of several properties – namely, multiple condominium units and their site within one condominium and site – and therefore both a single unit and the building as a whole are marketable, the value of the condominium as a whole and the value estimated by combining the values of each single unit may differ. Therefore, it is important to specify clearly in the appraisal report that the subject is valued as one property consisting of several condominium units and its site, or valued based on separately estimated single unit values.

2) Special Interests

The appraisal report must describe not only the relations between the client and parties involved in the securitization, but also whether there are interests of the appraiser or appraisal firm in the subject property, connections or special interests[51] with parties related to the subject property, capital, personal, or business ties[52] between the client and appraiser or appraisal firm involved in the valuation, capital, personal, or business ties between the parties for disclosure or submission and the appraiser or appraisal firm involved in the valuation. If any such relations exist, the details need to be provided. (If the parties for disclosure or submission are not determined or names are not yet known, this should be stated in the report.)

---

[51] If a certified public accountant uses the appraisal report, the interests between relevant parties can be checked for conformity with the following: "The auditor should check whether there is potential impairment of fair accounting by interviewing the company they work for. Interests herein include situations where the company directly or indirectly influences the fairness of the accountants, namely, regarding the employment and business relationship between the accountants and the company as well as the company's shares held by the appraisers and special rights specified in the contract." (extracted from Audit Standard Committee Report No. 14 "Use of Professionals")

[52] See Article 9-2 VIII of Appraisal Standards (General Topics)

Ⅶ 鑑定評価報告書

　鑑定評価報告書の内容は、不動産鑑定業者が依頼者に交付する鑑定評価書の実質的な内容となるものであるが、不動産証券化における鑑定評価報告書は、鑑定評価書を通じて依頼者のみならず一般投資家を含めた広範な第三者に対しても影響を及ぼすものであり、さらには適正な不動産投資市場の発展の基礎となるものであるから、その作成に当たっては誤解の生ずる余地を与えないよう留意するとともに、特に鑑定評価額の決定の理由については依頼者その他第三者に対して十分に説明し得るものとするように努めなければならない。

　なお、証券化対象不動産の鑑定評価は、不動産鑑定評価基準に則った鑑定評価であるため、鑑定評価書には不動産の鑑定評価に関する法律第39条第1項に基づく同法施行規則第38条及び不動産鑑定評価基準総論第9章・各論第3章に定める事項を記載する。

1　基本的事項
(1)　対象不動産の確定
　対象不動産が複数あり、一棟の区分所有建物及びその敷地内における複数の区分所有建物及びその敷地である場合など、単独並びに一体の両方で市場性を有する不動産である場合には、一括評価の鑑定評価額と単体評価の合計鑑定評価額が異なる可能性があるため、複数の区分所有建物及びその敷地について一括評価を前提とするのか、単独評価を前提とするのかを鑑定評価の条件として明確に記載しなければならない。

(2)　利害関係
　依頼者と証券化関係者との関係だけでなく、その不動産の鑑定評価に関与した不動産鑑定士又は当該不動産鑑定士が所属する不動産鑑定業者の対象不動産に関する利害関係又は対象不動産に関し利害関係を有する者との縁故若しくは特別の利害関係[51]の有無及びその内容[52]、依頼者と鑑定評価に関与した不動産鑑定士又は当該不動産鑑定士の所属する不動産鑑定業者との間の特別の資本関係、人的関係及び取引関係の有無及びその内容、開示・提出先と鑑定評価に関与した不動産鑑定士又は当該不動産鑑定士が所属する不動産鑑定業者との間の特別の資本関係、人的関係及び取引関係の有無及びその内容（ただし、開示・提出先が未定の場合や開示先の具体的名称が明らかでない場合は、その旨）について記載する必要がある。

---

[51] 公認会計士が鑑定評価書を利用する際の利害関係の確認は、次の内容に準拠して行っている。「監査人は、会社に対する質問等により専門家の業務の客観性を損なうような状況の有無を検討しなければならない。このような状況には、専門家が会社に雇用されている場合や会社の依頼により業務に従事している場合のほか、株式の所有、契約上の権利等によって会社が直接又は間接的に専門家の業務の客観性に影響を与えるような利害関係が含まれる。」（監査基準委員会報告書第14号「専門家の業務の利用」抜粋）

[52] 不動産鑑定評価基準総論第9章第2節Ⅷ

3) **Management Method based on Asset Securitization Plan**

In order to estimate the market value based on special considerations for the securitization under the Asset Securitization Law of Japan or Investment Trust and Investment Corporation Law, the management method of the subject property, which will be the conditions of the valuation, such as the asset securitization plan, should be described in the appraisal report. If the management method is determined in the asset securitization plan, examine the method and confirm that it is legally permissible and physically possible..

2. Information and Issues to be Confirmed
1) Site Inspection

The valuation of securitized properties requires site inspections with the client or the inspection guide named by the client, including internal inspection of the subject property, and interviews with the building manager of the subject. Issues confirmed by the appraiser with the client and/or the building manager clarify the scope of responsibilities of the appraiser at the time of dispute..It also affects the accuracy of the appraisal. Therefore, it should be described in detail in the appraisal report to avoid misunderstanding by the client or third parties.

The below items should be included in the appraisal report for the confirmation of the subject property:

(a) Date of Site Inspection

This is the date of the site inspection that was conducted to confirm the condition of the subject property as of the date of value. Other than this, the preparatory or additional inspection conducted before or after the date of inspection should also be included when necessary.

(b) Name of Appraiser who Conducted Site Inspection

If the valuation was conducted by more than one appraiser, names of all appraisers who participated in the site inspection should be provided.

(c) Name and Occupation of Inspection Guide and Building Manager of Subject Property

Inspection guide refers to a party appointed by the client to attend the site inspection and give a tour of the subject property. Building manager refers to a party who manages the subject property (e.g., senior managers of the property management company of the subject property), who are interviewed about legal rights associated with the subject property and the history of expansion or renovation.

(d) Inspection Coverage (including whether internal inspection was conducted) and Issues Confirmed at Site Inspection

The area that was inspected or measured and area that could not be inspected should be described. Details confirmed at the site inspection and through interview with the building manager, such as the area, structure, internal and exterior, rights, laws and regulations, use of asbestos, seismic adequacy, and history of maintenance, extension and renovation of the subject property, should also be described.

If part of the subject building or land could not be inspected because the subject

(3) 資産流動化計画等による運用方法

　資産流動化法又は投信法による証券化で特定価格を求める場合には、資産流動化計画等の鑑定評価の前提条件となる対象不動産の運用方法について鑑定評価報告書に記載する必要がある。資産流動化計画や資産信託流動化計画において運用方法が策定されている場合はその内容を検討し、それが合法的で実現性が認められることを確認すべきである。

2　資料及び確認事項
(1) 実地調査

　証券化対象不動産の鑑定評価においては、依頼者又はその指示を受けた者の立会いのもとでの対象不動産の内覧を含む実地調査と対象不動産の管理者からの聴聞が必要である。不動産鑑定士が依頼者及び対象不動産の管理者を通じて行った確認事項は、鑑定評価に係るトラブルの際における責任の範囲を明確にするとともに、鑑定評価の精度にも影響することから、依頼者その他第三者に誤解を生じさせないようにできる限り詳細に鑑定評価報告書に記載する。

　なお、対象不動産の確認について、次の事項を鑑定評価報告書に記載する必要がある。

① 実地調査を行った年月日

　価格時点における対象不動産の状態の確認として、対象不動産を実地に確認した日。その他、事前又は事後に予備的又は補足として行った調査日も必要に応じ記載する。

② 実地調査を行った不動産鑑定士の氏名

　対象不動産について複数の不動産鑑定士で鑑定評価を行った場合には、実地調査を行ったすべての不動産鑑定士の氏名

③ 立会人及び対象不動産の管理者の氏名及び職業

　立会人とは、依頼者の指示に基づき実地調査に立会い、対象不動産を案内した者をいい、対象不動産の管理者とは、対象不動産の権利関係、増改築等の履歴等についてヒアリングを行った対象不動産の管理者（対象不動産の管理を行っている会社の役職員等）をいう。

④ 実地調査を行った範囲（内覧の有無を含む。）及び実地調査により確認した内容

　対象不動産について視認及び計測を行った範囲又は実地調査を行えなかった範囲を記載した上で、実地調査及び対象不動産の管理者からの聴聞により確認した内容として、対象不動産の面積、構造、内外装、権利関係、公法上の規制、アスベスト使用の有無等、耐震性、修繕・増改築の履歴等を記載する。

　対象不動産の一部が、賃貸又は営業中であったり、物理的な要因で建物の一部や敷地の一部の確認を実施することができなかった場合には、その範囲及び理由を記載するとともに、確認できなかった部分についての現状確認のための状況推定根拠（竣工図面、他の類似の建物部分の実地調査、管理者等へのヒアリング等）を記載する。継続評価において内覧の全部又は一部を省略した場合もその旨を記載する。

is leased, the tenant is operating a business, or due to physical reasons, the area and reasons, and list the rationale for estimation of the condition of the area that could not be inspected (e.g., completion drawings, inspection of similar places within the building, interviews with the building manager) should be described. If all or part of the site inspection was omitted because it is a periodic valuation, it should be describe accordingly in the appraisal report.

2) **Engineering Report**

The appraiser should confirm the following items listed in the engineering report provided by the client, and include items confirmed in the appraisal report.[53]

(a) License and Name of Appraiser who Conducted Valuation

(b) Attributes of Engineering Report
- Name of Client who Requested Engineering Report

  Generally, investigation for an engineering report is requested by the client of the valuation to the professional firm. In most cases it is not prepared by the client of the valuation.

  Accordingly, the appraiser should check whether the client of the engineering report is the same as the client of the valuation. If they are different, it is necessary to check the background and reasons why they are different, as well as whether the report is a draft version or final version report.

- Name of Professional who Prepared Engineering Report

  It is necessary to check the name of the professional, firm, and license (technical license related to the investigation) of the engineering report. If part of the investigation is outsourced, it is also necessary to check the name of the professional who undertook the task.

- Date of Investigation and Date of Preparation of Engineering Report

  The engineering report, in principle, is prepared based on the conditions as of the date of investigation. Therefore, it is considered effective only as of the date of investigation. Accordingly, if the engineering report was prepared a long time prior, the appraiser should judge whether to use it, taking into account the period and changes in conditions of the subject property since its issue.

(c) How Engineering Report was Obtained and How to Use Engineering Report for Valuation
- From Whom the Engineering Report was Obtained (Name, Position, etc.)

  It is important to check the name, position, company, etc. of the person who provided the engineering report.

  If there is more than one engineering report, information on each of the report should be included. (Same applies to all the items in (c))

- Date when the Appraiser Obtained Engineering Report

  To avoid complications regarding receipt of an engineering report, the date the appraiser received it should also be included in the appraisal report, together

---

[53] Even if the new engineering report is not available or is insufficient for the valuation, the appraiser is required to include the items checked.

(2) エンジニアリング・レポート
　依頼者から受領したエンジニアリング・レポートのうち以下の項目に係る記載内容を確認し、確認した内容を鑑定評価報告書に記載しなければならない[53]。
ア　鑑定評価を担当した不動産鑑定士の資格及び氏名
イ　エンジニアリング・レポートの基本的属性
　ア）エンジニアリング・レポートに係る調査の依頼者
　　エンジニアリング・レポートは、依頼者自らが作成することはほとんどなく、依頼者が専門機関に調査を委託することが一般的である。
　　したがって、エンジニアリング・レポートの依頼者が鑑定評価の依頼者と同じかどうか、異なる場合にはその背景や理由を確認するとともに、当該レポートがドラフトか最終版かについても確認する必要がある。
　イ）エンジニアリング・レポートの作成者
　　エンジニアリング・レポートの作成者の氏名、所属会社及び資格（調査事項に関連する専門的な技能等に関するもの）を確認する。この場合において、エンジニアリング・レポートを作成するための調査の一部が他者に委託されている場合には、その委託先である作成者についても同様に取り扱いものとする。
　ウ）エンジニアリング・レポートの調査が行われた日及び作成された日
　　エンジニアリング・レポートに記載された内容は、基本的には当該レポートを作成するために調査を行った時点の状況に基づくものであり、その意味で調査した時点でのみ有効であるものと考えられる。したがって、作成から期間が経過している場合における当該エンジニアリング・レポートを鑑定評価において活用するか否かについては、期間経過の程度及びその間の対象不動産の物的状況等の変化の程度を勘案して、不動産鑑定士が個別に判断しなければならない。

ウ　エンジニアリング・レポートの入手経緯、対応方針等
　ア）エンジニアリング・レポートの入手先（氏名及び職業等）
　　エンジニアリング・レポートの提示を受けた相手の所属、氏名及び役職等の入手先の担当者の属性を確認する必要がある。
　　なお、エンジニアリング・レポートが調査内容に応じて複数あるときは、それらの全てについて記載する（ウのなかの以下の項目についても同様である）。
　イ）エンジニアリング・レポートを入手した日
　　後日、エンジニアリング・レポートの授受について疑義が生じることを防ぐために、エンジニアリング・レポートの入手先とともに入手した日を記録しておく必要がある。
　ウ）エンジニアリング・レポートの作成者からの説明等の有無等

---

[53] 新たなエンジニアリング・レポートがない場合や記載その内容が鑑定評価を行ううえで不十分な場合においても、確認した内容を鑑定評価報告書に記載することが必要である。

with the name of person who provided it.
- Explanation from Professional who Prepared Engineering Report

It is useful and advisable to receive explanation from the issuer of the engineering report to better understand its contents, especially at a time when there are concerns regarding its contents

If such explanation is provided, details of the explanation should be recorded.
- How to Use Engineering Report Provided by Client in Valuation

In order to estimate the value of securitized properties, the appraiser should not merely take the information from the engineering report. The appraiser should examine and analyze the information objectively, and independently judge its validity before using it for valuation.

Accordingly, not only when the appraiser uses data other than that in the engineering report but also when judging that the engineering report is sufficient for use in the valuation, the decision and rationale must be detailed in the appraisal report[54].

(d) Investigation for Technical Property-Specific Value Influences that Appraiser Thinks it is Required for Valuation

The means for investigating technical property-specific value influences in the valuation must be described. Means by A or B should be described.

A. Using the engineering report provided by the client

B. Using results of the investigation by the appraiser, including use of other engineering reports requested by the appraiser (including revisions based on the engineering report provided by the client)
- Public and Private Laws and Restriction (including compliance inspection)

It should be describe how the appraiser checked the certificate of building confirmation, certificate of inspection, and compliance issues; whether by A or B above. The compliance inspection is a required item in the Building Condition Investigation Report; one of the reports indicated by BELCA. The appraiser should make an individual judgment on the items in the engineering report before using this information.

If the appraiser sought the opinions of lawyers or other professionals when the restriction of private laws associated with the subject property was difficult to judge, it is also regarded as B above.
- Maintenance Plan and Reproduction Cost

Maintenance plan and reproduction cost are the required items of The Building Condition Investigation Report, which is one of the engineering reports defined by BELCA; therefore, by carefully examining the details of the engineering report provided by the client, it can be used in the valuation. Also note that the reproduction cost in the engineering report may not have the same definition as

---

[54] In such a case, the acceptable examples of rationale would be "The building condition report basically conforms with the new BELCA Guidelines" or "Land-use history has been conducted for soil contamination risk, and the result was the same as the assessment of soil contamination risk (phase I)."

エンジニアリング・レポートの作成者から説明を受けることは、当該エンジニアリング・レポートの内容についての理解を深めるうえで有益であるので、特にエンジアニリング・レポートの内容に疑問点がある場合には、作成者から調査結果について説明を受けることが望ましい。

なお、エンジニアリング・レポートの作成者から説明を受けた場合には、その旨及びその内容を記録する必要がある。

エ）依頼者から入手したエンジニアリング・レポートについて鑑定評価を行う上での対応方針等

証券化対象不動産の鑑定評価を行うに当たっては、不動産鑑定士はエンジニアリング・レポートの内容を鵜呑みにするのではなく、鑑定評価への活用に際してはその内容を客観的に検討・分析のうえ、その妥当性を主体的に判断するというプロセスを踏む必要がある。

したがって、エンジニアリング・レポートの内容をそのまま鑑定評価に活用せずに別の資料等に依る場合だけでなく、エンジニアリング・レポートの内容を鑑定評価において活用するに足るものであると判断した場合にも、その旨及び判断根拠を鑑定評価報告書に記載しなければならない[54]。

エ　当該鑑定評価に必要と不動産鑑定士が考える専門性の高い個別的要因調査

専門性の高い個別的要因調査について、下記AまたはBのいずれで対応したのかを記載する。

A　依頼者から提供されたエンジニアリング・レポートを活用

B　不動産鑑定士から他の専門家に調査を依頼して入手したエンジニアリング・レポートの活用を含む、不動産鑑定士の調査により対応（依頼者から提供されたエンジニアリング・レポートの内容を基に修正した場合を含む。）

ア）公法上及び私法上の規制、制約等（法令遵守状況調査を含む）

特に建築確認済証、検査済証の有無、重大な法令違反の有無について、A、Bどちらで対応したかを記載する。なお、法令遵守状況調査については、BELCAの定義するエンジニアリング・レポートの1つである「建物状況調査報告書」の必須項目となっているため、依頼者から提供されたエンジニアリング・レポートの内容を自ら判断し、活用する。

対象不動産に係る私法上の制約等について、判断が容易でない場合に、弁護士等の他の専門家の意見を求めた場合もBに該当する。

イ）修繕計画、再調達価格

BELCAの定義するエンジニアリング・レポートの1つである「建物状況調査報告書」の必須項目であるため、依頼者から提供されたエンジニアリング・レポートの内容を十分吟味のうえ、活用することができる。また、エンジニアリング・レポートの再調達価格は、必ずしも鑑定評価上の再調達原価と内容が同じでないことにも留意する。

ウ）有害な物質（アスベスト等）の使用調査

特にアスベスト、PCBについては、BELCAの定義するエンジニアリング・レポートの1つである「建物環境リスク評価報告書（フェーズⅠ）」の必須項目である。アスベストの調査においては、依頼者から提供されたエンジニアリング・レポートを自ら判断し、活用する。

また、PCB使用機器の有無の調査においては、実地調査及び依頼者や建物管理者へのヒアリングに加え、エンジニアリング・レポートを自ら判断し、活用する。

---

[54] この場合における判断根拠については、例えば、「建物状況調査報告書については、おおむねBELCAの新ガイドラインに合致している」、「土壌汚染については地歴調査等を実施したが、結果については土壌環境リスク評価報告書（フェーズⅠ）と一致している」といった記載が可能である。

the reproduction cost estimated in the appraisal.
- Use of Hazardous Substances (Asbestos, etc.)

Asbestos and PCB are required items of The Assessment of Environment Risk of Building (Phase I), which is one of the engineering reports designated by BELCA. For the investigation of asbestos, the appraiser evaluates the provided engineering report before using this information.

For the investigation for PCB, the appraiser evaluates the provided engineering report before using the data, in addition to the site inspection, and interviews the client and building manager.
- Investigation of Soil Contamination

Investigation of soil contamination is the Assessment of Soil Contamination Risk (Phase I), one of the engineering reports designated by BELCA. The appraiser must examine and judge the provided engineering report before using this information.
- Analysis of Earthquake Risk

This is included in the engineering report designated by BELCA. The appraiser evaluates the engineering report prepared by the earthquake risk professionals and provided by the client before using this information.
- Seismic Adequacy Investigation

Though the engineering report designated by BELCA includes the inspection of the structure in the Building Condition Investigation, seismic investigation is not included therein. As such, it is necessary to judge by using the above mentioned B, and find out whether the subject building is based on the old or new seismic construction regulations based on its building completion year.

If the subject building is based on the old seismic standards, the next step is to find via an interview with the client whether reinforcement has been made in accordance with the Act on Promotion of Seismic Retrofitting of Buildings. If the building is reinforced, with the cooperation of the client, the seismic assessment results should be used as engineering report. In the case reinforcement works had been conducted, report on seismic assessment result and report on reinforcement work are deemed as an engineering report. If these reports were obtained by the client, it is deemed as A.
- Underground Object Investigation

Underground object investigation is not included in the engineering report designated by BELCA. As an investigation report of underground objects by professional is unlikely to have been obtained, it is generally handled with B.

(e) The appraiser should give the details and rationale for why A or B was chosen for each item in (d) for the investigation of technical property-specific influences for valuation.

The confirmed information should be described in a list form indicated in Specific Standards Chapter 3, Appendix 1 and attached to the appraisal report, or the same information to be included within the appraisal report.

In such cases, if the engineering report provided by the client does not satisfy

エ）土壌汚染調査

　　BELCAの定義するエンジニアリング・レポートの1つである「土壌環境リスク評価報告書（フェーズⅠ）」に該当するため、依頼者から提供されたエンジニアリング・レポートの内容を十分吟味のうえ、自ら判断し、活用する。

オ）地震リスクに関する分析

　　BELCAの定義するエンジニアリング・レポートに含まれるため、依頼者から提供された地震リスクの専門家の作成したエンジニアリング・レポートを自ら判断し、活用する。

カ）耐震性調査

　　BELCAの定義するエンジニアリング・レポートには関連項目として建物状況調査に構造概要調査があるものの耐震性の調査は含まれないため、まず建物の竣工年から、旧耐震基準に基づく建物かどうかをBにより判定することが必要である。

　　その結果、旧耐震基準に基づく建物であった場合は、さらに耐震改修促進法に準拠した補強工事が実施されているかどうかを、依頼者へのヒアリングを中心に調査し、実施している場合には、依頼者の協力の下、耐震診断結果の報告書を耐震性調査におけるエンジニアリング・レポートとして活用する。なお、耐震診断が実施されている場合の耐震診断結果の報告書や耐震補強工事の状況の報告書はエンジニアリング・レポートに該当し、これらが依頼者から受領した資料である場合にはAに該当する。

キ）地下埋設物調査

　　BELCAの定義するエンジニアリング・レポートには含まれず、専門家の調査報告書を取得できる場合は稀なため、一般的にはBで対応する。

オ　鑑定評価に必要となる専門性の高い個別的要因に関する調査についての不動産鑑定士の判断
　　前記エの各項目において、不動産鑑定士の判断としてAの場合、Bの場合の内容及び根拠等を記載する。

　　確認した内容についての鑑定評価報告書への記載については、基準各論第3章別　表1で例示されたところを参考に表形式で確認内容を記載のうえ鑑定評価報告書に添付するか、同様の内容を鑑定評価報告書のなかで記載するものとする。

　　この場合において、依頼者より提示されたエンジニアリング・レポートが、対象不動産の

requirements of valuation of securitized properties due to issues related to the physical or legal confirmation of property-specific value influences, the appraiser should personally conduct a study (including a request for investigation to other professionals; such a report is also one of the engineering reports) or request additional investigation (including a new engineering report) from the client.

3. **Analysis of Value Influences**
   1) **General Value Influences**

   Information collected for general value influences analysis and its result, including the macro-economy (business climate, prices, and interest rates) and real estate investment and market sentiment in securitized properties market (supply-demand of real estate investment and securitized properties, entry and withdrawal of real estate funds, changes in investors' expected rate of return, and fund-raising conditions), that would largely influence the activity of market participants in the real estate market, including securitized properties (sales and lease market) should be described.

   2) **Area-Specific Value Influences**

   Differences in potential buyer demographics based on the scale and use of the real estate property (what determines buyer's activities and price tendencies) in the area where the subject property is located, as well as identification of primary market, and supply-demand conditions, price of real estate and taking rent trends of alternative and competing properties within the primary market should be described.

   3) **Property-Specific Value Influences**
   (a) Soil Contamination

   In the appraisal of securitized properties, a conclusion should be reached on soil contamination influences, which requires investigation by a professional. Accordingly, all investigation results (scope and contents of the investigation) including the studies of the engineering report and the appraiser's own study and how they influence the final appraisal value should be described.

   (b) Buried Archaeological Artifacts

   Costs related to excavation may be an unexpected expense for the investor after investment. The appraiser should check whether the subject property is located in an area recognized as containing cultural, archeological artifacts, and describe the outcome in the appraisal report. If the subject property is located in such an area, the influence of such buried archeological artifacts should be described.

   (c) Underground Objects

   Findings should be described in the investigation of the underground object.

   (d) Boundary Confirmation

   Determination of boundary and cross-boundary issues should be confirmed with the client, and if such issues are visible, observe the condition at the site inspection and describe the result in the appraisal report.

   (e) Compliance of Building

   Laws and regulations that buildings and attached equipment must comply with, cover a broad range of areas. The administrative authority is the only organization

個別的要因の物的及び法的確認等、証券化対象不動産の鑑定評価に当たって必要と判断される項目を満たしていない場合は、不動産鑑定士の調査（不動産鑑定士が自ら他の専門家に依頼して行う調査（この調査報告書もエンジニアリング・レポートの一つである。）も含む。）で補うか、追加調査（エンジニアリング・レポートの再取得を含む。）を依頼者に求める必要がある。

3　価格形成要因の分析
(1)　一般的要因
不動産証券化等の不動産市場（売買市場及び賃貸市場）における市場参加者の行動に大きな影響を及ぼす要因である景気、物価、金利等のマクロ経済に係る指標、また、不動産投資や不動産証券化市場における市況感（不動産投資及び不動産証券化の対象となる不動産の需給状況、不動産ファンド等の参入及び退出の状況、投資家の期待利回り及び資金調達環境の変化等）等の一般的要因の分析において収集した資料及びその分析結果を記載する。

(2)　地域要因
対象不動産の存する地域に係る不動産投資及び不動産証券化市場についての、不動産の規模、用途等による需要者層（需要者の行動や価格に関する判断基準）の違い、同一需給圏の範囲の把握や同一需給圏における代替、競争等の関係にある不動産の需給状況、不動産価格、成約賃料等の動向等について記載する。

(3)　個別的要因
① 土壌汚染に関する事項
　証券化対象不動産の鑑定評価においては、土壌汚染の価格への影響については結論が必要であり、そのために必要な専門家による調査が前提となる。したがって、鑑定評価報告書においては、エンジニアリング・レポート及び不動産鑑定士の独自調査を含むすべての調査結果の概要（調査範囲及び内容）とそれに基づき価格への影響をどのように結論づけたかを記載する。

② 埋蔵文化財に関する事項
　発掘調査に係わる費用は、投資家にとって、投資後の予期せぬ支出となるため、不動産鑑定士は、対象不動産が周知の埋蔵文化財包蔵地に該当するかどうか調査を行い、結果について鑑定評価報告書に記載する。なお、埋蔵文化財包蔵地に該当する場合は、それが、価格に与える影響について理由を付して記載する。

③ 地下埋設物に関する事項
　地下埋設物に関して、調査し確認できた内容を記載する。

④ 境界確定に関する事項
　境界確定及び越境の有無については、依頼者に確認するとともに、実地調査時に目視で可能な越境については確認し、その結果を記載する

⑤ 建物等の遵法性に関する事項
　建物及び付属設備が遵守すべき法律等は多岐にわたる一方、その遵法性の最終判断を下すことができるのは行政当局である。したがって、遵法性について確定的、断定的な判断や表現は

that can give final judgment on compliance issues regarding such laws. Accordingly, the appraiser should avoid conclusive or assertive decisions and expressions on such issues. The appraiser should clearly describe the coverage of the engineering report and investigation conducted by the appraiser, and the rationale for the judgment of compliance issues.

Specifically, a lack of compliance or emergency repair should be remedied, but if the remedy of the subject property has not been completed, the appraiser should at least describe in the appraisal report the owners willingness to remedy it and its feasibility.

If the cost required for remedy is substantially small in comparison to the appraisal value, and the appraiser determines it does not have a large influence on the value formation of the subject property, the rationale of the decision should be described in the appraisal report.

(f) Seismic Adequacy and Earthquake Risk

Since judgment in relation to seismic adequacy and earthquake risk requires high expertise, it is difficult for the appraiser to give a conclusive judgment.

Therefore the appraiser should avoid conclusive and affirmative decisions and expressions, and instead to the extent possible use language identical to that in the engineering report or report showing results of seismic assessment conducted under the Act on Promotion of Seismic Retrofitting of Buildings.

(g) Asbestos

In the valuation of securitized properties, the appraiser should conduct investigation of the following and include outcomes in the appraisal report if necessary.
- Structure and use of building, whether it is a fire protection district or not
- Date of completion (building age, date of renovation including spraying)
- Whether site inspection (visual) was conducted, whether sampling inspection was conducted
- Confirmation of the materials used in the internal and external finishing by referring to the design drawings, etc.
- Interviews with relevant parties
- Whether law-based public investigation for asbestos was conducted, and details of the investigation

Since investigation of asbestos requires high expertise, it is difficult for the appraiser to give a conclusive judgment.

Therefore the appraiser should avoid conclusive and affirmative decisions and expressions, and instead judgment (estimation) of hazardous substances should be based on the provided engineering report and the appraiser should in the appraisal report clearly describe what (s)he investigated as well as the judgment and rationale.

If the appraiser decides the value influence is not substantial, the accompanying rationale should be described in the appraisal report.

(h) PCB

Regarding the investigation of PCB-containing equipment, the appraiser should

避けるとともに、違法性に関する判断については、エンジニアリング・レポート等の調査範囲とその内容及び不動産鑑定士の行った調査又は確認の範囲と内容を明記し、違法性の判断を行った根拠等を明確に記載する。

特に、違法性に欠ける事項又は緊急修繕事項の是正の必要があるが、未だ是正されていない建物について鑑定評価を行う場合には、少なくとも是正を行う意思と実現性について確認した内容を鑑定評価報告書に記載する。

なお、是正に要する費用が鑑定評価額に比して小さく、対象不動産の価格形成に大きな影響を与えないと判断できる場合には、その判断した根拠を記載する。

⑥ 耐震性及び地震リスクに関する事項

耐震性及び地震リスクは、専門性が高いため、不動産鑑定士が確定的な判断を行うことが困難である。

したがって、耐震性及び地震リスクについて確定的、断定的な判断や表現は避けるとともに、できる限りエンジニアリング・レポートや耐震改修促進法に基づく耐震診断結果の記載を忠実に表現するよう留意する。

⑦ アスベストに関する事項

証券化対象不動産の鑑定評価において、不動産鑑定士は次のような調査を行うこととされており、必要に応じてその調査内容を鑑定評価報告書に記載する。

ア 建物の構造及び用途、防火地域か否か等
イ 施工時期（築年、吹き付け等を行った改修時期等）
ウ 現地調査（目視）を行ったのか、サンプリング調査まで行ったのか
エ 設計図書等による内装、外装等の使用材料の確認
オ 関係者へのヒアリング
カ 法令等に基づく石綿に係る公的調査の有無及び内容

アスベストの調査は、専門性が高いため、不動産鑑定士が確定的な判断を行うことが困難である。

したがって、アスベストについて確定的、断定的な判断や表現は避けるとともに、有害物質の有無に関する判断（推定）については、提出されたエンジニアリング・レポートに基づき、さらに、どのような調査及び確認を行ったのかを明記し、当該判断や推定を行った根拠等を明確に記載する。

なお、価格に対する影響が大きくないと判断できる場合には、その判断した根拠を記載する。

⑧ PCBに関する事項

PCB使用機器の有無の調査においては、実地調査及び依頼者や建物管理者へのヒアリング

describe the findings gained at site inspection, interview with the client and building manager, and contents of the engineering report, if necessary.

If the appraiser decides this value influence is not substantial, the accompanying rationale should be described in the appraisal report.

4) **Unknown Issues**

If any issues exist regarding value influences on the subject property that could not be clarified through professional investigation (engineering report, etc.) due to limitation of materials or lack of information, as well as for the case that the clue of the existence of such issue could not be clarified, they should be detailed and the valuation should to the extent possible and with the available information be conducted based on the rational estimation of the value influences within the scope of the appraisers ability. Appraisers should clearly describe the coverage and contents of investigation that they conduct, and those by professionals and via estimated information.

4. Application of Valuation Method

In order to apply the DCF method, the appraiser should provide an understandable explanation of the items described in Specific Standards Chapter 3, by referring to its Appendix 2 of Specific Standards Chapter 3 (example of DCF sheet).

The Year 1 and future cash flow in the DCF method are generally estimated based on the rent-roll, lease agreements, and required cost for the operation as provided by the client, and then the future changes should be estimated referring to the information obtained by the appraiser. Appraisers should detail how they analyzed and judged, along with the rationale.

It is necessary to be described clearly in the appraisal report how interest rate trend, market analysis, and uncertainty of cash flow of the subject property are reflected in the estimation of capitalization rate and discount rate, by providing the rationale such as comparables of securitized properties.

Rationale and validation depending on how the data is used (below A, B, or C) in the estimation of value indicated by the income capitalization approach, such as the DCF method, should also be described, as shown below.

For example, it should be described that in the estimation of rental income, the Year 1 and 2 cash flows were projected to be the same as the provided rent-roll, but the annual changes for years beyond were projected based on the rent-roll figure revised in accordance with the data obtained (market rent, vacancy rate, and supply-demand trend).

- A. Directly used the cash flow data associated with the subject property provided by the client
- B. Used the revised figure based on the cash flow data associated with the subject property provided by the client
- C. Used the cash flow data associated with the subject property obtained directly by the appraiser

5. Reconciliation of Indicated Values

During the process of reviewing and reconciliation of indicated values derived from in-

内容、エンジニアリング・レポート等の内容を必要に応じ記載する。

なお、価格に対する影響が大きくないと判断できる場合には、その判断した根拠を記載する。

(4) 不明事項

エンジニアリング・レポート等の専門家の調査を行っても、資料収集の限界や資料の不備等により、対象不動産の価格形成要因について不明事項が存する場合には、当該事項の存否の端緒が確認できない場合を含め、調査し得た範囲から不動産鑑定士の調査分析能力の範囲内で価格形成上の影響について合理的な推定を行って鑑定評価を行う必要がある。この際に、不動産鑑定士が自ら行った調査の範囲及び内容、専門家による調査の範囲及び内容、並びに推定の内容について明確に記載する。

4 鑑定評価手法の適用

DCF法の適用に当たっては、基準各論第3章別表2（DCF法シート）として例示されている様式を参考に、基準各論第3章等において記載すべきこととされている事項を、依頼者等に理解しやすく記載する必要がある。

一般に、DCF法の適用における収益費用の初年度の査定及び将来予測は、依頼者から入手したレントロールや賃貸借契約書、維持管理に係る費用明細等に基づき、それら数値がどのように変動するかを自ら入手した資料を参考に判断することにより行うが、このような将来収益費用の予測をどのような資料やデータに基づき、どのように判断及び分析し、それをどのように査定や予測に結びつけたかという判断根拠を明確にし、できる限り具体的に鑑定評価報告書に記載する必要がある。

還元利回り、割引率等の査定については、金利動向、市場分析結果、対象不動産の純収益の不確実性をどのように反映させたかを、証券化対象不動産等の取引事例等の判断根拠とした資料とともにできるだけ明確に鑑定評価報告書に記載する必要がある。

さらに、DCF法等による収益価格を求める際に採用する資料を次に定める区分に応じて、その妥当性や判断の根拠等を鑑定評価報告書に明記しなければならない。

例えば、貸室賃料収入について、初年度から2年度までの予測は、依頼者から入手したレントロール記載の数値が継続するものとして予測するが、翌期以降については、自ら入手した資料（市場賃料、空室率、需給動向に係る資料）に基づき、依頼者から入手したレントロール記載の数値を修正し、年間変動率を予測する旨記載することがあげられる。

ア　依頼者から入手した対象不動産に係る収益又は費用の額その他の資料をそのまま　採用する場合

イ　依頼者から入手した対象不動産に係る収益又は費用の額その他の資料に修正等を　加える場合

ウ　自らが入手した対象不動産に係る収益又は費用の額その他の資料を採用する場合

5 試算価格の調整

収益還元法、原価法、取引事例比較法等により求めた各試算価格から鑑定評価額の決定に至るま

come capitalization, cost, and sales comparison approaches to determine the final appraisal value, if income value and other values result in difference it should be described why there is such difference, by referring to such issues as limitations in approaches and result of market analysis.

Particularly, differences in values indicated by the DCF method (including development of a leasehold property) and direct capitalization method and differences in values indicated by the cost approach and sales comparison approach should be clearly explained and the rationale for the final appraisal value should be described.

6. Appraisal Value

1) If value is increased due to merger with adjacent property

If the value of the subject property is increased due to a merger with an adjacent property, and the market value based on special considerations[55] which shows the investment profitability is estimated, the assemblage value, which is not estimated assuming conditions of market value based on special considerations, and the market value of the subject as a single property should also be shown in the appraisal report.

2) If market value based on special considerations and market value are concluded to be equal

If the market value based on special considerations and the market value are determined to be the same, and the appraisal approaches to estimate one of the values is omitted, the appraiser should detail the reasons for determining the values to be the same, along with assumptions used in the estimation, such as the management plan and market analysis.

3) If value of land and building are to be separately shown

In the valuation of a tenant-occupied building and its site, if the value of land and building are shown as a breakdown of the combined value they should be practically treated as having the same definition as partial valuation.

The appraiser should not include the breakdown of value of land and building that are derived by simply calculating the value based on the ratio of land and building values or deducting the building value estimated in the process of the cost approach to derive at land value, because the reader of the appraisal report may mistakenly view such values as the appraisers opinions.

7. Appendix

The items that should be confirmed with the client (below (a)), and the items that should be recorded and saved (below (b)) must be documented and attached to the appraisal report as appendices, together with the valuation schedule[56].

(a) Items that should be confirmed with the client in relation to valuation schedule
- Purpose and background of the valuation request

---

[55] Estimate the value for typical investors based on the assumption that the adjacent land is combined and considering increases in value.

での検討状況、試算価格の調整において、収益価格と他の試算価格との開差が認められる場合には、その理由について手法の限界や市場分析結果との関連等を含め記載する。

特に、DCF法（開発賃貸型を含む）により査定した収益価格と直接還元法により査定した収益価格との関連及び原価法や取引事例比較法等で求めた試算価格との関連について明確にしつつ、収益価格や鑑定評価額を決定した理由を鑑定評価報告書に記載しなければならない。

6 鑑定評価額

(1) 隣接不動産の併合等により増分価値が生じる場合

隣接不動産との併合等により増分価値が生じる場合において、投資採算価値を表す特定価格[55]を求めるときには、特定価格としての条件を付加しない限定価格、単独の不動産としての正常価格を併記しなければならない。

(2) 特定価格と正常価格が一致すると判断される場合

特定価格と正常価格が一致すると判断され、一方の価格を求める手法の適用を省略した場合には、特定価格と正常価格が一致する旨と一致すると判断した理由について、評価の前提となる運用計画や市場分析等の観点からなるべく詳細に記載する。

(3) 土地建物の内訳価格を記載する場合

貸家及びその敷地等の複合不動産の鑑定評価額について、内訳価格として土地及び建物の価格を記載する場合には、部分鑑定評価と実質的に同義のものとして取り扱った上で記載しなければならない。

不動産鑑定士として判断を伴わずに、単なる計算結果として積算価格における土地建物の価格比や積算価格を求める過程で求めた建物価格を控除して土地価格を求める方法によって求めた内訳価格を鑑定評価報告書に記載することは、その価格が不動産鑑定士の意見であるものと誤解されるおそれがあるので、行うべきではない。

7 付属資料

処理計画の策定に関して依頼者に確認した、以下のアの依頼者に確認すべき事項に関して、イの記録、保管すべき事項については、鑑定評価を行うに際して記録を作成し、策定した処理計画を記載した書面とともに附属資料として鑑定評価報告書に添付することとされている[56]。

ア 処理計画の策定に関し依頼者に確認すべき事項
　ア）鑑定評価の依頼目的及び依頼が必要となった背景
　イ）対象不動産が前記Ⅰ2「対象とする鑑定評価の範囲」に定めるアからエのいずれに係るも

---

[55] 一体としての不動産を前提に、増分価値等を考慮して求めた投資採算価値として求める。。

- Subject property falls into which category specified in (a) through (d) of I-2 Scope of Appraisal for Securitized Properties
- Items included in engineering report and the date of receipt of the report
- Items included in required data for the DCF method and others and date of receipt of the data
- Whether the appraiser received an explanation from the issuer of the engineering report
- Coverage of the site inspection, including the internal inspection, of the subject property
- Other items required for determination of the valuation schedule

(b) Regarding (a), items that should be recorded and saved
- Date of confirmation
- Name of appraiser who confirmed the items: In the valuation of securitized properties, the appraiser who confirmed the items may not be the same as the appraiser in charge of the valuation of the subject property. The role and accountability of each appraiser should be made clear.
- Name and occupation of counterparty: name, company name, position, and relation with the client
- What has been confirmed and how it is reflected in the valuation schedule: notes should be taken about what has been confirmed with the client and how it is reflected in the appraisal process. If the initial information provided by the client was insufficient and the client and appraiser negotiated for the acquisition of further information, also record these procedures.
- If the appraisal process needs to be changed in line with revision of the confirmed items, it should be indicated what has to be changed: If (a) needs to be revised due to changes in situation or negotiations with the client, and the appraisal process needs to be changed accordingly (e.g., revisions in coverage of the subject, additional information, or securitization scheme, causing changes in basis of value, appraisal approaches, or changes in numbers used in calculation), record the details.

8. Draft Report

If a draft report is requested before concluding the final appraisal value, it should be sufficiently careful not to confuse the third party using the draft report since this report before concrete assumption or with insufficient information may result in a value different from the final appraisal value or the property-specific influence may differ from the final report.

More specifically, the following should be done.

---

[56] This is because if any failures were found in the provided information, these items will be evidence as they are important in terms of responsibility of the appraisers and appraisal companies.

Also note that the names of the documents used in the valuation being listed in the appraisal report may be sufficient; therefore it is not required to attach these documents to the report.

のであるかの別
　ウ）エンジニアリング・レポートの主な項目及び入手時期
　エ）DCF法等を適用するために必要となる資料その他の資料の主な項目及び入手時期
　オ）エンジニアリング・レポートの作成者からの説明の有無
　カ）対象不動産の内覧の実施を含めた実地調査の範囲
　キ）その他処理計画の策定のために必要な事項
イ　前記アに関し記録、保管すべき事項
　ア）確認を行った年月日
　イ）確認を行った不動産鑑定士の氏名：証券化対象不動産の鑑定評価においては評価担当の不動産鑑定士と異なる場合も多いので、不動産鑑定業者内での役割分担、責任の所在を明確にすること。
　ウ）確認の相手方の氏名及び職業：氏名、会社名、役職、依頼者との関係等
　エ）確認の内容及び当該内容の処理計画への反映状況：前記アの内容について、依頼者から確認した内容とともに、その内容によりどのような手順で評価作業を行ったか、について記録する。依頼者より当初示された内容が十分なものでなく、交渉を行った場合には、その経緯も記録する。
　オ）確認の内容の変更により鑑定評価の作業、内容等の変更をする場合にあっては、その内容：依頼者の事情の変化又は依頼者との交渉等により前記アの内容に変更があった場合に、評価作業を変更する必要が生じた場合（対象不動産の範囲や追加資料の提供、証券化スキームの変更等による、求める価格の種類、適用手法、適用数値の変更等）には、その内容を記録する。

8　ドラフト

　鑑定評価額決定前におけるドラフトの開示を求められた場合には、鑑定評価の前提条件や資料が整わない段階におけるドラフトの内容は、対象不動産の評価額や個別的要因が最終的な鑑定評価書と異なることとなる可能性が大きいので、提出に当たっては利用する第三者に誤解の生じることの無いように十分に留意する。
　具体的には、次のような対応をとる必要がある。
　ア　表紙を含め、全頁にドラフトである旨の表示を行う。

---

[56] これらは、依頼者から提供された資料に不備があった場合の証拠となるものであり、不動産鑑定士及び不動産鑑定業者の責任にかかわる重要な資料となるものであるので、不動産鑑定士からの提示を受けて、不動産鑑定業者が鑑定評価書の写しその他の書類の一つとして保管すべきものとなる。なお、鑑定評価書には、最終的に活用した資料名について記載すれば足りると考えられるので、これらの記録は鑑定評価書への添付までを求めているものではない。

- Insert "draft" for all pages, including the front page.
- No signature by appraiser
- Insert the date of draft valuation, instead of the date of completion of the appraisal process.
- Clearly describe that the conditions of the subject property and relevant data may differ from those in the final appraisal report, and for this reason the final appraisal value may differ.
- List the items that are not available at the date of issuance of the draft report, but will be obtained by the issuance of the final report.
- Do not provide the report in a file format that the client can revise.

イ 不動産鑑定士の署名又は記名は行わない。
ウ 鑑定評価を行った日に代えてドラフトとしての評価を行った日を明記する。
エ 対象不動産の状況、資料等について、最終的な鑑定評価書で採用するものとの違いを明確に記載し、鑑定評価額が変わる可能性があることを明確に記載する。
オ ドラフト提示時点における不明事項(最終的には確認する事項)を記載する。
カ 依頼者等が修正可能なファイル形式等では提示しない。

VIII. Periodic Valuation

Periodic valuation refers to regularly (annually or semiannually) conducted revaluation of real estate by the same appraiser who previously conducted appraisal of the real estate in accordance with the Appraisal Standards[57].

Periodic valuation in this case includes not only appraisal compliant with, but also valuation not compliant with the Appraisal Standards. It must be noted that periodic valuation can be conducted as a valuation not compliant with the Appraisal Standards only in limited cases, such as omitting an internal inspection or applicable appraisal approaches under certain requirements[58].

1. General Considerations in Periodic Valuation

In periodic valuation of securitized properties, in addition to maintaining full consistency with the previous valuation, the following must be considered (the same applies to non-periodic valuation):

- Procedures for valuation request and application of appraisal process regarding periodic valuation are generally the same for the newly requested valuation.

  Regarding specific value influences on the building (history of expansion, renovation, or major repair, and legal revisions for architecture), however, some changes may be identified since the previous valuation. Therefore, at the time of accepting the valuation request, it is necessary to confirm with the client if there have been any changes in building status since.

- In periodic valuation, a new engineering report prepared in accordance with the date of value may not be obtained, unlike at the time of acquisition of the subject property. However, if there have been major changes in specific value influences on the building such as expansion, renovation, or major repair, it is desirable to request that the client provide an updated engineering report. Even if no major changes exist in specific value influences on building, the abovementioned request is desirable if roughly three to five years has elapsed since the engineering reports preparation.

- In confirming the terms and conditions of building lease agreements, confirmation is necessary whether there have been changes in the conditions of the continued agreements. Along with that, by utilizing previously provided information, part of the confirmation process may be omitted; for instance, only changed agreements need to be checked since the date of value of the previous valuation. In periodic valuation, if unknown matters or their answers are found later, these must be reflected in the next valuation.

---

[57] An example of periodic valuation is the valuation for properties deemed as specified assets under the Investment Trust and Investment Corporation Law, which is regularly requested at each fiscal term during the investment period.

[58] When a valuation is limited to the client's internal use and the value is not to be published, if approval is obtained from all parties for disclosure and submission, the valuation will be conducted in accordance with the Valuation Guidelines and other relevant guidelines.

Ⅷ　継続評価等

　過去に同一の不動産鑑定士が不動産鑑定評価基準に則った鑑定評価を行ったことがある不動産の再評価であって、定期的（一年ごと又は半年ごと）に鑑定評価を行う場合を継続評価[57]という。
　この場合における継続評価には、不動産鑑定評価基準に則った鑑定評価だけでなく、不動産鑑定評価基準に則らない価格調査が含まれるが、価格調査として継続評価を行うことができるのは、一定の要件のもとに内覧の実施又は適用する手法を省略する場合等[58]限られることに留意する。

1　継続評価における一般的留意事項

　証券化対象不動産について継続評価を行う場合においては、前回評価との整合性を十分に検討することのほか、次の点に留意する必要がある（継続評価ではない再評価についても同様）。
　　ア　継続評価に係る依頼の受託及び評価の手順等については、基本的には新規に鑑定評価を依頼される場合と変わることはない。
　　　　ただし、建物に係る個別的要因（増改築又は大規模修繕の有無、建築等に関する法令の改正等）については、前回評価以降に変化していることがあるので、依頼の受託時において依頼者に建物状況の変化の有無等について確認を行う必要がある。
　　イ　継続評価では、対象不動産の取得時とは異なり、価格時点に合わせて作成された新たなエンジニアリング・レポートが入手できないことがあるが、建物の増改築又は大規模な修繕等の建物に係る個別的要因に大きな変更があった場合には、エンジニアリング・レポートを再取得するように依頼者に要請することが望ましい。
　　　　また、建物に係る個別的要因に大きな変更がない場合においても、エンジニアリング・レポートの作成後おおむね3年から5年経過しているときには同様の取扱いとする。
　　ウ　建物に係る賃貸借契約内容等の確認に当たっては、継続している契約について条件等に変更がないことを依頼者に確認のうえ、前回評価の価格時点以降に変更になった契約についてのみ賃貸借契約書の確認を行うなど以前提示を受けた資料を活用することにより、賃貸借契約書等の確認の一部を省略することができる。
　　　　なお、継続評価を行っている場合において、後日不明事項が発生したとき及び不明事項の内容が判明したときには、次回の評価においてその内容を反映しなければならない。

---

[57] 継続評価の例としては、投信法の特定資産にかかる不動産等の運用期間中の各決算期に評価する場合があり、定期的に評価が依頼される。
[58] 調査価格等が依頼者の内部における使用にとどまる場合、調査価格等が公表されない場合ですべての開示・提出先の承諾が得られた場合には、価格等調査ガイドライン及びこれに関連する実務指針等に従って価格調査を行うことになる。

2. Considerations in Periodic Valuation for an Appraisal not Compliant with the Appraisal Standards

1) Internal Inspection

Site inspection should be conducted for periodic valuation as in a valuation not conducted in a past and is a new valuation compliant with Specific Standards Chapter 3 and relevant Notes (hereinafter "new valuation")[59]. The internal inspection may, however, be omitted if the date of value is less than one year from the date of value of new valuation or periodic valuation in which the site inspection was conducted in the same manner as the new valuation[60] and no major changes in the subject propertys specific value influences, such as physical status or tenants, are found.

When the internal inspection is omitted, the periodic valuation must be conducted as a valuation not compliant with the Appraisal Standards.

2) Approaches to be Applied

In periodic valuation, if there have been no major changes in the subject propertys general and/or area-specific value influences[61], apart from property-specific value influences, after the date of value of the valuation conducted in accordance with Specific Standards Chapter 3 and relevant Notes, as a minimum the income capitalization approach must be applied and other applicable approaches for the valuation may be omitted.

If, however, the securitized properties is a vacant lot (including when a building is scheduled for demolition) or non-rental real estate, for which the value indicated by the income approach is not necessarily emphasized, the appraisal approach applied to determine the final appraisal value in the latest appraisal compliant with the Appraisal Standards must be applied in the periodic valuation (but other applicable approaches may be omitted, including the income capitalization approach).

If other applicable approaches are omitted, the periodic valuation must be conducted as a valuation not compliant with the Appraisal Standards, the same as when omitting an internal inspection.

3) Contents of the Final Report

- When periodic valuation is conducted without internal inspection or applicable appraisal approaches or the opinion of value is given via different procedures than those specified in the Appraisal Standards, the following must be stipulated next to the final value in the final report:

---

[59] In periodic valuation, if a site inspection with an internal inspection is conducted, the changed part from the effective date of the previous valuation can mainly be inspected with reference to the relevant data provided by the building manager.

[60] In determining considerable changes in specific value influences of the subject property, it is necessary to consider the site, building, and relevant rights including the lease of the subject property, along with the "Basic Policy on Periodic Valuation of Securitized Properties."

[61] In determining substantial changes in general and area-specific value influences of the subject property, along with the "Basic Policy on Periodic Valuation of Securitized Properties," a full analysis must be conducted regarding creation or revision of a system that can affect the subject property's use or profitability, or changes in the market and area characteristics.

2 価格調査として継続評価を行う場合における留意事項

(1) 内覧の実施

実地調査に関しては、継続評価でも、原則として過去に評価を行っていない不動産について基準各論第3章等に従って新規の鑑定評価を行う場合（以下「新規評価」という。）と同様に実施すべきである[※59]。ただし、価格時点が、同一の不動産鑑定士が新規評価又は新規評価と同等に実地調査を行った継続評価の価格時点から1年未満であって、対象不動産の物的状況やテナントの状況等の個別的要因に重要な変化がない場合[※60]には、内覧の実施を省略することができる。

なお、内覧の実施を省略した場合においては、当該継続評価は価格調査として行わなければならない。

(2) 適用する手法

継続評価においては、基準各論第3章等に従って行った鑑定評価の価格時点以降に、対象不動産の個別的要因のほか、当該不動産の価格形成に影響を与える一般的要因及び地域要因に重要な変化がないと認められる場合[※61]には、鑑定評価手法のうち少なくとも収益還元法は適用するものとし、当該評価において適用可能と認められる他の手法を省略することができる。

ただし、証券化対象不動産が更地である場合（建物を取り壊す予定である場合を含む）や賃貸用不動産以外の不動産であって、必ずしも収益価格が重視されないものであるときには、直近に行われた不動産鑑定評価基準に則った鑑定評価における鑑定評価額の決定において重視された鑑定評価手法は少なくとも適用する必要がある（収益還元法を含め、当該評価において適用可能と認められる他の手法を省略することができる）。

なお、適用可能と認められる他の手法を省略した場合には、内覧の実施を省略する場合と同様、当該継続評価は価格調査として行わなければならない。

(3) 成果報告書の記載事項

ア　内覧の実施又は適用する手法を省略して継続評価を行った場合その他不動産鑑定評価基準に定める手順と異なる手順で価格調査を行った場合には、成果報告書の調査価格が記載されている箇所の近傍に「不動産鑑定評価基準に則った鑑定評価とは結果が異なる可能性がある旨」及び「成果報告書に記載された以外の目的での使用及び記載されていない者への調査価格の開示は想定していない旨」について記載する。

---

[59] 継続評価において内覧の実施を含む実地調査を行う場合、前回評価の価格時点からの変更部分に関し、管理者から提示された建物管理報告書等の関連資料を参照しつつ、当該部分を中心に内覧を行うことも可能である。

[60] 対象不動産の個別的要因についての重要な変化の有無に関する判断に当たっては、「証券化対象不動産の継続評価の実施に関する基本的考え方」を踏まえて、対象不動産に係る敷地、建物及び賃貸借等の権利関係等の観点から検討を行う必要がある。

[61] 対象不動産の一般的要因及び地域要因についての重要な変化の有無についても、「証券化対象不動産の継続評価の実施に関する基本的考え方」を踏まえて、対象不動産の利用方法又は収益性に影響を与えるような制度の創設・変更、市場特性や地域特性の変化等について十分に分析のうえ判断すべきである。

- "The result may be different if appraisal is conducted in accordance with the Appraisal Standards."
- "This report does not assume disclosure of the final value other than for the stated purpose and to parties other than those specified."

● Also, if the following are omitted, confirming there have been no major changes since the appraisal compliant with the Appraisal Standards was conducted, the rationale for the omission must be described in the report.
- The subject propertys specific value influences with omission of internal inspection
- The subject propertys specific, general, or area-specific value influences with omission of appraisal approaches
- If the periodic valuation is conducted with omission of applicable appraisal approaches, not the basis of value but the approaches applied must be stated in the report.

3. Valuation not compliant with the Appraisal Standards other than Periodic Valuation

1) Properties including uncompleted buildings assuming completion

Regarding securitization of development properties, when an investment corporation acquires the subject building and its site after the completion of the building based on a forward commitment, valuation may be requested under the assumption of completion of the uncompleted building of the property. In such a case, the progress of the construction for the already constructed portion of the building must be properly checked along with the unconstructed portion with the above assumptions[62].

2) When not compliant with the Appraisal Standards for a valid reason

With the assumption of the development or ongoing construction is completed as of the date of value, if the valuation cannot comply with the Appraisal Standards because the certificate of inspection is not issued or approval for tentative use is not confirmed, the value of the securitized properties can be obtained as a valuation not compliant with the Appraisal Standards.

In such a case, the final report must be prepared in accordance with the Valuation Guidelines, but it is not necessary[63] to state in the final report that "The result may be different if appraisal is conducted in accordance with the Appraisal Standards". Also,

---

[62] Valuation conducted for a property with an uncompleted building under the assumption of its completion must be in accordance with the Appraisal Standards other than for identifying the physical characteristics and ownership and interests regarding the uncompleted building.

[63] If the building is regarded as nearly complete, there is generally considered to be no difference in the result from when it is estimated in an appraisal compliant with the Appraisal Standards since the only difference is the absence of the certificate of inspection or approval for tentative use at the time of the valuation. The valuation was in the first place conducted because appraisal compliant with the Appraisal Standards could not be conducted. As such, these results cannot be compared with one another. Even with the building nearly complete, it must be verified by a site inspection, etc. if it conforms to the drawings and specifications approved by construction confirmation.

イ　内覧の実施を省略する場合における対象不動産の個別的要因、又は適用する手法を省略する場合における対象不動産の個別的要因並びに一般的要因及び地域要因について、不動産鑑定評価基準に則った鑑定評価が行われた時点と比較して重要な変化がないと認められ、それらを省略した場合には、その根拠を成果報告書に記載しなければならない。また、適用する手法を省略して継続評価を行った場合には、価格の種類ではなく、適用した手法を成果報告書に記載する。

3　継続評価以外の価格調査

(1)　未竣工建物を含む不動産の竣工を前提とする場合

開発型証券化に関連する場合、投資法人がフォワード・コミットメントにより建物の竣工後に当該建物及びその敷地を取得する場合等には、未竣工建物を含む不動産の竣工を前提として価格調査を依頼されることがあるが、この場合においては、物的確認が可能な建物の既施工部分に係る工事の進捗状況を確認するとともに、想定上の条件等を付した未施工部分についても適切に確定する[※62]

(2)　やむを得ず不動産鑑定評価基準に則ることができない場合

価格時点において造成工事中又は建設工事中の工事が完了していることを前提とする場合において、検査済証の交付又は仮使用の承認を得ていないためにやむを得ず不動産鑑定評価基準に則ることができないときは、不動産鑑定評価基準に則らない価格調査として証券化対象不動産の価格を求めることができる。

この場合においては、価格等調査ガイドラインに従って成果報告書への記載を行うことになるが、成果報告書への記載事項のうち、「不動産鑑定評価基準に則った鑑定評価とは結果が異なる可能性がある旨」の記載は要しない[※63]。また、成果報告書には、適用する手法ではなく、求める価格の種類を記載することができる。

62　未竣工建物を含む不動産の竣工を前提として価格調査を行う場合には、当該未竣工建物に係る物的確認及び権利の態様の確認以外の部分については、不動産鑑定評価基準に則る必要がある。

63　建物が実質的に完成しているといえる状態の場合には、価格調査の時点において検査済証の交付又は仮使用の承認を得ていないだけであり、通常は不動産鑑定評価基準に則った鑑定評価と結果が異なることはないと考えられる。また、そもそも不動産鑑定評価基準に則ることができないため価格調査を行ったものであり、不動産鑑定評価基準に則った鑑定評価の結果と比較することはできない。なお、この場合においても、実質的に完成している建物が建築確認を受けた設計図書どおりのものであることを実地調査等によって確認すべきことはいうまでもない。

in the final report, the basis of value may be described, instead of describing the approaches to be applied.

Effective Date

The Guidelines will be applied to valuation under contracts made and entered into on and after January 1, 2010. This does not preclude applications before the effective date.

適用時期
　本実務指針は、平成22年１月１日以降に契約を締結する業務から適用する。ただし、当該日以前から適用することを妨げない。

V

Reference Materials

参考資料

V-1

Act on Real Estate Appraisal

July 16, 1963 Law No. 152
Final revision: March 31, 2006 Law No. 10

不動産の鑑定評価に関する法律

昭和38年7月16日法律第152号
最終改正：平成18年3月31日法律第10号

V - 1. Act on Real Estate Appraisal

CHAPTER 1. GENERAL PROVISIONS

Article 1. Purpose
The purpose of this law is to prescribe the necessary matters regarding licensed real estate appraisers (LREA) and real estate appraisal business, and thereby to contribute to the formation of suitable values for land, etc.

Article 2. Definitions
1. In this law, "real estate appraisal" means evaluating the economic value of real estate (land, buildings, and related rights other than ownership; the same applies below) and expressing the result of such evaluation as a monetary value.
2. In this law, "real estate appraisal business" means the business of providing real estate appraisal services upon the request of another person and for compensation, regardless of whether these services are provided by the business operator or by another person engaged to provide the services.
3. In this law, "real estate appraisal business operator" means a person who is registered under Article 24.

第1章　総　則

（目的）
第1条　この法律は、不動産の鑑定評価に関し、不動産鑑定士及び不動産鑑定業について必要な事項を定め、もつて土地等の適正な価格の形成に資することを目的とする。

（定義）
第2条　この法律において「不動産の鑑定評価」とは、不動産（土地若しくは建物又はこれらに関する所有権以外の権利をいう。以下同じ。）の経済価値を判定し、その結果を価額に表示することをいう。
2　この法律において「不動産鑑定業」とは、自ら行うと他人を使用して行うとを問わず、他人の求めに応じ報酬を得て、不動産の鑑定評価を業として行うことをいう。
3　この法律において「不動産鑑定業者」とは、第24条の規定による登録を受けた者をいう。

CHAPTER 2. LICENSED REAL ESTATE APPRAISERS (LREAs)

Section 1. General Provisions
Article 3. LREA operations
1. An LREA performs real estate appraisals.
2. An LREA may engage in the business of investigating and analyzing the factors affecting the objective value of real estate, or of providing consultation regarding real estate utilization, transactions, and investment, using the name of "LREA." However, this shall not apply if such operations are restricted under other laws.

Article 4. LREA qualifications
A person who has passed the LREA examination, completed practical training as prescribed in Article 14-2, and obtained approval by the Minister of Land, Infrastructure and Transport as prescribed in Article 14-23 is qualified to become an LREA.

Article 5. Duties of an LREA
An LREA must conscientiously and faithfully perform the operations specified in Article 3 (hereinafter "appraisal and related operations"), and must not commit any act that would injure the reputation of LREAs.

Article 6. Confidentiality
An LREA shall not divulge any secret information learned in relation to appraisal and related operations without a justifiable reason. The same shall apply even after the person is no longer an LREA.

Article 7. Maintaining and improving knowledge and skills
An LREA must strive to maintain and improve the knowledge and skills which are needed for appraisal and related operations.

Section 2. LREA Examination (Omitted)

Section 3. Practical Training (Omitted)

Section 4. Registration (Omitted except for Articles 15 and 16)
Article 15. Registration
To become an LREA, a person who is qualified to become an LREA shall have his/her name, date of birth, address, and any other matters specified by order of the Ministry of Land, Infrastructure and Transport recorded in the LREA register maintained by the Ministry of Land, Infrastructure and Transport.

Article 16. Grounds for disqualification
A person to whom any of the following applies may not obtain LREA registration.
 (a) A minor.
 (b) A person who has been adjudged incompetent or quasi-incompetent.
 (c) A person who has been declared bankrupt and has not been reinstated.
 (d) A person who has received a sentence of imprisonment or greater severity, if less

第2章　不動産鑑定士

第1節　総則

(不動産鑑定士の業務)
第3条　不動産鑑定士は、不動産の鑑定評価を行う。
2　不動産鑑定士は、不動産鑑定士の名称を用いて、不動産の客観的価値に作用する諸要因に関して調査若しくは分析を行い、又は不動産の利用、取引若しくは投資に関する相談に応ずることを業とすることができる。ただし、他の法律においてその業務を行うことが制限されている事項については、この限りでない。

(不動産鑑定士となる資格)
第4条　不動産鑑定士試験に合格した者であつて、第14条の2に規定する実務修習を修了し第14条の23の規定による国土交通大臣の確認を受けた者は、不動産鑑定士となる資格を有する。

(不動産鑑定士の責務)
第5条　不動産鑑定士は、良心に従い、誠実に第3条に規定する業務(以下「鑑定評価等業務」という。)を行うとともに、不動産鑑定士の信用を傷つけるような行為をしてはならない。

(秘密を守る義務)
第6条　不動産鑑定士は、正当な理由がなく、鑑定評価等業務に関して知り得た秘密を他に漏らしてはならない。不動産鑑定士でなくなつた後においても、同様とする。

(知識及び技能の維持向上)
第7条　不動産鑑定士は、鑑定評価等業務に必要な知識及び技能の維持向上に努めなければならない。

第2節　不動産鑑定士試験　(省略)

第3節　実務修習　(省略)

第4節　登録(第15条及び第16条以外は省略)

(登録)
第15条　不動産鑑定士となる資格を有する者が、不動産鑑定士となるには、国土交通省に備える不動産鑑定士名簿に、氏名、生年月日、住所その他国土交通省令で定める事項の登録を受けなければならない。

(欠格条項)
第16条　次の各号のいずれかに該当する者は、不動産鑑定士の登録を受けることができない。
　一　未成年者
　二　成年被後見人又は被保佐人
　三　破産者で復権を得ない者
　四　禁錮以上の刑に処せられた者で、その執行を終わり、又は執行を受けることがなくなつた日

than three years have elapsed since the completion of that sentence or exemption from the execution of sentence.
(e) A civil servant who has received a disciplinary discharge, if less than three years have elapsed since discharge.
(f) A person whose registration has been canceled under Article 20, Paragraph 1, Item (d) or Article 40, Paragraph 1 or 3, if less than three years have elapsed since cancellation.
(g) A person who has been prohibited from performing appraisal and related operations under Article 40, Paragraph 1 or 2, if that person's registration has been canceled under Article 20, Paragraph 1, Item (a) during the period of prohibition, and that period has not yet been completed.

から３年を経過しないもの
五　公務員で懲戒免職の処分を受け、その処分の日から３年を経過しない者
六　第20条第１項第４号又は第40条第１項若しくは第３項の規定による登録の消除の処分を受け、その処分の日から３年を経過しない者
七　第40条第１項又は第２項の規定による禁止の処分を受け、その禁止の期間中に第20条第１項第１号の規定に基づきその登録が消除され、まだその期間が満了しない者

CHAPTER 3. REAL ESTATE APPRAISAL BUSINESS

Section 1. Registration (Omitted except for Articles 22, 25 and 33)

Article 22. Registration of real estate appraisal business operators

1. A person wishing to operate a real estate appraisal business shall obtain registration in the register of real estate appraisal business operators maintained by the Ministry of Land, Infrastructure and Transport if he/she will establish offices in two or more prefectures, or otherwise, in the register maintained by the prefecture where his/her office is located.
2. The effective period of the registration of real estate appraisal business operators shall be five years.
3. If the person wishes to continue operating a real estate appraisal business after expiration of the effective period under the preceding paragraph, he/she shall obtain a renewal registration.
4. If application for renewal registration has been filed, but no decision on the application has been issued by the expiration of the effective period under Paragraph 2, then the former registration shall remain in effect from the expiration of that effective period until the date when a decision is issued.
5. In the case of the preceding paragraph, when renewal registration is obtained, the effective period of that registration shall begin on the day after expiration of the effective period of the former registration.

Article 25. Denial of registration

The Minister of Land, Infrastructure and Transport or the prefectural governor shall deny registration if any of the following applies to the registration applicant, or if any important matters are falsified or important facts are omitted on the registration application or documents appended to that application.

(a) A person who has been declared bankrupt and has not been reinstated.
(b) A person who has received a sentence of imprisonment or greater severity, or has been sentenced to a fine for a violation of this law or a violation regarding appraisal and related operations, if less than three years have elapsed since the completion of that sentence or exemption from the execution of sentence.
(c) A person subject to Article 16, Item (f) or (g).
(d) A person whose registration has been canceled under Article 30, Paragraph 1, Item (f) or Article 41, if less than three years have elapsed since cancellation.
(e) A person who has been ordered to suspend operations under Article 41, if Article 29, Paragraph 1, Item (a) applies during the period of suspension, and the person's registration has been canceled under Article 30, Item (a) or (b), and that period has not yet been completed.
(f) A person who has been adjudged incompetent or a minor, lacking the business capacity of an adult, if any of the preceding items applies to that person's legal representative.

第3章　不動産鑑定業

　　　第1節　登録（第22条、第25条及び第33条以外は省略）
（不動産鑑定業者の登録）
第22条　不動産鑑定業を営もうとする者は、2以上の都道府県に事務所を設ける者にあつては国土交通省に、その他の者にあつてはその事務所の所在地の属する都道府県に備える不動産鑑定業者登録簿に登録を受けなければならない。
2　不動産鑑定業者の登録の有効期間は、5年とする。
3　前項の有効期間の満了後引き続き不動産鑑定業を営もうとする者は、更新の登録を受けなければならない。
4　更新の登録の申請があつた場合において、第2項の有効期間の満了の日までにその申請に対する処分がなされないときは、従前の登録は、同項の有効期間の満了後もその処分がなされるまでの間は、なお効力を有する。
5　前項の場合において、更新の登録がなされたときは、その登録の有効期間は、従前の登録の有効期間の満了の日の翌日から起算するものとする。

（登録の拒否）
第25条　国土交通大臣又は都道府県知事は、登録申請者が次の各号のいずれかに該当する者であるとき、又は登録申請書若しくはその添付書類に重要な事項について虚偽の記載があり、若しくは重要な事実の記載が欠けているときは、その登録を拒否しなければならない。
一　破産者で復権を得ない者
二　禁錮以上の刑に処せられ、又はこの法律の規定に違反し、若しくは鑑定評価等業務に関し罪を犯して罰金の刑に処せられ、その執行を終わり、又は執行を受けることがなくなつた日から3年を経過しない者
三　第16条第6号又は第7号に該当する者
四　第30条第6号又は第41条の規定により登録を消除され、その登録の消除の日から3年を経過しない者
五　第41条の規定による業務の停止の命令を受け、その停止の期間中に第29条第1項第1号に該当し、第30条第1号又は第2号の規定に基づきその登録が消除され、まだその期間が満了しない者
六　営業に関し成年者と同一の行為能力を有しない未成年者又は成年被後見人で、その法定代理人が前各号のいずれかに該当するもの
七　法人で、その役員のうちに第1号から第5号までのいずれかに該当する者のあるもの

(g) A corporation, if any of items (a) through (e) applies to any of the corporation's executives.

Article 33. Prohibition of unregistered operations
Parties that have not obtained registration as a real estate appraisal business operator shall not operate a real estate appraisal business.

Section 2. Operations
Article 35. LREA appointment
1. A real estate appraisal business operator who is not an LREA shall appoint at least one full-time LREA for each office of that business. The same shall apply for any office where a real estate appraisal business operator who is an LREA will not him/herself perform real estate appraisals.
2. If a real estate appraisal business operator has an office that comes into violation of the preceding paragraph, that operator must take the necessary steps within two weeks for conformity with the provisions of that paragraph.

Article 36. Prohibition of appraisal by non-LREAs
1. A person who is not an LREA shall not perform real estate appraisal in connection with the operations of a real estate appraisal business operator.
2. A real estate appraisal business operator shall not cause any person who is not an LREA, or a person who is subject to a disciplinary measure under Article 40, Paragraph 1 or who is prohibited from performing appraisal and related operations under Article 40, Paragraph 2, to perform real estate appraisal and related operations in connection with that business.

Article 37 (Omitted)

Article 38. Confidentiality
A real estate appraisal business operator shall not divulge secret information learned in relation to business operations without a justifiable reason. The same shall apply even after the operator has discontinued the real estate appraisal business.

Article 39. Appraisal document, etc.
1. A real estate appraisal business operator shall issue an appraisal document, stating the final opinion of value and other matters specified by order of the Ministry of Land, Infrastructure and Transport, to the party requesting appraisal of real estate.
2. On the appraisal document, the LREA involved in the appraisal of that real estate shall enter his/her signature and seal and indicate his/her qualifications.
3. The real estate appraisal business operator shall retain a copy of the appraisal document and other documentation as specified by order of the Ministry of Land, Infrastructure and Transport.

（無登録業務の禁止）
第33条　不動産鑑定業者の登録を受けない者は、不動産鑑定業を営んではならない。

第2節　業務
（不動産鑑定士の設置）
第35条　不動産鑑定士でない不動産鑑定業者は、その事務所ごとに専任の不動産鑑定士を1人以上置かなければならない。不動産鑑定士である不動産鑑定業者がみずから実地に不動産の鑑定評価を行なわない事務所についても、同様とする。
2　不動産鑑定業者は、前項の規定に抵触するに至つた事務所があるときは、2週間以内に、同項の規定に適合させるため必要な措置をとらなければならない。

（不動産鑑定士でない者等による鑑定評価の禁止）
第36条　不動産鑑定士でない者は、不動産鑑定業者の業務に関し、不動産の鑑定評価を行つてはならない。
2　不動産鑑定業者は、その業務に関し、不動産鑑定士でない者又は第40条第1項に不動産の鑑定評価を、第2項の規定による禁止の処分を受けた者に鑑定評価等業務を行わせてはならない。

第37条　削除

（秘密を守る義務）
第38条　不動産鑑定業者は、正当な理由がなく、その業務上取り扱つたことについて知り得た秘密を他に漏らしてはならない。不動産鑑定業者がその不動産鑑定業を廃止した後においても、同様とする。

（鑑定評価書等）
第39条　不動産鑑定業者は、不動産の鑑定評価の依頼者に、鑑定評価額その他国土交通省令で定める事項を記載した鑑定評価書を交付しなければならない。
2　鑑定評価書には、その不動産の鑑定評価に関与した不動産鑑定士がその資格を表示して署名押印しなければならない。
3　不動産鑑定業者は、国土交通省令で定めるところにより、鑑定評価書の写しその他の書類を保存しなければならない。

CHAPTER 4. OVERSIGHT

Article 40. Disciplinary measures for improper appraisals, etc.

1. If an LREA has intentionally prepared an unjust or improper appraisal or committed another unjust or improper act with regard to appraisal and related operations (hereinafter "improper appraisal, etc."), then as a disciplinary measure, the Minister of Land, Infrastructure and Transport may prohibit the LREA from performing appraisal and related operations for a period of up to one year, or may cancel the registration of that LREA. The same shall apply if the LREA has violated Article 6 or Article 33.
2. If an LREA has committed an improper appraisal, etc. because of failure to use due caution, then as a disciplinary measure, the Minister of Land, Infrastructure and Transport may issue a reprimand or prohibit the LREA from performing appraisal and related operations for a period of up to one year.
3. If an LREA violates a prohibition under the two preceding articles, the Minister of Land, Infrastructure and Transport may cancel the registration of that LREA.

Article 41. Supervisory disposition of real estate appraisal operators

If any of the following applies to a registered real estate appraisal business operator, the Minister of Land, Infrastructure and Transport or the prefectural governor may issue a reprimand, order the suspension of all or a portion of that business for a period of up to one year, or cancel the operator's registration.

(a) If the operator has violated this law or a measure taken by the Minister of Land, Infrastructure and Transport or the prefectural governor on the basis of this law.

(b) If an LREA who is engaged in operations of that real estate appraisal business operator has been subjected to a disciplinary measure under the preceding article, for reasons which were the responsibility of the real estate appraisal business operator.

Article 42. Action requirement regarding improper real estate appraisals, etc.

If there are grounds for reasonable suspicion that an LREA has committed an improper appraisal, etc., then any person may report those circumstances to the Minister of Land, Infrastructure and Transport or the governor of the prefecture in which the real estate appraisal business operator employing that LREA is registered, appending documentation; and may request that appropriate measures be taken.

Article 43. Procedures for disciplinary measures, etc.

(Omitted)

Article 44. Public notice of disciplinary measures, etc.

If the Minister of Land, Infrastructure and Transport or a prefectural governor has taken disciplinary measures under Article 40 or Article 41, then public notice to this effect shall be issued as specified by government decree.

Article 45. Reporting and inspections

1. If deemed necessary by the Minister of Land, Infrastructure and Transport or a prefectural governor in order to ensure the proper administration of real estate appraisal bus-

第4章　監　督

（不当な鑑定評価等についての懲戒処分）
第40条　国土交通大臣は、不動産鑑定士が、故意に、不当な不動産の鑑定評価その他鑑定評価等業務に関する不正又は著しく不当な行為（以下「不当な鑑定評価等」という。）を行つたときは、懲戒処分として、1年以内の期間を定めて鑑定評価等業務を行うことを禁止し、又はその不動産鑑定士の登録を消除することができる。不動産鑑定士が、第6条又は第33条の規定に違反したときも、同様とする。
2　国土交通大臣は、不動産鑑定士が、相当の注意を怠り、不当な鑑定評価等を行つたときは、懲戒処分として、戒告を与え、又は1年以内の期間を定めて鑑定評価等業務を行うことを禁止することができる。
3　国土交通大臣は、不動産鑑定士が、前2項の規定による禁止の処分に違反したときは、その不動産鑑定士の登録を消除することができる。

（不動産鑑定業者に対する監督処分）
第41条　国土交通大臣又は都道府県知事は、その登録を受けた不動産鑑定業者が次の各号のいずれかに該当するときは、その不動産鑑定業者に対し、戒告を与え、1年以内の期間を定めてその業務の全部若しくは一部の停止を命じ、又はその登録を消除することができる。
一　この法律又はこの法律に基づく国土交通大臣若しくは都道府県知事の処分に違反したとき。
二　不動産鑑定業者の業務に従事する不動産鑑定士が、前条の規定による処分を受けた場合において、その不動産鑑定業者の責めに帰すべき理由があるとき。

（不当な鑑定評価等に対する措置の要求）
第42条　不動産鑑定士が不当な鑑定評価等を行つたことを疑うに足りる事実があるときは、何人も、国土交通大臣又は当該不動産鑑定士がその業務に従事する不動産鑑定業者が登録を受けた都道府県知事に対し、資料を添えてその事実を報告し、適当な措置をとるべきことを求めることができる。

（懲戒処分等の手続）
第43条　省略

（懲戒処分等の公告）
第44条　国土交通大臣又は都道府県知事は、第40条又は第41条の規定による処分をしたときは、政令で定めるところにより、その旨を公告しなければならない。

（報告及び検査）
第45条　国土交通大臣又は都道府県知事は、不動産鑑定業の適正な運営を確保するため必要がある

iness, the Minister may demand the necessary reports from all real estate appraisal business operators, or a prefectural governor may demand the necessary reports from all real estate appraisal business operators registered in that prefecture; or the Minister or governor may order their staff members to enter the premises of the offices or other locations related to those businesses and inspect ledgers and records related to the businesses (including electromagnetic records, if those ledgers and records were prepared or stored in electromagnetic form).
2. Staff members conducting an on-site inspection under the preceding paragraph shall carry certification of their identities, and shall present such certification if requested by a related person.
3. The authority to conduct on-site inspections under Paragraph 1 shall not be construed as having been approved for criminal investigations.

Article 46. Counsel and advice

If deemed necessary by the Minister of Land, Infrastructure and Transport or a prefectural governor in order to ensure the proper administration of real estate appraisal business or to promote the sound development of such business, the Minister or governor may provide the necessary counsel or advice regarding real estate appraisal business to the real estate appraisal business operators registered with the Minister or governor.

と認めるときは、国土交通大臣にあつてはすべての不動産鑑定業者について、都道府県知事にあつてはその登録を受けた不動産鑑定業者について、その業務に関し必要な報告を求め、又はその職員にその業務に関係のある事務所その他の場所に立ち入り、その業務に関係のある帳簿書類（その作成又は保存に代えて電磁的記録の作成又は保存がされている場合における当該電磁的記録を含む。）を検査させることができる。

2　前項の規定により立入検査をしようとする職員は、その身分を示す証明書を携帯し、関係人の請求があつたときは、これを提示しなければならない。

3　第1項の規定による立入検査の権限は、犯罪捜査のために認められたものと解釈してはならない。

（助言又は勧告）
第46条　国土交通大臣又は都道府県知事は、不動産鑑定業の適正な運営の確保又はその健全な発達を図るため必要があるときは、その登録を受けた不動産鑑定業者に対し、その営む不動産鑑定業に関し必要な助言又は勧告をすることができる。

CHAPTER 5. MISCELLANEOUS PROVISIONS

Article 47. Examiners
(Omitted)

Article 48. LREA organizations, etc.
Associations and foundations whose purpose is to help maintain and enhance the position of LREAs and to advance and improve business operations related to real estate appraisal, and which have been specified by order of the Ministry of Land, Infrastructure and Transport, shall submit the information required by order of the Ministry of Land, Infrastructure and Transport to the Minister of Land, Infrastructure and Transport or the prefectural governor, as specified by order of the Ministry of Land, Infrastructure and Transport.

Article 49
Associations and foundations which have submitted information under the preceding article must provide training for LREAs as specified by government decree.

Article 50
If deemed necessary by the Minister of Land, Infrastructure and Transport or a prefectural governor in order to ensure the proper implementation of real estate appraisal or to promote the sound development of real estate appraisal business, the Minister or governor may require reports from the associations and foundations which have submitted information under Article 48, or provide them with counsel or advice.

Article 51. Prohibition of name usage
Persons who are not LREAs may not use the name of LREA.

Article 52. Exclusions regarding farmland, etc.
Acts constituting any of the following shall not be included in real estate appraisal under this law.
 (a) Evaluating the transaction price of farmland, pastureland, or forestland (not including the case of transactions in which the land will not be used for a different purpose than farmland, pastureland, or forestland).
 (b) Calculating the insurable value or indemnity amount for a building subject to property insurance.
 (c) Appraising a building as a service of a registered architect's office (not including the office of a registered wooden building architect) under the Registered Architect Law (Law No. 202 of 1950).

Article 53. Special exception for applications by methods using electronic data processing systems
(Omitted)

Article 54. Delegation of authority
(Omitted)

Article 55. Classification of clerical operations
(Omitted)

第5章　雑　則

（試験委員）
第47条　省略

（不動産鑑定士等の団体）
第48条　不動産鑑定士の品位の保持及び資質の向上を図り、あわせて不動産の鑑定評価に関する業務の進歩改善を図ることを目的とする社団又は財団で、国土交通省令で定めるものは、国土交通省令で定めるところにより、国土交通大臣又は都道府県知事に対して、国土交通省令で定める事項を届け出なければならない。

第49条　前条の規定による届出をした社団又は財団は、政令で定めるところにより、不動産鑑定士に対する研修を実施しなければならない。

第50条　国土交通大臣又は都道府県知事は、不動産の鑑定評価の適正な実施の確保又は不動産鑑定業の健全な発達を図るため必要があるときは、第48条の規定による届出をした社団又は財団に対し、報告を求め、又は助言若しくは勧告をすることができる。

（名称の使用禁止）
第51条　不動産鑑定士でない者は、不動産鑑定士の名称を用いてはならない。

（農地等に関する適用除外）
第52条　次の各号のいずれかに該当する場合においては、当該評価等の行為は、この法律にいう不動産の鑑定評価に含まれないものとする。
　一　農地、採草放牧地又は森林の取引価格（農地、採草放牧地及び森林以外のものとするための取引に係るものを除く。）を評価するとき。
　二　損害保険の目的である建物の保険価額又は損害塡補額を算定するとき。
　三　建築士法（昭和25年法律第202号）による建築士事務所（木造建築士事務所を除く。）の業務として、建物につき鑑定するとき。

（電子情報処理組織を使用する方法により行う申込み等の特例）
第53条　省略

（権限の委任）
第54条　省略

（事務の区分）
第55条　省略

CHAPTER 6. SANCTIONS

Article 56
A person to whom any of the following applies shall be sentenced to imprisonment of up to one year, a fine of up to one million yen, or both.
 (a) A person who has obtained registration as a real estate appraisal business operator by deceit or other improper means.
 (b) A person who has operated a real estate appraisal business in violation of Article 33.
 (c) A person who has operated a business in violation of an order to suspend operations under Article 41.

Article 57
A person to whom any of the following applies shall be sentenced to imprisonment of up to six months, a fine of up to five hundred thousand yen, or both.
 (a) A person who has divulged secret information in violation of Article 6, Article 14-13, Paragraph 1, or Article 38.
 (b) A person who has divulged LREA examination questions in advance or improperly scored an LREA examination.
 (c) A person who has violated an order to suspend practical training operations under Article 14-16.
 (d) A person who has obtained LREA registration by deceit or other improper means.
 (e) A person who has performed real estate appraisal in violation of Article 36, Paragraph 1.
 (f) A person who has performed real estate appraisal, or appraisal and related operations, in violation of Article 36, Paragraph 2.
 (g) A person who has performed appraisal and related operations in violation of prohibition under Article 40, Paragraph 1 or 2.

Article 58
A person to whom any of the following applies shall be sentenced to a fine of up to three hundred thousand yen.
 (a) A person who has discontinued all practical training operations without obtaining approval under Article 14-10.
 (b) A person who has failed to keep a register, failed to enter the required information in the ledger, made false entries in the ledger, or failed to retain the ledger, in violation of Article 14-17.
 (c) A person who has failed to submit a report or submitted a falsified report when asked to submit a report under Article 14-19.
 (d) A person who has refused, obstructed, or challenged an inspection under Article 14-20.
 (e) A person who has failed to submit a report under Article 14-22 or submitted a falsified report.
 (f) A person who has closed or opened an office in violation of Article 26, Paragraph 1.

第6章　罰　則

第56条　次の各号のいずれかに該当する者は、1年以下の懲役若しくは100万円以下の罰金に処し、又はこれを併科する。
一　偽りその他不正の手段により不動産鑑定業者の登録を受けた者
二　第33条の規定に違反して、不動産鑑定業を営んだ者
三　第41条の規定による業務の停止の命令に違反して、業務を営んだ者

第57条　次の各号のいずれかに該当する者は、6月以下の懲役若しくは50万円以下の罰金に処し、又はこれを併科する。
一　第6条、第14条の13第1項又は第38条の規定に違反して、秘密を漏らした者
二　不動産鑑定士試験に関し、事前に試験問題を漏らし、又は不正の採点をした者
三　第14条の16の規定による実務修習業務の停止の命令に違反した者
四　偽りその他不正の手段により不動産鑑定士の登録を受けた者
五　第36条第1項の規定に違反して、不動産の鑑定評価を行つた者
六　第36条第2項の規定に違反して、不動産の鑑定評価又は鑑定評価等業務を行わせた者
七　第40条第1項又は第2項の規定による禁止の処分に違反して、鑑定評価等業務を行つた者

第58条　次の各号のいずれかに該当する者は、30万円以下の罰金に処する。
一　第14条の10の許可を受けないで、実務修習業務の全部を廃止した者
二　第14条の17の規定に違反して帳簿を備えず、帳簿に記載せず、若しくは帳簿に虚偽の記載をし、又は帳簿を保存しなかつた者
三　第14条の19の規定による報告を求められて、報告をせず、又は虚偽の報告をした者
四　第14条の20の規定による検査を拒み、妨げ、又は忌避した者
五　第14条の22の規定による報告をせず、又は虚偽の報告をした者
六　第26条第1項の規定に違反して、事務所を廃止し、又は設けた者
七　第27条第1項の規定に違反して、変更の登録を申請せず、又は虚偽の申請をした者
八　第28条の規定に違反して、書類の提出を怠り、又は虚偽の記載をして書類を提出した者
九　第45条第1項の規定による報告を求められて、その報告をせず、若しくは虚偽の報告をし、又は同項の規定による立入検査を拒み、妨げ、若しくは忌避した者
十　第51条の規定に違反して、不動産鑑定士の名称を用いた者

(g) A person who has failed to apply for a change registration or submitted a falsified application, in violation of Article 27, Paragraph 1.
(h) A person who has failed to submit documentation or submitted documentation containing false statements, in violation of Article 28.
(i) A person who has failed to submit a report or submitted a falsified report when asked to submit a report under Article 45, Paragraph 1, or who has refused, obstructed, or challenged an on-site inspection under the same paragraph.
(j) A person who has used the name of LREA in violation of Article 51.

Article 59
If a representative of a corporation, or an agent, employee, or other individual engaged by a corporation or person, has committed an act violating Article 56, Article 57, Item (f), or Article 58, Items (f) through (i) with regard to the operations of that corporation or person, then in addition to punitive measures for the violator, the corporation or person will also be fined under the relevant article.

Article 60
An administrative fine of up to two hundred thousand yen shall be imposed on any person who has failed to retain financial statements, etc., failed to enter the necessary information, or entered falsified information in the financial statements, etc. in violation of Article 14-11, Paragraph 1, or who has refused a request under any item of Paragraph 2 of that article.

Article 61
An administrative fine of up to one hundred thousand yen shall be imposed on any person who has violated Article 19, Paragraph 1 or Article 29, Paragraph 1.

Supplementary Provisions
(Omitted)

第59条　法人の代表者又は法人若しくは人の代理人、使用人その他の従業者が、その法人又は人の業務に関し、第56条、第57条第6号又は前条第6号から第9号までの違反行為をしたときは、その行為者を罰するほか、その法人又は人に対しても、各本条の罰金刑を科する。

第60条　第14条の11第1項の規定に違反して財務諸表等を備えて置かず、財務諸表等に記載すべき事項を記載せず、若しくは虚偽の記載をし、又は正当な理由がないのに同条第2項各号の規定による請求を拒んだ者は、20万円以下の過料に処する。

第61条　第19条第1項又は第29条第1項の規定に違反した者は、10万円以下の過料に処する。

附　則　省略

V-2

Land Price Publication Act

June 23, 1969 Law No.49
Final revision: June 2, 2004 Law No.66

地価公示法

昭和44年6月23日法律第49号
最終改正：平成16年6月2日法律第66号

(note) Land Price Publication Act is the same as Public Notice of Land Prices in Ⅰ.

Chapter 1. General Provisions

(Purpose)
Article 1   The Act aims to provide the guideline for land price in open market transactions and to help estimate appropriate compensation for land expropriation for public use and, in all, to contribute to set appropriate land price through the selection of the representative land in city and its outskirts, etc., and the publication of its fair price.

(The Responsibility of Parties in Land Transaction)
Article 1-2   Parties in land transaction in a city and its outskirts, etc., shall refer to the published price of the representative land that has a similar use value to the concerned land as the price criteria.

第1章　総則

（目的）
第1条　この法律は、都市及びその周辺の地域等において、標準地を選定し、その正常な価格を公示することにより、一般の土地の取引価格に対して指標を与え、及び公共の利益となる事業の用に供する土地に対する適正な補償金の額の算定等に資し、もつて適正な地価の形成に寄与することを目的とする。

（土地の取引を行なう者の責務）
第1条の2　都市及びその周辺の地域等において、土地の取引を行なう者は、取引の対象土地に類似する利用価値を有すると認められる標準地について公示された価格を指標として取引を行なうよう努めなければならない。

Chapter 2. The Procedure of Publication of Land Price

(Decision on the Representative Land Price, etc.)
Article 2.1 The Land Appraisal Committee shall annually have more than two licensed real estate appraisers and/or licensed assistant real estate appraisers according to the Ordinance of the Ministry of Land, Infrastructure, and Transport (MLIT) to appraise the representative land in the city planning area (prescribed by Article 4.2 of the Act of City Planning Area, except the restricted areas designated by Article 12.1 of the National Land Use Planning Act.) The Committee shall, then, inspect the result and decide the fair price of the concerned representative land per unit area on the certain date after making necessary adjustment. The Committee shall publish this fair price.

2.2 "The fair price" in the previous provision is defined as the price in a normal transaction of a piece of land (Except the transaction for farmland, pasture, and forest. However, the transaction for farmland, pasture, and forest in order to convert them into other uses is included.) In the cases where buildings and other structures are on the concerned land, or surface rights or other rights restrict the use of the concerned land or income from it, the fair price shall be decided without considering above-mentioned conditions.

(The Selection of the Representative Land)
Article 3 Under the Ordinance of the MLIT, the Land Appraisal Committee shall select a group of lands that have normal use and surroundings in the areas of similar use value ased on natural and social conditions as the representative land for Article 2.1.

(The Criteria for the Appraisal of the Representative Land)
Article 4 In appraising the representative land under Article 2.1, licensed real estate appraisers and/or licensed assistant real estate appraiser shall, under the Ordinance of the MLIT, consider the amount estimated from transaction price and rent of adjacent and similar lands and the estimated cost to develop the land of similar utility to the concerned land.

(The Submission of the Appraisal Report)
Article 5 The licensed real estate appraisers and/or licensed assistant real estate appraisers who conducted appraisal under Article 2.1 shall submit the appraisal report including the estimated price and other details prescribed by the Ordinance of the MLIT to the Land Appraisal Committee.

(The Publication of the Representative Land Price)
Article 6 The Land Appraisal Committee shall publish the subjects listed below in the government official newsletters promptly after the decision on the fair price per unit area of the representative land under Article 2.1.

第２章　地価の公示の手続

(標準地の価格の判定等)
第２条　土地鑑定委員会は、都市計画法（昭和43年法律第100号）第４条第２項に規定する都市計画区域その他の土地取引が相当程度見込まれるものとして国土交通省令で定める区域（国土利用計画法（昭和49年法律第92号）第12条第１項の規定により指定された規制区域を除く。以下「公示区域」という。）内の標準地について、毎年１回、国土交通省令で定めるところにより、２人以上の不動産鑑定士の鑑定評価を求め、その結果を審査し、必要な調整を行つて、一定の基準日における当該標準地の単位面積当たりの正常な価格を判定し、これを公示するものとする。
２　前項の「正常な価格」とは、土地について、自由な取引が行なわれるとした場合におけるその取引（農地、採草放牧地又は森林の取引（農地、採草放牧地及び森林以外のものとするための取引を除く。）を除く。）において通常成立すると認められる価格（当該土地に建物その他の定着物がある場合又は当該土地に関して地上権その他当該土地の使用若しくは収益を制限する権利が存する場合には、これらの定着物又は権利が存しないものとして通常成立すると認められる価格）をいう。

(標準地の選定)
第３条　前条第１項の標準地は、土地鑑定委員会が、国土交通省令で定めるところにより、自然的及び社会的条件からみて類似の利用価値を有すると認められる地域において、土地の利用状況、環境等が通常と認められる一団の土地について選定するものとする。

(標準地についての鑑定評価の基準)
第４条　不動産鑑定士は、第２条第１項の規定により標準地の鑑定評価を行うにあたつては、国土交通省令で定めるところにより、近傍類地の取引価格から算定される推定の価格、近傍類地の地代等から算定される推定の価格及び同等の効用を有する土地の造成に要する推定の費用の額を勘案してこれを行わなければならない。

(鑑定評価書の提出)
第５条　第２条第１項の規定により標準地の鑑定評価を行つた不動産鑑定士は、土地鑑定委員会に対し、鑑定評価額その他の国土交通省令で定める事項を記載した鑑定評価書を提出しなければならない。

(標準地の価格等の公示)
第６条　土地鑑定委員会は、第２条第１項の規定により標準地の単位面積当たりの正常な価格を判定したときは、すみやかに、次に掲げる事項を官報で公示しなければならない。
　一　標準地の所在の郡、市、区、町村及び字並びに地番

(1) The location and lot number of the representative land, including section, village, town, ward, city, and county
(2) The price of the representative land per unit area and the date when the decision was made
(3) The acreage and description of the representative land
(4) The current use of the representative land and its adjacent land
(5) The other items prescribed by the Ordinance of the MLIT

(Sending and Peruse of the Official Record, etc., of the Published Price)
Article 7.1 When the Committee made the publication under the previous provision, it shall promptly send the document with published information and map of the each concerned representative land on the same prefecture where the concerned representative land is located, to the heads of the municipal government of the concerned village, town, city (including special ward of Tokyo Metropolis and ward under the Local Autonomy Law, Article 252-19.1. Same as under the following provision).

7.2 The head of the concerned municipal government of the village, town, and city shall, under the Cabinet Orders, provide the document and map of the representative land for public peruse at the each local government office.

7.3 The documentation and procedure recognized as duty of the each municipal government by the previous provision, shall be classified as category 1 of statutory entrusted affairs under Article 2.9 (1) of the Local Autonomy Law.

二　標準地の単位面積当たりの価格及び価格判定の基準日
三　標準地の地積及び形状
四　標準地及びその周辺の土地の利用の現況
五　その他国土交通省令で定める事項

(公示に係る事項を記載した書面等の送付及び閲覧)
第7条　土地鑑定委員会は、前条の規定による公示をしたときは、すみやかに、関係市町村（都の特別区の存する区域にあつては特別区、地方自治法（昭和22年法律第67号）第252条の19第1項の指定都市にあつては当該市の区。次項において同じ。）の長に対して、公示した事項のうち当該市町村が属する都道府県に存する標準地に係る部分を記載した書面及び当該標準地の所在を表示する図面を送付しなければならない。
2　関係市町村の長は、政令で定めるところにより、前項の図書を当該市町村の事務所において一般の閲覧に供しなければならない。
3　前項の規定により市町村（特別区を含む。）が処理することとされている事務は、地方自治法第2条第9項第1号に規定する第1号法定受託事務とする。

Chapter 3. The Validity of the Published Price

(The Working Rule for the Land Appraisal by licensed Real Estate Appraisers etc.)

Article 8   In appraising the land in the city planning area of Article 2.1, licensed real estate appraisers and/or licensed assistant real estate appraisers shall employ the published price of the representative land under Article 6 as the criteria to estimate the fair price (prescribed by Article 2.2) of the concerned land.

(The Working Rule for Estimating Land Price to acquire the land to use for Public works)

Article 9   Parties in the business entitled to expropriate land under the Land Expropriation Act and other laws shall employ the published price as the criteria to decide the price (including cash consideration to nullify the surface right and other rights that restrict the use of the concerned land or income from it when they purchase the concerned land in the city planning area under Article 2.1 for their business use (or when they purchase the land and nullify the rights in case that there are surface rights or other rights that restrict the use of the concerned land or income from it.)

(The Working Rule for Estimating the Compensation Price for the Land Expropriation)

Article 10   In order to calculate the appropriate price for the land under the in the city planning area of Article 2.1, under Article 71 of the Land Expropriation Act, at the time of notifying the approval to the project, they shall consider the land price estimated from the published price as the criteria.

(The Meaning of Published Price as the Criteria)

Article 11   For Article 8, 9, and 10, appraisers shall employ published price as the criteria for appraising the concerned land. This means that the factors such as location, acreage, and surroundings that affect objective value of land shall be compared to each other between the concerned land and one, two, or more representative lands of similar use value, and based on this comparison, the estimated price of the concerned land shall be balanced with the published price of the chosen representative land. In the case that a building or structure exist on the concerned land, or surface rights or other rights restrict the use of the concerned land or income from it, the price shall be estimated without considering these conditions or restrictions.

第3章　公示価格の効力

(不動産鑑定士の土地についての鑑定評価の準則)
第8条　不動産鑑定士は、公示区域内の土地について鑑定評価を行う場合において、当該土地の正常な価格(第2条第2項に規定する正常な価格をいう。)を求めるときは、第6条の規定により公示された標準地の価格(以下「公示価格」という。)を規準としなければならない。

(公共事業の用に供する土地の取得価格の算定の準則)
第9条　土地収用法(昭和26年法律第219号)その他の法律によつて土地を収用することができる事業を行う者は、公示区域内の土地を当該事業の用に供するため取得する場合(当該土地に関して地上権その他当該土地の使用又は収益を制限する権利が存する場合においては、当該土地を取得し、かつ、当該権利を消滅させる場合)において、当該土地の取得価格(当該土地に関して地上権その他当該土地の使用又は収益を制限する権利が存する場合においては、当該権利を消滅させるための対価を含む。)を定めるときは、公示価格を規準としなければならない。

(収用する土地に対する補償金の額の算定の準則)
第10条　土地収用法第71条の規定により、公示区域内の土地について、当該土地に対する同法第71条の事業の認定の告示の時における相当な価格を算定するときは、公示価格を規準として算定した当該土地の価格を考慮しなければならない。

(公示価格を規準とすることの意義)
第11条　前3条の場合において、公示価格を規準とするとは、対象土地の価格(当該土地に建物その他の定着物がある場合又は当該土地に関して地上権その他当該土地の使用若しくは収益を制限する権利が存する場合には、これらの定着物又は権利が存しないものとして成立すると認められる価格)を求めるに際して、当該対象土地とこれに類似する利用価値を有すると認められる1又は2以上の標準地との位置、地積、環境等の土地の客観的価値に作用する諸要因についての比較を行ない、その結果に基づき、当該標準地の公示価格と当該対象土地の価格との間に均衡を保たせることをいう。

Chapter 4. Land Appraisal Committee

(The Establishment of the Committee, etc.)
Article 12   The Land Appraisal Committee (referred as the Committee below) shall be established under the MLIT in order to carry out the authorization by the Act and the Act concerning the Real Estate Appraisal (including corresponding application by the Act concerning the Special Examination for Real Estate Appraiser and Assistant Real Appraiser, Article 12.)
12.2   The Committee can ask for information, opinion, explanation, and other necessary items that are essential to conduct the Committee's duties, to the heads of concerned administrative and municipal institutions.

Article 13   Deleted

(Organization)
Article 14.1   The Committee shall consist of seven members.
14.2   Six members shall be the part-time members.

(The Committee Members)
Article 15.1   The Committee members shall be appointed by the Minister of the MLIT from those who have both knowledge and experiences of real estate appraisal and land systems. They shall be approved by both the House of Representatives and the House of Councillors as well.
15.2   When the Committee member's term was completed or a position becomes vacant but the approval from both Houses is unavailable due to the closed Diet sessions or dissolution of the House Representatives, the Minister of the MNLIT can appoint members from those with the qualification, in spite of the previous provision.
15.3   A member who was appointed by the Minister of the MLIT under the previous provision shall be approved by both Houses in the first Diet session after their appointment. If he/she is not approved by the Houses, the Minister of the MLIT shall dismiss the appointed person.
15.4   One of the conditions listed below shall disqualify a Committee member.
(1)   Bankruptcy without restoration of rights
(2)   Execution of penalty (the confinement or above)
15.5   The term of a member shall be three years. The term of a supplementary member shall be the rest of the former member's.
15.6   A member can be appointed another term.
15.7   A member shall leave the Committee when he/she becomes disqualified by one of the conditions prescribed by Article 15.4.
15.8   With the approval of both Houses, the Minister of the MLIT can dismiss a Commit-

第4章　土地鑑定委員会

(設置等)
第12条　この法律及び不動産の鑑定評価に関する法律(昭和38年法律第152号。不動産鑑定士特例試験及び不動産鑑定士補特例試験に関する法律(昭和45年法律第15号)第12条において準用する場合を含む。)に基づく権限を行わせるため、国土交通省に、土地鑑定委員会(以下「委員会」という。)を置く。
2　委員会は、その所掌事務を行うため必要があると認めるときは、関係行政機関の長及び関係地方公共団体に対し、資料の提出、意見の開陳、説明その他必要な協力を求めることができる。

第13条　削除

(組織)
第14条　委員会は、委員7人をもつて組織する。
2　委員のうち6人は、非常勤とする。

(委員)
第15条　委員は、不動産の鑑定評価に関する事項又は土地に関する制度について学識経験を有する者のうちから、両議院の同意を得て、国土交通大臣が任命する。
2　委員の任期が満了し、又は欠員を生じた場合において、国会の閉会又は衆議院の解散のために両議院の同意を得ることができないときは、国土交通大臣は、前項の規定にかかわらず、同項に定める資格を有する者のうちから、委員を任命することができる。
3　前項の場合においては、任命後最初の国会において両議院の事後の承認を得なければならない。この場合において、両議院の事後の承認が得られないときは、国土交通大臣は、直ちに、その委員を罷免しなければならない。
4　次の各号のいずれかに該当する者は、委員となることができない。
　一　破産者で復権を得ないもの
　二　禁錮以上の刑に処せられた者
5　委員の任期は、3年とする。ただし、補欠の委員の任期は、前任者の残任期間とする。
6　委員は、再任されることができる。
7　委員は、第4項各号の一に該当するに至つた場合においては、その職を失うものとする。
8　国土交通大臣は、委員が心身の故障のため職務の執行ができないと認めるとき、又は委員に職務上の義務違反その他委員たるに適しない行為があると認めるときは、両議院の同意を得て、これを罷免することができる。

tee member who is unable to carry out his/her duties due to physical or mental disorder, or who is proved to be in the breach of his/her duties or have performed unsuitably as a member.

(The Chairperson of the Committee)
Article 16.1   The Committee shall have a chairperson who is mutually elected.
16.2   The chairperson shall direct and represent the Committee.
16.3   In the case when the chairperson is unable to perform his/her duties due to an accident, the member appointed by the chairperson beforehand shall substitute for the chairperson and carry out his/her duties.

(Meeting)
Article 17.1   The chairperson shall call for the committee meeting.
17.2   The Committee shall not convene and make decisions, unless the chairperson and more than three members are present.
17.3   The decision for proceedings shall be made by majority of the present members. When the votes are equally divided, the chairperson shall make a decision.
17.4   In the case when the chairperson is unable to perform his/her duties due to an accident, for Article 17.2, the substitute member prescribed by Article 16.3 shall be regarded as the chairperson.

(The Duties of the Member)
Article 18.1   The member shall keep secret, confidential information that comes to his/her knowledge in the course of carrying out his/her duties during and after his/her term.
18.2   A member shall not take a position in a political party or political groups, and shall not participate positively in political activities during the term.
18.3   A fulltime member shall not engage in activities with remuneration, business, or services with monetary profit, except when the Minister of the MLIT gives permission.

(The Compensation for the Members)
Article 19   The compensation for the members shall be prescribed separately by the law.

Article 20   Deleted

(Reference to the Cabinet Orders)
Article 21   The other necessary matters regarding the Committee shall be prescribed by the Cabinet Orders besides prescribed by the Act.

(委員長)
第16条　委員会に委員長を置き、委員の互選によつてこれを定める。
2　委員長は、会務を総理し、委員会を代表する。
3　委員長に事故があるときは、あらかじめその指名する委員が、その職務を代理する。

(会議)
第17条　委員会は、委員長が招集する。
2　委員会は、委員長及び3人以上の委員の出席がなければ、会議を開き、議決をすることができない。
3　委員会の議事は、出席者の過半数でこれを決し、可否同数のときは、委員長の決するところによる。
4　委員長に事故のある場合の第2項の規定の適用については、前条第3項に規定する委員は、委員長とみなす。

(委員の服務)
第18条　委員は、職務上知ることのできた秘密を漏らしてはならない。その職を退いた後も、同様とする。
2　委員は、在任中、政党その他の政治的団体の役員となり、又は積極的に政治運動をしてはならない。
3　常勤の委員は、在任中、国土交通大臣の許可のある場合を除くほか、報酬を得て他の職務に従事し、又は営利事業を営み、その他金銭上の利益を目的とする業務を行つてはならない。

(委員の給与)
第19条　委員の給与は、別に法律で定める。

第20条　削除

(政令への委任)
第21条　この法律に定めるもののほか、委員会に関し必要な事項は、政令で定める。

Chapter 5. Miscellaneous Provisions

(Entry upon the Land)
Article 22.1   One who is ordered or assigned by the Committee or its member to conduct appraising or deciding the price under Article 2.1 or selecting a representative land under Article 3 can enter upon the land occupied by others in order to measure and survey the land to the extent as much as needed.
22.2   One who enters upon the land occupied by others, under the previous provision, shall notify the entry to the occupier by three days before the entry.
22.3   One who enters, under Article 22.1, upon the land occupied by others with buildings or enclosed by fences or railings, etc., shall notice of the entry to the occupiers beforehand.
22.4   One shall not enter upon the land prescribed by the previous provision before sunrise or after sunset, unless the occupier approved.
22.5   The occupier of the land shall not refuse or hinder the entry under Article 22.1 without justifiable excuses.
22.6   One who enters upon the land occupied by others under Article 22.1 shall have the proper identification with him/her and show it when asked for by the concerned party.
22.7   The form of the identification shall be prescribed by the Ordinance of the MLIT.

(The Compensation for Loss Caused by Entry upon the Land)
Article 23.1   The Minister of the MLIT shall compensate for the loss caused by entering upon the land under Article 22.1.
23.2   In order to compensate the loss prescribed by the previous provision, the Minister of the MLIT and the party having loss shall discuss the matter together.
23.3   In a case that the parties of the previous provision are unable to reach settlement, either of the parties can file for a decision to the Expropriation Committee under Article 94.2 of the Land Expropriation Act.

(The Duty of Keeping Secret)
Article 24   The licensed real estate appraiser and/or licensed assistant real estate appraiser who conducted appraisal shall keep secret, confidential information that he/she came to know in the course of appraising without justifiable excuses.

(The Order for Appraisal)
Article 25   The Committee can order licensed real estate appraisers and/or licensed assistant real estate appraisers to appraise representative lands when the Committee recognizes it necessary for Article 2.1.
25.2   The licensed real estate appraiser and licensed assistant real estate appraiser who carried out the appraisal of representative lands under the previously prescribed order

第5章　雑則

（土地の立入り）
第22条　委員又は委員会の命を受けた者若しくは委任を受けた者は、第2条第1項の規定による鑑定評価若しくは価格の判定又は第3条の規定による標準地の選定を行なうために他人の占有する土地に立ち入つて測量又は調査を行なう必要があるときは、その必要の限度において、他人の占有する土地に立ち入ることができる。
2　前項の規定により他人の占有する土地に立ち入ろうとする者は、立ち入ろうとする日の3日前までに、その旨を土地の占有者に通知しなければならない。
3　第1項の規定により、建築物が所在し、又はかき、さく等で囲まれた他人の占有する土地に立ち入ろうとするときは、その立ち入ろうとする者は、立入りの際、あらかじめ、その旨を土地の占有者に告げなければならない。
4　日出前又は日没後においては、土地の占有者の承諾があつた場合を除き、前項に規定する土地に立ち入つてはならない。
5　土地の占有者は、正当な理由がない限り、第1項の規定による立入りを拒み、又は妨げてはならない。
6　第1項の規定により、他人の占有する土地に立ち入ろうとする者は、その身分を示す証明書を携帯し、関係人の請求があつたときは、これを提示しなければならない。
7　前項に規定する証明書の様式は、国土交通省令で定める。

（土地の立入りに伴う損失の補償）
第23条　国土交通大臣は、前条第1項の規定による立入りにより他人に損失を与えたときは、その損失を受けた者に対して、通常生ずべき損失を補償しなければならない。
2　前項の規定による損失の補償については、国土交通大臣と損失を受けた者とが協議しなければならない。
3　前項の規定による協議が成立しないときは、国土交通大臣又は損失を受けた者は、国土交通省令で定めるところにより、収用委員会に土地収用法第94条第2項の規定による裁決を申請することができる。

（秘密を守る義務）
第24条　第2条第1項の規定により標準地の鑑定評価を行つた不動産鑑定士は、正当な理由がなく、その鑑定評価に際して知ることのできた秘密を漏らしてはならない。

（鑑定評価命令）
第25条　委員会は、第2条第1項の鑑定評価のため必要があると認めるときは、不動産鑑定士に対し、標準地の鑑定評価を命ずることができる。
2　前項の規定に基づく命令により標準地の鑑定評価を行つた不動産鑑定士に対しては、国土交通省令で定めるところにより、旅費及び報酬を支給する。

shall be provided with the expense for transportation and remuneration according to the provision of the Ordinance of the MLIT.

(The Exception of the Act concerning Real Estate Appraisal)
Article 26   The appraisal for representative lands by licensed real estate appraisers and/or licensed assistant real estate appraisers under Article 2.1, shall not be included in the appraisal prescribed by the Act concerning Real Estate Appraisal, Article 2.2.

(Examination and Discussion, etc., by The National Land Council)
Article 26-2.1   The National Land Council (NLC) shall examine and discuss the essential matters of real estate appraisal responding to the inquiry by the Minister of the MLIT.
26-2.2   The NLC can deliver opinions on the matters prescribed by the previous provision to the Minister of the MLIT.

(不動産の鑑定評価に関する法律の特例)
第26条　不動産鑑定士が第2条第1項の規定により行う標準地の鑑定評価についての不動産の鑑定評価に関する法律の適用に関しては、当該標準地の鑑定評価は、同法第2条第2項に規定する不動産の鑑定評価に含まれないものとする。

(国土審議会の調査審議等)
第26条の2　国土審議会は、国土交通大臣の諮問に応じ、不動産の鑑定評価に関する重要事項を調査審議する。
2　国土審議会は、前項に規定する重要事項について、国土交通大臣に意見を述べることができる。

Chapter 6. Penal Provisions

Article 27　One who committed one of the crimes listed below shall be penalized with up to six month imprisonment with hard labor, or up to a 50,000 yen fine, or both.
(1) Making false appraisal in estimating the representative land prescribed under Article 2.1
(2) Violation of Article 24; breaking the secret that came to be known while appraising the representative land

Article 28　One who violated Article 22.5, and refused or hindered the entry under Article 25.1 shall be penalized with up to a 100,000 yen fine.

Article 29　When the appraiser who was appointed under Article 25.1 to conduct appraising the representative land neglects to carry out the appraisal without justifiable excuses, or fails to submit the appraisal report under Article 5, he/she shall be penalized with up to a 10,000 yen fine.

Supplementary Provisions
(Omitted)

第6章　罰則

第27条　次の各号のいずれかに該当する者は、6月以下の懲役若しくは50万円以下の罰金に処し、又はこれを併科する。
　一　第2条第1項の規定による標準地の鑑定評価について、虚偽の鑑定評価を行なつた者
　二　第24条の規定に違反して、標準地の鑑定評価に際して知ることのできた秘密を漏らした者

第28条　第22条第5項の規定に違反して、同条第1項の規定による土地の立入りを拒み、又は妨げた者は、50万円以下の罰金に処する。

第29条　第25条第1項の規定により標準地の鑑定評価を命ぜられた者が、正当な理由がなく、鑑定評価を行わないとき、又は第5条に規定する鑑定評価書を提出しないときは、10万円以下の過料に処する。

附則（省略）

V-3

Real Estate Appraisal Standards and Guidance Notes on the Real Estate Appraisal Standards

Revised on July 3, 2002
Final revision: March 31, 2010
Ministry of Land, Infrastructure, Transport and Tourism

不動産鑑定評価基準及び不動産鑑定評価基準運用上の留意事項

平成14年7月3日全部改正
最終改正:平成22年3月31日
国 土 交 通 省

Real Estate Appraisal Standards

GENERAL STANDARDS (GS):

CHAPTER 1. FOUNDATIONS OF REAL ESTATE APPRAISAL ··············254
  Section 1. Real Estate and Its Value ··············254
  Section 2. Characteristics of Real Estate Value ··············254
  Section 3. Appraisal of Real Estate ··············256
  Section 4. Responsibility of LREAs ··············256

CHAPTER 2. USE CATEGORIES AND PHYSICAL DEVELOPMENT & TITLE CATEGORIES OF REAL ESTATE ··············258
  Section 1. Real Estate Use Categories ··············258
  Section 2. Physical Development & Title Categories ··············259

CHAPTER 3. INFLUENCES ON REAL ESTATE VALUE ··············261
  Section 1. General Value Influences ··············261
  Section 2. Area-Specific Value Influences ··············262
  Section 3. Property-Specific Value Influences ··············264

CHAPTER 4. PRINCIPLES OF REAL ESTATE VALUE ··············267

CHAPTER 5. BASIC APPRAISAL PROBLEM ··············269
  Section 1. Identification of the Subject Property ··············269
  Section 2. Identification of the Date of the Value Opinion ··············270
  Section 3. Identification of the Type of Value or Rental Value ··············270

CHAPTER 6. MARKET AREA ANALYSIS AND PROPERTY ANALYSIS ··············273
  Section 1. Market Area Analysis ··············273
  Section 2. Property Analysis ··············276

CHAPTER 7. APPRAISAL METHOD ··············278
  Section 1. Appraisal Approaches for Determining Real Estate Value ··············278
  Section 2. Appraisal Approaches for Determining Real Estate Rental Value ··············289

CHAPTER 8. APPRAISAL PROCESS ··············294
  Section 1. Identification of Basic Appraisal Problem ··············294
  Section 2. Identification of Client, Parties for Submission, and Interests/Ties ··············294
  Section 3. Drafting of a Processing Plan ··············295
  Section 4. Identification of the Subject Property ··············295
  Section 5. Gathering and Organizing of Data ··············295
  Section 6. Review of Data and Analysis of Value Influences ··············296
  Section 7. Application of Appraisal Method ··············296

不動産鑑定評価基準

総　論

第1章　不動産の鑑定評価に関する基本的考察 …………………………………………254
- 第1節　不動産とその価格 ……………………………………………………………254
- 第2節　不動産とその価格の特徴 ……………………………………………………254
- 第3節　不動産の鑑定評価 ……………………………………………………………256
- 第4節　不動産鑑定士の責務 …………………………………………………………256

第2章　不動産の種別及び類型 …………………………………………………………258
- 第1節　不動産の種別 …………………………………………………………………258
- 第2節　不動産の類型 …………………………………………………………………259

第3章　不動産の価格を形成する要因 …………………………………………………261
- 第1節　一般的要因 ……………………………………………………………………261
- 第2節　地域要因 ………………………………………………………………………262
- 第3節　個別的要因 ……………………………………………………………………264

第4章　不動産の価格に関する諸原則 …………………………………………………267

第5章　鑑定評価の基本的事項 …………………………………………………………269
- 第1節　対象不動産の確定 ……………………………………………………………269
- 第2節　価格時点の確定 ………………………………………………………………270
- 第3節　鑑定評価によって求める価格又は賃料の種類の確定 ……………………270

第6章　地域分析及び個別分析 …………………………………………………………273
- 第1節　地域分析 ………………………………………………………………………273
- 第2節　個別分析 ………………………………………………………………………276

第7章　鑑定評価の方式 …………………………………………………………………278
- 第1節　価格を求める鑑定評価の手法 ………………………………………………278
- 第2節　賃料を求める鑑定評価の手法 ………………………………………………289

第8章　鑑定評価の手順 …………………………………………………………………294
- 第1節　鑑定評価の基本的事項の確定 ………………………………………………294
- 第2節　依頼者、提出先及び利害関係等の確認 ……………………………………294
- 第3節　処理計画の策定 ………………………………………………………………295
- 第4節　対象不動産の確認 ……………………………………………………………295
- 第5節　資料の収集及び整理 …………………………………………………………295
- 第6節　資料の検討及び価格形成要因の分析 ………………………………………296
- 第7節　鑑定評価方式の適用 …………………………………………………………296

Section 8. Reconciliation of the Indicated Value or Rent ··296
Section 9. Determination of the Final Opinion of Value ···297
Section 10. Preparation of the Appraisal Report ··297

CHAPTER 9. APPRAISAL REPORT ···298
Section 1. Guidelines for Preparing Appraisal Report ···298
Section 2. Report Contents ··298
Section 3. Addenda to Appraisal Reports ··300

SPECIFIC STANDARDS(SS) :
CHAPTER 1. APPRAISAL OF REAL ESTATE VALUE ··301
Section 1. Land ···301
Section 2. Built-Up Property ···306
Section 3. Buildings ···309

CHAPTER 2. APPRAISAL OF REAL ESTATE RENTAL VALUE ·······························311
Section 1. Building Sites ··311
Section 2. Built-Up Property ··312

CHAPTER 3. APPRAISAL OF REAL ESTATE VALUE SUBJECT TO SECURITIZATION ···313
Section 1. Basic Approach to Securitization-Properties ···313
Section 2. Drafting a Work Plan for the Appraisal ··314
Section 3. Investigating Property-Specific Value Influences acting on the
           Securitization-Property ··315
Section 4. Application of DCF method ··317

第8節	試算価格又は試算賃料の調整	296
第9節	鑑定評価額の決定	297
第10節	鑑定評価報告書の作成	297

第9章　鑑定評価報告書 ……298
第1節　鑑定評価報告書の作成指針 ……298
第2節　記載事項 ……298
第3節　附属資料 ……300

各　論
第1章　価格に関する鑑定評価 ……301
第1節　土地 ……301
第2節　建物及びその敷地 ……306
第3節　建物 ……309

第2章　賃料に関する鑑定評価 ……311
第1節　宅地 ……311
第2節　建物及びその敷地 ……312

第3章　証券化対象不動産の価格に関する鑑定評価 ……313
第1節　証券化対象不動産の鑑定評価の基本的姿勢 ……313
第2節　処理計画の策定 ……314
第3節　証券化対象不動産の個別的要因の調査等 ……315
第4節　ＤＣＦ法の適用等 ……317

V - 3. Real Estate Appraisal Standards

Guidance Nates on the Real Estate Appraisal Standards

Guidance Note I on GS. Chap. 2 : USE CATEGORIES AND PHYSICAL DEVELOPMENT & TITLE CATEGORIES OF REAL ESTATE ·················324

Guidance Note II on GS. Chap. 3 : INFLUENCES ON REAL ESTATE VALUE ···············326
  1. Property-Specific Value Influences on Land ·················326
  2. Property-Specific Value Influences on Buildings·················327
  3. Property-Specific Value Influences on Built-Up Property ·················327

Guidance Note III on GS. Chap. 5 : BASIC APPRAISAL PROBLEM ·················328
  1. Identification of the Subject Property ·················328
  2. Identification of the Date of the Value Opinion ·················329
  3. Identification of the Type of Value to be Determined by the Appraisal ·················329

Guidance Note IV on GS. Chap. 6 : MARKET AREA ANALYSIS AND PROPERTY ANALYSIS ·················332
  1. Performing the Market Area Analysis ·················332
  2. Performing the Property Analysis ·················334

Guidance Note V on GS. Chap. 7 :   APPRAISAL METHOD ·················335
  1. Appraisal Approaches for Determining Real Estate Value ·················335
  2. Appraisal Approaches for Determining Rent ·················346

Guidance Note VI on GS. Chap. 8 : APPRAISAL PROCESS ·················347
  1. Identification of Client, Parties for Submission, and Interests/Ties ·················347
  2. Review of Data and Analysis of Value Influences ·················348

Guidance Note VII on SS. Chap. 1 : APPRAISAL OF REAL ESTATE VALUE ·················349
  1. Building Sites ·················349
  2. Built-Up Property ·················352

Guidance Note VIII on SS. Chap. 2 : APPRAISAL OF REAL ESTATE RENTAL VALUE ·················354
  1. Building Sites ·················354
  2. Built-Up Property ·················354

Guidance Note IX on SS. Chap. 3 : APPRAISAL OF REAL ESTATE VALUE SUBJECT TO SECURITIZATION ·················355
  1. Guidance on Basic approach regarding securitization properties ·················355
  2. Guidance on Drafting a processing plan ·················355
  3. Guidance on Investigating property-specific influences on the securitization property ·················355
  4. Guidance on Application of the DCF method ·················356

不動産鑑定評価基準運用上の留意事項

Ⅰ 「総論第2章　不動産の種別及び類型」について ……………………………324

Ⅱ 「総論第3章　不動産の価格を形成する要因」について ………………………326
　1．土地に関する個別的要因について …………………………………326
　2．建物に関する個別的要因について …………………………………327
　3．建物及びその敷地に関する個別的要因について …………………327

Ⅲ 「総論第5章　鑑定評価の基本的事項」について ………………………………328
　1．対象不動産の確定について …………………………………………328
　2．価格時点の確定について ……………………………………………329
　3．鑑定評価によって求める価格の確定について ……………………329

Ⅳ 「総論第6章　地域分析及び個別分析」について ………………………………332
　1．地域分析の適用について ……………………………………………332
　2．個別分析の適用について ……………………………………………334

Ⅴ 「総論第7章　鑑定評価の方式」について ………………………………………335
　1．価格を求める鑑定評価の手法について ……………………………335
　2．賃料を求める鑑定評価の手法について ……………………………346

Ⅵ 「総論第8章　鑑定評価の手順」について ………………………………………347
　1．依頼者、提出先及び利害関係等の確認について …………………347
　2．資料の検討及び価格形成要因の分析について ……………………348

Ⅶ 「各論第1章　価格に関する鑑定評価」について ………………………………349
　1．宅地について …………………………………………………………349
　2．建物及びその敷地について …………………………………………352

Ⅷ 「各論第2章　賃料に関する鑑定評価」について ………………………………354
　1．宅地について …………………………………………………………354
　2．建物及びその敷地について …………………………………………354

Ⅸ 「各論第3章　証券化対象不動産の価格に関する鑑定評価」について …………355
　1．証券化対象不動産の基本姿勢について ……………………………355
　2．処理計画の策定について ……………………………………………355
　3．証券化対象不動産の個別的要因の調査について …………………355
　4．ＤＣＦ法の適用等について …………………………………………356

GENERAL STANDARDS (GS)

CHAPTER 1. FOUNDATIONS OF REAL ESTATE APPRAISAL

It is of foremost importance for the Licensed Real Estate Appraiser (LREA) to fully understand what is involved in the appraisal of real estate, why appraisals are necessary, what role appraisal fulfills in the economy, and what is required of LREAs and LREA candidates.

Section 1. Real Estate and Its Value
Real estate ordinarily refers to land and improvements upon the land. Because of its utility, land is the indispensable basis of all human activity. Real estate reflects the relationship between the various uses people make of the land and the lives and activities of people. The relationship takes concrete configuration in the manner in which real estate is composed and the manner in which it contributes to human needs.

The interaction of physical, social, economic and governmental factors helps determine the configuration of real estate, which accounts for its economic value. The economic value of real estate in turn represents the main criterion in the selection of its optimal configuration.

The value of real estate is typically indicated in terms of the economic value or monetary amount that results from the interaction of the following elements:
  (1) the recognized utility of that real estate,
  (2) the relative scarcity of that real estate, and
  (3) the effective demand for that real estate.

The economic value of real estate is basically determined by physical, social, economic and governmental factors that influence the above three elements. The relationship between real estate value and these four factors has a dual nature, in that the value of real estate is formed under the influence of these factors while at the same time value itself exerts an influence on these factors since it also becomes a criterion in the selection of real estate.

Section 2. Characteristics of Real Estate Value
Although the degree to which real estate contributes to the lives and activities of citizens is expressed as its specific value, land has special characteristics that set it apart from other ordinary assets. Included among these characteristics are:
  (1) fixity of geographical location, immovability, durability, finite nature of supply, and non-fungibility ; physically speaking, land parcels cannot be substituted for or interchanged with one another.
  (2) changeable social and economic utility and status (potential uses may be competitive or complementary; uses may also be changed), and physical adaptability (land parcels can be divided or consolidated).

The social and economic utility of real estate depends on whether the characteristics of a land parcel meet the specific physical and socio-economic requirements of the intended use. The type of use and the social and economic utility of the real estate change according to changes in these requirements.

In addition, because all real estate shares common physical and socio-economic attributes, each real estate product represents a component of a regional or local market, depending upon or complementing other real estate products in that market, competing with or supporting similar real estate products in that market, and demonstrating its social and economic utility through these relationships.

Although various types of regional and local real estate markets differ according to their size, composition, and functions, all markets are identified in terms of their land use, and premised on the relationship to specific physical and socio-economic requirements in the same manner as individual real estate products. While regional and local markets have characteristics that distinguish them from other regional and local markets, they also maintain a mutual relationship with markets in other regions, and occupy a social and economic ranking through that mutual relationship.

Because of the special characteristics of real estate, real estate value can be distinguished from the value of other ordinary assets.

(1) The value of real estate represents value in exchange. But real estate value is also indicated by rent paid as compensation for the rights to occupy and use real estate. A correlation between value in exchange and rent can be observed in the relationship between capital investment and dividends.

(2) The value of real estate reflects compensation paid for the ownership interest in a fee simple. The right to use or occupy a leased fee estate can be leased for compensation in the form of rent, which represents economic profit to the lessor. In situations where two or more property rights pertain to, or lessor profits derive from, the same real estate, the value (or rental value) can be estimated for each property right and lessor profit.

(3) The regional or local market for a real estate product is not static, but rather in a state of continuous change, expanding or contracting, concentrating or dispersing, growing or declining. Judging whether or not the use of real estate is optimal requires continuous review with respect to whether or not the real estate is able to maintain optimal utility over the passage of time, even if it may currently be under optimal use. Thus, the value (or rent) of real estate normally depends on long-term considerations, extending from the past into the future. The current value (or rent) is an extension of yesterday, a reflection of tomorrow, and in a process of continuous change.

(4) The sale price of real estate is normally formed on the basis of the specific circumstances of the transaction. Moreover, the sale price is also influenced by the individual attributes of the real estate. It may be extremely difficult for ordinary persons to determine the market value of real estate from sales prices. Thus, the appraisal activities of expert LREAs are essential for determining the market value of real estate.

Section 3. Appraisal of Real Estate

Because the characteristics of real estate differ from those of other ordinary assets, it is necessary to rely on the activities of appraisers to determine its fair value (or market value).

Real estate appraisal involves estimation of the economic value of the subject real estate in terms of a monetary amount. This process consists of determining an indication of the level of value and/or rent that the real estate is capable of sustaining within a series of value parameters. It comprises the following steps:

(1) gaining an accurate perception of the real estate to be appraised;
(2) adequately gathering and organizing all required data;
(3) fully understanding those factors that form the value of the real estate along with those principles relating to real estate value;
(4) applying appraisal techniques while;
(5) analyzing all relevant information that has been gathered and organized, and considering the effects of physical, social, economic and governmental factors on the subject real estate; and finally
(6) reaching a final judgment regarding the economic value of the subject property in terms of a monetary amount.

How well this process is performed depends on the abilities of the person carrying out the successive stages of the appraisal as well as the extent to which those abilities have been applied. In addition, it also depends on the quality of the gathering and organization of requisite data and the degree of skill in analyzing and interpreting those data. Thus, appraisals can only be rationally and objectively performed when they are done by skilled specialists, having sophisticated knowledge, extensive experience and proven judgmental skills, and who are also able to apply these capabilities in a systematic and comprehensive manner.

The objective of real estate appraisal is to estimate a fair value, or indication of the probable market value of real estate in a market rationally operating under a given set of actual economic circumstances. When performed by skilled experts as exemplified by the professional work of LREAs, a real estate appraisal can be considered to be the judgment or opinion of an expert with respect to real estate value.

Since real estate appraisal also reflects the fair or equitable value of the subject property within a series of value parameters, its social and public significance can be considered to be extremely broad.

Section 4. Responsibility of LREAs

Land utilization and transactions involving land should be conducted in the spirit of the stipulations pertaining to land in the *Basic Land Act*. In particular, land should not become the target of speculative transactions. LREAs must conduct real estate appraisals in compliance with this stipulation.

LREAs are recognized by the Real Estate Appraisal Act as being persons charged with the appraisal of real estate, who have the status of capable and knowledgeable specialists, and who have been granted that status by demonstrating specific qualifications. Thus, LREAs are required to fulfill the trust and expectations of society. They must understand the social and public significance of real estate appraisal, be aware of their own responsibility, and perform their appraisal activities in an accurate and sincere manner.

In order to accomplish this, LREAs have to conduct real estate appraisals impartially in accordance with proper moral conduct and stipulations of the law; they must not be engaged in any acts that would damage the trust society has vested in them as specialized professionals. In addition, LREAs and LREA candidates must not disclose to other persons any confidential matters ascertained during the course of fulfilling their duties without proper cause, and must strive to uphold their reputation by strictly observing the guidelines indicated below.

(1) Since accurate appraisals can only be developed through the systematic integration of sophisticated knowledge, extensive experience and proven judgmental skills, efforts must be made to improve appraisal skills through continuous study and training.

(2) Not only must appraisers be able to provide clients with easily understandable and impartial explanations of appraisal results, but practical efforts should also be taken to raise the level of trust in real estate appraisals by educating the public with respect to real estate appraisal and the practice thereof.

(3) In undertaking a real estate appraisal, the appraiser should maintain a fair and reasonable attitude regardless of his / her own self interests or any other reasons.

(4) In performing a real estate appraisal, a professional specialist must take special care to consider every detail.

(5) In the case of appraisal assignments that are thought to exceed the limits of one's own capabilities or which involve associations or special interests that might impair obtaining a fair or impartial appraisal, the appraiser should, as a matter of principle, not accept such appraisal assignments.

V - 3. Real Estate Appraisal Standards

CHAPTER 2. USE CATEGORIES AND PHYSICAL DEVELOPMENT & TITLE CATEGORIES OF REAL ESTATE

In the appraisal of real estate, it is necessary to analyze the characteristics of the market area in which the subject real estate is located. It is also important to identify the use and physical development & relevant legal title of the subject real estate based on the market area characteristics of the area.

Thus, the identification of real estate is a dual concept, comprising a use category and a physical development & title category. Since these two categories essentially determine the economic value of real estate, it is only possible to conduct an accurate appraisal of real estate after first analyzing both categories.

The *use category* of real estate refers to real estate as classified with respect to one of three broad land uses, while the *physical development & title category* of real estate refers to real estate as classified according to its physical state of development and legal title and interests (i.e., freehold, leased fee, leasehold, etc.).

Section 1. Real Estate Use Categories
I Categories Describing the General Land Use in a Area

Categories describing the general land use in a district or area are divided into *building site areas, agricultural areas* and *forestland areas.*

Building site areas refer to areas, which make up lots for buildings and structures used for living, commercial activities and industrial production. The use of building sites must qualify as the rational use of a site in terms of physical, social, economic and governmental criteria. Building site areas can be further broken down into *residential areas, commercial areas* and *industrial areas*. In turn, residential areas, commercial areas and industrial areas may be further broken down according to their size, specific characteristics and functions.

Agricultural areas refer to areas used for agricultural production, i.e., for activities involving cultivation. The use of agricultural sites must be the rational use of a site in terms of physical, social, economic and governmental criteria.

Forestland areas refer to areas used for forestry production, i.e., for activities involving the planting and growing of trees, bamboo or special forest products. The use of forestland areas must be the rational use of the land in terms of physical, social, economic and governmental criteria.

Furthermore, it should be noted that some building site areas, agricultural areas and forestland areas may be undergoing transition from one use category to another use category. Some building site areas and agricultural areas may also be undergoing transition from one use sub-category to another use sub-category within each classification.

II Land Use Categories

Land use categories are identified according to the use category of the district or area. These are divided into building sites, agricultural land, forestland, sites with interim use, and lots in a transitional area. Land use categories may be further subdivided into use sub-categories in each of the classifications.

Building sites refer to land located in a building site area, which may be further broken down into residential, commercial, and industrial land. Residential land refers to land located in a residential area; commercial land refers to land located in a commercial area; and industrial land refers to land located in an industrial area.

Agricultural land refers to land located in an agricultural area.

Forestland refers to land located in a forestland area (excluding standing trees and bamboo).

Sites with interim use refer to land located in an area undergoing transition from one use category to a different use category. Interim use areas are divided into building sites with an interim use, agricultural land with an interim use, forestland with an interim use and so on.

Lots in a transitional area refer to land located in a building site area or agricultural area that is undergoing transition from one use sub-category to a different use sub-category.

Section 2. Physical Development & Title Categories

The following provides examples of the classification of both building sites and built-up properties according to their physical development & title categories.

I Building Sites

Building sites are classified as 1) vacant land, 2) land portion of built-up property, 3) leasehold interests in land, 4) leased fee interests in land, and 5) sectional superficies (air/underground rights).

Vacant land refers to building sites on which no buildings or other improvements stand and which are not subject to any legal or deed restrictions. (Editor's Note: vacant land connotes freehold ownership of land with no buildings or restrictions to it.)

The land portion of built-up property refers to a building site, on which buildings stand. A freehold interest in the land portion of built-up property denotes that the building(s) and lot belong to the same owner and are used by the same owner. The land should not be subject to legal or deed restrictions.

A leasehold interest in land (*shakuchiken*) refers to the interest of the tenant or lessee who holds a ground lease. Ground leases are typically held by the owners of the buildings that occupy leased sites and are classified into two types: the right to be granted by lease contract (*chinshakuken*) which are usually not registered and the right of superficies (*chijoken*) which are usually registered. Leasehold interests are defined in the *Land Lease and Building Lease Law*. (Editor's Note: An important distinction between a regular ground lease and the right of superficies is that the tenant holding a regular ground lease needs the consent of the landlord to transfer or sublease, but a holder of the right of superficies can transfer or sublease without the landlord's consent. In Japan, there are both land and building registries. Buildings are registered, but regular ground lease are usually not. However, if the tenant holds the right of superficies, the tenant's interest is registered, and his / her position is thereby enhanced.)

A leased fee interest in land refers to the leased fee estate in a building site. The owner of the building on the site is a lessee of the land on which the building stands while the building site owner/lessor holds the leased fee interest in the land.

Air/underground rights refer to sectional superficies established in vertical space under the ground or in the air. These rights make possible the conveyance of interests in the structures occupying such space.

II Built-Up Property (Buildings and the Sites on Which They Stand)

Title to buildings and the sites on which they stand is divided into the following categories: 1) the ownership interest in an owner-occupied building and its site, 2) the ownership interest in a tenant-occupied building and its site, 3) the ownership interest in the building on leased land, and 4) the ownership interest in a condominium unit.

The ownership interest in an owner-occupied building and its site refers to the ownership interest in a building and building lot where the building owner and lot owner are the same, and the property is not subject to legal or deed restrictions.

The ownership interest in a tenant-occupied building and its site refers to a building and site where the building owner and lot owner are the same, but the building is leased, i.e., the owner of the lot and building holds a leased fee interest in the building.

The ownership interest in the building on leased land refers to a situation where the ownership right to a building is held by someone with a ground lease to the site upon which the building stands. (A landlord or lessor holds title to, and leased fee interest in, the land on which the building stands.)

The ownership interest in a condominium unit refers to: exclusively-owned area stipulated in Article 2, Paragraph 3 of the *Law for Unit Ownership, etc. of Building* (the *Law for Condominium*); co-ownership of common areas stipulated in Article 2, Paragraph 4 of said Act; and co-ownership of the underlying site stipulated in Article 2, Paragraph 6 of said Act.

CHAPTER 3. INFLUENCES ON REAL ESTATE VALUE

Influences on the value of real estate (henceforth called "value influences") refer to those influences that affect the utility of real estate, its relative scarcity, and the effective demand for real estate. Although real estate value is formed as a result of the interaction of numerous value influences, those value influences themselves tend to change continuously. Thus, in the appraisal of real estate, it is necessary to accurately understand how market participants view value influences, and to evaluate the effect of these influences on the utility of, scarcity of, and effective demand for real estate by adequately analyzing market changes, industry trends and the interrelationships among value influences.

Value influences are divided into general value influences, area-specific value influences and property-specific value influences.

Section 1. General Value Influences

General value influences refer to value influences that have an effect on the real estate industry, the economy, and price levels. These are broadly classified into physical, social, economic, and governmental value influences.

The following lists provide major examples of general value influences.

I   Physical Value Influences
1. Geological features
2. Soil
3. Topography
4. Geographical location
5. Climate

II   Social Value Influences
1. Population
2. Family size and household formation
3. Urbanization and infrastructure development
4. Education and social welfare
5. Real estate transactions and practice (brokerage services, tenancy, and so forth)
6. Architectural styles
7. Availability and dissemination of information
8. Lifestyles

III   Economic Value Influences
1. Savings, consumption, investment and foreign trade balance
2. Fiscal and monetary conditions
3. Commodity prices, wages, employment and corporate activity
4. Taxation
5. Corporate accounting system
6. Technological innovations and industrial base

V - 3. Real Estate Appraisal Standards

    7. Transportation system
    8. Globalization
Ⅳ Governmental Value Influences
    1. Land use planning and regulation
    2. Building codes and required disaster prevention safeguards
    3. Policies relating to building sites (building setbacks, building density) and housing developments
    4. Real estate taxation
    5. Regulations applying to real estate transactions

Section 2. Area – Specific Value Influences
Area-specific value influences refer to influences that have an overall effect on the formation of the value of real estate in a specific market area. Area-specific influences include those features that give an area its character, i.e., size, land use, function, and so forth. Area-specific and general value influences may often overlap.
Ⅰ Building Site Areas
1. Residential areas
The following list provides major examples of area-specific value influences in residential areas.
    (1) Climate including sunlight, temperature, humidity and wind direction
    (2) Street width and structure
    (3) Distance from the city center and availability of transportation
    (4) Location of commercial facilities
    (5) Waterworks, city gas service, garbage disposal and sewers
    (6) Development of telecommunications infrastructure
    (7) Location of public institutions and utilities
    (8) Presence of nuisances such as sewage treatment plants
    (9) Risk of flooding, landslides and other natural disasters
    (10) Noise, air pollution, and soil contamination
    (11) Lot size, layout and utilization
    (12) Residences, hedges, landscaping and street appearance
    (13) Quality of the natural environment including scenic views
    (14) Land use planning and regulation
2. Commercial Areas
The following list provides examples of major market-specific value influences in commercial areas, and supplements the area-specific value influences listed in the section on residential areas above.
    (1) Types, sizes and concentration of commercial or service facilities
    (2) Quality and size of trade and customer profile
    (3) Availability of transportation for customers and employees
    (4) Convenience in loading and unloading of merchandise
    (5) Street accessibility and additional features such as covered arcades
    (6) Business types and competition

- (7) Entrepreneurship and financial resources of business owners in the subject area
- (8) Volume of automobile and / or pedestrian traffic
- (9) Provision of parking facilities
- (10) Degree of governmental assistance and regulation

3. Industrial Areas

The following list provides examples of major area-specific value influences in industrial areas, and supplements the market-specific value influences listed in the section on residential areas above.

- (1) Provision of arterial roads, railroads, harbors, airports and other transport networks
- (2) Availability of a work force
- (3) Location of consumer market(s) and industrial suppliers
- (4) Power, water and drainage costs
- (5) Location of related industries
- (6) Risk of water pollution and air pollution
- (7) Degree of governmental assistance and regulation

II Agricultural Areas

Major examples of area-specific value influences in agricultural areas are indicated below.

1. Climate including sunlight, temperature, humidity, wind and rain
2. Topography including rolling ground, elevated highland and flat lowland areas
3. Soil
4. Water utilization and water quality
5. Risk of flooding, landslides and other natural disasters
6. Adequacy of roads
7. Location of rural communities
8. Location of distribution center(s) and farms
9. Distance from consumer market(s) and availability of transport facilities
10. Degree of governmental assistance and regulation

III Forestland Areas

Major examples of area-specific value influences in forestland areas are indicated below.

1. Climate including sunlight, temperature, humidity, wind and rain
2. Altitude and topography
3. Soil
4. Adequacy of roads
5. Availability of a work force
6. Degree of governmental assistance and regulation

Regarding areas in rapid transition from one use category to a different use category, greater emphasis should be placed on area-specific value influences affecting the use category following the transition. In the case of a gradual transition, however, the market-specific value influences affecting the use category prior to the transition should be emphasized.

Section 3. Property — Specific Value Influences

Property-specific value influences refer to those influences that give real estate its individuality and form the value of individual properties. Property-specific value influences are broken down according to land use classification.

I Property — Specific Value Influences on Land

1. Building Sites

(1) Residential Land

Major examples of property-specific value influences on residential land are indicated below.

① Topography, geology and ground soil
② Sunlight, wind, dryness and dampness
③ Lot width, depth, size and shape
④ Land elevation in relation to the elevation of the facing street (corner lots will face two streets)
⑤ Width and condition of the facing street
⑥ Layout and network of the facing street
⑦ Distance from transportation
⑧ Proximity to commercial facilities
⑨ Proximity to public institution and utilities
⑩ Proximity to nuisances such as sewage treatment plants
⑪ Condition of adjacent real estate and surroundings
⑫ Availability of waterworks, city gas service, garbage disposal, and sewers
⑬ Development of telecommunications infrastructure
⑭ Presence of archeological artifacts buried on the site and condition of any underground structures
⑮ Presence and extent of soil contamination
⑯ Regulations or restrictions stipulated in public laws and private deeds

(2) Commercial Land

Major examples of property-specific value influences on commercial land are indicated below.

① Topography, geology and ground soil
② Lot width, depth, size and shape
③ Land elevation in relation to elevation of the facing street (corner lots will face two streets)
④ Width and condition of the facing street
⑤ Layout and network of the facing street
⑥ Proximity to center of commercial area
⑦ Proximity to main means of transportation
⑧ Location in conformity with customer flow
⑨ Condition of adjacent real estate and surroundings
⑩ Availability of waterworks, city gas service, garbage disposal and sewers
⑪ Availability of telecommunications infrastructure
⑫ Presence of archeological artifacts buried on the site and condition of any un-

　　　　derground structures
⑬　Presence and extent of soil pollution
⑭　Regulations or restrictions stipulated in public laws and private deeds

(3) Industrial Land

Major examples of property-specific value influences on industrial land are indicated below.

① Topography, geology and ground soil
② Lot width, depth, acreage and shape
③ Land elevation in relation to the elevation of the facing street (corner lots will face two streets)
④ Width and condition of the facing street
⑤ Layout and network of the facing street
⑥ Proximity to main means of transportation used by commuting employees
⑦ Location of arterial roads, railroads, harbors, airports and other transport networks
⑧ Availability of electrical power and other motive power resources
⑨ Adequacy of water sources and drainage facilities (and whether these facilities show any deferred maintenance)
⑩ Availability of waterworks, city gas service, garbage disposal and sewers
⑪ Development of telecommunications infrastructure
⑫ Presence of archeological artifacts buried on the site and condition of any underground structures
⑬ Presence and extent of soil pollution
⑭ Regulations or restrictions stipulated in public laws and private deeds

2. Agricultural Land

Major examples of property-specific value influences on agricultural land are indicated below.

(1) Sunlight, dryness, dampness and rainfall
(2) Soil
(3) Presence and condition of farm roads
(4) Irrigation and drainage
(5) Ease of cultivation
(6) Proximity to rural communities
(7) Proximity to shipping sites
(8) Potential risks of natural disaster
(9) Regulations or restrictions stipulated in public laws and private deeds

3. Forestland

Major examples of property-specific value influences on forestland are indicated below.

(1) Sunlight, dryness, dampness and rainfall
(2) Altitude above sea level and topography
(3) Soil
(4) Ease of carrying out and transporting the lumber
(5) Ease of management

(6) Regulations or restrictions stipulated in public laws and private deeds

4. Sites with Interim Use and Lots in Transitional Area

Regarding sites with an interim use and lots in a transitional area, greater emphasis should be placed on property-specific value influences affecting the land use category following the transition. In the case of a gradual transition, however, the property-specific value influences affecting the land use category prior to the transition should be emphasized.

II Property−Specific Value Influences on Building

Major examples of property-specific value influences on building are indicated below.
1. Age of the structure (and whether it is a new structure, an extension, a reconstruction or relocation)
2. Area, height, type of construction and materials
3. Design and functionality
4. Construction quality and dimensions
5. Earthquake resistance, fire resistance and compliance with other building performance standards
6. Maintenance and management
7. Presence of harmful substances and extent of contamination
8. Degree the building conforms to its environment
9. Regulations or restrictions stipulated in public laws and private deeds

III Property−Specific Value Influences on Built−Up Property (Buildings and the Underlying Sites)

In addition to those examples indicated in I and II above, major examples of property-specific value influences on buildings and building sites include the building layout, available parking lots, ground paths, gardens on the lot, and the overall compatibility between building and site, especially in regard to the size of the building relative to the dimensions of the site.

Property-specific value influences on leased real estate include how well the property is operated. Major examples are indicated below.
1. Status of the lessee and provisions of the lease contract
2. Occupancy level of the leased property
3. Quality of planned repairs and management program as well as the extent of their implementation

CHAPTER 4. PRINCIPLES OF REAL ESTATE VALUE

The value of real estate is formed by the interaction of various factors affecting the utility of the real estate, its relative scarcity, and the effective demand for that real estate. When the process of value formation is studied, basic economic laws or principles can be observed therein. Since the essence of real estate appraisal is the analysis of the value formation process as it pertains to a specific real estate product, these basic principles serve as necessary guidelines for any appraisal. The principles underlying the formation of real estate value are discussed below. An appraiser should study the operation of these principles to reach a conclusive judgment of the value of a real estate product.

Although these principles are based on general economic laws, they are identified and discussed within the specific context of appraisal.

It should be further noted that these principles are not independent of one another, but rather are directly or indirectly related.

I Principle of Supply and Demand

While the value of a commodity is determined by the relationship between the supply of and demand for that commodity, the value of that commodity may also have an effect on the supply of and demand for the commodity.

The value of real estate is determined by the relationship between supply and demand, but real estate also has physical characteristics and socio-economic characteristics that differ from the attributes of other commodities. The effect of these additional characteristics is reflected in the dynamics of real estate supply and demand and the formation of real estate value.

II Principle of Change

In general, the value of a commodity varies according to changes in the factors that form its value.

The value of real estate is also formed within a continuous process of change that reflects a succession of various cause and effect relationships between value influences. The value influences themselves undergo constant change. Thus, in appraising real estate, the dynamic cause and effect relationships between factors should be understood. In particular, the process of change must be analyzed in order to determine the highest and best use of real estate (see paragraph IV below).

III Principle of Substitution

In cases where two or more commodities are interchangeable, the value of such commodities is determined by the mutual effect they exert on one another.

The value of real estate is also formed in relation to the value of other substitute real estate products.

IV Principle of Highest and Best Use

The value of real estate is analyzed on the premise of the potential best use of the real estate, i.e., the use under which the real estate will achieve its maximal utility (henceforth called "highest and best use"). The highest and best use is an objective indicator of that use, which under actual socio-economic circumstances, is both rational and legally permissible and that is also practicable by a person possessing the common sense and ordinary capabilities to operate the property under that use.

It should be further noted that the actual use of a certain property is not necessarily the highest and best use of that real estate. A use based on irrational or personal circumstances may result in under-utilization of the real estate.

V Principle of Balance

It is necessary for the constituent elements of real estate to be in balance in order for the real estate to achieve its maximum profitability or highest amenity level. Thus, in order to estimate the highest and best use of real estate, it is necessary to analyze whether or not such a balance has been achieved.

VI Principle of Increasing or Decreasing Returns

When an investment is continuously increased by a definite amount, the gross income to the investment increases with each increment. However, although the income corresponding to each increment increases up to a certain point, it eventually reaches the point of diminishing returns where it begins to decrease.

This principle applies to additional capital investment in real estate as well.

VII Principle of Income Allocation

Gross income that is generated from the combination of land, capital, labor, and management (coordination) may be allocated to each of these elements. Therefore, that portion of gross income remaining after the other portions have been allocated to capital, labor and management (coordination) may be attributed to the land, provided the allocation has been properly carried out.

VIII Principle of Contribution

The degree to which each component of real estate contributes to income generated by the overall real estate has an effect on total real estate value.

This principle is especially useful in considering the feasibility of additional investment in the real estate when the appraiser determines the highest and best use of the real estate.

IX Principle of Conformity

It is necessary for real estate to conform to its environment in order to achieve its maximum profitability or highest amenity level. Thus, an appraiser must analyze whether or not that real estate is in conformity with its environment when the appraiser determines the highest and best use of the real estate.

X Principle of Competition

In general, excess profit stimulates competition, while excess competition reduces profit and may ultimately eliminate it. With respect to real estate, a competitive relationship is also observed both between real estate products and between real estate products and other commodities striving to realize excess profit through their utilization. Thus, the value of real estate is formed as a result of this competition.

XI Principle of Anticipation

The value of a commodity is determined in anticipation of future profitability.

The value of real estate is also influenced by anticipation on the part of market participants and whatever changes they foresee in value influences.

CHAPTER 5. BASIC APPRAISAL PROBLEM

Basic to the appraisal of real estate, is an identification of 1) the subject property, 2) date of value opinion, and 3) the type of value or rent estimated.

Section 1. Identification of the Subject Property

In performing a real estate appraisal, the appraiser must identify the physical characteristics of the land and/or building to be appraised as well as the property rights to be appraised, i.e., fee simple estate, leased fee estate, leasehold estate or other property rights.

Identification of the subject real estate involves clearly distinguishing the subject of the appraisal from other real estate and specifying the location, dimensions, use, and relevant ownership rights. These features should ultimately be verified by LREAs by confirming that the description of the subject property and its actual use conform with the specifications and objectives of the appraisal assignment.

I Requirements for the Subject Identification

The items required for an identification of the subject real estate are its physical characteristics and the relevant property rights.

The subject identification must verify physical characteristics such as the location and dimensions of the subject property (to ensure that the physical features of the real estate correspond to the real estate described in the client's specifications), and the legal estate in the subject property, e.g., fee simple (freehold ownership) or leasehold interest. The four possible aspects of physical real estate with which appraisal assignments deal:

1. Where the real estate is to be appraised "as is." The real estate may constitute land alone or a combination of land and buildings. Some assignments will call for the appraisal of the real estate "as is," i.e., the appraisal of the land component or the combined real estate components.

2. In situations where the real estate is a combination of land and buildings, but only the land is the subject of the appraisal, the value of the freehold interest in the site can be estimated, assuming the buildings did not exist. The value estimated in such an appraisal is referred to as *site value as if vacant*.

3. Where the real estate to be appraised is the "residual" site or the "residual" building. In situations where the real estate is a combination of land and building(s), and only one component (either the land or the building component) of that real estate is the subject of appraisal, the value estimated is referred to as the *severance value*. (Editor's Note: Unlike site value above, the severance value of land or building components is estimated based on the fact that the other property component exists.)

4. Where the real estate to be appraised is an assemblage or subdivision of real estate. Where the subject of an appraisal is the result of a consolidation or subdivision of real estate, the appraisal will necessarily be premised on that consolidation or

subdivision, and the value estimated in the appraisal is referred to as *assemblage value or component value*.

II Assumptions of Area-Specific or Property-Specific Value Influences

Although there are cases where a client may request the appraiser to make certain assumptions or limiting conditions with respect to the effect of area-specific or property-specific value influences on the property identified as the subject, such assumptions and limiting conditions imposed by a client must be reasonable, realistic, and legitimate. The appraiser will proceed objectively whether or not the results of the valuation jeopardize the benefits of an involved party (i.e., the client) or third party.

In general, where the assumptions and limiting conditions imposed with respect to area-specific value influences are reasonable, they are limited primarily to matters involving official agencies with the authority to alter, revise or abolish planning projects and regulations. (Editor's Note: For example, assumptions regarding the likelihood that a district will be rezoned from residential to commercial use or that a public utility plant will be constructed are only deemed reasonable when the appraiser has a good idea of how the authority with the power to approve or deny the change will act.)

Section 2. Identification of the Date of the Value Opinion

Since value influences change with the passage of time, the value of real estate is only valid on the day to which the valuation refers. Thus, in performing a real estate appraisal, it is necessary to identify the reference date of the real estate valuation; this date is referred to as *the date of the value opinion*. An additional benchmark, *the date of the opinion on rent* is the first day of each period (Editor's Note: In Japan, mostly monthly rent) for which the rental income is to be determined.

The date of the value of opinion may be current (i.e., a current value opinion), in the past (i.e., a retrospective value opinion) or in the future (i.e., a prospective value opinion), based on the data used to perform the appraisal.

Section 3. Identification of the Type of Value or Rental Value

A real estate appraisal performed by LREAs must determine that the value definition is appropriate to the assignment and then develop an estimate of that value.

I Value (Capital Value)

The value determined by a real estate appraisal is generally *market value*. However, there are other defined values such as *assemblage* or *component market value, market value based on special considerations*, and *non-market value*, which may also be determined according to the purpose and conditions of the client's specifications for the appraisal. Therefore, the type of value to be estimated should always be properly assessed and clarified in line with the purpose and conditions of the client's specifications. It should be further noted that there are cases where the purpose of the appraisal requires an estimate of the market value of the real estate based on special considerations.

1. Market Value

Market value refers to the probable value that would be formed for the marketable real estate in a market that satisfies conditions associated with a rational market under ac-

tual socio-economic circumstances. A market that satisfies the conditions associated with a rational market under actual socio-economic circumstances refers to a market that satisfies the conditions listed below.
(1) The market participants must be acting on their own free will, and be able to enter or leave the market as they wish.

Motivated by the desire to maximize their returns while exhibiting wise and prudent behavior, market participants will satisfy the requirements listed below:
① No special motivation causes them to sell off or to initiate buying.
② They have only access to ordinary knowledge and information, required to conduct transactions involving the subject property or in the subject property market.
③ They have expended the labor and costs normally considered necessary to conduct transactions.
④ They premise value on the highest and best use of the subject property.
⑤ Purchasers have ordinary access to procuring funds (financing).
(2) There must be no special curbs on transactions that restrict market participants nor any extraordinary incentives that induce participants to sell off or initiate buying.
(3) The subject property must be exposed in the market for an appropriate period of time.

2. Special Value

Special value refers to the appropriate value of the marketable real estate in a limited-market of buyers and sellers, created as a result of consolidation including land acquisition or subdivision of real estate. Thus, synergistic or component value is premised on a limited-market concept.

Examples of situations in which synergistic or component value is determined are indicated below.
(1) a sale by a landlord (lessor) or purchase by a leaseholder (lessee) of a site for the purpose of consolidating the ownership interest with the leased fee interest in land.
(2) a sale or purchase for the assemblage purpose with adjacent real estate.
(3) a sale or purchase of real estate where the manner in which the real estate is subdivided is deemed to be irrational.

3. Value for Regulated Purposes (VRP)

Value for Regulated Purposes (VRP) refers to the appropriate economic value of the marketable real estate, but does not necessarily satisfy all conditions on which market value is premised. Such valuations are performed in compliance with the requirements of laws and ordinances.

Examples of cases in which Value for Regulated Purpose Appraisal is determined are listed below.
(1) where the investment profitability value is premised on valuation for a typical investor based on a specific operation management scheme performed in accordance with the *Asset Liquidation Law* and the *Investment Trust and Investment Corporation Law*.
(2) where the value determined is premised on valuation for quick sale purposes. The

Civil Rehabilitation Law governs such valuations.
(3) where the value determined is premised on the continuation of a business. Such valuations come under the *Corporate Reorganization Law* or the *Civil Rehabilitation Law*.

(Editor's Note: Value for Regulated Purposes (VRP) may be divided into two categories: market value and value other than market value (see Part1: chap. 2. I . Japan-3) : the value under the Asset Liquidation Law and the Investment Corporation Law, is the market value assuming an operation management scheme which reflects the expectation of a typical investor. It refers to the investment profitability value of the subject property under the securitization regulations, but represents those of a typical investor rather than a specific investor in the market.)

4. Value of Special-Purpose Property

Value of Special-Purpose Property refers to the appropriate economic value of real estate such as cultural assets that are generally not marketable. Non-market value is premised on the continuation of the existing use of the real estate.

Examples of situations in which non-market value is determined include valuations of structures that have been designated as cultural assets, and temples and public facilities, the operation of which is expected to continue in its present state. Appraisals of such facilities are performed with an emphasis on their preservation.

II Rental Value

The rent generally determined by real estate appraisal is either *market rent* or *rent under a renewed lease*. However, since there are also situations in which *synergistic or component rent* must be determined according to the purpose and conditions specified by the client, such a rent should be properly assessed and clarified.

1. Market Rent

Market rent is the appropriate rent (market rent under new lease) reflecting the probable economic value of the real estate. Market rent is the rent that would be negotiated in a new lease agreement granting the rights to use or benefit from real estate interests; such rights may be conveyed by means of leases contract, right of superficies, or easements. Market rent is premised upon the same market concept as market value.

2. Special Rent

Special rent, like synergistic or component value, is also premised upon limited-market concept. The synergistic or component rent refers to the appropriate indication of the probable economic value of the real estate, i.e., the rent that would be negotiated in a new lease agreement.

Examples of situations in which synergistic or component rent may be determined are listed below.

(1) leases granting the right to use adjacent real estate (bringing two parcels under the same use).
(2) leases of parcels of real estate that have been subdivided in an irrational manner.

3. Rent under Renewed Lease

Rent under a renewed lease is the appropriate indication of the probable economic value of the real estate, i.e., the rent that would be negotiated between the involved parties to extend the term of a real estate lease.

CHAPTER 6. MARKET AREA ANALYSIS AND PROPERTY ANALYSIS

In performing analyses of the subject market area and the subject property, the appraiser must accurately understand what specific effects general value influences exert upon the area and property.

Section 1. Market Area Analysis
I The Concept of Market Area Analysis
Market area analysis refers to the investigation and analysis of the type of area the subject property is located in, the characteristics of the area, the characteristics of the market for the subject property, and how such characteristics influence land use and the formation of real estate value in the area.

II Application of Market Area Analysis
1．Market Area Characteristics
Particularly important in market area analysis is the identification of land use in the area (henceforth called "market area category"). In the broadest sense, the market area is generally the area including the subject neighborhood and similar or comparable neighborhoods in the vicinity. The subject neighborhood and these similar or comparable neighborhoods constitute the primary market area.

The typical or standard land use of real estate in a neighborhood determines the specific neighborhood characteristics, and provides information as to the relative ranking of, and real estate values in, neighborhoods of the same land use. The typical or standard land use also serves as a strong indicator for determining the highest and best use of each piece of real estate located in that neighborhood.

No market area is static, and market-specific value influences that form area characteristics are also continuously changing. Thus, in performing a area analysis, trends indicating whether the current use will continue or change must also be analyzed and assessed once the characteristics of the market for the subject property have been determined.

(1) Market Area Category
① Subject Neighborhood

A *subject neighborhood* refers to an area where most of the real estate, including the subject property, is under a common land use classification. In other words, a neighborhood is an aggregation of real estate having a defined area within a urban or rural area and used for residency, commercial activities, industrial production, or other human activities. The characteristics of a neighborhood are capable of directly affecting the formation of the value of the subject property.

Neighborhoods undergo change in accordance with the extent of change in market-specific value influences shaping the characteristics of those neighborhoods.

② Similar or Comparable Neighborhood

A *similar or comparable neighborhood* refers to a neighborhood having characteristics that are similar to the characteristics of the subject neighborhood. The real estate in that neighborhood resembles the real estate in the subject neighborhood because of common use.

(2) **Market Area**

The *market area* typically refers to an area in which other properties may be substituted for the subject property and where the other real estate exerts an effect on the formation of the subject's value. This area, which may include several neighborhoods, has a broad extent and is defined by the range of neighborhoods similar to the subject neighborhood.

In general, real estate in the neighborhood and real estate in similar neighborhoods located within the market area have a substitutive or competitive relationship, based on the similarity of the market-specific value influences to which the real estate is subject regardless of whether or not these neighborhoods are adjacent to each other.

In addition, even real estate located outside the neighborhood or outside similar neighborhoods but situated within the market area may have a substitutive or competitive relationship with the subject real estate because of similarities in use, size, grade and other characteristics.

Since the extent of the market area differs according to the preferences of users as to type, size and other attributes of the real estate, it is necessary to accurately understand those user preferences in order to properly define the market area.

The following discussion covers basic matters requiring particular attention in defining the market area.

① **Building Sites**

a. **Residential Land**

The market area typically includes other neighborhoods from which it is possible to commute to the city center. However, the number of such neighborhoods tends to be constricted by preferences for specific areas.

Furthermore, it should be noted that neighborhood preferences attributable to reputation, quality and so forth may also affect the specific neighborhoods included in the market area.

b. **Commercial Land**

The market area for properties in highly commercial districts tends to include other competitive districts with respect to the income generated from broad commercial support areas. The market area for properties in highly commercial districts typically covers a broad area including properties in other highly commercial districts with similar income-producing attributes.

The market area for properties in ordinary commercial districts tends to include other competitive districts with respect to income generated from narrow commercial support areas. The market area for properties in ordinary commercial districts tends to be more confined because of preferences within individual areas.

c. **Industrial Land**

The market area for large-scale and infrastructure-dependent properties in industrial districts typically includes other industrial districts with similar advanced transportation facilities that allow large-volume conveyance of raw materials and products. Such big properties in industrial districts require nearby infrastructure such as harbors, ports, high-speed transportation networks and other facilities. Thus, the market area of this type of industrial district tends to be nationwide.

On the other hand, the market area for medium- and small-scale and consumer market-oriented properties in industrial areas typically includes other industrial districts with similar cost levels in terms of producing and marketing products. Such smaller properties in industrial districts require proximity to a consumer market of sufficient size.

d. Land in a Transitional Area

The market area for land in transitional areas typically coincides with the market area for the land use category to which the land in the transitional area is expected to change. However, where transition is gradual, the market area tends to be the same as the market area for the land use category prior to transition.

② Agricultural Land

The market area for a parcel of agricultural land typically includes those areas that can be used for the same kind of farming operations.

③ Forestland

The market area for forestland typically includes those areas that can be used for the same kind of timber growing operations.

④ Sites with Interim Use

The market area for sites with an interim use typically includes the market area for the land use category to which the land with an interim use is expected to change. However, where the changeover is gradual, the market area tends to be the same as the market area for the land use category prior to the change.

⑤ Built-Up Property

The market area of buildings and building sites typically includes the market area of land use corresponding to the use of the subject lot. However, there are some situations where the market area of the property may not match with that of the underlying site due to its specific use, size, grade, and other attributes of the subject lot.

2. Market Characteristics Relating to the Subject Property

To understand the characteristics of the market for the subject property in a market area analysis, it is important to know the attributes of market participants in the market area, their reasons for selecting real estate under the specific use, and how they consider the effect of value influences. It is also necessary to understand supply and demand trends in the market area.

Not only should specific market characteristics be reflected in an assessment of the predominant land use in the neighborhood, but they should also be considered in the application of appraisal techniques and various adjustments made to value indications or rent estimates.

Section 2. Property Analysis
I The Concept of Property Analysis
The value of real estate is determined on the premise of the highest and best use of the real estate. Therefore, in performing a real estate appraisal, it is necessary to determine the highest and best use of the subject property. Subject property analysis refers to investigating the effect of property-specific value influences on the use of the subject property and the formation of its value, and thereupon determining the highest and best use of the subject property.

II Application of Property Analysis
1. Guidelines for Analyzing Property-Specific Value Influences
Each property-specific value influence individually contributes to the formation of the market value of the subject property. Therefore, in analyzing property-specific value influences, it is important to accurately determine what types of property-specific influences typical users of the Property would focus upon when considering to purchase or lease the subject property as well as the competitiveness of the subject property and its relative inferiority or superiority in regard to comparable real estate.

The results of an analysis of property-specific value influences should also be considered in the application of appraisal techniques and in the reconciliation of value indications or rent estimates.

2. Guidelines for Determining the Highest and Best Use of Property
In determining the highest and best use of real estate, special consideration should be given to the following points.

(1) The use of the real estate is that which would probably be employed by a person possessing the common sense and ordinary capabilities to operate the property under that use.

(2) The use will allow for the continuous generation of income far into the future.

(3) The time at which utility can be adequately demonstrated is at some anticipated point in the future.

(4) The highest and best use of individual real estate is typically subject to the restrictions imposed by the characteristics of the neighborhood. In performing a subject property analysis, it is necessary to assess the relationship between the subject's use and the typical or standard use of real estate in the neighborhood. There is always the possibility that the subject's use may differ from the standard use depending on the subject's location, size, environment and so forth. In such situations, the highest and best use of the property should be determined after analyzing property-specific value influences in regard to each potential use.

(5) Value influences are in a state of constant change. Thus where it may be reason-

ably anticipated that changes in market-specific value influences will affect the formation of the subject's value, the highest and best use of the subject property should be determined in view of the possibility that the use of the subject property may also change.

In determining the highest and best use of a building and building site, special consideration should be given to the following matters.
(6) Where the actual use of the building does not correspond to the highest and best use of the site as if vacant, it is necessary to consider the costs and time required to realize the highest and best use of the site as if vacant. In some of these cases, the highest and best use of improved property may not be the same as the highest and best use as if vacant.
(7) The economic value that would result from continuation of the current use of the building should be rigorously compared to the costs that would be incurred to demolish the building or alter its use.

CHAPTER 7. APPRAISAL METHOD

There are three approaches to real estate appraisal: the cost approach, the sales comparison approach, and the income capitalization approach.

The cost approach focuses on the cost required to reproduce the real estate (called reproduction cost new) including the costs of site preparation, construction and so forth. The sales comparison approach focuses on sales data or lease data from the sale or leasing of comparable real estate. The income capitalization approach focuses on the income generated from the real estate. Each method attempts to determine the value of, or rent for, the real estate.

The approaches to real estate appraisal may be classified according to approaches used to determine real estate value, and approaches used to determine real estate rental value. The value or rent determined through the application of an appraisal approach is referred to as the *indicated value* or *indicated rent*.

Section 1. Appraisal Approaches for Determining Real Estate Value

The basic appraisal approaches for determining the value of real estate are divided into cost, sales comparison, and income capitalization approaches. There is also a fourth approach, subdivision development analysis, which utilizes concepts from the above three approaches.

I General Guidelines for Determining Value Indications

1. The Correlation between General Value Influences and the Application of the Appraisal Approaches

General value influences are value influences that affect the formation of the overall value of the real estate. Not only must general value influences be considered at each step in the application of the appraisal approaches, but they must also be kept in mind when reviewing the validity of the value estimate.

2. Gathering and Selecting Data

The data required for applying the appraisal approaches consists of construction data in the cost approach, comparable sales data in the sales comparison approach, and income data in the income capitalization approach (such data is henceforth called comparable data). Comparable data should be gathered in large volume and in an orderly manner, based on a rational plan appropriate to the application of each appraisal approach. Data should not be compiled from speculative transactions.

Comparable data should satisfy all of the requirements indicated below.

(1) Comparable Real Estate Data Pertaining to:
① *Comparable real estate*. Comparable real estate should be located in the neighborhood, a comparable neighborhood in the primary market area, or when otherwise unavoidable, an area in the vicinity of the neighborhood (these are generally known as comparable neighborhoods in the primary market

area).
② *Real estate in a substitutive or competitive relationship with subject that is located in the primary market area.* Where the highest and best use of the subject property differs from the typical or standard use in the neighborhood, comparable data may include real estate in a substitutive or competitive relationship with the subject that is located in the primary market area (henceforth called substitutive or competitive real estate in the primary market area).

(2) *Comparable data.* Comparable data should reflect transactions closed under normal circumstances or else should be amenable to adjustment so as to reflect transactions closed under normal circumstances.

(3) *Comparable data* should allow adjustment for changes in price levels and market conditions over time.

(4) *Comparable data* should allow for comparison of market-specific value influences and comparison of property-specific value influences.

3. Adjustment for Conditions of Sale

Comparable data must be suitably adjusted when the transactions, from which the comparable data were compiled, were closed under special circumstances that affected the comparable property's value.

(1) For example, comparable sales data may reflect special circumstances that hasten selling or precipitate buying. Such special circumstances are attributable to the characteristics of the real estate market, the capabilities of the involved parties to the transaction, and any special motivation those parties may be acting upon. Nevertheless, the conditions under which the comparables were transacted must be rigorously investigated.

(2) Special circumstances refer to circumstances that do not satisfy conditions characterizing a rational market operating under actual socio-economic circumstances. Market value is necessarily premised upon the existence of a rational market.

4. Time Adjustment

In situations where a change in the price level is observable between the date of a transaction from which comparable data was compiled and the date of the value opinion, the value of the comparable data must be adjusted to the price level on the date of the value opinion.

5. Comparison of Area-Specific Value Influences and Property-Specific Value Influences

The value of comparable data reflects both area-specific and property-specific influences. Therefore, it is necessary to compare area-specific and property-specific value influences on the subject property and comparable property in cases where the comparable property is located in a similar neighborhood within the same market area, or is in a substitutive or competitive relationship with the subject property and located in the same primary market area. On the other hand, if the comparable property is located in the subject neighborhood, it is necessary to compare only property-specific influences on the subject property and comparable property.

II Cost Approach
1. Concept

The cost approach to value first determines the reproduction cost of the subject property on the date of the value opinion. Where the improvement is not a new structure, an estimate of accrued depreciation must be deducted from the reproduction cost (a value indication determined by this approach is called the value indicated by the cost approach). Where the property combines a building and building site, an estimate of the land value is added to the estimate of depreciated reproduction cost of the building to arrive at the total property value.

The cost approach is applicable in situations where the subject property is a building or building and building site and it is possible to determine the reproduction cost and properly estimate accrued depreciation. Where the subject property is only land, the cost approach can be applied if the reproduction cost of the land can be properly determined.

If the subject is a property under construction or a proposed property that does not currently exist, the cost approach can only be applied when the appraiser is able to determine the reproduction cost on the date of the value opinion.

2. Application Method
(1) Concept of Reproduction Cost

Reproduction cost refers to the total cost required to reproduce a duplicate of the subject property as of the date of the value opinion.

In situations where it is difficult to determine the reproduction cost of the subject property because of changes in building materials, construction methods and so forth, replacement cost may be determined. *Replacement cost* is the cost, at current prices as of the date of the value opinion, to construct a building of utility equivalent to that of the subject property, using modern materials and current design and layout standards.

(2) Methodology for Determining Reproduction Cost

Reproduction cost is determined by adding the ordinary incidental expenses (such as planning fees and building permits), borne directly by the builder, to the standard construction costs paid by the builder to the contractor, assuming the contractor will deliver the finished building to the builder in a state that allows immediate use in accordance with the construction contract.

Replacement cost is the total cost of constructing another property having equivalent utility to that of the subject property. Replacement cost is determined by adding the ordinary incidental expenses, borne directly by the builder, to the standard construction costs paid by the builder to the contractor.

① The reproduction cost of land is determined by adding the standard site preparation costs of the subject land and the ordinary incidental expenses, borne directly by the builder, to the standard acquisition cost of the raw land.

When the cost approach is applied to land, infrastructure development (roads, utility lines) and site improvements transform the social and economic environment, and strongly affect the price level of the land. By comparing market-specific value influences acting upon the subject land immediately after the preparation of the building site with market-specific value influences acting upon the subject land as of the date of the value opinion, an appraiser can determine the increment in land value that corresponds to the change in market-specific value influences.

② The reproduction cost of a building and building site is determined by first estimating the reproduction cost of the land (if the site is located in a built-up area where the reproduction cost cannot be determined, the value of the freehold interest in the land can be determined by the sales comparison and income capitalization approaches) or by estimating the value of a leasehold interest in the land, and then adding the depreciated reproduction cost of the building to that value.

③ Direct and indirect methods are used to determine reproduction cost. Either method may be applied depending on the degree of reliability of the construction data gathered, or both methods may be used together.

 a. The direct method is a method for directly determining the reproduction cost of the subject property.

  The direct method determines the reproduction cost of the subject property by 1) investigating the category, grade and volume of materials used and the kinds and duration of the required labor; 2) estimating the direct construction costs based on the unit price on the date of the value opinion in the area where the subject property is located; 3) adding to this estimate all indirect construction costs and a general management fee that includes a reasonable profit for the contractor; and 4) finally adding the ordinary incidental expenses borne directly by the builder.

  In situations where the appraiser knows the value of the raw land, direct and indirect construction costs required to prepare the actual site for construction, general management expenses (including a reasonable profit for the contractor), incidental expenses borne directly by the builder, and building specifications (including category, grade, volume, time and unit price) for the subject property, the appraiser can determine the reproduction cost by analyzing and appropriately updating the specifications, and adjusting for changes over time as required.

 b. The indirect method is a method for determining the reproduction cost of the subject property indirectly from real estate similar to the subject property and located in the same or a similar neighborhood within the primary market area, or from other substitutive or competitive real estate in the primary market area.

  In situations where the appraiser knows the value of the raw land, the direct and indirect construction costs of the real estate, general management expenses (including a reasonable profit for the contractor), incidental expenses borne directly by the builder, and the building specifications (including category, grade, volume, time and unit price) for comparable property, the appraiser can use the indirect method to determine the reproduction cost of the subject property by analyzing and suitably updating these specifications, adjusting for changes over time as required, and comparing both market-specific value influences and property-specific value influences.

3. Accrued Depreciation

The purpose of estimating accrued depreciation is to determine an appropriate deduction to apply to the reproduction cost of the subject property in order to arrive at the indicated value of the subject on the date of the value opinion.

The amount of accrued depreciation may be determined by an itemized and comprehensive analysis of the subject property according to the following types of depreciation.

(1) Types of Accrued Depreciation

Accrued Depreciation is broken down into physical deterioration, functional obsolescence and economic obsolescence.

It should be noted that these three types of accrued depreciation are not independent of one another, but rather are mutually related and interactive.

① Physical Deterioration

Examples of physical deterioration include wear and tear from the use of the real estate, deterioration occurring over the passage of time or resulting from natural causes, and incidental damage.

② Functional Obsolescence

Examples of functional obsolescence affecting real estate include uncompatibility between building and site, bad design, outdated form, and inadequate facilities of reduced capacity.

③ Economic Obsolescence

Examples of economic obosolescence include non-complementarity between the real estate and its environment resulting from neighborhood decline, non-conformity between the real estate and its surroundings, or a decline in the marketability of the real estate vis-a-vis either real estate in a substitutive or competitive relationship with the subject or other real estate in the vicinity.

(2) Methods of Estimating Accrued Depreciation

The two methods indicated below are used to determine the total depreciation in a property. Generally, these two methods are used in conjunction with one another.

① Methods of Estimating Accrued Depreciation over a Period

Methods of estimating accrued depreciation over a period consist of the straight-line method and the declining balance method. The decision as to which of these methods should be used is made according to the actual situation of the subject property.

When applying these methods, the appraiser should give greater weight to the remaining economic life of the property rather than its actual age.

In situations where the subject property is composed of two or more divisible components, and the respective depreciation periods or remaining economic lives of these components are different, how depreciation in each component is to be assessed and how salvage value and land value are to be estimated at the termination of the period should be decided according to the actual situation of the subject property.

② **Methods Based on Observation**
Accrued Depreciation may be estimated on the basis of direct observation. The appraiser investigates the functionality of the design, layout and facilities of the subject property; its maintenance and management; the condition of any repairs; how well the property conforms with the surrounding environment, and other possible factors contributing to accrued depreciation.

Ⅲ Sales Comparison Approach
1. Concept

The sales comparison approach uses data on the sales of comparable properties to determine the subject property's value. First, the appraiser gathers a large amount of comparable sales data, from which the most appropriate data are selected. The market prices negotiated in the comparable sales are adjusted for differences in sales conditions or changes occurring over the passage of time, if required. Market-specific and property-specific value influences are then compared to get value indicated by the sales comparison approach.

The sales comparison approach is applied when there is an availability of sales data involving comparable properties in the neighborhood or a similar neighborhood within the primary market area, or sales data involving substitutive or competitive real estate in the primary market area.

2. Application Method
(1) Gathering and Selection of Data

Since the sales comparison method uses comparable sales data found in the market as the basis for estimating value, the appraiser must first gather a large amount of comparable sales data.

Comparable sales data is gathered from data on real estate located in the neighborhood or similar neighborhoods within the primary market area. In situations where the highest and best use of the subject differs from the typical or standard use in the neighborhood, the selection of comparable sales data on real estate in a substitutive or competitive relationship with the subject will be unavoidable. In any case, comparable sales data must be found within the vicinity of the neighborhood and primary market area and satisfy all of the requirements indicated below.

① the data should reflect normal circumstances under which transactions are closed or else the data should be amenable to adjustment to reflect normal circumstances.

② the data should allow adjustment for changes in price levels and market conditions over time.

③ the data should allow comparison of market-specific value influences and comparison of property-specific value influences.

(2) Sales Condition and Time Adjustments

When comparable sales data reflect special circumstances affecting the sale price, an appropriate adjustment must be made. When a period of time has lapsed since the time of a comparable sale, and a change in the price level has occurred during that period, the value of the comparable sale must be adjusted to the price level on the date of the value opinion.

In making a time adjustment, the appraiser adjusts the sale price after determining the rate of growth in the value of land or buildings under the same land use classification as the comparable real estate in the neighborhood or a similar area, which has gone through a process of appreciation or decline in value similar to the neighborhood.

(3) Comparison of Market-Specific Value Influences and Property-Specific Value Influences

A sale price reflects both market-specific and property-specific value influences. Therefore, it is necessary to compare market-specific and property-specific value influences on the subject property and comparable property when the comparable real estate is located in a similar neighborhood within the same primary market area, or when it is in a substitutive or competitive relationship with the subject real estate and is located in the same primary market area. On the other hand, if the comparable property is located in the subject neighborhood, it is only necessary to compare property-specific value influences on the subject property and the comparable property.

To facilitate the comparison of market-specific value influences and property-specific value influences, the appraiser might identify a benchmark site subject to typical property-specific value influences in each area.

(4) Allocation Method

Situations will arise where comparable sales data is selected from real estate with two components, while the subject property has only one of two. The value of the extra component of the comparable property must be estimated first, and them must be deducted from the overall sale price to generate a comparable price for the subject property.

Alternatively, an allocation method may be used. Ratios between the values of property components as reflected by the comparable sales data can be developed on the basis of sales prices or development costs. The sale price derived from the comparable data is then multiplied by the percentage for the common component of the subject and comparable properties.

IV Income Capitalization Approach
1. Concept

The income capitalization approach estimates the total present value of the adjusted net operating income or net cash flow (NCF) that the subject property is expected to generate in a future period (a value indication derived from this approach is called the value indicated by the income approach).

The income capitalization approach is applicable for determining the value of lease-based properties and owner-occupied properties for business operation.

The formation of real estate value generally reflects the profitability of the given real estate, and income represents the essence of the economic value of real estate. Thus, the income capitalization approach cannot be applied to real estate that does not have general marketability, such as structures designated as cultural assets. However, it can be applied to owner-occupied residential properties upon the assumption that these properties are being leased.

Furthermore, when there is a precipitous increase in the sale price of land, a considerable disparity between the sale price and the value indicated by the income approach may result. In such situations, the income capitalization approach should be utilized to verify sale prices, which tend to be somewhat speculative.

2. Methods for Determining Value Indicated by the Income Approach

There are two basic methods for determining value indicated by the income approach. One method, called direct capitalization, applies a capitalization rate directly to net cash flow (NCF); the other method, discounted cash flow (DCF), discounts the net cash flow (NCF) generated over the typical holding period together with the reversionary value at the end of the holding period. Each income stream is discounted to present value at the time it is generated. All the discounted income streams are then added up.

These methods are basically represented by the following formulas.

(1) Direct Capitalization Method

$$P = \frac{a}{R}$$

where

P : Subject property value indicated by the income approach
a : Net cash flow (NCF) for one period
R : Capitalization rate

(2) DCF Method

$$P = \sum_{k=1}^{n} \frac{a_k}{(1+Y)^k} + \frac{P_R}{(1+Y)^n}$$

where

P : Subject property value indicated by the income approach
a_k : Net cash flow (NCF) for each period
Y : Discount rate
n : Holding period (or analysis period in cases where resale is not assumed, as is understood hereinafter)
P_R : Reversionary value

The reversion refers to the value of the subject property at the end of the holding period, and is basically represented by the following formula.

$$P_R = \frac{a_{n+1}}{R_n}$$

where

a_{n+1} : Net cash flow (NCF) for period n+1
Rn : Capitalization rate at the end of the holding period (terminal capitalization rate)

3. Application Methodology

(1) Net cash flow (NCF)

① Concept of Net Cash Flow (or Adjusted Net Operating Income)

Net cash flow (NCF) refers to the reasonable income to the real estate. NCF represents the portion of gross income remaining after allocations have been made for the contributions of capital (excluding capital converted into real estate), labor

V - 3. Real Estate Appraisal Standards

and management (coordination). (Editor's Note: Economic theory understands income-producing real estate as a product that combines four elements: land, capital (excluding capital converted into real estate), labor and management (coordination).)

② **Calculation of Net Cash Flow**

The net cash flow (NCF) of a subject property is typically determined by subtracting total expenses from the total income generated in one year. In addition, net cash flow (NCF) varies depending on the manner in which gross income and total costs are regarded, i.e., either as perpetual (level) NCF or non-perpetual (variable) NCF, or as NCF before depreciation allowance or NCF after depreciation. It should also be noted that the variability in NCF is closely related to selection of the method (direct capitalization or DCF) for determining value indications by the income approach and the method for determining capitalization rates or discount rates.

Furthermore, in direct capitalization, the net cash flow (NCF) used may, in some cases, be the subject property's first-year NCF and, in other cases, a stabilized NCF.

The net cash flow (NCF) of the subject property should be appropriately estimated by carefully analyzing each detailed line item in regard to past developments and future trends. The appraiser's analysis must be based on a direct understanding of the subject property's gross income and total related costs. The outlook for increased earnings and particularly the anticipated limits on earnings growth must be examined carefully.

The Discounted Cash Flow method explicitly indicates periodic or annual net cash flow (NCF), the reversion, and the times at which these income streams are generated. Thus, it is necessary to thoroughly investigate the outlook for net cash flow (NCF).

In the application of direct capitalization, the net cash flow (NCF) of the subject property may be indirectly determined on the basis of the net cash flow (NCF) of real estate similar to the subject property, located in the subject neighborhood or similar neighborhoods within the same primary market area, or the NCF of real estate in a substitutive or competitive relationship with the subject, located within the same market area. In such cases, it is necessary to compare respective area-specific value influences and property-specific value influences and appropriately adjust the net cash flow (NCF) of the comparable properties.

  a. **Calculation of Gross Income and Commentary**

    (a) **Lease－based property or owner－occupied property for business operation**

      For lease-based property, gross income generally includes nominal rent, interest earned on refundable deposits, interest earned and amortization of non-refundable deposits, and other income such as parking revenue. For owner-occupied property for business operation, gross income is the gross earning generated by sales.

      In applying the DCF method to leased-property, the appraiser must give special attention to the provisions of the lease agreement(s), and changes in the rents and the occupancy rates of the leased space for each period.

(b) **Highest and Best Use of vacant land is for lease-based development**

The gross income that is likely to be generated by the built-up property is appropriately estimated by assuming the leased building as the highest and best use of the subject property.

b. **Calculation of Total Expenses and Commentary**

Where the subject property is a lease-based property or where construction of a leased building represents the highest and best use of the land (see paragraph a-(b) above), the total expenses of the subject property include depreciation (excluded where net cash flow (NCF) is determined before depreciation allowance), maintenance and management fees (including maintenance costs, management fees and repair expenses), real estate taxes (property taxes, city planning tax) and insurance premiums, and other miscellaneous expenses. Where the subject real estate is an owner-occupied property for business operation, the total expenses of the property include cost of purchases and sales, general and administrative cost. In applying the DCF method, the appraiser must give special attention to the times that expenses, such as large-scale repairs, occur during the holding period.

(2) **Capitalization and Discount Rates**

① **Concept of Capitalization and Discount Rates**

The capitalization rate and discount rate both reflect the profitability of real estate, and although they are both used in the income approach to determine the indicated value, they are basically different, as is explained below.

The (overall) capitalization rate is the rate used in direct capitalization where property value is determined from the net cash flow (NCF) for a single period. In DCF analysis, the terminal capitalization rate is applied to estimate the reversion or anticipated property value at the end of the holding period. Capitalization rates incorporate a component for the uncertainty accompanying anticipated change in future income.

The discount rate is a rate used in DCF analysis to calculate the present value of income to be generated in the future. The discount rate excludes any component for uncertainty, accompanying anticipated change in the net cash flow (NCF) and reversion that are forecast over consecutive periods according to the income outlook.

② **Selecting and Supporting the Capitalization Rate and Discount Rate**

a. **Commentary on Determining Capitalization Rate and Discount Rates**

Since both the capitalization rate and discount rate are closely related to the profitability of comparable assets and investment yields in the financial market, the appraiser must investigate trends in the returns on real estate and other investments.

Moreover, since the capitalization rate and discount rate tend to differ according to region and property type and grade, both rates must be appropriately determined by analysis of area-specific value influences and property-specific value influences acting upon the subject property.

b. Methods for Determining Capitalization Rates

Examples of methods used to determine capitalization rates are provided below.

(a) Determination by Comparison with Comparable Sales Data on Similar Real Estate

This method determines the capitalization rate by making adjustments to market-derived capitalization rates for differences occurring over the time since the transaction involving the comparable property was closed, for the special circumstances of the transaction, and for changes in market-specific value influences and property-specific value influences.

(b) Determination by Means of Band of Investment Method based on Equity – Mortgage Ratio

The capitalization rate may be determined by weighting and averaging the respective capitalization rates for components of a capital investment (loan and equity) required for the acquisition of the subject property.

(c) Determination from Capitalization Rates for Land and Building Components

Where the subject property comprises a building and building site, the capitalization rate may be determined by weighting and averaging the respective capitalization rates for physical components (land and building) according to the respective ratios between the components.

(d) Determination from the Relationship with the Discount Rate

The capitalization rate may be determined by considering the growth rate in the subject property's net cash flow (NCF) based on the discount rate applied.

c. Methods for Determining Discount Rates

Examples of methods used to determine discount rates are provided below.

(a) Determination by Comparison with Comparable Sales Data on Similar Real Estate

This method determines the discount rate by making adjustments to market-derived discount rates for differences occurring since the time the transaction was concluded, for the special circumstances of the transaction, and for changes in market-specific value influences and property-specific value influences. Adjustments are based on the discount rate determined from comparable sales data on the subject property and similar real estate.

(b) Determination by Means of Discount Rates on Loans and Equity (Band of Investment Method Based on Equity – Mortgage Ratio)

The discount rate may be determined by weighting and averaging the respective discount rates for components of a capital investment (loan and equity) required for the acquisition of the subject property.

(c) **Determination Based on the Uniqueness of the Real Estate Investment Relative to Yields on Financial Assets**

This method determines the discount rate by considering the uniqueness of the subject property as an investment in terms of risk, non-liquidity, management difficulty, and asset security relative to yields on bonds and other financial assets.

(3) **Basis for Selecting the Application of Direct Capitalization or DCF**

The appraiser must decide whether it is appropriate to apply direct capitalization or DCF analysis according to the availability of data, the title category of the subject property, and the purpose of the client's request.

Section 2. Appraisal Approaches for Determining Real Estate Rental Value

There are several appraisal approaches for determining the rent paid for real estate. Where the rent is to be established for a new lease, acceptable methods include the summation approach, the rental data comparison approach, and the income analysis approach; where the rent is to be established for a renewed lease, acceptable methods include the rental disparity analysis approach, the yield approach, the trend approach, and the rental data comparison approach.

I General Commentary on Determining Rental Value

In a rental appraisal, the appraiser normally estimates the real rent to be paid to the lessor of the subject property over the period of payment. However, the appraiser may estimate the nominal rent in addition to the real rent, if the client requests him/her to do so and provides him/her with: 1) the specifics of the payment period and timing; and 2) information on paid deposits, such as *kenrikin*, a non-refundable deposit on residential space; *shikikin*, a refundable security deposit on residential space; and hoshokin, a refundable security deposit on commercial space.

1．Real Rent and Nominal Rent

Real rent refers to all reasonable economic compensation payable to the lessor over the period of payment regardless of the specific form in which the rent is paid. Real rent represents gross rent, i.e., net rent plus miscellaneous expenses normally required to operate the real estate (called "operating expenses").

Nominal rent refers to rent paid at the time of each scheduled installment. It is the real rent less the interest on the deposits and the amortization of non-refundable deposits, provided the lessor has received deposits such as *kenrikin*, *shikikin*, and *hoshokin*, specified in the lease contract.

Furthermore, although it is common practice for utility expenses, cleaning and sanitation costs as well as heating and cooling costs to be paid each month in the form of so-called added rent or as common area charges for leased space, it must be noted that some portions of these payments can be equivalent to rent.

2．Determination of Nominal Rent

When the lessee has paid deposits stipulated in the lease, the nominal rent is determined by deducting the interest earned on the deposits and the amortization of non-refundable deposits from the effective rent.

The interest earned and the amortization of non-refundable deposits should be appropriately determined based on the circumstances, including changes in the value of the subject property during the lease period.

The appraiser may determine the investment yield by comparing various investment returns, such as the expected yield on real estate, the market-derived capitalization rate, the interest on long-term deposits, the yield on government and corporate bonds, and the interest paid on loans from financial institutions, while bearing in mind differences in the kinds of deposits specified in the lease contract, the specific term and rental payments negotiated, and the type and condition of the subject property.

3. Calculation Periods for Rent

For leased building sites and leased properties comprising buildings and building lots, one-month units are generally used to calculate the rent determined by an appraisal. One-year units are used for calculating rent for other types of land.

II Appraisal Approaches for Determining the Market Rent under New Lease

1. Summation Approach

(1) Concept

The summation approach first determines the base value of the subject property on the date of the value opinion; the base value is then multiplied by the anticipated yield, and operating expenses are added to the resulting amount to arrive at gross rent (the rent estimated by this method is called rent indicated by the summation approach).

The summation approach is applicable where the base value of the subject property, the anticipated yield, and the operating expenses can be accurately determined.

(2) Application

① Base Value

The base value serves as the basis of the subject property's value to be used for determining the indicated rent by the summation approach; base value is determined by the cost and the sales comparison approaches.

② Anticipated Yield

Anticipated yield is the ratio between the anticipated net cash flow (NCF) to the capital invested in the leased real estate.

The method for determining anticipated yield is the same as the method for determining the capitalization rate in the income capitalization approach. In this particular application, special attention should be given to the characteristics of the rent.

③ Operating Expenses

Examples of expenses that are included in the total estimate of operating expenses for leased real estate are provided below.

 a. Depreciation
 b. Maintenance and management fees (including maintenance costs, management fees and repair expenses)

c．Real estate taxes (including property taxes and city planning tax)
　　d．Insurance premiums (including premiums for fire, machinery, boiler and other insurance)
　　e．Allowance for collection loss
　　f．Vacancy allowance

2．Rental Data Comparison Approach
(1) Concept
In the rental data comparison approach, the appraiser first gathers data on a large number of new leases in order to select actual real rents (actual real rent refers to the total economic compensation to the real estate as reflected in the rent). Then, if required, the appraiser makes adjustments to the comparable rents with regard to lease condition and time factor. Finally, the appraiser compares the subject property with the comparables in terms of market-specific and property-specific value influences to arrive at the indicated rent (the rent determined by this approach is called rent indicated by the rental data comparison approach).

The rental data comparison approach is applicable where there is an availability of leasing data on comparable properties in the neighborhood or similar neighborhoods in the primary market area, or leasing data on properties in a substitutive or competitive relationship with the subject property, located in the primary market area.

(2) Application
① Gathering and Selection of Data
The process of gathering and selecting lease data is the same as in the sales comparison approach. In this particular application, the lease data should be selected from lease contracts with similar terms and rental payments.

② Comparing Lease Conditions, and Changes in Rent Levels, and Market－specific and Property－specific Value Influences
The comparative procedures (i.e., the comparisons between the subject and comparable properties for different conditions of lease and rent levels over the time since the comparable transactions took place as well as the comparisons of market-specific and property-specific value influences) are the same as in the sales comparison approach.

3．Income Analysis Approach
(1) Concept
The income analysis approach determines the indicated rent for a non-leased income-producing property on the basis of its net income after depreciation. This is the net income attributable to the subject property over a fixed period. The appraiser adds operating expenses to the net income to estimate the indicated rent (the rent determined by this approach is called rent indicated by the income analysis approach).

The income analysis approach is applicable where the net income attributable to owner-occupied property for business operation can be properly determined.

(2) Application
① Calculation of Net Income
The procedure for calculating net income is the same as that for calculating net cash

flow (NCF) in the income capitalization approach. In this particular application, special attention must be paid to the characteristics of the imputed rent.

② Methodology for Determining an Indication of Rent by the Income Analysis Approach

In the income analysis approach, the appraiser estimates the subject property's indicated rent by adding the net income to the expected operating expenses, assuming the property is being leased.

In some cases, the appraiser can conclude an indication of the rent (net rent plus operating expenses) by analyzing the total revenues and expenses of the subject non-leased income-producing properties.

Ⅲ Appraisal Approaches for Determining Rent under Renewed Lease

1. Rental Disparity Analysis Approach

(1) Concept

The rental disparity analysis approach arrives at the reasonable market rent of the subject property by adding an estimated increase to, or deducting an estimated decrease from, the actual rent. The increased or decreased amount is obtained by first determining the difference between the reasonable market rent and the actual real rent or actual nominal rent. The appraiser then estimates the portion of the difference assignable to the lessor by a thorough analysis of lease terms, contract negotiations and so forth. Finally, the assignable amount is either added to, or deducted from, the actual rent.

(2) Application

① The reasonable real rent based on the economic value of the subject property is the market rent assumed on the date of the value opinion. The reasonable real rent may be determined by the summation approach or the rental data comparison approach.

Where deposits have been paid to the lessor as a condition of the lease contract, the reasonable nominal rent based on the economic value of the subject property is determined by deducting the interest earned and/or the amortization of deposits, such as *kenrikin*, *shikikin*, and *hoshokin* from the effective rent.

② The economic benefit or disadvantage assignable to the lessor is determined by analyzing a wide range of factors that may account for a difference between reasonable market rent and actual rent. The appraiser analyzes general value influences and market-specific value influences, and examines the contractual matters indicated below.

  a. The years passed and the remaining lease term
  b. Background factors at the time the lease contract was negotiated and relations between the tenant and landlord up to the present
  c. Degree to which the lessor or tenant contributes to the neighborhood

2. Yield Approach

(1) Concept

The yield approach arrives at an estimate of gross rent by adding operating expenses to base value multiplied by the rental yield rate under a renewed lease.

(2) **Application**
① The methods of determining base value and operating expenses in the yield approach are the same as in the summation approach.
② The rental yield rate under a renewed lease is based on the ratio of net rent to base value at the time the current rent was negotiated. It may be determined by thoroughly comparing 1) yield rates reflected in the data, including the yield at the time the contract was signed and each time the rent was revised, 2) the growth rate in base value, and 3) yield rates reflected in comparable data on similar properties in the neighborhood or similar neighborhoods in the primary market area, or comparable rental data on real estate in a substitutive or competitive relationship with the subject, and located in the primary market area.

3. Trend Approach
(1) **Concept**
The trend approach arrives at an estimate of gross rent by adding operating expenses on the date of the value opinion to the net rent, at the time the current rent was negotiated, which is multiplied by a trend factor for the growth rate in rent.

Where it is possible to determine a trend factor for the actual real rent or actual nominal rent since the time the current rent was agreed upon, the appraiser can arrive at the indicated rent by directly multiplying the current rent by the trend factor.

(2) **Application**
① A trend factor represents the amount of change in rent corresponding to changes in economic conditions between the time the current rent was agreed upon and the date of the value opinion. It may be determined by a thorough analysis of various indicators, including changes in land and building values, changes in commodity prices and changes in income level.
② The method for determining operating expenses is the same as in the summation approach.

4. Rental Data Comparison Approach
The rental data comparison approach is applied the same way as the rental data comparison approach for determining rent under a new lease.

V - 3. Real Estate Appraisal Standards

CHAPTER 8. APPRAISAL PROCESS

Real estate appraisal requires a planned, orderly process based on realistic understanding and reasonable judgment. This process typically includes 1) identifying basic appraisal problem, 2) drafting a processing plan, 3) identifying of the subject property, 4) gathering and organizing data, 5) reviewing data and analyzing value influences, 6) applying appraisal methodologies, 7) reconciling the indicated values or indicated rents, 8) determining the final value opinion, and 9) preparing the appraisal report. The appraiser carries out these steps in an orderly manner.

Section 1. Identification of Basic Appraisal Problem
Basic appraisal matters include clear confirmation of the intentions of the client with respect to the purpose of the appraisal and any limiting conditions.

Section 2. Identification of Client, Parties for Submission, and Interests/Ties
The following matters should be confirmed along with the confirmation of the client's intentions specified in the previous section.
Ⅰ　Client and parties for submission other than the client, if any
Ⅱ　Interests/ties associated with appraisers and appraisal firms involved in the valuation
　1. Interests/ties of appraisers or appraisal firms involved in the valuation regarding the subject property
　　The presence of interests between appraisers involved in the valuation (all appraisers involved in the valuation; the same applies hereinafter) or appraisal firms involved in the valuation (the appraisal firms in which the appraisers belong to; the same applies hereinafter) and the subject property or parties who have connections or special interests in the subject property, and details of such interests, should be clarified.
　2. Ties between the client and appraisers or appraisal firms involved in the valuation
　　The presence of are any special capital, personal or business ties between the client and appraisers or appraisal firms involved in the valuation and details of such ties should be clarified.
　3. Ties between the parties for disclosure/submission and appraisers or appraisal firms involved in the valuation
　　The presence of any special capital, personal, or business ties between the parties for disclosure of the appraised value or parties for submission of the appraisal report other than the client and appraisers or appraisal firms involved in the valuation and details of such ties should be clarified. If the parties for disclosure / submission are not determined or unknown, indicate that accordingly.

Section 3. Drafting of Processing Plan
A processing plan must be drafted in an orderly manner in respect to the appraisal matters identified above (i.e., with respect to verifying the description of the subject property, gathering and organizing data, reviewing data and analyzing value influences, applying appraisal methodologies, adjusting the indicated values and indicated rents, and determining the final value opinion) according to the quality and quantity of work to be done and processing abilities required.

Section 4. Identification of the Subject Property
To identify the subject property, the elements of the subject property's identification, as confirmed in the first step above, must be checked. These include the subject property's physical characteristics and ownership and interests. This step is carried out by means of sufficient investigation, including a property inspection, interviews, confirmation of public data, and so forth.

I Identification of the Physical Characteristics of the Subject Property
To identify the physical characteristics of the subject property, the subject property and property components must be compared with identification data (see Section 4-I below) and checked by site inspection to confirm the location, lot number, area and so forth; in addition to the above items, the appraiser must confirm the house number, structure and use of buildings.

The appraiser also has to ascertain whether the components of the subject property registered in the real property registry book differ in any way from the actual circumstances.

II Identification of Ownership and Interests
To identify ownership and interests, the appraiser must check the title to the subject property, as physically described above in paragraph I, against identification data. All titles to or interests in the subject property must be confirmed.

Section 5. Gathering and Organizing of Data
Since the results of an appraisal depend on the data that is used, the gathering and selection of data must be performed in a dependable manner through site inspection, interviews and confirmation of public data. This step of the appraisal process should be based on a rational plan appropriate to the appraisal assignment, and should produce objective and valid data.

Data required for appraisals can generally be categorized as indicated below.

I Property Identification Data
Property identification data refers to the data required to identify the physical characteristics of, and title encumbrances on, the real estate. Examples of identification data include the land registry book, drawings of the land or building, photographs, and maps showing the location of the real estate.

II Data on Value Influences
This category of data refers to data that reflects a variety of value influences. Data on value influences may be divided into data pertaining to general value influences, data pertaining to market-specific value influences, and data pertaining to property-specific value in-

V − 3. Real Estate Appraisal Standards

fluences.

General and market-specific data should be routinely gathered in an organized manner for a broad range of value influences. Property-specific data should be appropriately gathered on different types of properties and property characteristics.

III Comparable Data

Comparable data refers to data relating to actual transaction prices or rents required to apply the appraisal approaches. Examples of comparable data include construction data, comparable sales data, income data and leasing data.

There are also cases in which the appraiser can refer to the previous appraisal values and asking prices of comparable properties.

Section 6. Review of Data and Analysis of Value Influences

The data gathered must be examined to determine whether it satisfies the needs of the appraisal assignment, and whether or not it is sufficiently reliable. In particular, the data should be reviewed to determine whether or not it describes properties similar to the subject property, suits the purpose of the assignment, and allows for proper analysis of value influences.

In analyzing value influences, the appraiser examines all the data that has been collected. After investigating general value influences, the appraiser studies market-specific and property-specific value influences to determine the highest and best use of the subject property.

In cases where the effect of influences on the value of the subject property cannot be clearly determined despite the appraiser's having undertaken all the required research, it may be necessary to rely on the results of the investigation of another professional. Sometimes, because of restrictions resulting from the client's request, the appraiser will only be able to perform the appraisal by imposing additional assumptions or limiting conditions with the consent of the client. In other cases, the appraiser will have to determine the effect of value influences on the subject property based on his / her own investigative and analytical capabilities. In such situations, it is necessary to report all additional assumptions imposed to perform the appraisal assignment and to arrive at the value estimate.

Section 7. Application of Appraisal Method

The appraisal method applied should be appropriate to the subject of the appraisal. As a general rule, all three methodologies, i. e., the cost approach, sales comparison approach, and income capitalization approach, should be employed. Where the type of subject property or circumstances involving the property's location or reliability of the data make it difficult to apply each of the three approaches, every possible effort should be made to incorporate concepts from all approaches.

Section 8. Reconciliation of the Indicated Value or Rent

Reconciliation of the indicated values or indicated rents refers to the task of reconsidering the value or rent indicated by each appraisal approach, and judging the persuasiveness of each indicated value or indicated rent. Upon completing this step, the appraiser can determine the opinion of value that serves as the final judgment of the appraisal.

In reconciling the indicated values or indicated rents, it is important for the appraiser to be able to explain value influences acting on the subject property in both a logical and empirical manner. Consequently, reconciliation is performed by objectively and critically reconsidering each stage of the appraisal process and judging the weight to be placed on each indicated value or indicated rent. Attention must be given to the matters listed below.

I **In reconsidering each indicated value or indicated rent, the following should be addressed:**
  1. the suitability of the data selected and reviewed
  2. the appropriateness of the data used in view of the principles of value applied in valuing the subject real estate
  3. the suitability of the analysis of general value influences as well as the analyses of the neighborhood and subject property
  4. the appropriateness of judgments pertaining to various adjustments made in applying each method
  5. the consistency of judgment applied to value influences commonly dealt with in each method
  6. the suitability of the correlation between unit price and total value

II **In forming judgments about the weight to be placed on each indicated value or indicated rent, the following should be addressed:**
  1. the consistency between the results obtained and each technique applied in the analyses of the neighborhood and subject property
  2. the relative reliability of the indicated value or indicated rent, based on the characteristics and/or limitations of the data used in applying each method

Section 9. Determination of the Final Opinion of Value

After having performed the procedures described above, the appraiser is able to determine a final opinion of value, considered to be reasonable and conscionable.

In compliance with Article 2, Paragraph 1 of the *Land Price Publication Act*, the published land price must be used as a standard for determining the market value of land in published land areas.

Section 10. Preparation of the Appraisal Report

The appraisal report is prepared after the final opinion of value has been determined.

CHAPTER 9. APPRAISAL REPORT

The appraisal report is a document containing the results of a real estate appraisal. Its purpose is to clearly present the judgment and opinion of the LREA, based on his or her specialized knowledge and experience, and to clarify the scope of the appraiser's liability.

Section 1. Guidelines for Preparing Appraisal Report

The primary objective of the appraisal report is to communicate the basis of the appraisal and the final value opinion, to explain the rationale for the final value opinion, and to indicate the extent of the liability of the LREA involved in the real estate appraisal. Thus, the appraiser should prepare the report by first organizing all data used in the appraisal process, and then clarifying matters relating to judgment of value influences, judgment in applying appraisal methodology, and so forth.

The contents of the appraisal report are the substance of the appraisal document presented to the client by the LREA's firm. (Editor's Note: The standards distinguish an appraisal report from an appraisal document although the contents of the two documents are identical. The report is presented to the client with the signature of the appraiser through the appraisal firms) The appraisal report has an effect on not only the client but also on third parties, and serves as a basis for an orderly real estate value formation. Thus, offering clarification to ensure there is no room for misunderstanding, every effort must be made in preparing the report to adequately explain to the client and third party readers the rationale for the final value opinion.

Section 2. Report Contents

The appraisal report must contain, as a minimum, the following items (I through IX), and address the other matters indicated below.

I Final Opinion of Value and Type of Value or Rental Value

In accordance with the function and conditions of the valuation as requested by the client, the appraiser may estimate special value, value for regulated purposes (VRP) or special rent in an assignment that might be to arrive at market value or market rent. When the appraiser chooses to do so, the appraiser must report the market value or market rent in parentheses after the appraised value or rent. When asked to estimate nominal rent, as defined in CHAPTER 7, Section 2-I-1, the appraiser must also indicate the type of rent beside the appraisal figure. If the nominal rent differs from the real rent, the appraiser also includes the real rent in parentheses after the nominal rent.

II Assumptions and Limiting Conditions of the Appraisal

Where deemed necessary, the report will not only clarify the rationale for imposing assumptions and limiting conditions regarding market-specific and property-specific value influences (and explain their validity in terms of the function of the appraisal and the client's request) but also indicate what the value would be if such assumptions had not been made.

Ⅲ Location of the subject property, lot number, category of land, house number, structure, use, area and the types of title encumbrances pertaining to the subject property

Ⅳ Correspondence between the Function and Conditions of the Appraisal and the Type of Value or Rent Estimated

The report must state the rationale for determining the type of value estimated according to the function and conditions of the appraisal. In particular, where the type of value is value for regulated purposes (VRP), the report must clearly indicate the relevant laws and ordinances, which call for the special considerations. Where the type of value is value of special-purpose property, the report must indicate the facts such as the property's designation as a cultural asset.

Ⅴ Date of the Value Opinion and Date of the Appraisal Report

Together with the date of the opinion of value and the date when the appraisal is completed, the report must indicate the date of the property inspection. This is important because questions about the actual state of the property may arise at a later date.

Ⅵ The Principal Reasons for the Final Opinion of Value

The principal reasons for selecting the final value opinion are discussed under the topics listed below.

1. Analyses of the Neighborhood of value and Subject Property

The appraisal report must include discussion of the following items: the location and character of the primary market area and neighborhood, the value influences acting on the subject property, market trends in the primary market area and the behavior of typical market participants in the primary market area, the superiority or inferiority of the subject property in relation to substitutive or competitive real estate, and the relative competitiveness of the subject property.

2. The Highest and Best Use of the Subject Property

The highest and best use of the subject property and how it was determined must be clearly described. Furthermore, where the highest and best use of a building and the building site are to be determined, the report must identify the highest and best use of the building site as though vacant.

3. The Application of the Appraisal Approaches

Where all three appraisal approaches cannot be applied, the reason for not doing so must be explained.

4. The Indicated Value or Indicated Rent

The report must explain the appraiser's reconciliation of the indicated values or indicated rents and the reason that the appraiser judged it to be persuasive.

5. Compliance with the Requirement to Report the Published Price of Land

6. Other Matters

Where the purpose of the appraisal is to determine nominal rent as discussed in CHAPTER 7, Section 2-I-1 of these Standards, the report must describe the relationship between that nominal rent and the effective rent.

Ⅶ Handling of Ambiguous Appraisal Matters and the Scope of the Investigation

The report must clearly indicate how matters were handled that could not be clarified because of limitations on, or insufficiency of, data at any stage of the appraisal process (e.g., in identifying the subject property, reviewing the data compiled, or analyzing value influences). LREAs must describe the scope and content of the investigations they themselves conducted, and when they made use of investigations conducted by other professionals, the scope and content of those investigations must be clearly indicated.

VIII Interests/ties associated with appraisers and appraisal firms involved in the valuation

1. Interests/ties associated with appraisers and appraisal firms involved in the valuation regarding the subject property

    The presence of are any special interests between the appraisers or appraisal firms involved in the valuation and the subject property or parties who have connections or interests in the subject property and details of such interests should be specified in the appraisal report.

2. Ties between the client and appraisers or appraisal firms involved in the valuation

    The presence of are any special capital, personal, or business ties between the client and appraisers or appraisal firms involved in the valuation and details of such ties should be specified in the appraisal report.

3. Ties between the parties for disclosure / submission and appraisers or appraisal firms involved in the valuation

    The presence of any special capital, personal, or business ties between the parties for disclosure / submission and appraisers or appraisal firms involved in the valuation and details of such ties should be specified in the appraisal report. (If the parties for disclosure / submission are not determined or unknown, indicate that accordingly.)

IX Names of appraisers involved in the valuation

X Names of client and parties for submission other than the client, if any

Section 3. Addenda to Appraisal Reports

Maps clearly showing the location of the subject property, drawings of the land and/or buildings, photographs and other identification data as well as comparable data may be attached to the appraisal report when appropriate.

Data acquired from the reports of investigations conducted by other professionals may also be attached to the appraisal report. However, such data may only be attached to the appraisal report when the consent of the professional, who complied it, has been obtained.

SPECIFIC STANDARDS (SS)

LREAs perform appraisals of individual properties on the basis of their own specialized knowledge, professional capabilities, and in accordance with General Standards. To ensure competent appraisals of specific property types, practitioners should employ techniques corresponding to those associated with the use and title categories of real estate discussed below.

CHAPTER 1. APPRAISAL OF REAL ESTATE VALUE

Section 1. Land
I Building Sites
1. Vacant Land

The final opinion of the value of vacant land is determined by reconciling the value indicated by the sales comparison approach (based on comparable sales data on both vacant land and land with owner-occupied improvements) and the value indicated by the income capitalization approach (when the appraiser can estimate the value of the improvements, using methods other than the income capitalization approach, and is also able to determine the expected building and land capitalization rates, the value of the land is developed by the land residual technique, which allocates the net operating income [NOI] to the property between the building and the land, and capitalizes NOI to the land.).

Where reproduction cost can be estimated, the final value opinion should be formed by reconciling value indications from the sales comparison, income capitalization, and cost approaches. In cases where the area of the subject land is larger than the area of the standard plot size for the neighborhood, the final value opinion should be determined by comparing the values that would result from the following alternative valuation methods (subdivision development analysis) :

(1) When a condominium or townhouse building is recognized as being the rational use, the value of the vacant land may be obtained by deducting the normal building construction costs and incidental expenses (to be borne directly by the builder) from the total sales price, assuming the construction of the building, which represents the highest and best use of the site as of the date of the value opinion.

(2) When subdivision is recognized as being the rational use, the value of the vacant land may be obtained by deducting the normal site preparation costs and incidental expenses (to be borne directly by the builder) from the total sales price, assuming the subdivision of the vacant land and creation of standard sized building sites as of the date of the value opinion (this approach is referred to as the subdivision development approach).

When applying allocation and land residual techniques, the appraiser should use comparable sales data and income data that reflect the prices paid for, or income generated by, the lot under its highest and best use.

2. Land Portion of Built-Up Property

The land portion of a built-up property refers to a building site on which an improvement stands. The utility of land in this category is recognized as being closely associated with the building. Thus, the land portion of built-up property is appraised on the basis of its severance value when the current use is deemed reasonable.

As a general rule, the upper limit on the value of the land portion of built-up property is set by the value of the land as though vacant. The appraised value of the land portion of built-up property is determined by reconciling the value indicated by the sales comparison approach (developed by the allocation method) with the value indicated by the income capitalization approach (developed by the land residual technique).

The appraiser should consider 1) whether there is any difference between the highest and best use of the property as improved and the site as though vacant, 2) the degree of difficulty in demolishing the improvements, and 3) how well the building suits the site.

3. Leasehold Interests in Land and Leased Fee Interests in Land

Since the value of the leasehold interest in land and the value of the leased fee interest in land are closely related, the appraiser should compare the two values. In particular, the appraiser should consider the matters indicated below.

① Leasing practices involving building sites, and the characteristics of the sales market of leasehold and leased fee interests may differ depending on the city, and even within the same city, depending on the area.

② The existence of a leasehold interest in land does not necessarily mean that the leasehold interest in the land has value. Furthermore, there are some cities or areas where the conveyance of leasehold interests in land is negotiated independently. While in other cities or areas, the conveyance of leasehold interests in land is negotiated in conjunction with building transactions.

③ The appraiser should consider the area where the leasehold interest in land is being conveyed, i.e.,

　a. Whether or not it is an area where leasehold interests bear value when they are originally contracted or transferred

　b. Whether or not it is an area where leasehold interests in land are conveyed by transactions that typically involve persons other than owners

　c. Whether or not it is an area where many leasehold interests in land are held by the owners of steel and concrete frame (solid) buildings

　d. Whether or not it is an area where tenants have a strong awareness of leasehold interests in land

　e. Whether or not it is an area where receipt of deposits is a common practice

　f. Whether or not it is an area where the seller or the buyer of a leasehold in land usually pays a transfer agreement fee

④ The appraiser should consider the forms of the leasehold interest in land, i.e.,

　a. Originally contracted or transferred,

　b. Whether a superficies or a regular ground lease

　c. Whether or not a sublease

- d. Whether the purpose is to own a steel and concrete frame (solid) building or a wooden frame (non-solid) building
- e. Whether it is primarily a building for residency or for commercial use
- f. The presence or absence of a stipulated lease term
- g. The presence or absence of special provisions
- h. Whether the contract is written or oral
- i. The presence or absence of title registration
- j. Periodic leasehold interests in land (periodic leasehold interests in land as stipulated in Section 2, Paragraph 4 of the *Land Lease and Building Lease Law*) (Editor's Note: A periodic lease on land is a land lease for a fixed term.)

(1) **Leasehold Interests in Land**
① **Value of Leasehold Interests in Land**
The value of a leasehold interest in land reflects the monetary value of the economic advantage, including the amortized amount of non-refundable deposits, attributable to the tenant, who leases the land based on the *Land Lease and Building Lease Law* (including the former *Ground Lease Law*).

The economic advantage attributable to the tenant includes a wide variety of benefits generated by use of the land. This advantage primarily consists of:
- a. Stability from being able to occupy the land for a long period of time and to enjoy the benefit from its exclusive use.
- b. The marketability of a leasehold interest in land supported by the present value of the difference between market rent and contract rent. The present value is calculated on the basis of the period during which that difference lasts. The market rent here reflects the market value of the site, in which the leasehold interest exists.

② **Appraisal of Leasehold Interests in Land**
The approach used for appraising leasehold interests in land differs according to the maturity of the leasing market.

  a. **Areas where a mature leasing market exists**
  The final opinion of the value of a leasehold interest in land is based on reconciling the value indications from four possible methods. These include: (i) the sales comparison approach (based on either comparable leasehold interests in land or comparable properties on leased land); (ii) the land residual technique (applied here to arrive at the value of the leasehold interest in land); (iii) the income capitalization approach (based on capitalizing the difference between the market rent and contract rent); and (iv) the leasehold ratio method (the ratio of a typical leasehold value to fee simple value in an area). The appraiser should place more weight on the first two methods in reconciling indicated values.

  The following matters should all be considered.
  (a) The potential for future revision of the rent and the amount of this revision
  (b) The forms of the leasehold interest in land (see above 3.- ④ -(a) through (j)) and the remaining economic life of the building

(c) The background to the contract negotiations (i.e., relations between the renter and the landlord), the lease period that has already elapsed, and the remaining period of the lease
(d) The amount of the deposit received in closing the contract and any related contract terms
(e) The expected amounts of future deposits and related contract terms
(f) The typical transaction pattern of leasehold interests in land (leasehold interests in the land alone or in land with improvements) and market-derived capitalization rates of ground leases
(g) The value of the site being leased (vacant land or the land portion of built-up property)

b. Areas where a mature leasing market does not exist

The final opinion of the value of the leasehold interest in land is mainly based on the value indicated by the land residual technique. The appraiser also considers 1) the value obtained by capitalizing the difference between the market and contract rent (based on the conditions set in the leasehold contract); and 2) the value obtained by deducting the value of the leased fee interest in the land from the value of the site being leased (vacant land or the land portion of built-up property).

In these situations, items (a) through (g) above should all be considered.

(2) Leased Fee Interests in Land

The value of a leased fee interest in land reflects the economic benefit to the lessor. The benefit is closely related to the value of the leasehold interest in land.

The economic benefit to the lessor refers to the present value of the net operating income generated over the lease period, i.e., the amount remaining after deducting operating expenses from the actual nominal rent paid for the building site, plus the present value of the reversion upon the termination of the ground lease.

The final opinion of the value of a leased fee interest in land is determined by reconciling the value indicated by the income capitalization approach (the total present value of net operating income (NOI) based on the actual nominal rent and the reversion), and the value indicated by the sales comparison approach. In these situations, items (1) - ② -a-(a) through (g) above should all be considered.

In addition, it should be noted that if the tenant acquires the leased fee interest in the land, the economic value of the land may increase. This is attributable to the building site's greater marketability, resulting from the fact that the building and building site now belong to the same owner.

4. Sectional Superficies

The value of sectional superficies is typically based upon the value of the land, on which the sectional superficies are established. The specific economic benefits that derive from the creation of such superficies help determine their value. The value of sectional superficies is a monetary amount, reflecting two components: the economic value of the superficies, i.e., the rights to air or subsurface space ("two- or three-dimensional division of space"); and the economic value of the surrounding space whose utilization is restricted by structures in the superficies space.

The final opinion of the value of sectional superficies is obtained by reconciling 1) the value indicated by the sales comparison approach based on analysis of contract data, 2) the value indicated by the income capitalization approach using a residual technique, and 3) the value developed by applying a vertical allotment ratio for sectional superficies, which is derived from comparable properties.

II Agricultural Land

Appraisals of agricultural land may be requested for transactions where the objective is to convert the agricultural land to another land use, e.g., the acquisition of land to be used for public works.

In such situations, the final opinion of the value of agricultural land is based on the values indicated by the sales comparison and income capitalization approaches. Where reproduction cost can be estimated, the final value opinion should be formed by reconciling the above value indications with the value indicated by the cost approach.

It should be noted that in acquisitions of agricultural land for public works, agricultural compensation is sometimes provided separately as compensation for the losses normally incurred in the land acquisition.

III Forestland

Appraisals of forestland may be requested for transactions where the objective is to convert the forestland to another land use, e.g., the acquisition of land to be used for public works.

In such situations, the final opinion of the value of forestland is based on the values indicated by the sales comparison and income approaches. Where reproduction cost can be estimated, the final value opinion should be formed by reconciling the above value indications with the value indicated by the cost approach.

It should be noted that in acquisitions of forestland for public works, there are cases in which forestation compensation is sometimes provided separately as compensation for the losses normally incurred in the land acquisition.

IV Building Sites with Interim Uses

The final opinion of the value of a building site with an interim use is determined by reconciling the value indicated by the sales comparison approach and the value indicated by the steps in the following method: (a) estimating the value of the subject site assuming all the site services are provided on the date of the value opinion; (b) deducting normal site preparation costs and normal incidental expenses (to be borne directly by the builder) from the estimated land value in (a); and (c) forecasting the time required to realize the land use conversion and adjusting the value derived in (b) accordingly. In particular, the appraiser should consider the effect of urban growth on the neighborhood as well as the following matters.

1. Government measures and/or regulations that facilitate or hinder conversion of the interim use building site to a building site ready to accommodate its next use
2. Current and anticipated construction of public and institutional facilities in the vicinity
3. Current and anticipated construction of housing, commercial facilities, and factories in the vicinity

4. How difficult the task of site preparation will be and how extensive the required site preparation will be
5. How effectively the site will be used as a building site following site preparation

When the interim use of a building site is anticipated to have a long duration, the final opinion of value is determined by placing the most emphasis on the sales comparison approach. The appraiser also looks at the value based on the original land use, considering the expected appreciation in value.

Section 2. Built – Up Property
I Owner – Occupied Building and Its Site

The final opinion of the value of an owner-occupied building and its site is determined by reconciling the values indicated by the cost, sales comparison and income capitalization approaches.

Where converting the use of the building or remodeling the building for another use is the highest and best use of an owner-occupied building and its site, the appraiser determines the value of the subject property after taking into account both the increase in economic value resulting from the change in use and the required remodeling costs.

Where demolition of the building is the highest and best use of an owner-occupied building and its site, the final opinion of value is determined by first deducting an estimate of the required expenses of demolition and removal of debris from the salvage value of the materials remaining after demolition of the building. The difference is added to the value of the lot under its highest and best use.

II Tenant – Occupied Buildings and Its Sites

In arriving at the final opinion of the value of a tenant-occupied building and its site, the appraiser places the most emphasis on the value indicated by the income capitalization approach (estimated as the total present value of both net operating income [NOI] generated from the actual effective rent and reversion). (In transactions where the seller does not pass on to the buyer part of the deposits that the seller received, the interest on and amortization of such portion of deposits are not included in the estimated NOI.) Then the appraiser compares this value with the values indicated by the cost and sales comparison approaches. All of the following matters should be considered.

1. The potential for future revision of rent and the amount of this revision
2. The amount of the deposit received in closing the contract and any related contract terms
3. The expected amounts of future deposits and related contract terms
4. Background to the contract negotiations (i.e., relations between the renter and the landlord), the lease period that has already elapsed, the remaining period of the lease, and the remaining economic life of the building
5. The typical transaction pattern of tenant-occupied buildings and its sites and the market-derived capitalization rates
6. Whether the tenancy in the leased building is residential or commercial, the form of the contract, whether or not the title is registered, whether or not there is a sublease, and whether or not it is a periodic building lease as stipulated in Article 38 of the

Land Lease and Building Lease Law (Editor's Note: A periodic lease on a building is a building lease for a fixed term.)

7. The value of the tenant's rights (leasehold interest in building only)

It should be noted that if the tenant acquires the leased building and building site, the economic value of the site may increase. This is attributable to the greater marketability of the building and building site, resulting from the fact that the building and building site now belong to the same owner.

Ⅲ Buildings on Leased Land

1. Owner－Occupied Buildings on Leased Land

The final opinion of the value of a building on land held in leasehold, where the leaseholder owns the building, is determined by reconciling the values indicated by the cost, sales comparison and income capitalization approaches. All the items indicated above in ⑴-②-a-(a) through (g) (the section on the Appraisal of Leasehold Interests in Land) should be considered.

2. Tenant－Occupied Buildings on Leased Land

In arriving at the final opinion of the value of a leased building on land held in leasehold, where the leaseholder to the land rents out the building, the appraiser places the most emphasis on the value indicated by the income capitalization approach (estimated as the total present value of both net operating income (NOI) generated from the actual effective rent and reversion). (In transactions where the seller does not pass on to the buyer part of the deposits that the seller received, the interest on and amortization of such portion of deposits are not included in estimated NOI). Then, the appraiser compares this value with the values indicated by the cost and sales comparison approaches.

The appraiser should consider all of the above indicated items ⑴-②-a-(a) through (g) (Leasehold Interests in Land) and 1 through 7 in Ⅱ Tenant-Occupied Buildings and Building Sites.

Ⅳ Condominium Units

1. Value Influences on Condominium Units

The following list identifies typical property-specific value influences on condominium units.

⑴ **Property－Specific Value Influences on the Building and Building Site where the Condominium Project is Located**

① **Influences on the Building**

a. The age of the structure (whether a new structure, an expansion/reconstruction, or relocation)
b. Building area, height, structure and materials
c. Design and functionality
d. Construction quality and volume
e. Type of entryway, availability of conference rooms and other facilities
f. The number of floors in the building
g. Intended usage and actual use of the building
h. Quality of the maintenance and management
i. Status of residents and mix of shops

j. Earthquake resistance, fire resistance and compliance with other building codes
k. Whether any harmful substance was used in the construction, how it was used and whether it has been removed

② **Influences on the Site**
a. The shape of the site and dimensions of any open space
b. Facilities on the site
c. The size of the site
d. Ownership and interests in the site

③ **Influences on the Building and Building Site**
a. Layout of the building and ancillary facilities on the site
b. Relationship between the building and site size
c. Any long-term repair project(s), the sufficiency thereof, and the amount of funds reserved for the repair project(s)

(2) **Property-Specific Value Influences on the Exclusively Owned Area**
① Floor level and location
② Sunlight, view and scenery
③ Interior finish and quality of maintenance and management
④ Area of the condominium unit, its floor plan and room layout
⑤ Whether adjacent real estate is in use and the nature of that use
⑥ Convenience of elevators and other common facilities
⑦ Unit entitlement to the fee simple/leasehold interest in the site
⑧ Amount of unpaid management and other fees by condominium owners

2. The Appraisal of Condominium Units

(1) Owner-Occupied Units

The final opinion of the value of an owner-occupied condominium unit, the exclusively owned portion of which is held in freehold by the condominium owner, is determined by reconciling the values indicated by the cost, sales comparison and income capitalization approaches.

The value indicated by the cost approach is developed on the basis of the depreciated cost of the building and the site value where the condominium unit is located. This figure is then multiplied by the distribution factor for the subject unit, determined from the utility ratio for each floor of the building and for each location on each floor.

(2) Tenant-Occupied Units

In arriving at the final opinion of value of a tenant-occupied condominium unit, the appraiser places the most emphasis on the value indicated by the income capitalization approach (estimated from the total present value of both the net operating income (NOI) generated from the actual real rent and reversion). (In transactions where the seller does not pass on to the buyer part of the deposits that the seller received, the interest on and amortization of such portion of deposits are not included in estimated NOI.) Then, the appraiser compares this value with the values indicated by the cost and sales comparison approaches.

The appraiser should consider all of the items 1 through 7 in II Tenant-Occupied

Buildings and Building Sites.

Section 3. Buildings

The utility of a building is closely related to the utility of the building site. It is common practice to appraise a building and building site as a single unit. Depending on the purpose and conditions of specific assignments, however, the building may be appraised separately for both marketable and non-marketable properties.

I Appraising Buildings for Marketable Properties

A building may be appraised alone by estimating its severance value, i.e., by breaking down the final opinion of value of the total property, in which the building and building site are integrated into a single unit.

The final opinion of the value of the building is determined by reconciling the values indicated by the cost approach, sales comparison approach based on the allocation method, and income capitalization approach using the building residual technique. (In order to employ the building residual technique, the appraiser estimates the value of the site using any methods other than the income capitalization approach. The expected land and building capitalization rates are determined. Then, after allocating the net operating income [NOI] attributable to the property between the building and the site, the appraiser capitalizes the NOI to the building.)

II Appraising Buildings for Non−Marketable Properties

In appraising buildings for non-marketable properties, the appraiser typically estimates value of special-purpose property. Non-marketable properties include cultural heritage buildings, religious buildings, and utilities and institutional properties. The primary premise of such appraisals is to assume continuation of the current usage. The final opinion of the value of such buildings is determined by the value indicated by the cost approach.

III Tenant's Rights

Tenant's rights involve those rights associated with leasehold estates in buildings, to which the *Land Lease and Building Lease Law*, including the former *Building Lease Law*, applies. (Editor's note: It should be kept in mind that where the tenant is paying less than market rent, the leasehold is able to realize its value.)

Only a few types of tenant's rights can be traded in the market. When estimating the value of such transferable tenant's rights, the appraiser places the most weight on the value indicated by the sales comparison approach. In the process of using the sales comparison approach, the appraiser must take into consideration the specific features of the subject and comparable tenant's right contracts. The value of a tenant's right may also be calculated by the following steps: (1) estimating the value of the subject property both as if owner-occupied and as is; (2) deducting the value as is from the value as if owner-occupied; and (3) determining, out of the difference, an appropriate amount as the tenant's right. Furthermore, where the value of the tenant's rights may be determined on a percentage basis, this value should also be accounted for. In any event, the appraiser should consider all of the items indicated above as 1 through 7 in II Tenant-Occupied Buildings and Building Sites.

On the other hand, even a non-tradable tenant's right can give rise to value in one kind of situation involving the tenant and the landlord. When the landlord requests the tenant to vacate the building, the landlord usually pays the tenant's moving costs and compensates the tenant for disruption of the tenant's business. Therefore, in this kind of situation, the tenant's right is deemed to be equivalent to the tenant's de facto loss because the tenant was forced to move out of the premises. In this case, the appraiser determines the value of the tenant's rights by reconciling the value indications derived from the following two methods. In the first method, the appraiser: (1) estimates the difference between the actual market rent under a new lease (i.e., the market rent required to lease a unit in a substitutive or competitive building) and the current actual nominal rent; (2) calculates the present value of that difference for each year of the duration the difference is expected to last; and (3) adds both the amount of deposits, which are considered to be prepaid rents and other appropriate items, to the present value calculated in (2). In the second method, the appraiser: (1) estimates the value of the subject property both as if owner-occupied and as is; (2) deducts the value as is from the value as if owner-occupied; and (3) determines, out of the difference, an appropriate amount as the tenant's right. In addition to the individual circumstances of the involved parties, the appraiser should consider all the items indicated as 1 through 7 in II Tenant-Occupied Buildings and Building Sites.

CHAPTER 2. APPRAISAL OF REAL ESTATE RENTAL VALUE

Section 1. Building Sites
I Determining Market Rent Under New Lease
To determine the market rent of a building site, an estimate of the reasonable rent must be in line with the economic value of the building site, based on its use and the conditions of the lease contract.

The final opinion of the market rent of the building site is determined by reconciling the rent indicated by the summation approach, the rent indicated by the rental data comparison approach, and the rent indicated by the allocation method of the rental data comparison approach. When the net income can be properly estimated, the appraiser also considers the rent indicated by the income analysis approach.

The final opinion of rent may be required under circumstances where the building site is to be combined with another site or is to be subdivided. The synergistic or component rent is determined by reconciling the rent indicated by the summation approach (where the base value represents the assemblage value of the building site combined with an adjacent building site, or the component value of the building site resulting from subdivision), and the rent indicated by the rental data comparison approach (rental data that pertains to building sites that were combined with adjacent building sites or have been subdivided). The appraiser considers the following matters in this type of assemblage or subdivision.
  1. Ownership and interests in the adjacent building sites
  2. Conditions in the lease contracts from which the data is gathered

II Determining Rent Under Renewed Lease
1. Revising Actual Nominal Rent upon an Existing Ground Lease Contract
The appraiser arrives at the final opinion of the rental value at which to renew the actual nominal rent in an existing ground lease contract by reconciling rental estimates derived from the rental disparity analysis approach, the yield approach, the trend approach, and rental data comparison approach. The appraiser should consider all of the following items in this type of rental valuation.
  (1) Contract conditions and background of the contract negotiations
  (2) Elapsed term and remaining life of the contract
  (3) Previous rent revisions
  (4) Whether a renewal charge is required
  (5) Rent paid for comparable building sites in the neighborhood or similar neighborhoods within the primary market area, or rent paid for substitutive or competitive building sites in the primary market area, and the amount by which these rents have been revised
  (6) Market trends in net rent as a proportion of gross rent
  (7) Market trends in yields on ground leases

(8) Trends in real estate taxes

There are several reasons for revising rent. These include renewal of the lease upon conclusion of the lease or contract term, transfer of the leasehold interest in the land to a third party, and periodic rental renewals during a lease term. In the first two cases, a lump sum payment, called either `renewal fee´ or `transfer fee´, is often paid to the landlord. The appraiser must take into account such a lump sum payment in determining the final opinion of rental value.

2. Revising Rent upon a Change in the Contract Terms

When a ground lease contract is amended (e.g., through the elimination of restrictions on building renovations/additions, or on the type of building structures), a higher rent can be charged by the landlord. When asked to perform a rental renewal appraisal in this situation, the appraiser first estimates the new rent based on the approaches explained in the section above (1. Revising Actual Nominal Rent Based on an Existing Ground Lease Contract) assuming there was no amendment. Then, the appraiser analyzes the expected increase in the value of the subject land and improvements resulting from the amendment. Finally, the appraiser estimates the growth in rental value associated with the increase in property value over the rent first estimated without assuming the amendment.

In addition to the items indicated above in 1, the appraiser should consider all of the following matters.

(1) Characteristics of the lease
(2) Details of changes in the contract terms
(3) Amounts paid for consent to change the lease terms

Section 2. Built – Up Property
I Determining Market Rent Under New Lease

To determine the market rent of a building and building site, the rental estimate must be in line with the economic value of the building and building site, based on its use and the conditions of the lease contract.

The appraiser arrives at a final opinion of the market rent of a building and building site by reconciling the rents indicated by the summation approach and the rental data comparison approach. When the net income from the property can be properly estimated, the appraiser also considers the rent indicated by the income analysis approach.

Where a portion of the building and building site is being leased, the appraiser arrives at a final value opinion of the market rent by considering the size and other attributes of the leased portion in relation to those of the entire building and building site.

II Determining Rent Under Renewed Lease

Estimates of the revision of actual nominal rent in existing lease contracts to buildings and building sites are done the same way as appraisals to determine rent under renewed leases to building sites.

CHAPTER 3. APPRAISAL OF REAL ESTATE VALUE SUBJECT TO SECURITIZATION

Section 1. Basic Approach to Securitization – Properties

I Definition of Securitization-Properties

In this chapter, the term ⹂securitization-properties″ refers to properties (including those held under trust beneficiary rights), which are subject to or likely to become subject to a real estate transaction of any of the following types.

(1) Assets undergoing liquidation as specified in the *Asset Liquidation Law (Shisan Ryudoka Ho)* ; real estate transactions involving investment trusts as specified in the *Investment Trust and Investment Corporation Law (Toshin Ho or Kaisei SPC Ho)* ; or real estate transactions undertaken by investment corporations as defined in that law.

(2) Real estate transactions related to contracts involving real estate syndication as defined in the Real Estate Syndication Act (Fudosan Kyodo Jigyo Ho).

(3) Real estate transactions generating income or profit, and undertaken for the main purpose of fulfilling obligations on securities as specified in the *Financial Instruments Trading Law (Kinsho Ho)*, Article 2, Paragraph 1, No. 5, No. 9 (which deals only with stock corporations established for the sole purpose of real estate trading, including limited companies (yugen kaisha), which survive as stock corporations under Article 2, Paragraph 1 of the *Law Concerning the Coordination, Etc. of Relevant Laws Relating to the Enforcement of the Corporation Act*), No. 14, or No. 16, or property rights considered to be securities under Paragraph 2, No. 1, 3, or 5 of that article.

The appraisal of securitization properties must be conducted as is prescribed in this chapter. A statement to this effect must be included in the appraisal report.

Even when appraising properties other than securitization properties, it is important that the appraiser endeavor to conduct the appraisal as is prescribed in this chapter for appraisals of a large-scale rental property held for investment purposes, and whenever it is considered necessary to protect the investor, purchaser, or other interested party.

II Responsibility of LREAs

(1) LREAs must always conduct appraisals in a manner giving full consideration to the proper procedures for the appraisal of securitization properties, while recognizing that they (LREAs) exert a significant influence on the decision making, not only of the persons requesting the appraisal of securitization properties (hereinafter referred to as ⹂clients″) but also of a wide range of investors and others, and also keeping in mind that they (LREAs) bear the important responsibility of upholding the public reputation of the real estate appraisal profession.

(2) When appraising a property for securitization purposes, the LREA should seek to facilitate the securitization, etc., of the property by providing the client with explanations of the data, procedures, and other matters related to the appraisal, thereby enhancing the client's understanding, and obtaining his cooperation. The LREA must also take care as to the way information is presented in the appraisal report in order

to make the content of the appraisal report on the securitization property easier for the client, persons holding interests in the securitization property, and others to understand and use in comparisons with reports on other properties. The LREA must be fully accountable, ensuring that the data and other informational materials used in the appraisal are available for disclosure.

(3) Whenever several LREAs are working jointly on the appraisal of a securitization-property, the roles of each LREA must be clearly defined, and all of the LREAs must work as a team to complete the appraisal assignment, sharing information on the overall appraisal and maintaining close and thorough collaboration.

Section 2. Drafting a Work Plan for the Appraisal
I Verifying the data needed to develop the work plan

When drafting a work plan for the appraisal, the LREA should verify with the client in advance matters related to the appraisal of a securitization property, in order to develop an appropriate and reasonable work plan that allows competent and reliable implementation of the appraisal. The verified information should be reflected in the work plan for the appraisal, and the plan should be changed whenever any change occurs in the information specified. Matters that should be verified include:

(1) Purpose of the request for the appraisal and background as to why the request was made.

(2) Classification of the subject property transaction under (1), (2), or (3) of Section 1, I above.

(3) Main subjects covered in the engineering report (an investigative report on the condition of the securitization property, conducted by a person having specialized knowledge of buildings, mechanical and electrical [M&E] systems, environmental matters, etc.; the same applies in Section 3 below), data needed to apply DCF analysis, and other relevant documents; and the time when these documents will be available.

(4) Whether there are explanatory comments from the preparer of the engineering report.

(5) Scope of the field surveys, including visual inspection of the interior of the subject property.

(6) Other matters needed to develop the work plan for the appraisal.

II Records of verified information

After verifying the matters listed in (1) through (6) of Section 2, I (1) above, records must be prepared for each of these items, and these records must be attached to the appraisal report as appendices. Included among these records are:

(1) Date verified

(2) Name of the LREA who verified the information

(3) Name and occupation of the person who provided the verification

(4) Content of the information confirmed, and whether it has been reflected in the work plan for the appraisal

(5) Details of any changes in the appraisal procedures or changes in the content of the

report, etc., which were made as a result of changes in the verified information

III Purpose of the request for the appraisal, and the relationship between the client and the parties involved in the securitization of the property

In many cases, a wide variety of parties are involved and hold complex interests in a securitization-property. The appraisal report must state the purpose of the request for the appraisal of the securitization property, the background as to why the request was made, and the following items concerning the interests of the client with regard to the securitization property.

(1) Whether the client holds interests in the securitization of the property (parties such as an originator, arranger, asset manager, lender, equity investor, special purpose company [SPC], corporate investor, or funding agency [referred to below as "parties involved in the securitization"] should be identified).

(2) Whether the client has capital ties or business connections to any of the parties involved in the securitization; and if so, the details of those relationships.

(3) The details of any other special interests between the client and any of the parties involved in the securitization.

Section 3. Investigating Property-Specific Value Influences acting on the Securitization-Property

I Investigation of property-specific value influences acting on the subject property

In the investigation of property-specific value influences acting on a securitization property, there must be a reliable and detailed confirmation of information about the physical and legal characteristics of the securitization property. The field survey for the requested appraisal of the securitization property, including the visual inspection of the interior of the subject property, must be conducted in the presence of the client (or persons designated by the client); and the data needed for the appraisal, including the identification of associated rights and interests, restrictions under public statute, the presence of toxic substances such as asbestos, determination of earthquake resistance, and the history of remodeling, expansion, etc., must be verified by means such as interviews with the manager, etc., of the subject property.

II Property inspection

The LREA must include the following matters relating to the field survey in the appraisal report.

(1) Date of the field survey.
(2) Name of the LREA who performed the field survey.
(3) Names and occupations of witnesses to the survey and managers of the subject property.
(4) Scope of the field survey (including whether or not the interior was visually inspected) and matters verified in the field survey.
(5) If it was not possible to perform any part of the field survey, the reasons must be stated.

III Handling of the engineering report, and the property investigation by the LREA

(1) In the appraisal of a securitization property, the LREA must ask the client to submit the engineering report required for the appraisal, and after analyzing and evaluating its content, the LREA must incorporate its conclusions in the appraisal. However, if no engineering report is submitted, or if its content is considered to be inadequate for use in the appraisal, the LREA must then take action such as conducting an independent investigation to substitute for the engineering report and thereby fulfill the requirements of the assignment; and the appraisal report must describe the results of that investigation as well as the reasons why it is considered to be appropriate.

(2) For example, the engineering report could be lacking or inadequate for use in reappraising a securitization property, which has previously been appraised, or the securitization property may be an empty lot (or one on which the buildings are to be demolished).

(3) The appraisal report must include a statement of what decision was made as to whether or not to use the content of the engineering report in the appraisal, along with the reasons for that decision. For all the items listed in the following table, the information specified must be included in the appraisal report. Appendix 1 provides a sample format for an appraisal report. The same applies in the case of the second statement at III(1) above (beginning with "however").

Item	Content
Basic information about the engineering report	· Name, etc., of the preparer of the engineering report · Date of the investigation undertaken for the engineering report, and date when the engineering report was prepared
How the engineering report was obtained, and how it was handled in the appraisal	· Party providing the engineering report (name, occupation, etc.) · Date obtained · Whether explanatory comments were obtained from the preparer of the engineering report · How the engineering report was handled in the appraisal
Method of investigation of property-specific influences, which is required for the appraisal	Statement as to whether the engineering report was used for the investigation of property-specific influences, or whether the LREA investigated these influences himself (the investigation may have also been done by another expert, at the request of the LREA): Property-specific influences to be investigated include: · Regulations and restrictions under public and private statutes (including the state of compliance with the law) · Renovation plan · Replacement cost · Building environment with regard to toxic substances, including asbestos · Soil pollution

	· Earthquake risk · Earthquake resistance · Buried structures or objects
LREA's conclusions about the method of investigation of property-specific influences, which is required for the appraisal	Decisions on whether to use the content of the engineering report or an investigation by the LREA of property-specific influences, along with the reasons for that decision, etc.

(4) Because the engineering report may need to be revised or supplemented owing to changes in the market environment for real estate securitization, the LREA must maintain close contact with the preparer of the engineering report, and must also endeavor to improve his own knowledge and understanding of engineering reports.

Section 4. Application of DCF method
When appraising the value of a securitization property by the income approach, DCF method must be applied. In addition, it is also appropriate to apply direct capitalization method for verification.

I Clarifying the procedure for applying DCF method
(1) The appraisal report must include statements regarding the suitability of the data used to determine the property's value by the income approach. Along with the reasons for the conclusion, these statements must indicate the following:
  ① Whether the data that was obtained from the client for the subject property, such as the income and expense amounts, has been used without modification.
  ② Whether the data that was obtained from the client for the subject property, such as the income and expense amounts, has been adjusted or modified.
  ③ Whether the LREA himself has obtained data for the subject property, such as the income and expense amounts.
(2) When DCF method is used to determine the value by the income approach, in addition to explaining the selection of the terminal capitalization rate, discount rate, forecasts of future income and expenses, and other individual items that have been assessed, the appraisal report must lay out the procedure by which that data was used to determine the value by the income approach and the reasons for using that procedure, clearly indicating such factors as the possibility of change in the economic situation, the specific comparables which were examined, and the logical consistency. When several LREAs work jointly to appraise a group of securitization properties, they must endeavor to ensure logical consistency among all of the subject properties with regard to the selection of terminal capitalization rates, discount rates, forecasts of future income and expenses, and other data used in applying DCF method.

V - 3. Real Estate Appraisal Standards

(3) The appraisal report must contain a clear statement of the relationship between the value indicated by the income approach, using DCF method (including verification by direct capitalization), and the indicated value using the cost approach, and sales comparison approach; and the appraisal report must also state the reasons for concluding the final opinion of value.

(4) The LREA must strive for greater accountability, endeavoring to improve his own knowledge and understanding in order to achieve further proficiency in the application of DCF method.

II Uniformity in income and expense items in DCF method

(1) When using DCF method to determine the value by the income approach, the income and expense amounts for the securitization property (hereinafter referred to as "income and expense items") must be entered in the appraisal report for each of several continuous time periods, classified according to the items shown in the following table. Each of the income and expense items should be accompanied by a breakdown of how the figures were calculated. When entering this data in the appraisal report, each item in the "Item" column of the following table should be defined as specified in the table.

	Item	Definition
Effective gross income	Potential gross income	When all or a portion of the subject property is rented or operated by a contractor, the recurring income (assuming full occupancy).
	Income from common area charges	Income collected under contracts with tenants for that portion of the recurring expenses in the maintenance, management, and operation of the subject property (including expenses for electricity, water, gas, regional heating and air conditioning, etc.), which apply to the common areas.
	Utility fee income	Income collected under contracts with tenants for that portion of the recurring expenses for electricity, water, gas, regional heating and air conditioning, etc., in the operation of the subject property, which apply to leased areas (assuming full occupancy).
	Parking fee income	Income from leasing the subject property's parking spaces to tenants, or from renting parking spaces by the hour.
	Other income	Other income from facility installation fees for signs, antennas, vending machines, etc., and income from lump-sum payments, which are not refundable, such as key money and renewal fees.
	Vacancy allowance	Decrease in each income item, based on predicted vacancies, periods it will take to replace tenants, etc.
	Collection losses allowance	Decrease in each income item, based on predicted debt collection losses.

Operating expenses	Maintenance and management expenses	Recurring expenses for the maintenance and management of the subject property, including building and mechanical and electrical (M&E) system management, security, and cleaning.
	Utility expenses	Expenses for electricity, water, gas, regional heating and air conditioning, etc., incurred in the operation of the subject property.
	Repair expenses	That portion of the expenditures for building and M&E system repair, renovation, etc., of the subject property, which is a recurring expense for ordinary building and M&E system maintenance and management, etc., or is expended to restore damaged building and M&E system portions to their original condition.
	Property management fees	Expenses for management services in the subject property.
	Tenant recruitment expenses, etc.	Expenses for rental agency services, advertising, etc., to recruit new tenants; and expenses for lease renewal or repeat leasing contracts with existing tenants.
	Real estate taxes	Property taxes (on land, buildings, and depreciable assets) and city planning taxes (on land and buildings).
	Casualty insurance premiums	Premiums for fire insurance on the subject property and accessory equipment; liability insurance for losses by third parties, etc., due to subject property defects or management failures, etc.
	Other expenses	Other expenses for ground rent, road occupancy and utilization, etc.
Net Operating Income		Operating income minus operating expenses.
Operating profit on lump-sum payments		Operating profit on security deposits and other lump-sum payments, which are f refundable deposits.
Capital expenditures		That portion of expenditures for building and M&E system repair, renovation, etc., which is recognized as increasing the value of the building, M&E system, etc., or strengthening its durability.
Net Cash Flow (Adjusted NOI)		Net operating income, plus operating profit on lump-sum payments, minus capital expenditures.

(2) When using DCF analysis to determine the value by the income approach, the LREA must identify and explain the income and expense items and their definitions to the client before obtaining the requisite data, and must check that each income and expense item corresponds to its specified definition.

(3) Appendix 2 is a sample format for an appraisal report when DCF analysis is applied. This format may be revised as is necessary to conform to the specific appraisal situation, based on factors such as the purpose and the category of the securitization property.

V - 3. Real Estate Appraisal Standards

Appendix 1

LREA		Affiliation	

Basic information about the engineering report and its acquisition

Basic information about the engineering report and its acquisition		Preparer	Client
	A		
	B		
	C		
	D		

How the submitted engineering report was handled in the appraisal; whether an additional investigation by the LREA was needed; results of the investigation by LREA, etc.	

Results of the investigation and preparer comments (Enter A, B, C, or D in the "Preparer" column)	Explanatory comments from the preparer	Item	Was the engineering report used, or did LREA conduct an investigation?
1. Building condition survey		Location overview	
		Building overview	
		M&E system overview	
		Structural overview	
		Regulations and restrictions under public and private statutes (state of compliance with the law)	
		Renovation/renewal history and plans	
		Emergency repair/renewal expenses	
		Short-term repair/renewal expenses	
		Long-term repair/renewal expenses	
		Replacement cost	
2. Building environment survey		Asbestos (Phase 1)	
		PCBs	
		Other	
3. Soil pollution risk assessment		Soil survey (Phase 1)	
4. Earthquake risk assessment		Simple analysis	
		Detailed analysis	

Buried structures or objects			
Building environment survey		Asbestos (Phase 2)	
Soil pollution risk assessment		Soil survey (Phase 2)	
		Environmental assessment, etc.	
Earthquake resistance survey		Earthquake resistance determination by architects, etc.	

Note: "Phase 1" indicates investigating the possible presence of toxic substances or pollutants by performing field surveys, collecting and analyzing data, and conducting interviews; "Phase 2" indicates confirming the presence or absence of toxic substances or pollutants by taking samples and conducting chemical analyses. "Simple analysis" indicates analysis by means of statistical methods, while "detailed analysis" indicates the use of analytical techniques.

Date of form completion		Name of property		Location of property	

Date investigated	Date prepared	Obtained from	Date obtained

Items used in appraisal, and reasons for doing so

V - 3. Real Estate Appraisal Standards

Appendix 2

Identification of the subject property

	Location and block number	Land category	Lot area			
Land						
Building	Location	House number	Structure	Purpose	Floor area	Date co...

			1	2	·	·	·	·	·	·
(a)	Effective gross income	Potential gross income								
(b)		Income from common area charges								
(c)		Rental income, including income from common area charges [(a)+(b)]								
(d)		Utility fee income								
(e)		Parking fee income								
(f)		Other income								
①		(c) + (d) + (e) + (f)								
		Vacancy allowance for (c) and (d)								
		Vacancy allowance for (e) and (f)								
(g)		Total vacancy allowance								
(h)		Collection losses allowance								
②	Effective gross income [①−(g)−(h)]									
(i)	Operating expenses	Maintenance and management expenses								
(j)		Utility expenses								
(k)		Repair expenses								
(l)		Property management fees								
(m)		Tenant recruitment expenses, etc.								
(n)		Real estate taxes — Land								
		Real estate taxes — Buildings								
		Real estate taxes — Depreciable assets								
(o)		Casualty insurance premiums								
(p)		Other expenses								
③		Operating expenses [(i)+(j)+(k)+(l)+(m)+(n)+(o)+(p)]								
④	Net operating income [②−③]									
(q)		Operating profit on lump-sum payments								
(r)		Capital expenditures								
⑤	Net cash flow [④+(q)−(r)]									
		(Reference)								
		Operating efficiency ratio (OER)								
		Balance of lump-sum payments (refundable deposits)								
		Compound present value rate								
(s)		Present value								
(t)		Total for (s) column								

Value indicated by the income approach ((t)+(x)) *	

(u)	Sale value ⑤ for n+1 years / z
(v)	Sale expenses
(w)	Reversionary value (u)-(v)
(x)	Current reversionary value
(y)	Discount rate
(z)	Terminal capitalization rate

Ⅴ－3．不動産鑑定評価基準

mpleted

n	Year after expiration of the preservation period (n+1)	Grounds for assessment		
		Assessment method	Anticipated changes	Additional comments
		If data obtained from the client or other informational materials were used, were any modifications made, or did the LREA use data which he had obtained himself? State the grounds for those decisions.		

	Reasons for conclusion	Additional comments
%		
%		

V − 3. Guidance Notes on the Real Estate Appraisal Standards

Guidance Notes on the General Standards (GS) and the Specific Standards (SS) of the Real Estate Appraisal Standards are provided below.

Guidance Note I on GS. Chap. 2 :
USE CATEGORIES AND PHYSICAL DEVELOPMENT & TITLE CATEGORIES OF REAL ESTATE

Classification of real estate by use category is an important step carried out through various procedures in the appraisal process, such as market area analysis, property analysis and the application of the appraisal approaches. Exact classification further enhances the accuracy of the appraisal. The following detailed categories should be considered in analyzing residential and commercial neighborhoods.

(1) **Residential Areas**
  ① Residential areas with an established reputation, characterized by large lots, blocks and plots in an orderly arrangement; abundant green space, and scenic views; rows of buildings of high-quality construction; and a remarkably pleasant residential environment.
  ② Residential areas in a pleasant residential environment, created primarily by residences of standard-quality construction on standard- sized lots.
  ③ Residential areas made up of concentrations of comparatively small single-family residences and low-rise apartment houses, or residential areas consisting primarily of residences but also containing a mix of shops, offices and small factories.
  ④ Rural community areas and residential areas that have not become a part of built-up urban areas; primarily consisting of conventional farmhouses (such rural communities may be located within commuting distance of urban areas).

(2) **Commercial Areas**
  ① **Prime Commercial Areas**
  Prime commercial areas are located in the centers or nodes of large cities (such as Tokyo and other major cities with the ward system) that draw clientele from over a large trade area. Prime commercial areas are characterized by a high concentration of comparatively large-scale, medium- or high-rise shops and offices. These areas may be further broken down into the following subcategories according to the specific features of the prime commercial area.
    a. **Prime Retail Areas**
    Areas with a high concentration of high-end shops with large sales volume.
    b. **Prime Office Areas**
    Areas with a high concentration of office buildings, occupied by government agencies, corporations and financial institutions.
    c. **Prime Areas of Retail/Office Mix**
    Areas with a high concentration of shops and offices.
  ② **Central Commercial Areas**
  Following prime commercial areas in order of magnitude, central commercial areas draw clientele from over a broad trade area, and are characterized by rows of shops

and offices, and high commercial concentration.

③ **Second‐tier Commercial Areas**
Second-tier commercial areas refer to commercial areas other than prime commercial areas, central commercial areas, neighborhood commercial areas (see below) or suburban roadside commercial areas (see below); these commercial areas are located in the city center or an urban node and consist of rows of shops, offices, and buildings with other uses.

④ **Neighborhood Commercial Areas**
Areas consisting of rows of shops that sell articles of daily consumption, primarily for neighborhood residents.

⑤ **Suburban Roadside Commercial Areas**
Areas consisting of rows of shops and businesses located along arterial roads (national highways, prefecture highways) outside cities.

Guidance Note II on GS. Chap. 3 : INFLUENCES ON REAL ESTATE VALUE

Particular attention should be given to the following items with respect to property-specific value influences relating to land, buildings, and buildings and building sites, discussed in Chapter 3 of the General Topics (Influences on the Value of Real Estate).

1. Guidance on Property-Specific Value Influences on Land

(1) The Presence of Buried Cultural Assets

There are situations where the presence of buried cultural assets, as defined in the *Cultural Properties Protection Law*, may have a considerable effect on the value of a site. This may be the result of excavation surveys required under the above law, the cessation and prohibition of activities that would alter the condition of buried cultural assets, the costs of changing building plans, or possible restrictions on land use.

Particular attention must be paid to the following matters regarding both the likelihood of cultural assets being buried on the subject property and their condition. In so doing, the appraiser must consider procedures mandated under the *Cultural Properties Protection Law* as well as the characteristics of the subject property.

① Whether or not the subject property is included in an area containing known buried cultural assets, as defined in the *Cultural Properties Protection Law*

② Whether or not measures such as registered excavation surveys or test drilling surveys have indicated the presence of buried cultural assets

③ Whether or not it has already been determined that buried cultural assets exist on the site (if an excavation survey had been conducted in the past, what were the findings and what measures were taken?)

④ Whether civil engineering work should be halted or the building design changed to protect important remains discovered in the course of a survey

(2) The Presence and Current Status of Soil Contamination

Soil contamination may have a considerable effect on the value of a site as a result of the cost incurred to remove the contaminants and possible restrictions on land use.

Particular attention must be paid to the following matters regarding the presence of contaminants on the subject property and their condition. In so doing, the appraiser must consider procedures mandated under the *Soil Contamination Measures Law* as well as the characteristics of the subject property.

① Whether or not the subject property includes a factory or business facility that uses harmful substances and falls under the category of a polluted site stipulated in Article 3 of the Soil *Contamination Measures Law*, and whether or not a factory or business facility that falls under the category stipulated in Article 3 of the above Act existed on the subject site before the law came into effect.

② Whether or not an investigation into the status of soil pollution on the subject site is required after operation of the factory or business facility that used harmful substances has ceased, in accordance with Article 3 of the *Soil Contamination Measures Law*, and whether or not a local governor has ordered a survey of the status of soil pollution under the provisions of Article 4 of the same Act.

③　Whether or not the subject property has been included in a designated area under Article 5 of the *Soil Contamination Measures Law*, and whether or not that designation was later repealed.

④　Whether or not a local governor, under the provisions of Article 7 of the *Soil Contamination Measures Law*, has ordered that measures be deployed to clean up pollution on the subject property.

2．Guidance on Property-Specific Value Influences on Buildings

(1)　Design, Facilities and Functionality

Particular attention must be given to typical floorplate size, ceiling height, floor loads, telecommunications facilities, air-conditioning facilities and electrical capacity.

(2)　Building Performance

The appraiser must ascertain whether the earthquake resistance of a building complies with earthquake resistance standards based on the *Building Standards Act*. In addition, for residential valuations, the appraiser should investigate the following items based on guidelines of the *Japan Home Performance Standards*, which were established under the *Housing Quality Assurance Law*: stability of the building structure, fire safety and the curing of deterioration, the level of maintenance and management, climate control and heating, air quality, lighting and visual environment, noise abatement, and special considerations for the elderly and handicapped.

(3)　Level of Maintenance and Management

Particular attention must be paid to the upkeep of depreciable items, among which are included the roof, exterior walls, floors, interior finish, electrical wiring, water and drainage facilities and sanitary facilities.

(4)　Presence of Harmful Substances and Current Status

The appraiser must check on the presence of asbestos insulation, the implementation of measures to prevent its dissipation, and the presence of polychloride biphenyls (PCBs) and the condition of their storage.

3．Guidance on Property-Specific Value Influences on Built-Up Property

(1)　Tenant Status and Lease Contract Provisions

Particular attention must be given to any history of arrears in rent or breaches of contract. Tenant attributes (e. g., industry type, company size), and the ratio of the rental area occupied by the anchor tenant relative to the total rentable area should also be investigated.

(2)　Quality of Repair Projects, Management Plans and Implementation

The appraiser must investigate any large-scale repair projects, the history of building repair projects, management bylaws, the property manager, and management services provided.

Guidance Note III on GS. Chap. 5 : BASIC APPRAISAL PROBLEM

1. Guidance on Identification of the Subject Property

(1) **Setting Assumptions and Limiting Conditions for the Appraisal**

The value of real estate sometimes cannot simply be determined on the basis of the actual use of the subject, ownership and interests in the property and value influences acting on the area or property. In order to reflect the attributes of various real estate transactions and to meet other requirements, the appraiser must make special assumptions and limiting conditions in certain appraisal assignments.

Setting assumptions and limiting conditions for the appraisal helps ensure that the identification of the subject property fits the specifications and the purpose of the client's request and that any additional conditions regarding specific value influences acting on the area or property are clear. Thus, setting assumptions and limiting conditions for the appraisal defines the scope of the appraisal as well as the scope of liability of the LREA, who performs the appraisal.

(2) **Procedures for Setting Assumptions and Limiting Conditions for the Appraisal**

Since the assumptions and limiting conditions for the appraisal are set by the specifications in the client's request, they are confirmed indirectly by the LREA when the real estate appraisal firm accepts the assignment. However, since the final value opinion may differ depending on the subject property identification and any conditions assumed with respect to value influences acting on the area and property, the LREA should directly confirm the specifications in the client's request.

① **Requirement for the Subject Identification**

The appraiser must consider how valid the specifications and purpose of the client's request are after identifying the subject property and confirming the attributes of the subject. Under ordinary circumstances, the appraiser may value the subject site as though vacant and free of encumbrances even if improvements occupy the site or restrictive covenants run with the site. However, when the appraisal is expected to significantly affect the benefits to involved parties or interested third parties, the appraiser should value the property as is (i.e., the appraiser should consider all the existing improvements and encumbrances on the property.) Examples of such situations include appraisals for mortgage origination and the issuing of securities based on mortgages.

② **Setting Additional Assumptions and Limiting Conditions Regarding Value Influences Acting on the Market Area or Subject Property**

Where assumptions are added:

    a. Additional conditions imposed must be agreed upon in the appraisal contract with the client, and there must be a reasonable certainty of said conditions being realized in view of the ability of involved parties to bring them about. Where additional assumptions are made with respect to market-specific value influences, the certainty of said conditions being realized should be confirmed directly with the responsible section of the authority involved in their realization.

b. "Legally permissible" means that additional assumptions and limiting conditions must comply with the stipulations of relevant laws and covenants.

c. Many parties rely on appraisals performed by LREAs. Involved parties and interested third parties include the client, persons with a close interest in the results of the appraisal, purchasers of securities issued on the basis of revenue generated by the real estate (the law mandates that such real estate must be appraised by an LREA) and purchasers of securities issued on mortgages approved on the basis of the conclusions of an appraisal.

Where it is recognized that additional assumptions or limiting conditions lack validity, such assumptions and limiting conditions must be revised and the client informed.

2. Guidance on Identification of the Date of the Value Opinion

A retrospective value opinion can only be performed when it is possible to confirm the attributes of the subject property at that point in time, and to gather data on value influences and comparable data required for the valuation. With the passage of time between the date of the value opinion and the date of the appraisal report, change will likely have occurred in the subject property and neighborhood. Thus, confirmation of the attributes of the subject property on the date of the value opinion (in cases where the property has undergone change during the interim) should be based on as much identification data as can be gathered for a point in time near the date of the value opinion.

A prospective value opinion assumes it is possible to identify the future attributes of the subject real estate, to forecast future value influences, and to determine the property's future highest and best use. Since all information gathered is necessarily limited to circumstances up to the date of the appraisal report, the results of a prospective appraisal can only be tentative, and as a general rule, prospective appraisals should not be performed. However, some situations will require a value opinion at some future date. Prospective appraisals can only be performed when sound appraisal procedures are assured.

3. Guidance on Identification of the Type of Value to be Determined by the Appraisal

(1) Market Value

Reasonable conditions under actual socio-economic circumstances are described below.

① Ordinary Ability of a Buyer to Procure Funds

The ordinary ability of a buyer to procure funds is understood within the context of normal or typical borrowing conditions (in terms of the loan-to-value ratio, the interest rate on the loan, and the amortization period of the loan) for the market in which the subject property is being acquired.

② Appropriate Market Exposure Time for the Subject Property

An appropriate exposure time on the market refers to the period of time required for information to disseminate among potential buyers prior to the acquisition of the subject property. The appropriate period of time differs according to supply and demand trends in the real estate market on the date of the value opinion as well as the type and nature of the subject property.

In addition, exposure implies that the subject property was placed on the market before the date of the value opinion. In other words, an exposure period does not mean the time between the date of the value opinion and the consummation of a sale.

(2) **Value for Regulated Purposes (VRP)**
① **In Compliance with Specific Laws and Ordinances**

The term "laws and ordinances" is a broad category, which includes government laws and ordinances, cabinet ordinances, ministerial ordinances, other regulations, proclamations, directives and notifications of government agencies, as well as supreme court rulings, the ordinances and regulations of local public entities, and corporate accounting and auditing standards. (see Part1 Chap.2. Ⅰ.Japan-3)

② **Examples of Situations Requiring Value for Regulated Purposes (VRP)**

The rationale for requiring VRP is discussed below. Basic appraisal procedure is also illustrated in the three examples that follow.

a. Where the purpose of the appraisal is to arrive at an indication of investment profitability value for investors as required under the *Asset Liquidation Law* or the *Investment Trust and Investment Corporation Law*.

In this case, the determination of investment profitability value is based on the value indicated by the income capitalization approach, which reflects the earning ability of the subject property. The purpose of such appraisals is to protect investors by disclosing the value of the real estate assets of investment corporations, investment trusts or special purpose corporation (collectively referred to as investment corporations) either at the time of the acquisition of the real estate assets or during the holding period.

When appraising a real property for investors corporation either at the time of acquisition or during the holding period, the appraiser must estimate its value based on an operation management scheme, which is disclosed to the investors. Therefore, the value does not necessarily satisfy all conditions for the highest and best use on which market value is premised. Thus, the VRP must be determined. It should also be noted that the value in appraisals, requested by investors for the disposal of real estate, is determined on the basis of market value.

The primary appraisal method used is Discounted Cash Flow Analysis (a method in the income capitalization approach). The final value opinion is determined by verifying the DCF indication against the value indicated by direct capitalization, and reconciling this figure with the values indi cated by the sales comparison approach and the cost approach.

b. Where appraisals are required for a quick sale under the *Civil Rehabilitation Law*

The determination of VRP is also required in the disposition of assets under the

Civil Rehabilitation Law. An appraiser must estimate a reasonable disposition value, considering the possibility of a quick sale of the subject property as well as the property type, its attributes, and the characteristics of the market.

Since the appraisal is premised on a quick sale, the value to be determined is VRP.

The final value opinion is determined by reconciling the values indicated by the sales comparison approach and income capitalization approach, premised upon the assumption of a quick sale. This figure is then verified against the value indicated by the cost approach. In situations where there is little comparable data, the final value opinion may be determined by adjusting the market value of the subject property (obtained by ordinary methods) downward to reflect the circumstance of the quick sale.

c. Where the purpose of the appraisal is to determine the value, premised on continuation of an enterprise, as required under the *Corporate Reorganization Law* and the *Civil Rehabilitation Law*

The *Corporate Reorganization Law* and the *Civil Rehabilitation Law* require an appraisal, which is based on the premise that the particular property is estimated as a part of the entity's continuing business.

Since the appraisal is premised upon the existing use of the subject property, which may not always represent the highest and best use, the value to be determined is VRP.

The final value opinion is generally determined from the value indicated by the income capitalization approach (based on the net cash flow (NCF) attributable to the real estate, as a portion of net cash flow (NCF) to the enterprise) compared with the value indicated by the sales comparison approach and verified against the value indicated by the cost approach.

> *Guidance Note IV on GS. Chap. 6 :*
> *MARKET AREA ANALYSIS AND PROPERTY ANALYSIS*

1. Guidance on Performing the Market Area Analysis
(1) Area Analysis of Subject Neighborhood

① Area analysis consists of investigating the neighborhood where the subject property is located, and ascertaining the characteristics of that neighborhood.

In analyzing the characteristics of the subject's market, the appraiser scrutinizes market-specific value influences, and identifies similarities and differences in influences affecting areas that surround the subject.

This process requires the analysis of an extensive area, including the subject's immediate neighborhood and other neighborhoods in the vicinity, to identify those areas in which the real estate is subject to common value influences.

② To ascertain the relative position of the subject neighborhood, the characteristics of the subject's market are first identified. Then, differences in area-specific value influences are assessed by comparing the area-specific value influences acting on similar neighborhoods in the subject's primary market area with market-specific value influences acting on the subject neighborhood. It is also useful to compare area-specific value influences acting on the subject neighborhood with market-specific value influences acting on other types of neighborhoods within the market.

③ Although the neighborhood analysis involves an investigation of data on value influences affecting the neighborhood where the subject property is located, the characteristics of the subject's market and specific value influences acting on the broader district that includes the neighborhood must be investigated prior to the neighborhood analysis. To accomplish this, data on value influences affecting a broad area must be routinely gathered and analyzed.

④ In analyzing area-specific value influences and trends or changes in market-specific value influences over the course of time, the appraiser must also identify trends in area-specific value influences affecting other areas surrounding the neighborhood as well as the degree to which those trends affect the neighborhood. The effects of such trends on the characteristics of the subject's market, and the use and value of land in the neighborhood should be understood.

With respect to interim use sites and lots in transitional areas, trends and changes in value influences affecting the surrounding areas serve as particularly useful indications of trends and changes in land use.

(2) Defining the Boundaries of the Neighborhood

To define the boundaries of the neighborhood, the appraiser should consider the following items, which influence basic land use and development readiness.

① **Natural Factors**
  a. **Rivers**
   Wide rivers may affect street grid patterns, the placement of buildings, and the

boundaries of contiguous areas.
b. Mountains and Hills
Mountains and hills not only affect street grid, building placement, and area unity; they can also have an effect on an area's sunlight, wind, dryness and dampness.
c. Topography, Geology and Soil
In addition to their effect on an area's sunlight, wind, dryness and dampness, the topography, geology and soil also have an effect on residential and commercial land use.

② Socio－Economic Factors
a. Political Boundaries
Political boundaries influence development readiness, and account for differences in the level of construction of streets, utilities, schools and other public facilities as well as in the real estate taxes levied.
b. Land Use Regulations
Land use regulations based on the *City Planning Act* and other laws affect land use.
c. Railways and Parks
Railway lines and parks may also influence the street grid, building placement, and area unity.
d. Roads
Similarly, wide roads may also affect the street grid, building placement, and area unity.

(3) **Characteristics of the Market for the Subject Property**
① Market Definition
a. The Attributes and Behavior of Market Participants in the Market Area
The appraiser should pay particular attention to the following matters in determining the attributes and behavior of market participants in the market area.

(a) In the case of commercial and industrial real estate, the attributes of market participants include the specific industries and businesses that make up the major demand and supply groups, and the form of legal entity (corporate or private individual). The extent of the area in which potential buyers are found must also be considered.

In the case of residential real estate, the attributes of market participants include the age, family composition and income level of the major demand and supply groups and the area in which potential buyers are found.

(b) The appraiser should also identify specific value influences that will be considered by market participants, whose attributes were explained in the above paragraph, when they make decisions involving property transactions, including price levels and other criteria.

b. Supply and Demand Trends in the Market Area
The appraiser should give special consideration to the following matters in determining supply and demand trends in the market area.

(a) Trends characterizing the supply of, and demand for, real estate similar to the subject property in terms of use, size and grade, and which is currently available in the market area.

(b) The effect of trends in the supply and demand situation (identified above) on the value of the subject property and how significant the effect of such trends is.

② **References and Publications Used**

To identify the characteristics of the subject's market, the appraiser must gather information on transactions (including the volume of transactions, sales prices, asking prices and offering prices) by routinely interviewing real estate firms, construction companies and financial institutions. It is also important to consult a wide range of publications relating to the local economy and transitions and trends in the real estate market, issued by public agencies, real estate firms, financial institutions and trade groups.

2. Guidance on Performing the Property Analysis

(1) Commentary on Analyzing Property–Specific Value Influences

The appraiser should address the following to determine the superiority or inferiority of the subject compared to real estate in a substitutive or competitive relationship, and the subject's competitiveness.

① The most popular price range for the same type of properties, and the attributes of the principal potential buyers

② Preferences of potential buyers as to property location, size, functions and surrounding environment

③ Number of inquiries about the subject property

(2) Commentary on Determining the Highest and Best Use

① **Important Pointers for Determining the Highest and Best Use: Premised on Changes Anticipated in Market–Specific Value Influences**

A high probability of the anticipated changes being realized within a specific timeframe must be supported by reliable data gathered at the time the appraisal is performed.

② **Important Pointers for Determining the Highest and Best Use of Building and Building Site:**

When demolition of the subject building or alteration of its use is assumed to be the highest and best use, the appraiser should compare the property's economic value after demolition or alteration against the required costs of demolition or alteration. The appraiser should also compare the property's economic value based on the assumption that the current use of the building were to continue unchanged.

a. The likelihood of demolition of the building or alteration of its use must be considered from the perspectives of physical possibility and legal permissibility.

b. Both the uncertainty of anticipated changes in income to the subject property, based on its increased competitiveness following demolition of the building or alteration of its use, and the expected amount of income lost during the alteration of use must be considered.

Guidance Note V on GS. Chap. 7 : APPRAISAL METHOD

1. **Guidance on Appraisal Approaches for Determining Real Estate Value**
   (1) **General Guidance on Determining Value Indications**
   ① **Selection of Comparables**
   　a. **In Situations Where the Appraiser Must Choose Comparables from Outside the Subject Neighborhood and Similar Neighborhoods**
   　　Such situations arise when most of the comparable sales data gathered in the subject neighborhood or similar neighborhoods nearby is significantly affected by special circumstances, and the appraisal cannot be performed without recourse to comparables in other areas.
   　b. **Selection of Comparables from Substitutive or Competitive Real Estate in the Market Area for a Subject Property with a Highest and Best Use That Differs from the Standard Property Use in the Market Area**
   　　The highest and best use of the subject property often differs from the standard property use in its neighborhood because the subject property is fairly unique and its use is rarely subject to the market-specific value influences of its neighborhood, as shown in the following examples.
   　　(a) Large-scale plots in a predominantly single-family residential district that are especially suitable for multi-family buildings due to the area's excellent location and development potential; in a nearby residential district large-scale multi-family buildings have already been developed.
   　　(b) Hotels drawing a broad clientele and conveniently accessible but located in districts of medium- and high-rise office building use.
   　　(c) Regional shopping centers along arterial roads, drawing patrons from over a broad trade area but located in residential areas.
   　　(d) Large-scale, highly competitive office buildings developed on tracts assembled from smaller lots in small- and medium-size office building districts.
   　c. **Commentary for Assessing a Substitutive or Competitive Relationship**
   　　Comparables selected from substitutive or competitive real estate in the primary market area (see the section (1)-①-b above) must satisfy the requirements indicated below.
   　　(a) Similarity to the subject property in terms of use, size and grade must be clearly observable.
   　　(b) The direct influence of the comparable property on the value of the subject property must be demonstrable.
   ② **Comparison of Market-Specific and Property-Specific Value Influences**
   　In selecting data on substitutive or competitive real estate in the primary market area, the appraiser should not only compare property-specific value influences, but

also the effect of market-specific influences on market characteristics.

(2) Guidance on Sales Comparison Approach

In applying the sales comparison approach, a large amount of comparable sales data must be gathered, and data must be selected that serves as a reliable indicator of value. To ensure the usefulness of that data, the appraiser should gather a wide range of information, including asking prices, offering prices and expert opinions in addition to comparable sales data.

Such information can be readily used for determining the price levels in the neighborhood as well as trends in land values.

① Gathering Data

Analysis of a large amount of comparable sales data is indispensable to identifying the special circumstances of individual transactions, determining the time adjustment, and deciding the effect of value influences on the value of the subject property. The comparable sales data selected provides the basis for the value indicated by the sales comparison approach while the reliability of the comparable sales data gathered determines the accuracy of that value indication.

The price of each sales comparable is affected by the use of the real estate, the appeal of the real estate, and the motives of the seller and buyer shaping the circumstances of the transaction. Thus, the appraiser must carefully analyze the circumstances of each transaction in the comparable sales data, the attributes of the involved parties (which are the same as the attributes of market participants described in Chapter IV of Guidance Notes to the Standards, "Chapter 6 of the General Topics: Neighborhood Analysis and Subject Property Analysis"), and trends in sales price levels.

② Adjustment for Conditions of Sale

To determine the need for, and magnitude of an adjustment for conditions of sale, a large amount of comparable sales data should be reviewed and analyzed. If it is determined that a conditions of sale adjustment is required, the appropriate adjustment will be based on the objective price level of the market in which the transactions took place.

Examples of special circumstances requiring adjustment for the conditions of sale are indicated below.

a. Special Circumstances Requiring a Downward Adjustment

(a) When transactions involve real estate, which has certain locational and/or operational advantages

(b) When transactions take place in markets characterized by atypical conditions, such as an extreme supply shortage or an overly optimistic outlook for the future

(c) When transactions occur between businesses or affiliated firms for the purpose of making profits on resale

(d) When transactions result in excessively high prices because buyers clearly lack information about, and knowledge of, the real estate

(e) When transactions include amounts other than compensation for the real estate, i.e., amounts equivalent to interest earned on the installment payments of the negotiated purchasing price, the costs of tenant removal (Editor's Note : e.g., when a landlord needs to demolish the existing building and rebuild the site), or compensation for early termination of agricultural production.

b．Special Circumstances Requiring an Upward Adjustment
(a) When transactions result in excessively low prices because sellers clearly lack information about, and knowledge of, the real estate
(b) When transactions take place under circumstances in which the property must be sold quickly, e.g., an inheritance or an employee transfer

c．Special Circumstances Requiring a Downward or Upward Adjustment
(a) When transactions, though conducted in a spirit of good will, take place between corporations under financial pressure or faced with bankruptcy; or when transactions are conducted between friends or relatives
(b) When transactions involve a property for which unreasonable site preparation costs or repair expenses are anticipated
(c) When the price has been established through arbitration, liquidation, auction sale or compulsory sale

③ Time Adjustment Factor
a．The time adjustment is determined by means of time-series analysis of a large quantity of data on comparable sales transacted prior to the date of the value opinion. The appraiser also takes into account trends in general value influences when estimating the time adjustment factor. General value influences to be examined include both socio-economic factors (such as growth in GDP, fiscal/monetary policies, public investment, building starts, and real estate sales) and governmental factors (such as land use regulations and tax policies).

b．The time adjustment should be determined as described in a. above, and references such as surveys of land values published by the central and prefectural governments should be consulted. However, in cases where suitable comparable sales data is lacking, the appraiser can also use other miscellaneous information such as trends in asking prices and offering prices, and market supply and demand.

(3) Guidance on Income Capitalization Approach
① Application of Direct Capitalization Method
a．Calculation of Net Cash Flow (NCF) for a Single Year

In direct capitalization, the net cash flow (NCF) for a single year and the capitalization rate applied to it must be determined in a consistent manner.

Namely, where an estimate of the net cash flow (NCF) for a single year reflects stabilized income over a certain period of time, a capitalization rate used must be developed on the same basis. In developing an estimate of net cash flow (NCF) to real estate that includes a building or other depreciable property component (to be referred to as buildings), the appraiser may calculate net cash flow (NCF) before depreciation (i.e., NCF from which depreciation has not been deducted). The appraiser should capitalize this estimated NCF by applying a capitalization rate appropriate to the NCF estimate.

$$P = \frac{a}{R}$$

where
P is the property value indicated by the income capitalization approach
a is the net cash flow (NCF) to the property before depreciation
R is the capitalization rate corresponding to net cash flow (NCF) prior to depreciation

On the other hand, where an estimate of the net cash flow (NCF) after depreciation (i.e., NCF from which depreciation has been deducted) is calculated, a capitalization rate appropriate to net cash flow (NCF) after depreciation must be used.

The straight-line method or sinking fund factor method is usually used to calculate the depreciation, but another method should be applied where the circumstances are appropriate.

$$P = \frac{a'}{R'}$$

where
P is the property value indicated by the income capitalization approach
a' is the net cash flow (NCF) to the property after depreciation
R' is the capitalization rate corresponding to net cash flow (NCF) after depreciation

The following formula is used to determine the capitalization rate corresponding to net cash flow (NCF) after depreciation, when the depreciation and the capitalization rate for net cash flow (NCF) before depreciation can be calculated.

$$R' = \frac{a'}{(a' + d)} \times R$$

where
R' is the capitalization rate corresponding to net cash flow (NCF) after depreciation
R is the capitalization rate corresponding to net cash flow (NCF) prior to depreciation
a' is the net cash flow (NCF) after depreciation
d is the depreciation

b. Land Residual Technique or Building Residual Technique

Where real estate includes land and building components, and the value of either the land or building may be determined by an approach other than the income capitalization approach, a residual technique (the land residual technique or building residual technique) is applied. This technique capitalizes the net cash flow (NCF) remaining after deduction of the net cash flow (NCF) attributable to the building or the land from the net cash flow (NCF) to the property.

Residual techniques are effective in cases where the net cash flow (NCF) generated by a building and building site (land) can be rationally allocated between the land and building.

The land residual technique should only be applied in situations where the buildings are of recent construction because the older the building, the more difficult it becomes to break out the net cash flow (NCF) attributable to the land from the net cash flow (NCF) to the overall property (building and building site). Even when the subject property is a freehold interest in land, this technique can be applied by assuming the construction of a leased building is the highest and best use of the land.

(a) **Land Residual Technique**

The formula below demonstrates how land value is determined by the land residual technique.

$$PL = \frac{a - B \times R_B}{R_L}$$

where

- P_L is the land value indicated by the land residual technique
- a is the net cash flow (NCF) to the building and building site before depreciation
- B is the building value
- R_B is the building capitalization rate
- R_L is the capitalization rate corresponding to that share of net cash flow (NCF) allocated to land (the allocation of NCF between land and building is based on NCF before depreciation)

(b) **Building Residual Technique**

The formula below demonstrates how building value is determined by the building residual technique.

$$P_B = \frac{a - L \times R_L}{R_B}$$

where

- P_B is the building value indicated by the building residual approach
- a is the net cash flow (NCF) to the building and building site before depreciation
- L is the land value
- R_L is the land capitalization rate
- R_B is the capitalization rate corresponding to that share of net cash flow (NCF) allocated to the building (the allocation of NCF between land and building is based on NCF before depreciation)

c. **Capitalization over a Definite Term**

Where the real estate includes land and building components, its value may be determined by multiplying an ordinary level annuity factor, developed on the basis of both an appropriate discount rate and the expected period of the income streams, by the net cash flow (NCF) before depreciation, based on the rental income to leased real estate or the income to business operations making use of real estate for purposes other than leasing. The formulas below demonstrate how value is determined by this method.

$$P = a \times \frac{(1+Y)^N - 1}{Y(1+Y)^N}$$

where

P is the value of the building and building site indicated by the income capitalization approach

a is the net cash flow (NCF) to the building and building site before depreciation

Y is the discount rate

N is the expected period of the income streams (i.e., the period during which income is anticipated, corresponding to the economic life of the building)

$\dfrac{(1+Y)^N - 1}{Y(1+Y)^N}$ is the ordinary level annuity factor

The present value of the building (assuming that the economic life of the building is longer than the income period), the present value of the land, and the present value of the costs to demolish the building less salvage value are added to, or subtracted from, the value of the property, derived by ordinary level annuity capitalization. This calculation is generally referred to as the Inwood Method.

The formulas below demonstrate the use of a discount rate based on this concept.

$$P = a \times \frac{(1+Y)^n - 1}{Y(1+Y)^n} + \frac{P_{Ln} + P_{Bn}}{(1+Y)^n} \quad \text{or}$$

$$P = a \times \frac{(1+Y)^N - 1}{Y(1+Y)^N} + \frac{P_{LN} - E}{(1+Y)^N}$$

where

P   is the value of the building and building site indicated by the income capitalization approach

a   is the net cash flow (NCF) to the building and building site before depreciation

Y   is the discount rate

N or n is the expected period of the income streams (period during which income is anticipated; N is the period coinciding with the economic life of the building while n indicates situations in which the period is shorter than the economic life)

P_{Ln} is the land value after n years

P_{Bn} is the building value after n years

P_{Ln} is the land value after N years

E   is the building demolition costs

Under the Hoskold method, on the other hand, a discount rate and a sinking fund factor, which is based on the safe rate, are used instead of ordinary level annuity capitalization shown above.

The formulas below demonstrate the use of a discount rate based on this concept.

$$P = a \times \cfrac{1}{Y + \cfrac{i}{(1+i)^n - 1}} + \cfrac{P_{Ln} + P_{Bn}}{(1+Y)^n} \quad \text{or}$$

$$P = a \times \cfrac{1}{Y + \cfrac{i}{(1+i)^N - 1}} + \cfrac{P_{Ln} - E}{(1+Y)^N}$$

where

P is the value of the building and building site indicated by the income capitalization approach

a is the net cash flow (NCF) to the building and building site before depreciantion

Y is the discount rate

i is the safe rate

N or n is the expected period of the income streams (period during which income is anticipated; N is the period coinciding with the economic life of the building while n indicates situations in which the period is shorter than the economic life)

$\cfrac{i}{(1+i)^n - 1}$ is the sinking fund factor

P_{Ln} is the land value after n years
P_{Bn} is the building value after n years
P_{Ln} is the land value after N years
E is the building demolition costs

d．Selecting and Supporting Capitalization Rates

The capitalization rate should be consistent with the anticipated return in the market. Since the capitalization rate includes expected change in the net operating income (NOI) to the subject property, the anticipated change must be accurately ascertained and reflected in the capitalization rate. The following methods are used for determining the capitalization rate. In some situations, only one of the following methods is employed while in others a combination of multiple methods may be employed. Sources such as the opinions of investors and well-established property indices should also be consulted, as required.

(a) Determination from Comparable Sales Data on Similar Real Estate

The gathering and selection of comparable sales data should comply with the procedure for applying the sales comparison approach as discussed in Chapter 7 of the General Topics, "Appraisal Methodology."

The appraiser must exercise caution as to whether the capitalization rate obtained from comparable sales data (to be referred to as the market-derived capitalization rate) corresponds to the net operating income (NOI) before or after depreciation. There are special factors that should also be noted with respect to net operating income (NOI) such as whether the property operation has not been stabilized immediately after new construction or remodeling. Comparable sales data, which cannot be reasonably adjusted, should not be used.

This method is particularly useful when it is possible to develop the capitalization rate from a large quantity of sales data on comparable sales that are highly similar to the subject property.

(b) **Determination by Means of the Band of Investment Method Based on Equity – Mortgage Ratio**

This method focuses on the procurement of funds by potential buyers with an ordinary capability for procuring funds to acquire real estate. As a method, it is superior at reflecting the return on real estate investments and trends in the financial markets during the process of fund procurement.

The following formula demonstrates the above method for determining the capitalization rate.

$$R = R_M \times W_M + R_E \times W_E$$

where

R is the capitalization rate
R_M is the mortgage capitalization rate
W_M is the ratio of the loan to total property value
R_E is the equity capitalization rate
W_E is the ratio of equity to total property value

(c) **Determination from Capitalization Rates for Land and Buildings**

This method is applied to properties that include land and building components. As a method, it is superior at reflecting return trends in a market where the yields on land and buildings are considered to be different.

The following formula demonstrates the above method for determining the capitalization rate.

$$R = R_L \times W_L + R_B \times W_B$$

where

R is the capitalization rate
R_L is the land capitalization rate
W_L is the ratio of land value to total property value
R_B is the building capitalization rate
W_B is the ratio of building value to total property value

(d) **Determination from the Relationship of the Capitalization Rate to the Discount Rate**

This method is effective where net cash flow (NCF) can be assumed to continue in perpetuity, and it can be assumed that net cash flow (NCF) will grow at a fixed rate.

The formula representing the relationship between the capitalization rate and discount rate appears below.

$R = Y - g$

where

R is the capitalization rate
Y is the discount rate
g is the growth rate in the net cash flow (NCF)

(e) Utilization of Debt Service Coverage Ratio

This method determines the capitalization rate by using the debt service coverage ratio (the value obtained by dividing the net cash flow (NCF) for a certain period by the amount of the principal repayment plus the interest paid in the same period), based on the mortgage capitalization rate and ratio of the loan to total property value. It considers the safety of debt service from the perspective of net cash flow (NCF) to the subject property.

It must be noted that the debt service coverage ratio used should be based on the average net cash flow (NCF) for the loan period. This method focuses on the procurement of funds by the purchaser of the real estate, and is effective where repayment of the loan is based only on income to the subject property.

The following formula demonstrates the above method for determining the capitalization rate.

$R = R_M \times W_M \times DSCR$

where

R is the capitalization rate
R_M is the mortgage capitalization rate
W_M is the ratio of the loan to total property value
DSCR is the debt service coverage ratio; the DSCR is normally required to be 1.0 or more

② Guidance on Application of Discounted Cash Flow Method

DCF anticipates and clearly specifies net cash flow (NCF) generated during multiple, consecutive periods as well as the reversionary value. As a method, it is superior at explaining the process of determining value indications by the income capitalization approach.

a. Calculation of Net Cash Flow (NCF) for Each Period

When the net cash flow (NCF) to buildings is calculated, net cash flow (NCF) before depreciation (i.e., the depreciation is not deducted from NCF) is used. The allowance for building depreciation is considered in the reversionary value.

(a) Calculation of Gross Income

Two methods may be used with respect to the treatment of refundable deposits received. One method assumes the total amount is entrusted to a repayment reserve, and the investment income is recorded as it is generated. Under the other method, the entire amount is recorded as revenue or expenditure at the time of receipt or refund.

(b) **Calculation of Total Expenses**
Two methods may be used to estimate costs such as large-scale repair expenses. Under one method, costs are recorded as a reserve for each period. Under the other method, costs are recorded when they are expected to be actually paid. The appraiser should forecast the timing of the expected expenditures by taking into account the attributes of the subject property.

b. Determination of the Discount Rate
The discount rate should reflect the yield in the market. Typically it is determined for one-year intervals. It should also be noted that the discount rate differs according to the degree of uncertainty over anticipated earnings.

The following methods are used for determining the discount rate. In some situations only one of the following methods is used while in others a combination of multiple methods may be used. Sources such as the opinions of investors and well-established property indices should also consulted, as required.

(a) **Determination from Data on Comparable Sales**
The gathering and selection of comparable sales data should comply with the procedure for applying the sales comparison approach discussed in Chapter 7 of the General Topics, "Appraisal Methodology."

The discount rate developed from comparable sales data is the internal rate of return (IRR) calculated on the basis of the sales price and income streams (IRR is the discount rate, at which the present value of future income and initial capital investment are equal). The appraiser should be able to forecast the net cash flow (NCF) of each period for the comparable property.

This method is particularly effective where a large amount of yield data can be gathered from comparable sales similar to the subject property.

(b) **Determination from Mortgage and Equity Discount Rates**
This method focuses on the cost of procuring funds by purchasers of real estate, and best reflects the yield on the real estate investment as well as trends in the financial markets during the process of fund procurement. The method should be based on ratios for the mortgage and equity to total property value, assumed by typical real estate investors.

The following formula demonstrates the above method for determining the discount rate.

$$Y = Y_M \times W_M + Y_E \times W_E$$

where

Y is the discount rate

Y_M is the mortgage discount rate

W_M is the ratio of the loan to total property value

Y_E is the equity discount rate

W_E is the ratio of equity to total property value

(c) **Determination by a Built-Up Rate** (Adding Risk Components Associated with the Individual Real Estate to the Assured Yield on Assets Such as

Bonds)
The yield on ten-year government bonds is typically used as a bench mark. The yield rates on corporate stocks and corporate bonds may also be used for comparative purposes.

Additional risk components associated with the individual real estate include the uncertainty related to the real estate investment, the non-liquidity of the investment, potential problems in the management of the real estate, and the security of the asset. The value of a real estate investment may change as the result of a natural disaster, modification in land use planning or regulation, inability to find a buyer at the desired time, or lack of requisite knowledge and experience with respect to leasing. Risks are also associated with the amount of revenue obtained, which may differ according to the quality of management. On the other hand, the indestructive nature of land provides a positive aspect.

This method is useful when the uncertainty associated with the anticipated income to the subject property can be ascertained and can be compared against the uncertainty of other financial assets.

c. Holding period

The assumed holding period should allow for accurate anticipation of the net operating income (NOI) of each period and the reversionary value. The length should be based on the period for which typical investors would retain a real estate investment and should not extend beyond the period that would generally be assumed for typical investors.

d. Determination of the Reversionary Value

At the termination of the holding period, the sales expenses required must be deducted from the reversionary value.

The reversionary value is determined by capitalizing the net operating income (NOI) for the (n + 1) period at the terminal capitalization rate. Anticipated change in net operating income (NOI) beyond the (n + 1) period as well as the uncertainty accompanying that anticipation must be accurately reflected both in the net operating income (NOI) of the (n + 1) period as well as in the terminal capitalization rate.

Where demolition of the building or a change in its use is planned after the end of the holding period, or where the building is so deteriorated that demolition is expected, the reversionary value must be determined in consideration of those required costs.

e. Determination of Terminal Capitalization Rates

Terminal capitalization rates must reflect market trends at the end of the holding period, anticipated change in income after that time, and the degree of uncertainty in that anticipation based on the capitalization rate for the property on the date of the value opinion.

2. Guidance on Appraisal Approaches for Determining Rent

(1) Summation Approach

The following matters should be considered in determining the base value of a property.

① **Determination of Rent for a Building Site (Ground Rent)**
   a. Where the lessee can use the site in line with the highest and best use as though vacant, the base value corresponds to the economic value of the freehold interest in the land.
   b. Where the highest and best use as though vacant cannot be anticipated from the provisions of the contract, the base value corresponds to the economic value of the site based on the provisions in the contract.

② **Determination of Rent for a Building and Building Site (Building Rent)**

The base value corresponds to the economic value of the building and building site, based on the premise that the present use of the building and building site will continue.

(2) Rental Data Comparison Approach

① **Selection of Data**
   a. Lease and other data should be selected from comparable properties that are as similar to the subject property as possible. The rent level typically differs according to whether the rent is paid under a new lease or under a renewed lease, and according to the use of the building.
   b. The appraiser should consider the following matters when assessing the similarity of contract provisions.
      (a) Form of the lease
      (b) Rental area
      (c) Lease term, period of the lease already elapsed and remaining period of the lease
      (d) Rental payments adjusted for deposits received
      (e) Period for which rent is calculated and method of payment
      (f) Matters pertaining to repairs and alterations
      (g) Portion of space leased and the use thereof (Editor's Note: e.g., Flex space in an industrial building may be used for office or industrial purposes; the appraiser should ascertain whether the lease includes both office and industrial space or only office space)

② **Comparison of Area-specific and Property-Specific Value Influences**

Comparison of market-specific value influences is useful in determining rent. However, there are some specific influences applicable only to rental values. Therefore, the boundaries and attributes of the market for the subject property may differ between rental value and property value assignments.

In comparing property-specific value influences for the determination of rent, the appraiser should pay special attention to the contract provisions as well as property-specific value influences acting on the land and building.

Guidance Note VI on GS. Chap. 8 : APPRAISAL PROCESS

1. Identification of Client, Parties for Submission, and Interests/Ties
(1) **Client and parties for submission other than the client, if any**
Confirmation of the parties for submission other than the client should be made in accordance with the purpose of the valuation. Details of the parties, such as their exact names, may not necessarily be required. In some cases, information useful for understanding how the report will be used, such as the reason for submission or attributes of the parties, may be sufficient. It therefore should be noted that information sufficient for understanding how the report will be used is required even if the exact names of the parties for submission are not known.

(2) **Interests/ties associated with appraisers and appraisal firms involved in the valuation**

① **Appraisers involved in the valuation**
The "appraisers involved in the valuation" refers to all appraisers involved in the valuation of the subject property. If part or all of the valuation process is subcontracted, the appraisers involved in the valuation in the subcontracted appraisal firms are also included.

② **Appraisal firms involved in the valuation**
The "appraisal firm involved in the valuation" refers to all appraisal firms with appraisers engaged in the valuation of the subject property.

③ **Ties between the client and appraisers or appraisal firms involved in the valuation**
Special ties between the client and appraisers or appraisal firms involved in the valuation that should be clarified, at the least, include the following. Other special ties important in judging the purpose of the valuation request or decision-making of clients, parties for disclosure or submission, and other parties should also be clarified.

   a. Special capital ties between the client and appraisal firms involved in the valuation (stated in ②; the same applies hereinafter) that should be clarified herein refer to if the client is a consolidated subsidiary or affiliated company (under the consolidated financial statement regulations) of the appraisal firm, or vice versa, in its previous business year (if financial statements are not prepared, the year before the previous business year is applied; the same applies in c.), or capital ties equivalent to or greater than this. The investment ratio and other factors that made this clarification necessary should be clarified.

   b. The special personal ties between the client and appraisal firms involved in the valuation that should be clarified herein refer to if the client or client's representative is the appraisal firm or appraisal firm's representative involved in the subject valuation, or personal ties equivalent to or greater than this. Factors that

made this clarification necessary should be clarified.
  c. The special business ties between the client and the appraisal firms involved in the valuation that should be clarified herein refer to if over 50% of the appraisal firm's liabilities are borrowed from the client, over 50% of the revenue (including that from business other than valuation services) of the appraisal firm is earned from the client, the valuation fees between the client and the appraisal firm are over 50% of the total fees the appraisal firm earns from valuation services in the previous business year, or other business ties equivalent to or greater than this. The ratio of the liabilities, revenue, and/or fees and other factors that made this clarification necessary should be clarified.
  d. The special capital ties between the client and the appraisers involved in the valuation refer to if the appraiser holds 20% or more voting rights of the client, or capital ties equivalent to or greater than this. The voting right ratio and other factors that made this clarification necessary should be clarified.
  e. The special personal ties between the client and the appraisers involved in the valuation refer to if the client or client's representative is the appraiser involved in the subject valuation, or personal ties equivalent to or greater than this. Factors that made this clarification necessary should be clarified.

④ **Ties between the parties for disclosure / submission and appraisers or appraisal firms involved in the valuation**

Rules specified in ③ are also applicable for ties between parties for disclosure / submission and appraisers or appraisal firms involved in the valuation. In this regard, the "client" in ③ should be replaced by "parties for disclosure / submission."

Please note that when specifying items in relation to VIII through X in section 2, Chapter 9 of the General Standards Chapter in the appraisal report, rules specified in (1) and (2) should also be referred to.

2. Review of Data and Analysis of Value Influences

(1) **The appraiser is able form an opinion regarding uncertain value influences based on the appraiser's own investigative and analytical capa<DH>bilities:**

(a) if comparable data exists to analyze those value influences; and (b) if it is possible to quantify the effect of those value influences based on the data, and the degree of value decrease can be reflected in the appraised value.

(2) **The appraiser can perform an appraisal assignment without consideration of uncertain value influences:**

either (a) if the appraiser is not able to ascertain evidence of any cause and effect relationship involved in those value influences by means of common sense and general scientific knowledge, or (b) if the appraiser is not able to confirm even a clue of their existence through ordinary investigation; and if the appraiser judges those uncertain value influences not to have any significant effect on the value of the subject property.

Guidance Note VII on SS. Chap. 1 : APPRAISAL OF REAL ESTATE VALUE

1. Guidance on Building Sites

(1) Vacant Land

The subdivision development analysis determines the value of vacant land by deducting respectively the building construction costs and incidental expenses (to be borne directly by the builder), and/or the land site preparation costs and incidental expenses (to be borne directly by the builder) at the date of the value opinion from the present value of the total sales revenue of the condominium building or subdivision development site. Since the land value of the condominium project typically differs according to the floor area ratio allowed in the zoning ordinance, the appraiser must prepare the design, layout and development schedule of the hypothetical condominium building by taking into account the land shape, frontage, and the Building Standards Act among other factors.

The formula below demonstrates the subdivision development approach.

$$P = \frac{S}{(1+r)^{n_1}} - \frac{B}{(1+r)^{n_2}} - \frac{M}{(1+r)^{n_3}}$$

where
- P is the land value indicated by the subdivision development analysis
- S is the total sales price
- B is building construction cost or land site preparation cost
- M is incidental expenses
- r is the discount rate
- n_1 is the period between the date of the value opinion and the time of the sale
- n_2 is the period between the date of the value opinion and the time of the payment of the construction fees
- n_3 is the period between the date of the value opinion and the time of the payment of incidental expenses

(2) Leasehold Interests in Land

The deposits paid by the tenant to the lessor with respect to the lease contract to a building site are typically classified into:

① refundable deposits, normally called *hoshokin;*
② non-refundable prepayments of rent, set as compensation for the leasehold interest in the land, normally called *kenrikin;* and
③ other deposits paid to obtain consent from the landowner, e.g., for transfer of the leasehold interest in the land.

The appraiser must individually assess whether or not each of these deposits constitutes a component in the value of a leasehold interest in land by considering the nature of the deposit and actual leasing practices regardless of what they may be called.

(3) Sectional Superficies

V - 3. Guidance Notes on the Real Estate Appraisal Standards

The following discussion covers important considerations in the appraisal of sectional superficies.

① **Economic Value Based on the Characteristics of Sectional Superficies**

In appraising sectional superficies, the appraiser must pay particular attention to economic value, based on the characteristics of sectional superficies described below.

    a. The economic value of the land, above or below which sectional superficies have been created, reflects the total utility above and below ground, generated by each of the buildable improvements based on the highest and best use. Thus, the economic value of sectional superficies may be ascertained by the ratio of the value of those sectional superficies to the economic value of the land, upon or under which those rights are created. The functional relationship of the sectional superficies to the total utility of the land becomes the focus of the appraisal.

    b. Sectional superficies are rights created to accommodate a structure or building in a portion of the space above or below land that belongs to another person. Their economic value is determined according to the specific structure, use, purpose of that use, and duration of the rights pertaining to the superficies.

② **Value Indicated by the Sales Comparison Approach Using Data on Sectional Superficies**

The sales comparison approach determines the value of sectional super ficies by comparing data gathered on sectional superficies, created in a manner similar to the subject, and located in the same neighborhood or similar neighborhood of the primary market area. After selecting appropriate data, the appraiser makes sales condition and time adjustments as required, comparing market-specific and property-specific value influences.

The appraiser must pay particular attention to the following matters when applying this approach.

    a. There are many situations where the economic value of the land, above or below which sectional superficies are created, is affected by spatial restrictions on land use imposed to preserve adjacent structures or buildings. Since the effect of these encumbrances is factored into the economic value of the sectional superficies created above or below that land, the data gathered on the creation of comparable rights, including restrictive encumbrances and the periods for which these rights are created, should be verified.

    b. The appraiser can estimate the growth rate for the time adjustment through an analysis of land value trends in the neighborhood of a comparable property or in a similar area considered to have undergone a change in land value close to that of the comparable neighborhood.

    c. In comparing market-specific value influences and property-specific value influences, the appraiser must pay particular attention to influences that are unique to sectional superficies, as indicated below.

        (a) With respect to market-specific value influences, the appraiser should consider market-specific influences acting on the neighborhood and on similar neighborhoods where other real estate may contribute to the utility of the sectional superficies; for example, parcels of land linked in a row such as the sectional superficies where subway tracks are laid.

(b) With respect to property-specific value influences acting upon sectional superficies, particularly important are the two-dimensional and three-dimensional locations, sizes, and shapes of above- and below-ground areas subject to the sectional superficies. The appraiser should consider the effect of spatial dimensions on value by assessing the two-dimensional and three-dimensional division of space in relation to the entire land, above or below which the sectional superficies have been created.

③ **Value Determined from a Sectional Superficies/Vacant Land Value Ratio**

The value of sectional superficies may be determined by gathering data on sectional superficies, which have been created in a manner similar to the subject property and which are located in the subject neighborhood or similar neighborhoods in the primary market area. After selecting appropriate data, the appraiser determines the ratio of the value of the sectional superficies (either at the time these rights were created or at the time they were transferred) to the value of the freehold interest in the land, above or below which the sectional superficies have been created, for each of the selected data.

The reasonable ratio for the subject property is chosen by analyzing the ratios of the comparable data. The value of the freehold interest in the land, above or below which the subject sectional superficies have been created, is then multiplied by the ratio to determine the value of the sectional superficies on the date of the value opinion.

In applying this approach, the appraiser should pay particular attention to the matters described in part c. of ② above.

④ **Value Indicated by the Income Capitalization Approach Using the Quasi-Land Residual Technique**

The quasi-land residual technique may also be used to determine the value of sectional superficies. In this technique, the appraiser first estimates the net operating income (NOI) attributable to the land, above or below which the sectional superficies have been created, using two different assumptions. Under the first assumption, the appraiser employs the highest and best use of the land as though vacant without considering the sectional superficies. Under the second assumption, the appraiser assumes the highest and best use of the land taking into account the sectional superficies, the difference between the two NOIs attributable to the land is then capitalized at an appropriate capitalization rate.

⑤ **Value Determined from the Vertical Allotment Ratio for the Land above or below Which Sectional Superficies Have Been Created**

An appraiser can estimate the value of sectional superficies by multiplying the value of the underlying site, as if vacant and free of any encumbrances, by the vertical allotment ratio, based on the contract for the sectional superficies. The appraiser further adjusts this estimated value according to the specific contract provisions to arrive at a final value estimate. The vertical allotment ratio refers to the ratio between: a) the value of the space in which the sectional superficies are created plus the value of the adjacent space, the development of which is restricted because of structures in the superficies' space (e.g., high-voltage power lines or subway tracts); and b) the value of the underlying site based on its highest and best use. In calculating the vertical allotment ratio for sectional superficies, the appraiser determines what economic share the space in question represents of the total value of buildable area, considered as the base value.

In applying this technique, the appraiser should pay particular attention to the matters indicated in part c. of section ② above.

(4) **Appraisal in situations such that where soil contamination on the subject site was verified**

Appraisal of real estate on which the presence of soil contamination has been verified should make use of investigations performed by environmental specialists to ascertain the extent of the contamination and the costs required for its removal.

However, if the requirements mentioned in section 1 of General Standards Chapter 5, and Guidance Note III are satisfied, the appraisal can be performed after obtaining the client's consent, with condition that assumes removal of the contamination.

In situations where it is possible to objectively determine the degree of value influences discussed in section 6 of General Standards Chapter 8 and Guidance Note VI, the appraiser can also perform the valuation by estimating the effect of the presence of soil contamination on the subject propety's value.

It should be further noted, however, that even after implementing measures for removal of soil contamination, the appraiser should still need to consider the stigma of this on the subject propety's value.

2. Guidance on Built-Up Property

(1) **Tenant-Occupied Building and Its Site**

Where the value of a tenant-occupied building and its site is to be determined by the income capitalization approach and the economic value of the deposit is relatively insignificant because of changes in the value of the land and building over the passage of time following the receipt of that deposit, the value is determined by capitalizing the net operating income (NOI), based on actual nominal rent, rather than actual effective rent.

(2) **Condominium Units**

An appraiser may confirm the physical characteristics of, and ownership and interests in, a condominium unit from land registry books, building drawing (or building documents when more detailed drawings are required), management bylaws, assessment rolls and survey drawings.

Some matters requiring special attention in the confirmation process are listed below.

① **Exclusively Owned Areas**
   a. Location, shape, size, structure and use of the condominium building
   b. Location, shape, size and use of the exclusively owned areas of the building
   c. Details of building appurtenances that go with the exclusively owned areas

② **Common Areas**
   a．Extent of common areas and co-ownership
   b．Common areas belonging to only some condominium unit owners
③ **Building Site**
   a．Location, shape and size of the site
   b．Title encumbrances upon the site
   c．Dimensions of the site assigned to the building where the subject condominium project is located
   d．Co-ownership of the site
④ **Management Fees**
   Amounts of the management fees and repair reserves.

Guidance Note VIII on SS. Chap. 2 :
APPRAISAL OF REAL ESTATE RENTAL VALUE

1. Guidance on Building Sites

In determining the market rent under new lease to a building site, the appraiser should pay special attention to the following matters.

(1) Where the highest and best use of the building site cannot be realized because of restrictions on use imposed by the lessor in the lease contract, the base value that is used for determining rent in the summation approach must consider the resulting decrease in economic value.

In assessing the anticipated yield, the appraiser must consider both the lagging nature of rent growth compared with the change in the land value and the degree of interdependence between rent and land value.

(2) The comparable rental data analyzed must include data on leases newly closed on a date near the date of the value opinion. The location of the comparable rental properties and other influences on the rent negotiated must be similar.

(3) Analysis of comparable rental data from similar lease contracts for the built-up property may provide an indication of the rent for building sites. The appraiser arrives at the indication of rent by deducting an amount equivalent to the actual real rent paid for portions other than the building site from the actual real rent paid for the total leased area of the building, including the building site. In selecting comparable data to determine the market rent for a building site, the appraiser should especially consider the similarity in contract provisions as well as in the highest and best use of the sites.

2. Guidance on Built-Up Property

Where a building is occupied by retail shops, only the core of the building and a portion of the building facilities may be constructed by the lessor (in such cases, leases to the tenants are called "skeleton leases"). The interior finish, exterior and a portion of the building facilities are often constructed by the tenant. The appraiser must keep this circumstance in mind when estimating the base value used to determine rent in the summation approach and selecting data used to determine rent in the comparable rental data approach.

Guidance Note IX on SS. Chap. 3 : APPRAISAL OF REAL ESTATE VALUE SUBJECT TO SECURITIZATION

1. Guidance on Basic approach regarding securitization properties
(1) A securitization property as defined in the Specific Standards, Chapter 3, Section 1, I must be appraised in accordance with Chapter 3 of the Specific Standards, even if this means reevaluating a property that has been previously appraised.

2. Guidance on Drafting a processing plan
(1) In some cases, the person verifying the data needed to draft the processing plan may be a different person than the LREA who is in charge of appraisal of the subject property. However, the LREA bears responsibility for this as part of the appraisal.

(2) If negotiations are conducted with the client when verifying the data needed to draft the processing plan, such as asking the client to submit information to facilitate a suitable appraisal, then the course of such negotiations must be included in the records of verified data. The records of verified data are appended to the appraisal report as supplementary information. It is not necessary to append these records to the appraisal document; however, they must be retained as data specified in Article 38, Paragraph 2 of the Real Estate Appraisal Act Enforcement Rules.

(3) If engineering reports, data needed for application of the DCF method, or other documents have been obtained multiple times, or if multiple field surveys of the subject property have been performed, then the matters confirmed at every stage and records from every stage are needed.

(4) The relationships between the client and the parties involved in securitization must be described, as stated in the Specific Standards, Chapter 3, Section 2, III. It is also necessary to state whether the LREA holds interests in the subject property and whether the LREA has relationships to any persons holding interests with regard to the subject property, in accordance with Chapter 9, Section 2 of the General Standards.

3. Guidance on Investigating property-specific influences on the securitization property
The following must be addressed in the investigation of property-specific influences on the securitization property.

(1) The LREA makes an independent decision as to whether to use the engineering report or not. When judging the appropriateness and accuracy of the engineering report, if necessary, the LREA must seek verification based on the views of architects or other experts. In some cases, an existing engineering report can be used; but in other cases, even if the engineering report formally states the required items, it may be inadequate for appraisal purposes, and investigation by an LREA may be required.

(2) The matters listed in the table in Specific Standards, Chapter 3, Section 3, III, (3) and the matters listed in Appendix 1 are only the necessary minimum of physical, legal, and other matters regarding the subject property which must be confirmed

for appraisal. It may be necessary to confirm additional items and details.
(3) The LREA should obtain the full engineering report from the client and obtain an explanation directly from the preparer of the engineering report, to the extent this is possible.
(4) The preparation of an engineering report is often a contracted service. In this case, the engineering report preparer should indicate the contract provider of survey services. When identifying the engineering report preparer in the appraisal report, the name of the contract provider of survey services must also be stated.

4. Guidance on Application of the DCF method

The following must be addressed in the application of the DCF method.
(1) When explaining the income and expense items and their definitions to the client, in order to improve the accuracy of the data that the client provides to the LREA, it is necessary to provide guidance such as indicating the correspondences between income/expense items and data concerning the management of real estate receipts and disbursements, including a detailed breakdown of how to calculate each item.
(2) The income and expense items should not include securitization-related expenses such as trust fees, business expenses of SPCs, investment corporations, funds, etc., or asset management fees (except for expenses related to specific properties). Since net cash flow is calculated prior to depreciation, no depreciation allowances are entered. Also, the breakdown of net operating income as defined in the table in the Specific Standards, Chapter 3, Section 4, II (1) may differ from that of NOI (net operating income) as the term is used in general disclosure documents related to securitization properties.
(3) Regarding the calculation of operating profit on lump-sum payments and capital expenditures, which account for the difference between net operating income and net cash flow, two of the income and expense items in the table in the Specific Standards, Chapter 3, Section 4, II (1), it is necessary to append a note concerning the approach for the yield of operating profit on lump-sum payments, and to ensure that the categories of capital expenditures and repair expenses conform to their handling under tax procedures.
(4) When the direct capitalization method is used for verification purposes in cases when the DCF method has been applied, the income and expense items must be used in the same way.

V-4

General Guideline for Real Estate Appraisers on Determination of Purpose and Scope of Valuation and Contents of Report

August 28, 2009
Ministry of Land, Infrastructure, Transport and Tourism

不動産鑑定士が不動産に関する価格等調査を行う場合の業務の目的と範囲等の確定及び成果報告書の記載事項に関するガイドライン

平成21年8月28日
国土交通省

V − 4. General Guideline for Real Estate Appraisers on Determination
of Purpose and Scope of Valuation and Contents of Report

Table of Contents

Ⅰ. **General Principles** ··360
　1. **Purpose of This Guideline** ···360
　2. **Definitions** ··360
　3. **Scope of This Guideline and Relatinship with the Standards** ········362
　4. **Distinction between Appraisal Compliant with the Standards
　　　and Any Other Valuation** ··362
　5. **Valuation with Special Assumptions** ······································362

Ⅱ. **Determination of Purpose and Scope of Valuation** ··················366
　1. **Client and Recipient of Report** ··366
　2. **Intended Use and Scope of Disclosure or Publication/Non-
　　　publication of Value Conclusion.** ··366
　3. **Interests** ··368
　4. **Basic Matters of Valuation** ··370
　5. **Procedures of Valuation** ··372
　6. **Passibility That the Results May Differ from Appraisal Compliant with
　　　the Standards (only if the valuation does not comply with the Standards)** ······374

Ⅲ. **Contents of Report** ···376
　1. **Value Conclusion** ···376
　2. **Client and Recipient of Report** ··376
　3. **Intended Use and Scope of Disclosure or Publication/Non-publication of
　　　Value Conclusion** ···376
　4. **Basic Matters of Valuation** ··378
　5. **Procedures of Valuation** ··378
　6. **Date of Valuation** ···380
　7. **Interests** ··380
　8. **Names of Real Estate Appraisers Involved in Valuation** ·············382

Ⅳ. **Mutatis Mutandis Application** ···384

Supplementary Provisions ···384

目　次

Ⅰ．総論 …………………………………………………………………………………361
　　1．本ガイドラインの趣旨 …………………………………………………………361
　　2．定義 ………………………………………………………………………………361
　　3．本ガイドラインの適用範囲及び不動産鑑定評価基準との関係………………363
　　4．不動産鑑定評価基準に則った鑑定評価とそれ以外の価格等調査との峻別等 ……363
　　5．特定の想定上の条件を付加した価格等調査について ………………………363

Ⅱ．業務の目的と範囲等の確定 ………………………………………………………367
　　1．依頼者及び成果報告書の提出先 ………………………………………………367
　　2．依頼目的、調査価格等が開示される範囲又は公表の有無等…………………367
　　3．利害関係等 ………………………………………………………………………369
　　4．価格等調査の基本的事項 ………………………………………………………371
　　5．価格等調査の手順 ………………………………………………………………373
　　6．不動産鑑定評価基準に則った鑑定評価と結果が異なる可能性がある旨
　　　（不動産鑑定評価基準に則らない場合に限る）…………………………………375

Ⅲ．業務の目的と範囲等に関する成果報告書への記載事項 ………………………377
　　1．調査価格等 ………………………………………………………………………377
　　2．依頼者及び成果報告書の提出先 ………………………………………………377
　　3．依頼目的、調査価格等が開示される範囲又は公表の有無等…………………377
　　4．価格等調査の基本的事項 ………………………………………………………379
　　5．価格等調査の手順 ………………………………………………………………379
　　6．価格等調査を行った年月日 ……………………………………………………381
　　7．利害関係等 ………………………………………………………………………381
　　8．価格等調査に関与した不動産鑑定士の氏名 …………………………………383

Ⅳ．不動産鑑定士が直接不動産の鑑定評価に関する法律第3条第2項の業務を行う場
　　合についての準用 …………………………………………………………………385

附　則 ……………………………………………………………………………………385

V - 4. General Guideline for Real Estate Appraisers on Determination of Purpose and Scope of Valuation and Contents of Report

I. General Principles

1. Purpose of This Guideline

This Guideline provides for the matters that a licensed real estate appraiser or an assistant real estate appraiser (hereinafter collectively referred to as "real estate appraiser") shall determine with a client as to the intended use and scope of valuation and the contents of a report, when performing valuation service as a business of the real estate appraisal service provider that the appraiser belongs to.

2. Definitions

The terms as used in this Guideline shall be defined as follows:

(1) The term "appraisal service" means the service set forth in Article 3, paragraph 1 of the Real Estate Appraisal Act (Act No. 152 of 1963).

(2) The term "value" means capital value or rental value.

(3) The term "document" means a paper or an electromagnetic record.

(4) The term "valuation" means the determination of value of real estate in a document. Valuation is either carried out as appraisal service or so-called "adjacent/peripheral service" set forth in Article 3, paragraph 2 of the Real Estate Appraisal Act.

(5) The term "client" means the one who requests a real estate appraisal service provider (in the case of adjacent/peripheral service, a real estate appraisal service provider or a real estate appraiser) to carry out valuation, including an asset manager or the like, who is virtually in the position of a client in the case of valuation of securitized real estate.

(6) The term "appraisal compliant with the Standards" means valuation carried out in accordance with all of the contents of the Real Estate Appraisal Standards (hereinafter referred to as "the Standards"). It does not include valuation that applies only a part of the Standards, such as the one that adopts only one of the appraisal approaches specified in the Standards where it is not difficult to adopt the others as well.

(7) The term "value conclusion" means the price/rent determined in the process or as a result of valuation.

(8) The term "report" means a written report of valuation in accordance with Part III of this Guideline.

(9) The term "publication/disclosure/submission" means broad publication of a value conclusion to general public, or disclosure of a value conclusion to a party other than the client, or submission of a report to a party other than the client.

(10) The term "recipient of disclosure/submission" means a party other than the client to whom a value conclusion is to be disclosed or a report is to be submitted.

Ⅰ．総論

1．本ガイドラインの趣旨

本ガイドラインは、不動産鑑定士及び不動産鑑定士補（以下「不動産鑑定士」という。）が、その所属する不動産鑑定業者が業として価格等調査を行う場合に、当該価格等調査の目的と範囲等に関して依頼者との間で確定すべき事項及び成果報告書の記載事項等について定めるものである。

2．定義

本ガイドラインにおける用語の定義は以下のとおりとする。

(1) 「鑑定評価等業務」とは、不動産の鑑定評価に関する法律（昭和38年法律第152号）第3条第1項の業務（鑑定評価業務）又は同条第2項の業務（いわゆる隣接・周辺業務）をいう。

(2) 「価格等」とは、不動産の価格又は賃料をいう。

(3) 「文書等」とは、文書又は電磁的記録をいう。

(4) 「価格等調査」とは、不動産の価格等を文書等に表示する調査をいう。なお、価格等調査は、不動産の鑑定評価に関する法律第3条第1項の業務（鑑定評価業務）の場合のほか、同条第2項の業務（いわゆる隣接・周辺業務）の場合がある。

(5) 「依頼者」とは、不動産鑑定業者（いわゆる隣接・周辺業務の場合は不動産鑑定業者又は不動産鑑定士）に価格等調査を求める他人をいい、証券化対象不動産の価格等調査の場合の実質的な依頼者となるアセットマネジャー等を含むものとする。

(6) 「不動産鑑定評価基準に則った鑑定評価」とは、不動産鑑定評価基準の全ての内容に従って行われる価格等調査をいい、例えば、他の手法の適用が困難でないにもかかわらず、不動産鑑定評価基準に定める鑑定評価の手法のうちの一のみを適用した価格等調査等不動産鑑定評価基準の一部分のみを適用・準用した価格等調査は含まれないものとする。

(7) 「調査価格等」とは、価格等調査の途中で、又は成果として求められる価格等をいう。

(8) 「成果報告書」とは、価格等調査の成果をⅢ．に従い書面に示したものをいう。

(9) 「公表・開示・提出」とは、調査価格等が不特定多数の者に広く公表されること、若しくは依頼者以外の者に開示されること、又は成果報告書が依頼者以外の者に提出されることをいう。

(10) 「開示・提出先」とは、調査価格等が開示される依頼者以外の者又は成果報告書が提出される依頼者以外の者をいう。

V - 4. General Guideline for Real Estate Appraisers on Determination
of Purpose and Scope of Valuation and Contents of Report

3. Scope of This Guideline and Relationship with the Standards

This Guideline shows the procedure that a real estate appraiser shall comply with when carrying out valuation, regardless of whether it is appraisal service or adjacent/peripheral service. In the case of appraisal compliant with the Standards, a real estate appraiser shall comply with this Guideline along with the Standards.

If a real estate appraisal service provider is subcontracted from another to undertake all or part of the valuation service requested by a client, this Guideline does not apply to such subcontracted valuation. However, the real estate appraiser shall endeavor, as necessary, to take measures equivalent to those under this Guideline.

Services separately provided under laws and regulations, such as the published land prices, prefectural land price surveys, roadside land prices, and assessed value of fixed assets tax, provided on requests from the state or local public entities, shall comply with the said laws and regulations, and shall not be subject to application of this Guideline.

4. Distinction between Appraisal Compliant with the Standards and Any Other Valuation

The Standards are the unified standards to be observed when a real estate appraiser appraises real estate, and its purpose is to be conducive to the appropriate operation of the real estate appraisal system, and thereby to contribute to the formation of fair values of real estate. Therefore, if a real estate appraiser carries out valuation, he/she shall, in principle, carry out appraisal compliant with the Standards. However, appraisal compliant with the Standards is not necessarily required in the following cases:

(i) Cases where the value conclusion is only for internal use by the client.
(ii) Cases where publication/disclosure/submission is to be made, but is not considered to materially affect the judgments of a third party or a recipient of disclosure/submission.
(iii) Cases where all of the recipients of disclosure/submission have agreed that the value conclusion is not to be published.
(iv) Cases where it is impossible to comply with the Standards.
(v) Other cases where there exists reasonableness of a departure from the Standards by taking into account II-2 (Intended Use and Scope of Disclosure or Publication/Non-publication of Value Conclusion).

5. Valuation with Special Assumptions

If valuation with any of the assumptions set forth in 1) through 4) below cannot be carried out in compliance with the Standards due to the said assumptions and the value conclusion, or the report is subject to publication/disclosure/submission (excluding the case where it is not considered to materially affect the judgments of a third party or a recipient of disclosure/submission), the said valuation shall be carried out in compliance with the Standards except for the related portions of Chapter 5, Section 1 (Identification of the Subject Property) and Chapter 8, Section 3 (Verification of the Subject Property) of the Standards:

(1) Valuation on the assumption that construction of the property with any uncomplet-

3．本ガイドラインの適用範囲及び不動産鑑定評価基準との関係

本ガイドラインは、不動産の鑑定評価に関する法律第3条第1項に規定する不動産の鑑定評価であるか、同条第2項に規定するいわゆる隣接・周辺業務であるかを問わず、価格等調査を行う場合に、不動産鑑定士が従うべき業務の方法等を示すものであり、不動産鑑定評価基準に則った鑑定評価を行う場合は、不動産鑑定評価基準のほか、本ガイドラインに従うものとする。

なお、他の不動産鑑定業者が依頼者から受注した価格等調査業務の全部又は一部について価格等調査を当該他の不動産鑑定業者から再受注する場合の当該再受注する価格等調査については、本ガイドラインは適用しない。ただし、必要に応じ、本ガイドラインに準じた措置を取るよう努めるものとする。

また、国又は地方公共団体が依頼する地価公示、都道府県地価調査、路線価、固定資産税評価等、別に法令等に定めるものは、当該法令等に従うものとし、本ガイドラインは適用しない。

4．不動産鑑定評価基準に則った鑑定評価とそれ以外の価格等調査との峻別等

不動産鑑定評価基準は、不動産鑑定士が不動産の鑑定評価を行うに当たっての統一的基準であり、不動産鑑定評価制度の適切な運用に寄与し、もって不動産の適正な価格の形成に資することを目的とするものであることから、不動産鑑定士が不動産の価格等を調査するに当たっては、不動産鑑定評価基準に則った鑑定評価を行うことを原則とする。ただし、①調査価格等が依頼者の内部における使用にとどまる場合、②公表・開示・提出される場合でも公表される第三者又は開示・提出先の判断に大きな影響を与えないと判断される場合、③調査価格等が公表されない場合ですべての開示・提出先の承諾が得られた場合、④不動産鑑定評価基準に則ることができない場合、又は⑤その他「Ⅱ．2．依頼目的、調査価格等が開示される範囲又は公表の有無等」等を勘案して不動産鑑定評価基準に則らないことに合理的な理由がある場合には、不動産鑑定評価基準に則った鑑定評価を行うことを必ずしも求めるものではない。

5．特定の想定上の条件を付加した価格等調査について

以下の(1)から(4)までの想定上の条件を付加した価格等調査が、当該条件を付加することによって不動産鑑定評価基準に則ることができなくなる場合であって、かつ、調査価格等又は成果報告書が公表・開示・提出されるとき（公表される第三者又は開示・提出先の判断に大きな影響を与えないと判断されるときを除く。）には、不動産鑑定評価基準「第5章鑑定評価の基本的事項第1節対象不動産の確定」、「第8章鑑定評価の手順第3節対象不動産の確認」のうち当該想定上の条件に係る部分以外は不動産鑑定評価基準に則るものとする。ただし、①調査価格等が公表されない場合で全ての開示・提出先の承諾が得られた場合、②その他「Ⅱ．2．依頼目的、調査価格等が開示される範囲又は公表の有無等」等を勘案して合理的な理由がある場合は、この限りでない。

(1) 未竣工建物を含む不動産の竣工を前提として行う価格等調査

V - 4. General Guideline for Real Estate Appraisers on Determination of Purpose and Scope of Valuation and Contents of Report

　　　　ed buildings would have been completed.
(2) Valuation without considering the possibility of soil contamination.
(3) Valuation without considering the possibility of existence of hazardous substances, such as asbestos, with regard to the building environment.
(4) Valuation without considering the possibility of existence of buried cultural property or underground installations.
　　　　However, this shall not apply to—
(i) Cases where the value conclusion is not to be published and all of the recipients of disclosure/submission have given their consent; and
(ii) Other cases where there exists reasonableness by taking into consideration II-2 (Intended Use and Scope of Disclosure or Publication/Non-publication of Value Conclusion).

When the assumptions set forth in (1) through (4) above are not considered to be appropriate from the standpoint of feasibility, legal compliance, or the risk of harming the interests of the related and third parties, valuation shall only be carried out if the attaching of the said assumptions is found to be reasonable after verifying the reasonableness in light of the intended use and the scope of disclosure or publication/non-publication, as prescribed in II-4-(5) and III-4-(5).

(2) 土壌汚染の可能性を考慮外とする価格等調査
(3) 建物環境についてアスベスト等の有害物質の存在の可能性を考慮外とする価格等調査
(4) 埋蔵文化財又は地下埋設物の埋蔵又は埋設の可能性を考慮外とする価格等調査

なお、対象不動産に係る上記(1)から(4)までの想定上の条件が、実現性、合法性、関係当事者及び第三者の利益を害するおそれがないか等の観点から妥当な想定上の条件に該当しないと判断される場合には、Ⅱ．4．(5)及びⅢ．4．(5)に規定するとおり、依頼目的、調査価格等が開示される範囲又は公表の有無等に照らして当該想定上の条件を付加することが合理的である理由を検証のうえ合理的と認められる場合に限り、当該条件を付加した価格等調査を行うものとする。

V – 4. General Guideline for Real Estate Appraisers on Determination
of Purpose and Scope of Valuation and Contents of Report

II. Determination of Purpose and Scope of Valuation

A Real Estate Appraiser in charge of determination of the intended use and scope of valuation hereinafter referred to as "real estate appraiser in charge of determination") shall confirm with a client and determine the following matters, before concluding the contract. A real estate appraisal service provider shall deliver a document that clearly describes the following matters to the client, before concluding the contract. In the case of changing any matters in the document after conclusion of the contract, the real estate appraiser in charge of determination shall confirm with the client and determine such changes and the real estate appraisal service provider shall deliver a document that clearly describes them to the client before the delivery of the report.

A real estate appraiser shall carry out valuation based on the contents indicated in the document.

1. Client and Recipient of Report
(1) The client of the valuation
(2) Any recipients of the report (other than the client)

2. Intended Use and Scope of Disclosure or Publication/Non-publication of Value Conclusion
(1) Intended Use

Examples are getting reference for sale and purchase, valuing collateral, valuing possessed assets such as real estate investment trust, applying the lower of cost or market (LCM) method to inventory, obtaining market value of leased property, and doing litigation.

(2) Scope of disclosure or publication/non-publication
  (i) Scope of disclosure, if the valuation conclusion is to be disclosed to any parties other than the client.
  (ii) A statement that the value conclusion is to be published to general public, when applicable.

If publication/disclosure/submission is to be made, but is not considered to materially affect the judgments of a third party, the reasonableness of the said consideration shall be verified; provided, however, that this shall not necessarily apply to appraisal compliant with the Standards.

(3) Need for obtaining consent when expanding the scope of publication or disclosure after valuation

If, after completion of valuation, the value conclusion originally planned to be withheld is to be published or the original scope of disclosure is to be expanded, it is necessary to obtain the consent of the real estate appraiser before the said publication or disclosure, by way of the client delivering a document to the real estate appraisal service pro-

Ⅱ．業務の目的と範囲等の確定

　価格等調査の業務の目的と範囲等の確定を担当する不動産鑑定士（「確定担当不動産鑑定士」という。）は、契約の締結までに、以下の事項を依頼者に確認した上で確定するものとする。不動産鑑定業者は以下の事項を明記した文書等を契約の締結までに依頼者に交付するものとする。また、契約の締結後に当該文書等に記載された事項を変更する場合には、確定担当不動産鑑定士は変更について依頼者に確認した上で確定し、不動産鑑定業者は、成果報告書の交付までに、変更を明記した文書等を依頼者に交付するものとする。

　不動産鑑定士は、文書等に記載された内容に従って価格等調査を行うものとする。

1．依頼者及び成果報告書の提出先
⑴　価格等調査の依頼者
⑵　依頼者以外の者に成果報告書を提出する場合は、当該提出先

2．依頼目的、調査価格等が開示される範囲又は公表の有無等

⑴　価格等調査の依頼目的
　売買の参考のための調査、担保評価のための調査、不動産投信等の保有資産の調査、棚卸資産の低価法適用のための調査、賃貸等不動産の時価評価のための調査、訴訟に使用するための調査など。

⑵　開示範囲又は公表の有無
　①調査価格等が依頼者以外の者に開示される場合にはその範囲、②不特定多数の者に広く公表される場合はその旨。
　なお、公表・開示・提出されるにもかかわらず、公表・開示・提出される第三者の判断に大きな影響を与えないと判断される場合は、当該判断が合理的である理由を検証するものとする。ただし、不動産鑑定評価基準に則った鑑定評価を行う場合には、必ずしも確定、明記することを求めない。

⑶　事後の公表・開示範囲の拡大の際の承諾の必要性
　価格等調査終了後に、①当初公表が予定されていなかった調査価格等について公表されることとなる場合や、②当初定めた開示範囲が広がる場合には、当該公表又は開示の前に依頼者が不動産鑑定業者に文書等を交付することにより、不動産鑑定士の承諾を得る必要があること。ただし、不動産鑑定評価基準に則った鑑定評価を行う場合には、必ずしも確定、明記することを求めない。

V - 4. General Guideline for Real Estate Appraisers on Determination
of Purpose and Scope of Valuation and Contents of Report

vider; provided, however, that this shall not necessarily apply to appraisal compliant with the Standards.
(4) Consent of recipients of disclosure/submission
If the value conclusion is not to be published, a statement is needed that all of the recipients of disclosure/submission have agreed that the valuation will not be appraisal compliant with the Standards.

3. Interests
(1) Interests of the real estate appraiser or the real estate appraisal service provider in the subject property
Any interests or connection of the real estate appraiser or the real estate appraisal service provider involved in valuation with the subject property or a party who has a stake in the subject property shall be noted.
(2) Interests between the client and the real estate appraiser or the real estate appraisal service provider
Any special capital interests, personal interests, and business interests between the client and the real estate appraiser or the real estate appraisal service provider involved in valuation shall be notedin the case of publication/disclosure/submission or appraisal compliant with the Standards.
(3) Interests between the recipient of disclosure/submission and the real estate appraiser or the real estate appraisal service provider
Any special capital interests, personal interests, and business interests between the recipient of disclosure/submission and the real estate appraiser or the real estate appraisal service provider involved in valuation shall be noted if the value conclusion is to be disclosed to a party other than the client or the report is to be submitted to a party other than the client. However, if the recipient of disclosure/submission is undecided or the name of the recipient is unclear, a statement of that fact shall be enough.
(4) Interests between the client and securitization-related parties
The following matters shall be noted concerning the interests between the client and the securitized property subject to valuation:
(i) Identification as to which type of interested party the client is: originator, arranger, asset manager, lender, equity investor, special purpose company,investment corporation, and fund (hereinafter referred to as "securitization-related party".
(ii) Any special capital interests, personal interests, and business interests between the client and the securitization-related parties.

In the following cases, description of the interests set forth in (2) and (3) above may be omitted unless performing appraisal compliant with the Standards:
(i) Where the fact is noted that the value conclusion is not to be published, and all of the clients and the recipients of disclosure/submission have agreed to the omission of the descriptions set forth in (2) and (3) above from the report.
(ii) Where publication/disclosure/submission is to be made, but is not considered to materially affect the judgments of a third party to whom the publication is made

(4)　開示・提出先の承諾

　　調査価格等が公表されない場合であって、全ての開示・提出先から不動産鑑定評価基準に則った鑑定評価としないことについて承諾が得られている場合は、その旨。

3．利害関係等

(1)　不動産鑑定士又は不動産鑑定業者の対象不動産に関する利害関係等

　　価格等調査に関与する不動産鑑定士又は当該不動産鑑定士が所属する不動産鑑定業者の①対象不動産に関する利害関係又は対象不動産に関し利害関係を有する者との縁故若しくは特別の利害関係の有無及び②その内容。

(2)　依頼者と不動産鑑定士又は不動産鑑定業者との間の関係

　　公表・開示・提出される場合又は不動産鑑定評価基準に則った鑑定評価を行う場合においては、依頼者と価格等調査に関与する不動産鑑定士又は当該不動産鑑定士が所属する不動産鑑定業者との間の①特別の資本的関係、人的関係及び取引関係の有無並びに②その内容。

(3)　開示・提出先と不動産鑑定士又は不動産鑑定業者との間の関係

　　調査価格等が依頼者以外の者へ開示される場合又は成果報告書が依頼者以外の者に提出される場合においては、開示・提出先と価格等調査に関与する不動産鑑定士又は当該不動産鑑定士が所属する不動産鑑定業者との間の①特別の資本的関係、人的関係及び取引関係の有無並びに②その内容。ただし、開示・提出先が未定の場合や開示・提出先の具体的名称が明らかでない場合は、その旨。

(4)　依頼者の証券化関係者との関係

　　証券化対象不動産に係る価格等調査の場合には、依頼者と証券化対象不動産との利害関係に関する次の事項。
　① 依頼者が証券化対象不動産の証券化に係る利害関係者（オリジネーター、アレンジャー、アセットマネジャー、レンダー、エクイティ投資家又は特定目的会社・投資法人・ファンド等をいい、以下「証券化関係者」という。）のいずれであるかの別
　② 依頼者と証券化関係者との資本関係、取引関係その他特別な利害関係の有無及びこれらの関係を有する場合にあっては、その内容

なお、以下の場合には、(2)及び(3)の関係を明記することを省略することができる。ただし、不動産鑑定評価基準に則った鑑定評価を行う場合には省略することはできない。
　① 調査価格等が公表されない場合で、全ての依頼者及び開示・提出先が、成果報告書への(2)及び(3)の記載を省略することについて承諾しており、その旨を確認・明記した場合。

　② 公表・開示・提出される場合で公表される第三者又は開示・提出先の判断に大きな影響を与えないと判断される場合。

V − 4．General Guideline for Real Estate Appraisers on Determination
　　　of Purpose and Scope of Valuation and Contents of Report

or of the recipient of disclosure/submission.

4．Basic Matters of Valuation

A real estate appraiser in charge of determination shall decide on appropriate basic matters of valuation in light of 1 through 3 above and clearly describe each of the following items:

(1) Subject property
  (i) The land or buildings subject to valuation.
  (ii) The ownership or other rights subject to valuation.
(2) Requirements for Subject Identification

The items required for an identification of the subject real estate are its physical characteristics and the relevant property rights.

The subject identification must verify physical characteristics such as the location and dimensions of the subject property (to ensure that the physical features of the real estate correspond to the real estate described in the client's specifications), and the legal estate in the subject property, e.g., fee simple (freehold ownership) or leasehold interest. The four possible aspects of physical real estate with which valuation assignments deal are listed below:

1) Where the real estate is to be valued "as is." The real estate may constitute land alone or a combination of land and buildings. Some assignments will call for the valuation of the real estate "as is," i.e., the valuation of the land component or the combined real estate components.

2) In situations where the real estate is a combination of land and buildings, but only the land is the subject of the valuation, the value of the freehold interest in the site can be estimated, assuming the buildings did not exist.

3) Where the real estate to be valued is the "residual" site or the "residual" building. In situations where the real estate is a combination of land and building(s), only one component (either the land or the building component) of that real estate can be the subject of valuation.

4) Where the real estate to be valued is an assemblage or subdivision of real estate. Where the subject of an valuation is the result of a consolidation or subdivision of real estate, the valuation will necessarily be premised on that consolidation or subdivision.

If a property assumed to be different from the "as is" is subject to valuation, the property shall be identified after clarifying (5) (Assumptions) below.

(3) Date of value conclusion

The date of a value conclusion may be classified into the following three, based on the data used to perform valuation:
  (i) The current point in time (i.e., current conclusion).
  (ii) A past point in time (i.e., retrospective conclusion).
  (iii) A future point in time (i.e., prospective conclusion).
(4) Valuation method or value type
  (i) The method to calculate the value.

4．価格等調査の基本的事項

確定担当不動産鑑定士は、1．から3．までに照らして適切な価格等調査の基本的事項を決定し、以下の項目ごとに明記する。

(1) 対象不動産
　①価格等調査の対象となる土地又は建物等並びに②価格等調査の対象となる所有権及び所有権以外の権利。

(2) 対象確定条件
　対象不動産（依頼内容に応じて次の1）から4）までのような条件により定められた不動産をいう。）の①所在、範囲等の物的事項及び②所有権、賃借権等の対象不動産の権利の態様に関する事項を確定するために必要な条件。

1) 不動産が土地のみの場合又は土地及び建物等の結合により構成されている場合において、その状態を所与として価格等調査の対象とすること。

2) 不動産が土地及び建物等の結合により構成されている場合において、その土地のみを建物等が存しない独立のもの（更地）として価格等調査の対象とすること。

3) 不動産が土地及び建物等の結合により構成されている場合において、その状態を所与として、その不動産の構成部分を価格等調査の対象とすること。

4) 不動産の併合又は分割を前提として、併合後又は分割後の不動産を単独のものとして価格等調査の対象とすること。

なお、現況と異なる不動産を価格等調査の対象とする場合には、後記「(5)想定上の条件」を明らかにした上で、想定する不動産を確定する。

(3) 価格等調査の時点価格等調査の基準日。なお、価格等調査の時点は、価格等調査を行う年月日を基準として①現在の場合（現在時点）、②過去の場合（過去時点）及び③将来の時点（将来時点）に分けられる。

(4) 価格等を求める方法又は価格等の種類
　①どのような方法で価格等を求めるのか。②ただし、不動産鑑定評価基準総論第5章第3節に

V − 4. General Guideline for Real Estate Appraisers on Determination
of Purpose and Scope of Valuation and Contents of Report

(ii) The type of value, if it falls under any one of the values (market value, special value, value for regulated purposes, value of special-purpose property, etc.) prescribed in Chapter 5, Section 3 of the General Principles of the Standards.

(5) Assumptions

Any assumptions shall be described, such as the one that construction of the property with any uncompleted buildings would have been completed and the one that there would be no possibility of soil contamination.

When adding assumptions that are not considered to be appropriate from the standpoint of feasibility, legal compliance, and the risk of harming the interests of the related and third parties, it is necessary to verify the reasonableness of the said assumptions in light of II-2 (Intended Use and Scope of Disclosure or Publication/Non-publication of Value Conclusion).

(6) Main differences from appraisal compliant with the Standards

Main differences from the basic matters under the Standards shall be noted if all or part of (1) through (5) above does not comply with them.

In addition, it is necessary to verify the reasonableness of the said differences in light of 2 (Intended Use and Scope of Disclosure or Publication/Non-publication of Value Conclusion).

5. Procedures of Valuation

A real estate appraiser in charge of determination shall set the appropriate procedures of valuation in light of 1 through 3 above and clearly describe them for each of the following items:

(1) Work schedule

Work schedule may be replaced with a process plan if the plan is provided to the client.

(2) Filed survey and its method

Whether or not a field survey (including an interior inspection) is conducted for the subject property, and the method of the survey (including the attributes of the witnesses or the property managers) shall be noted.

(3) Method of gathering and organizing date

Method of gathering and organizing main data necessary for valuation in light of the intended use, such as the following, shall be noted:

(i) Whether to use data offered by the client as they are or on the judgment of the real estate appraiser.
(ii) Whether the real estate appraiser is to independently gather data, and if so, the scope thereof.
(iii) Whether to use data from research conducted by other experts, such as an engineering report, and if so, whether the data is used as it is or based on the judgment of the real estate appraiser.

(4) Method of valuation to be adopted

(i) Whether or not to adopt cost approach, comparison approach, and income approach.

規定する価格又は賃料の種類（正常価格、限定価格、特定価格、特殊価格等）のいずれかに該当する場合は、当該価格又は賃料の種類。

(5) 想定上の条件
　未竣工建築物を含む不動産の竣工を前提として行う価格等調査や土壌汚染の可能性を考慮外とする価格等調査など、想定上の条件を付加する場合は、その内容。

　なお、実現性、合法性、関係当事者及び第三者の利益を害するおそれがないか等の観点から妥当な想定上の条件に該当しないと判断される想定上の条件を付加する場合には、「2．依頼目的、調査価格等が開示される範囲又は公表の有無等」等に照らして当該想定上の条件を付加することが合理的である理由を検証するものとする。

(6) 不動産鑑定評価基準に則った鑑定評価との主な相違点及びその妥当性
　(1)から(5)までの全部又は一部が不動産鑑定評価基準に則らない場合は、不動産鑑定評価基準における基本的事項との主な相違点。
　なお、併せて「2．依頼目的、調査価格等が開示される範囲又は公表の有無等」等に照らした当該相違点の合理的な理由を検証するものとする。

5．価格等調査の手順

確定担当不動産鑑定士は、1．から3．までに照らして適切な価格等調査の手順を決定し、以下の項目ごとに明記する。

(1) 調査スケジュール
　調査スケジュール。ただし、処理計画を策定し、依頼者に交付する場合は、これを調査スケジュールに代えることができる。

(2) 実地調査の有無及びその方法
　対象不動産の実地調査の有無及び実地調査を行う場合の立ち会いの有無、内覧の有無（立会人又は管理者の属性を含む。）等対象不動産の実地調査の方法。

(3) 資料の収集及び整理の方法
　①依頼者から提供された資料をそのまま使用するのか、②依頼者から提供された資料を不動産鑑定士が判断して使用するのか、③不動産鑑定士が独自調査を行うのか及び独自調査を行う場合の範囲、④エンジニアリング・レポート等他の専門家の行う調査の使用の有無及び使用する場合に提供されたものをそのまま使用するのか、提供されたものを不動産鑑定士が判断して使うのか、不動産鑑定士が自ら発注して取得するのかなど、依頼目的等にかんがみ価格等調査に当たって必要となる主な資料の収集及び整理方法。

(4) 適用する価格等調査の手法
　① 原価方式、比較方式、収益方式の各方式の適用の有無及び②他の方法を採用する場合の当該手法。

V - 4. General Guideline for Real Estate Appraisers on Determination
of Purpose and Scope of Valuation and Contents of Report

(ii) Any other approaches to be adopted.
(5) Main differences from appraisal compliant with the Standards
Main differences from the procedures under the Standards shall be noted if all or part of (1) through (4) above does not comply with them.

In addition, it is necessary to verify the reasonableness of the said differences in light of 2 (Intended Use and Scope of Disclosure or Publication/Non-Publication of Value Conclusion).

6. Possibility That the Results May Differ from Appraisal Compliant with the Standards (only if the valuation does not comply with the Standards)

Possibility shall be noted that the results may differ from appraisal compliant with the Standards if all or part of the basic matters of valuation are to be different from appraisal compliant with the Standards as described in 4-(6) or the valuation procedures are to be different from appraisal compliant with the Standards as described in 5-(5), after deciding appropriate basic matters and procedures in light of 1 through 3, based on 4 and 5 above.

(5) 不動産鑑定評価基準に則った鑑定評価との主な相違点及びその妥当性

　(1)から(4)までの全部又は一部が不動産鑑定評価基準に則らない場合は、不動産鑑定評価基準における手順との主な相違点。

　なお、併せて「2．依頼目的、調査価格等が開示される範囲又は公表の有無等」等に照らした当該相違点の合理的な理由を検証するものとする。

6．不動産鑑定評価基準に則った鑑定評価と結果が異なる可能性がある旨（不動産鑑定評価基準に則らない場合に限る）

　4．及び5．に基づき、1．から3．までに照らして適切な価格等調査の基本的事項及び手順を決定した結果、4．(6)に記載したとおり価格等調査の基本的事項の全部若しくは一部を不動産鑑定評価基準に則った鑑定評価と異なることとした場合又は5．(5)に記載したとおり価格等調査の手順を不動産鑑定評価基準に定める手順と異なることとした場合には、これらの相違点があることにより不動産鑑定評価基準に則った鑑定評価とは結果が異なる可能性がある旨。

V – 4. General Guideline for Real Estate Appraisers on Determination of Purpose and Scope of Valuation and Contents of Report

III. Contents of Report

A real estate appraiser who is in charge of preparing a report (hereinafter referred to as "real estate appraiser in charge of preparation") shall prepare a report containing at least the matters set forth in 1 through 8 below, and a real estate appraisal service provider shall deliver it to the client and the recipient of submission.

In addition, a reminder on the results of the service as indicated in 1) and 2) below shall be put on a place easy to be found in a report, such as a place close to a value conclusion—

(ⅰ) If matters other than those set forth in Chapter 5 of the General Principles of the Standards have been decided as the basic matters of the valuation;

(ⅱ) If any of the procedures set forth in Chapter 8 of the General Principles and Chapter 3 of the Specific Principles of the Standards has been omitted; and

(ⅲ) In any other cases where the basic matters or procedures of valuation differ from those specified in the said chapters:

1) There is a possibility that the results may differ from appraisal compliant with the Standards, since all or part of the basic matters of valuation differ from appraisal compliant with the Standards as described in 4-(6), or the procedures of valuation differ from the ones set forth in the Standards as described in 5-(2).

2) The valuation has been undertaken on the premise that it will be used for only the intended use indicated in 3 and with only the scope as described in 2 and 3, and it does not assume any use other than that set forth in 3 or any disclosure other than that set forth in 3.

1. Value Conclusion

2. Client and Recipient of Report
(1) The Client of the valuation
(2) Any recipients of the report (other than the client)

3. Intended Use and Scope of Disclosure or Publication/Non-publication of Value Conclusion
(1) Intended Use

Examples are getting reference for sale and purchase, valuing collateral, valuing possessed assets such as real estate investment trust, applying the lower of cost or market (LCM) method to inventory, obtaining market value of leased property, or doing litigation.

(2) Scope of disclosure or publication/non-publication

(ⅰ) Scope of disclosure, if the value conclusion is to be disclosed to any parities other than the client.

Ⅲ．業務の目的と範囲等に関する成果報告書への記載事項

　成果報告書の作成を担当する不動産鑑定士（「作成担当不動産鑑定士」という。）は、価格等調査を行った場合、最低限以下の１．から８．までの事項を記載した成果報告書を作成し、不動産鑑定業者はこれを依頼者及び提出先に交付するものとする。

　また、①価格等調査の基本的事項として不動産鑑定評価基準総論第５章に定める事項以外を定めた場合又は②不動産鑑定評価基準総論第８章及び各論第３章に定める手順を省略した場合等価格等調査の基本的事項又は手順がこれらの章に定める価格等調査の基本的事項又は手順と異なる場合の成果報告書には、以下の１）及び２）のような業務の成果物の性格や取扱いについて、調査価格等の近傍など分かりやすい場所に記載するものとする。

1） 本価格等調査では、４．(6)に記載したとおり価格等調査の基本的事項の全部又は一部が不動産鑑定評価基準に則った鑑定評価と異なる、又は、５．(2)に記載したとおり価格等調査の手順が不動産鑑定評価基準に定める手順と異なることから、不動産鑑定評価基準に則った鑑定評価とは結果が異なる可能性がある旨。
2） 本価格等調査は、３．に記載された依頼目的で使用されること、及び開示・提出先の範囲又は公表の有無は２．及び３．に記載されたとおりであることを前提としたものであり、３．に記載された以外の目的での使用及び３．に記載されていない者への調査価格等の開示は想定していない旨。

１．調査価格等

２．依頼者及び成果報告書の提出先
(1) 価格等調査の依頼者
(2) 依頼者以外に提出される成果報告書については、当該提出先

３．依頼目的、調査価格等が開示される範囲又は公表の有無等

(1) 価格等調査の依頼目的
　売買の参考のための調査、担保評価のための調査、不動産投信等の保有資産の調査、棚卸資産の低価法適用のための調査、賃貸等不動産の時価評価のための調査、訴訟に使用するための調査など。

(2) 開示範囲又は公表の有無
　①調査価格等が依頼者以外の者に開示される場合にはその範囲、②不特定多数の者に広く公表される場合はその旨。ただし、不動産鑑定評価基準に則った鑑定評価を行った場合には、必ずし

V - 4. General Guideline for Real Estate Appraisers on Determination
of Purpose and Scope of Valuation and Contents of Report

(iii) A statement that a value conclusion is to be published to general public.
These are not necessarily required for the appraisal compliant with the Standards.
(3) Reasoning that the judgments of a third party are not materially affected by publication/disclosure/submission.

If publication/disclosure/submission is to be made, but is not considered to materially affect the judgments of a third party, a statement of that fact and the reasoning of such consideration are needed.

(4) Need for obtaining the consent when expanding the scope of publication or disclosure after valuation

If, after completion of valuation, the value conclusion originally planned to be withheld is to be published or the original scope of disclosure is to be expanded, it is necessary to obtain the consent of the real estate appraiser before the said publication or disclosure, by way of the client delivering a document to the real estate appraisal service provider; provided, however, that this shall not necessarily apply to appraisal compliant with the Standards.

(5) Consent of the recipients of disclosure/submission

A statement is needed that all of the recipients of disclosure/submission have agreed that the valuation will not be appraisal compliant with the Standards.

4. Basic Matters of Valuation

(1) Subject property
(2) Requirements for the subject identification as determined under II-4-(2).
(3) Date of the value conclusion as determined under II-4-(3)
(4) Valuation method or the type of value as determined under II-4-(4)
(5) Assumptions
  (i) Any assumptions added.
  (ii) Reasonableness of the assumptions that are not considered to be appropriate from the standpoint of feasibility, legal compliance, and the risk of harming the interests of the related and third parties, in light of 3 (Intended Use and Scope of Disclosure or Publication/Non-publication of Value Conclusion).
(6) Main differences from appraisal compliant with the Standards
  (i) Main differences from the basic matters under the Standards, including the matters set forth in (1) through (5) above.
  (ii) The reasonableness of the said differences in light of 3 (Intended Use and Scope of Disclosure or Publication/Non-publication of Value Conclusion) if all or part of II-4 (Basic Matters of Valuation) does not comply with the Standards.

5. Procedures of Valuation

(1) Treatment of unclear matters and scope of investigation

Treatment of unclear matters due to the limitation of data collection and deficiency of data shall be described: whether such matters were excluded from consideration while clearly stating their ambiguousness, or a real estate appraiser made a reasonable presumption, carried out separate research, or used the result of research by another ex-

も記載することを求めない。

(3) 公表される第三者又は開示・提出先の判断に大きな影響を与えないと判断される理由
　公表・開示・提出されるにもかかわらず、公表される第三者又は開示・提出先の判断に大きな影響を与えないと判断される場合は、①その旨及び②当該判断が合理的である理由。ただし、不動産鑑定評価基準に則った鑑定評価を行った場合には、必ずしも記載することを求めない。

(4) 事後の公表・開示範囲の拡大の際の承諾の必要性
　価格等調査終了後に、①当初公表が予定されていなかった調査価格等について公表されることとなる場合や、②当初定めた開示範囲が広がる場合には、当該公表又は開示の前に依頼者が不動産鑑定業者に文書等を交付することにより、不動産鑑定士の承諾を得る必要がある旨。ただし、不動産鑑定評価基準に則った鑑定評価を行った場合には、必ずしも記載することを求めない。

(5) 開示・提出先の承諾
　全ての開示・提出先から不動産鑑定評価基準に則った鑑定評価としないことについて承諾が得られている場合は、その旨。

4．価格等調査の基本的事項
(1) 対象不動産
(2) Ⅱ．4．(2)により確定した対象確定条件
(3) Ⅱ．4．(3)により確定した価格等調査の時点
(4) Ⅱ．4．(4)により確定した価格等を求める方法又は価格等の種類
(5) 想定上の条件
　① 付加した想定上の条件。
　② 実現性、合法性、関係当事者及び第三者の利益を害するおそれがないか等の観点から妥当な想定上の条件に該当しないと判断される想定上の条件を付加した場合には、「3．依頼目的、調査価格等が開示される範囲又は公表の有無等」等に照らして当該想定上の条件を付加したことが合理的である理由。
(6) 不動産鑑定評価基準に則った鑑定評価との主な相違点及びその妥当性の根拠
　「Ⅱ．4．価格等調査の基本的事項」の全部又は一部が不動産鑑定評価基準に則らない場合は、①(1)から(5)までの事項を含め不動産鑑定評価基準における基本的事項との主な相違点及び②「3．依頼目的、調査価格等が開示される範囲又は公表の有無等」等に照らした当該相違点の合理的な理由。

5．価格等調査の手順
(1) 調査上の不明事項に係る取扱い及び調査の範囲
　資料収集の限界、資料の不備等によって明記することができなかった事項が存する場合の調査上の取扱い（例えば、不明である旨を明記して考慮外としたのか、不動産鑑定士が合理的に推定して調査を行ったのか、不動産鑑定士が別途調査を行ったのか、他の専門家等が行った調査結果等を活用したのかなど）。

V – 4. General Guideline for Real Estate Appraisers on Determination
of Purpose and Scope of Valuation and Contents of Report

pert.
(2) Main differences from appraisal compliant with the Standards
 (i) Main differences from the procedures under the Standards.
 (ii) The reasonableness of the said differences in light of 3 (Intended Use and Scope of Disclosure or Publication/Non-publication of Value Conclusion) if all or part of II-5 (Procedures of Valuation) does not comply with the Standards.

6. Date of Valuation

In addition to the date when valuation is completed, the date of a field survey shall be noted. If a field survey is not made, that fact shall be stated.

7. Interests

(1) Interests of the real estate appraiser or the real estate appraisal service provider in the subject property

Any interests or connection of the real estate appraiser or the real estate appraisal service provider involved in valuation with the subject property or a party who has a stake in the subject property shall be noted.

(2) Interests between the client and the real estate appraiser or the real estate appraisal service provider

Any special capital interests, personal interests, and business interests between the client and the real estate appraiser or the real estate appraisal service provider involved in valuation shall be noted, in the case of publication/disclosure/submission or appraisal compliant with the Standards.

(3) Interests between the recipient of disclosure/submission and the real estate appraiser or the real estate appraisal service provider

Any special capital interests, personal interests, and business interests between the recipient of disclosure/submission and the real estate appraiser or the real estate appraisal service provider involved in valuation shall be noted if the value conclusion is to be disclosed to a party other than the client or a report is to be submitted to a party other than the client. However, if the recipient of disclosure/submission is undecided or the name of the recipient is unclear, a statement of that fact shall be enough.

(4) Interests between the client and securitization-related parties

The following matters shall be noted concerning the interests between the client and the securitized property subject to valuation:
 (i) Identification as to which type of securitization-related party the client is.
 (ii) Any special capital interests, personal interests, and business interests between the client and the securitization-related parties.

In the following cases, the description of the interests set forth in (2) and (3) above may be omitted unless performing appraisal compliant with the Standards:
 (i) Where the fact is noted that the value conclusion is not to be published, and all of the clients and the recipients of disclosure/submission have agreed to the omission of the descriptions set forth in (2) and (3) above from the report.

(2) 不動産鑑定評価基準に則った鑑定評価との主な相違点及びその妥当性の根拠「Ⅱ．5．価格等調査の手順」の全部又は一部が不動産鑑定評価基準に則っていない場合は、①不動産鑑定評価基準における手順との主な相違点及び②「3．依頼目的、調査価格等が開示される範囲又は公表の有無等」に照らした当該相違点の合理的な理由。

6．価格等調査を行った年月日

価格等調査を行った年月日のほか、実際に現地に赴き対象不動産の現況を確認した場合はその年月日。実際に現地に赴いていない場合はその旨。

7．利害関係等

(1) 不動産鑑定士又は不動産鑑定業者の対象不動産に関する利害関係等
価格等調査に関与した不動産鑑定士又は当該不動産鑑定士が所属する不動産鑑定業者の①対象不動産に関する利害関係又は対象不動産に関し利害関係を有する者との縁故若しくは特別の利害関係の有無及び②その内容。

(2) 依頼者と不動産鑑定士又は不動産鑑定業者との間の関係
調査価格等が公表・開示・提出される場合又は不動産鑑定評価基準に則った鑑定評価を行った場合においては、依頼者と価格等調査に関与した不動産鑑定士又は当該不動産鑑定士が所属する不動産鑑定業者との間の①特別の資本的関係、人的関係及び取引関係の有無並びに②その内容。

(3) 開示・提出先と不動産鑑定士又は不動産鑑定業者との間の関係
調査価格等が依頼者以外の者へ開示される場合又は成果報告書が依頼者以外の者へ提出される場合においては、開示・提出先と価格等調査に関与した不動産鑑定士又は当該不動産鑑定士が所属する不動産鑑定業者との間の①特別の資本的関係、人的関係及び取引関係の有無並びに②その内容。ただし、開示・提出先が未定の場合や開示先の具体的名称が明らかでない場合は、その旨。

(4) 依頼者の証券化関係者との関係
証券化対象不動産に係る価格等調査の場合には、依頼者と証券化対象不動産との利害関係に関する次の事項。
① 依頼者が証券化関係者のいずれであるかの別
② 依頼者と証券化関係者との資本関係、取引関係その他特別な利害関係の有無及びこれらの関係を有する場合にあっては、その内容

なお、以下の場合には、(2)及び(3)の関係を記載することを省略することができる。ただし、不動産鑑定評価基準に則った鑑定評価を行った場合には省略することはできない。
① 調査価格等が公表されない場合で、全ての依頼者及び開示・提出先が、成果報告書への(2)及び(3)の記載を省略することについて承諾しており、その旨を確認・記載した場合。

V - 4. General Guideline for Real Estate Appraisers on Determination
of Purpose and Scope of Valuation and Contents of Report

(ii) Where publication/disclosure/submission is to be made, but is not considered to materially affect the judgments of a third party to whom the publication is made or of the recipient of disclosure/submission, and the matter set forth in 3-(3) has been described.

8. Names of Real Estate Appraisers Involved in Valuation

Names of all the real estate appraisers involved in valuation shall be listed, including the ones who belong to the real estate appraisal service provider that took on all or part of the service as a subcontractor.

② 公表・開示・提出される場合で公表される第三者又は開示・提出先の判断に大きな影響を与えないと判断され、3．(3)の事項を記載した場合。

8．価格等調査に関与した不動産鑑定士の氏名

他の不動産鑑定業者に業務の全部又は一部を再委託した場合の当該不動産鑑定業者の不動産鑑定士を含め、価格等調査に関与した不動産鑑定士全員の氏名。

V − 4. General Guideline for Real Estate Appraisers on Determination of Purpose and Scope of Valuation and Contents of Report

IV. Mutatis Mutandis Application

This Guideline shall apply mutatis mutandis if a real estate appraiser performs valuation, as the service set forth in Article 3, paragraph 2 of the Real Estate Appraisal Act, by direct request from a client.

Supplementary Provisions

1. This Guideline is effective from January 1, 2010, and shall apply to the valuation for which a contract is concluded on or after the the said day.

2. The Ministry of Land, Infrastructure, Transport and Tourism shall review the execution status of this Guideline as needed, and take necessary measures based on the results of the review.

Ⅳ. 不動産鑑定士が直接不動産の鑑定評価に関する法律第3条第2項の業務を行う場合についての準用

　本ガイドラインは、不動産鑑定士が直接依頼者から不動産の鑑定評価に関する法律第3条第2項の業務として価格等調査を依頼されて当該価格等調査を行う場合に準用するものとする。

附則
1. このガイドラインは、平成22年1月1日から施行し、同日以後に契約を締結する価格等調査から適用する。

2. 国土交通省は、このガイドラインの施行の状況について、必要に応じ、随時検討を加え、その結果に基づいて必要な措置を講ずるものとする。

V-5

Guidance Notes on the General Guideline for Real Estate Appraisers on Determination of Purpose and Scope of Valuation and Contents of Report

August 28, 2009
Ministry of Land, Infrastructure, Transport and Tourism

不動産鑑定士が不動産に関する価格等調査を行う場合の業務の目的と範囲等の確定及び成果報告書の記載事項に関するガイドライン運用上の留意事項

平成21年8月28日
国 土 交 通 省

V - 5. Guidance Notes on the General Guideline for Real Estate Appraisers on Determination of Purpose and Scope of Valuation and Contents of Report

Table of Contents

Ⅰ. **General Principles** ··390
  1. **Note on "2. Definitions"** ··390
  2. **Note on "3. Scope of This Guideline and Relationship with Standards"** ······390
  3. **Notes on "4. Distinction between Appraisal Compliant with the Standards and Any Other Valuation"** ································390
Ⅱ. **Determination of Purpose and Scope of Valuation** ···············398
  1. **Notes on the preamble** ···398
  2. **Note on "1. Client and Recipient of Report"** ··················398
  3. **Notes on "2. Intended Use and Scope of Disclosure or Publication/Non-publication of Value Conclusion"** ···············398
  4. **Notes on "3. Interests"** ··400
  5. **Notes on "4. Basic Matters of Valuation"** ·······················404
  6. **Note on "5. Procedures of Valuation"** ····························404
Ⅲ. **Contents of Report** ···406
  1. **Note on the preamble** ··406
  2. **Notes on "3. Intended Use and Scope of Disclosure or Publication/Non-publication of Value Conclusion"** ··············406
  3. **Notes on "4. Basic Matters of Valuation"** ·······················406
  4. **Note on "5. Procedures of Valuation"** ····························408
  5. **Note on "7. Interests"** ···408
  6. **Note on "8. Names of the Real Estate Appraisers Involved in Valuation"** ······408
Supplementary Provisions ···408

目　次

- Ⅰ．総論関係 ··391
  - 1．「2．定義」関係 ···391
  - 2．「3．本ガイドラインの適用範囲及び不動産鑑定評価基準との関係」関係 ········391
  - 3．「4．不動産鑑定評価基準に則った鑑定評価とそれ以外の価格等調査との峻別等」関係 ··391
- Ⅱ．業務の目的と範囲等の確定関係 ··399
  - 1．前文関係 ··399
  - 2．「1．依頼者及び成果報告書の提出先」関係 ···399
  - 3．「2．依頼目的、調査価格等が開示される範囲又は公表の有無等」関係 ···········399
  - 4．「3．利害関係等」関係 ··401
  - 5．「4．価格等調査の基本的事項」関係 ···405
  - 6．「5．価格等調査の手順」関係 ··405
- Ⅲ．業務の目的と範囲等に関する成果報告書への記載事項関係 ····························407
  - 1．前文関係 ··407
  - 2．「3．依頼目的、調査価格等が開示される範囲又は公表の有無等」関係 ···········407
  - 3．「4．価格等調査の基本的事項」関係 ···407
  - 4．「5．価格等調査の手順」関係 ··409
  - 5．「7．利害関係等」関係 ··409
  - 6．「8．価格等調査に関与した不動産鑑定士の氏名」関係 ·······························409
- 附　則 ··409

V - 5. Guidance Notes on the General Guideline for Real Estate Appraisers on Determination of Purpose and Scope of Valuation and Contents of Report

General Notes on the General Guideline on Determination of Purpose and Scope of Valuation and Contents of Report (hereinafter referred to as the "Guideline") are provided below:

I. General Principles

1. Note on "2. Definitions"
Valuation subject to the Guideline

Even if it is not the ultimate goal to show the value to a client, a third party to whom the publication is made, or a recipient of disclosure/submission, the valuation in which the value is indicated in the course of service, such as providing consultation on use, transactions, and investment of real estate by using the value, shall be subject to the Guideline.

2. Note on "3. Scope of This Guideline and Relationship with the Standards"
Application to valuation subcontracted from another real estate appraisal service provider

The second paragraph premises that if a real estate appraisal service provider who has undertaken valuation from a client (referred to as "original service provider") subcontracts all or part of it to another one (referred to as "subcontracted service provider"), a real estate appraiser of the original service provider is supposed to determine the intended use and scope of valuation with the client according to the Guideline. On such premise, the Guideline need not be further applied to the valuation undertaken by the subcontracted service provider from the original service provider.

3. Notes on "4. Distinction between Appraisal Compliant with the Standards and Any Other Valuation"
1) Internal use by the client

"Internal use by the client" includes the use for internal decision-making on sale and purchase or on financing by an officer or employee of the client when it is a company or a financial institution.

Meanwhile, submitting a report or a value conclusion to an external attorney or accountant is not considered to be internal use by the client in a strict sense. However, for instance, if client company A shows a report or a value conclusion to auditing firm B, and the report or the value conclusion is to be only used internally by auditing firm B, there can be reasonableness for deeming that it is equivalent to internal use and may allow for valuation that is not compliant with the Standards. Even in such cases, when predicted in advance, it is necessary that such fact be determined and clearly described pursuant to II-2-(2) of the Guideline.

In addition, if it is highly predictable beforehand that the scope of publication or disclosure will be expanded after the delivery of the report, it is necessary to determine and clearly describe that effect in advance pursuant to II-2-(2) of the Guideline and to

不動産鑑定士が不動産に関する価格等調査を行う場合の業務の目的と範囲等の確定及び成果報告書の記載事項に関するガイドライン（以下「価格等調査ガイドライン」という。）運用上の留意事項は以下のとおり。

Ⅰ．総論関係

1．「2．定義」関係
価格等調査ガイドラインの対象とする価格等調査について
　依頼者、公表される第三者又は開示・提出先に対して価格等を示すことを最終的な目的としていなくても、価格等を求め、それを利用して不動産の利用、取引又は投資に関して相談に応じるなど、その業務の過程で価格等を示すものは価格等調査ガイドラインの対象とする価格等調査に含まれる。

2．「3．本ガイドラインの適用範囲及び不動産鑑定評価基準との関係」関係
他の不動産鑑定業者から再受注する価格等調査への適用について

　なお書きの趣旨は、依頼者から価格等調査を受注した不動産鑑定業者（「元受注業者」という。）が当該価格等調査の全部又は一部を他の不動産鑑定業者（「再受注業者」という。）に委託する場合に、元受注業者に所属する不動産鑑定士が価格等調査ガイドラインに従い依頼者との間で当該価格等調査の目的と範囲等を確定することを前提としており、その前提の範囲内においては、再受注業者が行う価格等調査については、元受注業者との間で改めて価格等調査ガイドラインを適用することとはしないものである。

3．「4．不動産鑑定評価基準に則った鑑定評価とそれ以外の価格等調査との峻別等」関係
1）依頼者の内部における使用の考え方について
　「依頼者の内部における使用」とは、依頼者が企業である場合にその役職員などが売買のために内部での意思決定に使用する、又は、依頼者が金融機関である場合にその役職員などが融資を行うために内部での意思決定に使用する場合などが考えられる。
　一方、社外の弁護士、会計士等へ提出する場合は厳密な意味での依頼者の内部における使用とはいえないが、例えば、価格等調査の依頼者であるＡ企業が、Ａ企業の監査人であるＢ監査法人に対して成果報告書や調査価格等を示す場合は、当該成果報告書や調査価格等がＢ監査法人の内部でのみ利用される場合は、内部における使用に準じたものとして合理的理由があると考えられ、不動産鑑定評価基準に則らない価格等調査が可能となる場合もあると考えられる。その場合でも、このような事態が事前に想定される場合には価格等調査ガイドラインⅡ．2．(2)に基づきその旨を確定・明記する必要がある。

　また、成果報告書の交付後に公表、開示される範囲が拡大されることが成果報告書の交付前から十分予想される場合には、価格等調査ガイドラインⅡ．2．(2)に基づきあらかじめこれを確定・明記するとともに、これを勘案して価格等調査の基本的事項や手順を適切に判断することが必要

V − 5. Guidance Notes on the General Guideline for Real Estate Appraisers on Determination of Purpose and Scope of Valuation and Contents of Report

appropriately determine the basic matters and procedures of valuation by taking it into consideration.

2) Case that does not necessarily require appraisal compliant with the Standards
Appraisal compliant with the Standards is not necessarily required in any of the cases set as in (i) through (v) of I-4 of the Guideline.

3) Cases where publication/disclosure/submission is considered to materially affect the judgments of a third party
The following (1) through (6) are the cases where publication/disclosure/submission is considered to materially affect the judgments of a third party, which means that appraisal compliant with the Standards shall be carried out in these cases unless it is impossible to do so:
(1) Valuation of the specified asset to be stated or recorded in —
  (i) The notice on subscription for preferred equity under Article 40 of the Act on Securitization of Assets;
  (ii) The notice on subscription for specified company bonds under Article 122 of the said Act; and
  (iii) The asset trust securitization plan under Article 226 of the said Act.
(2) Valuation of the specified asset for —
  (i) A settler company of an investment trust under Article 11 (including the cases where applied mutatis mutandis pursuant to Article 54) of the Act on Investment Trust and Investment Corporations; and
  (ii) An asset management company under Article 201 of the said Act.
(3) Verification of the value of a property contributed in kind in lieu of the inspection by an inspector at the time of —
  (i) Incorporation of a company under Article 33 of the Companies Act;
  (ii) Issuance of shares for subscription under Article 207 of the said Act; and
  (iii) Exercise of new share subscription right under Article 284 of the said Act.
(4) Verification of the value of a property contributed in kind in lieu of the inspection by an inspector at the time of public offering of fund subscription under Article 137 of the Act on General Incorporated Associations and General Incorporated Foundations.
(5) Valuation at the time of acquisition or sale of real estate in a "non-statutory securitization scheme," which means the raising of capital through a scheme to issue securities (including deemed securities) for the purpose of distributing to the investors proceeds gained by managing real estate backing the securities (excluding those pertaining to specific purpose companies and investment corporations under

である。

2) 不動産鑑定評価基準に則った鑑定評価を行うことを必ずしも求めない場合について

『①調査価格等が依頼者の内部における使用にとどまる場合、②公表・開示・提出される場合でも公表される第三者又は開示・提出先の判断に大きな影響を与えないと判断される場合、③調査価格等が公表されない場合ですべての開示・提出先の承諾が得られた場合、④不動産鑑定評価基準に則ることができない場合、又は⑤その他「Ⅱ．２．依頼目的、調査価格等が開示される範囲又は公表の有無等」等を勘案して不動産鑑定評価基準に則らないことに合理的な理由がある場合』のいずれかに該当すれば、不動産鑑定評価基準に則った鑑定評価を行うことを必ずしも求めるものではない。

3) 公表される第三者又は開示・提出先に大きな影響を与えると判断される場合について

以下の(1)から(6)は、公表される第三者又は開示・提出先に大きな影響を与えると判断される場合である。したがって、(1)から(6)については、不動産鑑定評価基準に則ることができない場合を除き、不動産鑑定評価基準に則った鑑定評価が行われるものである。

(1) 資産の流動化に関する法律第40条における募集優先出資の引受申込者への通知、同法第122条における募集特定社債の引受申込者への通知及び同法第226条における資産信託流動化計画に記載又は記録するための特定資産である不動産の評価

(2) 投資信託及び投資法人に関する法律第11条（第54条において準用する場合を含む。）における投資信託委託会社等による特定資産の価格等の調査及び同法第条における資産運用会社による特定資産の価格等の調査の際の評価

(3) 会社法第33条における会社設立時、同法207条における募集株式の発行時及び同法284条における新株予約権が行使された時の検査役の検査に代わる現物出資財産等の価額の証明

(4) 一般社団法人及び一般財団法人に関する法律第137条における基金引受けの募集時の検査役の検査に代わる現物拠出財産の価額の証明

(5) 法定外証券化スキーム（合同会社と匿名組合契約を用いて組成した私募ファンドなど、不動産を裏付け資産として当該不動産の運用による収益を投資家に配分することを目的に有価証券（みなし有価証券を含む。）を発行する仕組み（資産の流動化に関する法律及び投資信託及び投資法人に関する法律に基づく特定目的会社、投資法人等に係るものを除く。）を利用して出資を募るものをいう。）における不動産の取得時又は譲渡時の評価

V − 5．Guidance Notes on the General Guideline for Real Estate Appraisers on Determination of Purpose and Scope of Valuation and Contents of Report

the Act on Securitization of Assets and the Act on Investment Trust and Investment Corporations), such as a private placement fund made up of a limited liability company and an anonymous association contract.
(6) Valuation of real estate collateral for application for issuance of mortgage securities (cf. Article 21-2 of the Ordinance for Enforcement of the Mortgage Securities Act).

The following (7) through (12) are the cases where publication/disclosure/submission is generally considered to materially affect the judgments of a third party:
(7) Valuation for denial of disposition of estate under bankruptcy law, which means judgment of appropriate sales price of real estate (cf. Article 161 of the Bankruptcy Act, Article 127-2 of the Civil Rehabilitation Act, and Article 86-2 of the Corporate Reorganization Act).
(8) Valuation for acquisition of lands for public use and use/disposition of public properties (cf. "Compensation Standards for Losses Associated with the Acquisition of Lands for Public Use" (Association of Liaison & Consultation for Land), "National Properties Assessment Standard" (Ministry of Finance), and "Public Property Rules" (local authorities)).
(9) Valuation of collateral (when the value exceeds a certain amount) (cf. "Inspection Manual for Deposit-Taking Institutions" (Financial Services Agency)).
(10) Valuation for verification of the appropriate sales price of lands and equipment in transactions between affiliated companies (cf. "The audit treatment of the reporting of profits from sales of lands and equipment in transactions between affiliated companies" (Audit Committee, Japanese Institute of Certified Public Accountants, Report No. 27 of August 8, 1977)).
(11) Valuation for use in litigation (valuation to be submitted as evidence by either the plaintiff or the defendant, or to be carried out upon the request of the court).
(12) Valuation of properties of a company to be reorganized under the Corporate Reorganization Act or a rehabilitation debtor under the Civil Rehabilitation Act (cf. Chapter 5, Section 3 of the General Theory of the Standards, Article 83 of the Corporate Rehabilitation Act, and Article 124 of the Civil Rehabilitation Act).

The above cases are listed for purposes of illustration and not limitation. Appropriate consideration must be made by taking into account the purpose of request, the scope of disclosure or submission, and the amount of value conclusion among others, as to whether or not publication/disclosure/submission materially affects the judgments of a third party.

4) Cases where there exists reasonableness of a departure from the Standards by taking into account II-2 (Intended Use and Scope of Disclosure or Publication/Nonpublication of Value Conclusion)
One of the examples that there exists reasonableness of a departure from the Standards by taking into account II-2 (Intended Use and Scope of Disclosure or Publication/

(6) 抵当証券の交付の申請に必要な担保不動産の評価
　　cf）抵当証券法施行細則第21条ノ2
　以下の(7)から(12)は、一般的には、公表される第三者又は開示・提出先に大きな影響を与えると判断される場合である。

(7) 倒産法制における否認要件（不動産等売却時の適正価格の判断）
　　cf）「破産法第161条」、「民事再生法第127条の2」、「会社更生法第86条の2」

(8) 標準地における公共用地の取得、国有・公有財産の使用や処分に伴うもの。cf）「公共用地の取得に伴う損失補償基準」（用地対策連絡協議会）、「国有財産
　　評価基準」（財務省）、「公有財産規則」（地方公共団体）

(9) 担保評価（一定額以上の場合）
　　cf）「預金等受入金融機関に係る検査マニュアル」（金融庁）
(10) 関連会社間取引に係る土地・設備等の売買の適正価格の証明としての評価
　　cf）「関係会社間の取引に係る土地・設備等の売却益の計上についての監査上の取扱い（昭和52年8月8日公認会計士協会監査委員会報告第27号）」

(11) 訴訟に使用するための評価（原告又は被告が証拠として提出する価格調査、裁判所の要請により行われる価格調査）
(12) 会社更生法における更生会社の財産評価、民事再生法における再生債務者の財産評価
　　cf）「不動産鑑定評価基準総論第5章第3節」、「会社更生法第83条」、「民事再生法第124条」

　なお、公表・開示・提出される場合であって、その調査価格等の大きさ等から公表される第三者又は開示・提出先に大きな影響を与えると判断される場合は以上の場合に限られないことから、依頼目的、開示・提出される範囲、調査価格等の大きさ等を勘案して大きな影響を与えないかどうかについて適切に判断することが必要である。

4) 「Ⅱ．2．依頼目的、調査価格等が開示される範囲又は公表の有無等」等を勘案して不動産鑑定評価基準に則らないことに合理的な理由がある場合について

　『「Ⅱ．2．依頼目的、調査価格等が開示される範囲又は公表の有無等」等を勘案して不動産鑑定評価基準に則らないことに合理的な理由がある場合』を例示すれば、調査結果が公表・開示・

V - 5. Guidance Notes on the General Guideline for Real Estate Appraisers on Determination of Purpose and Scope of Valuation and Contents of Report

Non-publication of Value Conclusion) is revaluation of a property for which —
 (ⅰ) Appraisal compliant with the Standards has been done;
 (ⅱ) A field survey has been or is to be performed by the same real estate appraiser; and
 (ⅲ) No significant changes have been found in land price indices (e.g., official land prices) and value influences (e.g., sales prices, rents, and yields) in light of its physical characteristics, relevant rights, usage, and location since the last appraisal compliant with the Standards.

提出され、公表される第三者又は開示・提出先に影響を与える場合でも、過去に不動産鑑定評価基準に則った鑑定評価が行われたことがある不動産の再評価を行う場合において、自ら実地調査を行い又は過去に行ったことがあり、当該不動産の不動産鑑定評価基準に則った鑑定評価が行われた時点と比較して当該不動産の物的状況や権利関係及び当該不動産の用途や所在地にかんがみて公示地価その他地価に関する指標や取引価格、賃料、利回り等の価格等形成要因に重要な変化がないと認められる場合が挙げられる。

V - 5. Guidance Notes on the General Guideline for Real Estate Appraisers on Determination of Purpose and Scope of Valuation and Contents of Report

II. Determination of Purpose and Scope of Valuation

1. Notes on the preamble
   1) Real estate appraiser in charge of determination
   A real estate appraiser in charge of determination is the one who sets appropriate basic matters and procedures of valuation in light of II-1 through 3 of the Guideline. He/she shall be involved in the valuation service.

   2) Timing of delivering a document that describes changes in any determined matters
   A real estate appraiser in charge of determination does not need to deliver to the client a document that describes a change every time it is made. Before the delivery of a report, however, he/she must determine the changes with the client, and the real estate appraisal service provider must deliver a document that lists them.

   3) Subject property
   A Document that describes the matters set forth in II of the Guideline need not be made for each property subject to valuation. It would be sufficient if the document is made for each contract or for any other suitable units, in consideration of the intended use, the value conclusion, and the scope of publication/disclosure/submission, among other factors.

2. Note on "1. Client and Recipient of Report"
   Recipient of a report (other than the client)
   As for the determination and description of a recipient of submission, the specific name of the recipient is not necessarily required, depending on the intended use. Matters would be sufficient that help realize the purpose of use, such as the purpose of submission and the attributes of the recipient. Even if submission/non-submission or the recipient is undecided, it is necessary to describe the presence or absence of the possibility of submission, the attributes of the prospective recipient, and the purpose of submission, and to determine the basic matters and procedures of valuation by taking them into consideration. If the recipient of submission becomes clear before the submission of a report and is found to be covered by the attributes that have been confirmed and determined, there is no need to deliver a new document that describes the contents specified in II-1-(2) of the Guideline.

3. Notes on "2. Intended Use and Scope of Disclosure or Publication/Non-publication of Value Conclusion"
   1) Scope of Disclosure or Publication/Non-publication
   As for the determination and description of the scope of disclosure, the specific name of the recipient is not necessarily required, depending on the intended use. Matters

Ⅱ．業務の目的と範囲等の確定関係

1．前文関係

1) 確定担当不動産鑑定士について

　確定担当不動産鑑定士は、価格等調査ガイドラインⅡ．1．から3．までに照らして適切な価格等調査の基本的事項及び手順を決定する不動産鑑定士であり、鑑定評価等業務に関与するものとする。

2) 確定した事項の変更を明記した文書等の交付の時期について

　確定担当不動産鑑定士は、変更の都度、依頼者に変更を明記した文書等を交付することは求められていないが、成果報告書の交付までに、変更について依頼者に確認した上で確定し、不動産鑑定業者は成果報告書とは別に変更を明記した文書等を交付する必要がある。

3) 業務の目的と範囲等の確定を行う対象となる不動産について

　価格等調査ガイドラインⅡ．の事項を明記した文書等は必ずしも価格等調査の対象となる不動産ごとに作成・交付する必要はなく、契約ごと等依頼目的や調査価格等又は成果報告書の公表・開示・提出の範囲等を勘案し適当と思われる単位で作成・交付すれば足りる。

2．「1．依頼者及び成果報告書の提出先」関係

依頼者以外の者に成果報告書を提出する場合の当該提出先について

　提出先の確定及び明記は、依頼目的等に応じ、必ずしも個別具体的な提出先の名称等は必要ではなく、提出の目的や提出先の属性等利用目的の把握に資するものでも足りる。このため、提出の有無や提出先が未定である場合にも、提出の可能性の有無及び提出の可能性がある場合の提出先の属性や提出目的について確認及び確定の上明記するとともに、これを勘案して価格等調査の基本的事項及び価格等調査の手順を決定することが必要である。また、成果報告書の提出までに判明した提出先が確認及び確定した属性等に含まれている場合には、価格等調査ガイドラインⅡ．1．(2)に定められた内容を確定して明記した文書等を改めて交付する必要はない。

3．「2．依頼目的、調査価格等が開示される範囲又は公表の有無等」関係

1) 調査価格等が開示される範囲又は公表の有無について

　開示される範囲の確定及び明記は、依頼目的等に応じ、必ずしも個別具体的な開示先の名称等は必要ではなく、開示の目的や開示先の属性等利用目的の把握に資するものでも足りる。このた

V − 5. Guidance Notes on the General Guideline for Real Estate Appraisers on Determination of Purpose and Scope of Valuation and Contents of Report

would be sufficient that help realize the purpose of use, such as the purpose of disclosure and the attributes of the recipient. Even if disclosure/non-disclosure or the recipient is undecided, it is necessary to describe the presence or absence of the possibility of disclosure, the attributes of the prospective recipient, and the purpose of disclosure, and to determine the basic matters and procedures of valuation by taking them into consideration.

Also, even if publication/non-publication is undecided, it is necessary to describe the presence or absence of the possibility of publication and whether the publication will cause no trouble, and to determine the basic matters and procedures of valuation by taking them into consideration.

2) Verification of reasoning that publication/disclosure/submission will not materially affect the judgments of a third party

The result of the verification of reasoning that publication/disclosure/submission will not materially affect the judgments of a third party need not be described in a document by the beginning of the service. It would be sufficient if indicated in a report pursuant to III-3-(3) of the Guideline.

3) Need for obtaining the consent when expanding the scope of publication or disclosure after valuation

In principle, the consent when expanding the scope of publication or disclosure after valuation shall be obtained from the real estate appraiser in charge of preparation.

4. Notes on "3. Interests"

1) Real Estate Appraiser involved in valuation

A real estate appraiser involved in valuation shall be all the ones involved, including the ones who belong to the real estate appraisal service provider that took on all or part of the service as a subcontractor.

2) Real estate appraisal service provider involved in valuation

A real estate appraisal service provider involved in valuation shall be all the ones that have the real estate appraisers set forth in 1) above engage in valuation.

3) Special capital interests, personal interests, and business interests

The interests to be noted in a document for a client shall at least include the followings:

① Interests between the client and the real estate appraisal service provider
 (i) Capital Interests
  Ratio of capital of the real estate appraisal service provider to that of the client, if both are affiliated with each other under the Accounting Principle for Consolidated Financial Statements.

め、開示の有無や開示先が未定である場合にも、開示の可能性があるか、開示の可能性がある場合の開示先の属性や開示目的について確認及び確定の上明記するとともに、これを勘案して価格等調査の基本的事項及び価格等調査の手順を決定することが必要である。

また、公表の有無が未定である場合についても、公表の可能性があるか又は公表されても支障がないかについて確定の上明記するとともに、これを勘案して価格等調査の基本的事項及び価格等調査の手順を決定することが必要である。

2) 公表・開示・提出される第三者の判断に大きな影響を与えないと判断される合理的理由の検証について

公表・開示・提出されるにもかかわらず、公表・開示・提出される第三者の判断に大きな影響を与えないと判断される場合は、当該判断が合理的である理由を検証するものとされているが、検証の結果については、業務開始までに文書等に明記することは要せず、価格等調査ガイドラインⅢ.3.(3)に基づき成果報告書に記載すれば足りる。

3) 事後の公表・開示範囲の拡大の際の承諾の必要性について

事後に公表・開示範囲が拡大する際の承諾は、原則として、作成担当不動産鑑定士の承諾とする。

4.「3.利害関係等」関係
1) 価格等調査に関与する不動産鑑定士について

価格等調査に関与する不動産鑑定士とは、他の不動産鑑定業者に業務の全部又は一部を再委託した場合の当該不動産鑑定業者の不動産鑑定士を含め、価格等調査に関与する不動産鑑定士全員をいう。

2) 価格等調査に関与する不動産鑑定士が所属する不動産鑑定業者について

価格等調査に関与する不動産鑑定士が所属する不動産鑑定業者とは、当該価格等調査に1)にいう不動産鑑定士を従事させている不動産鑑定業者のすべてをいう。

3) 明記すべき特別の資本的関係、人的関係及び取引関係について

依頼者に交付する文書等に明記すべき関係の有無及び内容は、最低限、以下に掲げる特別の関係の有無及び内容である。ただし、以下に掲げるもののほか、依頼目的、公表・開示・提出される範囲及び公表される第三者又は開示・提出先の判断に与える影響の大きさ等にかんがみ必要な特別の関係がある場合は、その旨を明記するものとする。
① 依頼者と不動産鑑定業者との間の関係
【資本的関係】
・不動産鑑定業者が依頼者の関連会社（連結財務諸表原則にいう関連会社をいう。以下同じ。）である、又は依頼者が不動産鑑定業者の関連会社である→その旨及び出資割合

V－5．Guidance Notes on the General Guideline for Real Estate Appraisers on Determination of Purpose and Scope of Valuation and Contents of Report

When to judge
- Between the date of confirmation/determination of submission of a report and the end of the last business year.
- At the end of the business year before last, if the financial statements for the last business year have yet to be prepared.

(ii) Personal Interests

Whether or not the real estate appraisal service provider or its representative is the client or its representative.

When to judge
- At the time of confirmation/determination.
- At the time of submission of a report.

(iii) Business Interests
- Ratio of loan(s) from the client to the entire debts of the real estate appraisal service provider, if it is more than half.
- Ratio of transactions with the client to the entire sales of the real estate appraisal service provider, if it is more than half.
- Ratio of transactions with the client to the entire orders of the real estate appraisal service provider for valuation services, if it is more than half.

When to judge
- Between the date of confirmation/determination of submission of a report and the end of the last business year.
- At the end of the business year before last, if the financial statements for the last business year have yet to be prepared.

② Interests between the Client and the Real Estate Appraiser

(i) Capital Interests

Ratio of voting rights of the real estate appraiser to those of the client, if it is more than 20%.

When to judge

Between the date of confirmation/determination of submission of a report and the end of the last business year.
- At the end of the business year before last, if the financial statements for the last business year have yet to be prepared.

(ii) Personal Interests

Whether or not the real estate appraiser involved is the client or its representative.

When to judge
- At the time of confirmation/determination.
- At the time of submission of a report.

③ Interests between the recipient of disclosure/submission and the real estate appraisal service provider or the real estate appraiser

① and ② above shall apply by replacing the term "client" with " recipient of disclosure/

〈判断時点〉
　確認・確定時及び報告書提出時から前事業年度末までの間で調査可能な時点、前事業年度の財務諸表等が未調製の場合は前々事業年度末

【人的関係】
・不動産鑑定業者又は不動産鑑定業者を代表する者が依頼者又は依頼者を代表する者である→その旨
〈判断時点〉
　確認・確定時、報告書提出時

【取引関係】
・不動産鑑定業者の負債の過半が依頼者からの借入れである→その旨及び割合
・依頼者との取引が不動産鑑定業者の全売上（兼業している場合はその業務に係るものも含む。）の過半を占める→その旨及び割合
・依頼者との取引が不動産鑑定業者の鑑定評価等業務受注額の過半を占める→その旨及び割合
〈判断時点〉
　確認・確定時及び報告書提出時から前事業年度末までの間で調査可能な時点、前事業年度の財務諸表等が未調製の場合は前々事業年度末

② 依頼者と不動産鑑定士との間の関係
【資本的関係】
・関与する不動産鑑定士が依頼者の議決権の20％以上を保有している→その旨及び割合

〈判断時点〉
　確認・確定時及び報告書提出時から前事業年度末までの間で調査可能な時点、前事業年度の財務諸表等が未調製の場合は前々事業年度末

【人的関係】
・関与する不動産鑑定士が依頼者又は依頼者を代表する者である→その旨〈判断時点〉
　確認・確定時、報告書提出時

③ 開示・提出先と不動産鑑定業者・不動産鑑定士との間の関係
　①及び②の「依頼者」を「開示・提出先」と読み替えて適用する。

V - 5. Guidance Notes on the General Guideline for Real Estate Appraisers on Determination of Purpose and Scope of Valuation and Contents of Report

submission."

If any other special interests are found to be practically equivalent to or stronger than those in ① through ③ above, they shall be noted pursuant to II-3-(2) or (3) of the Guideline.

5. Notes on "4. Basic Matters of Valuation"
1) Verification of reasonableness of the assumptions

"Reasonableness" in the second paragraph of II-4-(5) of the Guideline shall be verified by considering whether it would be appropriate under normal social conventions to add the assumptions in light of the intended use, the scope of disclosure, and the publication plan even though that leads to a departure from the Standards. The consideration need not be described in a document by the time of beginning of the service and would be sufficient if indicated in a report pursuant to III-4-(5) of the Guideline.

2) Verification of reasonableness of the differences from the basic matters under the Standards

"Reasonableness" in the second paragraph of II-4-(6) of the Guideline shall be verified by considering whether it would be appropriate under normal social conventions to allow the differences from the basic matters under the Standards in light of the intended use, the scope of disclosure, and the publication plan even though that leads to a departure from the Standards. The consideration need not be described in a document by the time of beginning of the service and would be sufficient if indicated in a report pursuant to III-4-(6) of the Guideline.

3) Verification of reasonableness of the assumptions and main differences from appraisal compliant with the Standards

Verification in the second paragraph of II-4-(5) of the Guideline is included in verification in the second paragraph of II-4-(6) of the Guideline. The former is prescribed for the purpose of confirmation.

6. Note on "5. Procedures of Valuation"
Verification of reasonableness of the differences from the procedures under the Standards

"Reasonableness" in the second paragraph of II-5-(5) of the Guideline shall be verified by considering whether it would be appropriate under normal social conventions to allow the differences in light of the intended use, the scope of disclosure or publication/non-publication even if there are differences between the procedures of valuation and those under the Standards. The consideration need not be described in a document by the time of beginning of the service and would be sufficient if indicated in a report pursuant to III-5-(2) of the Guideline.

なお、①から③の他、実質的にこれらと同等程度以上の特別の関係があると認められる場合についても、価格等調査ガイドラインⅡ．3．(2)又は(3)に基づき明記するものとする。

5．「4．価格等調査の基本的事項」関係
1) 想定上の条件を付加することが合理的である理由の検証について

　価格等調査ガイドラインⅡ．4．(5)のなお書きに規定する「想定上の条件を付加することが合理的である理由を検証する」とは、当該想定上の条件を付加して不動産鑑定評価基準に則った鑑定評価以外の価格等調査を行ったとしても、依頼目的、調査価格等が開示される範囲又は公表の有無等に照らして当該想定上の条件を付加することとした判断が社会通念上合理的であるかを検証するものである。なお、検証の結果については、業務開始までに文書に明記することは要せず、価格等調査ガイドラインⅢ．4．(5)に基づき成果報告書に記載すれば足りる。

2) 不動産鑑定評価基準における基本的事項との相違点の合理的な理由の検証について

　価格等調査ガイドラインⅡ．4．(6)のなお書きに規定する「相違点の合理的な理由を検証する」とは、価格等調査の基本的事項と不動産鑑定評価基準における基本的事項とに相違が存在しても、依頼目的、調査価格等が開示される範囲又は公表の有無等に照らして当該相違点が妥当であるとした判断が社会通念上合理的であるかを検証するものである。なお、検証の結果については、業務開始までに文書に明記することは要せず、価格等調査ガイドラインⅢ．4．(6)に基づき成果報告書に記載すれば足りる。

3) 想定上の条件の付加及び不動産鑑定評価基準に則った鑑定評価との主な相違点についての合理的理由の検証について

　価格等調査ガイドラインⅡ．4．(5)のなお書きに規定する「検証」は、価格等調査ガイドラインⅡ．4．(6)のなお書きに規定する「検証」に含まれるが、(5)では確認的に規定しているものである。

6．「5．価格等調査の手順」関係
不動産鑑定評価基準における手順との相違点の合理的な理由の検証について

　価格等調査ガイドラインⅡ．5．(5)のなお書きに規定する「相違点の合理的な理由を検証する」とは、価格等調査の手順と不動産鑑定評価基準における手順とに相違が存在しても、依頼目的、調査価格等が開示される範囲又は公表の有無等に照らして当該相違点が妥当であるとした判断が社会通念上合理的であるかを検証するものである。なお、検証の結果については、業務開始までに文書に明記することは要せず、価格等調査ガイドラインⅢ．5．(2)に基づき成果報告書に記載すれば足りる。

V - 5. Guidance Notes on the General Guideline for Real Estate Appraisers on Determination of Purpose and Scope of Valuation and Contents of Report

III. Contents of Report

1. Note on the Preamble
Real estate appraiser in charge of preparation
A real estate appraiser in charge of preparation shall be the one who decides on the substantial matters in a report and gets involved in the valuation service.

2. Notes on "3. Intended Use and Scope of Disclosure or Publication/Non-publication of Value Conclusion"
1) Scope of disclosure or publication/non-publication
As for the scope of disclosure, the specific name of the recipient is not necessarily required, depending on the intended use. Matters would be sufficient that help realize the purpose of use, such as the purpose of disclosure and the attributes of the recipient.

2) Need for obtaining the consent when expanding the scope of publication or disclosure after valuation
In principle, the consent when expanding the scope of publication or disclosure after valuation shall be obtained from the real estate appraiser in charge of preparation.

3. Notes on "4. Basic Matters of Valuation"
1) Reasonableness of the assumptions
"Reasonableness" in III-4-(5)-(ii) of the Guideline shall be the grounds for which it is appropriate under normal social conventions to add the assumptions in light of the intended use, the scope of disclosure, and the publication plan even though that leads to a departure from the Standards.

2) Reasonableness of the differences from the basic matters under the Standards
"Reasonableness" in III-4-(6) of the Guideline shall be the grounds for which it is appropriate under normal social conventions to allow the differences from the basic matters under the Standards in light of the intended use, the scope of disclosure, and the publication plan even though that leads to a departure from the Standards.

3) Reasonableness of the assumptions and main differences from appraisal compliant with the Standards
"Reasonableness" in the second paragraph of III-4-(5)-(ii) of the Guideline is included in "reasonableness" in III-4-(6)-(ii) of the Guideline. The former is prescribed for the purpose of confirmation.

Ⅲ．業務の目的と範囲等に関する成果報告書への記載事項関係

1．前文関係
作成担当不動産鑑定士について
　作成担当不動産鑑定士とは、成果報告書の実質的な記載内容を決定する不動産鑑定士であり、鑑定評価等業務に関与するものとする。

2．「3．依頼目的、調査価格等が開示される範囲又は公表の有無等」関係

1) 開示範囲又は公表の有無について
　開示範囲の記載は、依頼目的等に応じ、必ずしも個別具体的な開示先の名称等は必要ではなく、開示の目的や開示先の属性等利用目的の把握に資するものでも足りる。

2) 事後の公表・開示範囲の拡大の際の承諾の必要性について
　事後に公表・開示範囲が拡大する際の承諾は、原則として、作成担当不動産鑑定士の承諾とする。

3．「4．価格等調査の基本的事項」関係

1) 想定上の条件を付加したことが合理的である理由について
　価格等調査ガイドラインⅢ．4．(5)②に規定する「想定上の条件を付加したことが合理的である理由」とは、想定上の条件を付加して不動産鑑定評価基準に則った鑑定評価以外の価格等調査を行ったとしても、依頼目的、調査価格等が開示される範囲又は公表の有無等に照らして当該想定上の条件を付加することとした判断が社会通念上合理的である理由である。

2) 不動産鑑定評価基準における基本的事項との相違点の合理的な理由について
　価格等調査ガイドラインⅢ．4．(6)に規定する「相違点の合理的な理由」とは、価格等調査の基本的事項と不動産鑑定評価基準における基本的事項とに相違が存在しても、依頼目的、調査価格等が開示される範囲又は公表の有無等に照らして当該相違点が妥当であるとした判断が社会通念上合理的である理由である。

3) 想定上の条件の付加及び不動産鑑定評価基準に則った鑑定評価との主な相違点についての合理的理由について
　価格等調査ガイドラインⅢ．4．(5)②に規定する「合理的である理由」は、価格等調査ガイドラインⅢ．4．(6)に規定する「合理的な理由」に含まれるが、確認的に規定しているものである。このため実現性、合法性、関係当事者及び第三者の利益を害する恐れがないか等の観点から妥当な想定上の条件に該当しないと判断される想定上の条件を付加する価格等調査においては、(5)又

V - 5. Guidance Notes on the General Guideline for Real Estate Appraisers on Determination of Purpose and Scope of Valuation and Contents of Report

4. Note on "5. Procedures of Valuation"
Reasonableness of the differences from the procedures under the Standards
"Reasonableness" in III-5-(2) of the Guideline shall be the grounds for which it is appropriate under normal social conventions to allow the differences in light of the intended use, the scope of disclosure and the publication plan even if there are differences between the procedures of valuation and those under the Standards.

5. Note on "7. Interests"
With regard to the interests to be noted in a report, see II 4.

6. Note on "8. Names of Real Estate Appraisers Involved in Valuation"
Valuation shall, regardless of whether or not it complies with the Standards, fall under the category of the service set forth in Article 3, paragraph (1) of the Real Estate Appraisal Act (appraisal service) as long as it evaluates the economic value of real estate and indicates the result as a monetary value. In this case, it should be noted that a report requires the signature and seal set forth in Article 39, paragraph (2) of the said Act, as an appraisal report set forth in paragraph (1) of the said Article.

Supplementary Provisions
These Notes is effective from January 1, 2010, and shall apply to the valuation for which a contract is concluded on or after the said day.

は(6)のどちらかに記載すれば足りる。

4．「5．価格等調査の手順」関係
　不動産鑑定評価基準における手順との相違点の合理的な理由について
　価格等調査ガイドラインⅢ．5．(2)に規定する「合理的な理由」とは、価格等調査の手順と不動産鑑定評価基準における手順とに相違が存在しても、依頼目的、調査価格等が開示される範囲又は公表の有無等に照らして当該相違点が妥当であるとした判断が社会通念上合理的である理由である。

5．「7．利害関係等」関係
　成果報告書に記載すべき利害関係等については、Ⅱ．4．「3．利害関係等」関係を参照することとする。

6．「8．価格等調査に関与した不動産鑑定士の氏名」関係
　価格等調査は、不動産鑑定評価基準に則っているか否かにかかわらず、不動産の経済価値を判定し、その結果を価額に表示しているかぎり、不動産の鑑定評価に関する法律第3条第1項の業務（鑑定評価業務）に該当するものであり、この場合、成果報告書は、同法第39条第1項の鑑定評価書として、同条第2項の署名押印が必要となることに留意する。

附　則
　この留意事項は、平成22年1月1日から施行し、同日以後に契約を締結する価格等調査から適用する。

V-6

Guidelines for Appraisal of Overseas Investment Real Estate

海外投資不動産鑑定評価ガイドライン

V - 6. Guidelines for Appraisal of Overseas Investment Real Estate

Guideline Objectives

These guidelines specify standard appraisal procedures for Japanese real estate appraisers (the only profession that is licensed and registered by the government by law. Hereinafter "Japanese Appraisers") to appraise overseas real estate for investment purposes.

As the globalization of the real estate market progresses, cross-border real estate investment is gaining momentum. In addition, real estate investment trust (REIT) markets have been set up in the past few years, and international competition in real estate markets is heightening rapidly.

In Japan's domestic market, there are no regulations that prohibit Japanese REITs (J-REITs) from acquiring overseas properties. The Tokyo Stock Exchange, however, has established criteria for J-REIT listing that prohibits the acquisition of overseas properties. This prohibition is said to be partly due to the lack of standards for overseas property valuation for Japanese Appraisers.

Further, the domestic real estate industry is actively looking into investing in overseas real estate assets from the perspective of diversifying the risks of portfolios concentrated in domestic real estate investment. The establishment of appropriate guidelines for appraising overseas properties is thus expected to promote the further healthy growth of real estate markets.

With the recent changes in the global real estate market stated above, these guidelines specify standards for Japanese Appraisers to perform appropriate collaborative or joint appraisals with overseas real estate appraisers, protecting the interests of investors and enhancing the reliability of appraisals.

I. Basic Procedures for Appraising Overseas Properties

A. When a Japanese Appraiser is to appraise overseas properties, he/she may
- travel to the country in which the property to be valued is located to perform a property appraisal on his/her own or
- perform a collaborative or joint appraisal with an overseas real estate appraiser (hereinafter "Overseas Appraiser").

It will be reasonable and practical to prepare an appraisal with an Overseas Appraiser as a supportive or collaborative staff that is familiar with the real estate market trends and social and economic conditions in the country in which the property is located.

Ⅴ－6．海外投資不動産鑑定評価ガイドライン

〔ガイドラインの目的〕
　本ガイドラインは、海外投資不動産についての不動産鑑定士による鑑定評価の標準的手法について示すものである。
　不動産市場のグローバル化が進む中、海外からの国内不動産への投資や国内企業や投資家による海外不動産への投資も活発化するとともに、各国でリート市場の開設が相次ぎ、不動産分野における国際間競争が厳しくなってきている。
　一方、我が国の不動産証券化市場においては、日本版不動産投資信託（Ｊリート）の運用対象資産に海外不動産を組み入れることを禁止する法令上の規定は存在しないが、東京証券取引所の上場規程はこれを禁止している。これについては、海外不動産について、これまで標準的な鑑定評価手法が確立していないこと等がその要因となっているとの声もある。
　また、国内不動産事業者は、不動産投資の国内集中に伴うリスクを分散させる観点から、海外不動産への投資に積極的になっており、その際に必要となる適正な鑑定評価の確保により、不動産市場の一層の健全な成長が期待できる。
　本ガイドラインは、以上を踏まえ、海外不動産への投資を行う際に不動産鑑定士が鑑定評価を行う場合において、投資家保護及び鑑定評価の信頼性の向上の観点から適正な鑑定評価が行われるよう、海外現地の不動産鑑定人との連携・共同作業のあり方、鑑定評価の手法等を示すものである。

Ⅰ　海外不動産の鑑定評価の基本的な実施方法
(1)　海外不動産の鑑定評価を依頼された場合には、
　・不動産鑑定士が海外現地（海外不動産の存する地域をいう。以下同じ。）に赴き鑑定評価を行う
　・海外現地の不動産鑑定人を補助員・共同作業員として鑑定評価を行うことが考えられるが、海外現地の市場動向、社会経済情勢等に精通している不動産鑑定人を補助員・共同作業員として鑑定評価を行うことが合理的かつ現実的である。

(2)　この際の鑑定評価は、不動産鑑定士が、
　・海外現地において専門職業家として認定又は公認された不動産鑑定人との連携・共同作業により、

V − 6. Guidelines for Appraisal of Overseas Investment Real Estate

B. In performing an appraisal, the Japanese Appraiser shall in principle complete an appraisal:

- through collaborative or joint work with an Overseas Appraiser who is certified or qualified as a specialist in the country in which the property is located; and
- in accordance with locally authorized or officially recognized real estate appraisal standards.

C. A Japanese Appraiser must fully understand the basic information needed to appraise overseas real estate properties, such as local real estate market trends, legal and taxation systems, appraisal standards, and the qualification system for appraisers. In addition, the Japanese Appraiser must review the work of the Overseas Appraiser, examining whether or not the work is appropriately and reasonably performed and confirming that the results of the work are also appropriate.

II. Agreement on Basic Procedures for Appraising Overseas Real Estate

In the appraisal of overseas real estate properties, the following basic appraisal procedures must be explained to the client and the client's written consent to them must be received.

1. Selection of an Overseas Appraiser according to Section III
2. Scope of work of the Japanese Appraiser and the OverseasAppraiser, and the allocation of responsibilities
3. Property inspections and other investigations into the attributes and characteristics of the real estate to be appraised
4. Currency unit to be used to express the appraisal value of the property
5. Receipt of technical reports (if any) on the conditions of the buildings, facilities and environment of the property to be appraised (often called Engineering Report (hereinafter "ER")

III. Selection of Overseas Appraisers

A. Japanese Appraisers shall understand overseas appraisal standards and overseas appraiser organizations (meaning organizations that grant licenses or titles to real estate appraisers; hereinafter the same). Overseas Appraisers shall be selected for collaborative or joint appraisal work from among Overseas Appraisers who are certified or qualified as specialists in the country after the Japanese Appraiser confirms the following minimum requirements:

1. Professional qualifications of the Overseas Appraiser and the overseas appraiser organization with which the appraiser is affiliated

> ・海外現地において認定又は公認された不動産の鑑定評価基準に基づき、鑑定評価を行うことが原則である。
>
> (3) 不動産鑑定士は、海外現地における不動産市場の動向、不動産に関連する法制・税制・鑑定評価基準、不動産鑑定人の資格制度等海外不動産の鑑定評価を行うために必要となる基礎的知識について十分に理解するとともに、海外現地の不動産鑑定人の作業が適切かつ合理的に行われていることを確認し、及びその作業成果が適正であることを検証しなければならない。

Ⅱ 海外不動産の鑑定評価の基本的な実施方法の確認

> 海外不動産の鑑定評価に当たっては、依頼者に対し、鑑定評価の基本的な実施方法として次の事項について説明し、書面による確認を得なければならない。
> ①Ⅲに定める海外現地の不動産鑑定人の選任
> ②海外現地の不動産鑑定人との連携・共同作業の内容及び役割分担
> ③実地調査その他対象不動産の確認の方法
> ④鑑定評価額の通貨の単位
> ⑤対象不動産に係る建築物、設備等の状況及び環境に関する調査の有無並びに当該調査が行われる場合にあってはその報告書の入手方法

Ⅲ 現地鑑定人の選任

> (1) 不動産鑑定業者は、海外現地の鑑定評価制度、不動産鑑定人団体(不動産鑑定人の資格・称号を付与する団体をいう。以下同じ。)等不動産の鑑定評価を巡る社会経済情勢について理解し、海外現地において専門職業家として認定又は公認された不動産鑑定人の中から、不動産鑑定士に少なくとも次の事項を確認させた上で、鑑定評価の連携・共同作業の補助員又は共同作業員を選任するものとする。
> ①不動産鑑定人としての資格及び所属する不動産鑑定人団体
> ②不動産鑑定人としての略歴及び実績
> ③依頼された鑑定評価に係る不動産取引の利害関係者以外の者であること

V - 6. Guidelines for Appraisal of Overseas Investment Real Estate

2. Broad knowledge and practical experience of the Overseas Appraiser as a real estate appraiser; and
3. No conflicts of interest in the transaction of the real estate to be appraised.

B. The Overseas Appraiser selected according to Subsection A may be a nonresident of the country in which the property is located, but should be familiar with social and economic conditions concerning real estate appraisal in the country in which the property is located. The Overseas Appraiser shall be capable of performing appraisals in the country based on the grounds that he/she has practical experience in making appraisals in that country.

C. The Overseas Appraiser must be selected by the Japanese Appraiser's office in order to smoothly perform collaborative or joint appraisal work. Should the client recommend a candidate to serve as the Overseas Appraiser, the Japanese Appraiser's office shall select the candidate only after determining that the candidate is appropriately qualified to perform the collaborative or joint work by confirming the candidate's resume, practical experience, professional qualifications as a real estate appraiser, and so forth.

IV. Property Inspections and Survey of Market Trends and Legal Restrictions

A. Property Inspections

The property to be appraised must be identified through a property inspection that includes an internal inspection of the buildings.

However, in case that a property were to be reappraised by the same Japanese Appraiser who has done the property inspections before and if it were recognized that there were no relevant legal, physical, economic and other factors' changes on the subject property nor in the neighboring area, the inspections of the subject property may be admitted through an inspection report submitted by the Local Appraiser.

B. Survey of local real estate market trends and legal restrictions on the property

The Japanese Appraiser must have a thorough understanding of overseas real estate market trends, legal and taxation systems on the property, and appraisal standards, before performing property inspections or when visiting the foreign locality, through reports or information supplied by the Overseas Appraiser. In evaluating market trends and legal restrictions, the Japanese Appraiser must bear in mind that the appraisal report or its summary can be disclosed to investors. It is necessary to obtain a sufficient amount of information, including a macroeconomic analysis of local markets and social, economic, and administrative factors affecting the property value, such as standard contract conditions, land ti-

(2) (1)により選任される不動産鑑定人(以下「現地鑑定人」という。)は必ずしも海外現地の国に居住する者であることを要しないが、当該海外現地の鑑定評価制度、不動産鑑定人団体等不動産の鑑定評価を巡る社会経済情勢について理解し、海外現地において鑑定評価を行った実績があるなど海外現地における鑑定評価を行うことができると認められる者でなければならない。

(3) 現地鑑定人の選任は、鑑定評価の連携・共同作業を円滑に行う上で不動産鑑定業者が行うことが必要である。依頼者が現地鑑定人の候補者を推薦した場合であっても、その者の不動産鑑定人としての略歴、実績、資格等を確認し、連携・共同作業を行う者として適切であると認められる場合に限り、不動産鑑定業者が選任するものとする。

Ⅳ 実地調査、市場動向、法令等の調査

(1) 対象不動産の実地調査

対象不動産の内覧の実施を含めた実地調査等により対象不動産の確認を行わなければならない。

ただし、既に鑑定評価が行われたことがある不動産の再評価をする場合において、自ら実地調査を行ったことがあり、当該不動産や周辺地域において価格形成要因に影響を与えるような変化がないと認められるときは、現地鑑定人等による実地調査の報告により確認を行うこととしても差し支えない。

(2) 海外現地における不動産の市場動向、不動産に関連する法令等の調査

海外現地における不動産市場の動向、不動産に関連する法制・税制・鑑定評価基準等については、実地調査に先立って又は海外現地において、現地鑑定人による報告及び価格形成要因に関連する資料の収集など自らの調査により十分に把握する必要がある。

これらの市場動向、法令等の調査については、鑑定評価書が投資家向けに開示されることも念頭に置き、海外現地における市場のマクロ的な経済分析、不動産取引の契約形態や慣行等の社会的・経済的・行政的な価格形成要因を含めて、十分な情報を収集・分析して鑑定評価報告書又は鑑定評価検証報告書に記載することが必要である。

(3) 対象不動産に関する他の調査

対象不動産に係る建築物、設備等の状況及び環境に関する調査(いわゆるエンジニアリング・レポートが作成される場合の調査)、土壌汚染の調査等が行われる場合には、当該調査に係る報告書を入手し、必要に応じて鑑定評価に活用しなければならない。

V - 6. Guidelines for Appraisal of Overseas Investment Real Estate

tle system and other practices in real estate markets. The Japanese Appraiser shall collect and analyze information regarding the property. The appraisal report or the appraisal review report must contain sufficient information analysis.

C. Other surveys of the property for valuation

If an ER is issued or a ground contamination survey or other examination is conducted, the Japanese Appraiser must obtain these reports and incorporate that information in the appraisal if necessary.

V. Collaborative or Joint Work with an Overseas Appraiser

A. Collaborative or Joint Work Procedures

The Japanese Appraiser shall work collaboratively or jointly with an Overseas Appraiser based on an appropriate allocation of responsibilities. Basically, either of the following two methods may be applied.

1. The Japanese Appraiser requests the Overseas Appraiser to collect and provide basic materials and other support considered to be necessary to complete the appraisal (hereinafter, "Overseas Appraisal Support Work"), and the Japanese Appraiser performs the appraisal by using the services of Overseas Appraisal Support Work (hereinafter, "Overseas Appraisal Support Method").
2. The Japanese Appraiser requests the Overseas Appraiser to prepare an appraisal report and performs the appraisal by reviewing the overseas appraiser's report (hereinafter, "Overseas Report Review Method").

B. Promotion of Collaborative or Joint Work

The Japanese Appraiser and the Overseas Appraiser shall smoothly and steadily perform collaborative or joint work through close discussions and coordination at each phase in the appraisal process by means of meetings in person, telephone conversations, and communication via the Internet. Thus, the Japanese Appraiser's office shall conclude a written contract with the overseas real estate appraisal office to which the Overseas Appraiser is affiliated. The contract should contain appropriate procedures for collaborative or joint work between the Japanese Appraiser and the Overseas Appraiser.

Ⅴ 現地鑑定人との連携・共同作業

(1) 現地鑑定人との連携・共同作業の方式

　不動産鑑定士は、現地鑑定人と適切な役割分担及び密接な連携の下、連携・共同作業を行うものとする。連携・共同作業の方式としては、主に、次の方式が考えられる。

①現地鑑定人に、鑑定評価を行うために必要となる基礎資料等の収集・提供その他の不動産鑑定士が行う鑑定評価の補助作業（以下「現地鑑定補助作業」という。）を依頼し、不動産鑑定士が現地鑑定補助作業に係る役務の提供を受けて鑑定評価を行う方式（現地鑑定補助方式）

②現地鑑定人に、鑑定評価の報告を依頼し、現地鑑定人が行った鑑定評価を不動産鑑定士が検証することにより鑑定評価を行う方式（現地鑑定検証方式）

(2) 現地鑑定人との連携・共同作業の推進方法

　不動産鑑定士は、現地鑑定人が行う鑑定評価の作業の内容及び各段階における成果等について、会議の開催、電話・インターネット通信等により、現地鑑定人と直接に意見交換等を行いながら、鑑定評価の連携・共同作業を円滑かつ確実に推進するものとする。このため、不動産鑑定業者は、書面により、現地鑑定人との連携・共同作業の実施に関する契約を現地鑑定人が所属する鑑定業者（以下「現地鑑定業者」という。）と締結するものとする。

V - 6. Guidelines for Appraisal of Overseas Investment Real Estate

	Overseas Appraisal Support Method	Overseas Report Review Method
Japanese Appraiser's office	1. Selection of the verseas Appraiser 2. Overall appraisal report (quality control)	1. Selection of the Overseas Appraiser 2. Overall Appraisal Report (quality control)
Japanese Appraiser	1. Confirmation of Local Basic Materials 2. Overall appraisal report	1. Review of the Overseas Appraisal Report 2. Appraisal review report on the Overseas Appraisal Report 3. Translation into Japanese of the Overseas Appraisal Report
Overseas Appraiser	1. Local Basic Materials	1. Overseas Appraisal Report

VI. Contract Specifics for Collaborative or Joint Work
A. Overseas Appraisal Support Method

In applying the Overseas Appraisal Support Method, the contract shall include provisions on the following.

1. Scope of contracted work

   - Specifics of Overseas Appraisal Support Work
   - Discussion and coordination of the Overseas Appraisal Support Work (by means of meetings in person, telephone conversations, and communication via the Internet)
   - Specifics of materials to be supplied at meetings

2. Professional qualifications of the Overseas Appraiser

   - Professional qualifications of the Overseas Appraiser who performs the Overseas Appraisal Support Work

3. Fees and expenses

4. Schedule

	現地鑑定補助方式	現地鑑定検証方式
不動産鑑定業者	①現地鑑定人の選任 ②鑑定評価書全体（品質管理）	①現地鑑定人の選任 ②鑑定評価書全体（品質管理）
不動産鑑定士	①現地基礎資料等の検証 ②鑑定評価書全体	①現地鑑定報告書の検証 ②現地鑑定報告書の鑑定評価検証報告書 ③現地鑑定報告書の日本語による翻訳文
現地鑑定人	①現地基礎資料等	①現地鑑定報告書

Ⅵ 現地鑑定人との連携・共同作業のための契約内容

(1) 現地鑑定補助方式

現地鑑定人との連携・共同作業を行うに当たっては、現地鑑定補助作業を行う者の資格・称号、現地鑑定補助作業の各段階における会議の開催、電話・インターネット通信等による意見交換、現地基礎資料等の作成要領及び提出期限、報酬等について契約を締結するものとする。その際の主な契約内容を例示すると次のとおりである。

①業務委託の範囲
・現地鑑定補助作業の内容
・現地鑑定補助作業を行うに当たっての意見交換の方法（会議の開催、電話・インターネット通信等）
・会議資料の内容等

②担当者の専門職業家としての資格
・現地鑑定補助作業を実際に担当する専門職業家の資格

③報酬及び費用

④日程
・会議の開催日、現地基礎資料等の説明を行う日、現地基礎資料等の提出日等連携・共同作業の具体的な日程
・期限厳守であること。

⑤現地鑑定人の責任範囲
・不動産鑑定士が作成する鑑定評価報告書（現地鑑定補助作業が反映された部分に限る。）の利用（依頼者等の利用）に対する現地鑑定人の責任の範囲

⑥その他
・情報の秘密保持等

V − 6．Guidelines for Appraisal of Overseas Investment Real Estate

- Details of the schedule for the collaborative or joint work, including dates of meetings, briefings on Local Basic Materials, and delivery of Local Basic Materials
- The deadline must be strictly observed

5. Scope of responsibility of the Overseas Appraiser

- Scope of the Overseas Appraiser's responsibility for users (the client and others) of the appraisal report prepared by the Japanese Appraiser (limited to portions incorporating the Overseas Appraisal Support Work)

6. Other provisions

- Confidentiality agreement and so forth

B. Overseas Report Review Method

In applying the Overseas Report Review Method, the contract shall include provisions on the following.

1. Scope of contracted work

- Specifics of the appraisal in accordance with the appropriate authoritative standard in the country in which the property is located
- Discussion and coordination for performing the appraisal (by means of meetings in person, telephone conversations, and communication via the Internet)
- Specifics of materials to be supplied at meetings

2. Professional qualifications of the Overseas Appraiser

- Professional qualifications of the Overseas Appraiser who performs the appraisal

3. Fees and expenses

4. Schedule

- Details of the schedule for the collaborative or joint work, including dates of meetings, briefings on the Overseas Appraisal Report, and delivery of the Overseas Appraisal Report
- The deadline must be strictly observed

(2) 現地鑑定検証方式

　現地鑑定人との連携・共同作業を行うに当たっては、現地鑑定人の資格・称号、鑑定評価手法、作業の各段階における会議の開催、電話・インターネット通信等による意見交換、現地鑑定報告書の作成要領及び提出期限、鑑定評価の報酬等について契約を締結するものとする。その際の主な契約内容を例示すると次のとおりである。

① 業務委託の範囲
　・対象不動産について、海外現地において認定又は公認された不動産の鑑定評価基準その他遵守すべき法令、規程等に基づき行う鑑定評価の内容
　・鑑定評価を行うに当たっての作業の各段階における意見交換の方法（会議の開催、電話・インターネット通信等）
　・会議資料の内容等

② 担当者の専門職業家としての資格
　・鑑定評価を実際に担当する専門職業家の資格

③ 報酬及び費用

④ 日程
　・会議の開催日、現地鑑定報告書の説明を行う日、現地鑑定報告書の提出日等連携・共同作業の具体的な日程
　・期限厳守であること。

⑤ 現地鑑定人の責任範囲
　・現地鑑定報告書の利用（依頼者等の利用）に対する現地鑑定人の責任の範囲

⑥ その他
　・情報の秘密保持等

V - 6. Guidelines for Appraisal of Overseas Investment Real Estate

5. Scope of responsibility of the Overseas Appraiser

- Scope of Overseas Appraiser's responsibility for users (the client and others) of the Overseas Appraisal Report

6. Other provisions

- Confidentiality agreement and so forth

VII. Review and Supplementary Surveys

A. Review of Local Basic Materials or Overseas Appraisal Report

The Local Basic Materials or the Overseas Appraisal Report supplied by the Overseas Appraiser must be reviewed in order to confirm the soundness, relevance, appropriateness, and reasonableness of the work. This review process should at minimum include the following.

1. Review of Local Basic Materials

- Professional qualifications of the Overseas Appraiser, and his/her professional affiliations
- Date of preparation of the Local Basic Materials, and date of the data
- Physical condition of buildings and title related to the property to be appraised
- Assumptions of the Local Basic Materials
- Whether appropriate and sufficient data has failed to be supplied
- Data sources

2. Review of Overseas Appraisal Report

- Professional qualifications of the Overseas Appraiser, and his/her professional affiliations
- Date of preparation of the Overseas Appraisal Report and the effective date of the appraisal and the date of the report
- Physical condition of buildings and title related to the property to be appraised
- Assumptions in the Overseas Appraisal Report
- Whether appropriate and sufficient data has failed to be supplied
- Data sources
- Consistency of the appraisal method with the requirements of the authoritative standards in the country in which the property is located

Ⅶ 現地基礎資料等又は現地鑑定報告書の検証及び追加・補完調査

(1) 現地基礎資料等又は現地鑑定報告書の検証

現地基礎資料等又は現地鑑定報告書について、現地基礎資料等の内容又は鑑定評価手法その他の鑑定評価の内容の合理性及び鑑定評価額の適正性等につき、検証しなければならない。その際の検証は、少なくとも次の事項を含まなければならない。

①現地基礎資料等の検証
　・現地鑑定人の資格・称号、所属する不動産鑑定人団体の確認
　・現地基礎資料等の作成された年月日及び資料データの時点の確認
　・対象不動産の物的事項、権利の態様等に関する事項の確認
　・現地基礎資料等の前提条件、調査範囲等の確認
　・資料データが明らかに不適切・不十分であると認められるかどうかの確認
　・資料データの出所の確認

②現地鑑定報告書の検証
　・現地鑑定人の資格・称号、所属する不動産鑑定人団体の確認
　・現地鑑定報告書の作成された年月日及び鑑定評価の基準日の確認
　・対象不動産の物的事項、権利の態様等に関する事項の確認
　・鑑定評価の前提条件・制限的条件、調査範囲等の確認
　・資料データが明らかに不適切・不十分であると認められるかどうかの確認
　・資料データの出所の確認
　・採用されている鑑定評価手法が、対象不動産が存する国又は地域において認定又は公認された不動産の鑑定評価基準に適合して行われているかの検証
　・価格形成要因の理解と合理性の検証
　・必要に応じて他の現地鑑定人による複数鑑定又は鑑定レビューなどによる検証

(2) 追加・補完調査

現地基礎資料等又は現地鑑定報告書の検証を行い、その結果、適正な鑑定評価を行う上で必要があると認めるときは、追加・補完調査を行うものとする。この場合には、不動産鑑定士が行うほか、海外現地の他の専門職業家を選任して行うことも考えられる。

- Sound analysis of price factors related to property value
- Preparation of another appraisal or an appraisal review by another Overseas Appraiser if necessary

B. Supplementary surveys

In addition to the review of the Local Basic Materials or the Overseas Appraisal Report, supplementary surveys shall be carried out when deemed necessary to perform a proper appraisal. In this case, the supplementary surveys shall be performed by the Japanese Appraiser or by another overseas expert or specialist in the country.

VIII. Appraisal Value

A. Overseas Appraisal Support Method

The Japanese Appraiser shall work collaboratively or jointly with the Overseas Appraiser in accordance with Sections I through VII and determine the appraisal value.

The appraisal value shall in principle be expressed in the currency unit of the country in which the property is located.

B. Overseas Report Review Method

The Japanese Appraiser shall work collaboratively or jointly with the Overseas Appraiser in accordance with Sections I through VII .If the Overseas Appraisal Report is judged to be appropriate, the Japanese Appraiser shall agree to the appraisal value. However, if the Overseas Appraisal Report is judged to be inappropriate, the Japanese Appraiser shall not agree to it, but shall determine the final appraisal value and state the grounds for his/her judgment.

The appraisal value shall in principle be expressed in the currency unit of the country in which the property is located.

Ⅷ　鑑定評価額の決定等

(1)　現地鑑定補助方式

　不動産鑑定士は、ⅠからⅦまでに定めるところにより、現地鑑定人との連携・共同作業を行い、適正と判断される鑑定評価額を決定するものとする。

　鑑定評価額の表示は、原則として、海外現地の通貨の単位によるものとする。

(2)　現地鑑定検証方式

　不動産鑑定士は、ⅠからⅦまでに定めるところにより、現地鑑定人との連携・共同作業を行い、現地鑑定報告書が適正なものであると判断する場合には鑑定評価額に同意するものとする。なお、同意しない場合には、その根拠を明らかにして適正と判断される鑑定評価額を決定するものとする。

　鑑定評価額の表示は、原則として、海外現地の通貨の単位によるものとする。

　鑑定評価額は、現地鑑定補助方式の場合にあっては不動産鑑定士が決定し、現地鑑定検証方式である場合にあっては不動産鑑定士が同意することとなる。いずれの場合においても、鑑定評価額について、不動産鑑定士として責任を有することとなる。

　現地鑑定検証方式で行う場合の同意については、不動産鑑定士が現地鑑定人の鑑定評価の各作業段階において意見交換を行うなど鑑定評価の作業に関わるため、最終的な鑑定評価額に同意することとなるのが通常であると考えられるが、何らかの理由で鑑定評価額の意見に相違が生じた場合には、不動産鑑定士がその根拠を明記して鑑定評価額を修正し、決定するものとする。

V − 6. Guidelines for Appraisal of Overseas Investment Real Estate

IX. Appraisal Document
The appraisal report or the appraisal review report shall be prepared in writing by the Japanese Appraiser.

A. Overseas Appraisal Support Method

In performing an appraisal using the Overseas Appraisal Support Method, the Japanese Appraiser shall prepare the appraisal report. The Local Basic Materials (original supplied by the Overseas Appraiser) shall be attached to the appraisal report.

B. Overseas Report Review Method

In performing an appraisal using the Overseas Report Review Method, the Japanese Appraiser shall prepare the appraisal review report. The Japanese Appraiser shall also prepare an appropriate Japanese translation of the Overseas Appraisal Report.

The written appraisal document shall consist of the appraisal review report (including supplementary surveys, if any) and the Overseas Appraisal Report (original report). A Japanese translation of the Overseas Appraisal Report shall be attached to the appraisal document.

X. Content of Appraisal Document
A. Report Content Policy

The appraisal document shall include matters deemed necessary in accordance with Japanese Real Estate Appraisal Standards (established by the government in 1969) to the extent possible.

If certain matters deemed necessary according to Japanese Real Estate Appraisal Standards are not considered to be factors in real estate transactions and are usually ignored in appraisal reports in the country in which the property is located, these matters may be left unstated. The reasons for leaving these matters unstated, however, must be recorded.

B. Content

The appraisal report or the appraisal review report shall include matters in Subsection 1 below since the Japanese Appraiser is performing the appraisal with an Overseas Appraiser. Furthermore, it shall include matters in Subsection 2 below

Ⅸ 鑑定評価報告書等の作成等

鑑定評価報告書又は鑑定評価検証報告書は、不動産鑑定士が作成するものとする。

(1) 現地鑑定補助方式

不動産鑑定士は、現地基礎資料等に基づき鑑定評価を行い、鑑定評価報告書を作成するものとする。また、現地基礎資料等(原文)を添付するものとする。

(2) 現地鑑定検証方式

不動産鑑定士は、現地鑑定報告書をⅦに従ってその内容を検証し、鑑定評価検証報告書を作成するものとする。また、現地鑑定報告書の日本語による翻訳文を作成し、原文の内容が正確に翻訳されているかを確認するものとする。

鑑定評価書は、鑑定評価検証報告書(追加・補完調査を行った場合にあっては当該調査報告書を含む。)及び現地鑑定報告書(原文)により構成し、現地鑑定報告書の日本語による翻訳文を添付するものとする。

Ⅹ 鑑定評価報告書等の記載事項等

(1) 記載事項の原則

不動産鑑定評価基準に照らして、必要な記載事項とされている内容をできる限り記載するものとする。

この場合において、不動産鑑定評価基準上記載すべき事項とされているものの、海外現地の不動産市場においては重視されず、現地鑑定評価報告書に記載されないことが通常である場合には記載しないこととして差し支えないが、その合理的理由を記載する必要がある。

(2) 追加的記載事項

鑑定評価報告書又は鑑定評価検証報告書の記載事項については、不動産鑑定士が現地鑑定人と連携・共同作業により鑑定評価を行うこと、海外現地の不動産市場の動向等について日本の投資家等が十分に把握していない場合が多いと考えられること等から、次の事項を追加的に記載するものとする。

①不動産鑑定士及び現地鑑定人の連携・共同作業の役割分担

当該鑑定評価に関する不動産鑑定士及び現地鑑定人のそれぞれの作業内容等役割分担について明記するものとする。

V - 6. Guidelines for Appraisal of Overseas Investment Real Estate

since Japanese capital market investors and other parties are usually unfamiliar with overseas real estate market trends.

1. Scope of work of the Japanese Appraiser and the Overseas Appraiser

   The scope of work of the Japanese Appraiser and the Overseas Appraiser shall be respectively stated.

2. Information on the overseas real estate market

   Since the appraisal document can be disclosed to investors, it shall include overall market analyses, information on real estate market practices and other social, economic, and administrative factors for property value in the country in which the property is located, in particular stating features that differ from those of Japan's real estate market.

   a) Overseas real estate market trends
      Basic real estate market trends of the regional real estate markets
   b) Legal and taxation systems concerning real estate transactions
      Title of the legal and taxation systems concerning real estate transactions
   c) Other information
      Differences in real estate market practices in the country in which the property is located

3. Content of review using the Overseas Report Review Method

   The appraisal review report shall include the specifics of review of the Overseas Appraisal Report, stating the opinions, reasons and conclusions in accordance with Section VII.

4. Appraisal value
   The appraisal value shall be stated in the currency unit of the country in which the property is located, and also stated in the currency of Japan (yen) converted by using the closing exchange rate on the effective date of the appraisal.

C. Signature and seal
   The appraisal report or the Overseas Appraisal Report shall be signed and sealed, respectively, by the Japanese Appraiser or the Overseas Appraiser.

②海外現地の不動産市場の動向に関する事項等
　　鑑定評価書が投資家向けに開示されることも念頭に置き、海外現地における市場のマクロ的な経済分析、不動産取引の契約形態や慣行等の社会的・経済的・行政的な価格形成要因に関する次の事項について、日本の不動産市場と異なる特徴等を踏まえつつ、必要かつ十分な情報を収集・分析して記載するものとする。
　ア　海外現地の不動産市場の動向に関する事項
　　　海外現地及びその周辺地域の不動産市場の動向を示す基礎資料等
　イ　海外現地の不動産に関連する法制、税制等に関する事項
　　　海外現地における不動産の権利関係、不動産取引に係る契約内容及び税制の相違等
　ウ　その他必要な事項
　　　海外現地における不動産取引に係る慣行の相違等

③現地鑑定検証方式における検証内容等
　　鑑定評価検証報告書には、現地鑑定報告書の検証内容について記載するものとし、Ⅶに定める検証すべき事項について、それぞれの検証内容、根拠等を明記するものとする。

④鑑定評価額
　　鑑定評価額を海外現地の通貨の単位で表示した場合においては、原則として、鑑定評価の基準日の為替レート（終値）及び当該レートにより換算した本邦通貨の単位での表示も併記するものとする。

(3)　署名押印
　　鑑定評価書にあっては不動産鑑定士が、現地鑑定報告書にあっては現地鑑定人が署名押印するものとする。

V - 6. Guidelines for Appraisal of Overseas Investment Real Estate

XI. Notes

Appraisals of overseas properties shall be performed in accordance with the Sections I through X. For performing appropriate appraisals by following these guidelines, the following requirements must be met in the country in which the property is located:

1. Property data, market information needed to perform the appraisal, price factor data for property value and any other information can be obtained.
2. A real estate appraiser who is affiliated to a professional organization that grants professional qualifications and provides guidance and education for its members can be selected.
3. Authorized or officially recognized real estate appraisal standards are maintained and disclosed as appropriate, and an overseas appraisal organization takes disciplinary actions (such as caution, suspension of title, revocation of title and so forth) in cases where its members fall seriously short of the standards expected of them.

Even in cases where Condition 2 and/or 3 above are not adequately met, the collaborative or joint work of real estate appraisal based on these guidelines may be performed with an Overseas Appraiser whose profession is qualified in other countries in which these conditions are satisfied.

If the requirements stated above are not satisfied, it is inappropriate to engage in overseas real estate appraisals and the client's request for such appraisal services should be declined.

XII. Status and Application of These Guidelines

These guidelines specify standards for Japanese Appraisers to perform appropriate collaborative or joint appraisals with Overseas Appraisers, protecting the interests of investors and enhancing the reliability of appraisals.

When Japanese private funds invest in overseas real estate or if J-REITs are allowed to include overseas real estate in the near future, the Japanese real estate market will be more integrated into the global real estate market. In particular, real estate appraisal by Japanese Appraisers is mandated for J-REITs in the Japanese regulations. Overseas property appraisals by Japanese Appraisers shall thus be regulated by the Real Estate Appraisal Law (Law No. 152 of 1963).

In this context, these guidelines shall have status equal to the Real Estate Appraisal Standards of Japan for overseas property appraisals. A misleading or fraudulent appraisal violating these guidelines shall be subject to disciplinary actions by the government.

XI　その他留意事項

　海外不動産の鑑定評価に当たっては、ⅠからⅩまでに定める手続きにより実施されるべきであり、その際には、海外現地の国又は地域において、

①鑑定評価を行うために必要となる事例資料、対象不動産の物的確認及び権利の態様等の確認に必要となる資料並びに価格形成要因に照応する資料その他不動産市場の動向を示す基礎資料があること。

②認定又は公認された不動産鑑定人の資格・称号を付与し、かつ、不動産鑑定人を指導育成する不動産鑑定人団体が存在していること。

③認定又は公認された不動産の鑑定評価基準を有し、これに逸脱するなど不正又は不当な鑑定評価が行われた場合には、不動産鑑定人団体により不動産鑑定人の資格・称号の使用停止・剥奪等の指導監督が行われること。

など適正な鑑定評価が行われるための制度が十分に整っていることが必要である。

　ただし、これらの要件のうち②又は③の要件が十分に整っていない国又は地域においても、これらの要件が整った他の国又は地域の資格・称号を有している者が現地鑑定人となる場合には、本ガイドラインに基づく不動産鑑定評価の連携・共同作業を推進することが可能である。

　以上の要件が満たされない海外不動産の鑑定評価については、鑑定評価の依頼を受けることは一般的には困難と考えられ、依頼の拒否も検討すべきである。

XII　本ガイドラインの位置づけ

　本ガイドラインは、海外不動産への投資を行う際に不動産鑑定士が鑑定評価を行う場合において、投資家保護及び鑑定評価の信頼性の向上の観点から適正な鑑定評価が行われるよう、現地鑑定人との連携・共同作業のあり方、鑑定評価の手法等鑑定評価の標準的手法について示すものである。

　一方、日本のプライベートファンドが海外不動産を組み入れる場合や、今後、Ｊリートによる海外不動産の組み入れが可能となった場合には、海外不動産と本邦不動産とで一つの不動産市場が形成されること、Ｊリートについては不動産鑑定士による鑑定評価が義務づけられていること等にかんがみ、不動産鑑定士が行うこれらの海外不動産の鑑定評価については、不動産の鑑定評価に関する法律（昭和38年法律第152号）に基づく指導監督を行うことが必要である。

　したがって、これらの鑑定評価については、本ガイドラインの内容は不動産鑑定評価基準と同等の位置づけとして取り扱うこととし、本ガイドラインを逸脱することにより不当な鑑定評価が行われた場合には、同法に基づく指導監督を行うものとする。

V - 6. Guidelines for Appraisal of Overseas Investment Real Estate

Appendix

	USA	UK	Australia	Singapore
Designations & Qualifications	①State Certified Apprasider/State Licensed Appraiser ② MAI (Commercial・Residential・Indutrial), SRPA (Commercial・Residential・Industrial), SRA (Residential)	MRICS (Member) FRICS (Fellow)	Certified Practising Valuer (CPV)	Singapore Institute of Valuers (SIV)
Organizations	①State Regulatory Agency (50 States) ②Appraisal Institute	Royal Institution Of Chartered Surveyors (RICS)	Australian Property Institute (composed of API members)	Singapore Institute of Surveyors and Valuers
Constituents	See above.	See above.	See above.	See above.
Membership	① Approx.95,000 ② Approx.6,000	Approx. 130,000 (121countries)	Approx. 7,500	Approx. 1,800
Appraisal Standards	US USPAP (Appraisal Foundation)	RICS Appraisal and Valuation Standards (RICS)	Professional Practice Standards (API/PINZ)	SISV Valuation Standards and Guidelines (SISV)

Ⅴ-6. 海外投資不動産鑑定評価ガイドライン

〔別表〕

	アメリカ合衆国	英国	オーストラリア	シンガポール
資格・称号	①州公証・公認鑑定人 ②MAI（商・住・工），SRPA（商・住・工），SRA（住）	MRICS (member) FRICS (fellow)	CPV Certified Practising Valuer	SIV Singapore Institute Of Valuers
登録機関	①州不動産鑑定評価委員会（50州） ②不動産鑑定協会（Appraisal Institute）	RICS Royal Institution of Chartered Surveyor	①州不動産鑑定評価委員会（APIのmemberから登録） ②API Australian Property Institute	Singapore Institute of Surveyors and Valuers
所属団体	同上	同上	同上	同上
人数	①約9万5千人 ②約6千人	約13万人（121カ国）	約7千5百人	約1千8百人
鑑定評価基準（基準作成団体）	USPAP (Appraisal Foundation)	RICS Appraisal and Valuation Standards (RICS)	Professional Practice Standards (API/PINZ)	SISV Valuation Standards and Guidelines (SISV)

V － 6．Guidelines for Appraisal of Overseas Investment Real Estate

Appendix

	Taiwan	Korea	Germany	Honk Kong
Designations & Qualifications	State Certified Real Estate Appraiser	Property Appraiser	Property Valuation Expert	MHKIS (Member) FHKIS (Fellow)
Organizations	Dept. of Land Administration	The Ministry Of Construction and Transportation (MOCT)	IfS-ZERT	Hong Kong Institute of Surveyors
Constituents	The Real Estate Appraiser's Association of the Republic of China	Korea Association of property (KAPA)	BVS (Association of Publicly appointed and Sworn Experts by chamber of commerce and court) BDGS (Munich)	See above.
Membership	Approx. 200	Approx. 2,500	Approx. 1,000	Approx. 1,400
Appraisal Standards	Regulations on Real Estate Appraisal (Dept. of Land Administration, Ministry of the Interior, Central Government)	The laws on Public Notice relating to Real Estate Pricing and Appraisal /The Ministerial Ordinances on Appraisal (MOCT)	WERTV (IFS-ZERT)	The HKIS Valuation Standards On Properties

〔別表〕

	台湾	大韓民国	ドイツ	香港
資格・称号	不動産估價師	鑑定評価士	Property Valuation Expert	MHKIS（member） FHKIS（fellow）
登録機関	市（地政局等）	国（建設交通部）	IfS-ZERT	Hong Kong Institute of Surveyors
所属団体	台北市（高雄市・台中市）不動産估價師公會・中華民國不動産估價師公會全國聯合會	韓国鑑定評価協会	BVS（地方商工会議所・裁判所指定鑑定人協会） BDGS（ミュンヘン）等	同上
人数	約2百人	約2千5百人	約1千人	約1千4百人
鑑定評価基準（基準作成団体）	不動産估價技術規則（中央政府内政部地政司）	不動産価格公示および鑑定評価に関する法令 鑑定評価に関する規則（建設交通部）	WERTV（IfS-ZERT）	the HKIS Valuation Standards on Properties（HKIS）

V-7

Guidelines Regarding Valuation Practice for Appraisal Firms

September 2009
Japanese Association of Real Estate Appraisal

不動産鑑定業者の業務実施態勢に関する業務指針

平成21年9月
社団法人日本不動産鑑定協会

V - 7. Guidelines Regarding Valuation Practice for Appraisal Firms

1. Purpose

Since valuation (hereinafter referring to the operation specified in Article 3, clauses 1 and 2 of the Act on Real Estate Appraisal) results affect a wide range of parties in addition to the client, need is seen for constructing a system that ensures further transparency and credibility, not only as appraisers but from an organizational standpoint as appraisal firms

These guidelines (hereinafter the "Guidelines") provide basic valuation considerations for the appraisal firms of the appraisers when conducting valuation, in order to promote smooth and appropriate operations and further transparency and credibility.

2. Scope of Application and Definition

Though the Guidelines should be applied to all real estate valuations, in light of the social climate, for the time being, the Guidelines will be applied only to valuations (hereinafter referring to valuation based on the Valuation Guidelines regarding Determination of Objectives and Scope of Work and Preparation of Final Valuation Report ["Valuation Guidelines"] prescribed by the Ministry of Land, Infrastructure, Transport and Tourism) used for securitization properties, or preparation of financial statements or corporate accounting[1].

The Guidelines are not applicable when valuation is requested by an appraisal firm other than which originally accepted the request from the client. However, necessary measures should be made in accordance with the Guidelines when required.

Terms defined in the Guidelines are in accordance with the Valuation Guidelines.

3. Structure of the Guidelines

The Guidelines consist of the following categories corresponding to the valuation process (see Attachment: Framework of the Guidelines within the Operation Process)
    1) General practice
    2) Accepting valuation requests
    3) Conducting valuation
    4) Quality control
    5) Information control

---

[1] Valuation for the purpose of preparation of financial statements refers to valuation as in II. Scope of Application of the Basics of Valuation for Financial Statements, indicated by the Ministry of Land, Infrastructure, Transport and Tourism.

Ⅴ-7. 不動産鑑定業者の業務実施態勢に関する業務指針

1．目的

　鑑定評価等業務（不動産の鑑定評価に関する法律第3条第1項又は第2項の業務をいう。以下同じ。）の結果が依頼者以外の広範囲の者に影響を及ぼすことにかんがみ、一層の透明性・信頼性を確保するために不動産鑑定士のみならず不動産鑑定業者の組織としての態勢作りを行うことが求められている。

　本業務指針は、不動産鑑定士が鑑定評価等業務を行うに際し、当該不動産鑑定士が所属する不動産鑑定業者の業務実施態勢に関する基本的事項を定め、業務を円滑かつ適切に行い、透明性・信頼性向上を目指すための業務上の指針として示すものである。

2．適用範囲及び定義

　本業務指針は、鑑定評価等業務全般を対象範囲とすべきであるが、社会の状況にかんがみ、当面の間は証券化対象不動産又は財務諸表の作成に利用される目的[※1]の価格等調査業務（国土交通省が定めた「不動産鑑定士が不動産に関する価格等調査を行う場合の業務の目的と範囲等の確定及び成果報告書の記載事項に関するガイドライン」（以下「価格等調査ガイドライン」という。）に基づく価格等調査に関する業務をいう。以下同じ。）を行う場合に適用する。

　なお、他の不動産鑑定業者が依頼者から受託した価格等調査業務を当該他の不動産鑑定業者から再受託する業務を行う場合については、本業務指針は適用しない。ただし、必要に応じ、本業務指針に準じた措置を取るよう努めるものとする。

　また、本業務指針における用語の定義は「価格等調査ガイドライン」によるものとする。

3．本業務指針の構成

　本業務指針は価格等調査業務の過程等に照応して、以下の区分に応じた指針から構成される（別紙1「業務過程における本業務指針の構成」参照）。

(1) 業務実施全般
(2) 価格等調査業務の受託
(3) 価格等調査業務の実施
(4) 品質管理
(5) 情報管理

---

[1] 財務諸表の作成に利用される目的の業務とは、国土交通省が定めた「財務諸表のための価格調査の実施に関する基本的考え方」の「Ⅱ．適用範囲」の定義による業務を指す。

V - 7. Guidelines Regarding Valuation Practice for Appraisal Firms

4. General practice

1) The appraisal firm must conduct all practice in accordance with relevant regulations and the Japanese Appraisal Standards ("Appraisal Standards")[2] , and implement appropriate policy and procedures according to the valuation process.
2) Upon conducting valuation, all board members, employees, temporary staff, and contractors (hereinafter collectively "Employees") of the appraisal firm must comply with the designed policy and procedures.
3) The appraisal firm must inform the Employees of the designed policy and procedures in a proper and timely manner. Therefore, as necessary, it must document the rules and instructions[3] of business policies and procedures.
4) The level of documentation regarding business policies and procedures should be moderated accordingly since it varies depending on attributes of the company's structure, such as its size.
5) The appraisal firm must check if the business policies and procedure are effectively implemented, and revise or improve them as necessary.

5. Accepting valuation requests

1) Upon accepting a request, the appropriateness for the appraisal firm must be checked by a party other than the party who received the request[4], and the request must be rejected when it is deemed inappropriate.
2) In screening of requests, judgment must be based on the written standards[5] prepared in advance.
3) When in the screening a valuation request is deemed appropriate, an agreement must be made with the client via a specified document. Documents stating the purpose and scope of business by the appraiser in charge of confirming the opinion of value request ("Confirmation Letter") must be issued before conclusion of the agreement.
4) Regarding the fee, it is desirable to set standards beforehand and present these to the client. In some cases a quotation may need to be provided.

---

[2] Such as considerations regarding application of the Japanese Appraisal Standards, Valuation Guidelines, and guidelines provided by Japanese Association of Real Estate Appraisal.

[3] Such as office regulations and business processing instructions

[4] The party who received the request may not be an appraiser in charge of confirming the valuation request. In such cases, the purpose and scope of valuation must be determined an appraiser in charge of confirming the valuation request.

[5] For examples of documentation, see Attachment 2.

4．業務実施全般

(1) 不動産鑑定業者は、法令等及び不動産鑑定評価基準等[※2]に従って、全ての業務が適切に実施されるように、業務実施の過程に応じて方針と手続を適切に策定し、実行する必要がある。

(2) 不動産鑑定業者における業務を行うに当たっては、役員・職員・臨時雇用者（アルバイト・パート雇用者）・派遣職員等（以下「職員等」という。）に対し、策定された方針と手続を厳正に遵守させなければならない。

(3) 不動産鑑定業者は、策定された方針と手続を職員等に適切かつ適時に周知しなければならない。そのためには、不動産鑑定業者は、業務実施等の方針と手続に関する規程・マニュアル等[※3]を必要に応じて文書化して定めるものとする。

(4) 業務実施等の方針と手続及び文書化の程度は、個々不動産鑑定業者の規模等の組織体制等に応じて異なるものであり、適切に行うものとする。

(5) 不動産鑑定業者は、業務実施等の方針・手続等の実施状況について、効果的に運用されているか否かを確認し、必要に応じて変更又は改善を行うものとする。

5．価格等調査業務の受託

(1) 業務の受託に当たっては、不動産鑑定業者として行うことが適切な業務であるかを、原則として受付担当者[※4]以外の者が審査し、不適切と判断されるものは業務を謝絶するものとする。

(2) 受託審査に当たっては、あらかじめ文書化された基準[※5]を定めることとし、それにより受託の適否を判定する。

(3) 受託審査において適切と認められた場合には、定められた書面により依頼者との間で契約を取り交わして、契約の締結までに確定担当不動産鑑定士により確定された業務の目的と範囲等を明記示した書面文書等（「確認書」）を交付するものとする。

(4) 業務報酬については、その基準をあらかじめ定めておき、依頼者等に明示することが望ましい。また、場合によっては見積書の発行等も行うこととする。

---

[2] 不動産鑑定評価基準運用上の留意事項、価格等調査ガイドライン、日本不動産鑑定協会の策定した実務指針等
[3] 職務規程、業務処理マニュアル等が考えられる。
[4] 受付担当者は、必ずしも確定担当不動産鑑定士とは限らない。その場合には、業務の目的や範囲等の確定は、確定担当不動産鑑定士を通して行うこととなる。
[5] 文書化された例示として別紙2のようなものが考えられる。

6. Conducting valuation

1) Conducting valuation by the concerned appraisers, etc. (including all concerned Employees) must follow the designed policy, procedures, and instructions.
   The policy, procedures, and instructions will be applied to the entire process, including valuation procedures.
2) Other than the above policy, appropriate gathering, organizing, and utilizing of data required in valuation must be provided to make it regularly available as an organization.
3) If providing a supervising appraiser, this person must operate as specified in the Guidelines Regarding Roles of Appraisers and Appraisal firms[6].
4) Secure the time and workforce required for the valuation and construct a system in which all appraisers involved in the valuation[7] can maintain their independence.
5) Valuation conducted under a business alliance must be in accordance with the Guidelines as well as the Guidelines Regarding Roles of Appraisers and Appraisal firms.
6) After accepting the request, if the client requests presentation of the value, etc. prior to submission of the final report, it must follow the procedures provided in advance. If such a request is made before the assumptions or data are fully prepared, it must be handled with the utmost caution.

7. Quality Control

1) In order to maintain and improve the quality of the final report in each valuation, the appraiser who signs the report, as a party in charge of valuation of a subject property, must follow the guidelines and procedures regarding valuation provided by the appraisal firm.
2) Other than quality control regarding valuation practice, policy, and proceduresfor report reviewing according to the valuation must be provided and well organized.
3) The report reviewing that should be specified in the policy and procedures as described in the above item 2 must involve one or more appraiser other than the signing appraiser (who should not be involved), and review items for the report[8] are as specified in the previous section.

---

[6] In an appraisal report to be submitted to the client, a principal task of the supervising appraiser is to lead the multiple appraisers involved in the preparation of the valuation and review its results.

[7] Regardless of whether it is the main part of the valuation

[8] For examples review for the report, see Attachment 3.

6．価格等調査業務の実施

(1) 価格等調査業務の実施は、関与不動産鑑定士等（業務に携わる全ての職員等を含む。）が業務内容に応じて定められた方針・手続・マニュアル等に従って行うものとする。この方針・手続・マニュアル等は鑑定評価の手順等における全ての業務実施過程を対象とする。

(2) 上記方針等のほか、価格等調査業務の実施において必要となる適切な資料の収集・整理・利用については、日頃から組織として行えるよう方針・手続を策定する。

(3) 総括不動産鑑定士を置く場合には、総括不動産鑑定士は「不動産鑑定士の役割分担等及び不動産鑑定業者の業務提携に関する業務指針」に規定する業務[※6]を行うものとする。

(4) 価格等調査業務の実施等に必要な人員・期間等を確保するとともに、当該業務[※7]に関わるすべての不動産鑑定士の独立を保てる態勢を構築する。

(5) 業務提携にて業務を行う場合には、この業務指針のほか「不動産鑑定士の役割分担等及び不動産鑑定業者の業務提携に関する業務指針」に従うものとする。

(6) 業務受託後に依頼者等から成果報告書の提出に先がけて価格等の提示を求められた場合には、あらかじめ定められた手続に従って対応するものとする。ただし、前提条件や資料が整わない段階における価格等の提示要請に対しては十分な留意が必要である。

7．品質管理

(1) 個々の業務における成果報告書の質を維持・向上させるために、署名不動産鑑定士は当該対象不動産の価格等調査を行う責任者として、不動産鑑定業者が定める価格等調査業務の実施に係る方針と手続に従うものとする。

(2) 価格等調査業務実施に係るもののほか、業務内容に応じた報告書審査等に対する方針・手続をあらかじめ策定するとともに、併せて態勢を整備するものとする。

(3) 上記(2)の方針・手続に定めるべき報告書審査は、署名不動産鑑定士以外の不動産鑑定士1名以上（この場合の審査鑑定士を報告書審査鑑定士という。）が担当することとし、報告書審査の項目等[※8]は前項により定めた内容によることとする。

---

[6] 総括不動産鑑定士は、依頼者に提出する鑑定評価書について、作成に係わる複数の不動産鑑定士を指揮するとともに、鑑定評価の結果を検証することを主たる業務とする。

[7] 価格等調査業務の核となる主たる部分に該当するか否かを問わない。

[8] 報告書審査項目の例示として別紙3のようなものが考えられる。

V - 7. Guidelines Regarding Valuation Practice for Appraisal Firms

8. Information Control

1) Business information (regardless of its form) among the appraisal firms is, in principle, confidential and the policy and procedures[8] to protect the information must be provided along with assignment of a person in charge.
2) Countermeasures must be taken to maintain the valuation division's independence from other divisions, such as providing physically separated room and controlling access to information.
3) Necessary countermeasures[9] must be taken to prevent appraisers from being involved in transactions of specified securities[10] by taking advantage of facts regarding the listed company that are learned through the valuation work before such facts are published.
4) In order to clarify interests between the appraisal firm or appraiser and the subject property, and the relationship between the appraisal firm or appraiser and the client, or parties for disclosure or submission, appropriate policy and procedures must be implemented, such as advising Employees to report necessary information on a daily basis. Along with such measures, full attention must be paid to protection of personal information.

9. Effective Date

The Guidelines will be applied to valuation used for securitization properties or preparation of financial statements or corporate accounting under contracts made and entered into on and after January 1, 2010. This does not preclude application before the effective date.

---

[9] Such as information security guidelines, document management guidelines, and policies

[10] As specified in Articles 163 and 166 of the Financial Instruments and Exchange Act, trading of specified securities refers to buying and selling, transferring for profit, receiving transfer, or derivatives transactions of the following: stocks, corporate bonds, preferred securities, subscription warrants for preferred securities, stock option warrants, exchangeable bonds.

[11] Insider trading regulations, for instance

8．情報管理

(1) 不動産鑑定業者内における業務情報（媒体を問わない）は原則業者外秘として、情報管理責任者を定め、情報を保護するための方針・手続[9]を定めることとする。

(2) 鑑定部門における他業種部門との独立性を維持するために、物理的区画・情報アクセス管理等の必要な態勢等を講じるものとする。

(3) 業務において知り得た上場会社等に関する重要事実を用いて、それらの公表前に特定有価証券等の売買等[10]を行わないように必要な措置[11]を講じるものとする。

(4) 不動産鑑定業者及び不動産鑑定士の対象不動産に関する利害関係又は依頼者及び開示・提出先との関係を明確にするためにも、個人情報保護に十分留意しつつ職員等に必要な報告を日頃から求めておく等、適切な方針・手続を策定する。

9．適用時期

本業務指針は、平成22年1月1日以降に契約を締結する証券化対象不動産又は財務諸表の作成若しくは企業会計に関連したに利用される目的の価格等調査業務から適用する。ただし、当該日以前から適用することを妨げない。

---

[9] 情報セキュリティ規程、文書管理規程の規程や指針等が考えられる。

[10]「特定有価証券等の売買等」とは、金商法第163条及び第166条の定義により、株券・社債券・優先出資証券・優先出資引受権証書・新株予約権証券・カバードワラント・他社株償還条項付債（EB債）等に係る売買、その他の有償の譲渡、若しくは譲受け又はデリバティブ取引をいう。

[11] インサイダー取引防止規程等が考えられる。

V - 7. Guidelines Regarding Valuation Practice for Appraisal Firms

Attachment 1: Framework of Guidelines within Operation Process

Ministry of Land, Infrastructure, Transport and Tourism

Japanese Association of Real Estate Appraisal

Real Estate Appraisal Committee Report - "Improving Valuation to Meet Changes in Society," prepared by the National Land Development Council

Valuation Guidelines
(including Considerations for Operations of the Guidelines)

Mainly Concerned with Appraisers

1. Guidelines for role of appraisers and business alliance of appraisal firms
   (Section in relation to role of appraisers)
2. Guidelines in relation to management of Opinion of Value Guidelines
   (Example of written format)
   - Example of report

Mainly Concerned with Appraisal Firms

1. Guidelines regarding business operation of appraisal firms
2. Guidelines regarding role of appraisers and business alliance of appraisal firms
   (Section in relation to business alliance with appraisal firms)
3. Guidelines regarding Preparing Engagement agreements for valuation assignments
4. Guidelines regarding management of Valuation Guidelines
   (Example)
   - Confirmation to Determine Purposes and Scope of Work

1. Guidelines regarding Appraisal of Securitized Properties ("Guidelines")
2. Guidelines regarding business operation of appraisal firms
   (Operational guidelines bylaw regarding business operation of appraisal firms when conducting appraisal of securitized properties)

Appraisal complies with the Appraisal Standards

Appraisal does not comply with the Appraisal Standards
(In some cases a valuation may be regarded as an appraisal under relevant laws)

Estimating Value is the Ultimate Objective

a. Cannot comply with the Appraisal Standards
   a) Forced by circumstances
   b) Given the condition that it cannot comply

b. Does not comply, although it could
   a) Estimate value for revaluation purpose of the same securitized property by the same appraiser
   - Omission of internal inspection
   - Application only of DCF method of income capitalization approach

Estimating Value is not the Ultimate Objective

a. Consulting use and utilization of real estate
b. Due diligence for collateral properties
c. Opinion on time adjustment, etc.

Specific Standards Chapter 3, etc.
(In the case of appraisal for securitized properties)

"Basic Policy on Periodic Valuation of Securitized Properties"

448

Ⅴ-7．不動産鑑定業者の業務実施態勢に関する業務指針

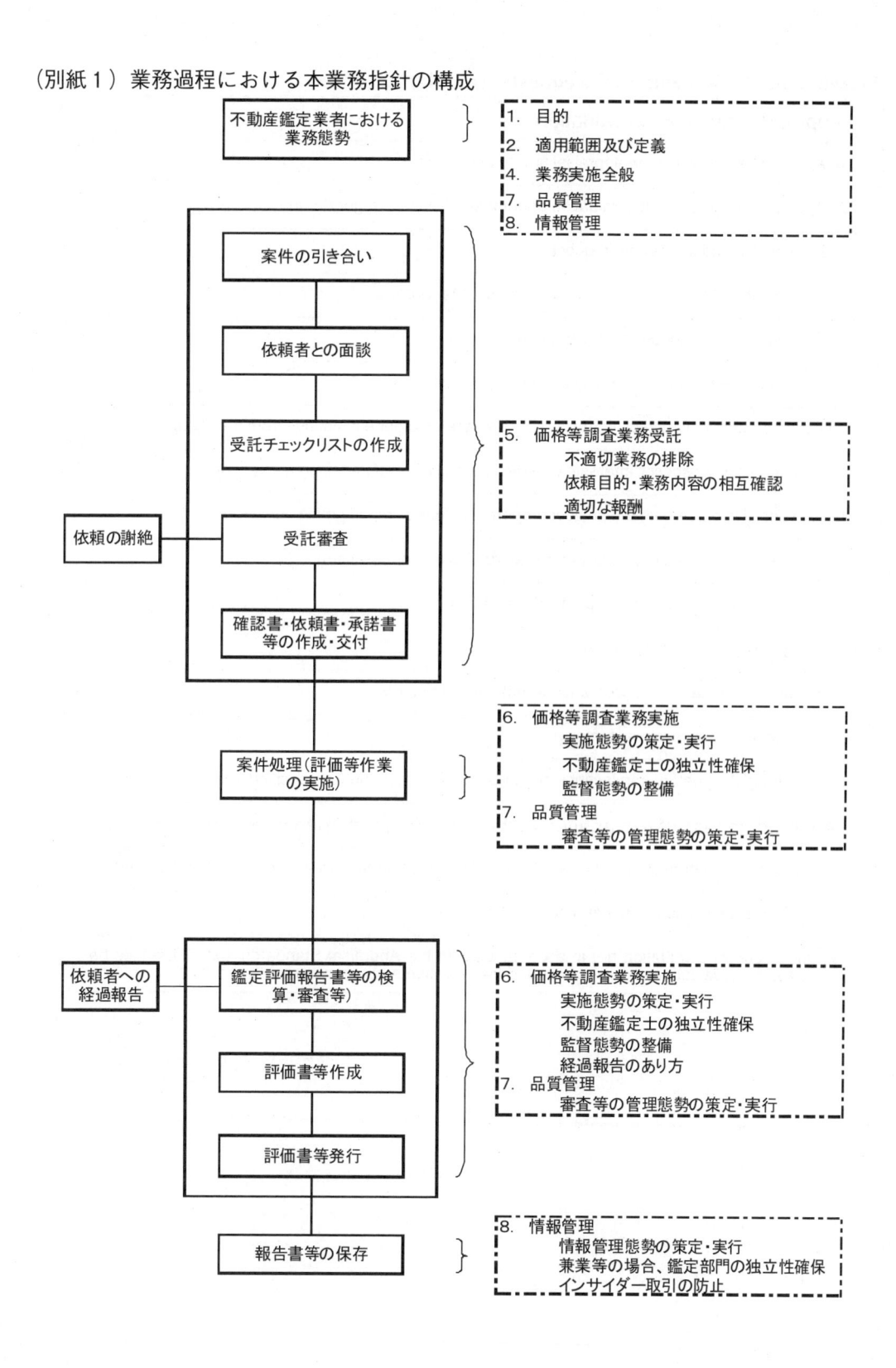

（別紙1）業務過程における本業務指針の構成

```
不動産鑑定業者における     1. 目的
業務態勢              2. 適用範囲及び定義
                    4. 業務実施全般
                    7. 品質管理
                    8. 情報管理

案件の引き合い

依頼者との面談

受託チェックリストの作成    5. 価格等調査業務受託
                       不適切業務の排除
                       依頼目的・業務内容の相互確認
依頼の謝絶 ─ 受託審査      適切な報酬

確認書・依頼書・承諾書
等の作成・交付

案件処理（評価等作業      6. 価格等調査業務実施
の実施）                 実施態勢の策定・実行
                       不動産鑑定士の独立性確保
                       監督態勢の整備
                    7. 品質管理
                       審査等の管理態勢の策定・実行

依頼者への    鑑定評価報告書等の検  6. 価格等調査業務実施
経過報告     算・審査等）          実施態勢の策定・実行
                              不動産鑑定士の独立性確保
                              監督態勢の整備
                              経過報告のあり方
          評価書等作成        7. 品質管理
                              審査等の管理態勢の策定・実行
          評価書等発行

報告書等の保存        8. 情報管理
                    情報管理態勢の策定・実行
                    兼業等の場合、鑑定部門の独立性確保
                    インサイダー取引の防止
```

Attachment 2: Screening of Requests (sample)

1. Appropriateness of the valuation	
1) Appropriate request for an appraisal firm to undertake	☐
2) Appropriate to conduct the valuation under the specified category* and type	☐
3) Reasonable and practicable request	☐
4) The valuation does not require cooperation of other experts	☐
5) Other experts will cooperate when needed	☐
6) No wrongful enticement upon accepting the request	☐
7) Accepted without wrongful instruction on the value or other estimations from the client	☐
8) No connection or special interests with the client. No fear of impairing fair valuation.	☐
9) No special interests with the subject property. No fear of impairing fair valuation.	☐
10) The valuation would not jeopardize social trust as an appraisal firm	☐
*Accordance with the Japanese Appraisal Standards	
2. Appropriateness of the Fee	
1) Provided explanation in accordance with the fee standards	☐
2) The fee in no way involves dumping	☐
3) No wrongful monetary transactions are involved other than the fee specified in the fee standards	☐
3. Appropriateness of explanation to the client (other than that regarding the fee)	
1) Explained the nature of the valuation (whether it is in accordance with the Appraisal Standards)	☐
2) Clarified the valuation status and obtained approval	☐
3) Upon accepting valuation not in accordance with the Appraisal Standards, the differences between such valuation and appraisal, and the valuation practice, were explained.	☐

（別紙２）受託審査項目例

1．受託する業務内容の適否	
①不動産鑑定業者として行うことが適当な業務である	☐
②当該区分（※）・類型として行うことが適当な業務である	☐
③無理なく実施できる業務である	☐
④他の専門家の協力を必要としない業務である	☐
⑤他の専門家の協力を必要とする場合、その協力を得ることができる	☐
⑥不当に依頼を誘引することなく受託している	☐
⑦対象不動産等の価格その他判断内容等について、依頼者等から不正な指示を受けることなく受託している	☐
⑧依頼者等との間に縁故または特別な利害関係等はなく、公平な鑑定評価を害する恐れのない業務である	☐
⑨対象不動産に関して特別な利害関係等はなく、公平な鑑定評価を害する恐れのない業務である	☐
⑩その他不動産鑑定業者としての社会的信頼を損なう危険等のない業務である	☐
（※）鑑定評価基準に則ったものか否かの区分	☐

2．報酬の適否	
①報酬基準等に従った説明を行った	☐
②不当なダンピング等のない報酬となっている	☐
③報酬基準等に定められた報酬以外の不正な金品等の授受が行われることなく受託している	☐

3．（報酬以外の）依頼者への説明の適否	
①業務の性格（鑑定評価基準に則る鑑定評価であるか否か等）の説明を行った	☐
②業務の具体的な状況を明示し、了解された	☐
③鑑定評価業務以外の受託に際しては、鑑定評価との相違及び業務の実施方法等の必要な事項の説明を行った	☐

Attachment 3: Review of valuation report (sample)

		Review Appraiser	Preparation Appraiser
1. Subject property and estimated value	1) If the valuation is not based on Appraisal Standards, the report explains that the estimated value may be different from appraisal value.	☐	☐
	2) If the valuation is not based on Appraisal Standards, the report explains that the valuation is not prepared assuming use other than intended use and disclosure to parties other than intended parties.	☐	☐
	3) There are no miscopies or misrepresentations (numeric) in the estimated value (appraisal value)	☐	☐
	4) All subject properties are included (match with the request form, confirmation letter, and register)	☐	☐
	5) Parties for disclosure and publication are appropriately listed (match with the request form and confirmation letter)	☐	☐
2. Basic items	1) Type of property (use, title) and type of value/rent are appropriate	☐	☐
	2) Assumptions are appropriately stated in terms of feasibility and legality, without excess or insufficiency, and with no conflict with relevant parties and third parties	☐	☐
	3) Date of value is appropriate (consistent with the dates of site inspection, valuation process, and issuance)	☐	☐
	4) Rationale for differences and validity is included	☐	☐
3. Confirming the subject property	1) There are no problems regarding confirmation of the subject, rights, and lease agreements	☐	☐
	2) The numbers used in the valuation are appropriate (check with the source)	☐	☐

Ⅴ-7.不動産鑑定業者の業務実施態勢に関する業務指針

(別紙3) 報告書等審査項目例等

報告書審査項目		審査担当鑑定士	作成担当鑑定士
1．対象不動産及び調査価格等	①鑑定評価基準に則らない場合、鑑定評価とは結果が異なる可能性がある旨の記載があるか	☐	☐
	②鑑定評価基準に則らない場合、目的外使用・範囲外開示等を想定していない旨の記載はあるか	☐	☐
	③調査価格等（鑑定評価額等）に転記ミス、誤記（桁違い）はないか	☐	☐
	④対象不動産の漏れはないか（依頼書・確認書・登記簿と整合しているか）	☐	☐
	⑤開示範囲・公表の有無等の記載は適切か（依頼書・確認書との整合）	☐	☐
2．基本的な事項	①不動産の種別・類型、価格・賃料の種類は適切か	☐	☐
	②条件は実現性、合法性、関係当事者及び第三者の利益を害さず、過不足なく、適切に付されているか	☐	☐
	③価格時点は適切か(実査日、鑑定評価を行った日、発行日との整合性等依頼書との照合)	☐	☐
	④鑑定評価との相違点・妥当性の根拠の記載があるか	☐	☐
3．対象不動産の確認	①物的確認、権利の確認、賃貸借契約内容の確認に問題はないか	☐	☐
	②採用数量の妥当性（確認資料との照合）	☐	☐
4．価格形成要因の分析	①市場分析は適切か（他の地域・用途の分析が記載されていないか）	☐	☐
	②対象不動産の行政的規制の記載に誤りはなく、適切か	☐	☐
	③土壌汚染・アスベスト・地下埋設物等の有無に係る判断・記載内容は適切か	☐	☐
	④画地条件の記載に誤りはなく、適切か	☐	☐
	⑤土地建物一体としての市場性の分析は適切か（手法適用の整合性）	☐	☐
	⑥土地、建物及びその敷地の最有効使用は適切か	☐	☐
	⑦都市計画図（用途地域・容積率等）・要因資料・ERとの照合	☐	☐
6．査定等	①価格等調査の方針はガイドライン・鑑定評価基準・確認書に照らし、必要十分な手法を適用しているか	☐	☐
	②手法不適用の理由は適切に記載されているか	☐	☐
	③価格査定において価格形成要因に係る説明は十分か、査定数値は適切か	☐	☐
	④DCF法において、収支変動の根拠説明、貸室等稼働率と水光費との関係、建物公租公課の経年減価は適切か	☐	☐
	⑤還元利回り・割引率・最終還元利回り、投下資本収益率、期待利回り等各種利回りは整合性が保たれ適切か	☐	☐

V − 7. Guidelines Regarding Valuation Practice for Appraisal Firms

4. Analysis of value influences	1) Market analysis is adequate (make sure analysis of the correct market area and type of use are described)		☐	☐
	2) Laws and regulations of the subject property are appropriately listed		☐	☐
	3) Judgment and description of soil contamination, asbestos, and underground structures are appropriate		☐	☐
	4) Description of site features is appropriate		☐	☐
	5) Market analysis of the land and building combined is appropriate (approaches are consistent)		☐	☐
	6) Highest and best use of the land or building and its site is appropriate		☐	☐
	7) Text and numbers in the report are checked with the city planning drawings (use zoning, FAR, etc.), data of factors, and engineering report		☐	☐
6. Estimation	1) The approaches considered sufficient in the guidelines, Appraisal Standards, and confirmation letter are applied for the estimation of opinion of value		☐	☐
	2) Reasons why some approaches are not applied are appropriately described.		☐	☐
	3) In the estimation of value, value influences are sufficiently explained and the estimated figures are appropriate		☐	☐
	4) In the DCF method, rationale for changes in cash flow, connection between the lease occupancy rate and utility charges, property tax, and deduction for age deterioration are appropriate		☐	☐
	5) Cap rate, discount rate, terminal cap rate, return on capital, expected cap rate, and other rates are consistent and appropriate		☐	☐

			業者最終確認者	作成担当鑑定士
		⑥土地残余法の想定建物、開発法の開発計画は適切か（CADを適用すべき案件は、適切に適用又は外注しているか）	☐	☐
		⑦査定ファイル等及び本文の加減乗除の再計算	☐	☐
		⑧査定ファイル及び要因資料との照合	☐	☐
		⑨本文と別表の照合	☐	☐
7．調査価格等の決定		①試算価格の再吟味及び説得力に係る判断が適切に行われているか	☐	☐
		②各試算価格の開差の理由及び調査価格等の決定説明は適切か	☐	☐
8．その他		①公示地、基準地の記載内容と官報・公報との照合	☐	☐
		②ERとの照合	☐	☐
		③確認資料・要因資料・査定ファイルとの照合	☐	☐

		業者最終確認者	作成担当鑑定士
成果物発行時の確認項目	成果物の内容確認		
	①原稿等の修正箇所は正しく反映されているか	☐	☐
	②誤字・脱字等はないか	☐	☐
	③落丁・誤綴り等はないか	☐	☐
	④附属資料の内容は適切か	☐	☐
	⑤記名鑑定士名の記載、署名鑑定士の署名はあるか	☐	☐
	⑥業者印・鑑定士印は押印されているか	☐	☐

	依頼書等の確認	業者最終確認者	確定担当鑑定士	作成担当鑑定士
	① 正式な依頼書を受領済みか	☐	☐	☐
	② 確認書・修正確認書は提出済みか	☐	☐	☐

V - 7. Guidelines Regarding Valuation Practice for Appraisal Firms

	6) Assumed building in the land residual method or development plan in the development method is appropriate (if CAD should be applied, is it applied appropriately or is it outsourced appropriately?)	☐	☐
	7) Recalculation of the estimation sheet and main body of the report	☐	☐
	8) Text and numbers in the estimation sheet are checked with the data on relevant factors	☐	☐
	9) The main body of the report is checked with the attachment	☐	☐
7. Concluding final value	1) Decisions based on review and persuasiveness of the indicated values are appropriate	☐	☐
	2) Final conclusion on differences in indicated values and estimated values are appropriately explained	☐	☐
8. Others	1) Text and numbers in the report are checked with the data on official land prices and authorities reports	☐	☐
	2) Text and numbers are checked with the engineering report	☐	☐
	3) Text and numbers are checked with the references, data of factors, and estimation sheet	☐	☐

Checklist for delivery of final report	Check the contents	Final Review	Preparation Appraiser
	1) Corrections have been appropriately reflected.	☐	☐
	2) There are no typographical errors or omissions	☐	☐
	3) There are no missing pages or binding errors	☐	☐
	4) Attached documents are appropriate	☐	☐
	5) Names of appraisers are listed. The report is signed by a signer (appraiser) of the report.	☐	☐
	6) The report is sealed by the appraisal firm and appraisers	☐	☐

	Check the order form	Final Review	Confirmed by appraiser	Preparation Appraiser
	1) Formal request form has been received	☐	☐	☐
	2) Confirmation letter and/or revised confirmation letter has been submitted.	☐	☐	☐

Ⅴ-7.不動産鑑定業者の業務実施態勢に関する業務指針

V − 7. Guidelines Regarding Valuation Practice for Appraisal Firms

Valuation of Securitization Properties
Administrative Instructions for Appraisal Firms

December 2009
Japan Association of Real Estate Appraisal

In the valuation of securitization properties, in addition to the Guidelines Regarding Valuation Practice for Appraisal Firms, the appraisal firm should also follow these administrative instructions.

1. "5. Accepting valuation requests"

1) Inappropriate valuation requests

The appraisal firm should ask the potential client to remedy or review the inappropriate request. If it is deemed impossible to conduct the requested valuation properly, as in the following examples, the appraisal firm should decline the request.

(a) Considering the type and volume of the subject property and the time allowed for the valuation process, the requested valuation is deemed difficult to conduct based on the team, available human resources, ability, and experience of the appraisal firm.

(b) The client determines the appraisal value or requests that the appraisal firm re-estimate the value until it reaches an agreeable number.

(c) The provided assumptions and information do not satisfy requirements of the Appraisal Standards and relevant Guidance Notes and separately stated Guidelines Regarding Appraisal of Securitization Properties

(d) There are interests or connections between the appraiser or appraisal firm involved in the valuation and the subject property or parties who have interests in the subject property, or there are special capital ties between the appraiser or appraisal firm involved in the valuation and parties for disclosure or submission of the appraisal report, and the appraisal firm's acceptance of the valuation request may damage public trust of the firm.

In order to avoid such difficulties with the client, the appraisal firm should prepare and show guidelines explaining that it does not accept inappropriate valuation requests.

2) Requesting support in collecting information upon acceptance of valuation request

In order to confirm the subject property for valuation of securitization properties, the appraisal firm should explain to the client that detailed investigation and information are required, and ask for support in collecting such information.

3) Requesting submission of report that shows coverage of engineering report

In order to accept a request for valuation of securitization properties, the appraisal

証券化対象不動産の鑑定評価業務を実施する場合における
不動産鑑定業者の業務実施態勢に関する業務指針細則

平成21年12月
社団法人日本不動産鑑定協会

証券化対象不動産の価格に関する鑑定評価業務を行う場合においては、不動産鑑定業者は、「不動産鑑定業者の業務実施態勢に関する業務指針」のほか、本細則に定めるところに従うものとする。

1．「5．価格等調査業務の受託」について

1) 不適切な依頼要請への対応等

不動産鑑定業者は、次のような不適切な依頼要請に対して、不適切な要請の是正や依頼内容の再検討を求めるほか、適切に業務を実施できないと認められる場合には依頼を謝絶する等の措置を講ずるものとする。

ア　対象不動産の内容、依頼件数、評価期間等と当該鑑定業者の組織、人員、能力、経験等に鑑み、適切な鑑定評価を行うことが困難と認められる鑑定評価依頼

イ　鑑定評価額を指定したり、依頼者の希望する鑑定評価額となるまで試算を求めたりするような鑑定評価依頼

ウ　不動産鑑定評価基準及び不動産鑑定評価基準運用上の留意事項並びに別途定める「証券化対象不動産の鑑定評価に関する実務指針」の規定を満たさない条件や資料提示による鑑定評価依頼

エ　対象不動産又は対象不動産に利害関係を有する者と鑑定評価に関与する不動産鑑定士（以下「関与不動産鑑定士」という。）又は不動産鑑定業者との間に利害関係、縁故関係等がある場合のほか、依頼者又は鑑定評価書が依頼者以外に開示・提出されるケースにおける当該開示・提出先と関与不動産鑑定士又は不動産鑑定業者との間に特別の資本的関係等がある場合などで、当該業務を受託することにより不動産鑑定業者の社会的信頼を損なう危険のある鑑定評価依頼

なお、不動産鑑定業者は、依頼者等とのトラブルを未然に防止するため、上記のような不適切な依頼要請を受けない旨を定めた受託指針をあらかじめ表明するよう努めなければならない。

2) 受託時における資料提供の協力の要請

不動産鑑定業者は、証券化対象不動産の鑑定評価の実施に当たり、対象不動産の確認等を行うためには、より詳細な調査や資料の収集が必要になることを依頼者に説明のうえ、必要な資料の提供等についての協力を求める必要がある。

3) エンジニアリング・レポートの依頼内容を記載した書面の提出の要請

証券化対象不動産に係る鑑定評価の受託に際し、不動産鑑定業者は、鑑定評価の依頼者から別途実施中若しくは実施予定のエンジニアリング・レポートに係る作成業務の内容について記載した書面（以下「エンジニアリング・レポート依頼内容報告書」という。）の提出を求める必要がある[※12]。

V - 7. Guidelines Regarding Valuation Practice for Appraisal Firms

firm should ask the client to provide the coverage of the engineering report that is under preparation or being scheduled[12].

The engineering report required for valuation of securitization properties should have the following specifications, which must be confirmed with the client.

(1) **Specifications of engineering report**
   (a) The coverage of the subject property in the engineering report and valuation should be the same, or the engineering report should cover the entire subject of the valuation.
   (b) If the engineering report covers a larger area than the subject of the valuation, the subject of the valuation should be clearly distinguished.
   (c) If the subject of the engineering report is a condominium or co-owned property, the replacement cost and repair and maintenance cost for the subject property of the valuation should be able to be easily found.
   (d) To prepare the engineering report, the preparer should conduct the site inspection and compliance investigation unless a legitimate reason prevents it.
   (e) The request for the engineering report should be made free of improper approach that hinders the independence of its preparer.
   (f) The date of the investigation and issuance of the engineering report must be clearly stated in the final engineering report.
   (g) Expenses for potential improvements of the facility in the future should not be included. Repair and maintenance costs should be based on the current building after completion of previous repairs and maintenance.

(2) **Items that should be confirmed with the client**
   The request form of the report of coverage of the engineering report should include items that must be confirmed with the client, including the specifications of the engineering report used in the valuation of securitization properties, date of submission of the final engineering report, and the request to the preparer of the engineering report.

   (a) Items that may influence the valuation process plan should be reported via a written document (electronic document is also acceptable). The appraisal report will not be issued before the issuance of the final engineering report.
   (b) If Specifics Chapter 3 of the Appraisal Standards and relevant Guidance Notes (hereinafter, "Specifics Chapter 3 and relevant Notes") were applied for the valua-

---

[12] Report of the coverage of the engineering report is required for the appropriate and smooth valuation of securitization properties. The appraisal firm requests the client's support in obtaining such documentation. In addition to the report of the coverage of the engineering report, copies of the engineering report order or specification sheet that lists the coverage are also acceptable.

Also note that if a report of the coverage of the engineering report (including copies of equivalent documents) was not submitted or the information was not sufficient, the appraisal firm should interview the client and confirm the coverage.

Ⅴ－7．不動産鑑定業者の業務実施態勢に関する業務指針

　なお、証券化対象不動産に係る鑑定評価で用いるエンジニアリング・レポートは、次に列挙される仕様等を備えるとともに、その仕様等について鑑定評価の依頼者への確認が必要となることに留意する。

(1)　エンジニアリング・レポートの仕様等
　ア　エンジニアリング・レポートの対象範囲が鑑定評価の対象範囲と同じであること、又は当該対象範囲を含むものであること。
　イ　エンジニアリング・レポートの対象範囲が鑑定評価の対象範囲よりも大きい場合には、鑑定評価の対象範囲が、その内訳として明確に判別できるようになっていること。
　ウ　区分所有物件や共有物件を対象とするエンジニアリング・レポートの場合には、当該建物の再調達価格や修繕・更新費用等の金額について、鑑定評価の対象となっている部分が容易に識別できるものであること。
　エ　エンジニアリング・レポートの作成に当たっては、特段の理由がある場合を除き、エンジニアリング・レポート作成者による現地調査・遵法性調査が行われたものであること。
　オ　エンジニアリング・レポートの発注に当たり、エンジニアリング・レポート作成者の独立性を損なう不適切な働きかけがなされていないこと。
　カ　エンジニアリング・レポートの最終版について調査年月日及び発行年月日が明記されていること。
　キ　修繕・更新費用は、過去の改修を含めた現状建物の竣工時の状態を前提とし、将来における機能向上を企図した改修費用が含まれていないこと。

(2)　鑑定評価の依頼者への確認事項
　　エンジニアリング・レポート依頼内容報告書の提出を要請する文書には、証券化対象不動産に係る鑑定評価で用いるエンジニアリング・レポートの仕様等のほか、依頼者からのエンジニアリング・レポートの最終版の提出時期やエンジニアリング・レポート作成者への要請等に関する依頼者への確認事項を記載する。

　ア　鑑定評価の処理計画に変更を及ぼす事項については、文書等（電磁的方法も含む）にて報告があること。また、エンジニアリング・レポートの最終版が提出されるまでは鑑定評価書を発行することはできないこと。
　イ　不動産鑑定業者から、不動産鑑定評価基準各論第3章及びこれに係る不動産鑑定評価基準運用上の留意事項（以下「基準各論第3章等」という。）を適用した鑑定評価を行ううえで必要と認められる要請があった場合には、エンジニアリング・レポート発注者として、エンジニアリング・レポート作成者に対して当該要請に添った適切な依頼を行うよう努めること。
　ウ　上記ア及びイの内容に添わない場合、不動産鑑定業者は鑑定評価業務の受託を謝絶する

---

[12] エンジニアリング・レポート依頼内容報告書の提出の要請は、証券化対象不動産に係る鑑定評価を適切かつ円滑に実施するために、依頼者に対し必要な協力を求めるという主旨であるので、提出を受ける書面については、エンジニアリング・レポート依頼内容報告書に代えて、エンジニアリング・レポートの発注書あるいは仕様書等依頼内容が記載された書面の写しでも差し支えない。
　なお、エンジニアリング・レポート依頼内容報告書（これに代わる書面の写しを含む）の提出がない場合又は当該書面の記載内容が十分でないと認められる場合には、聴聞等の方法により依頼者に依頼内容を確認するものとする。

V - 7. Guidelines Regarding Valuation Practice for Appraisal Firms

tion, and the appraisal firm requested required items related to this, the client of the valuation, as the party requesting the engineering report, should request that the preparer of the engineering report prepare an engineering report according to such a request.
(c) If the client of the valuation does not follow (a) and (b), the appraisal firm can decline the valuation request.

See Attachment for an example of the request form of the report of coverage of the engineering report.

2. "6. Conducting valuation"

1) Appraiser involved in valuation of securitization properties

The appraisal firm should appoint an appraiser who has completed the securitization training given by the Japan Association of Real Estate Appraisal[13] for the valuation of securitization properties.

2) Valuation of multiple properties

When the client requests valuation of multiple properties and more than one appraiser take part in the project, the appraisal firm should clarify the role of each appraiser, determine the valuation schedule, and develop a system by which appraisers can share information.

In such a case, the roles of appraisers and signatures and names of appraisers in the appraisal report should be written in accordance with the separately stated Guidelines Regarding Roles of Appraisers and Appraisal firms.

3) Draft Report

If the client requests a draft report before conclusion of the final value, the appraisal firm should pay substantial attention so as not to cause confusion to the third party since the value of the subject property and property-specific value influences in the draft report may differ from the final report. Use the following list to avoid confusion:
  (a) Insert "draft" for all pages, including the front page.
  (b) Do not provide the signature of the appraiser.
  (c) Insert the date of draft valuation, instead of the date of completion of the valuation process.
  (d) Clearly describe that the conditions of the subject property and relevant data may differ from the final appraisal report, and for this reason the final value may differ.
  (e) List the items not available at the date of issuance of the draft report, but which will be obtained by the issuance of the final report.

---

[13] As a minimum prerequisite, the appraiser should have completed obligatory training on the Appraisal Standards and Guidelines regarding securitization properties. In addition to the obligatory training, appraisers who continuously receive training to update and expand their knowledge of valuation of securitization properties are preferred.

場合もあり得ること。

なお、エンジニアリング・レポート依頼内容報告書の書式を例示すれば別紙のとおりである。

2.「6．価格等調査業務の実施」について

1）関与不動産鑑定士

不動産鑑定業者は、証券化対象不動産の鑑定評価の実施に当たっては、社団法人日本不動産鑑定協会が実施する証券化研修等を修了している者[※13]が関与不動産鑑定士となるよう努めるものとする。

2）複数不動産の評価体制等

不動産鑑定業者は、同一依頼者からの複数物件の鑑定評価を複数の不動産鑑定士がチームで担当する場合には、一連の鑑定評価を行う複数の不動産鑑定士の役割分担を明確にした上で処理計画を策定し、常に情報を共有できる体制を整備する必要がある。

また、複数の不動産鑑定士が分担して一つの証券化対象不動産の鑑定評価を行う場合には、受付等の依頼者との協議、エンジニアリング・レポート等の資料の確認、実地調査等のそれぞれの担当する役割を明確にした上で、それぞれの作業から得られた情報を全員が常に共有し、密接かつ十分な連携を保って適切な鑑定評価を行える体制を整備しなければならない。

なお、これらの場合において、鑑定評価書への役割分担の明示、不動産鑑定士の署名・記名の別等については、別途定める「不動産鑑定士の役割分担等及び不動産鑑定業者の業務提携に関する業務指針」に従うものとする。

3）鑑定評価書のドラフト

不動産鑑定業者は、鑑定評価額決定前におけるドラフトの開示を求められた場合において、ドラフトに記載された内容は、対象不動産の鑑定評価額や個別的要因が最終的な鑑定評価書と異なることとなる可能性があるので、ドラフトの提出に当たっては次のような措置を講じ、利用する第三者に誤解の生じることの無いように十分に留意しなければならない。

ア　表紙を含め、全頁にドラフトである旨の表示を行うこと。
イ　不動産鑑定士の署名又は記名は行わないこと。
ウ　鑑定評価を行った日に代えてドラフトとしての評価を行った日を明記すること。
エ　対象不動産の状況、資料等について、最終的な鑑定評価書で採用するものとの違いを明確に記載し、鑑定評価額が変わる可能性があることを明確に記載すること。
オ　ドラフト提示時点における不明事項（最終的には確認する事項）を記載すること。
カ　依頼者等が修正可能なファイル形式等では提示しないこと。

---

[13] 少なくとも証券化対象不動産に関する不動産鑑定評価基準及び実務指針等に関する義務的研修を修了していることが必要であり、これに加えて証券化対象不動産の鑑定評価に関する知識の更新・拡充のための研修を継続的に受講していることが望ましい。

(f) Do not provide the report in a file format that the client can revise.

Also note that the appraisal firm should keep a record of the submission of the draft report and keep the draft report until the issuance of the final report[14].

4) Appraisal report
(1) If Specifics Chapter 3 and relevant Notes are applied
If Specifics Chapter 3 and relevant Notes are applied for the valuation of securitization properties, insert on the front page or in the main body of the appraisal report that the subject property falls under a securitization properties as stated in Specifics Chapter 3 and therefore Specifics Chapter 3 and relevant Notes were applied (also insert the appraisal value), so that the client and other parties can easily recognize this fact.

Though it is a securitization properties, if Specifics Chapter 3 and relevant Notes were not applied[15], describe why, as well as the fact that the appraisal report cannot be used for the transaction of securitization properties in the appraisal report.

(2) Explaining the valuation to the client
Since the appraisal report of securitization properties will be used as a reference by many parties involved in the investment or loans for the securitization properties, the appraisal firm should prepare the analysis and rationale in the report so that it is understandable not only to the client but to other parties involved.

Also note that if valuation of multiple properties was requested by one client, analysis of value influences of each subject property (increase or decrease factors, cap rate, etc.), valuation approaches, and applied methods should be uniform and consistent among each appraisal report.

5) Management of documents
(1) Filing the attached documents
The appraisal firm is obliged to keep a copy of the appraisal report, drawings that can identify the subject property, photographs, and other relevant documents for five years. In the valuation of securitization properties, the engineering report provided by the client and the data required for the DCF method are also included in the relevant documents that should be stored. The appraisal firm should manage these documents with appropriate information control.

---

[14] It is required to organize data used in the draft report and be ready to explain the differences between the draft report and final appraisal report. The draft report is, however, not the subject of required storage of documents as specified in Article 39-3 of the Real Estate Appraisal Act and Article 28-2 of the Rules of Practice of Real Estate Appraisal Act.

[15] I. 3. of the Guidelines Regarding Appraisal of Securitization Properties describe cases where it is acceptable to not apply Specifics Chapter 3 and relevant Notes though the subject property falls under the definition of securitization properties, such as its being a valuation requested by a seller that owns the property for sale to an unknown buyer, not for securitization, but was later acquired by a party involved in securitization.

なお、不動産鑑定業者は、ドラフトの提出履歴について記録するとともに、鑑定評価書の発行まで当該ドラフト等を保管する必要がある[14]。

4）鑑定評価書

(1) 基準各論第3章等を適用した旨の記載

証券化対象不動産について基準各論第3章等を適用して鑑定評価を行った場合には、依頼者等に一見してその旨が分かるように、鑑定評価書の表紙又は本文（鑑定評価額等の記載を含む）の前に、基準各論第3章規定の証券化対象不動産に該当し、基準各論第3章等を適用したものであることを明確に記載する必要がある。

証券化対象不動産に該当するにも関わらず、基準各論第3章等を適用しない場合[15]には、その理由及び「当該鑑定評価書が不動産証券化の取引等に関して用いることができない」旨を鑑定評価書に記載する必要がある。

(2) 鑑定評価書の依頼者等への説明

証券化対象不動産に係る鑑定評価書は、証券化対象不動産への投資、融資に係る多くの利害関係者の参考資料として用いられるので、不動産鑑定業者は、依頼者のみならず証券化対象不動産に係る利害関係者その他の者が鑑定評価の調査内容や判断根拠を把握することができるようにする必要がある。

また、同一の依頼者から同時に複数物件の鑑定評価を依頼された場合には、各対象不動産の価格形成要因に対する判断（増減価要因の格差や利回り等）や評価手法の適用方法等について、複数の鑑定評価書相互間の統一性や整合性の確保に留意しなければならない。

5）資料の管理態勢

(1) 付属資料の保管

不動産鑑定業者は、鑑定評価書の写しのほか、対象不動産等を明示するに足りる図面、写真その他の資料を5年間保存する義務が課されているが、証券化対象不動産の鑑定評価においては、依頼者より提示を受けるエンジニアリング・レポートやDCF法を適用するために必要となる資料がこれに該当する。不動産鑑定業者は、これらの資料を適切な情報管理の下で保管する態勢をとる必要がある。

(2) 依頼者への確認事項

不動産鑑定士が行う処理計画の策定に関し、依頼者に確認した、以下のアの依頼者に確認すべき事項に関して、イの記録、保管すべき事項については、これらは依頼者から提供された資料に不備があった場合の証拠となるものであり、不動産鑑定士及び不動産鑑定業者の責任にかかわる重要な資料となるものであるので、不動産鑑定士からの提示を受け、不動産鑑

---

14 最終的な鑑定評価書との相違について、活用した資料を含め、説明できるようにしておく必要がある。ただし、ドラフトについては、不動産の鑑定評価に関する法律第39条第3項及び同法施行規則第38条第2項に規定する保存義務までを求めるものではない。

15 「証券化対象不動産の鑑定評価に関する実務指針」Ⅰ.3では、形式的に証券化対象不動産に該当しても基準各論第3章等を適用しないことができる場合として、証券化目的のない売主からの買主未定の売却目的の鑑定評価依頼において、後日、証券化関係者が購入することとなった場合などの例示をあげている。

V − 7. Guidelines Regarding Valuation Practice for Appraisal Firms

(2) **Items to be confirmed with the client**
In order to determine the valuation schedule, the appraiser confirms the items specified in the below section A. Of these, the items listed in below B should be written down and stored by the appraisal firm together with a copy of the appraisal report and other documents, in accordance with the appraiser's instruction. This is because if any deficiencies are found in the provided information, these items will serve as evidence as they are important documents in relation to responsibility of the appraisers and appraisal firms.
Also note that listing in the appraisal report the names of the documents used in the valuation may be sufficient, and therefore these documents may not need to be attached to the report.

  A. Items to be confirmed with the client for the valuation process plan
   (a) Purpose and background of the valuation request
   (b) Under which of the categories specified in (a) - (d) of I. 2. Scope of Appraisal for Securitization Properties of Guidelines Regarding Appraisal of Securitization Properties the subject falls
   (c) Items included in the engineering report and date of its receipt
   (d) Items included in the required data for the DCF method and other information and its date of receipt
   (e) Whether the appraiser received an explanation from the issuer of the engineering report
   (f) Coverage of the site inspection including the internal inspection of the subject property
   (g) Other items required for determination of the valuation process plan

  B. Regarding A., items that should be written down and stored
   (a) Date of confirmation
   (b) Name of appraiser who confirmed the items: In the valuation of securitization properties, the appraiser who confirmed the items may not be the same as the appraiser in charge of the valuation of the subject property. The role and accountability of each appraiser should be made clear.
   (c) Name and occupation of counterparty in the confirmation: Name, company name, position, and relation with the client
   (d) What has been confirmed and how it is reflected in the process plan: Regarding the above A., take notes on what has been confirmed with the client and how it is reflected in the valuation process. If the initial information provided by the client was insufficient and the client and appraiser negotiated for further information, also record the progress.
   (e) If the valuation process has to be changed in accordance with revision in the confirmed items, indicate what has to be changed: If the above A. is revised due to changes in situation or negotiation with the client, and the valuation process has to be changed accordingly (e.g., changes in the coverage

定業者が鑑定評価書の写しその他の書類とともに保管する必要がある。
　なお、鑑定評価書には、最終的に活用した資料名について記載すれば足りると考えられるので、これらの記録は鑑定評価書への添付までを求めているものではない。

　　ア　処理計画の策定に関し依頼者に確認すべき事項
　　　ア）鑑定評価の依頼目的及び依頼が必要となった背景
　　　イ）対象不動産が前記Ⅰ2「対象とする鑑定評価の範囲」に定めるアからエのいずれに係るものであるかの別
　　　ウ）エンジニアリング・レポートの主な項目及び入手時期
　　　エ）DCF法等を適用するために必要となる資料その他の資料の主な項目及び入手時期
　　　オ）エンジニアリング・レポートの作成者からの説明の有無
　　　カ）対象不動産の内覧の実施を含めた実地調査の範囲
　　　キ）その他処理計画の策定のために必要な事項

　　イ　前記アに関し記録、保管すべき事項
　　　ア）確認を行った年月日
　　　イ）確認を行った不動産鑑定士の氏名：証券化対象不動産の鑑定評価においては評価担当の不動産鑑定士と異なる場合も多いので、不動産鑑定業者内での役割分担、責任の所在を明確にすること。
　　　ウ）確認の相手方の氏名及び職業：氏名、会社名、役職、依頼者との関係等
　　　エ）確認の内容及び当該内容の処理計画への反映状況：前記アの内容について、依頼者から確認した内容とともに、その内容によりどのような手順で評価作業を行ったか、について記録する。依頼者より当初示された内容が十分なものでなく、交渉を行った場合には、その経緯も記録する。
　　　オ）確認の内容の変更により鑑定評価の作業、内容等の変更をする場合にあっては、その内容：依頼者の事情の変化又は依頼者との交渉等により前記アの内容に変更があった場合に、評価作業を変更する必要が生じた場合（対象不動産の範囲や追加資料の提供、証券化スキームの変更等による、求める価格の種類、適用手法、適用数値の変更等）には、その内容を記録する。

of the subject, additional information, or securitization scheme that cause changes in type of value, valuation approaches, or changes in numbers used for the calculation), record the details.

(3) Draft Engineering Report

If the draft engineering report is used for the valuation process, the appraiser should obtain and check the final engineering report before concluding the appraisal value.

The appraisal firm should keep a record of the receipt of draft report and store it until the issuance of the final appraisal report.

3. "7. Quality Control"

Review of the appraisal report

The appraisal firm should determine in advance the policy and procedures for review of an appraisal report, and review the appraisal report accordingly. During the review, it is required to check whether the report is prepared in accordance with the separately stated Guidelines Regarding Appraisal of Securitization Properties.

4. Using these administrative instructions for valuation

1) Valuation which cannot be in accordance with the Appraisal Standards

The valuation of securitization properties should, in principle, be conducted in accordance with the Appraisal Standards. However, if this is not possible, an appraisal report not in accordance with the Appraisal Standards is allowed in exceptional situations.

In such cases, these administrative instructions should be applied in the process, in the same manner as the appraisal in accordance with the Appraisal Standards[16].

2) Revaluation

Revaluation refers to the periodic valuation (e.g., annual or semiannual) of property in which the previous valuation was conducted by the same appraiser in accordance with the Appraisal Standards. Revaluation includes not only valuation in accordance with the Appraisal Standards, but appraisal not in accordance with the Appraisal Standards. However, in any case, the appraisal form should use these administrative instructions.

Nevertheless, the following items do not require confirmation with the client and are not necessarily included in the report in the revaluation.

---

[16] For example, the opinion of value should be based on the assumption that current improvements or construction are completed as of the date of value, but the certificate of inspection or permission for tentative use are not yet obtained. Such cases may be rare.

(3) エンジニアリング・レポート等のドラフト

エンジニアリング・レポート等の資料については、ドラフトを入手して作業を進める場合であっても、鑑定評価額を決定する前までに最終版を確認しなければならない。

なお、不動産鑑定業者は、エンジニアリング・レポート等のドラフトの受領履歴について記録し、鑑定評価書の発行までの間、当該ドラフト等を保管する。

3．「7．品質管理」について

報告書審査

不動産鑑定業者は、鑑定評価書の審査等に関する方針及び手続きをあらかじめ策定のうえ、適切に報告書審査を実施することとなっている。この場合における報告書審査に当たっては、鑑定評価書の内容が別途定める「証券化対象不動産の鑑定評価に関する実務指針」に適合しているかどうかを確認する必要がある。

4．価格調査への本細則の準用

1）不動産鑑定評価基準に則ることができない価格調査

証券化対象不動産については、不動産鑑定評価基準に則った鑑定評価を行うことが原則であるが、不動産鑑定評価基準に則ることができない場合には例外的に不動産鑑定評価基準に則らない価格調査が認められている。

この価格調査のうち、やむを得ず不動産鑑定評価に則ることができない場合の価格調査においては、不動産鑑定業者は、不動産鑑定評価基準に則った鑑定評価と同様、本細則を準用して業務を実施するものとする[16]。

2）継続評価の場合

過去に同一の不動産鑑定士が不動産鑑定評価基準に則った鑑定評価を行ったことがある不動産の再評価であって、定期的（例えば、一年ごと又は半年ごと）に評価を行う場合を継続評価という。この場合における継続評価には、不動産鑑定評価基準に則った鑑定評価だけでなく、不動産鑑定評価基準に則らない価格調査が含まれるが、いずれの場合であっても、不動産鑑定業者は、本細則を準用して業務を実施するものとする。

ただし、継続評価を行う場合においては、以下の事項に関しては、依頼者への確認及び成果報告書の記載は要しない。

---

[16] 価格時点において、現在造成工事中又は建築工事の工事が完了したものとしての価格調査であるが、検査済証又は仮使用の承認が得られていない場合など、当該価格調査は極めて限定的と考えられる。

V − 7. Guidelines Regarding Valuation Practice for Appraisal Firms

    A.
      Items regarding the engineering report:
      1. 3) Requesting submission of report that shows coverage of engineering report
      2. 5) (2) A. Items to be confirmed with the client for the valuation schedule
      (c) Items included in the engineering report and date of its receipt
      (e) Whether the appraiser received explanation from the issuer of the engineering report
      (However, the appraiser should basically use these administrative instructions as usual if expansion, renovation, or large-scale maintenance was conducted, there were changes in laws that cause large changes in value formation of property, or the client again requested a new engineering report.)
    B.
      2. 4) (1) Text stating that Specifics Chapter 3 and relevant Notes were applied.
      (However, if revaluation is conducted in accordance with the Appraisal Standards, use these administrative instructions as usual and insert text stating that Specifics Chapter 3 and relevant Notes were applied)[17].

Effective from:
These administrative instructions will be applied to valuation contracts made and entered into on and after January 1, 2010. This does not preclude application before the effective date.

---

[17] If the revaluation is conducted as an opinion of value not based on the Appraisal Standards, do not insert text stating that the report is based on Specifics Chapter 3 and relevant Notes. Also, since the revaluation omits part of the valuation process based on the assumption that the previous valuation was conducted based on the Appraisal Standards with application of Specifics Chapter 3 and relevant Notes, and since it estimates the value of securitization properties during the holding period, insertion of "the appraisal report cannot be used for the transaction of securitization properties in the appraisal report" is not required.

ア　エンジニアリング・レポートに関する事項のうち、1.3）エンジニアリング・レポート依頼内容報告書の提出の要請、及び2.5）(1)ア処理計画の策定に関し依頼者に確認すべき事項のうち、ウ）エンジニアリング・レポートの主な項目及び入手時期、オ）エンジニアリング・レポートの作成者からの説明の有無（ただし、増改築工事又は大規模修繕の実施、関連法令等の大規模な変更等建物に関する価格形成の大きな変更があった場合など、依頼者がエンジニアリング・レポートの再入手を行う場合には、原則どおり本細則を準用する。）
イ　2.4）(1)基準各論第3章等を適用した旨の記載（ただし、不動産鑑定評価基準に則った鑑定評価として継続評価を行う場合には、原則どおり本細則を準用し、基準各論第3章等を適用した旨の記載する。）[17]

適用時期
　本細則は、平成22年1月1日以降に契約を締結する業務から適用する。ただし、当該日以前から適用することを妨げない。

以上

---

[17] 不動産鑑定評価基準に則らない価格調査として継続評価を行う場合、成果報告書に基準各論第3章等を適用した旨の記載は行わない。また、当該継続評価は、基準各論第3章等を適用した不動産鑑定評価基準に則った鑑定評価を過去に行っていることを前提として、一定の要件のもとに手続き等の一部を省略しているもので、あくまでも証券化対象不動産の保有時における価格を把握することを目的とするものであるため、「当該成果報告書が不動産証券化の取引等に関して用いることができない」旨を敢えて記載する必要はない。

Attachment: Report of coverage of engineering report

Month Day, Year

(Name of the client of the valuation)

(Name of the appraisal company) (Seal)

Submission of Report of Coverage of Engineering Report

The report of the coverage of the engineering report is a document the client submits to the appraisal firm upon accepting a request for appraisal of securitization properties.

Upon accepting the valuation request, the client is required to obtain an engineering report that satisfies the specifications listed in item 1 below, and the appraisal firm is required to confirm with the client the items listed in 2. Please fully understand these and request an engineering report.

1. Specifications of the engineering report
    1) Coverage of the subject property in the engineering report and valuation should be the same, or the engineering report should cover the entire subject of the valuation.
    2) If the engineering report covers a larger area than the subject of the valuation, the subject of the valuation should be clearly distinguished.
    3) If the subject of the engineering report is a condominium or co-owned property, the reproduction cost and repair and maintenance cost for the subject property of the valuation should be able to be easily defined.
    4) To prepare the engineering report, the preparer should conduct the site inspection and compliance investigation unless a legitimate reason prevents it.
    5) The request for the engineering report should be made free of improper approach that hinders the independence of its preparer.
    6) The date of the investigation and issuance of the engineering report must be clearly stated in the final engineering report.
    7) Expenses for potential improvements of the facility in the future should not be included. The repair and maintenance costs should be based on the current building after completion of previous repairs and maintenance.

2. Items that should be confirmed with the client
    1) Items that may influence the valuation process plan should be reported via a written document (electronic document is also acceptable). The appraisal report will not be issued before the issuance of the final engineering report.
    2) If the Specifics Chapter 3 of the Appraisal Standards and relevant Guidance Notes were applied for the valuation, and the appraisal firm requested required items related to this, the client of the valuation, as the party requesting the engineering report, should request that the preparer of the engineering report prepare an engineering report according to such a request.
    3) If the client of the valuation does not follow 1) and 2), the appraisal firm can decline the valuation request.

（別　紙）エンジニアリング・レポート依頼内容報告書

平成　年　月　日

〔不動産鑑定評価等依頼者〕

_____　御中

〔不動産鑑定業者〕

_____　印

エンジニアリング・レポート依頼内容報告書のご提出のお願い

　エンジニアリング・レポート依頼内容報告書は、不動産鑑定業者が証券化対象不動産に係る鑑定評価等業務を受託する際に、鑑定評価等依頼者にご提出いただくものとなります。
　なお、鑑定評価等業務の受託に当たっては、下記1に列挙される仕様のエンジニアリング・レポート（以下「ER」という。）の入手、及び下記2に列挙される鑑定評価等依頼者への確認が必要となりますので、これらの点を十分ご理解のうえERをご発注いただけますようお願い致します。

記

1　ERの仕様
(1) ERの対象範囲が鑑定評価等の対象範囲と同じであること、又は当該対象範囲を含むものであること。
(2) ERの対象範囲が鑑定評価等の対象範囲よりも大きい場合には、鑑定評価等の対象範囲が、その内訳として明確に判別できるようになっていること。
(3) 区分所有物件や共有物件を対象とするERの場合には、当該建物の再調達価格や修繕・更新費用等の金額について、鑑定評価等の対象となっている部分が容易に識別できるものであること。
(4) ERの作成に当たっては、特段の理由がある場合を除き、ER作成者による現地調査・遵法性調査が行われたものであること。
(5) ERの発注に当たり、ER作成者の独立性を損なう不適切な働きかけがなされていないこと。
(6) ERの最終版について、調査年月日及び発行年月日が明記されていること。
(7) 修繕・更新費用は、過去の改修を含めた現状建物の竣工時の状態を前提とし、将来における機能向上を企図した改修費用が含まれていないこと。

2　鑑定評価等依頼者への確認事項
(1) 鑑定評価等の処理計画に変更を及ぼす事項については、文書等（電磁的方法も含む）にて報告があること。また、鑑定評価書等の発行前に必ずERの最終版が交付されること。
(2) 不動産鑑定業者から、不動産鑑定評価基準各論第3章に則った鑑定評価等を行ううえで必要と認められる要請があった場合には、ER発注者として、ER作成者に対して当該要請に沿った適切な依頼を行うよう努めること。
(3) 上記(1)及び(2)の内容に添わない場合、不動産鑑定業者は鑑定評価等業務の受託を謝絶する場合もあり得ること。

V - 7. Guidelines Regarding Valuation Practice for Appraisal Firms

Month Day, Year

(Name of the appraisal company)

(Name of the client of the valuation) (Seal)

Report of Coverage of Engineering Report

We, (name of the client of the valuation) request from (name of the appraisal firm) the valuation of securitization properties listed at the end of this report. For the valuation, we request or plan to request the engineering report concerning the properties as follows. Please contact regarding any unclear areas in this report or the engineering report.

1. Parties requesting and preparing the engineering report

    Requesting party

Company name	
Address	
Division, contact person	
Telephone, e-mail	
Notes	

    Preparing party

Company name	
Address	
Division, contact person	
Telephone, e-mail	
Organization membership	

2. Coverage of engineering report

    1) Type of ownership of subject property of valuation

    ☐ Fee simple   ☐ Condo-ownership   ☐ Joint-ownership   ☐ Other

    2) If the above is condo-ownership or joint-ownership, the coverage of the engineering report and valuation are:

    ☐ the same   ☐ different (specified below)

    Describe the differences:

    3) Are there any other special instructions regarding the coverage?

☐	No	
☐	Yes: allocation of costs required for FF&E	Based on these, which party actually paid for what in the subject property of the valuation will be reflected in the engineering report ☐Yes ☐No
☐	Yes: regarding which party will conduct improvements of the property	
☐	Yes, but other than the above	

474

Ⅴ-7. 不動産鑑定業者の業務実施態勢に関する業務指針

平成　年　月　日

〔不動産鑑定業者〕

　　　　　　　　　　　　　　　御中

〔不動産鑑定評価等依頼者〕

　　　　　　　　　　　　　　　　　　　印

エンジニアリング・レポート依頼内容報告書

　今般、貴鑑定事務所に対し、末尾記載証券化対象不動産の鑑定評価等を依頼しておりますが、同不動産に関し、下記の内容にてエンジニアリング・レポート（以下「ER」と略す）を依頼予定、又は依頼済みですのでご報告申し上げます。なお、本書及び弊社提示ERの内容等につきご不明点等がございましたら、弊社を通じてご照会下さい。

1　ER発注者及びER作成者

〔ER発注者〕

社　名	
住　所	
部署・担当	
電話番号・E-mailアドレス	
備　考	

〔ER作成者〕

社　名	
住　所	
部署・担当	
電話番号・E-mailアドレス	
加入団体	

2　ERの対象範囲

(1) 鑑定評価等の対象となる建物の権利形態
　　□ 完全所有権　　□ 区分所有　　□ 共　有　　□ その他

(2) 上記が区分所有又は共有の場合、ERの対象範囲と鑑定評価等の対象範囲は　　□ 同　じ　　□ 以下の点で異なる

　　具体的な相違点：

(3) その他、対象範囲についての特記事項は
　　□ 特にない
　　□ FF&E負担区分であり、
　　□ 甲・乙工事区分であり、　　　これに基づく鑑定評価等対象範囲の現実の負担内容はERに
　　□ あるが、上記例示以外の内容であり、　　□ 反映する　　□ 反映しない

　　特記事項ある場合における
　　対象範囲・負担内容の判断根拠：

3　ERの調査内容等

(1) ERの作成方法

　① 作成基準（BELCAガイドライン活用の有無等）
　　□ 鑑定評価等発注時点におけるBELCAガイドラインの最新年版を活用
　　□ 上記ガイドラインとは、以下の点が異なる

　　具体的な相違点：

　② BELCAガイドラインにおける修繕・更新費用区分との相違
　　□ BELCAガイドラインの区分と同じ
　　□ BELCAガイドラインの区分とは、以下の点が異なる

　　具体的な相違点：

475

V－7. Guidelines Regarding Valuation Practice for Appraisal Firms

If "Yes," describe the rationale to determine the coverage and cost of the subject property:

3. Details of investigation for engineering report

   1) How to prepare the engineering report

      (a) Standard (whether BELCA Guidelines are used)

      ☐ The latest BELCA Guidelines as of the request of valuation are used.

      ☐ The guidelines used are different from the latest in terms of the following:

      Describe the differences:

      (b) Whether the allocation of repair and maintenance costs is the same as in the BELCA Guidelines

      ☐ Same as BELCA Guidelines

      ☐ Different from BELCA Guidelines in terms of the following:

      Describe the differences:

      (c) Of the items listed in 1 through 4 of Appendix 1 of Specifics Chapter 3 of the Appraisal Standards, which items will be omitted

	Omitted		If "Yes," give reasons and describe in details
1 Building conditions	☐ No	☐ Yes	
2 Environmental risk of building	☐ No	☐ Yes	
3 Soil contamination risk	☐ No	☐ Yes	
4 Seismic risk	☐ No	☐ Yes	

   2) Special instructions

      (1) Special instructions regarding repair and maintenance costs

         (a) All repair and maintenance costs that should be reflected in the engineering report

         ☐ All will be reflected   ☐ Part of it will be removed for the reasons specified below

☐ Because it is borne by the seller as specified in the purchase agreement	☐ Because it is borne by the tenant as specified in the lease agreement.	☐ None of the above
Describe the reason in details:		

         (b) Apart from the above, are there any special instructions regarding the repair and maintenance costs available as of today?

         ☐ No   ☐ Yes

      (2) Special instructions other than the repair and maintenance cost

         (a) Special instructions regarding the items specified in the BELCA Guidelines available as of today (except for repair and maintenance costs)

	Special instructions		If "Yes," give reasons and details
1 Building conditions	☐ No	☐ Yes	

Ⅴ-7.不動産鑑定業者の業務実施態勢に関する業務指針

③ 不動産鑑定評価基準各論第3章別表1(別添)の調査内容1～4のうち、省略される項目

項目	省略の有無	省略「有」の場合にはその理由と具体的な省略内容
1 建物状況調査	□無 □有	
2 建物環境調査	□無 □有	
3 土壌汚染リスク評価	□無 □有	
4 地震リスク評価	□無 □有	

(2) 特記事項

① 修繕・更新費用に関する特記事項

(ア) 本来ERに反映すべき修繕・更新費用の　□ 全てを調査結果に反映する　□ 一部を、以下の理由により調査結果から除外する

□ 売買契約に基づき売主負担となるため	□ 賃貸借契約に基づき借主負担となるため	□ 左記以外：

具体的な除外内容：

(イ) 上記のほか、現時点で判明している「修繕・更新費用に関する特記事項」

□無　□有：

② 修繕・更新費用以外の調査に関する特記事項の有無

(ア) 現時点で判明している「BELCAガイドラインの調査項目に関する特記事項」(修繕・更新費用以外)

項目	特記の有無	特記「有」の場合にはその理由と具体的内容
1 建物状況調査	□無 □有	
2 建物環境調査	□無 □有	
3 土壌汚染リスク評価	□無 □有	
4 地震リスク評価	□無 □有	

(イ) 現時点で判明している「BELCAガイドラインの調査項目以外の項目に関する追加調査事項」

項目	追加調査の有無	追加調査「有」の場合にはその具体的内容
1 地下埋設物除去費用	□無 □有	
2 建物環境調査（フェーズⅡ等）	□無 □有	
3 土壌汚染リスク評価（フェーズⅡ等）	□無 □有	
4 耐震性調査	□無 □有	
5 上記以外のその他	□無 □有	

＊ 上記に拘わらず、調査の進捗により別途調査項目の追加が必要になる場合には、適切に対応する予定である。

4 上記のほか、現時点で判明しているER作成者への特別な指示事項

指示事項	具体的内容

5 ERドラフト及び最終版の提出時期(予定)

ドラフト	平成　年　月　日頃
最終版	平成　年　月　日頃

6 鑑定評価等対象不動産の表示

NO.	物件名称	所在地(住居表示)	物件用途
1			
2			
3			
4			

以　上

477

V − 7. Guidelines Regarding Valuation Practice for Appraisal Firms

2 Environmental risk of building	☐ No	☐ Yes	
3 Soil contamination risk	☐ No	☐ Yes	
4 Seismic risk	☐ No	☐ Yes	

(b) Special instruction regarding the items <u>NOT</u> specified in the BELCA Guidelines available today

	Additional investigation		If "Yes," give details
1 Cost required for removal of underground structures	☐ No	☐ Yes	
2 Environmental risk of building (Phase II, etc.)	☐ No	☐ Yes	
3 Soil contamination risk (Phase II, etc.)	☐ No	☐ Yes	
4 Seismic risk	☐ No	☐ Yes	
5 Others	☐ No	☐ Yes	

Regardless of the above, if additional investigation is required during the progress, we will appropriately conduct such investigation.

4. Special instructions to the preparer of the engineering report other than the above available as of today

Instructions	Describe in details

5. Date of submission of draft and final engineering report (scheduled)

Draft Report	Month Day, Year
Final Report	Month Day, Year

6. Subject properties of the valuation

No.	Property	Location (address)	Use
1			
2			
3			
4			

V-8

Japanese-English Glossary

日英用語対照表

V-8. Japanese-English Glossary

No	JAPANESE 日本語	ENGLISH 英訳	Used in "Japan Real Estate Appraisal in a Global Context" 『不動産鑑定評価の国際化』
1	不動産鑑定評価基準	Real Estate Appraisal Standards	Real Estate Appraisal Standards
2	不動産鑑定評価	real estate appraisal	real estate appraisal
3	鑑定評価	appraisal	appraisal
4	不動産鑑定士	licensed real estate appraiser	licensed real estate appraiser
5	取引価格	sales price	sales price
6	土地	land	land
7	建物	buildings	building improvements
8	価格形成要因	value influences (influences on the value of real estate)	value influences (influences on the value of real estate)
9	一般的要因	general value influences	general value influences
10	地域要因	area-specific value influences	area-specific value influences
11	個別的要因	property-specific value influences	property-specific value influences
12	最有効使用	highest and best use	highest and best use
13	鑑定評価の基本的事項	basic elements of valuation	basic appraisal problem
14	対象不動産の確定	identification of the subjet property	identification of the subject property
15	対象不動産	subject property	subject property
16	対象確定条件	premises of the subject identification	requirements for the subject identification
17	想定上の条件等	assumptions	assumptions
18	価格時点	date of value	date of the value opinion
19	価格の種類	basis of value	type of value
20	価格	value	value
21	正常価格	market value	market value
22	市場価値	market value	market value
23	限定価格	assemblage or component value	assemblage or component market value
24	特定価格	market value based on special consideration	market value based on special considerations
25	投資採算価値	value for typical investors	investment profitability value

480

26	特殊価格	value of special-purpose property	non market value
27	鑑定評価手法	appraisal approaches	appraisal approaches
28	原価法	cost approach	cost approach
29	積算価格	value indicated by the cost approach	value indicated by the cost approach
30	再調達原価	reproduction cost	reproduction cost
31	取引事例比較法	sales comparison approach	sales comparison approach
32	比準価格	value indicated by the sales comparison approach	value indicated by the sales comparison approach
33	収益還元法	income capitalization approach	income capitalization approach
34	収益価格	value indicated by the income capitalization approach	value indicated by by the income approach
35	DCF法	DCF method	DCF method
36	直接還元法	direct capitalization method	direct capitalization method
37	鑑定評価の手順	appraisal process	appraisal process
38	鑑定評価の基本的事項の確定	identification of basic elements of valuation	identification of basic appraisal problem
39	処理計画の策定	appraisal schedule	drafting of processing plan drafting a work plan for the appraisal
40	対象不動産の確認	verification of subject property	identification of the subject property
41	実地調査	site inspection	property inspection
42	資料の収集及び整理の方法	gathering and organizing of data	gathering and organizing of data
43	資料の検討及び価格形成要因の分析	review of data and analysis of value influences	review of data and analysis of value influences
44	鑑定評価方式の適用	application of appraisal approach	application of appraisal method
45	試算価格の調整	reconciliation of value indications (reconciliation of indicated value)	reconciliation of the indicated value
46	試算価格	indicated value	value indications indicated value
47	鑑定評価額の決定	determination of the final appraisal value	determination of the final opinion of value

V-8. Japanese-English Glossary

48	鑑定評価額	appraisal value	final opinion of value
49	鑑定評価報告書の作成	preparation of the appraisal report	preparation of the appraisal report
50	鑑定評価書	appraisal report	-
51	鑑定評価報告書	appraisal report	appraisal report
52	鑑定評価の条件	assumptions	assumptions and limiting conditions of the appraisal
53	鑑定評価の依頼目的	purpose of the valuation	function and conditions of the appraisal
54	鑑定評価を行った日	date of completion of the valuation process	date of the appraisal report
55	実地調査を行った日（実地調査日） 実地調査を行った年月日	date of site inspection	date of the property inspection
56	不動産鑑定評価基準各論第3章 各論第3章	Specific Standards Chapter 3	Specific Standards Chapter 3
57	証券化対象不動産	securitized property (securitised real estate)	securitiization-propreties
58	地震リスク	earthquake risk	earthquake risk
59	耐震性 （耐震性調査）	seismic adequacy	earthquake resistance
60	地下埋設物	underground objects	buried structures of objects
61	不動産鑑定評価基準運用上の留意事項	Guidance Notes on the Real Estate Appraisal Standards	Guidance Notes on the Real Estate Appraisal Standards
62	目的	purpose	purpose
63	証券化対象不動産の鑑定評価に関する実務指針	Guidelines Regarding Appraisal of Securitized Properties	-
64	実務指針	guidelines	-
65	不動産鑑定業者	real estate appraisal firms	-
66	不動産鑑定士が不動産に関する価格等調査を行う場合の業務の目的と範囲等の確定及び成果報告書の記載事項に関するガイドライン	General Guidlline for Real Estate Appraisers on Determination of Purpose and Scope of Valuation and Contents of Report	-

67	価格等調査ガイドライン	Valuation Guidelines	-
68	価格等調査	valuation	-
69	証券化対象不動産の継続評価の実施に関する基本的考え方	Basic Policy on Revaluation of Securitized Property (Real Estate)	-
70	継続評価の基本的考え方	Basic Policy on Revaluation	-
71	不動産鑑定評価基準に則った鑑定評価	appraisal compliant with the Appraisal Standards	-
72	不動産鑑定評価基準に則らない価格等調査	valuation partially compliant with the Appraisal Standards	-
73	再評価	revaluation	-
74	「業務の目的と範囲等の確定に係る確認書」	Confirmation to Determine Purposes and Scope of Work	-
75	開示	disclosure	-
76	公表	publication	-
77	DCF法（開発賃貸型）	DCF method (development of a leasehold property)	-
78	事業経営の影響の大きい用途の不動産	operational property	-
79	継続評価	revaluation	-
80	内覧	internal inspection	-
81	周辺業務	adjacent/periperal service	-
82	調査価格	final value	-

V-9

Related Taxation issues etc

関連税制等

V - 9. Related Taxation issues etc

Tax system on land acquisition

Tax items	Taxpayer	Object of taxation	Tax base	Tax rate	Special rules, etc.
Registered license tax (National tax)	Applicant for registration	Registration concerning preservation, transfer and others of ownership	Value at registration (Assessed value of fixed assets tax)	Registration of transfer Main rule: 2% Registration of ownership preservation Main rule: 0.4%	*The tax concerning residential buildings should be reduced as follows: - Registration of transfer by sales transaction: 0.3% - Registration of ownership preservation: 0.15%
Real estate acquisition tax (Prefectural tax)	Individual or corporation that acquired real estate	Land and building	Price at acquisition (Assessed value of fixed assets tax)	Main rule: 4%	*Special rule on tax base concerning residential buildings - New houses: Deductible by 12 million yen *Special rule on tax amount for residential lands
Inheritance tax (National tax)	Individual who acquired property by inheritance or bequest	All inherited properties including lands	Value at acquisition (Assessed value of inheritance tax)	Progressive tax rate of 10-50%	Progressive tax rate of 10-50% Special rule should be applied to a land up to 240 m² (up to 400 m² for residential land for commercial use). [For residence] - A relative living together continues to live: 80% reduction - Others: 50% reduction [For commercial (except for real-estate lending)] - In the case of continuing the business: 80% reduction - Others: 50% reduction [For real-estate lending] 50% reduction * Extension of applicable period of special rule on conversion of agricultural land, etc. in the specially designated urbanization area, on which tax payment is postponed. - In the case of converting land to a

① 土地の取得に係る税制

税目	納税義務者	課税対象	課税標準	税率	主な特例等
登録免許税 (国税)	登記等を受ける者	所有権の保存、移転等に係る登記等	登記時の価額 (固定資産評価額)	売買に係る所有権移転の登記 2％ 所有権保存の登記 0.4％ 所有権の信託の登記 0.4％	＜参考＞ ● 住宅用家屋の特例 ○ 所有権移転の登記0.3％ ○ 所有権保存の登記0.15％
不動産取得税 (都道府県税)	不動産を取得した個人又は法人	土地及び家屋	取得時の価格 (固定資産評価額)	本則4％	＜参考＞ ● 住宅に係る課税標準の特例 ○ 新築住宅1,200万円控除 ○ 既存住宅新築時期に応じ一定額控除
相続税 (国税)	相続又は遺贈により財産を取得した個人	土地を含めたすべての相続財産	取得時の価額 (相続税評価額)	10～50％の累進税率	● 小規模宅地等の課税の特例 特例適用対象面積240m²まで（事業用宅地については400m²まで） ［居住用］ ○ 同居親族が居住継続80％減額 ○ その他50％減額 ［事業用（除不動産貸付用）］ ○ 事業継続80％減額 ○ その他50％減額 ［不動産貸付用］50％減額 ○ 納税猶予中の特定市街化区域農地等の転用特例の延長 ○ 賃貸住宅等の敷地として転用する場合、納税猶予を継続、一定期間経過後免除

V－9．Related Taxation issues etc

					rental housing site, the postponement of tax payment is continued, and after a prescribed period, the tax payment is exempted.

Tax system regarding possession of land

Tax items	Taxpayer	Object of taxation	Tax base	Tax rate	Special rules, etc.
Fixed assets tax (Municipal tax)	Owner of fixed assets	Lands, buildings and depreciable assets	Price of fixed assets (Assessed value of fixed assets tax)	Standard tax rate 1.4% Limited tax rate 2.1%	*Special rule concerning tax base for residential land - General residential land: 1/3 of the price - Small-scale residential land: (Up to 200 m^2) 1/6 of the price
City planning tax (Municipal tax)	Owner of a land or a building in the specially designated urbanization area, etc.	Land and building	Same as fixed assets tax	Limited tax rate 0.3%	*Special rule on tax base for residential lands - General residential land: 2/3 of the price - Small-scale residential land (residential land of max. 200 m^2): 1/3 of the price

Tax system on transfer of land

Tax items		Period of possession	Within 5 years (short period)	Exceeding 5 years (long period)
Individual	Acquisition by transfer		30% of gain from the transfer (+ 9% of inhabitant tax)	Taxable transfer income Separate taxation of 15% without exception (+ 5% of inhabitant tax)
	Business income or other income		Additional tax should not be applied.*	Ordinary general taxation
Corporation tax			Additional tax should not be applied.*	Additional tax should not be applied.*

② 土地保有に係る税制

税目	納税義務者	課税対象	課税標準	税率	主な特例等
固定資産税（市町村税）	固定資産の所有者	土地、家屋及び償却資産	固定資産の価格（固定資産評価額）	標準税率 1.4%	• 住宅用地の課税標準の特例 ○ 一般住宅用地価格の1/3 ○ 小規模住宅用地（200m^{2}まで）価格の1/6
都市計画税（市町村税）	市街化区域等に所在する土地、家屋の所有者	土地、家屋	固定資産税と同じ	制限税率 0.3%	• 住宅用地の課税標準の特例 ○ 一般住宅用地価格の2/3 ○ 小規模住宅用地（200m^{2}までの住宅用地）価格の1/3

③ 土地の譲渡に係る税制

税目		所有期間 5年以内（短期）	5年超（長期）
個人	譲渡所得	譲渡益の30%（＋住民税9%）	課税譲渡所得 一律15%分離課税（＋住民税5%）
個人	事業所得又は雑所得	次の①と②のいずれか多い額（注1） ①譲渡益の40%（＋住民税12%） ②総合課税による上積税額（注2）×110%	通常の総合課税
法人税		通常の法人税に加え、10%の税率で課税（注1）	通常の法人税に加え、5%の税率で課税（注1）

Copyright reserved by the
JAPANESE ASSOCIATION OF REAL ESTATE APPRAISAL
SVAX TT Bldg., 3-11-15, Toranomon Minato-ku Tokyo 105-0001, Japan
Tel : 03 (3434)2301
URL http://www.fudousan-kanteishi.or.jp

Published by **JUTAKU-SHIMPOSHA, INC.**
TAM Bldg., 1-4-9, Nishishimbashi Minato-ku Tokyo 105-0003, Japan

英語で読む証券化対象不動産の鑑定評価の実務
Practical Guidance on Investment (Securitized) Real Estate Appraisal

2011年7月6日　初版発行

　　　　　　　　　　　　　　　　　㈳日本不動産鑑定協会
　　　　　　　　　　　編 著 者　証券化鑑定評価委員会
　　　　　　　　　　　　　　　　　証券化グローバル化対応委員会
　　　　　　　　　　　発 行 者　中　野　博　義
　　　　　　　　　　　発 行 所　㈱住　宅　新　報　社

編 集 部　　〒105-0003　東京都港区西新橋1-4-9（ＴＡＭビル）
　　　　　　　　　　　　　　　電話（03）3504－0361
出版販売部　〒105-0003　東京都港区西新橋1-4-9（ＴＡＭビル）
　　　　　　　　　　　　　　　電話（03）3502－4151
大 阪 支 社　〒541-0046　大阪市中央区平野町1-8-13(平野町八千代ビル)
　　　　　　　　　　　　　　　電話（06）6202－8541㈹
　　　　　　　　　　　ウェブサイト　http://www.jutaku-s.com/

©2011　JAPANESE ASSOCIATION OF REAL ESTATE APPRAISAL
Printed in Japan　ISBN978-4-7892-3393-4　C2030
印刷・製本／亜細亜印刷
定価はカバーに表示してあります。落丁本・乱丁本はお取り替えいたします。

本書の全部または一部を無断で複写複製（コピー）することは、著作権法上での例外を除き、禁じられています。